To –

Larry Swindell

In appreciation !

From
Dick Crews
Jan. 6, 1992

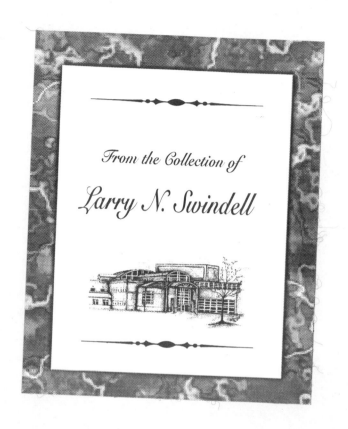

UNCLE TOM'S CABIN AND AMERICAN CULTURE

HARRIET BEECHER STOWE

Uncle Tom's Cabin
and
American Culture

THOMAS F. GOSSETT

SOUTHERN METHODIST UNIVERSITY PRESS • 1985

The paper in this book meets the standards for permanence
and durability established by the Committee on Production
Guidelines for Book Longevity of the Council on Library
Resources.

LIBRARY OF CONGRESS CATALOGUING-IN-PUBLICATION DATA

Gossett, Thomas F., 1916–
    Uncle Tom's cabin and American culture.

    Bibliography: p.
    Includes index.
    1. Stowe, Harriet Beecher, 1811–1896.   Uncle Tom's
cabin.   2. Slavery and slaves in literature.   3. Afro-
Americans in literature.   4. Race relations in
literature.   I. Title.
PS2954.U6G67   1985   813'.3   83-17245
ISBN 0-87074-189-6

For Henry Nash Smith—
with affection and gratitude

UNCLE TOM'S CABIN AND AMERICAN CULTURE is the last book to be printed on the Miehle M 41 letterpress owned by the SMU Printing Department. The press was purchased by the University of Arkansas after World War II and brought to Southern Methodist University in 1969. SMU Press expresses its appreciation for many years of excellent service and wishes to thank individually the craftsmen who produced this book: James Roe, Linotype operator; Allen Dickson, floor and lock-up man; Noe Verver, pressman; Pepe Perico, proofreader; and Art Watson, supervisor.

Contents

ILLUSTRATIONS

Preface

Harriet Beecher Stowe's *Uncle Tom's Cabin* is often dismissed as a sentimental novel without literary merit. And it certainly does have its sentimental side with its extended death scenes and with other characteristics stereotypical of melodrama. What a careful reader will notice, however, is that for all its sentimentality about some things—the devotion of a father for his almost angelic child, for example—the novel is not at all sentimental about political and social institutions. Many critics have testified to the comprehensive grasp Stowe had of the complex matter of American slavery. The novel deals with all the major issues. It shows, for one thing, that the white North was almost equally as culpable as the white South in maintaining an inherently barbarous system.

In addition to human compassion, Stowe had a sense of humor. It is an old-fashioned, but nonetheless real, humor. This is an important trait because the tone of the novel is such that it does not rule out the possibility that slavery might be abolished by peaceful means. As to its literary faults, *Uncle Tom's Cabin* does have them—especially of style and sometimes even of ordinary problems of syntax. Yet these faults are not sufficient to overrule the novel's merits.

The first part of this study is an examination of Stowe's early life

and the circumstances that led her from a largely introverted and with-
drawn youth to a major public role in the antislavery struggle. The
second part deals with the actual writing of *Uncle Tom's Cabin* and
analyzes in some detail its themes. The third part examines reactions to
the novel in the North, in the South, and abroad from the time it was
published in 1851–1852 until the end of the Civil War. The fourth part
examines the widespread reactions to *Uncle Tom's Cabin*, the play, during approximately the same period. The next two sections of the book
deal with the period from the end of the Civil War to the present time.
The fifth part examines the critical reputation of *Uncle Tom's Cabin*
as a novel, while the sixth part deals with productions of the play based
upon the novel.

A generation or two after the defeat of the Confederacy, white critics
in both the North and the South began to form what seemed for a time
a consensus of opinion with regard to *Uncle Tom's Cabin*. They often
agreed with one another that Stowe had been right about slavery—or
at least right in her conviction that it ought to be abolished. They also
agreed with one another, however, on the point that she had had too
high a conception of the innate intellectual, moral, and temperamental
qualities of the blacks. She had made them much better, a good many
white critics argued, than blacks really are. It was an age in which innate
traits of racial character were accepted as a self-evident fact by a great
many people. This view was strongly held until at least the 1920s.

In more recent years, an almost directly opposite opinion has developed. The strongest criticisms of *Uncle Tom's Cabin* have come from
writers and scholars—many of them black—who have argued that the
novel has done at least as much harm as good because it portrays blacks
as inherently servile. She made them, these critics argued, worse than
blacks really are. Still more recently, Stowe has attracted a number of
critics—all of them, as yet, white—who have strongly defended her. I
consider myself to be among this latter group.

The play was one of the great hits of all times and may have had a
greater number of performances than all of its dozen closest rivals in
popularity in the United States put together. After the Civil War, productions of the play lost much of their antislavery emphasis and became
largely comic treatments of blacks with heavy infusions of sentimentality
and melodrama. Thus, the defects of the play were much worse than
those of the novel.

I wish to thank Edgar T. Thompson and Charles E. King for having read the complete manuscript. I also wish to thank the following people who have read one or more of the chapters—Warren T. Carr, John A. Carter, Jr., J. Rodney Meyer, Lee H. Potter, David L. Smiley, Henry S. Stroupe, John E. Via, Edwin G. Wilson, and W. Buck Yearns, Jr. I have strongly benefited from discussing problems of the study with Alonzo W. Kenion, William M. Moss, and E. Bruce Kirkham. The Reference Department of the Z. Smith Reynolds Library of Wake Forest University was very helpful in finding obscure references for me. I also benefited from the help I received at the Harvard University libraries, the American Antiquarian Society, the Boston Athenaeum, the New York Public Library, the Enoch Pratt Library in Baltimore, the Library of Congress, the University of Virginia Library, Duke University Library, and the library of the University of North Carolina at Chapel Hill. Most helpful were Joseph S. Van Why and Diana Royce of the Stowe-Day Foundation Library in Hartford, Connecticut.

I am indebted to Wake Forest University for providing me with a Reynolds Research Leave for a semester and for several summer grants. I am also grateful for a summer grant from the National Endowment for the Humanities and one from the Visiting Scholar Fund at Duke University.

Margaret Hartley of the Southern Methodist University Press worked with me on the book until the time of her death in August 1983. I am indebted to her both for her encouragement and for many helpful suggestions. I am also indebted to Charlotte T. Whaley, who undertook the editing of the last sections of the manuscript after the death of Mrs. Hartley.

Mildred K. Garris did some of the typing for me. Herman J. Preseren took photographs of some of the illustrations. I benefited from the work and the enthusiasm of a number of part-time undergraduate student assistants too numerous to name individually.

The greatest help of all came from my wife Louise.

UNCLE TOM'S CABIN AND AMERICAN CULTURE

I

The Early Years
1811-1826

HARRIET BEECHER STOWE was born in the little town of Litchfield in northwestern Connecticut on June 12, 1811. Litchfield had been for many years a stronghold of the Federalist party and of Calvinist orthodoxy. Lyman Beecher (1775-1863), Harriet's father, was an able man with many oddities and contradictions of character. At the time when Harriet was born he was already well known, and he was to become a national figure, sometimes even being described—at least by his friends—as the most famous clergyman in America. He was a battler for the Lord and for the old orthodoxy of New England against the tides of modernism and especially against Unitarianism. His defenses of orthodoxy were by no means inflexible, however, and he could sometimes give ground on theological questions as well as on other matters. Neither was he the dour man that his theology might suggest to the modern mind. Like Jonathan Edwards, he carried within his religion not only the God of wrath but also the God of infinite love and mercy. For him, it was the latter God who was more important. In addition, he had a sense of humor. Though he never rejected predestination outright, he interpreted the doctrine in such a way as to make it less absolute. When all eleven of his children who grew to maturity rejected Calvinism in most of its distinctive doctrines, they did so with no feelings of rancor toward their father. It could be argued that they were merely doing what Lyman Beecher's temperament, if not his theology, encouraged them to do—think for themselves.[1]

It was easy to love a father who allowed his children to climb into his bed in the morning and wake him by pulling on his nose. He would then pretend that he did not dare to get up because there was a terrible beast hiding under the bed. He would not even put his toe outside the covers until he had been assured by the children, over and over again, that they had looked everywhere and no beast was to be found. Frequently he played games with his children. One of his particular talents was to make work and play almost synonymous and to join with the children in performing household chores.[2]

Lyman Beecher had the knack of teaching his children without seeming to do so. At an early age, for example, the children were introduced to religion. He did not merely present them with a catechism to be memorized. Religion was something to be felt, it is true, but it was also something to be understood and debated. At the supper table he might take a position on some doctrinal question and encourage the children to challenge his ideas. Harriet described his method:

Occasionally he would raise a point of theology . . . and ask the opinion of one of his boys, and run a sort of tilt with him, taking up the wrong side of the question; for the sake of seeing how the youngster would practice his logic. If the party on the other side did not make a fair hit at him, however, he would stop and explain to him what he ought to have said. "The argument lies so, my son; do that, and you'll trip me up." Much of his teaching to his children was in this informal way.

Though Harriet did not say that she herself took part in these lessons, it is obvious that she learned a good deal from them. When she grew up, she was able to combine two qualities not readily associated with one another in the nineteenth-century view of woman. She had in abundant supply all the love of children and family which a woman was supposed to have. On the other hand, she had a clear understanding of the rules of logic. *Uncle Tom's Cabin* would show both of these qualities. Many a proslavery advocate must have thought he could easily demolish the arguments of a sentimental novel written by a woman. If he was clever enough, he would usually discover that his arguments had been anticipated.[3]

Calvinism did not prove an obstacle to the optimism and energy of Lyman Beecher. He was willing to accept as a fact that the elect who would go to heaven were a small, perhaps an infinitesimal, percentage even of communities which aspired to be Christian, but he did not despair. He would save as many people as he could. He came near convincing himself that nobody, certainly nobody he knew, need go to hell. The sternness of Calvinism is evident in his thought but chiefly as a final trump card. Salvation was available, apparently to all who did not delight in their wickedness. Harriet may have been thinking of her father when she created the Reverend Mr. Avery, a character in her novel *Oldtown Folks* (1869):

Mr. Avery was a firm believer in hell, but he believed also that nobody need go there, and he was determined, so far as he was concerned, that nobody should go there if he could help it. Such a tragedy as the loss of any one soul in his parish he could not and would not contemplate for a moment; and he had such a firm belief in the truths he preached, that he verily expected with them to save anybody that would listen to him.

In his view, even Calvinist theology was flexible. When "original minded sheep" would not be enticed into the fold by entering its gate, Mr. Avery would "loosen a rail or tear off a picket, and let the sheep in, it being his impression, after all, that the sheep are worth more than the sheepfold." Of her father himself, Harriet could say that though he believed in total depravity, "yet practically he never seemed to realize that people were unbelievers for any other reason than want of light, and that clear and able arguments would not at once put an end to skepticism." In an expansive mood she would even refer to Lyman Beecher as "my blessed father, for many years so true an image of the Heavenly Father."[4]

It is easy to see that Lyman Beecher had an attractive side both as father and as teacher. The effect of his theology may have been, however, to make his children think they had a latitude in their own thinking which did not in fact exist. The special twist he gave to Calvinist theology would have been a trial to an adult who was emotionally mature and also an accomplished logician. An impressionable child was almost wholly unequipped to deal with it. On the one hand, Lyman told his children that they had freedom of choice with regard to ideas. They should "receive no opinions upon trust." "Dare to think for yourself," he proclaimed. "Let no creed bind you because it is reputed orthodox, until you perceive its agreement with the Scriptures; but then, though every where spoken against, adopt it." He could encourage in them what at first seems to be an almost Emersonian self-reliance, because he was certain that it would lead nowhere but to his own modified Calvinist orthodoxy. The catch was, of course, "agreement with the Scriptures." The children were not supposed to challenge that. The result was that Lyman gave his children freedom in such a way as to make it almost useless to them. If they tampered with Scripture, which meant in effect if they tampered with his interpretation of it, they would immediately find themselves faced with the prospect of hell. Lyman never seems to have recognized that he took away with his left hand what he had offered with his right. His son Edward underwent a spiritual crisis while he was a student at Yale, one which showed signs of ending in religious skepticism. Lyman no longer talked about freedom. Instead, he warned Edward of the terrible consequences of a wrong decision. "What shall it profit you," he wrote, "though you should gain all knowledge and lose your own soul?" In another letter, he was even more emphatic. "Oh my dear son," he pleaded, "agonize to enter in. You *must go* to heaven; you *must not* go to hell!"[5]

Lyman had a profound effect upon the characters and opinions of his children, and, predictably, not all of his influence was good. When they were young he maintained a strict discipline and did not hesitate to spank them. As they grew older, however, he never forced his opinions on them in any obvious way. Though he would sometimes argue or even plead with his children, these were not his usual methods. Harriet would speak years later of the "moral oxygen" of her father's household. He simply assumed that the children could do no other than share his religious commitment. Once they became converted, the children might have the illusion that they were permitted a considerable latitude. As it worked out, however, they were free only to decide how they would make their commitment to religion felt. To ask whether the soul had all the obligations that Lyman said it did was off limits. As a practical matter, their freedom consisted in their being allowed to decide which branch of religious endeavor they would enter.[6]

Confronted with a father like this, the children were helpless. All seven of his sons who lived to maturity became ministers. Two of them apparently could not stand the strain. After three nervous breakdowns, George shot himself in 1843. The death was listed as accidental, but it probably was not. James went to sea and became an officer on a clipper ship. Like Jonah, he knew he was resisting a powerful will. "Oh, I shall be a minister," he is reported as saying. "That's my fate. Father will pray me into it." And he did become one, but the decision, like that of George, was probably a mistake. In 1886, twenty-three years after his father's

death, James also committed suicide. Charles was another son who resisted for a time his father's will. His difficulty was not merely in becoming a minister but in sustaining a religious faith at all. He became
a cotton clerk and a music teacher in New Orleans, thus helping to fur-
nish Harriet with information which she would use in *Uncle Tom's
Cabin*; but he too was reclaimed for the ministry. The other sons—
William, Edward, Henry Ward, and Thomas—all became ministers,
almost as a matter of course.[7]

Of Lyman Beecher's four daughters who grew to maturity, only Mary,
one of Harriet's two older sisters, elected to live a life limited to marriage
and domesticity. She lived to the age of ninety-five, longer than any of
the other Beecher children, and one reason for her long life may have
been that she was not a battler like the others. Catharine, Harriet's other
older sister, was involved all her life in reforms, chiefly those concerned
with the education of women. She was opposed, however, to woman
suffrage. Isabella, Harriet's younger half-sister, was an enthusiastic advocate of woman suffrage and an important figure in the early history of
the movement. It may be charitable to describe her as extremely eccentric.
At one point, she believed she had been informed in a heavenly vision
that she was the twin sister of Jesus Christ. This kind of aberration did
not, however, prevent her from having a sensible side and exerting a
remarkable influence.[8]

Roxana Foote Beecher, Lyman's first wife and Harriet's mother, died
in 1816. Since Harriet was only five years old at the time, she retained
only a bare memory of her mother, chiefly of a single incident. While
her mother was away from home, Harriet had discovered some tulip
bulbs in the house and, not knowing what they were, had eaten them.
Her mother had gently and sorrowfully explained to her what beautiful
flowers she had destroyed. Later in life, Harriet wrote a letter to her son
Charles in which she spoke of "the angelic mother whom I scarcely knew
in the world, and who has been to me only a spiritual presence through
life." On another occasion, she said that the saintly mother of the character Augustine St. Clare in *Uncle Tom's Cabin* was based upon her
memories of her own mother. It is probable that Roxana also affected
her children, especially her daughters, in another way. She had come
from a cultivated family, her father having read all the books of the
public library of the small Connecticut town in which they lived. She
had tied books in French to her distaff so that she could read while
she spun flax. In her letters to Lyman, she wrote of poetry and of

science. She was excited at the "discovery that the fixed alkalies are metallic oxyds." On one occasion, she proposed the question of who was the greater general, Alexander or Hannibal. Her example probably influenced Catharine to assume as a matter of course that a woman should be educated, and Catharine in turn influenced Harriet on this point.[9]

Part of the good side of Lyman Beecher was that, unlike many orthodox Protestant clergymen of his time, he did not object to imaginative literature. He had his doubts about novels, but he struggled to overcome them. When George asked his father for permission for Harriet and himself to read the novels of Sir Walter Scott, Lyman considered the matter carefully. Then he made what Harriet later called an "*ex cathedra*" pronouncement. "George," she remembered Lyman Beecher as saying, "you may read Scott's novels. I have always disapproved novels as trash, but in these is real genius and real culture, and you may read them." George and Harriet liked *Ivanhoe* so much that during one summer they read it through seven times, and both of them could quote whole scenes of it from memory. Lyman himself joined in the reading of Scott and thought up still another project from which the whole family might profit. "I have the image of my father still as he sat working the apple-peeler," Harriet recalled. " 'Come, George,' he said, 'I'll tell what we'll do to make the evening go off. You and I'll take turns and we'll see who'll tell the most out of Scott's novels . . .' ." And so Lyman and George took Scott's novels one by one, reciting incidents from them. These performances, Harriet said, "kept the eyes of the children wide open, and made the work go without flagging." She did not say that her father had also asked her to recite incidents from Scott, but neither is there any indication that she may have felt resentment at being left out. At an early age, she may already have been used to it.[10]

Less than a year after the death of Roxana, Lyman—never one to remain long a widower—met Miss Harriet Porter in Boston. A week later he proposed, and not long afterward Harriet Porter became his wife. In later years, Harriet Beecher Stowe tried to be fair in her memories of her stepmother, but she obviously had not been strongly drawn to her. Her stepmother was "a lady of great personal elegance and attractiveness, of high intelligence and moral culture," Harriet wrote, but the task of being the wife of Lyman, the stepmother of his children, and the mother of her own children had been a tax upon her strength. "Her nature and habits were too refined and exacting," said Harriet, "for the bringing up of children of great animal force and vigor, under the strain and pressure of straitened circumstances." Though Lyman Beecher was an important man in the community, he was not well paid. His salary at Litchfield was for many years only $800 a year. Even this modest sum was sometimes delayed, being dependent upon financial pledges made by members of his congregation. Inevitably the family budget was strained. Harriet Porter Beecher, under the stress of family cares, became melancholy. Harriet remembered that her stepmother had the custom of taking each child of the family into her bedroom on Sunday evenings for long and serious religious talks. "She gave an impression of religion," said Harriet, "as being like herself, calm, solemn, inflexible, mysteriously sad and rigorously exacting."[11]

It may have been partly the emotional poverty of her early years which led Harriet to read with appreciation the works of Sir Walter Scott. It was probably not Scott's tales of knights and ladies which principally influenced her. As Henry F. May observes, the Scott most important to her was the man who wrote stories which dealt with the lives of humble people—as in *The Heart of Midlothian*, for example. In addition, Scott is the probable source for the theme of the homeless traveler as found in *Uncle Tom's Cabin*. Charles H. Foster says that Scott may have influenced her as "a writer of the expanded tale of travel. His characters are always on the move." Edmund Wilson made a similar point, saying that the wanderings of the characters of the novel "progressively and excitingly reveal, like the visits of Chichikov in Gogol's *Dead Souls*, the traits of a whole society." It is John William Ward who has most clearly pointed out, however, why the theme of travel is important in *Uncle Tom's Cabin*:

. . . Mrs. Stowe organized her fiction around one of the universal motifs in human experience, the story of a journey that metamorphoses itself into a symbolic quest, a search for the meaning of life inside. As one stands back from *Uncle Tom's Cabin* and regards it whole, one sees how deeply the novel is characterized by movement, how pervasively it presents a world of people in constant motion. It is a world threatened by instability, a world of individuals seeking a resting place, seeking no less than a home. The only moments of rest in the novel are tied closely and immediately to home and the moments of bliss in the novel, like the Quaker settlement, are domestic.

As Ward suggests, family instability is one of the great evils of slavery. "The tragedy of the Negro is that he has, quite literally," says Ward, "no home. The pathos of the Negro slave's world lies in this elemental fact.

The bare rudiments of human community are not there for the Negro: husband and wife, mother and child, again and again are torn one from the other. The Negro's world is defined by separation and loneliness, a terrible solitude."[12]

Lyman Beecher also read Milton's *Paradise Lost* aloud to his children. In this he showed a curious contradiction between his temperament and his theology. "With all that was truly great among men," Harriet recalled many years later,

he [Lyman] felt a kindred sympathy. Genius and heroism would move him even to tears. I recollect hearing him read aloud Milton's account of Satan's marshaling his forces of fallen angels after his expulsion from heaven. The description of Satan's courage and fortitude was read with such evident sympathy as quite enlisted me in his favor. . . .[13]

Another work which she read as a child may have influenced Harriet. This was *Don Quixote*, a copy of which, disintegrated into forty or fifty fragments, she found in her father's library "amid Calls, Appeals, Sermons, Essays, Reviews, Replies, and Rejoinders." It seemed to her "like the rising of an enchanted island out of an ocean of mud." There is a great distance, of course, between Harriet's moral earnestness and Cervantes's relative detachment. The two may not be so far apart, however, as might be supposed. Like most of the Beechers, Harriet had a sense of humor. Cervantes may have helped to keep her—at least most of the time—from the doctrinaire and self-righteous qualities of many reformers.[14]

Harriet probably read Cotton Mather's *Magnalia Christi* as a child. If she did, she was almost certainly excited by his tales of witches and of ferocious Indians, but she was probably also impressed by his pride in the "chosen people" of New England. On this point, we have only indirect evidence. There is a little girl character in her *Poganuc People* (1878) who reads Cotton Mather, and the narrator of the novel says, "No Jewish maiden ever grew up with a more earnest faith that she belonged to a consecrated race, a people especially called and chosen of God for some great work on earth. Her faith in every word of the marvels related in this book was fully as great as the dear old credulous Dr. Cotton Mather could have desired." If Harriet felt as this character did, we can see her reformist zeal taking shape long before it had a specific object.[15]

Harriet read at least one book of which Lyman Beecher probably would not have approved. She found in the home of her Aunt Esther a volume of Byron's poetry. Harriet read *The Corsair* and later recalled how "astonished and electrified" she was, and how she "kept calling to Aunt Esther to hear the wonderful things that I found in it." She was puzzled by Byron's reference in the book to "one I loved enough to hate." She asked Aunt Esther what the phrase meant. Aunt Esther, probably recognizing the intrusion of sexuality, replied evasively, "Oh, child, it's one of Byron's strong expressions." Lyman Beecher himself admired Byron, although chiefly he regarded him as a soul with a need to be saved. When Byron died, Lyman said, "Oh, I'm sorry that Byron is dead. I did hope he would live to do something for Christ. What a harp he might have swept." As unlikely as any achievements by Byron in that direction may seem to us, the reaction was characteristic of Lyman. Harriet, too, was distressed over Byron's death. Years later she recalled that she had gone out upon a hill to pick strawberries. She "lay down among the daisies, looking up into the blue sky, and wondered how it might be with his soul."[16]

Harriet would soon become too busy to have much time to admire Byron. When she was thirteen, she was pressed into the service of her sister. Catharine Beecher, eleven years older than Harriet, had founded the Hartford Female Seminary in 1823. With her ability and her openness to new methods of education, Catharine was to develop a school which would become well known far beyond the borders of New England, one which was, in fact, a landmark in the history of the education of women. Although the school had a modest beginning in a single room over a harness shop, it soon became a success and moved to better quarters. Harriet was no older than some of the pupils, but Catharine needed her too much to allow her to confine herself to being a student. She was something between a teaching assistant and a full-fledged teacher. In moving from Litchfield to Hartford, Harriet was thrown more upon her own resources. Catharine was not unkindly, but she had great demands upon her time and could spend little of it with Harriet. She set Harriet to learning a Latin grammar, largely without help. If necessary, Harriet could learn Latin by herself.[17]

It was about this time that Harriet wrote what was meant to be a classical verse drama. *Cleon* was a play named after a hero who, as Forrest Wilson has pointed out, reflects the influence of Byron. He also foreshadows the hero Augustine St. Clare in *Uncle Tom's Cabin*. The Cleon of the play is an athletic and fiery Greek youth, a winner in the Olympic games. He leaves his native country and goes to Rome, where he becomes a member of the court of Nero. We learn by genteel indirection that Cleon has had a profligate past. He has, however, been converted to Christianity, and now lives an exemplary life. Juvenile as the drama is, it illustrates what was to become a major theme in Harriet's fiction—a noble man or woman encounters in the world an evil which can be neither vanquished nor acquiesced to. At this stage of her development, Harriet could not bring herself to allow Nero to destroy Cleon. He sends Cleon to the torture chamber to make him renounce his faith but counteracts his orders in hopes of persuading him of the foolishness of his belief. At first, Cleon listens to the arguments of Nero; but he cannot bear to hear Jesus described as "a crazy Jew." Cleon says:

> I could sit still and hear myself reviled,
> But not my Sovereign!

As a compromise, Nero proposes that Cleon retain his religious faith but make no public profession of it. At this point Harriet laid down the unfinished work.[18]

When Catharine discovered that Harriet was writing a verse drama, she "pounced" on her younger sister and told her not to waste her time. She set Harriet to the formidable task of reading Joseph Butler's *The Analogy of Religion, Natural and Revealed, to the Constitution and Course of Nature.* In addition, Catharine employed a private tutor for Harriet, a Miss Degan who had been born in Italy, to give her private lessons in French and Italian, apparently with a view of preparing her to teach these subjects. When she was fourteen years old, Harriet was already teaching Butler's *Analogy* to a class of girls no younger than herself. She was obliged, she later said, "to master each chapter just ahead of the class I was teaching."[19]

Though she was probably overworked, Harriet suffered chiefly from the conviction that she was unregenerate and therefore damned. It was true that she had confessed her faith in Christ and was ostensibly a committed Christian. This was not, however, nearly enough for Calvinist theology. Her son, Charles Stowe, would later describe the more wrenching ordeal which lay ahead for her. The fact that the lamb had submitted was almost irrelevant, he said. Now it must be "chased all over the lot by the shepherd, great stress being laid, in those days, on what was called being 'under conviction.'" Charles Stowe told how Harriet went to the pastor of a church in Hartford with the hope of obtaining spiritual guidance. He turned out to be an advocate of the bleakest kind of Calvinist orthodoxy. One of the tortures to which a novice might be subjected was to ask him what his response would be if it should turn out that God had already decided to damn him. The expected reply was that one should be willing to suffer an eternity in hell without complaint, that is, to be damned for the glory of God. Charles Stowe reconstructed the conversation of the pastor and the child on the subject as his mother had told it to him. The minister put the terrible question in this way: "Harriet, do you feel that if the universe should be destroyed (awful pause) you could be happy with God alone?" Charles Stowe said that his mother struggled to absorb the meaning of the question and managed to answer, "Yes, sir." And then came the real point. "You realize, I trust, in some measure at least," said the pastor, "the deceitfulness of your heart, and that in punishment for your sins God might justly leave you to make yourself as miserable as you have made yourself sinful. . . ." To this, Harriet could only stammer out another "Yes, sir."[20]

There is some mystery in this story, since there is evidence that Lyman Beecher himself deplored this kind of logic. Later, when he became a minister in Boston, Lyman was said to have overheard a seminary student from Andover catechizing a convert. He asked the convert if she was willing "to be damned for the glory of God." At this point, Lyman was said to have interrupted the catechism and to have demanded of the student, "Well, sir, would you be willing?" "Yes, sir, I humbly hope I should be," the student replied. "Well, then, sir," Lyman is reported to have said, "you *ought* to be damned." Whether Charles Stowe misunderstood this early experience of Harriet's, whether Lyman really did combat this particular point of theology, whether his rejection of this doctrine came later are all questions to which there are no clear answers.[21]

Probably the major source of Harriet's troubles as an adolescent was that her father's modifications of Calvinism—what Henry Ward Beecher would call his father's "alleviated Calvinism"—did not much change the original doctrine. Lyman tried, for example, to comfort the parents of unbaptized infants, which Calvinist theology had traditionally consigned to hell. Lyman conceded that such infants were "justly liable to future punishment," but he argued that there was some hope that God might decide to save them. His interpretation of the Calvinist doctrine of election was no more encouraging. Optimistically, he argued that a person is free to choose salvation or damnation. Then he added that God may accept or reject the sinner's decision. Election having been banished from the front door has come in again at the back. Since Lyman was convinced that hell is "a real place full of real fire," the matter of salvation was especially agonizing. Even the charm of Lyman for his children was partially a snare, because behind it lay a grim theology which gave one little hope.[22]

One can hardly come away from a study of Lyman Beecher without reaching two quite different conclusions. One is that he was a remarkably good and able man. The other is less reassuring. He was engaged in a lifelong effort to modify the doctrines of Calvinism so that they would be more attractive to the climate of opinion of his time. In the process, he probably caused his children more anguish than comfort. They were led to think that their father's version of religion was more different from Calvinism than in fact it was. The kind of agonies which the children suffered are suggested by the experience of Catharine, whose fiancé was drowned. He was a church member and had shown every sign of being a committed Christian, but he had not undergone an experience of conversion, and thus Lyman could give Catharine no real hope that her fiancé had not gone to hell. Then there was the experience of Lyman's son Edward. He was the father of a son who was a congenital idiot. For the next forty years, Edward suffered from the idea that perhaps the defective son represented a sign of God's displeasure. His condition might be a punishment for the attempts of Edward himself to purge Calvinism of some of its doctrines. In later years Robert Ingersoll would describe Lyman Beecher as "one of the wardens of the Puritan penitentiary." Lyman was undoubtedly doing his best to reinterpret Calvinism to make it less objectionable. In some respects he was all the more a warden because he kept assuring the inmates that their prison was not a prison at all.[23]

Some of the letters of Harriet as an adolescent suggest her despair. When she was fourteen, she wrote to Edward, "My whole life is one continued struggle. I do nothing right. I yield to temptation almost as soon as it assails me. My deepest feelings are very evanescent. I am beset behind and before, and my sins take away all my happiness." In later years she came near mastering the defects of Calvinism. In her fiction, she would argue the inconsistency of predestination with the idea of a loving God. She would turn humor and folk wisdom against it. On the other hand, she never did wholly divest herself of pessimism concerning the odds in favor of predestination. Calvinism was associated in her mind not merely with the idea of divine election but with determinism generally. Sometimes the events of the world seemed to reveal to her a terrible inner logic of their own, and she would conclude that there is almost nothing a person can do to deflect them from their course. On the matter of slavery, she could neither wholly believe the idea that God in his own good time would abolish it nor have any sustained faith in purely human efforts to do so. Her difficulty is indicated by something which sometimes puzzled her readers. She could convincingly show the horrors of slavery. What she could not do was to imagine a process, a series of steps, by which slavery could be abolished.[24]

Lyman Beecher also caused Harriet difficulties of a different kind. Even when she was a small child, he recognized her unusual intelligence; but his chief reaction to it was to reflect that in a girl child it was wasted. In one of his household work projects, Lyman observed that Harriet went about the task assigned to her with such energy and intelligence that he was amazed. He "wished Harriet was a boy." If she had been, he added, "she would do more than any of them." In a letter written in 1819 when Harriet was eight years old, Lyman expressed a similar idea. "Harriet is a genius," he wrote. "I would give a hundred dollars if she was a boy. She is as odd as she is intelligent and studious." The child knew that her qualities would be more appreciated if she were a boy. She labored to fulfill the irrelevant requirement in an attempt to seem to be like one. When she carried wood, she said, "I remember putting on a little black coat which I thought looked more like the boys, working almost like one possessed . . . till in the afternoon all the wood was in." The fact that three of his daughters turned out to be women of achievement and of independent mind may suggest that Lyman was more flexible than these stories of his wishing Harriet were a boy would suggest. It is known that as a young man Lyman had read Mary Wollstonecraft's *Vindication of the Rights of Women*, but there is no indication of his opinion of it.[25]

About the time that Harriet was born, the Beecher family had an experience which demonstrated to them the evils of slavery. Aunt Mary, her mother's sister, had married John James Hubbard, a merchant in Jamaica whom she had met while he was visiting in New England. When she accompanied him to Jamaica, she discovered that he was the father of several mulatto children by slave women. A year later, Mary left her husband permanently, returning to New England horrified by slavery and particularly by the sexual license which it permitted. She died several weeks before Harriet was two years old, and thus Harriet was unlikely to have remembered her. What she apparently later recalled was the retelling by members of the Beecher family of Mary's accounts of her life in Jamaica. "What she [Mary] saw and heard of slavery," Harriet wrote many years later, "filled her with constant horror and loathing. She has said that she often sat by her window in the tropical night, when all was still, and wished that the island might sink in the ocean, with all its sin and misery, and that she might sink with it." Mary's experience with slavery probably influenced one of Harriet's major themes in her anti-slavery fiction—the wrongs women suffered from slavery.[26]

Another of Harriet's recollections of a discussion of slavery came definitely from her own memory. In 1851, while she was writing *Uncle Tom's Cabin*, Frederick Douglass complained to her concerning the general lack of interest in slavery in the northern churches. Harriet wrote him a soothing letter with the theme that there had been more concern than he realized. As an example, she recalled that when she was a child of nine, her father on the occasion of the passage by Congress of the Missouri Compromise of 1820 had preached a sermon upon slavery. "[O]ne of the strongest and deepest impressions on my mind," she said, "was that made by my father's sermons and prayers, and the anguish of his soul for the poor slave at that time." He had pleaded with the Lord for the cause of " 'poor, oppressed, bleeding Africa,' that the time of her deliverance might come; prayers offered with strong crying and tears, which indelibly impressed my heart and made me what I am from my very soul, the enemy of all slavery." As it turned out, however, Lyman would always be remarkably lukewarm as an enemy of slavery. For him, abolition was one of those projects which God might have in mind for the future but which the Christians of his own time need not become unduly exercised about.[27]

As a child, Harriet had only a few associations with blacks. There were two young black girls who were bound apprentices in the Beecher household in Litchfield. They left when Harriet was five years old, probably too soon for her to remember them clearly. She did refer briefly to two other blacks in the nearby household of her Aunt Harriet, another sister of her mother. Aunt Harriet, an Episcopalian, taught Harriet and her own daughter Mary the catechism. Harriet and Mary were made to sit "bolt upright at . . . [Aunt Harriet's] knee," but "black Dinah and Harvey the bound-boy were at a respectful distance behind us." Aunt Harriet had strong feelings about the precedence of rank and she "always impressed it upon her servants 'to order themselves lowly and reverently to all their betters'. . . ." Harriet humorously recalled that this was "a portion of the Church Catechism which always pleased me, particularly when applied to *them*, for it insured their calling me 'Miss Harriet,' and treating me with a degree of consideration which I never enjoyed in the more democratic circle at home."[28]

In the mind of the Beecher family at the time of Harriet's childhood, racial caste may have been mixed with the idea of moral contagion. In a biographical sketch of Henry Ward Beecher, published in 1868, Harriet recalled that he had not been allowed to play with a black child who lived near by in Litchfield. "The only association of doubtful character forbidden to Henry," she said, "was Ulysses Freeman, a poor, merry, softly giggling negro boy, who inhabited a hut not far off. . . ." The reason for this prohibition, she added, was that it was "feared"—she did not say by whom—that Ulysses might teach Henry "something that he ought not to know." Harriet did not criticize her parents on this issue.[29]

The religious tradition in which Harriet grew up had not been deeply involved with the issue of slavery. Such antislavery sentiment as had existed in the North had come more from the influence of the Quakers than from the traditional Protestant churches. On the other hand, we can sense that if there were any way to arouse the energy which Calvinist Christians were capable of, the results might be remarkable. The slaveholders of the South might have as much to fear from such Christians as Charles II did from the Puritans of England. The course of antislavery still had a long way to travel, but at the time when Harriet was a child there were already a few indications of the direction it might take.

II

Hartford and Boston

1826-1832

IN 1826, WHEN HARRIET was fifteen years old, Lyman Beecher accepted a call to the Hanover Church in Boston. His mission there was to revive the Congregational churches; what that principally meant was to combat the Unitarians. Especially exasperating to Congregational and Presbyterian churches was the fact that the Unitarian church was partly the outgrowth of ideas which had originally been espoused by the older denominations. Calvinists had generally prided themselves upon their logic. When the Unitarians rebelled against Calvinism, they rejected most of its theological dogmas but not its rationalism. For the Unitarians, the flaw of the Calvinists was that they were not logical enough. For the Calvinists, the authority of the Bible was absolute—logic might interpret the scriptures but not deny their truth. The Unitarians subjected the Bible itself to "logical" analysis, accepting what seemed to them reasonable and rejecting what did not. They were willing to accept God as an all-loving and all-powerful authority. On the other hand, he was not a "Trinity" but a single being. Once the idea that inconvenient scripture could be rejected had been established, the Unitarians were free to develop a religion more at home with ideas of philosophical inquiry and of science. A Unitarian could be "religious" without troubling himself much with the issue of whether his ideas squared with those in the Bible.

Religion was made more intellectually respectable but at the same time purged of much of its passion. The Unitarians did not, for example, agonize over salvation; they did not believe in it at all in any sense which was not purely rational. The former terrors of hell virtually disappeared.

The stronghold of the Unitarians was Boston, but even there they did not outnumber the orthodox church members. On the other hand, they were frequently wealthy and influential and thus exerted more power than their numbers would indicate. Lyman Beecher might not seem, at first glance, to have been the clergyman to lead the campaign of the orthodox churches to conquer these aristocrats. He had never paid much attention to his personal appearance. His wife and daughters had always had the task of seeing that he appeared in the pulpit with his cravat tied straight, his hair brushed and combed, and his shoes polished. In addition, he used folksy stories in his sermons and sometimes adopted a provincial pronunciation for the sake of humor. Years later, James Russell Lowell would create the character Hosea Biglow of his *Biglow Papers* who would satirize the proponents of the Mexican War and of slavery in dialect verse. Lowell's position in society was unquestioned, but when Lyman Beecher used such words as "natur'" and "creeter" in his sermons, it is probable that important members of the community winced. William Ellery Channing, the leader of the Unitarians, recognized that upperclass Boston was sometimes snobbish. A man who betrayed in "brogue or uncouth tones his want of cultivation," said Channing, could not take the place among Unitarians "to which, perhaps, his native good sense entitled him." Lyman was not uncouth, but neither was he the kind of man usually admired by genteel members of the upper class.[1]

Lyman was intelligent enough to recognize that orthodoxy would not succeed with cultivated Bostonians through the straightforward sermons he had preached in Litchfield. He might have decided at this point to lambaste privilege and corruption among the upper classes, with the implication that the Lord's anointed were members of the middle and lower classes. Instead, he attempted to conciliate those Unitarians who were willing to listen to him. The nature of some of his work is indicated by his writing in a letter to his son Edward of two "young ladies," a "young man of intelligence," and another "intelligent young man," all of whom were Unitarians but troubled enough about the validity of their beliefs to discuss them with him. To Catharine he wrote that he was creating "no small stir upon the Unitarians" and had "great hopes for the future."[2]

On one issue which would turn out to be important, Lyman agreed with his principal opponent, Channing. Both men were convinced that though slavery was an evil it could be brought to an end only gradually and with the consent of the slaveholders themselves. Thus, both men were disturbed when William Lloyd Garrison established the *Liberator* in Boston in 1831 and began to advocate immediate emancipation. As a young man, Channing had been the tutor of the son of a prominent Virginia family in Richmond. This experience, while not making him an apologist for slavery, had given him at least some recognition of how firmly embedded the institution was in the South and how difficult it would be to abolish it. He hoped nonetheless to convince the white people of the South that slavery was wrong, but he hoped that discussion of it would not involve ugly confrontations with proslavery factions.[3]

Garrison was an intense spirit who threw himself into the battle against slavery with a vigor which exhilarated the immediate emancipationists, infuriated the white South, and dismayed those who hoped for compromise and gradual abolition. Born in Newburyport, Massachusetts, Garrison came from a poor and unstable family. His father, a shoemaker, was a drunkard who deserted his family. William Lloyd Garrison himself was self-educated. He had developed an interest in writing and controversy by his work setting type for newspapers. By the time he came to choose an occupation, there was no doubt that it would be that of a reformer. The only uncertainty was which reforms he would advocate. At one time or another he espoused temperance, the observance of the Sabbath, antitobacco, antigambling (he was opposed even to raffles at church fairs), and pacifism. In time, he decided not to spread himself too thin among reforms, and thus he eventually concentrated on abolition. He settled in Boston in 1830, and on January 1, 1831, there appeared the first issue of the *Liberator*, a weekly which never in its thirty-five-year history had a large number of subscribers but which was destined to exert a great influence. Seldom has there been an editorial statement in the first issue of a publication which indicated more clearly what its readers might expect:

I am aware, that many object to the severity of my language; but is there not cause for severity? I *will be* as harsh as truth, and as uncompromising as justice. On this subject I do not wish to think, or speak, or write, with moderation. No! no! Tell a man whose house is on fire, to give a moderate alarm; tell him to moderately rescue his wife from the hands of a ravisher; tell the mother to gradually extricate her babe from the fire into which it has fallen;—but urge me not to use moderation in a cause like the present. I am in earnest—I would not equivocate—I will not excuse—I will not retreat a single inch—AND I WILL BE HEARD.[4]

Since Garrison could not find an antislavery church in Boston, he was a member of none. Later his children would say that he often attended Lyman Beecher's church and that he considered himself a member of it "as much as any." At the beginning of their acquaintance and for several years afterward, Garrison and Lyman Beecher were friendly though wary with one another. In 1829, Garrison paid tribute to Lyman. "As a divine," he said, "Lyman Beecher has no equal." The chief source of Lyman's strength, Garrison believed, was "Truth—TRUTH—delivered in a childlike simplicity and affection." Lyman Beecher and Garrison had certain qualities in common. Both of them, for example, strongly emphasized logical debate. Thomas Wentworth Higginson later noted that Garrison's "vocabulary," for all its emotion, never abandoned an emphasis on reason and that his method of approach was "the logical result of that stern school of old-fashioned Calvinism in which he had been trained." In certain respects, Beecher might almost seem to be a mentor of Garrison. "Controversy has always been the great instrument of recovering individuals and communities from the dominion of error," he said on one occasion. "Abuses never reform themselves. Depravity never purifies itself."[5]

The major difference between the two men was that Lyman Beecher used more caution than Garrison in choosing his causes. In Litchfield, Beecher had organized the Connecticut Society for the Reformation of Morals, its purpose being to protect society against "Sabbath-breakers, rum-sellers, tippling folk, infidels, and ruff-scuff." In Boston, he organized a society to outvote the minions of Satan in the form of whiskey drinkers and Sabbath breakers. Members of his Hanover Association of Young Men were sent into the city primary elections with instructions to counteract the influence of "smoking loafers" and to work for the removal of liquor stands from the Boston Common on Sundays. It is true that Lyman was capable of arousing opposition. He was so strongly associated with the cause of temperance that when the Hanover Street Church burned the local firemen refused to help save it because of their resentment of his efforts to restrict the sale of liquor. He did have a killjoy side. He was the leader, for example, in a campaign to prohibit

Sunday steamboat excursions from Boston to Nahant. Garrison himself had once advocated two of Beecher's causes—temperance and opposition to Sabbath breaking—but he later came to feel that both issues were unimportant and, in fact, were put forward as substitutes for such genuine reforms as abolition.[6]

Beecher and Garrison attempted to influence each other. In 1830, Garrison made a fiery abolition speech and Lyman was in the audience. After the address, he approached the platform and attempted to convince Garrison that she should be more moderate. "Your zeal is commendable," Lyman is said to have told him. "But you are misguided." If only Garrison would be less vehement, Lyman assured him, he might become the Wilberforce of America. Such an ideal was impossible for Garrison to achieve. Even if he had been temperamentally similar to Wilberforce, which he was not, he was situated differently. Wilberforce had had high connections in the British government and among influential people generally. In addition, he was a member of Parliament during most of his career. Garrison, by contrast, was a man without an established position, influential friends (at least for a long time), or money.[7]

Several years later, Catharine Beecher would publicly make the charge against Garrison that he damaged the antislavery cause by his intemperate language. She compared him unfavorably to the leaders of abolition in England. Garrison was eloquently defended by Richard Hildreth, the author of *The Slave; or Memoirs of Archy Moore* (1836), the best of the early abolition novels:

[L]et us grant the fact that the anti-slavery leaders are ever so inferior in character to Wilberforce and Clarkson; that certainly is rather the misfortune of the abolitionists, than their fault, and perhaps it is not so much proof that their cause is bad, as that it is unpopular. They have been obliged to take such leaders as offered. Have they not called upon [Lyman] Beecher . . . and other men of immaculate character, to come over and help them, and have they not held back? The priest and the scribe declining to act, it becomes necessary to be content with publicans and sinners.[8]

On one occasion, Garrison attempted directly to enlist the aid of Lyman Beecher in the abolition crusade. This encounter Harriet described many years later in an essay which included one of her rare critical comments about her father. She said that Lyman listened courteously to the plea of Garrison but objected that he himself had so many " 'irons in the fire' that he could not think of putting in another." "Then," Harriet reported Garrison as replying, "*you had better let all the others go, and attend to this one alone."* Time had shown, Harriet said, "that the young printer saw further than the sages of his day." In another encounter, Garrison is said to have asked Lyman whether slavery was not a national sin. Lyman agreed that it was. "Well, then, in accordance with your doctrine of immediate repentance," Garrison is quoted as replying, "is it not the duty of the nation to repent immediately of the sin of slavery and emancipate the slaves?" In exasperation, Lyman is said to have replied, "Oh, Garrison, you can't reason that way! Great economic and political questions can't be solved so simply. You must take into account what is expedient as well as what is right."[9]

Lyman kept hoping for conciliation between the North and South, a conciliation which would lead to a plan for gradual abolition. He himself was convinced that American blacks ought to return to Africa. "Were it in my power to put an end to slavery immediately, I would do it," he said in a characteristic statement,

but it is not. I can only pursue the measures best calculated, in my judgment, to get the slaves out of bondage in the shortest time, and the best manner; and this, as I view the subject, is to make emancipation easy instead of difficult, to make use of the current of human fears and passions and interests when they may be made to set in our favor instead of attempting to row up-stream against them.

On one occasion, he described Garrisonian abolitionists as "men who would burn down their houses to get rid of the rats."[10]

Lyman was a member of the American Colonization Society. This was an organization which had been founded in 1817 with two rather different motives. One was to Christianize Africa by founding a homeland for American blacks there; the other was—though it was seldom openly admitted—to rid the United States of as many blacks as possible. Through the efforts of the society, the new African colony of Liberia had been founded.

The society encountered opposition from groups which were very different from one another. Slaveholders were frequently suspicious of it, thinking it provided refuge for reformers whose true mission would eventually turn out to be abolition. Free blacks protested that the real purpose of the society was to banish them from the country. They also argued that if free blacks emigrated to Liberia, their absence from the United States would bind the chains more securely upon black slaves. Garrison attacked the colonizationists with all his power. He argued that those slaves who were sent to Liberia would probably be old and worn-out. The plan would enable the slaveholders to evade the duty of taking care of slaves who had spent their lives working for them.[11]

Catharine was the first member of the Beecher family to become involved in attempts to help oppressed peoples. Women, she believed, were naturally the guardians of benevolence, and thus she encouraged her students to express their concern for people who were persecuted or who suffered from natural disasters. They sent bandages and other supplies to the Greeks in their war for independence against the Turks. In this country, when the state of Georgia began expelling the Cherokee Indians from their homelands and sending them on the "Trail of Tears" to the West, Catharine formed a woman's auxiliary to aid several Boston ministers who opposed the removal. To arouse support for the Indians, she wrote a pamphlet, *To the Benevolent Women of the United States*, which was widely distributed. Professor Benjamin Silliman of Yale read it and said that it was worthy of the elder Pitt. Harriet, still a teen-ager, was amused by the appellation and began calling Catharine "old Mrs. Pitt."[12]

Abolition was not, however, one of the reforms which Catharine undertook herself or recommended for her students. It was too controversial. She had two ideals for women which were not wholly consistent with one another. They should be benevolent and humanitarian; on the other hand, they should avoid controversy. They might appeal to the altruism of the nation, but they were not supposed publicly to castigate their opponents. The cause of the Indians in Georgia she apparently considered as unlikely to arouse animosity in New England, and therefore she could afford to support it. But slavery was a different matter.

Harriet was apparently too young to take any part in the humanitarian causes espoused by Catharine. In addition, she was still absorbed in her despair over her unredeemed soul. "I wish I could die young and let the remembrance of me and my faults perish in the grave," she wrote when she was fifteen to Catharine, "rather than live a life of trouble to everyone. How perfectly wretched I often feel—so useless, so weak, so destitute of all energy!" In an attempt at least to appear cheerful, she counterfeited good spirits so enthusiastically that Lyman Beecher rebuked her for it.[13]

Harriet might have resigned herself patiently to the contradictions of Calvinism as beyond human understanding; this is what many people did. Even as an adolescent, however, she showed a hint of the rebel to come. God seemed to give man the irresistible urge to sin, she complained, and then damned him for it. To Edward she wrote a letter which skirted outright skepticism:

The wonder to me is, how all the ministers and all Christians can feel themselves so inexcusably sinful when it seems to me we all come to the world in such a way that it would be miraculous if we did not sin. Mr. Hawes always says in prayer, "We have nothing to offer in extenuation of any of our sins," and I always think when he says it, that we have everything to offer in extenuation. The case seems to me exactly as if I had been brought into the world with such a thirst for ardent spirits that there was just a possibility, though no hope, that I should resist, and then my eternal happiness made dependent on my being temperate. Sometimes when I try to confess my sins I feel that after all I am more to be pitied than blamed, for I have never known the time when I have not had a temptation within me so strong that it was certain I should not overcome it. This thought shocks me, but it comes with such force, and so appealingly to all my consciousness, that it stifles all sense of sin.[14]

Harriet was capable even of charging God with being deliberately unfair. In the Book of Job, "God seems to strip a dependent creature of all that renders life desirable," she wrote to Edward, and then to find it odd that Job complained. Instead of "showing mercy and pity" to Job, God had appeared in a whirlwind and "overwhelmed him by a display of his power and justice." A God who "sympathizes with his guilty, afflicted creatures, would not have spoken thus." Drawing back from the implication of infidelity, she found a refuge in the religion of the New Testament. There, "in the character of Jesus Christ," she found "a revelation of God as merciful and compassionate; in fact just such a God as I need."[15]

Lyman Beecher had encouraged his children to think deeply and to argue logically, secure in his belief that his own theological system would hold. We find Harriet obeying his injunction in a way which probably would have dismayed him if he had been fully aware of it. She probably knew better than to bring such questions to him; at least, there is little evidence that she did. A woman like this would hardly be likely, when twenty-two years later she came to write Uncle Tom's Cabin, to accept piously the biblical arguments advanced in support of slavery. Already in Harriet there was a mind and spirit engaged in a radical quest for truth. She had a willingness to give her intellect the free play which explains her later power more than does her Christian piety, more perhaps—in some respects—than does her humanitarian concern.

Probably more important than theological speculation for Harriet was the fact that, even when she was eighteen, she was already thinking seriously about the problems of writing an acceptable style. To her friend and fellow teacher, Mary Dutton, Harriet wrote in 1830 of her plans to teach a class in composition:

I am quite busy preparing for my composition class—have been reading Rasselas & writing a little in imitation of Dr. Johnson's style—think it is improving me by giving me a command of language—The man writes as if some Fairy had spell bound [*sic*] him & given him the task of putting every word in his great dictionary in his book as a means of release—I have been spouting at Catharine respecting "*general & transcendental truths*" & "errors of exaggeratory declamation" ever since. For half an hour I was quite "ove rotundo" & could not even shut a closet door except in a double antithesis— My plan this summer is to have the young ladies imitate the style of various authors & read the English Classics—Respecting composition I think that never yet have time & attention been enough given to it to have it well taught—I mean it shall be this summer.

In the same letter she spoke of her plans to write a series of "Sketches of female characters," but there is no record of her having done so.[16]

Harriet profited from the intensity of the Beecher commitment to ideas and to human welfare, however limited or even wrong some of these ideas may seem to us now. In addition, she had a quality which her brothers and sisters and her father did not have strongly developed. For them, the ideas themselves were the important thing, and how they were expressed was decidedly secondary. Harriet was more than they a reader of imaginative literature and, in addition, though not yet committed to the career of a writer she was at least interested in it.

III

Cincinnati

1832-1850

IN 1832, WHEN HARRIET was twenty-one, Lyman Beecher embarked on a new crusade—that of saving the West. He was called to be president of Lane Seminary in Cincinnati, a new institution which he himself had played a major part in establishing. The Unitarians had not, it is true, been routed from New England. On the other hand, it was generally agreed that Lyman had rallied and invigorated the conservative Protestant churches. One of his friends said of him that "no minister in New England" was "so uniformly dreaded and hated by Unitarians as Dr. B." Another friend, Dr. Nathaniel Taylor, pastor of the Centre Church of New Haven, thought Lyman had been so successful as a champion of orthodoxy in Boston that he ought to stay there. "Truth and the interests of religion" demanded, Taylor said, that Lyman should work where he had clearly shown a special talent. From the point of view of his reputation, staying would probably have been the better course for Lyman, though he could not foresee this result. He was fifty-seven years old. If he had stayed, he would probably have ended his career as a figure of honor rather than—as it turned out—one badly bruised in battle.[1]

There was no doubt, however, that Lyman preferred going to Cincinnati to staying in Boston. With the enthusiasm of his temperament he transferred the chief responsibility for his going to the West to God.

"When the Lord calls I will go," Lyman said in one of his sermons, "and I will send my children." Apparently it was not necessary to bother the Lord with so minor a decision as that of whether the children should go, and they themselves were unlikely to object. Thus it happened that most of the children went with their father—"terrible as an army with banners," as one of them humorously put it. At one time or another, all the children of Lyman Beecher lived in what is now the Middle West, with the exception of his nonactivist daughter, Mary, who had married a lawyer and settled down in Hartford. Even before Lyman had decided to go to the West, he was certain of the overwhelming importance of winning the region for the orthodox Protestant faith. "If we gain the West, all is safe," he wrote to Catharine in 1830; "if we lose it, all is lost."[2]

Cincinnati was then a city of 30,000 people—the third largest in the United States. It was already a place of fine houses and churches, and it would be one of the few cities in the United States admired by Charles Dickens when he visited this country in 1842. Catharine went with her father on a preliminary trip and wrote back enthusiastically to Harriet, "I know of no place in the world where there is so fair a prospect that makes social and domestic life pleasant." She also found the women she met in Cincinnati to be "intelligent, New England sort of folks." Cincinnati was, she thought—though on this point she would prove to be quite wrong—"a New England city in all its habits."[3]

For one thing, the economic interests of Cincinnati were seen by its citizens to lie primarily in a different direction from those of New England. Much of the trade of the city was along the Ohio and Mississippi rivers, and thus the economy of the city was closely allied with that of some of the southern states. The economic concerns of the city were clearly seen when the railroads began to build. The city's leaders were more interested in establishing a link with the Carolinas and Georgia than with the northeastern states. Most New Englanders who came to live in Cincinnati quickly learned that it was not prudent to express too strongly the opinion that slavery might not be a legitimate institution.[4]

Lyman came to Cincinnati prepared to fight one battle, observes one of his biographers, only to find himself obliged to fight another. It was abolition which proved to be the major issue in Cincinnati, not the saving of the West from irreligion, profligacy, and Catholicism. Theodore Weld, the student destined to lead the revolt against Lyman, had the traits of an authentic prophet. He had a "severity" combined with a "deep wild gloom" of manner. He was twenty-eight years old when he enrolled at Lane Seminary. That he was older than most college students is less surprising than it might seem. Late conversions have always meant that seminaries have a larger number of older students than most other schools. Weld was not much older than many of the other students at Lane, and some of them were as old as thirty-five. He lived an exemplary personal life. He was not yet married but later would become the husband of Angelina Grimké, the daughter of a prominent slaveholding family in the South but destined to be one of the leading figures of the abolition movement.[5]

The question for Theodore Weld was simply whether slavery was right or wrong. If it was wrong, then it should be combatted with all the resources at the command of Christians. Glowing with ardor but also fortified with the New England tradition of logical debate—he was born in Massachusetts—Weld began at Lane to attempt to persuade the other students to his point of view. He organized small groups for discussions of slavery. Men who "sympathized together" in their "abhorrence of slavery selected each his man to instruct, convince and enlist in the cause." Thus, Weld later wrote, "we carried one after another." In time, the individual groups came together. Now the antislavery students were ready to hold a meeting of the entire student body at which the question of slavery would be discussed. What evolved was not a debate, exactly, but a protracted session in which anyone who cared to speak was allowed to stand and express his opinions. In all this, Weld was clearly the leader. He was an accomplished orator. He had a deep and resonant voice; he knew how to speak with fluency and precision; he emphasized the issue and only incidentally his own relation to it.[6]

Weld had carefully studied the arguments for and against slavery. It was an age of oratory and perhaps this fact can partially explain that in one of the discussions he "held the floor for eighteen hours." He overwhelmed the audience with arguments. "His speech," one member of the audience said, "was a thesaurus, giving the origin, history, effects, both upon the despot and the victim, of slavery." The result was virtually inevitable. Slavery was censured; colonization was censured; and immediate emancipation was approved. The vote among the student body was unanimous.[7]

It was bad enough for the students to do this in a city where proslavery sentiment was strong. It was worse to put their principles into practice with regard to the equality of the races. "We have formed a large and efficient organization for elevating the colored people in Cincinnati," Weld wrote to Arthur Tappan, the New York merchant who had espoused and financed abolition causes,

have established a Lyceum among them, and lecture three or four evenings a week on Grammar, Geography, Arithmetic, Natural Philosophy, etc. Besides this, an evening free school for teaching them to read, is in operation every week-day evening, and we are about establishing one or two more. . . . I visited this week about thirty families and found some of the members of more than half . . . were in bondage.

Cautious people might regard Weld as foolhardy, but he was not oblivious to the possibility that his activities and those of the other students might lead them into serious trouble. "May God make us more humble, fearless, unflinching, full of faith, and of the Holy Ghost, full of sympathy for suffering humanity," he wrote, "and rejoicing that we are counted worthy to suffer shame for his name."[8]

Probably more potentially dangerous than the principles of the students were their friendly associations with blacks in Cincinnati. "If I ate in the City," Weld wrote to Lewis, the brother of Arthur Tappan and also a wealthy New York merchant and a friend of abolition, "it was at their [the blacks'] tables. If I slept in the City it was in their homes. If I attended parties, it was *theirs—weddings—theirs—Funerals—theirs —Sabbath School Bible classes—theirs*." The statement was not quite as daring as it seemed because Weld did not publicize in the white community his attendance at black gatherings. In the same letter he warned Lewis Tappan that the abolitionists should always keep as their primary goal the destruction of slavery and remember that such "collateral" goals as meetings with blacks were secondary. "There are times," he said, "when we may refrain from making *public visible demonstrations* about difference of color in practical exhibitions, when such demonstrations would bring down persecution on . . . [the blacks]."[9]

In addition to his influence with the students, Weld would become a formidable opponent of Lyman Beecher for another reason. He had powerful friends in Arthur and Lewis Tappan, men who had helped to endow Lane Seminary; Arthur had also been one of the men who had supported Lyman for the post as president. After Lyman had come to Cincinnati, however, Arthur Tappan had undergone a significant change of opinion with regard to colonization. For one thing, he discovered that some of the emigrants to Liberia had become more interested in importing liquor than missionaries from the United States. He began to wonder whether colonization, which he formerly considered to be "this splendid scheme of benevolence," might not be something quite different. He doubted whether the chief motive of the colonizationists had been to free the slaves. Colonization might be, he reflected, "a device of Satan to rivet still closer the fetters of the slaves." His suspicion became a settled conviction. "I now believe," he wrote, "that . . . [colonization] had its origin in the single motive to get rid of the free colored people, that the slaves . . . [might] be held in greater safety." Arthur Tappan had urged Theodore Weld to enroll at Lane Seminary as a student. Since Tappan's position with regard to colonization came to be virtually identical with that of Weld and quite different from that of Lyman Beecher, it was obvious that Lyman would have to act circumspectly.[10]

Calvin Stowe, who would become Harriet's husband, would write of Lyman Beecher after his death that he had possessed "not a little of the old Connecticut prejudice about blacks." Stowe taught at Lane Seminary for eighteen years while Lyman was president and was in a position to know, but there is evidence that Lyman was less prejudiced than this remark would indicate. Lane Seminary had, for example, admitted a black student as early as 1832. James Bradley was a former slave who had "purchased his own body," that is, earned a sufficient sum from wages which his master had allowed him to keep to buy his freedom. When Bradley, probably through a desire not to offend the code of racial caste, had stayed away from a reception for the students at the home of the president, Lyman was genuinely disturbed. He is reported to have said that "if he had thought of . . . [Bradley's] feeling so, he would have gone to him personally and told him he *must* come." One black student may not appear to be a large number, but Bradley was then one of the very few blacks who had been allowed to enroll in an institution of higher learning in this country. The same year that Bradley enrolled at Lane, Charles B. Ray, a black, enrolled at Wesleyan College in Connecticut, but because of student protests he was obliged to withdraw.[11]

Lyman was not inflexible in his attitude to the students' discussions on slavery. He himself at first agreed to take part in the debates. Caution may have been the reason for his changing his mind and sending Catharine in his place. Lyman was chiefly concerned that the activities of the students off campus might lead to serious trouble for both them and the seminary. He commended them for trying to help the blacks in Cincinnati, but he urged them to be careful not to arouse "the slumbering demon of pro-slavery fanaticism." "Said I," he later recalled, "you . . . [will] defeat your own object. . . . If you want to teach colored schools, I can fill your pockets with money; but if you visit in families and walk with them in the streets, you will be overwhelmed." The students, for their part, showed themselves receptive to cautionary advice. They argued that rumors which had them associating freely with blacks were untrue. "[I]f any member of the Seminary had, at any time, walked with a colored young lady either in the city or out of it," they said in a prepared statement, "no one of us had any knowledge of it."[12]

Lyman's warnings to the students were understandable. Cincinnati had a history of hostility and violence toward blacks. In 1804 and 1807, Ohio had passed laws requiring free blacks entering the state to post bonds as a guarantee of their good behavior and to prove their freedom by a court certificate. For twenty years or so the laws were not stringently enforced. As more blacks moved into the city, however, the whites became restive. In 1829, blacks had come to constitute about 10 percent of the population. Suddenly the city announced that the blacks must either post bonds or leave within thirty days. Impatient mobs of lower-class whites began to attempt to hurry the departure of the blacks by attacking them on the streets and by rampaging through "Buckstown" and destroying their homes. Respectable Cincinnati sat by and did nothing. A large number of blacks, at least eleven hundred and perhaps twice as many as that, left the city, some of them settling in Canada.[13]

In 1834, when the crisis over the students' espousal of abolition came to a head, Lyman obviously confronted a dilemma. If he supported the students, he risked being dismissed and perhaps even seeing the destruction of Lane Seminary by a mob. If he did not support the students, he would probably lose their loyalty. There is at least a chance that he might have worked out a compromise with the students, but the Lane trustees intervened. While Lyman was traveling in the East to raise funds, they appointed a special committee to study the problem. There were two societies concerned with slavery on the campus, one which advocated immediate emancipation and another which, up until the time when its members had been converted to abolition by Weld, had advocated colonization. The committee of the trustees recommended that both societies be abolished. The students had not come to Lane Seminary to agitate, they said, but to study. They should not become involved in advocating reforms "upon which able men, and pious Christians differ." If the students persisted in discussing the subject of slavery, they would "unsettle the judgement, and unfit the mind for genial and useful intercourse with mankind." From the community they could expect only "a heated torrent of unextinguishable rancor." Accordingly, the trustee committee recommended that no mention at all of antislavery be allowed among the students unless it was specifically authorized by the faculty. The prohibition extended not merely to public meetings but also to individual discussions among the students "when assembled at their meals, or on ordinary occasions. . . ." In addition, the students must cease their efforts to aid the black community. Any student who would not agree to comply with the new regulations should be dismissed. The trustees met and passed the recommendations of the special committee with only one dissenting vote.[14]

When forced to choose between the students and the trustees, Lyman chose—like many another college president—the trustees. The students must submit to the new rules against free discussion and free association, he said, or leave. The students left. In October, 1834, virtually all of them walked out of Lane Seminary. In a three-day period, forty of the students requested permission to leave. Lyman tried to repair the damage. He persuaded the trustees to rescind the prohibition against free discussion. It was too late; the students refused to come back. Most of them enrolled at the recently organized Oberlin Collegiate Institute in northern Ohio. Soon afterward, Arthur Tappan in New York provided funds for Oberlin with a "princely liberality." Theodore Weld was shrewd enough to know that a more telling point against Lane Seminary than its attitude to slavery would be its denial of freedom of speech. He argued that "*free* discussion . . . is a DUTY, and of course a RIGHT." At Lane Seminary, "free discussion" had been "prohibited *by law*."[15]

Toward Theodore Weld, Lyman Beecher would have an ambivalent attitude. A battler himself, he could admire—at least to some extent—other battlers. Eventually he would pay tribute to Weld's "talents, and piety, and moral courage, and energy," and he could speak of his own pride in the fact that he had "never quarrelled" with him. On the other hand, at the time of the departure of the students from Lane, Lyman was bitter. "[A]ll our difficulties were originated and continued by the instrumentality of an influential member of the Abolition Society," he said, "with the express design of making the institution subservient to the cause of abolition. . . ." This person had been willing, Lyman said, to sacrifice "the prosperity of the seminary itself." The fact that he was willing to do so could only be described as "monomania."[16]

Lyman's position in the dispute at Lane is something of a puzzle. He had always said he encouraged his children to think logically and to allow their minds to move from premises to conclusions without being aghast at where logic might lead them. He may have thought that he would be there to steer the minds of his children in the direction in which he thought they ought to go. About the students, Lyman probably had a feeling not essentially different from the one he had toward his own children. They were to think boldly and freely except, apparently, when such thinking might lead them in a direction which he strongly disapproved. Or perhaps another factor entered here. Lyman was a great persuader and conciliator, but he was fundamentally an institutional man. If he could not make the institution bend, he would go along with it. Thus, when the trustees spoke out against freedom of discussion of slavery, Lyman was willing to acquiesce to them and to insist that the students do so.[17]

At the time of the troubles at Lane Seminary, Harriet said about them, so far as we know, nothing at all, not even in her private letters. Because the Beechers nearly always stood together when attacked by outsiders, it is unlikely that she would have said anything even if she had been much older and more independent of her father. With their strong convictions, it might seem almost inevitable that the Beechers would quarrel with one another. They rarely did and almost never in public. When *Uncle Tom's Cabin* was published, Wendell Phillips praised it. He could not resist making a point against Lyman Beecher, however, as the man who had long opposed the abolitionists. He mentioned Lyman's role in stifling free discussion at Lane. Unwilling to remain silent in the face of this attack upon her father, Harriet wrote a letter to Phillips and gave him permission to publish it. She said that the Lane trustees had passed their resolutions when her father and Calvin Stowe were in New England. When they returned to Cincinnati they found "such a state of feeling" among the trustees "that they had no choice, except to throw up their professorships, or to submit to them." Lyman Beecher had sensibly chosen, she said, "to submit temporarily to those regulations. So much for that." Though she admired Theodore Weld, when she was forced to choose between him and her father, the decision was in favor of her father. "With all credit to my good brother Theodore," she wrote in her letter to Phillips, "I must say that prudence is not his forte, and that there was a plentiful lack of that useful article in all those worthy reformers. . . . It seems to me that it is not necessary always to present a disagreeable subject in the most disagreeable way possible, and needlessly to shock prejudices. . . ."[18]

Phillips wrote to Theodore Weld and asked him concerning Stowe's version of events at Lane Seminary. By this time, Weld had retired from the antislavery struggle, but he still retained a bitter memory of the role of Lyman Beecher at Lane Seminary. To Phillips' question as to whether Stowe's statements concerning her father's position were correct, Weld replied, "Partly correct, but *substantially not.* Technically Dr. B 'did not silence the discussion in Lane Seminary.'" Weld compared Lyman's position with that of Paul in the stoning of Stephen in the Bible and of Calvin in the burning of Servetus. Neither Paul nor Calvin had been actually responsible for the deaths of the two men, said Weld, but they had "consented" to them. Dr. Beecher had "assured me privately," said Weld, "that he was heartily with me in principle except upon [illegible word] but *publicly* he was on the side of the trustees." Weld said that he had "implored the Doctor to proclaim it [his opposition to the position of the trustees] to the housetops. His answer was, 'It would blow me sky high.'" Phillips did not publish Weld's letter. In a reply to Stowe, which was published, he merely questioned whether the influence of Lyman Beecher had "ever been distinctly felt on the slave's side." He said that Beecher's "first public explicit word in behalf of the Anti-slavery cause is yet to be uttered."[19]

Harriet would have been more frank if she had admitted that Lyman Beecher's role in antislavery had not, as she knew very well, been anything to be proud of. Lyman's silence on the issue of the ban on free discussion at Lane Seminary in 1834 was generally interpreted to mean that he sided with the trustees. In his letter to Phillips in 1853, Weld said that when he left Lane in 1834 and began to lecture on slavery "along the Ohio river," he found "the Doctor's course respecting the discussions in the Seminary quoted every where by professing Christians as a reason for refusing to give me a hearing." Soon afterward, Lyman's opposition to the free discussion of slavery became more definite. In December, 1834, two months after the departure of the students from Lane, he was in Boston attempting to prevent the Congregational churches of the state from any association with the abolitionists. He was one of the founders of the American Union for the Relief and Improvement of the Colored Race. The apparent purpose of this organization was to demonstrate that the churches had a concern for the blacks and thus to prevent William Lloyd Garrison from pre-empting the issue of their welfare. Though it sponsored praiseworthy projects, the important thing about the society was that it did not endorse abolition. In 1835, Lyman proposed to the Congregational Association of Connecticut that its churches close their pulpits to "itinerant agents and lecturers" who preached "erroneous or questionable" sentiments, a euphemism for abolition. The association unanimously approved the motion, and a few weeks later Lyman offered a similar motion to the Congregational Association of Massachusetts, which also approved it. Thus in two states the denomination which was numerically the most powerful put itself on record in effect as being unwilling to listen to abolition arguments.[20]

In addition to helping quell the discussion of abolition at Lane Seminary, Lyman Beecher insisted that his children should not take sides publicly on the slavery issue. "As to abolition, I am still of opinion," he wrote to his son William in 1835,

that you ought not, and need not, and will not commit yourself as a partisan on either side. The cause is moving on in Providence, by the American Union, and by colonization, and by [Benjamin] Lundy [a colonizationist] in Texas . . . and I hope and believe that the Abolitionists as a body will become more calm and less denunciatory, with the exception of a few he-goat men, who think they do God service by butting everything in the line of their march which does not fall in or get out of the way.

In addition, Lyman made sure that abolition would not again become a problem at Lane Seminary. In 1840, he said, "Our trustees and faculty are not abolitionists, and our students are conservative rather than ultra." He assured a correspondent that "young men from the South will not be annoyed here or disqualified for usefulness at home."[21]

Harriet was to have more trouble than Catharine in defining the role she would play. Apparently she did not dream in the 1830s that it would include public controversy. She was too introspective, too detached, and perhaps too reflective to assume easily even the relatively modest public role played by Catharine. Although by this time she probably no longer thought she was condemned to hell, she was still plagued by other painful questions. In 1832, she wrote in a letter to one of her friends, Georgina May, that as "this inner world of mine has become worn out and untenable, I have at least concluded to come out of it and live in the eternal [external?] one, and to give up the pernicious habit of meditation . . . and try to mix in society somewhat as another person would . . ." Referring to a motto on a sundial, she said she had decided "to count no hours but unclouded ones, and to let all the others slip out of my memory. . . . Instead of shrinking into a corner to notice how other people behave, I am holding out my hand to the right and to the left, and forming casual or incidental acquaintances with all who will be acquainted with me." She admitted that she was having only a limited success in this endeavor.[22]

Sometimes, Harriet recognized that her difficulties were accentuated by the fact that she was a woman and that as such society had imposed severe restraints upon her. In another letter to Georgina May in 1833, Harriet again commented on her struggle to find a proper role:

Recently I have been reading the life of Madame de Staël and "Corinne." I have felt an intense sympathy with many parts of that book, with many parts of her character. But in America feelings vehement and absorbing like hers become still more deep, morbid, and impassioned by the constant habits of self-government which the rigid forms of our society demand. They are repressed, and they burn inward till they burn the very soul, leaving only dust and ashes. It seems to me the intensity with which my mind has thought and felt on every subject presented it has had this effect. It has withered and exhausted it, and though young, I have no sympathy with the feelings of youth. All that is enthusiastic, all that is impassioned in admiration of nature, of writing, of character, in devotional thought and emotion, or in the emotions of affection, I have felt with vehement and absorbing intensity,— felt till my mind is exhausted, and seems to be sinking into deadness. Half of my time I am glad to remain in listless vacancy, to busy myself with trifles, since thought is pain, and emotion is pain.[23]

In 1836, Harriet married Calvin Stowe, a few months before her twenty-fifth birthday. It was well past the time when most young women then could have much hope of marriage, and for Harriet the prospects had been especially bleak. Calvin was apparently the only man who had ever shown any romantic interest in her. He had been born in 1802 of a poor family in Natick, Massachusetts. Originally apprenticed to a paper-maker, Calvin had won a scholarship and had gone to Bowdoin College. There he was almost the only Christian in a largely skeptical student body. He studied for the ministry at Andover and became a professor of Greek at Dartmouth. One of his many eccentricities was that he insisted on having in his pockets at all times a copy of the Greek New Testament and of Dante's *Divine Comedy*. He became acquainted with Lyman Beecher in Boston. When Lyman became president of Lane Seminary, he brought Calvin Stowe with him to be a professor there.

At the time, Calvin was married; but his young wife, Eliza, died—probably of cholera—in 1834. Harriet had known Eliza, had been, in fact, deeply fond of her.[24]

Calvin was a man of real ability but with his share of weaknesses. He was a genuine scholar in his field of Hebraic studies. He was personally engaging, with a vein of humor which was noticeable in his dialect stories which featured the wit of New England rural characters. He was a great success as a teacher. He was generally sympathetic with the ambitions of Stowe* when she became a writer, and her later fame did not apparently arouse jealousy in him. His weaknesses were hypochondria, feelings of hopelessness under stress, gluttony—eventually he would become enormously fat—and a lack of resolution and skill in handling practical problems. He could sometimes be almost childishly helpless. One indication of his lack of resolution was that when Lyman Beecher decided to support the trustees' ban on discussion of slavery at Lane Seminary, he did not himself tell the students of his decision. Instead, he sent Calvin to tell them. The incident probably shows the extent to which Calvin was dominated by his father-in-law. Stowe seems to have felt a genuine affection for Calvin. He himself may never have realized that his position as head of the family was anomalous. With unconscious irony he wrote an article, published in 1869, entitled "The Woman Question and the Apostle Paul." He argued that because of her "peculiar dependence on man," there was "an obligation to respect and obedience on the part of the wife, since men cannot protect and defend those who will not trust in them, and be guided by them." All the evidence would suggest that though Stowe was willing to discuss matters with Calvin, she made her own decisions.[25]

From the point of view of his own future, Calvin would have been well advised when the troubles came to Lane Seminary to look for a position elsewhere, since it was obvious that the school would for some years go through a very lean period. He finally resigned in 1850, sixteen years after the departure of nearly all the students. He did not leave, in fact, until a year after his resignation, because he was asked to stay on at Lane until a replacement could be found for him. When he did leave, Calvin was forty-nine years old. His new position was a modest one at Bowdoin College, his alma mater in Brunswick, Maine. What Lyman Beecher seems to have done was to insist, possibly without ever having to trouble himself to state the issue in words, that his son-in-law remain

* From this point on Harriet Beecher Stowe will be referred to as Stowe.

at Lane Seminary until he was himself ready to retire. In 1850, when he was seventy-five years old, Lyman did retire, the same year that Calvin resigned his professorship there. Whatever Lyman's intention, the fact was that the Stowes lived a life of cramped poverty from the time of their marriage in 1836 until 1852, when *Uncle Tom's Cabin* became a runaway best seller. During that time they had seven children.[26]

Aside from the issue of slavery, Lyman and some of his children had other troubles in Cincinnati. In 1835, the year after the debacle at Lane, Lyman was tried for heresy by the Cincinnati synod of the Presbyterian church. Originally a Congregationalist, Lyman had become a Presbyterian when he became president of Lane Seminary. The differences in doctrine between the two denominations were not great, but they were sufficient to make some local Presbyterians suspicious of even the mild reservations which Lyman had expressed concerning such doctrines as predestination. The attempt to censure Lyman failed, but the synod did admonish him for incautious statements. Even though he was acquitted of all charges, however, it was still true that there was a faction among the Presbyterians who had no use for Lyman Beecher nor for Lane Seminary.[27]

Still another difficulty which the Beechers encountered in Cincinnati was the fact that they too strongly represented a single element within the city, the New England element. Some New Englanders who had emigrated to Cincinnati realized that harmony among the groups was based upon the assumption that no one faction would insist too much on its own peculiarities. The Beechers apparently thought that the New England element was the important one and were puzzled when they discovered that many Cincinnatians resisted so obvious a fact. To the Beechers, the West and Cincinnati as a part of the West were the Macedonian hinterland. In 1834, Lyman made a trip to New England and appealed for money for Lane on the assumption that the West, unless the orthodox New England churches came to the rescue, would succumb to frontier barbarism or, equally disastrous, would become Catholic. He spoke of the "limited means of education [in the West], and of the importance of introducing the social and religious principles of New England among them." One of his addresses with this theme was paraphrased in the eastern papers, which in turn were read in Cincinnati. Local people did not enjoy seeing themselves described as if they were saved from barbarism only by the attention of such men as Lyman Beecher, and there was complaint of his patronizing attitude.[28]

The New England element represented by the Beechers also seemed to many Cincinnatians too narrowly pious. In addition to being president of Lane Seminary, Lyman was pastor of the Second Presbyterian Church. It troubled him that his parishioners did not forbid social dancing as orthodox churches in New England generally did. He tried to convince the members of his congregation that it was wrong for them to allow young people to dance. One of the elders to whom he wrote a letter of complaint about dancing at balls wrote him a stinging reply. He said that he did not regard it as a matter of importance "whether our children are made to romp with a measured or unmeasured step around our parlor." His letter added something like an insult. Dancing at family affairs was denounced, he said, only by those people for whom it was a "novelty" or "above their rank."[29]

The hostility of important elements of upper-class Cincinnati society to the Beechers was also encountered by Catharine. As a woman, she was even more vulnerable than her father to the snubs of society in Cincinnati. She failed just as Lyman did to understand that Cincinnati was not Hartford and that the West was not merely an extension of New England. She moved to assert the dominance of the New Englanders in the Semi-Colon Club, the local literary society. First she proposed that the club's motto should be "The March of Intellect." It might seem a harmless slogan, but to her opponents in the club it had the implication that intellect had clearly marched from New England. Then she began a campaign among highly placed acquaintances in Cincinnati to exclude from the club James Hall and Daniel Drake, men who had not hesitated to express the opinion that the West could afford to be independent of eastern influence and could create a civilization of its own. As a result of Catharine's efforts to exclude others from the club, she herself became unpopular in Cincinnati society. One effect of her decline in status was that her school for girls failed and had to be closed.[30]

For all their virtues, the Beechers did not move easily and gracefully in society. For them, the good and the true were more important than the beautiful. After *Uncle Tom's Cabin* was published, an anonymous writer who said that he had been a student at Lane Seminary wrote an account of his impressions of the Beecher family for a British magazine. "Their movements and gestures have much of the abruptness and want of grace common in Yankee land," he said, "where the opera and dancing school are considered as institutions of Satan." All the members of the Beecher family had facial features which were "large and irregular," said the writer. The Beecher men had a "certain manly beauty," but the Beecher women were "scarcely redeemed from homeliness" by the "expression of intelligence which lights them up, and fairly sparkles in the bluish-grey eyes."[31]

Both Catharine and Harriet as young women had handicaps in upper-class society. Not all their intellectualism could make them conversant with what was said and what was worn in genteel society. When Harriet became famous, Richard Henry Dana, Jr. remembered that at some time in the late 1820s, when he was a boy about twelve or thirteen years old, Catharine and Harriet had come to visit the Dana home in Cambridge, Massachusetts. At the time Harriet was "a young lady of about eighteen." Dana was already aware of the conventions of upper-class society. He and his brother, who was three years younger than he, had not been wholly favorably impressed by the sisters. In both "style of manner" and "dress," they were, he remembered, "careless, . . . inattentive to what we had been sedulously taught as 'the Minor Morals.' " In addition, "there was a want of reverence in their religious exercises, & a familiarity in their manner of speaking of the Most High & of the Saviour which shocked us in Church, as much as their want of refinement did in society." Of the two sisters, the Dana brothers liked Harriet better than Catharine. "Miss Catharine Beecher had the family failings strongly marked, & the more objectionable being in a woman; but we were quite won by Miss Harriet. . . ." Dana wrote. "Though not handsome, there was something very pleasing about her. She too was rather careless of dress & manner & absent minded, but feminine, kind, & with a quick apprehension of humor, which pleased us very much."[32]

Though not as badly off as Catharine, Harriet too was handicapped as a girl and as a young woman by her undeveloped social graces and by the religious tradition in which she was reared. After the death of Stowe, Julia Ward Howe admitted that she had not liked *Uncle Tom's Cabin* when she had first read it. She mentioned that she had not liked the book's excessive piety and its orthodox religious bias, but it may also have troubled her that Harriet had come from the wrong sort of New England society. Years after she had become famous, Stowe attended a social gathering in Hartford. Howe saw her there and remembered a little condescendingly that Stowe had improved her opportunities by acquiring a greater knowledge of what ladies should wear. "Mrs. Stowe had by this time become familiar with conventional society," Howe wrote. "She wore a becoming dress of light gray silk, and her dark ringlets were held in place by a silver comb or coronet." When she lived in Cincinnati, Stowe was well aware of the snubs which Catharine encountered. Since she herself was more shy and introspective, it is not surprising that she assumed a far less public role.[33]

In 1836, Cincinnati proved that Lyman's fears of violence against people who openly expressed abolitionist opinions had been justified. James G. Birney was a more moderate figure than William Lloyd Garrison and one with a more substantial place in society. He had been born in Kentucky in 1792, the son of a wealthy slaveholder. He was educated at the College of New Jersey, later to become Princeton, and became a lawyer and a man of considerable prestige in Huntsville, Alabama, where he served a term as mayor. In 1826, Birney had become a colonizationist. In 1834, he freed his own slaves and in the same year, influenced by Theodore Weld, he became an abolitionist. He attempted to found an antislavery paper in Danville, Kentucky, but under the threat of violence he moved to Cincinnati. Then the first issue of his paper, the *Philanthropist*, appeared January 1, 1836. It was moderate in tone. It denied any intention of stirring up rebellion among the slaves. It said that slavery was a question which ought to be discussed, and it invited people of all shades of opinion to contribute to its pages. Its motto, "We are very guilty concerning our brother. . . . [T]here is this distress come upon us," was apparently meant to suggest that the whole of American society was implicated in the guilt of slavery, not merely the slaveholders themselves.[34]

All the moderation of Birney did not save the *Philanthropist* from violence. Leading figures of Cincinnati warned him of what might happen. Judge Jacob Burnet told him publicly that if a mob attacked the paper it would probably include two-thirds of the city's property holders. The first violence occurred on July 12, 1836, when the press was damaged but not destroyed. When the paper continued to be published, the mob formed again on the night of July 30, and this time it did a more thorough job. It took the press and threw it into the Ohio River. Then it went to the homes of Birney and of his associate editor. When they were not to be found, the mob moved into the "Little Africa" area of Cincinnati. Some of the houses of the blacks it destroyed; at others it contented itself with ripping off doors and windows and ravaging the interiors. The destruction went on for four hours with the police nowhere in sight. At midnight the mayor of Cincinnati appeared. He spoke to the mob, saying, "We have done enough for one night. . . . The abolitionists

themselves must be convinced by this time what public sentiment is."
The mayor then helped the mob search a hotel where Birney was
thought to be hiding, but he was not there.[35]

It may have been the violence of the proslavery faction in Cincinnati
against Birney more than the controversy at Lane Seminary over Theodore Weld and the other dissident students which led Stowe to recognize
how evil the institution of slavery was and how difficult it would be
to eradicate. After her death, her son, Charles E. Stowe, recalled that
she had said to him:

I saw for the first time clearly that the institution of slavery was incapable
of defence, and that it was for that reason that its supporters were compelled
to resort to mob-violence. I saw that it was . . . incompatible with our free
institutions and was confident that it was doomed, and that it would go,
but how or when I could not picture to myself. That summer and fall opened
my eyes to the real nature of slavery as they had never been opened before.[36]

The lesson which Catharine Beecher drew from the destruction of
Birney's press was apparently different. In 1837 she published a pamphlet, *An Essay on Slavery and Abolitionism with Reference to the Duty
of American Females*. The occasion of her pamphlet was the decision of
Angelina Grimké to tour cities of the North giving antislavery lectures.
Grimké was probably chosen for attack because she represented views
concerning women which were almost the direct opposite of Catharine's.
Grimké had coupled her antislavery agitation with a protest against the
exclusion of women from the ranks of abolition. In taking this stand, she
was opposing Catharine's conviction that women should stay out of discussions of public questions. It may have been that Catharine thought
by attacking Grimké and by taking a conservative position with regard
to agitation against slavery she might regain some of her lost prestige
in Cincinnati.[37]

In her pamphlet, Catharine developed the idea that women should
help to regenerate society; but their influence must be largely private
and indirect. "A man may act on society, by the collision of intellect,
in public debate," she said; "he may urge his measures by a sense of
shame, by fear, and by personal interest; he may coerce by the combination of public sentiment; he may drive by physical force, and he does not
outstep the boundaries of his sphere." On the other hand, it would be
wrong for a woman to do any of these things. "Woman is to win everything by peace and love and by making herself so much respected,
esteemed, and loved," she said, "that to yield to her opinions and to

gratify her wishes, will be the free-willing offering of the heart." A woman who proceeded in this way could work wonders. "All the sacred protection of religion, all the generous promptings of chivalry, all the poetry of romantic gallantry," she argued, "depend upon woman's retaining her place as dependent and defenseless, and making no claims, and maintaining no rights but what are the gifts of honor, rectitude, and love." What woman should do, Catharine concluded, was to persuade the male members of her family or male friends to take up publicly causes which she herself could express only in private.[38]

To abolitionists generally, Catharine complained that they should not criticize slavery unless they were thoroughly familiar with it. If they were opposed to slavery, they should first travel to the South and examine the institution closely at first hand. Otherwise, the southerners would justly object to criticism of their institution by people who knew little about it and that by hearsay. It apparently did not occur to Catharine that the southerners might not take kindly to those northerners who had come visiting their region with the purpose of studying slavery. Catharine also argued that the abolitionists should speak only in peaceful and loving terms to the South. To this argument, Richard Hildreth made a spirited reply. "The truth is," he wrote,

that the discussion of all great questions, whether moral, religious, or political, generate party spirit and angry passions. . . . Yet it is not the less necessary to speak and to act. The measures of the abolitionists produce precisely the same discord which must necessarily be produced by all measures that come into conflict with custom, prejudice, and self-interest.[39]

In her pamphlet, Catharine strongly attacked William Lloyd Garrison. She questioned whether his commitment to Christianity was genuine. Though "he professes a belief in the Christian religion," said Catharine, he "is an avowed opponent of most of its institutions." Catharine did not name those institutions; one wonders whether she may not unconsciously have assumed that one of them was Lyman Beecher himself. Garrison poured scorn on most of the church bodies because they did not attack slavery, but he was not antireligious. What Catharine was doing was to suggest that abolitionism, or at least too vehement an expression of it, was linked to infidelity.[40]

The extent to which the children of Lyman Beecher would be able to stay out of dangerous controversies over slavery depended, in part, on what happened to their friends who were more actively engaged in antislavery activities than they were. It was Edward Beecher, who had become president of Illinois College in Jacksonville, who was to have the first close brush with the violence which the expression of antislavery opinion might entail. Edward was a friend of Elijah Lovejoy, a man who was not an immediate emancipationist. He had begun as a colonizationist and proposed that slavery be abolished "at such distant period of time as may be thought expedient." How far he was from the idea of racial equality is suggested by his argument that one of the virtues of colonization was that it might be a means "eventually for ridding the country altogether of a colored population. . . ." Lovejoy's first paper, the *Observer*, was established in St. Louis. In 1836, a mob had broken into the jail there and had seized a black man and burned him at the stake. When Lovejoy condemned this atrocity, his press was destroyed. Lovejoy moved his paper to Alton, Illinois, across the Mississippi River and twenty-five miles north of St. Louis. He criticized the leniency of the charge which the judge in St. Louis gave to the grand jury concerning the destruction of his press. Stubbornly he ignored both the advice of his friends and the threats of his enemies concerning what might happen if he continued to publish his paper. Except for not believing in nonresistance, Lovejoy was the almost perfect martyr. He did not revile his enemies. "I know I am but one and you are many," Edward Beecher quoted him as saying to his opponents. "My strength would avail but little against you all. You can crush me if you will; but I shall die at my post, for I cannot and will not forsake it." And die he did. In defending the press with firearms against a mob on the night of November 7, 1837, he was shot and killed. Edward Beecher had been with Lovejoy the day before the attack and had returned from Alton to Jacksonville, convinced that the crisis was over and that there would be no violence.[41]

Edward Beecher had gradually moved toward at least a theoretically abolitionist position. He said he had changed from "gradual emancipation" to "immediate emancipation" in 1835, but he meant merely a change in his private convictions. He was dissatisfied with the "spirit" of immediate abolitionists, with their tendency "of pushing true principles to an extreme." Accordingly, he had resolved "to join no society—and to speak as an individual, if I spoke at all." Until the death of Lovejoy, he chose not to speak at all. What shocked Edward as much as the killing of Lovejoy was his sudden glimpse of how indifferent a society might be to injustice. He discovered that the predominant opinion even in the North was that Lovejoy was more to be blamed than the people who had killed him. Most of the supposedly "wise and good" people, Edward said, were "unsparing in their censure of the sufferers." After Lovejoy's death, Edward conceded, some arguments for "certain abstract principles of free inquiry were expressed," but "the full tide of indignation" was "reserved for the audacious man, who dared to speak and act as a free man," and his "penalty" was "declared to be deserved." Edward came near despair. He wondered whether "as a nation we are radically unsound and lost. . . ." Though he drew back from this conclusion, he recognized that the death of Lovejoy was "the result of principles neither superficial nor accidental. They penetrate to the very vitals of society; and indicate a crisis in our national life."[42]

In Baynard R. Hall's *Frank Freeman's Barbershop*, one of the many anti-*Uncle Tom's Cabin* novels published in the 1850s, an incident occurs which is apparently meant to be the killing of Lovejoy, though he is not named. The omniscient narrator justifies the killing because the abolitionist agitator had resisted his attackers by force and had fired upon them. "Lynch law is, unquestionably, a very gingerly thing to handle," he says, but "where applied with some show of reason, it is yet a cat with more than nine tails." If society refuses in all circumstances to permit lynching, the narrator argues, it will suffer evils which will be "destructive of everything else." On the other hand, if society recognizes that lynchings may sometimes be necessary it will benefit from its common sense. For one thing, "the advocates of 'Higher Law,' will, we presume, have some respect for 'Lynch Law.' "[43]

Mob action which Lyman Beecher had feared in 1834 at Lane Seminary came closer to reality in 1841 when the school was doing nothing to provoke the anger of proslavery factions. A riot between Irishmen and blacks had broken out in Cincinnati and there were several days of street fighting. A rumor was circulated among the rioting whites that some of the blacks had taken refuge at Lane Seminary. Luckily, the school was three miles distant from the center of town, there had been recent rains, and the only road was unpaved and uphill all the way. Faced with the possibility of a physical attack, Lane prepared to defend itself. Lyman later gleefully recalled his telling the students "that they had the right of self-defense, that they could arm themselves, and if the mob came they could shoot." Lest he be thought unduly violent, Lyman added, "I told them not to kill 'em, just to aim low" and "hit 'em in the legs!" The exhortation proved to be unnecessary because the mob never reached the Seminary.[44]

Before the children of Lyman Beecher could play a major role in the antislavery struggle, several changes would have to take place. One was that his sons and daughters would have to divest themselves of his moral and intellectual tutelage. Another was that those Beechers who would be active in the antislavery struggle—Stowe, Henry Ward, and Edward—would have to return to the East where abolitionists were more respectable. A third change, the most intangible but the most important of the three, was that Stowe would have to develop, from a background which was in most respects unpromising, the characteristics of an imaginative writer.

IV

Harriet Beecher Stowe in Cincinnati

1836-1850

CATHARINE AND STOWE represented two ways in which women in the nineteenth century might approach a public career. In spite of her taking the position that women ought not to agitate publicly the questions of the day, Catharine was obliged to some extent to do this herself. Her interest in education for women was certain to encounter controversy, and she had no male relatives or friends sufficiently interested in the question to fight the necessary battles for her. In order to convince the public of the desirability of educating women, Catharine was sometimes reduced to humiliating stratagems. When she formed an organization with the purpose of advocating education for women, neither she nor any other woman could be president of it without incurring the charge of being too forward. She asked the unwilling Calvin Stowe to accept the presidency. In order to induce him to accept, she also enlisted the aid of Stowe, who in turn cajoled Calvin. In addition, Catharine wrote to her friends and asked them to urge him to accept without telling him that she had asked them. In spite of her efforts to state her ideas modestly and to work through influential men, Catharine herself was often written off as a busybody and as a querulous old maid.[1]

The extent to which Stowe consciously chose a different role from that of Catharine we can only conjecture. Her own methods were different, but the differences may be chiefly due to the fact that she was a writer and did not need, except in rare instances, to work through organizations. In addition, Stowe achieved a public career after having done everything that a nineteenth-century woman could reasonably be expected to do. She "went through." She married, had seven children, and struggled with all the problems of maintaining a household and rearing a family. It was hard on her to have two or three different careers. Since women then were supposed to be frequently ill and subject to nervous disorders, it is difficult to distinguish the real from the factitious case. Certainly Stowe had enough stress put upon her to justify complaints. One of her difficulties was Calvin Stowe himself. He was, if anything, worse than she in occasionally succumbing to moods of black melancholy. Harriet, for her part, complained of ill health and exhaustion during most of her writing career, but her complaints were most acute during the first fifteen years of her married life, before she had written anything which was especially noteworthy.[2]

Dolefully, Stowe wrote to Calvin in 1842, when she was thirty-one years of age, that their best years were over and that there was little apparently for them to do except to prepare for decrepit old age and death:

Now by the grace of God I am resolved to come home [she was writing from Buffalo] & live for God. It is time to prepare to die—the lamp has not long to burn—the hour is flying—all things are sliding away & eternity is coming. Will you dear husband join with me in simplicity & earnestness to live a new life . . .[?] Why look at it[?]—Life is half gone! What have we done? We are both of us no longer young[.] We both of us have already the sentence of death in our members—the grey hair will never become black again but the black hair will become grey. Nay[,] I feel in myself changes that I know will not *change back.* I see steps that I have taken downward that I shall not retrace—& are we ready to take the exceeding & eternal weight of glory[?] What have we done & suffered for Christ[?] . . . Let us . . . give ourselves wholly to Christ, to *know* him, the power of his death[,] the fellowship of his sufferings—if by any means we may attain unto the renunciation from the dead.[3]

When Calvin assumed a similarly dire tone, on the other hand, Stowe sometimes reacted with a brisk humor. When she was taking "the water cure" at a spa in Brattleboro, Vermont, in 1847, he must have written a truly horrendous account of his troubles. "I received your most melancholy effusion," she replied, "and I am sorry to find it's just so. I entirely agree and sympathize. Why didn't you engage the two tombstones—one for you and one for me?" Then she scolded him gently. "To see things as through a glass darkly," she said, was his "infirmity." He should seek to bear his present trouble as if it were a "toothache, or a driving rain, or anything else that you cannot escape." Having given this good advice, Stowe in the same letter returned to her own troubles. ". . . I have suffered from an overwhelming mental depression," she said, "a perfect heartsickness. All I wanted was to get home and die. Die I was very sure I should, at any rate, but I suppose I was never less prepared to do so." Stowe would sometimes complain to other people of Calvin's hypochondria. She wrote to a sister-in-law that Calvin had written to her of his being "all but dead," and of his conviction that he would never see his family again. He wondered how she would manage after his death, admired her courage, and warned her to be prudent since she would be left with very little money. "I read the letter," Stowe wrote to her sister-in-law, "and poke it into the stove, and proceed. . . ."[4]

If the Stowes did not always bear their burdens patiently, they could at least usually confide in and help one another. Stowe did not like the climate of Cincinnati, especially the hot summers, and on one occasion she wrote to Calvin while he was away concerning the discouragements of housekeeping:

My dear Husband,—It is a dark, sloppy, rainy, muddy, disagreeable day, and I have been working hard (for me) all day in the kitchen, washing dishes, looking into closets, and seeing a great deal of that dark side of domestic life which a housekeeper may who will investigate too curiously into minutiae in warm, damp weather, especially after a girl who keeps all clean on the *outside* of cup and platter, and is very apt to make good the rest of the text in the *inside* of things.

I am sick of the smell of sour milk and sour meat, and sour everything, and then the clothes *will* not dry; and no wet thing does, and everything smells mouldy; and altogether I feel as if I never wanted to eat again.

In addition, her health was bad again. "I suffer with sensible distress in the brain, as I have done more or less since my sickness last winter, a distress which some days takes from me all power of planning or executing anything," she said, "and you know that, except this poor head, my unfortunate household has no mainspring, for nobody feels any kind of responsibility to do a thing in time, place, or manner, except as I oversee it."[5]

The worst of Stowe's sorrows was the death of one of her children, the eighteen-month-old Samuel Charles Stowe, who died of a cholera epidemic which killed thousands of people in Cincinnati in the summer of 1849. Calvin was again away from home, this time taking the water cure himself in Vermont, and Stowe told him not to come back until the epidemic was over. Of the baby's death, she wrote:

At last it is over, and our dear little one is gone from us. He is now among the blessed. My Charley—my beautiful, loving, gladsome baby, so . . . sweet, so full of life and hope and strength—never was he anything to me but a comfort. . . . Many an anxious night have I held him to my bosom and felt the sorrow and loneliness pass out of me with the touch of his little warm hands. Yet I have just seen him in his death agony, looking on his imploring face when I could not . . . mitigate his cruel suffering—do nothing but pray in my anguish that he might die soon.

Even at the time, however, Stowe could recognize that others in Cincinnati were suffering. "I write as though there were no sorrow like my sorrow," she said; "yet there has been in this city, as in the land of Egypt, scarce a house without its dead."[6]

Calvin Stowe had problems which he may not have communicated fully to his wife, but he did write to Lyman Beecher about them. "I try to be spiritually minded," he said, "and find in myself a most exquisite relish, and deadly longing for all kinds of sensual gratification—I think of the revival ministers who have lived long in licentiousness with good reputation, and then been detected,—and ask myself, who knows whether there be any real piety on earth."[7]

Stowe may have known that Calvin was sometimes strongly tempted. On returning from a trip, Henry Ward Beecher preached a sermon of "unexpected falls among high places in the church and the need of prayers." When Stowe heard him, "a horrible presentiment crept over" her. She wrote to Calvin:

I thought of all my brothers and of you—and could it be, that as I am gifted with a most horribly vivid imagination, in a moment imagined—nay saw as in a vision all the distress and despair that would follow a fall on your part. I felt weak and sick—I took a book and lay down on the bed, but it pursued me like a nightmare—and something seemed to ask if your husband [was?] any better *seeming* than so and so!—I looked in the glass and my face which since spring has been something of the palest was so haggard that it frightened me. The illusion lasted a whole forenoon and then evaporated like a poisonous mist—but God knows how I pity those heart wrung women—wives worse than widows, who are called to lament that the grave has *not* covered their husbands—the father of their children. . . . What terrible temptations lie in the wake of your sex—till now I never realized it—for tho I did love you with an almost insane love before I married you I never knew yet or felt the pulsation which showed me that I could be tempted in that way—there never was a moment when I felt anything by which you could have drawn me astray—for I loved you as I now love God —and can conceive of no higher lover—and as I have no jealousy,—the most beautiful woman in the world could not make me jealous as long as she only *dazzled the senses*—but not to look or think too freely on womankind. If your sex would guard the outworks [*sic*] of *thought*, you would never fall and when so dizzying [and?] so astounding are the advantages which Satan takes it scarce is implying a doubt to say "be cautious". . . .[8]

Some biographers and critics of Stowe have argued that she developed a sympathy for slaves because she was, in a real sense, a slave herself— a slave to family cares, household chores, and ill health. The thesis may be true, but it is difficult to prove. The death of her own child did lead her to reflect on the greater sorrows of those black slave mothers who had their children sold away from them. "I wrote what I did," she explained to the Earl of Shaftesbury concerning *Uncle Tom's Cabin*, "because as a woman, as a mother, I was oppressed & broken hearted, with the sorrows & injustice I saw. . . ." In addition there may have been some connection between her worries over her own husband's possible infidelity and her recognition that slavery may frequently have involved men having children by slave women, children who almost inevitably would be slaves themselves.[9]

Whatever relation her own problems would have to the writing of *Uncle Tom's Cabin*, her early stories and articles show no especial concern with them. She went about writing with an eye to the demands of the magazine and gift book market. "*I do it for the pay*," she said frankly. She did insist that her work was important enough that she must have a definite place for it. "If I am to write I must have a room to myself that will be my room . . . ," she demanded of Calvin. She wrote tales of religious piety, occasional sentimental tales of people who suddenly discovered long-lost lovers or relatives, stories of New England rural life, children's stories which emphasized morality and the idea of obeying one's parents, a children's geography, and numerous essays and reviews in which temperance, morality, anti-Catholicism, and the evils of dancing and going to the theater were among the themes. Her writings gave little evidence of what was to come. Occasionally there would be a salty rural New England character who showed promise of developing into something genuine. There was virtually nothing in her early writings about slavery.[10]

One of the major themes of Stowe's early writing was the glory of New England civilization. She rarely argued the region's superiority to other sections of the country; she simply assumed it. In her first published book, *Primary Geography for Children* (1833), she emphasized the importance of the New England states in forming an American civilization. It was the aim of the early Puritans in New England, she said, "to train up their children to be industrious, and honest, and truthful, and obedient to all the laws of God in the Bible; and they took especial care that their children should have good schools." The result was that "the descendants of the Pilgrim Fathers in New England have been distinguished for their reverence for the Bible, for their good schools, and for their industrious habits." It was these qualities which explained the fact that "no people in the world have been more prosperous in every kind of business than those in New England, for God always makes those most prosperous who are most obedient to his laws in the Bible." Thus it was not surprising that people in New England "own more ships, in proportion to their numbers, than [those in?] any other country; and manufactures . . . abound over New England. . . ."[11]

Baynard R. Hall, in his anti-*Uncle Tom's Cabin* novel, *Frank Freeman's Barber Shop* (1852), would complain of some unnamed New England antislavery writer whose children's books were written for the region's "self-glorification." These books portrayed New England as "the exact center of the earth," he said, and "the religion and morals of the world" were "pushed up or down according to the new sliding scales of their never sufficiently rectified theologies and philosophies." It is probable that Hall was thinking of Stowe's geography book. There is some truth in what he says. Stowe seemed to judge a group by estimating how near to or how far from the standards of the New Englanders it was. New Yorkers "are chiefly descended from people who came from New England," and they have "valued good schools and . . . trained their children to reverence the Bible and to be industrious." She noted that New York had first been settled by the Dutch, but that is all she said about them. Of the Quakers, she said that "they were a very benevolent and honest people, and were as careful as the New England people to have good schools." People in the northwestern states and territories had emigrated from "the Eastern and Middle states" and were "chiefly educated" by the people of those regions. One of Stowe's earliest published stories, "A New England Sketch," insistently sounded the note of regional pride. The narrator says that he will write of his "own New England—the land of bright fires and strong hearts; the land of deeds and not of words; the land of fruits and not of flowers—the land often spoken against, yet always respected—'the latchet of whose shoes, the nations of the earth are not worthy to unloose.' "[12]

In her antislavery fiction, Stowe would nearly always be too shrewd to assert or imply the idea of New England superiority, would portray faults in its people, and would insist that it share the guilt of slavery. On the other hand, there are indications that this was merely a stratagem. The essential superiority of New England comes out again and again in her fiction throughout her writing career. Part of the region's virtues she attributed to its cold and bracing climate. In *Agnes of Sorrento* (1862), the narrator reflects on what causes explain the superiority of northern Italians to southern Italians. The fifteenth-century men of Florence are described by the narrator of the novel as "of a large grave, earnest mould. What the Puritans of New England wrought out with the severest earnestness in their reasonings and their lives," the narrator says, "these early Puritans of Italy embodied in poetry, sculpture, and painting." The southern part of Italy was different. It had "gorgeous scenery," but its beauty was "more favorable to voluptuous ecstasy than to the severe and grave warfare of the true Christian soldier." It was a climate similar to that in which Circe had "made men drunk with her sensual fascinations, till they became sunk in the form of brutes." It was "a lotus-eater's paradise" where the sun served to "melt the energy of the will, and to make existence either a half doze of dreamy apathy or an awaking of mad delirium." It was not from "dreamy, voluptuous Southern Italy that the Italian race received any vigorous impulses," the narrator says. "These came from more northern regions. . . ." Stowe sometimes had a tendency to explain away the wrongful acts of members of "northern races" when they were criticized. In one of her other books she complained of the unbalanced view of those who had emphasized too much that side of John Calvin which had led him to acquiesce to the execution of Servetus by burning at the stake and that side of the New England Puritans which had led them to engage in "witch persecutions."[13]

Stowe would sometimes admit that New Englanders, like other people, might have faults, but they were faults which she frequently regarded with indulgence. Augustine St. Clare, the benevolent southern slaveholder in *Uncle Tom's Cabin*, had spent much of his youth living in New England and he would observe that New Englanders relish their family pride as much as southerners do. In one of her essays, Stowe herself mildly criticized "certain elderly dames in Hartford" who knew "their genealogical tables as well as their Bibles." On the other hand, she sometimes seemed to think that family pride is more pardonable in New England than it is elsewhere. Some Boston family records go back to the seventeenth century, the narrator of her novel, *Pink and White Tyranny* (1871), observes. "Being of a Puritan nobility," he says, "they have an ancestral record of unworldly faith and prayer and self-denial, of incorruptible public virtue, sturdy resistance of evil, and pursuit of good."[14]

Slavery in early New England, Stowe would argue in later years, had been different from slavery in the South. It had died out because it "never suited the genius of the people." She gave no weight to the possibility that climate, the nature of the land, and the economic system might have made slavery difficult to maintain there. Many New Englanders from the first were opposed to slavery, she said, "from conscientious scruple." Others "despised the rude, unskilled work of barbarians." In addition, the New Englanders had tended to think of their slaves as subordinate workers. "If there were [*sic*] a black man or black woman or bound girl," she said—possibly remembering that her parents had had black bound apprentices, "they were emphatically only the *help*, following certain portions of their toils." The New England slaveholders were essentially "head workers." This description of the nature of slavery in New England might have been news to the slaves there. If Stowe thought it was applicable to the black "bound apprentices" of her parents, she may have been wrong. The apprentices had already departed before she was old enough to remember them clearly. Catharine, who did remember them, said that they "did all the work of the family except the washing till the year mother died in Litchfield." This was in 1816, when Stowe was five years old.[15]

Another theme in Stowe's early writing was anti-Catholicism. On this subject, she followed the lead of her father and of her brother Edward. Their campaign against Catholics had at least some characteristics of Stowe's later campaign against slavery. It was not that individual Catholics were evil. The trouble was with the nature of the Catholic church itself. Because it claimed exclusive rights, it was a danger to free institutions everywhere. Later on, when she was attacking slavery, Stowe would employ a similar line of argument. Individual slaveholders might have the highest conscience and probity, but the system of slavery itself was necessarily evil. The effect of the strategy was, of course, to imply that both Catholicism and slavery were beyond the reach of reform. The only way in which Catholics and advocates of slavery could answer the charges against them, according to this method of reasoning, was to abandon their institutions entirely. With regard to slavery, the evaluation was accurate. With regard to Catholicism, however, the argument was a mere stratagem. Stowe did not, it is true, advocate persecution of Catholics, though it is odd—to say the least—that when Catholics in this country were sometimes being violently persecuted, she said nothing about it. Although she wrote only one anti-Catholic essay, there are a good many anti-Catholic comments in her writings up until the late 1850s, when she apparently changed her opinion.[16]

In 1854, Stowe would censure American Catholics for their indifference to slavery, a charge which could have been made against her, with equal propriety, only a few years before. A Catholic woman in Europe had written to her, she said, and asked her why in *The Key to Uncle Tom's Cabin* she had not included the Catholic clergy as among the opponents of slavery. "I am sorry to be obliged to make the reply," Stowe wrote, "that in America the Catholic clergy have never identified themselves with the anti-slavery cause, but in their influence have gone with the multitude."[17]

In time, Stowe would become more tolerant of Catholics. In 1860, when she was in Italy, she discussed Catholicism with Elizabeth Barrett Browning, who recorded what she said in a letter to a friend. "I find it impossible to believe that God *cares* to which church a man belongs," Mrs. Browning remembered Stowe as saying. She wrote of Stowe, "She is a woman of remarkable largeness of mind & heart, especially considering the sectarian influence she was born & educated under. . . ." After the Civil War, Stowe advised Protestant women employers of Irish servant girls not to try to shake their religious faith. "The general purity of life and propriety of demeanor of so many undefended young girls cast yearly upon our shores, with no home but their church and no shield but their religion," she said, "are a sufficient proof that this religion exerts an influence over them not to be lightly trifled with." Moreover, "there is a real unity even in opposite Christian forms; and the Roman Catholic servant and the Protestant mistress, if alike possessed by the spirit of Christ, and striving to conform to the Golden Rule, cannot help being one in heart, though one go to mass and the other to meeting." On this issue as on others, Stowe overcame the prejudices of her early years and developed more tolerant views.[18]

Another sign of Stowe's provincial narrowness at the beginning of her writing career can be seen in her reactions to literature. This trait is seen particularly in her comments on Charles Dickens. In 1843, she wrote a long essay on Dickens which showed how unwilling she was to see ministers or religion satirized or to admit that genuine goodness might exist which has no relation to religion. Dickens, we might have thought, would represent more of a challenge to her than it turned out that he did. She did like some things about his writings, but chiefly her attitude was one of strong disapproval.

Stowe praised Dickens for his "generous, warm heart" and for the fact that the welfare of his lower-class characters was as important to him as that of his upper-class ones. She was shocked, however, that in *The Pickwick Papers* Dickens could introduce a clergyman character, the Reverend Mr. Tiggins, who showed up drunk at a temperance meeting. She also objected to a burlesque by the character Sam Weller of the expression "born again." This was a term, she said, which "first had its origin with Jesus Christ." The fact that he "attached to it a most solemn significance" meant that it involved "all that was highest and deepest in our religious interests. . . ." She would not be surprised, she said, if in some future work Dickens should treat the Day of Judgment as if it were "a theme of scurrilous jesting." In addition, Stowe accused Dickens of writing "for fame and money. . . ." It was a charge which would later be made against her when *Uncle Tom's Cabin* was published. She objected to the fact that in *Oliver Twist* Dickens had introduced to his young readers the "foul and muddy current" of criminal society in England. She also objected to the fact that the good characters, especially the good child characters, in Dickens's stories had no specifically religious motivation, and she pointed particularly to Oliver Twist and Little Nell.[19]

In her essay on Dickens, Stowe made one of her few public references to slavery before *Uncle Tom's Cabin*. She mentioned the visit of Dickens to the United States in which he "said and did so many foolish and extravagant things," and she censured him for singling out one great evil of American society, that of slavery, and ignoring other evils equally serious:

Mr. Dickens is immeasurably shocked at the system of slavery, and really sets himself in an attitude of considerable moral sublimity in his remarks upon the subject—and why? Because of the amount of misery and suffering to man, his dearest interests involved in the system. Why is Mr. Dickens so extremely alive to the interests of humanity in one point of view, and not in another, that he can burlesque temperance speeches, temperance hotels, and temperance societies, while he rejoices to add his mite to the efforts that are making against slavery? The most charitable conclusion to be made in the case, is, that Mr. Dickens, being . . . a person of no very profound habits or capacity for reflection on moral subjects . . . gives . . . full way to the floating, idle prejudice which pervades men of that class generally, making amends for it by very virtuous and cheap abhorrence of certain other men, who act precisely in the same way, on another point of equally vital interest to humanity.

If Dickens had read this criticism and had been familiar with Stowe's writings up to this point, he might well have replied that it could be at least as serious an offense to do what she had done. She had written about the evils of liquor but had never publicly mentioned the evils of slavery.[20]

During the troubles of 1836 when James G. Birney's press was destroyed in Cincinnati, Henry Ward Beecher became editor of the newspaper, the *Cincinnati Journal and Western Luminary*. His editorial position was not abolitionist, but he was sometimes critical of slavery. Stowe wrote a series of anonymous articles for the newspaper defending Birney's right to express his opinions, though not necessarily endorsing the opinions themselves. She imagined a debate between two men, one for Birney and the other against him. The anti-Birney man says that he believes in freedom of the press in most instances but Birney's opinions are too dangerous to be allowed. The following dialogue begins with the statement of the pro-Birney speaker:

"That is to say, so *you* think them. There are a large class of people in the nation who are just as sure they are not. Now, how is the Constitution to be worded: 'Every man in the State may speak, write, print, and publish his own sentiments on any subject, provided that nobody in the nation thinks they are dangerous?' "

"Pshaw!" said my friend. "Of course, no law could run that way; but there is a point, you know, where all men of sense are pretty much agreed."

"Then," said I, "perhaps you would recommend that the Constitution should provide that every man may print and publish his sentiments, except in cases where all men are *pretty much agreed* that they are dangerous?"

"Why," said my friend, after an uneasy silence of a few moments, "really you are getting to be quite a warm abolitionist. I had no idea that you were so much inclined to favor Birney."[21]

In 1843, Stowe published a collection of her stories and essays. It was entitled *The Mayflower; or, Sketches of Scenes and Characters among the Descendants of the Pilgrims.* The book consisted mainly of stories for children. It contained one oblique reference to slavery. In an essay, after humorously relating the problem a woman might have in directing the labors of a hired girl in the home, Stowe reflected on the choices open to the middle-class housewife: "What shall we do? Shall we go for slavery, or shall we give up houses, have no furniture to take care of, keep merely a bag of meal, a porridge-pot, and a pudding stick, and sit in our tent door in real patriarchal independence? What shall we do?" Ten years later, after the success of *Uncle Tom's Cabin,* a new edition of *The Mayflower* was published, but the allusion to slavery was omitted.[22]

Stowe's first antislavery story, "Immediate Emancipation," appeared in the *New York Evangelist* in 1845. In one respect, the short story anticipated one of the devices of *Uncle Tom's Cabin,* one which was substantially different from that of most other antislavery fiction. There is a slaveholder in the story who is presented in an almost wholly favorable light. This young southerner comes up to Cincinnati with his slave. Sam, the slave, takes advantage of being in a free state and runs away. Alfred B---, the southern slaveholder, inquires among the black servants in his hotel concerning Sam's whereabouts. One of the servants says, "Them boys was mighty apt to show the clean heel when they come into a free State." Alfred is angry with Sam, but is also grieved because he "really loved the fellow." At this point in the story, the narrator imagines a "scornful zealot" among the abolitionists as scoffing, " 'Loved him!' . . . a slaveholder love his slave!" "Yes, brother," replies the narrator, "why not?" Alfred had, in fact, loved Sam from his childhood. He "had always redressed his grievances, fought his battles, got him out of scrapes, and purchased for him, with liberal hand, indulgences to which his comrades were strangers. He had taken pride to dress him smartly; and as for hardship and want, they had never come near him."[23]

Alfred discovers that Sam may have been helped to escape by a Mr. Simmons, a local Quaker who is a tailor. (One wonders whether Stowe had read the antislavery writings of that other Quaker tailor, John Woolman.) The man who tells Alfred that Simmons may have helped in the escape describes him as "a meddlesome, canting Quaker rascal, that all these black hounds run to, to be helped into Canada, and nobody knows where all." Alfred goes to Simmons, determined to have it out with him, but is surprised to discover a mild-mannered man who attempts to placate him. Simmons tells Alfred that no matter how benevolent he is as a master he may die and thus Sam may be sold to a cruel owner. With unrealistic suddenness, Alfred accepts this argument and agrees to free Sam. Having been hiding in the back of the tailor shop, Sam comes out and says, "Oh, massa I want to be a free man." Alfred writes out a legal paper giving Sam his freedom and then adds some useful advice. He tells Sam to be "obedient as you were when a slave" and "to perform all the duties that are required of you, and do all you can for your future welfare and respectability." Then the narrator of the story speaks directly to the reader, "[A] man who has had the misfortune to be born and bred a slaveholder," he says, "may be enlightened, generous, human, and capable of the most disinterested regard to the welfare of his slave." One may wonder what would happen when the South ran out of high-minded young slaveholders. The more important point may be, however, that slavery as a subject for Stowe was at last out in the open.[24]

In the private letters which Stowe wrote during the Cincinnati years from 1832 to 1850, there are, if anything, even fewer comments about slavery than in her published writings. In 1834, she went on a journey from Cincinnati to New England to see Henry Ward Beecher graduate from Amherst College. She described the travelers on a stagecoach in Ohio in a letter home and paraphrased briefly a debate which occurred between two men on the subject of slavery:

Yet our friend, withal, is of Irish extraction, and I have seen him aroused to talk with both hands and a dozen words in a breath. He fell into a little talk about abolition and slavery with our good Mr. Jones, a man whose mode of reasoning consists of repeating the same sentence at regular intervals as long as you choose to answer it. This man, who was finally convinced that Negroes were black, used it as an irrefragable argument to all that could be said, and at last began to deduce from it that they might just as well be slaves as anything else, and so he proceeded until the philanthropy of our friend was roused, and he sprung up all lively and oratorical and gesticulatory and indignant to my heart's content. I like to see a quiet man that can be roused.

This kind of comment was so rare in Stowe's early writings that it deserves some attention. She did not specifically praise the abolition arguments of the traveler of Irish extraction. She praised his enthusiasm and commitment, but not specifically his position with regard to slavery. She was not yet ready definitely to espouse the cause of antislavery. On the other hand, she did satirize the response of the proponent of slavery.[25]

There is evidence that Stowe hoped for a movement which would press for something less drastic than immediate emancipation. In 1837, when she was visiting in the village of Putnam, Ohio, in the home of her brother William, she wrote to Calvin concerning the abolition activities there:

The good people here, you know, are about half Abolitionists. A lady who takes a leading part in the female society in this place, yesterday called and brought Catharine the proceedings of the Female Anti-Slavery Convention.

I should think them about as ultra as to measures as anything that had been attempted, though I am glad to see a better spirit than marks such proceedings generally.

Today I read some in Mr. Birney's *Philanthropist*. Abolition being the fashion here, it is natural to look at its papers.

It does seem to me that there needs to be an *intermediate society*. If not, as light increases, all the excesses of the abolition party will not prevent humane and conscientious men from joining it.

Pray, what is there in Cincinnati to satisfy one whose mind is awakened on this subject? No one can have the system of slavery brought before him without an irrepressible desire to do something, and what is there to be done?[26]

Soon after her marriage in 1836, Stowe had a black servant whom she had assumed to be free. Suddenly the young woman came from town to her home and confessed the truth, that she was an escaped slave and was being pursued by slave catchers. Calvin and Henry Ward Beecher engineered the escape of this woman. Armed with pistols, they drove her to the farm of an abolitionist twelve miles from Cincinnati. There she was hidden until it was safe for her to proceed north to freedom.[27]

In the fall of 1834, Stowe visited—apparently for the first and only time—a slave state. At the time she was a teacher in Catharine's Western Female Institute. She went to Kentucky with Mary Dutton, a fellow teacher at the school, spending a few days with the family of one of the pupils there. The home of the pupil was not on a plantation but was a house in the small town of Washington; it is unlikely that any slaves lived there. During the time when she was in Kentucky, Stowe may have visited a plantation, but there is no direct evidence of it. At one of the places she visited, at least, there were slaves in the household. Mary Dutton recalled, years later, Stowe's reaction to these slaves:

Harriet did not seem to notice anything that happened, but sat much of the time as though abstracted in thought. When the negroes did funny things and cut up capers, she did not seem to pay the slightest attention to them. Afterwards, however, in reading "Uncle Tom," I recognized scene after scene of that visit portrayed with the most minute fidelity, and knew at once where the material for that portion of the story had been gathered.[28]

In her later years, Stowe probably exaggerated the amount of direct experience she had had with slavery. In 1886, she wrote a letter to James Lane Allen saying that, in accompanying her father on his travels, she had "visited somewhat extensively in Kentucky, and there became acquainted with those excellent slaveholders delineated in 'Uncle Tom's Cabin.' I saw many counterparts of the Shelbys—people humane, conscientious, just, and generous, who regarded slavery as an evil and were anxiously considering their duties to the slave." Stowe's memory for exactness of detail was never good, and it became much worse in her old age.[29]

Southern critics of *Uncle Tom's Cabin* complained sometimes, when it first appeared, of the slight knowledge Stowe had of slavery, and they would have complained much more if they had known that her direct experience with the South had been limited to a single brief visit to Kentucky. In addition, historians and literary critics have sometimes argued that her lack of direct knowledge of slavery means that her novel is seriously flawed. The error in this assumption may be that it discounts the importance of a creative imagination. In his essay, "The Art of Fiction," Henry James made the point that it is insight which counts for a writer far more than amount of experience. James mentioned a woman who had written a novel with French Protestant characters. Someone asked her where she had learned so much about French Protestants. She replied that her experience had been limited to a single and seemingly minor incident. In Paris, she had once passed a doorway of a house and had seen inside a group of Protestants seated about a table. "The glimpse was a picture," said James; "it lasted only a moment, but that moment was experience." Stowe, too, may well have the ability to make a little experience count for much.[30]

In 1879, Stowe herself, in the introduction of a new edition of

Uncle Tom's Cabin, spoke of the many years in which she had said nothing about slavery and came near admitting that she did not even think much about it:

[I]t was a sort of general impression upon her mind, as upon that of many humane people in those days, that the subject was so dark and painful a one, so involved in difficulty and obscurity, so utterly beyond human hope or help, that it was of no use to read, or think, or distress one's self about it. There was a class of professed abolitionists in Cincinnati and the neighboring regions, but they were unfashionable persons and few in numbers. Like all asserters of pure abstract right as applied to human affairs, they were regarded as a species of moral mono-maniacs, who, in the consideration of one class of interests and wrongs, had lost sight of all proportion and all good judgment. Both in church and in state they were looked upon as "those that troubled Israel."[31]

One might conclude from this explanation that the chief reason Stowe did not pay much attention to antislavery in the early years of her writing career was that it was "unfashionable." More important, probably, was the fact that it was dangerous to be an abolitionist in Cincinnati at the time when she lived there. It may be that the very lateness of her opposition to slavery gave it an added strength when it came. The convictions which led to the writing of *Uncle Tom's Cabin* probably developed slowly and quietly. The novel may have been all the more powerful because of the pent-up emotions which produced it.

In 1849, a series of events began which would greatly influence Stowe's career and contribute to making the writing of *Uncle Tom's Cabin* possible. In that year, Calvin at last resigned from his position at Lane Seminary and accepted a teaching post at Bowdoin College in Brunswick, Maine. He stayed on at Lane until a replacement could be found for him. That turned out to be eighteen months later, in March, 1851. Stowe was eager to leave as soon as possible. She departed for Maine in the spring of 1850 with three of their five children and with another baby on the way. She had never liked Cincinnati and was delighted to be leaving it. Soon the slavery issue would develop a powerful new impetus with the passage of the Fugitive Slave Law. Even so, Stowe might not have been able to write *Uncle Tom's Cabin* if something else had not happened. Catharine Beecher would generously decide to give Stowe a year of her life and come to Brunswick to help manage the household while Stowe was engaged in composition. Stowe, though busy enough, would still have time to nurture her indignation, sort out her memories, and write the novel.[32]

V

Stowe's Ideas of Race

TO SAY THAT STOWE was a racist in the sense that she freely assigned innate temperamental and intellectual qualities to both races and nationalities (assuming that they were races too) is not to say much. In the middle of the nineteenth century and, in fact, well into the twentieth, the tendency to explain the character of peoples on the basis of race was extremely widespread. The historians, the scientists and social scientists (or ancestors of what would now pass for them), and the imaginative writers of the time nearly all utilized race as a means of classifying peoples and nations. As a discipline, cultural anthropology did not then exist, and in its absence race and racism frequently served as a crude equivalent. More important than whether any figure of the nineteenth century was a racist—virtually everybody was, by modern standards— is the question of what kind of racist. As an aid in deciding what may be difficult cases, a rule of thumb is often useful. What nineteenth-century writers thought of race itself is often less important than what they thought should be done about such differences among races as they believed to exist.

Stowe never did work out a systematic statement of her theories of race. Often she will stop in a discussion of a particular subject—slavery, the role of blacks or of European immigrants in this country, or treatment of Indians—and deliver some comment on the innate character of the races. Her opinions on this matter do not seem to have changed significantly over her entire career as a writer. It is true that the blacks in *Uncle Tom's Cabin* (1852) give the reader more occasion for confidence in their innate abilities than do those in her other antislavery novel, *Dred: A Tale of the Swamps* (1856). As we shall see, she went through a time in the middle 1850s—after it became clear that even the great success of *Uncle Tom's Cabin* in the North and abroad would not have any effect in changing opinion in the South—when she apparently faltered in her conviction that most blacks have sufficient innate ability to serve as equal citizens in a free society. Later, she returned to her more usual attitude, one in which she argued that whites and blacks both have their peculiar virtues and faults, with the implied conclusion that these tend to cancel one another out and thus make both equally suitable for freedom.

Because she wrote fiction, Stowe's ideas are sometimes less easy to detect than they otherwise would be. What any writer of fiction, or at least any good writer, believes about race or anything else is often difficult for a reader to classify. Bald statements of principle in her nonfiction sometimes turn out to be attenuated when we examine the characters who we may think are supposed to represent these principles. As a writer, Stowe worked on a deeper level when she was creating characters than when she was enunciating principles. The result is that the black characters frequently represent the vagaries of human character much more than they do racist theory.

On the surface, Stowe's ideas of race were fairly definite. What she frequently did was to assign certain innate traits to races or nations— she apparently had no clear idea of a difference. She did not say how one recognizes that a particular trait is racial. Like most people of her time, she regarded racial character as something so obvious that no one would dream of denying it. Some of her comments on race seem on first reading to be extremely prejudiced. At the time, however, the criticism most frequently directed against her was that she did not accentuate the differences among races sharply enough. In terms of political and social policy, she was racially tolerant. Though later she would come to think that Reconstruction in the South should proceed slowly in granting political and other rights to blacks, this was a special case which had to do with how much change the white South could absorb in a short period of time. She did not want to hang legal or social liabilities upon anyone because of his race. On the other hand, she thought innate racial differences to be a fact of life which cannot be ignored. From this premise, the reader finds himself catapulted into a system of thought in which one racial trait or another is likely to pop up in her writings at almost any point.

In describing the supposed innate racial traits of the blacks, Stowe often wrote as if she had in mind the idea of defending them against charges which she rarely specified. She listed what she considered to be their virtues and left it to the reader to fill in their defects. Her comments on the nature of black racial traits eventually convey a fairly clear notion of what she believed black defects to be, even though she did not often state them clearly. For her the virtues of the blacks were obvious. They have warmth, kindliness, attachment to family, patience, meekness; they have richly emotional natures which make them susceptible to art, music, and religion. They have a sense of humor. They have a physical hardihood which enables them to work long hours in the hot sun. On the other hand, they suffer from both a lack of intelligence and a lack of resolution—Stowe's usual word for that latter trait was "unenterprising." They are not often handsome, and if they are it is usually the result of white intermixture.

Even the virtues of blacks often turn out to be ambiguous. At least, they are not the kinds of virtues which are likely to get them very far. Their meekness may be related to their lack of will, their susceptibility to emotion may mean that they are deficient in logic, and even their sense of humor may mean that they are more likely to adapt themselves to a bad situation than to attempt to change it.

Stowe had little to say in her writings about race as a discipline of special study. The extent to which this was a disadvantage is hard to judge. Both in Europe and in the United States there was then a widespread search going on within the scientific community to measure and classify human races. Skin color, shape and size of crania, size and alleged differences in the conformation of brains, differences in hair, what would now be called differences in intelligence—all these subjects were being studied to discover ways in which races might differ from one another. As a scientific endeavor, there was, of course, nothing wrong with the idea of pursuing such research, though a good many people erroneously assumed that a scale of racial differences had already been established, and they proceeded to assign definite mental and temperamental differences to particular races. Virtually all of these ideas of race are now wholly discounted. Race is apparently not the definite fact which early theorists generally assumed it to be, and thus it can not be submitted to any accurate scale of measurement. If Stowe had read much of the "science" of race of her time, which she probably had not, she might have learned to be more cautious in assigning racial traits, especially those involving mental and emotional characteristics. It is only fair to add, however, that many of the scientists of the time were at least as liberal as she in pasting labels upon races.

On occasion, Stowe was close to the assumption that some human qualities—intelligence, for example—are not racial at all. The degradation of slavery, she believed, had prevented the blacks from developing their latent ability. In 1858, she hailed the academic achievements of three black students at the Sorbonne. They were from Haiti and had won the first prizes in Greek, Latin, and Rhetoric. They had excelled in "the most conspicuous theater of modern Europe," said Stowe, and one reason for their success had been "the absolute and philosophic superiority to the prejudice of races" in France. She did not go on to argue, however, that blacks have no inherent temperamental differences from other races:

The Africans as a race are exceedingly approbative. They are sensitive to kindness or unkindness. They need a warm, kindly atmosphere to grow in, as much as tropical plants. The pitiless frosts and pelting storms of scorn, ridicule, contempt, and obloquy which have fallen upon them could not have found a race more sensitive, more easily beaten back and withered.[1]

Often, Stowe apparently thought that lack of education and of proper motivation were all that stood in the way of black achievement. She sometimes recognized that the role demanded of a person in a society is not necessarily a key to his real character. On one occasion, she quoted the letter of an unidentified "friend"—probably a northern woman—who was visiting in the South and who commented on one of the slaves assigned to be her maid in a white household. "Her whole appearance, as she goes giggling and curtseying about," wrote the correspondent, "is perfectly comical, and would lead a stranger to think her really deficient in intellect. This, however, is by no means the case. During our two months' acquaintance with her, we have seen many indications of sterling good sense, that would do credit to many a white person with ten times her advantages."[2]

The ambivalent side of Stowe's views with regard to the intelligence of blacks can often be inferred from her attempts to explain the exceptional ability of an individual black. Sometimes she ascribed such ability to the fact that a particular black was a descendant of a superior African tribe. This kind of explanation was slightly better than the common one—which Stowe herself was not above utilizing—of attributing black intelligence to some white ancestor. It had the defect, however, of relegating most of the blacks to an innately inferior status. Frederick Douglass had once seen a picture of Remeses II, the Egyptian pharoah, in a history book and had been struck by its resemblance to his mother. Later, Douglass developed the theory that the ancient Egyptians were blacks, or at least that they had had heavy black intermixture. Stowe drew a different conclusion, that the ancestors of Douglass in Africa may have, in the distant past, belonged to a tribe which had been improved by the infusion of white intermixture:

The face alluded to is copied from a head of Ramases, the great Egyptian king of the nineteenth dynasty. The profile is European in its features, and similar in class to the head of Napoleon. . . . The mother of Douglass must have been one of that Mandingo tribe of Africans who were distinguished among the slaves for fine features, great energy, intelligence and pride of character. The black population of America is not one race. If slaveholders and kidnappers had been busy for years in Europe stirring up wars in the different countries, and sending all the captives to be sold in America, the mixture of Swedes, Danes, Germans, Russians, Italians, French, might all have gone under the one head of *Whitemen*, but they would have been none the more of the same race. The negroes of this country are a mixture torn from tribes and races quite as dissimilar. The Mandingo [the name of the tribe from which Douglass was supposedly descended] has European features, a fine form, wavy, not woolly hair, is intellignt, vigorous, proud and brave. The Guinea negro has a coarse, animal head, is stupid, dirty, cunning. Yet the argument on negro powers is generally based on some such sweeping classification as takes the Guinea negro for its type.[3]

George Harris, the nearly white slave in *Uncle Tom's Cabin*, escapes to Canada and reflects on how he will spend the rest of his life. He thinks of going to Haiti but decides not to do so because the island is peopled by an inferior tribe of the blacks. "[I]n Hayti they had nothing to start with," Harris reflects to himself. "A stream cannot rise above its fountain. The race that formed the character of the Haytiens was a worn-out effeminate one; and, of course, the subject race will be centuries in rising to anything." In reading this kind of analysis, one wonders how many blacks in the United States are descended from Mandingoes and how many from the same tribes of blacks as those who had been brought to Haiti. If Mandingoes are extremely rare among the blacks, both in the United States and in Africa, then George Harris might encounter absolute barriers to progress when—at the end of *Uncle Tom's Cabin*—he departs for Liberia to help establish a new civilization there.[4]

On many occasions, Stowe praised blacks for being jolly, cheerful, gregarious, and affectionate, with the implication that these qualities are inherent. Many of the blacks in her stories have such traits. Black Caesar, a character in her short story, "Captain Kidd's Money," is one of them. He is shown in the barn hatcheling flax, "sometimes gurgling and gigling [*sic*] to himself with an overflow of that interior jollity with which he seems to be always full." A black in New England, says the narrator of the story, "was a curious contrast to everybody around him in the joy and satisfaction that he seemed to feel in the mere fact of being alive." In *The Minister's Wooing*, the narrator pays tribute to the role of blacks in stimulating the imaginations of white children in New England. "In families, the presence of these exotics was a godsend to the children," says the narrator, "supplying from the abundant outwardness and demonstrativeness of their nature that aliment of sympathy so dear to childhood, which the repressed and quiet habits of New England education denied. Many and many a New Englander counts among his pleasantest early recollections the memory of some of these genial creatures, who by their warmth of nature were the first and most potent mesmerizers of his childish mind."[5]

There is nothing wrong, of course, with warmth and geniality unless they imply other qualities less admirable. That they do imply such qualities is an idea which if we read enough of the writings of Stowe we can scarcely miss. Though she sometimes allowed for the role of a culture or of institutions in determining the character of peoples, the emphasis is more frequently upon heredity. "The Neapolitans remind one of the plantation negroes," she wrote in one of her travel letters from Italy, "a merry, rollicking, ragged, careless set, to whom it is sufficient to lie in the sun and sing. They have such a passion for gay colors and musical sounds, and such a flexibility of motion and a sense of the dancing and singing element in nature. They are all of the faun tribe, as conceived by Hawthorne." Gaiety does not necessarily imply kindliness. The Neapolitans are cruel to animals, "not from malice or ferocity but from sheer idle inconsiderateness. Nobody considers them, why should they consider anybody? They overload and beat horses in the most shocking way." Since Italians are white, one might think that

Stowe was aware she was describing a cultural rather than a racial difference. This explanation is unlikely, since, as we have seen, in the nineteenth century nation and race were often almost interchangeable terms.[6]

Stowe seldom provided the reader with any real insight as to how she distinguished between those qualities which are racial and therefore innate and those which are the product of a particular culture. Like many other people of her time, she had obviously not thought much about the distinction. In general, the reader eventually learns to distinguish by a rough rule of thumb when a trait is acquired, in her opinion, and when it is innate. If it definitely is evil, it is acquired; if it is not a serious fault it is racial and innate. To those people who said that blacks are by nature thievish, Stowe spoke of "the benumbing effects of slavery." To the charge that they are inherently lascivious, she pointed to the faults of slavery, especially the instability of family life. On the other hand, she was willing to let pass almost any generalization which argued that blacks are inherently genial and carefree, with the implied corollary that they are also immature and unreliable.[7]

In addition to their being jolly, Stowe thought, the blacks have an emotional intensity which makes them susceptible to the arts—especially music, dancing, painting, and oratory. Blacks, she believed, are perfectly attuned to music. They inherit a susceptibility not merely to music but to a highly special kind. In her novel, *Dred*, one of the blacks plays upon a dulcimer, and the narrator thinks at once of a racist explanation. "The air was one of those inexpressibly odd ones," he reflects, "whose sharp, metallic accuracy of rhythm seems to make the delight which the negro race feels in that particular element of music."[8]

In addition to being inherently musical, blacks are—as Stowe saw them—natural dancers. "Dancing is the one thing which every negro man or woman can do well by nature," she said. "The merest lout among them becomes graceful as a dancer, and it appears that dancing is selected as the one thing to be given up when the postulant thinks of joining the church." No black was identified as a painter or sculptor in her writings; Stowe probably had never met such a black. She did mention the susceptibility to a painting shown by one of her black servants and thought she was describing a racial trait. The servant was one whom Stowe had hired in Florida when she lived there a number of winters after the Civil War. The black woman was particularly impressed by a reproduction of Raphael's *Madonna of the Veil* hanging on the wall of

the Stowe home. Minnah, the servant, knelt before the picture "in a kind
of ecstatic trance" and said: "O good Lord! If there ain't de Good Man
when he was a baby! How harmless he lies there! So innocent! And here
we be, we wicked sinners, turning our backs on him, and going to the Old
Boy. Lord, O Lord! we ought to be better than we be, we sartain ought."
"It is only one of many instances we have seen," Stowe said of this
incident, "of the overpowering influence of works of art on the im-
pressible nervous system of the negro."[9]

Though Stowe sometimes spoke as if the blacks have the seeds of
imaginative genius within them which need only encouragement to
grow, the examples she gave rarely bore out this conviction. What black
characters in her fiction usually display is a taste for garish colors, for
simple melodies, and for inflated rhetoric. There are no examples in
her fiction of a black with unquestionable aesthetic talent.

The supposed innate capability of blacks for music, dancing, oratory,
and the visual arts is apparently related, in Stowe's mind, to her conviction of their aptitude for religion. Both "racial" traits apparently
spring from the same imaginative exuberance. In 1876, she described
the singing of blacks in a rural church in Florida and reflected on its
meaning in terms of racial peculiarities. "Singing grows to be an ecstasy,
a perfect intoxication [for the blacks]," she said; "it takes possession
of the whole man, and the 'shout' as it is called, is a sort of rhythmic
dance, in which the tropic blood of old African origin asserts more
fervid life powers." She argued that blacks sing like birds when they are
hungry or in trouble. "It takes a good deal of philosophic thought to
understand the differences of races," she concluded, and "that what suits
one race may not suit another." Black songs and dances which are a
mere "curiosity" to whites, she thought, have the "power to stir the
very deepest and best feelings of the colored race. . . . The Spirit of
God understands all languages, all races, and speaks to every man in
the tongue wherein he was born."[10]

Sometimes Stowe accounted for the supposed emotional exuberance
of blacks in especially odd and unfamiliar ways. She suggested that
blacks share the emotional qualities of "Oriental races," by which she
apparently meant principally the Jews. Blacks, she said, "will laugh,
weep, and embrace each other convulsively, and sometimes become entirely paralyzed and cataleptic." She was not certain whether this trait
"betrays" their "tropical origin" or whether it is the result of the "fact"
that blacks, Jews, and other members of "Oriental races" all come from

hot climates. At least, all these "races" share qualities with one another. "Like the Hebrews of old and the Oriental nations of the present," she said, "they [the blacks] give vent to their emotions with the utmost vivacity of expression, and their whole bodily system sympathizes with the movements of their minds."[11]

The blacks, Stowe was convinced, have certain mysterious and perhaps even magical powers which are closely associated with their religious natures. "Mesmerists have found," she said, "that the negroes are singularly susceptible to all that class of influences which produce catalepsy, mesmeric sleep, and partial clairvoyant phenomena." Since Stowe herself, after the death of her son in a drowning accident in 1858, took up spiritualism and especially the variety which involved conversations with the dead, it is probable that she took the abilities of blacks in this respect quite seriously. She found it significant that a belief in "the evil eye" was found among blacks, saying that such beliefs represent their "peculiarity of constitution." Pharaoh's magicians in the Bible, she believed, were "Africans." Even in modern Africa, she said, magic was still performed "with a degree of skill and success which can only be accounted for by supposing peculiarities of nervous constitution [among the blacks] quite different from those of the whites." When blacks are converted to Christianity, she believed, they necessarily bring their racial traits along with them. For the blacks, "the powerful stimulant of the Christian religion" has "very peculiar features." They have "visions," they hear "heavenly voices," they receive "mysterious sympathies and transmissions of knowledge from heart to heart without the intervention of the senses, or what the Quakers call being 'baptized into the spirit' of those who are distant."[12]

Another inherent trait of blacks, according to Stowe, is their imitativeness, their lack of a positive stamp of their own. "The negro is imitative," she stated flatly on one occasion, "and is very much what the influences around him make him." When she was motivated by this conviction, she would sometimes create black characters in her fiction who seem scarcely, if at all, different from the happy blacks of southern fiction of the time. Her carefree, imitative blacks are more often found in her New England stories than in her southern ones. In *The Minister's Wooing* (1859), for example, the narrator says that the eighteenth-century New England clergyman "not unfrequently had his black shadow, a sort of African Boswell, who powdered his wig, brushed his boots, defended and patronized his sermons, and strutted compla-

cently about as if through the virtue of his blackness he had absorbed
every ray of his master's dignity and wisdom." In *Poganuc People*
(1878), Colonel Davenport, a New Englander, reviews the local militia
while he is seated upon a white horse. "[J]ust behind him, also mounted,
was old Cato," says the narrator, "with his gold-laced hat and plume,
his buff breeches and long-tailed blue coat. On the whole, this solemn
black attendant formed a striking and picturesque addition to the scene."
Sam Lawson, the village humorist narrator of Stowe's short story "The
Parson's Horse-Race," describes another such black:

"Cuff was the doctor's nigger man, and he was nat'lly a drefful proud
critter. The way he could swell and strut and brag about the doctor and
his folks and his things! The doctor used to give Cuff his cast-off clothes;
and Cuff would prance round in 'em, and seem to think he was a doctor of
divinity himself, and had the charge of all natur."[13]

When Stowe was describing the supposedly good racial qualities
of the blacks, the reader may sometimes wonder whether they are not,
in reality, faults or at least virtues which are suitable chiefly for menial
laborers. One of the "traits" of blacks which she described was their
supposed ability to work for long hours in the hot sun as whites could
not. After the Civil War, she described the nature of work in the fields
of Florida in such a way as to imply that virtually all of it would have
to be done by black laborers. Clearing up scrub palmetto was a task
which was particularly onerous. "Only those black men, with sinews of
steel and nerves of wire,—men who grow stronger and more vigorous
under those burning suns that wither the white man,—" she was convinced, "are competent to the task." The modern reader may interpret
such a remark as a sign of virulent racism, since it implies that outdoor
labor in the hot sun is the peculiar talent of the black. Such a reader
should realize that this idea could be held in the nineteenth century
not merely by a white but by a black and by an abolitionist black at
that. William Wells Brown wrote, in 1863, "All time has shown that
the negro is the best laborer in the tropics." In addition to thinking that
black men are especially suited to work in the fields, Stowe also thought
that black women have a racial trait which makes them good cooks.
In *Uncle Tom's Cabin*, a slave woman is described as "a native and essential cook, . . . cooking being an indigenous talent of the African race. . . ."
The traits of both black men and black women, as Stowe described them,
would lead the reader to assume that she thought blacks especially suited
by their racial traits to perform menial labor.[14]

Rather than stating the faults of blacks directly, Stowe sometimes allowed her readers to infer them. George Harris, the fiery mulatto of *Uncle Tom's Cabin*, inherits his "high, indomitable spirit," the narrator tells us, from his white father who belonged to "one of the proudest families of Kentucky. . . ." This way of putting it suggests that it would be unlikely for him to have such a spirit if he had no white intermixture. In the same novel, the narrator tells us that blacks "are not naturally daring and enterprising, but home-loving and affectionate." The coupling of favorable and unfavorable traits is probably an attempt to soften the impact of implying strongly that the blacks are naturally defective in will and may even be cowardly. It is true that Stowe elsewhere expressed a quite different opinion on the question of whether blacks can be courageous. She wrote an introduction in 1855 to *The Colored Patriots of the American Revolution*, a book by the black author William C. Nell. In this essay, she criticized those people who had assumed that blacks are "deficient in energy and courage." Nell's book, she said, would "redeem the character of the race from this misconception, and show how much injustice there may often be in a generally admitted idea."[15]

There is no character of unmixed black ancestry in Stowe's fiction who is outstandingly handsome. At first the descendants of the princely African tribe, the Mandingoes, seem to be exceptions. There are only two such characters in her fiction—Dred and Milly in the novel *Dred.* Elsewhere Stowe suggested, however, that the Mandingoes may have acquired somehow, in their distant African past, a substantial white intermixture. How much of their beauty and intelligence they owe to their black racial heritage is, therefore, debatable. It is the quadroons and mulattoes among her characters, especially her black women characters, who monopolize beauty. In *Uncle Tom's Cabin*, George Harris's mother is said to have had only a slight black intermixture. She was "one of those unfortunates of her race marked out by personal beauty to be the slave of the passions of her possessor, and the mother of children who may never know a father." Eliza Harris, in the same novel, is an example of a beauty who is apparently the result of white intermixture. The narrator of the novel says that the "natural graces in the quadroon are often united with beauty of the most dazzling kind, and in almost every case with a personal appearance prepossessing and agreeable." Although not all the fully black characters in her fiction are ugly, they are only rarely described as handsome. An ugly black, on the

other hand, apparently never has any white intermixture. Stowe described
a black cook in her Florida home after the Civil War, for example, as
"like some uncanny gnome laughing at our perplexities." In addition,
scattered through the writings of Stowe are comparisons of blacks to
animals and birds. In her novel *The Minister's Wooing* (1859) there is
a reference to a courtyard where "three black wenches, each with a
broom, pretended to be sweeping, but were in fact chattering and laughing, like so many crows."[16]

About other nonwhite races, Stowe did not have much to say. Other
nonwhite racial and national groups also suffer, however, from the
ambivalence of her attitudes. In her geography for children, for example,
she said that Indians are a people who "think a great deal of dress"
and who paint their bodies with bright colors. She described vividly
the Indian method of scalping enemies. "These Indians [there are draw-
ings of them in the book] are very fierce and cruel," she said, "and it
was with such as these that our forefathers had to contend for a great
many years." Indian men "spent most of their time in war and hunting
and made the women raise the corn and do the work." She may not
have fully shared her sister Catharine's objections to the removal of the
Cherokee Indians from Georgia. "North of Texas is a vast country, a
large portion of which has been set apart for the various tribes of
Indians," she said. "They have been removed from various parts of the
country and settled in this territory. Here good missionaries have been
aiding them to have schools, to establish themselves in settled towns
and to live comfortably as white people." There was no suggestion in
the geography that the English or American settlers in this country had
ever mistreated the Indians, but the Spaniards had done so. They "treated
. . . Indians very wickedly. They took away their lands and made slaves
of them and behaved to them with the greatest cruelty." The result
was that a great many Indians in those parts of the United States which
had formerly been Spanish territory were "scattered over the country,
a lazy and miserable people."[17]

In some of Stowe's New England stories, there are minor Indian
characters toward whom the white characters feel a mixture of fascination, pity, and repugnance. In *Oldtown Folks* (1869), the narrator re-
calls the early mission work for Indians of the Puritan clergyman John
Eliot. "He taught them [the Indians] agriculture, and many of the arts
and trades of civilized life," says the narrator. "But he could not avert
the doom which seems to foreordain that those races shall dry up and

pass away with their native forests." One of the characters in this novel is a missionary to Indians. Parson Lathrop attempts to carry on the work of John Eliot. "[H]e talked to them of the evil of drunkenness and lying and idleness, and exhorted them to be temperate and industrious," says the narrator, "and when they, notwithstanding his exhortations, continued to lead an unthrifty, wandering life, he calmly expressed his conviction that they were children of the forest, a race destined to extinction with the progress of civilization, but continued his labors for them with automatic precision."[18]

John Eliot would probably have been surprised to learn from Stowe that he, though unsuccessful in converting Indians or in persuading them to accept the ways of whites, was nonetheless successful in convincing white New Englanders to feel kindly toward them. He himself had a good many complaints on this particular point and censured the cruelty of the whites toward Indians, but the narrator of *Oldtown Folks* sees things differently. "The traditions of tenderness, pity, and indulgence which the apostle Eliot had inwrought into the people of his day in regard to the Indians," says the narrator, still existed in the New England of the present. The "roving people" had "established rights in every household, which . . . no one ever thought of disowning. The wandering Indian was never denied a good meal, a seat by the kitchen fire, a mug of cider, and a bed in the barn." New Englanders did what they could for the Indians but apparently because of the inherent faults of the race the aid extended to them was largely in vain. The Indians were "always falling into want, and needing to be helped," says the narrator, "hanging like a tattered fringe on the thrifty and well-kept petticoat of New England society."[19]

Sometimes Stowe came near suggesting that ferocity might be an inherent trait of the Indians. In a biographical sketch of Philip H. Sheridan, published in 1868, she described his work as "subduing" the Apache Indians on a western reservation. Once Sheridan had stopped singlehandedly a quarrel among these Indians. "These turbulent savages have no more self-control than so many tigers," Stowe said, "and in a moment their knives were out, and a battle-royal was opened." The Indians could recognize, however, the personal qualities of Sheridan. "Their wild, keen instincts appreciate courage and energy, sense and kindness, quite as readily as do civilized men," she said. She may have been influenced by the fact that her nephew, Lieutenant Frederick Beecher, the son of her brother Charles, was killed in a battle between a

U.S. Army unit and a band of Indians in Colorado in 1868.[20]

In her later years, Stowe apparently came to think that Indians were not necessarily designed for extinction by factors beyond anyone's control and could, in fact, be civilized and educated. In 1877, she visited an Indian school in St. Augustine, Florida. Many of the students there had been brought from the West. She said that one of the Indians she saw there was "a woman so distinguished for fiend-like fierceness and atrocity [*sic*] that it was not deemed safe to leave her on the frontier." Another was the wife of an Indian chief and, "for an Indian . . . a handsome woman." The teachers at the school had, considering their difficulties, done wonders for their pupils. "The Indian face is naturally a stern and hard one," she said, "but as they [*sic*] gathered round their teacher and return her morning greeting the smiles on these faces made them seem even handsome." Among the pupils were adults "docile and eager, with books in hand," some of them men who had formerly been "foremost in battle and bloodshed." Stowe concluded her essay on the school with a plea that the government should provide education for all Indians.[21]

Other nonwhite races besides blacks and Indians play a small part in Stowe's writings. In her geography for children, it was the Chinese who came off best. They are "ingenious and industrious," she said, "and a great portion are taught to read." In addition, they are "trained to be respectful to their parents and rulers." Even with these virtues, however, the Chinese are still "a very thievish, deceitful, and debased people." Even worse are the South Sea islanders. She said they are among "the fiercest and cruelest" of peoples, "some of them being cannibals." She called the attention of her children readers to a drawing in the geography of a chief of one of the islands of Polynesia with a group of his counselors around him. "You see," she said to the children, "how stupid and brutal they look."[22]

In one of Stowe's New England stories, "A Student's Sea Story," the evil of a Malay character is presented as if it were related to his racial traits. The story is told by Jim Larned, who recounts the murder of his friend, Bill Jones, who had owned an oyster smack in New England. Jim recites the events which have led to the murder:

"Well, Bill had a fellow on his smack that I never liked the looks of. He was from the Malays, or some foreign critter, or other; spoke broken English; had eyes set kind o' edgeways in his head: homely as sin he was, and I always mistrusted him. 'Bill,' I used to say, 'you look out for that fellow;

don't you trust him. If I was you, I'd ship him off short metre.' But Bill, he only laughed. 'Why,' says he, 'I can get double work for the same pay out of that fellow; and what do I care if he ain't handsome?' I remember how chipper an' cheery Bill looked when he was sayin' that just as he was going down to New York with his load of oysters. Well, the next night I was sound asleep in Aunt Jerusha's front chamber that opens out towards the Sound, and I was waked right clear out of my sleep by Bill's voice screaming to me. I got up and run to the window and looked out, and I heard it again, plain as anything: 'Jim! Jim! Help, help!' It wasn't a common cry, neither; it was screeched out, as if somebody was murdering him. I tell you, it run through my head for weeks afterwards."

Later, Jim learns that Bill was indeed murdered by the Malay who stole his money and ran away. If Stowe had remembered Chaucer's "Nun's Priest's Tale," she might have had Bill point out in the dream how the Malay could be found.[23]

Stowe also had a good many essentially racist ideas about the different white peoples in Europe. Chiefly, she divided the whites in Europe between "southern races" and "northern races." In her geography for children, she explained that the people "in the southern part of Europe" are "gay and lively with very strong feelings—they love and hate and do everything else with all their hearts." She thought that her children readers would find the southern Europeans "most agreeable to talk and play with," but the northern Europeans would be "the best to advise and instruct you." Elsewhere, she mentioned another apparent racial trait of the southern Europeans. It was to be found in the emphasis on proportion and order in the architecture of Greece and Rome. Her own preference was for the architecture of "the northern races." She referred to the "forest-like firmament, glorious in holiness" of the interior of Strasbourg Cathedral. In such architecture she was convinced that she could see the "earnest northern races, whose nature was a composite of influences from pine forest, mountain, and stone, expressing, in vast proportions and gigantic masonry, those ideas of infinite duration and existence which Christianity opened before them."[24]

These "northern races," she believed, had largely disappeared in France. Without telling us how she knew, she assumed that they were the people who had designed and built the Gothic cathedrals and were also the ones who later became Huguenots. When a "Jezebel de Medici" had massacred the Huguenots, France had begun to decline. She had been "drained . . . of her lifeblood," but her folly had enriched the racial heritage of England and America. It was significant, Stowe thought, that an "expelled French refugee became the theological leader of Puritanism in England, Scotland, and America; and wherever John Calvin's system of theology had gone, civil liberty had gone with it."[25]

In the 1840s and 1850s there was much talk in the United States—in connection with westward expansion—of the supposedly resistless element of the Anglo-Saxons' character which impelled them to conquer other "inferior" races. Stowe believed that this trait was real and that it had a strong influence in the development of American slavery. In dealing with members of their own race, she said, the Anglo-Saxons have a good deal of altruism. "[T]here is in Anglo-Saxon blood," she argued, "a vigorous sense of justice, as appears in our *habeas corpus*, our jury trials and other features of state organization. . . ." She thought she could sense a racial difference between the "bosom of a military despotism" in Louis Napoleon's France and the "blessed reality" of "liberty" in England and America. "Oh, never, never let us lose that treasure," she exhorted, "of which the Anglo-Saxon race are now almost the sole guardians." When the Anglo-Saxons have problems among themselves, she said, their "aggressiveness" is "tempered . . . with the elements of gentleness and compassion. . . ." On the other hand, she was convinced that the Anglo-Saxons in dealing with people of a different race from themselves often lose their inherent kindliness. "I think a better story[,] on the whole, can be made out for the Romans," she said, "than for us. Witness the [Anglo-Saxon] treatment of the Chinese, of the tribes of India and of our own American Indians." The strongest traits of Anglo-Saxons, she believed, are "energy and indomitable perseverance. . . ." These qualities had let them to an almost equal impulse to evil and to good. "In short, the Anglo-Saxon is efficient, in whatever he sets himself about," she said "whether in crushing the weak or lifting them up." One hardly knows what to make of a racial trait which is equally at home in helping or destroying members of other races.[26]

Two other great qualities of the Anglo-Saxons, she believed, are honesty and forthrightness. The narrator of her novel *Pink and White Tyranny* (1871) develops this theme. "The Anglo-Saxon race have, so to speak," the narrator says, "a worship of truth; and they hate and abhor lying with an energy which leaves no power of tolerance." This supposed love of truth made the Anglo-Saxons more trustworthy than other races. They were especially remarkable for their fidelity to the marriage vow. In one of her later novels, *We and Our Neighbors* (1875), Stowe developed the theme that "Anglo-Saxon" women should develop feelings of compassion for "fallen women," but she seemed to think that in doing so they would have to overcome a trait in themselves which was probably racial—a horror of sexual immorality. Aunt Maria is an elderly white woman character in the novel who takes grim pleasure in contemplating disasters which may happen to women who have "gone wrong." "For the sins of women," says the narrator, "Aunt Maria had the true ingrained Saxon ferocity which Sharon Turner describes as characteristic of the original Saxon female in the earlier days of English history, when the unchaste woman was pursued and beaten, starved and frozen, from house to house, by the merciless justice of her sisters." Throughout English history, the narrator sweepingly concludes, this uncompromising rejection of immoral women has been strongly implanted in the Anglo-Saxons. Whether it is implanted in Anglo-Saxon men as well as in women is not specifically stated.[27]

The bad racial qualities of the Anglo-Saxons, Stowe thought, are their materialism, their lack of appreciation of beauty, and their cold natures which make it difficult for them to be friendly. "Oddly enough," she said, "a race [the Anglo-Saxon] born of two demonstrative, outspoken nations—the German and French—has an habitual reserve that is like neither." She sometimes urged Americans and Englishmen to try to combat the lack of genial virtues within themselves, but at other times she equated their silent tendencies with a blunt honesty which she admired. The narrator of the story "Little Foxes" admits that the Anglo-Saxons are frequently morosely silent but thinks none the less of them for it. He is convinced that

those races of men that are most distinguished for outward urbanity and courtesy are the least distinguished for truth and sincerity, and hence the well-known alliterations, "fair and false," "smooth and slippery." The fair and false Greek, the polished and wily Italian, the courteous and deceitful Frenchman, are associates which, to the strong, downright, courageous Anglo-Saxon, make up-and-down rudeness and blunt discourtesy a type of truth and honesty.

And the narrator goes on to argue that in French novels the characters frequently treat other people with outward civility but are nonetheless cruel to them.[28]

The Anglo-Saxon race is "cool, logical, and practical," Stowe said, and thus it has little patience with impulsive and emotional races. God had a reason for making the Anglo-Saxons hardy, domineering, and logical, she believed, in order to enable them to fulfill their peculiar mission in the world, the conquest of new lands and the development of stable institutions of government. On the other hand, God had also recognized the defects of the Anglo-Saxons and had attempted to compensate for them by giving the race a religion which was expressed in a language that reflected the impulsive feelings of races different from themselves. Thus God had given the Bible to the Anglo-Saxons, said Stowe, "with a foresight of their peculiar character and dominant position in the earth." He gave it to them "in the fervent language and with the glowing imagery of the more susceptible and passionate Oriental races." In general, the Anglo-Saxons had not, she believed, taken the hint. They had followed the promptings of their own sternly matter-of-fact and logical natures rather than those of emotion and love which were found in the Bible.[29]

It was this very logic and resolution of the Anglo-Saxons, said Stowe, which made them more unsuitable than other white "races" to be owners of slaves. When they accepted an institution, they were not content with half-measures. In this country, for example, they had gone about the task of enslaving blacks with a thoroughness which other races would never have thought of attempting. They had worked out a system which deprived the blacks of any protection of law and which made them completely dependent upon the kindliness of their white masters or upon whatever social pressures might be exerted upon white masters by their white neighbors. The reason that American slavery was worse than other systems of slavery was to be found, therefore, in the racial traits of the Anglo-Saxons. They are, she said, "a more coldly and strictly logical race, and have an unflinching courage to meet the consequences of every premise which they lay down, and to work out an accursed principle, with mathematical accuracy, to its most accursed results." Just how "logical" these principles were could readily be grasped by anyone, she said, who examined carefully American laws with regard to slavery. It was not because "judges are inhuman or partial," she concluded, "that they announce from the bench, in the calmest manner, decisions which one would think might make the earth shudder, and the sun turn pale." William Lloyd Garrison had a conception of the innate traits of Anglo-Saxons quite similar to that of Stowe. He was convinced, however, that it was rigorous application of law and not the language of love and emotion which was needed to combat these tendencies of the race. "We, Anglo-Saxons, being somewhat ferocious and exceedingly stubborn in our nature," he wrote to a friend just before the onset of the Civil War in 1861, "need 'line upon line, and precept upon precept,' to make us noble and good toward each other, and to those whose place in the scale of mankind is lower than our own."[30]

Where do Stowe's ideas of race come from? On this point, she gave us little help. In the nineteenth century, race theories proliferated and thus it is almost impossible to assign accurate sources for them. Ideas about Anglo-Saxons as representing the virtues of steadiness, courage, and fidelity are widespread in the works of Sir Walter Scott, works which we know Stowe had read. Her own emphasis on the virtues of middle-class Americans probably owed a good deal to the descriptions of the yeoman Saxons in his novels. The "hard and dominant Anglo-Saxon" theme in her writings suggests the debates of the time over manifest destiny and westward expansion. The comparison of the earnest and thoughtful "races" of northern Europe with the colorful, carefree, voluptuous, and artistic "races" of southern Europe was an idea empha-sized in Madame de Stael's *Corinne* (1807), a novel which we also know Stowe had read.

Stowe employed phrenology in her fiction, but only to explain the traits of individual characters, not those of races. In *The Minister's Wooing* (1859), one of her New England novels, there is a Mr. Scrobbs, a man engaged in the African slave trade in the eighteenth century. He matter-of-factly tells of shooting those blacks who had resisted being taken as slaves. He is "a square-built individual, a man of about forty, whose round head, shaggy eyebrows, small, keen eyes, broad chest, and heavy muscles showed a preponderance of the animal and brutal over the intellectual and spiritual." By contrast, Doctor Hopkins, a clergyman character in the novel, has a "forehead" which shows "the squareness of ideality giving marked effect to the outline." His head indicates that he is capable of "subtle refinements of argument and exalted ideas of morals." This is no doubt a prejudiced way of looking at people, but it is not racism.[31]

After the Civil War, a mild kind of Darwinism occasionally ap-peared in the writings of Stowe, and some of it had racist implications. In 1873, she argued that the seemingly arbitrary favor of God for certain peoples in the Old Testament was related not so much to a regard for them as individuals as to an awareness that they carried within themselves the seeds of a superior genetic stock. Thus, God had favored Sarah over Hagar because of his concern for the future of the Israelites. Of the "race" of Sarah, the "final outcome and perfected flowering was to spring forth Jesus, spoken of as the Branch of this sacred tree. For the formation of this race, we see a constant choice of the gentler and quiet elements of blood and character, and the persistent rejection of that which is wild, fierce, and ungovernable." It was not that God felt an antipathy to those persons he felt obliged to reject. "The thoughtful, patient, meditative Isaac is chosen; the wild, hot-blooded, impetuous Ishmael is rejected—not as in themselves better or worse, but as in relation to their adaptation to a great purpose of future good of mankind." And yet Stowe did not apply this idea of Darwinian selection to races generally.[32]

A source for Stowe's ideas on the racial traits of blacks may have been the public lectures of Alexander Kinmont, a young man who lived in Cincinnati at a time when she also lived there. There is no evidence that she knew him, but there is a striking similarity between some of his ideas on race and hers, especially in the conviction which they shared that it is the inherent meekness of the blacks which gives them a special talent for religion. The lectures were given in Cincinnati in the winter of 1837-38. Kinmont died suddenly in September, 1838, but shortly afterward some unknown person or persons edited and published the lectures. The reason the editor's name was omitted may have been that though Kinmont was a gentle and noncombative person, he had ideas about race and slavery which might have aroused opposition in Cincinnati. The book is entitled *Twelve Lectures on the Natural History of Man, and the Rise and Progress of Philosophy.*[33]

Though he was reared in poverty in Scotland, Kinmont had been given a good education. When he was thirteen, he came under the influence of an Englishman who taught him classical and modern languages and mathematics. He received a scholarship at the University of St. Andrews and pursued his studies there, receiving a master of arts degree. He emigrated to the United States and came, eventually, to Cincinnati where he was known as an excellent teacher in a private school for boys. Earlier in life, he had undergone a religious crisis and for a time had become skeptical and despairing. He was attracted to the ideas of Emmanuel Swedenborg, however, and for the remaining years of his life his religious faith never wavered.[34]

Kinmont's major idea with regard to race was that each race has been entrusted by God with some earthly mission peculiar to it. Logic and the ability to organize affairs are virtues in which the Anglo-Saxons particularly excel. They are one of the "northern races" of Europe, races

which have less "intuition" than the "southern races" but more practicality and common sense. Though it was Galileo, a member of the
"southern races" of Europe, who first grasped the nature of the laws
of motion, Kinmont said, it was Newton, a member of one of the
"northern races," who had worked them into a coherent system.[35]

As much as Kinmont admired the white races, he was convinced
that the blacks represent a potentially higher development. The whites
excel in rationality, logic, and action; the blacks excel in love and
emotion. The "Caucasian" had been destined by God "to reflect the
luster of the divine wisdom, or, to speak more properly, the divine
science," but the blacks would build "a far nobler civilization." They
embody "the splendor of the divine attributes of mercy and benevolence
in the practice and exhibition of all the milder and gentler virtues."
Even those qualities which the Caucasians regard as unimportant in
blacks may be the basis of their later superior development. The
"natural talent for music with which they are preeminently endowed,"
he said, "will help them create a civilization in which the attributes
of love and benevolence will be paramount." The "light-hearted" nature of the blacks, their "want of solicitude about the future," may seem
to be a "vice" to the Caucasians, he conceded, but it is nonetheless the
basis of that perfect trust in God recommended in the Sermon on the
Mount. Because there "is more of the child, of the unsophisticate nature
in the negro race than in the European," explained Kinmont, there is
also a greater approximation to the divine nature. What chiefly distinguishes the blacks from the whites is their "willingness to serve," he
said, and this is "the most beautiful trait of humanity, which we, from
our [the white race's] own innate love of dominion, and in defiance
of the Christian religion, brand with the name of servility, and abuse
not less to our dishonor than to their injury." Though both the whites
and the blacks have important special missions which come from God,
that of the blacks is the higher one. The "Caucasian" would continue
to flourish as a "versatile genius," but the black would create a civilization which would represent "the very type itself of affection and of
gentleness."[36]

Kinmont did not directly argue that the blacks ought to go back
to Africa, but this idea was strongly implied in some of his lectures.
Blacks are naturally attached to their "homeland" in Africa, he said,
and have no desire to go elsewhere. The "Caucasian" had "dragged"
the black, "contrary to his genius and inclination, from his native re-

gions, and in America he is an exile." It is Africa which is "the appropriate and destined seat of his future glory and civilization. . . ." In the "sweet and mellow light" of Africa would flower "the attributes of divine beneficence" of the blacks. There they would create a civilization "from the cultivation of innocence, simplicity and virtue." It would be a more "enduring civilization than that of the whites, because it would be "the only right kind, but the latest in arriving at perfection. . . ."[37]

As we shall see, the parallels between Kinmont's ideas of race and those of Stowe are remarkable. Uncle Tom might be said to represent a foreshadowing of the kind of black who would create this noble African civilization. Like Kinmont, Stowe would see Africa as the home of a future high civilization, higher in fact than that of the whites in Europe and America. Like Kinmont, she would argue that the blacks ought to return to Africa. At least, this would be her position when she wrote *Uncle Tom's Cabin*.

It is instructive to compare Stowe's ideas concerning slavery with those concerning race. She was a better critic of the institution of slavery than she was of theories of race. With regard to slavery, she had a shrewd intelligence and a knowledge of human nature. A careful reading of *Uncle Tom's Cabin* will disclose that she anticipated most of the objections which proslavery opinion would bring against it. The charge frequently made against her that she was sentimental needs a good deal of qualification. The chief weakness of a truly sentimental writer is to dissolve into tears when the occasion calls for a clear appraisal, and she was not sentimental in this sense.[38]

The most serious weakness of Stowe's approach lies in an area which was scarcely visible at all to her contemporaries or to her readers for generations afterward. It was her legacy of race theory and especially her conception of the innate meekness and humility of the black which would eventually cause the most trouble. As an argument for the ending of slavery, the emphasis upon these supposed traits was probably an advantage, because it suggested that the blacks would not be troublesome when they were freed. For readers who might not be convinced by this argument, she had another in reserve—the idea that the blacks should be induced, by what means she does not say, to return to Africa. There, she thought, their superior qualities would enable them to create a superior civilization.

Most of the difficulties of Stowe's racial theories would not become obvious until long after the Civil War, when there was no longer any serious talk of sending the blacks back to Africa. Though some blacks recognized from the first that Uncle Tom was not a satisfactory image for the ideal black, the large-scale rejection of him and of *Uncle Tom's Cabin* generally among blacks would not occur until nearly a hundred years later, not in fact until after World War II. The delay would be caused principally by the fact that for many years after the Civil War any black who wrote about *Uncle Tom's Cabin* was likely to be strongly aware of the tremendous influence of the novel in convincing the North of the evils of slavery. It was sometimes said, in fact, that *Uncle Tom's Cabin* was the greatest single influence in giving blacks their freedom. In the face of this conviction, it is understandable that a full-scale attack upon the racial image of Uncle Tom among blacks was a long time coming. When it did come, it was all the stronger—in fact so strong that many black readers (and many white ones, for that matter) would reject *Uncle Tom's Cabin* completely.

VI

The Writing of Uncle Tom's Cabin

STOWE LEFT CINCINNATI and moved to Brunswick, Maine, in the spring of 1850. It would be nearly a year after that, however, before she would begin the actual writing of *Uncle Tom's Cabin*. Her seventh and last child, named Charles Edward after her baby son who had died in 1849, was born in July, 1850. Calvin was obliged to return to Cincinnati in the fall of that year to remain until a replacement could be found for him at Lane Seminary. When she first went to Brunswick, Stowe had little time for literary composition. For one thing, she had to set up a new household. The new place did offer advantages, however, for writing an antislavery novel. Slavery was no longer only a few miles away, as it had been in Cincinnati, but her distance from it may have enabled her to see the subject with a broader perspective. One of the advantages of the new place was that its people were not likely to regard antislavery with horror. If there had been any possibility that she might have become more reconciled to slavery because it was far away, the passage of the Fugitive Slave Law in 1850 made any such development virtually impossible.

Citizens in the free states were required by the Constitution to return fugitive slaves. What was new in the Fugitive Slave Law of 1850 was the suspension of judicial process. The task of returning runaways

was taken out of the hands of the courts and turned over to federal commissioners. All the pursuing slaveholder or his agent had to do was to
present an affadavit of ownership to the commissioner, who was em-
powered either to declare the runaway free or to turn him over to the
person who claimed to own him. Common legal safeguards, such as a
judicial hearing or a jury trial, were absent. If a commissioner decided
that a person was not a slave, he was paid five dollars. If he decided a
person was a slave, he was paid ten dollars. The reason given for one
fee being greater than the other was that returning the slave would require more paper work than freeing him. The difference in fees convinced
many antislavery people that the commissioners were being bribed to
rule against an alleged runaway in doubtful cases. The law did not
merely make it more difficult for runaway slaves to escape; it also posed
a potential threat to a great many people, and especially to free blacks.
If a federal commissioner ruled that a person was a runaway slave,
there was no way that he could appeal to the courts.[1]

Most of what we know about the composition of *Uncle Tom's Cabin*
comes from information which was written many years later. These
accounts, especially those of Stowe herself, frequently have an apoca-
lyptic character which makes it difficult for the reader to sort out either
her motives for writing the book or the process by which she composed
it. Two events should be distinguished. The decision to enter the antislavery battle and the decision to write *Uncle Tom's Cabin* did not happen simultaneously. In one sense, the decision to enter the antislavery
struggle went back to 1845 when Stowe had published the short story,
"Immediate Emancipation," but that story had simply been an appeal
to southerners to free their slaves. In August, 1850, she published another story in which her treatment of the issue of slavery was more
urgent and uncompromising. The story appeared in a magazine several
months before she began the writing of *Uncle Tom's Cabin*.

The story is entitled "The Freeman's Dream: A Parable." Written
in language which suggests the Bible, it relates the capture by slave-
catchers of a family of fugitive slaves in a northern state. The slaves
encounter a northern white man on a road. The husband and father of
the slave family appeals to the white man to aid him and his family.
The white man considers responding to the appeal but decides against it:

The man was not hard, and his heart misgave him when he looked on
the failing eye and the toil-worn face—when he saw the worn and trembling
hands stretched forth; but he bethought him of human laws, and he feared

to befriend him, and he hardened his heart, and set his face as a flint, and bade him pass on, and trouble him not.

And it was so that after he passed on, he saw the pursuers come up with him, and the man and woman could not escape, because they were weary and footsore, and there was no strength in them. And the man heard their screams, and saw them bound and taken by them that would not show mercy.

As dramatic as it is, this scene is much less so than what follows. The northern white man has a vision of divine retribution against himself. It is not wholly clear whether this vision is real or merely a dream:

[I]t seemed to him that the sky grew dark, and the earth rocked to and fro, and the heavens flashed with a strange light, and a distant rush, as of wings, was heard, and suddenly, in mid heavens, appeared a sign of the Son of Man, with his mighty angels. Upward, born from the earth towards the great white throne and Him that sat thereon, before whose face the heavens and the earth fled away.

Thus, the northerner is summoned before God to answer for the offense of having obeyed an earthly law which was in conflict with a divine one. We are not told the penalty which this man suffers for his transgression. The story goes on to upbraid those

who seem to think that there is no standard of right and wrong higher than an act of Congress, or an interpretation of the United States Constitution. It is humiliating to think that there should be in the church of Christ men and ministers who should need to be reminded that the laws of their Master are above human laws which come in conflict with them; and that though heaven and earth pass away, His Word shall not pass away.[2]

In terms of its effectiveness as an antislavery argument, "The Freeman's Dream" is notably weak. Calling down divine retribution upon one's opponents is risky business and is likely to result in nothing more than having them appeal to the same divine power. Stowe probably recognized later that the degree of her effectiveness as an opponent of slavery would not be in proportion to the amount of horror and indignation she felt. Compared with this crude effort, *Uncle Tom's Cabin* would be a masterpiece of persuasion. There would be horror and indignation in it too, but these qualities would be expressed in such a way as to make the reader more likely to feel them himself.

Toward the end of 1850, Mrs. Edward Beecher, Harriet's sister-in-law, wrote a letter to her. "If I could use a pen as you can," she is quoted as saying, "I would write something that would make this whole nation feel what an accursed thing slavery is." One of Stowe's children, who is not named, is the authority for having remembered the effect of the letter upon his or her mother. When Stowe read the passage aloud to the family, she rose from her chair, crushed the letter in her hand, and with an expression on her face which deeply impressed the child said: "I will write something. I will if I live." The "if I live" is significant. Up until the time of her great success, Stowe took a gloomy view of her own health. She apparently thought that she might not live long. It may have been that this conviction lent a special urgency to the task of writing the novel. After she became a celebrity, her health greatly improved. She still suffered from fatigue and nervousness, but she never again had a serious illness until she died at the age of eighty-five.[3]

To Calvin, who was still in Cincinnati, Stowe wrote a letter in which she repeated her determination to write the novel. "As long as the baby sleeps with me nights I can't do much at any thing—but I shall *do it at last.* I shall write that thing if I live. . . ." Later in the letter she expressed her horror at the Fugitive Slave Law. "What do all you folks think about the slave law and about the stand taken by Boston ministers generally except Edward[?]" Apparently speaking of those Boston clergymen who refused to speak out against the Fugitive Slave Law and Daniel Webster who openly supported it, she said, "To me it is incredible—amazing—mournful. . . ." Her Aunt Mary who had married the slaveowner in Jamaica had sometimes thought that the island would sink under the weight of the iniquity of slavery. Now, Stowe said something similar. "I feel as I could be willing to sink with it [the United States], were all this sin and misery to sink in the sea. . . ." She still had her faith in her father's ability to respond to crises. "I wish Father would come to Boston and preach on the Fugitive Slave law as he once [in Litchfield when she was a child] preached on the slave trade. . . . Mrs. Judge Reeves was crying in one pew and I in another. I wish some Martin Luther would arise to set this community right."[4]

In the midst of the excitement, Stowe had her domestic duties to think of. To Calvin Stowe in Cincinnati, she wrote about the difficulties of caring for the family and the house in Brunswick. The stoves were inadequate; if she sat by the fire in the parlor her back froze. When she had a headache, there was no place during the day where she could lie down to take a nap without being disturbed. "Overhead is the schoolroom[,] in the next room the dining room, and the girls practice there two hours a day; & if I lock my door and lie down some one is sure to be at it before a half hour is through." She thought it would be difficult to meet their expenses. "God shall enable us to come thro notwithstanding," she said, "but I don't want to feel obliged to work as hard every year as I have this—I can earn two hundred by writing[,] but I don't want to feel that I *must* and when weary with teaching children, and tending the baby, buying provisions, settling bills, cutting out clothes still to feel that I *must* write a piece for some paper." In spite of her difficulties, she mentioned that she was thinking of writing something on the subject of slavery. "I am projecting a sketch for the [*National*] 'Era' of [on?] the capabilities of liberated blacks to take care of themselves," she told him. "Can't you find out for me how much Willie Watson has paid for the redemption of his friends—and get me any items in figures of that kind that you can pick up in Cincinnati[?]."[5]

It was probably about this time, in January, 1851, that Henry Ward Beecher visited Harriet and the two had a conversation about what each one planned to do to combat slavery. In a letter written many years later to George Eliot, Stowe mentioned this visit. Henry Ward did not arrive until nearly midnight, and the two sat up until dawn to exchange opinions and formulate plans. "Henry told me then that he meant to fight that battle in New York," Stowe wrote; "that he would have a church that would stand by him to resist the tyrannic dictation of Southern slaveholders." She told him of her own plans. "I said: 'I, too have begun to do something; I have begun a story, trying to set forth sufferings and wrongs of the slaves.'" As the most successful member of the Beecher family, pastor of a wealthy church in Brooklyn, Henry Ward may have been a little patronizing to his sister. "'That's right, Hattie,'" Stowe quoted him as saying; "'finish it and I will scatter it thick as the leaves of Vallambrosa. . . .'" As well known as he was, Stowe would outdistance him in reputation. As Forrest Wilson pointed out in his biography of Stowe, she "scattered her own leaves of Vallambrosa."[6]

Not long afterward, probably in February of 1851, Stowe imagined the character of Uncle Tom. During a communion service at the First Parish Church in Brunswick, she had what she could only describe as a "vision" of the scene which illustrated the worst possible evil of slavery—death by torture. Stowe said that she wrote out a scene of Uncle Tom's being whipped to death and read it to her two sons, Henry and Frederick, then twelve and ten years old. The children wept and one of them exclaimed, "Oh, mamma! slavery is the most cruel thing in the world."[7]

There is another story about how Stowe imagined the scene containing the death of Uncle Tom which would seem to be inconsistent with this one. Mrs. John T. Howard, a parishioner in Henry Ward Beecher's church, was one of Stowe's friends. She said Stowe told her that the scene of the death of Uncle Tom came to her only when she arrived at that part of the novel and not before she had begun the writing of it. Stowe told her, Mrs. Howard said, of the process by which she came to imagine the death scene. She was approaching the end of the novel when she and Calvin were visiting in Andover, Massachusetts, where he had been offered a professorship. The purpose of their visit, in this account, was to search for a house in which they would live when they should come to Andover. After a morning's inspection of houses, the Stowes returned to a boardinghouse for lunch. Afterward, the two went to their room for a rest. Just as Stowe was about to lie down, however, an idea flashed into her mind of how to write Uncle Tom's death scene. Mrs. Howard attempted to reconstruct what she remembered Stowe as saying at this point:

[S]uddenly arose before me the death scene of Uncle Tom. . . . I sat down at the table and wrote nine pages of foolscap paper without pausing, except long enough to dip my pen into the inkstand. Just as I had finished, Mr. Stowe awoke. "Wife," said he, "have you not lain down yet?" "No," I answered, "I have been writing, and I want you to listen to this and see if it will do." I read aloud to him with the tears flowing fast. He wept, too, and before I had finished, his sobs shook the bed upon which he was lying. He sprung up saying, "Do! I should think it would do!" and folding the sheets he immediately directed and sent them to the publisher, without one word of correction or revision of any kind. I have often thought . . . that if anything had happened to that package in going, it would not have been possible for me to have reproduced it.[8]

In the introduction to the 1879 edition of *Uncle Tom's Cabin*, Stowe told how she had written the whipping scene of Uncle Tom before anything else in the novel and how she had read it to her children. When she read this account, Mrs. Howard remembered what Stowe had previously told her and asked her about the contradiction. As Mrs. Howard told the story, Stowe denied that there was any inconsistency between the two accounts. "[B]oth are true," Mrs. Howard quoted her as saying, "for I had entirely forgotten that I had ever written that sketch, and I suppose that I had unconsciously woven it in with the other." There is another difficulty, however, in the way of our accepting this account. Annie Fields, in her edition of *Life and Letters of*

Harriet Beecher Stowe, published in 1897 after Stowe's death, said that Calvin Stowe received no inkling of his being considered for an appointment to the Andover Seminary faculty until months after *Uncle Tom's Cabin* had been published and, therefore, the scene in the boardinghouse in Andover could not have taken place.[9]

It is possible to conclude from these differing accounts that Stowe was simply careless with the truth. Elizabeth Barrett Browning probably knew nothing about these discrepancies. When she met Stowe in 1857, however, she wrote a letter to a friend about her. She praised her but noted that she had "a mouth which wants something in frankness. . . ." Of course, the observation proves nothing. Mrs. Browning—like Stowe herself—was susceptible to the fad of determining human character by physical traits. In addition, both of them took spiritualist séances seriously. Stowe was probably not lying when she gave these different accounts of writing the scene of the death of Uncle Tom. People who live in a world of imagination are more prone than other people, probably, to mistake their ideas for facts. In the main, Stowe managed to keep fact and fiction separated in her mind, but every now and then there was a perceptible slip.[10]

One of Stowe's ideas about the composition of *Uncle Tom's Cabin* has called forth a good deal of mirthful comment from critics. This was her conviction that it was not she but God who wrote the book. One of the accounts of her making this claim placed the incident at a time when she was an old woman and failing mentally. In her edition of *The Life and Letters of Harriet Beecher Stowe* (1897), Annie Fields inserted a note which recounted a tale of an elderly sea captain who met Stowe on the streets of Hartford while she was out for a stroll:

"When I was younger," said he respectfully, holding his hat in his hand while he spoke, "I read with a great deal of satisfaction and instruction *Uncle Tom's Cabin*. The story impressed me very much, and I am happy to shake hands with you, Mrs. Stowe, who wrote it." "I did not write it," answered the white-haired old lady gently, as she shook the captain's hand. "You didn't?" he ejaculated in amazement. "Why, who did, then?" "God wrote it," she replied simply. "I merely did his dictation." "Amen," said the captain reverently, as he walked thoughtfully away.[11]

The idea that God wrote *Uncle Tom's Cabin* may suggest that Stowe had been possessed with a prolonged spell of religious hysteria. As the nation moved toward war after the novel was published, she did sometimes become emotional and strident. Perhaps she did not always clearly distinguish between God's voice and her own. When she was writing the novel, however, there is no evidence that she thought God was guiding her pen. On the other hand, there is plenty of evidence in her writings to show that she believed that God gives specific missions to people on earth. One of the themes of Lyman Beecher had been that a person might find himself a deputy of God in carrying out divine tasks. The selection of a person as God's emissary need not imply an endorsement of that person's merit. Lyman could go to Cincinnati as a response to the Lord's command to save the West for Christianity. "That he believed himself personally deputed by the Creator to carry out these plans," said his great-grandson Lyman Beecher Stowe in 1934, "inevitably gave him implicit confidence in their rightness." And yet something saved Lyman Beecher from self-righteousness. He apparently thought that the will of God is unspecific about how a mission is to be carried out. Thus he was not obsessed with the idea of his own importance. In his mission of saving the West for Christianity, he was nearly always willing to listen to other people, to compromise on nonessential issues, and to maintain a healthy sense of his own fallibility.[12]

Several years before she wrote *Uncle Tom's Cabin*, Stowe examined the puzzling matter in the Bible of how God might sometimes choose the most unlikely people to perform specific tasks for him. In the Old Testament, for example, it was difficult to see Jacob as a suitable person to accomplish the great mission which God had given to him:

Gentle, affectionate, but entirely devoid of courage, either physical or moral; accomplishing his purpose always by adroit and sagacious, rather than by straight-forward and decided means; always managing and prudent, but sometimes sinking into duplicity, he seems at first to be a character in no way remarkable for positive excellence. But divine preferences are not to be regarded simply as indications of personal feeling, but founded on the fitness of the individual to accomplish a present design. The plan of God in just that crisis, required a man qualified to raise a large, peaceable family in the midst of adverse and contending tribes; and the whole history of Jacob shows that he was admirably adapted to this.

God comes across to the reader of this passage as rather like a shrewd Yankee casting about for the best way to get a thing done and not too much concerned about the ethics involved. It is worth noting, however, that the fact of Jacob's being given an important mission is no endorsement of his character. It seems probable that Stowe did not imagine that if God chose *Uncle Tom's Cabin* to help end slavery the choice involved the conferring of any particular sanctity or authority on the novel, and certainly none on herself.[13]

When *Uncle Tom's Cabin* caused a great stir in the world, it occurred to Stowe that the purposes of the Lord might be at work, but she was careful to add that she thought of herself as wholly fallible and prone to error. Her comments on the subject suggested an attitude toward God rather like that expressed by writers in prefaces of their works toward people to whom they are indebted for help but who, they hasten to add, are not responsible for any errors. To an admirer in Scotland, Stowe wrote:

That Christian hearts in good old Scotland should turn so warmly to me seems to me like a dream; yet it is no less a most pleasant one. For myself, I can claim no merit in that work which has been the cause of this. It was an irresistible outburst and had no more merit in it than a mother's wailing for her first born. The success of the work, so strange, so utterly unexpected, only astonishes me. I can only say that this bubble of my mind has risen on the mighty stream of a *divine purpose*, and even a bubble can go far on such a tide. . . .

In a reply to a letter of congratulations from the Earl of Shaftesbury, Stowe expressed a similar idea. "I can only see that when a Higher Being has purposes to be accomplished," she said, "he can make even 'a grain of mustard seed,' the means."[14]

Something different from its success in spreading antislavery opinion may have caused Stowe to think God had a hand in the writing of *Uncle Tom's Cabin*. Like other writers of fiction, she was apparently puzzled about how the characters and events of the novel could have so seemingly real an existence. Howard Mumford Jones made the valid point, in 1962, that her explanation of how she wrote the novel had "a certain hallucinatory fascination." "Many a writer, once his book is out," said Jones, "has a queer feeling that somebody else wrote it." Nothing in Stowe's previous writings approached *Uncle Tom's Cabin* in depth of passion or in the ability to persuade. The characters range through its pages: people of different stations, different sections, different civilizations even, and yet many of them are effectively drawn as individual people. Stowe herself noted how a character could have the strange quality of taking on a life of its own independently of the author's intention. She made this point when Edward Beecher expressed an older brother's cautionary concern that she might allow her great success to turn her head. Her friend Mrs. John Howard recorded her memory of Stowe's response to Edward's warning when his letter was read aloud:

She dropped her [hair]brush from her hand and exclaimed with earnestness, "Dear soul, he need not be troubled. He doesn't know that I did not write that book!" "What!" said I, "you did not write Uncle Tom?" "No," she said, "I only put down what I saw." "But you have been at the South, have you?" I asked. "No," she said, "but it all came before me in visions, one after another, and I put them down in words." But being still skeptical, I said, "Still you must have arranged the events." "No," said she, "your Annie approached me for letting Eva die. Why, I felt it as a death in my own family, and it affected me so deeply that I could not write a word for two weeks after her death." "And did you know," I asked, "that Uncle Tom would die?" "Oh, yes," she answered, "I knew that he must die from the first, but I did not know *how*. When I got to that part of the story, I saw no more for some time."

The imaginative creation of *Uncle Tom's Cabin*, like that of all works of art, is a mystery. In attempting to explain it, Edward Wagenknecht has perceptively used a phrase of Henry James, "the suddenly determined absolute of perception." The phrase may come as near as anything to indicating how Stowe could have written a novel so much more powerful than anything else she ever wrote.[15]

Whether her conviction that God had written *Uncle Tom's Cabin* came chiefly from her religious faith or whether it came from her inability to understand how one could create reality in fiction, it had some unfortunate consequences. To introduce the intentions of God into a political issue is dangerous enough. To introduce them in connection with one's own contribution to the debate is worse. Luckily, the idea that God may have written *Uncle Tom's Cabin* did not strongly occur to Stowe until the great furore over the novel had largely passed. If skeptical critics had suspected she had such a conviction, they would have been even more impassioned in their responses.

Though *Uncle Tom's Cabin* often has a strongly emotional tone, it is not messianic. What gives the novel its continuing power is chiefly that the characters in it are recognizable as human beings reacting in complex ways to their experience. It is directed against slavery and not against the white South, and it concedes the North's complicity in guilt. It also concedes the point that many white southerners attempt to alleviate the cruelties and injustices of slavery which they believe they are helpless to abolish or even substantially to change. Most important of all, the novel is directed to the nation, not alone to the North.

That it was not received in this spirit says more about the excited state of opinion of the time than it does about the novel. Though Stowe would come to believe that God may have written *Uncle Tom's Cabin*, or at least had something to do with the writing of it, the novel fortunately makes no such claim for itself.

That Stowe did not begin writing *Uncle Tom's Cabin* as a command from God is strongly suggested by the fact that she apparently had at first no intention of writing a full-length novel. She wrote Dr. Gamaliel Bailey, the publisher of the *National Era* in Washington, D.C., that her story would extend through three or four numbers of the weekly journal and that it would be ready within two weeks. Actually, the story was to run for forty issues. Dr. Bailey paid her $300 for the story, which would have been a good price if it had been no longer than it was projected to be. Later he asked her to name an additional figure for the extended length of the novel. She suggested the very modest figure of $100, and he paid it to her.[16]

Even though she thought the story would not be a long one, she recognized that it was more important than anything she had done before. She said of it to Dr. Bailey:

[It will be] a series of sketches which give the lights and shadows of the "patriarchal institution," written either from observation, incidents which have occurred in the sphere of my observation, incidents which have occurred in the sphere of my personal knowledge, or in the knowledge of my friends. I shall show the *best side* of the thing, and something *faintly approaching the worst.*

Up to this year I have always felt that I had no particular call to meddle with this subject, and I dread to expose even my own mind to the full force of its exciting power. But I feel now that the time is come when even a woman or a child who can speak a word for freedom and humanity is bound to speak. . . .

My vocation is simply that of a *painter*, and my object will be to hold up in the most lifelike and graphic manner possible Slavery, its reverses, changes, and the negro character which I have had ample opportunity for studying. There is no arguing with *pictures*, and everybody is impressed by them, whether they mean to be or not.[17]

At one point in her letter to Dr. Bailey, Stowe showed that she understood that it might take something more than persuasion to end slavery. "The Carthagenian women in the last peril of their state cut off their hair for bow-strings to give to the defenders of their country," she said, "and such peril and shame as now hangs over this country is worse than Roman slavery, and I hope every woman who can write will not be silent. . . ." The militant note is probably merely figurative, but it is nonetheless significant. Persuasion which is not backed up by a determination not to yield beyond a certain point is almost certain to fail. This is not the fault of Stowe but a tragic fact of human history. If she is to be blamed, it is for not knowing what no one else then knew either—that the price in the bloodshed of war might be almost unimaginably high.[18]

A major source of the strength of *Uncle Tom's Cabin* is its humor. It was not a vein which Stowe had done much with in her previous writings, and it was almost wholly absent in the antislavery fiction of other writers. She seems to have recognized that many people might concede the evils of slavery without feeling obliged to do anything about them or even to read about them. Humor was a way of establishing the reality of the characters of the novel, especially that of the blacks. Once the reader came to recognize these characters as human beings struggling with an institution which gave all the power over their lives to their owners, his sympathy for them would become less abstract and more personal. In the 1879 introduction to *Uncle Tom's Cabin*, Stowe described this aspect of her approach:

[S]he was convinced that the presentation of slavery alone, in its most dreadful forms, would be a picture of such unrelieved horror and darkness as nobody could be induced to look at. Of set purpose, she sought to light up the darkness by humorous and grotesque episodes and the presentation of the milder and more amusing phases of slavery, for which her recollection of the never-failing wit and drollery of her former colored friends in Ohio gave her abundant material.[19]

Though humor is a source of the strength of *Uncle Tom's Cabin* as an antislavery novel, it is also the occasion for some ambivalence in the perceptions of the modern reader. A major source of the humor in the novel is to be found in its black characters. One can see them not as buffoons but as people who are forced to develop stratagems for self-protection and sometimes for survival. It is true that Stowe has enough racism in her writings to make the modern reader wonder whether this explanation will always suffice. He may wonder sometimes whether the black characters in the novel are meant to show the inherent stupidity of the race. Yet many of the stratagems of the black characters show considerable ingenuity. When they do not choose the best methods of achieving their ends, the reason may be ignorance rather than stupidity.

For their ignorance, they can scarcely be blamed. The reader does not finish reading *Uncle Tom's Cabin* with the conviction that the black characters in it are inherently stupid.

The chief surprise which the novel is likely to give a modern reader is that for all its clichés of exhortation, for all its vehement moral purpose, it still has power. The characters are generally drawn carefully in such a way as to think and act in a credible manner. In the passion of her moral argument, Stowe does not lose sight of the major task of a novelist—to conjure up a world, a fictional world but one which is believable. Sometimes critics have assumed that it was the subject of antislavery which made *Uncle Tom's Cabin* a powerful novel. It is perhaps more nearly true to say the opposite—that because *Uncle Tom's Cabin* was a powerful novel, antislavery became a powerful cause.

VII

Uncle Tom's Cabin
Part I

UNCLE TOM'S CABIN is a novel with two plots, and the relationship between them is not fully clear until almost its last pages. One story is that of Uncle Tom, a black with no white intermixture, the slave of Mr. Shelby, a Kentucky plantation owner. Mr. Shelby gets into financial trouble and is obliged to sell two of his slaves, one of whom is Uncle Tom. Though he has a wife and children, Uncle Tom submits without protest to being sold away from them. Mr. Haley, a slavetrader and his new owner, takes him to New Orleans. On the way there, Tom performs a heroic deed. Evangeline, or Eva, the ethereal little daughter of Augustine St. Clare, falls overboard from the deck of a river steamer and Tom rescues her from drowning. In gratitude, St. Clare purchases Tom. In New Orleans, Tom becomes the coachman and house servant of the St. Clare family and is well treated. After the deaths of Eva and St. Clare, however, the cruel Marie St. Clare, Augustine's wife and Eva's mother, sells Tom. He becomes the slave of Simon Legree, who has a plantation in a remote section of the state on the Red River. There Legree savagely maltreats his slaves, and he eventually whips Tom to death.

The other story in the novel is that of George and Eliza Harris and of their little son, Harry. These characters have a large amount of white intermixture and can, in fact, pass as whites. Eliza and Harry, like Tom, are owned by Mr. Shelby, but George is owned by a Mr. Harris. Resenting George's intelligence and ability, Harris assigns him menial tasks and allows his adolescent son to whip him with switches, the purpose being to break his spirit. At the beginning of the novel, George decides to run away to Canada with the hope of later purchasing his wife and child. After George runs away, Eliza discovers that Shelby has sold her child Harry as well as Uncle Tom to a slave trader. She flees in terror with Harry and performs the dramatic but improbable feat of crossing the Ohio with a child in her arms by leaping from ice floe to ice floe. There are no dogs to chase her. These would be added when *Uncle Tom's Cabin* became a play. Later, Eliza and Harry join George Harris and all three escape to Canada.

Even critics favorably disposed to *Uncle Tom's Cabin* were sometimes puzzled about its having two plots. This particular arrangement was unknown in novels then, though about twenty years later Leo Tolstoy was to use it in *Anna Karenina* and it has since become a familiar device. An advantage of using two plots was that it enabled Stowe to explore attitudes toward slavery in both the South and the North. Tom's experience with three different slave masters represents, roughly, the major differences among the conditions of slaves in the South. At one extreme is the kindly Augustine St. Clare; at the other is the evil Simon Legree, with Shelby representing the middle between the two—he is generally kindly but submits fairly casually to the separation of families even when he is confronted with what is apparently only a temporary shortage of cash. The plot involving George, Eliza, and Harry Harris, on the other hand, enabled Stowe to involve the North directly in slavery. The family encounters a wide range of northern opinion on slavery in their flight to Canada.

Tom is quite different, of course, from George Harris. One can interpret this difference to mean that Tom is more nearly Christian than George is. Remembering all that Stowe had said about the "docile" and inherently meek blacks, however, one wonders to what extent Tom's virtues are merely evidence of his innate racial character. Some of his "virtues" are likely to appear to the modern reader as defects. His Christian love and trust preclude, for example, his having any strong sense of his own rights. Quite different from Tom is the mulatto George Harris. That Harris owes his willingness to take his own part to his white intermixture is not something which Stowe merely implies. The narrator of the novel states the idea with considerable definiteness. Thus, *Uncle Tom's Cabin* does not merely explore differences in attitude toward slavery between white southerners and white northerners. It also explores the ideas and attitudes of two races, white and black, which Stowe regarded as fundamentally different from one another. These differences can be most clearly recognized, perhaps, in her portrayal of those blacks who have substantial white intermixture and those blacks who have none at all.

In addition to having two plots, *Uncle Tom's Cabin* is different in another way from virtually all other novels of any period or place. It has no love story. From the standpoint of its power in the antislavery struggle, this omission was undoubtedly an advantage. People who strongly objected to reading novels objected to them principally because of their romantic love stories. *Uncle Tom's Cabin* could not be rejected for this reason. As one reviewer pointed out, it is "destitute of that which is the ordinary resource of the writers of fiction—the adventure of two lovers." The only other novel the reviewer could think of which did not have a love story was *Robinson Crusoe*.[1]

Another curiosity of *Uncle Tom's Cabin* is to be found in its title. The cabin which appears in the early pages of the novel soon disappears, and Tom never sees it again. As a symbol of the family, however, the cabin serves to direct the attention of the reader to one of the chief evils of slavery—the fact that it separates families. The use of the cabin in the title was an astute device on Stowe's part, especially in a society which strongly maintained, at least in principle, a respect for the family as one of its highest ideals. *Uncle Tom's Cabin* showed how hollow this commitment was under slavery.

Tom himself is obviously intended to be the novel's major weapon against slavery. To the modern reader, he certainly does seem excessively meek. On the other hand, he is not the quavering white-headed old man he would become in nearly all the dramatic adaptations of the novel. The Tom of the novel is "a large, broad-chested, powerfully made man, of a full glossy black and with a face whose truly African features are characterized by an expression of steady good sense, united with much kindliness and benevolence." His religion is not a mere subterfuge for personal weakness. There is "something about him . . . self-respecting and dignified, yet united with a confiding and humble simplicity." He is much concerned for the welfare of Aunt Chloe, his wife, and he is a loving father. "Law, now!" he says of his children, "they are so full of tickle all the while, they can't behave themselves."[2]

It is not possible to discover with any certainty how much of his meekness Tom owes to his religion and how much to his race. All religions celebrate virtues which are frequently honored in the breach, and in the nineteenth century the differences between what people said they admired and what they actually admired may have been greater even than is now the case. Generally, Tom can be taken as a portrait of what Stowe thinks a Christian is supposed to be. His response to the knowledge that he will be sold away from his family has not a trace of expressed resentment in it. "I'm in the Lord's hands," he says; "nothin' can go furder than he lets it;—and thars *one* thing I can thank him for. It's me that's sold and going down [the river], and not you [his wife] nur the chil'en. Here you're safe; what comes will come only on me, and the Lord he'll help me—I know he will." Tom speaks "with a thick utterance, and with a bitter choking in his throat,—but he spoke brave and strong." And to avoid the possibility that the reader may not have sufficiently realized the point, the omniscient narrator of the story says, "Ah, brave, manly heart,—smothering thine own sorrow to comfort thy beloved ones."[3]

The modern reader is likely to note at once that Tom has racial qualities which now connote a degrading stereotype, but he may pass over too quickly the fact that Tom has religious traits which Stowe sincerely admired—and not just in blacks. Thus, the probability is that Stowe would be intensely surprised, were she alive now, to discover the opinion that she had denied Tom humanity by making him excessively meek. Late in the novel, Tom shows great strength of character and chooses probable death by torture rather than the denial of his faith and the betrayal of his fellow slaves who are in hiding. It is significant that some readers of *Uncle Tom's Cabin* in the 1850s also thought Tom was excessively noble, but they did not often condemn the nobility itself. The reason may have been that it was a more "religious" age and thus the value of a Christian martyr was less likely to be challenged. What they generally complained of was that nobody could attain to such nobility, and especially that no black could. Thus, they thought Stowe had evaluated the character of Tom as too high, not too low.

The God of Tom is significantly different from the God of Calvinism, even from those attenuations of Calvinism developed by Lyman Beecher. A revolution had apparently taken place in the religious conceptions of Stowe by the time she wrote *Uncle Tom's Cabin*. She did not lose her admiration for Calvinist logic, probity, and firmness of resolution. She saw New England as the source of the highest ideals of America because, traditionally, its people had combined an obedience to God with self-discipline and hard work. On the other hand, it becomes apparent—particularly in the virtues of Tom—that respect for God, logic, probity, and firmness of resolution are not in themselves the highest virtues. The highest virtue is Christian love, and without it the other virtues scarcely matter.

One critic has suggested that Stowe was probably influenced by the ideas of Charles Finney and the movement known as Christian perfectionism. Finney was a Presbyterian revivalist and one of the opponents of Lyman Beecher. He was opposed to what he regarded as old-fashioned Calvinist orthodoxy's shriveling effect upon the Christian convert. Calvinism placed the individual believer in direct confrontation with God. The question at issue was nothing less (and frequently nothing more) than the salvation of his soul. The convert might urgently desire salvation, but all he could do to achieve it was to throw himself upon the mercy of God and hope that he was one of the elect. Finney called this the "can not religion," since the will of the convert was not the decisive issue. In its place, Finney substituted a religion which gave the convert the right to choose whether he would be saved or damned. Tom shares with Finney a rejection of the idea that one cannot choose salvation. On the other hand, he differs from Finney on an important point. The terrors of hell as preached by Finney fully matched those of Jonathan Edwards himself. Tom, on the other hand, emphasizes the love and mercy of God. He does not deny the existence of hell; he simply never mentions it. Thus, the whole idea of the fear of punishment as a part of his theology is absent. Tom's religion amounts to the proposition that since God loves mankind, people should love one another.[4]

If Stowe admired Charles Finney or was converted to his version of Christianity, she did not say so. There is apparently no mention of him in her writings. On the other hand, there is a shift in attitude toward religion in the articles she wrote in the 1840s for religious magazines. Some of the earlier essays have a painful literalness—don't drink, don't dance, don't go to the theater, don't patronize art if, however beautiful it may be, your doing so may set a bad example for others. Gradually, in the place of these admonitions, the reader finds an emphasis upon Christian love as the distinguishing factor of true religion. The question becomes not what one does but why one does it. There was a new steadiness and calmness in all this. Instead of exhibiting an obsessive concern for her own salvation as she did in her early letters, she reached out to express sympathy for the problems of other people.

Though she did not mention Charles Finney, Stowe did show a great enthusiasm for someone else who may have influenced her in formulating the character of Tom. This was François de Salignac de la Mothe Fénelon (1651-1715), the French theologian and spiritual adviser. Fénelon has many modern admirers. Austin Warren has said that he was "doctrinally . . . rigorous" but in "tone and style . . . lucid, gracious, tender, affectionate." As a spiritual adviser, he had the "ability to deal with each person in terms of that person's temperament and situation." Aldous Huxley called him the Proust of spiritual psychology. Stowe overcame her prejudice against Catholicism to the point that she could pay a strong tribute to him. In the same article in which she praised him she also praised John Calvin for his "calm, cold logic," his "severe vehemence." It is obvious, however, that she cared more for Fénelon than she did for Calvin. It may seem odd that Stowe could feel a sympathy for two such different men, but the divergent qualities which Calvin and Fénelon possessed are also found in her and may be a source of her strength as a writer. Henry F. May may be exaggerating when he says that the "overt religious content" of *Uncle Tom's Cabin* is "in the tearful revivalistic vein," but there is no doubt that he is right when he says "the mark of Calvinism" is also in the novel. It is "its harsh realism about human nature that gives the book its lasting bite." The reader learns in reading the novel that the charge of sentimentalism against it needs to be much qualified. In 1973, Kenneth S. Lynn made the valid point that Stowe "aroused emotions not for emotions' sake alone—as the sentimental novelists notoriously did—but in order to facilitate the moral regeneration of an entire nation." She was, he said, "a sentimentalist with a vengeance—and the clichés she invokes in *Uncle Tom's Cabin* are not an opiate but a goad."[5]

Sometimes Tom himself appears to be a Fénelon, though stripped of Fénelon's learning and wit. The two have in common a quietism and a patience under suffering. The great interest which Stowe took in Fénelon and her sensitivity to his virtues are probably a sign that she took Tom and his religion with equal seriousness. He cannot be dismissed casually as a fake saint. Like Fénelon, Tom sees God as a loving Father. Tom has none of the niggling Calvinist anxiety concerning the fate of his own soul. On the other hand, with his eyes firmly

on a future life in heaven, he regards his earthly misfortunes as not of
ultimate importance. One of the quotations from the Bible which he
finds comforting is, "We have here no continuing city, but we seek one
to come; wherefore God himself is not ashamed to be called our God;
for he hath prepared for us a city." Tom has some of Fénelon's ability
to be a spiritual adviser to others, whether it be to an intellectual like
his master Augustine St. Clare or to his fellow slaves. Toward the end
of the novel, the persecuted slaves on the Simon Legree plantation begin
to call him Father Tom.[6]

Even so, Tom's nobility puts a strain on the modern reader, and this
is not merely because this age is less religious than that of the America
of the middle of the nineteenth century. Quite simply, Tom is *too* noble.
When Shelby sells him away from his wife and children, Tom has no
words of criticism for his master's inhumanity. Aunt Chloe, Tom's wife,
impresses us more favorably because she rightly feels resentment toward
Shelby for selling her husband. Speaking apparently of Shelby, she says
to Tom, "Them as sells heart's love and heart's blood to get out thar
scrapes, de Lord'll be up to 'em!" But to her complaint, Tom replies,
"Chloe! now, if ye love me, ye won't talk so, when perhaps jest the
last time we'll ever have together! And, I'll tell ye, Chloe, it goes agin
me to hear one word again Mas'r. Wan't he put in my arms a baby?
—it's natur I should think a heap of him." Aunt Chloe might logically
have answered that it was also "nature" to resent an undeserved injury,
but she does not.[7]

In making Tom meek and forgiving and in arguing that these are
qualities which blacks have naturally, Stowe did not apparently realize
that she might be depriving both Tom and the blacks generally of any
merit for their virtues, which may be simply a part of their racial character. Later in the novel, Augustine St. Clare, Tom's subsequent master,
would say to him, "It seems to be given to children, and poor honest
fellows, like you, to see what we can't"; and Tom replies in Biblical
language, "O Mas'r, haven't you read how he hides from the wise and
prudent, and reveals unto babes . . .?" In *The Key to Uncle Tom's
Cabin*, Stowe stated the thesis of the spiritual character of the blacks
most explicitly. "The negro race is confessedly more simple, docile,
childlike, and affectionate, than other races," she said; "and hence the
divine graces of love and faith, when in-breathed by the Holy Spirit, find
in their natural temperament a more congenial atmosphere." This was
obviously meant as a compliment, but if the blacks are like this because

of their racial character it is difficult to see how they deserve credit for it. As we shall see, Stowe did not hold the "good" whites in the novel to any such standard of virtue and holiness; they are, we suspect, presented as all the more admirable because they do not take the blows of fate meekly.[8]

A number of actual persons have been suggested as models for Tom in the novel. The best known of these was the Reverend Josiah Henson, an escaped slave who fled to Canada, organized a community of blacks there into a joint stock company which had a considerable success, and wrote—or had ghost-written for him—an account of his life which was first published in 1849. Stowe herself wrote an introduction for the 1858 revised edition of this work, but she said nothing in it of Henson's being a model for Tom. Neither did Henson precisely make this claim for himself, but he allowed others to make it for him. In 1882, Stowe wrote a letter to the *Indianapolis* [Ind.] *Times* in which she acknowledged that some of the events of *Uncle Tom's Cabin* had come from the Henson autobiography. "After I had begun the story," she said, "I got, at the Anti-Slavery Rooms in Boston, the autobiography of Josiah Henson and introduced some of its most striking incidents into my story." By this time Henson had traveled to England and had been received by Queen Victoria as the model for the character of Uncle Tom. Of this event, Stowe said, "The good people of England gave my simple good friend Josiah Henson enthusiastic welcome, though he was alive and well, and likely long to live, and the Uncle Tom of the story was buried in a martyr's grave." Earlier in the letter, she said, ". . . I will say that the character of Uncle Tom was not the biography of one man." She probably recognized that in the process of developing a character for fiction, the actual person on whom the character is based undergoes considerable change.[9]

When we turn to the autobiography of Josiah Henson, we can hardly avoid reflecting that, in some respects, it is too bad that Uncle Tom was not more like him. Henson has not always fared well, it is true, with his critics. He has been accused of having been cruel to his fellow slaves, of having helped his master evade his creditors by leading a group of his slaves to another state, and of being dishonest in his financial dealings when he became free. Kenneth S. Lynn has called him "a self-publicizing, arrogant man who had a history of mistreating fellow slaves." These charges are not easy to substantiate, but they may be true. On the other hand, Henson has sometimes elicited admiration from other critics, especially black scholars, who see him as a better man than Tom. One black critic complains, "It is one of the ironies of American history that Josiah Henson, the prototype of 'Uncle Tom,' should have been in his total life so much the opposite of what Harriet Beecher Stowe's fictional projection of a segment of his life ultimately came to make of him." Stowe herself was willing to concede that Josiah Henson might have virtues which were superior to those of Tom. "The real history of Josiah Henson," she said in a letter of 1876, "in some points goes even beyond that of Uncle Tom in his heroic manhood."[10]

Henson was born a slave in Maryland in 1789. When he was a young man he was so severely beaten by the overseer of a neighboring plantation that his shoulder blades were broken. Until the end of his life he was never able to lift his hands as high as his head. Henson was converted by a white Methodist minister to a religion of love and forgiveness. He was trusted so much by his master that he was commissioned to take a group of slaves from Maryland to Kentucky without any white supervision. The master wished to remove his slaves in order to prevent their being seized by his creditors in payment for his debts. When the group reached Cincinnati, some of the slaves wished to escape, but Henson convinced them that to do so would be a betrayal of trust. Later he came to repent of having persuaded them to remain in slavery. Some of them were sold away from their families, a few to especially cruel masters. Then Henson's master took him to New Orleans and there attempted to sell him. The only thing which prevented the sale was that the master became seriously ill and required the nursing services of his slave. Repenting of his desire to sell Henson, the master returned to Kentucky with him. Even so, Henson was thoroughly disillusioned and resolved to escape. He took his wife and children with him to Canada, and the family suffered severe hardships in their flight. Later Henson made a series of trips back to Kentucky to help other slaves to escape.[11]

Henson, like Tom in the novel, was a large and powerfully built man. Also like Tom, he had a cheerfulness of disposition and a willingness to regard his problems philosophically and to hope for the best. He himself had absorbed some of the ideas of race prevalent at the time. "Ours is a light-hearted race," he wrote. In spite of his kindliness and good humor, Henson was in other ways different from Tom. For one thing, he had more of the wisdom of the serpent. Tom could only suffer and endure, but Henson could shrewdly devise plans for avoiding trouble. On his trip from Canada to Kentucky to help slaves escape, he employed a trick to keep from being questioned. He wrapped a cloth around his face, pretending that he was in such pain that he could not speak. He was a good businessman. Understanding that the blacks in Canada could not prosper merely as hired laborers, he persuaded a group of them to pool their resources, buy land, build a sawmill, and establish classes in practical subjects for their children. He may have shown all too much ability. He was charged with using the group's money for his own purposes. After he protested his innocence, a committee appointed to examine into the matter acquitted him of wrongdoing. Questions continued to be raised, however, concerning his honesty. In any event, he managed to combine some reputation for goodness with a knowledge of how to survive under adverse conditions.[12]

On one occasion, Stowe came near to denying, at least by implication, that any black without white intermixture could use his freedom wisely. In the novel itself, Tom—who has no white intermixture—certainly does deserve to be free. There is a strong implication that if he were a free man he would be a responsible citizen. In one of her prefaces to *Uncle Tom's Cabin*, Stowe seemed to suggest a quite different opinion. Late in 1852, the Leipzig firm of Tauchnitz published a European edition of *Uncle Tom's Cabin* in English and asked Stowe to write a special preface for it. By this time, there had been many reviews of the novel, some of which had argued that though slavery obviously was an evil institution it did not necessarily follow that blacks were fit for freedom. Stowe's reply was to emphasize the idea that a large number of American slaves had white intermixture. "It has been said that the slave population is entirely unfit for freedom and incapable of it and that such characters as are described in the book are fictitious exaggerations and impossibilities," she said in her preface. "Whatever may be said of the African race by itself, the slave population of America is now to a very wide extent a *mixed race* in whose veins the best of Anglo-Saxon blood is circulating—characters like that [*sic*] of George Harris and Eliza are by no means uncommon among slaves." The phrase "whatever may be said of the African race by itself" would seem to leave Tom and the other blacks in the novel without white intermixture as among those who are, at best, doubtful material for good citizenship. One can argue that this was a mere debating point and that Stowe did not mean to say that blacks without white intermixture are unfit for freedom. She herself was apparently unaware that she had cast doubt on the fitness for freedom of Tom or any other wholly black person. In the same paragraph she argued that Tom's nobility was entirely possible. As proof she quoted from the will of a slaveholder which praised the character of a slave and gave him his freedom. Yet the earlier comment should warn the reader that there is an ambivalence in Stowe's conceptions of the inherent character of blacks and that he should expect inconsistencies.[13]

Stowe may have been aware that Tom's extreme goodness might make it difficult for readers to accept him as genuine. Perhaps recognizing that readers might reject him for this reason, she may have sought to contrast Tom with other black characters in the novel with less exalted traits. Some of them are presented humorously. Before the tragedy of Tom's separation from her occurs, Aunt Chloe, Tom's wife, is largely a comic character. Early in the novel, George Shelby, the master's teenage son, risks Aunt Chloe's wrath by telling her that one of his friends has said that their family cook is better than she is. Though the incident is meant to be humorous, it leads Aunt Chloe to reflect upon what would appear to be the inherent difference of races. Aunt Chloe and Mrs. Shelby, her mistress, came near a serious disagreement over how to make a crust for a chicken pie when the Shelbys were planning to entertain a guest, General Knox. Aunt Chloe relates a difference of opinion she had with her mistress:

"Now, Missis, she wanted me to do dis way, and she wanted me to do dat way; and, finally, I got kinder sarcy and says I, 'Now, Missis, do jist look at dem beautiful white hands o' yourns, with long fingers and all a sparkling with rings, like my white lillies when de dew's on 'em; and look at my great black stumpin hands. Now, don't ye think dat de Lord must have meant me to make de pie-crust, and you to stay in de parlor?' Dar! I was jist so sarcy, Mas'r George."

"And what did mother say?" said George.

"Say—why, she kinder larfed in her eyes—dem great handsome eyes o'hern; and says she, 'Well, Aunt Chloe, I think you are about in the right on it,' says she; and she went off in de parlor. She oughter racked me over de head for bein' so sarcy; but dar's what 't is. I can't do nothin' with ladies in de kitchen!"

Of course, Chloe's opinions are not necessarily Stowe's, and Stowe may merely be showing how the system of values of slavery has been absorbed by many of the slaves themselves. On the other hand, the narrator of the novel says elsewhere that black women have an inherent knack for

cooking. Thus the reader may wonder whether Stowe thought that blacks
are especially suited, not for slavery certainly, but at least for menial
labor.[14]

Sam is another slave in the Shelby household. He is second in
status to Tom but completely different in character. He knows how to
assume an air of almost idiotic innocence when he stands to benefit
from it. At first, he seems to be close to the Jim Crow stereotype. In
riding his horse, he expresses his high spirits by "all sorts of super-
natural howls and ejaculations." He has a trick of sitting backward on
the horse "with his face to the horse's tail and sides, and then, with a
whoop and a somerset," he ends up in the right position, and completely changes his manner. ". . . [D]rawing on a grave face," he
begins to lecture Andy, another slave, "in high-sounding tones for laughing and playing the fool." At one point, Sam is rebuked by Shelby for
not performing his duties properly. The omniscient narrator comments,
"Now, there is no more use in making believe to be angry with a negro
than with a child; both instinctively see the true state of the case,
through all attempts to affect the contrary; and Sam was in no wise
disheartened by this rebuke, though he assumed an air of doleful gravity,
and stood with the corners of the mouth lowered in most penitential
style."[15]

When Sam learns that Tom is to be sold, he immediately begins to
speculate on what the change will mean for his own future. "Yes, it's
an ill wind blows nowhar," he says. "Now, dar, Tom's down—well,
course der's room for some nigger to be up—and why not dis nigger?"
He sees himself as replacing Tom as the future right hand man of his
master. Perhaps other slaves will black his boots and he will always
have a pass in his pocket, "as grand as Cuffee." When Eliza escapes
with her child, Mrs. Shelby is obliged to pretend in the presence of
Mr. Haley, the slavetrader, that she hopes the two will be captured; but
Sam recognizes the truth that Mrs. Shelby really hopes they will escape.
Assigned to help Haley catch the runaways, Sam decides to try to make
him think he is being helpful but to mislead him as much as he dares.
Later Sam explains to Andy that in frustrating Haley's plans he was
obeying his "conscience":

"Dat ar was conscience, Andy; when I thought of gwine arter Lizzy, I
railly spect mas'r was sot dat way. When I found Missis was sot to contrary, dat ar was conscience *more yet*—cause fellers allers get more by
stickin' to Missis' side,—so yer see I's persistent either way, and stick up to

conscience, and holds on to principles. . . . [W]hat's principles good for, if
we isn't persistent, I wanter know?"

In 1966, Anthony Burgess would comment on this passage. "The speech
is the speech of a whole tradition of fictional negroes, not excluding
film and music-hall," he said, "but the argument is that of the modern
African politician." It is also the argument of shrewd and self-interested
people of any race anywhere.[16]

George and Eliza Harris have more white intermixture than black,
and therefore both of them can pass as whites among people who do
not know their origins. One of the arguments of proslavery apologists
was that the institution would be wholly wrong for whites but that it
was suitable for blacks because of their supposed inferior traits. Stowe's
reply was to portray some of the slaves as almost completely white.
George Harris's white father had been a man of the highest social class.
"From one of the proudest families in Kentucky . . . [George] had inherited a set of fine European features, and a high indomitable spirit."
He is also intelligent. When he is rented out to the owner of a bagging
factory, he invents a machine for cleaning hemp which is so successful
that his employer praises him for it to his master. Praise of George
merely makes his master more cruel to him. In order that George will
not "take on airs," his master requires him to perform "the meanest
drudgery on the farm." In this instance slavery not merely fails to reward merit; it penalizes it. That slavery is less suited for whites than it is
for blacks is, of course, a racist argument. It was one of those many
occasions when Stowe apparently thought that she was pointing out a
"fact" which virtually no one would deny.[17]

Eliza Harris, George's wife, represents still another danger of slavery
—the likelihood that women slaves will be used to gratify the sexual
passions of white men. Eliza is the beautiful quadroon or octoroon, the
woman who is herself the product of interracial sex and who serves as
a temptation to white men. This is, of course, one of the standard situations of antislavery fiction. Many antislavery novelists did, in fact, handle
the theme of illicit sexuality more explicitly than Stowe did in *Uncle
Tom's Cabin*. Eliza suggests a comparison with Cassy, the heroine of
Richard Hildreth's *The Slave, or Memoirs of Archy Moore*, an antislavery novel published in 1836. Born in Massachusetts, Hildreth (1807-
1865) was a lawyer, a writer on political and reform issues, a historian,
a newspaperman, and the author of this one novel. His histories have
scarcely survived, but his novel has had a long life and still attracts

readers. He wrote it after spending eighteen months from 1834 to 1836 in Florida, where he had gone to recover his health. In some respects, *The Slave* requires fewer concessions from the modern reader than does *Uncle Tom's Cabin*.[18]

In *The Slave*, Cassy belongs to Colonel Moore, the owner of a plantation in Virginia and the master of many slaves. Some of his slave children on the plantation are almost completely white. He recognizes none of them as belonging to him and has no intention of giving any of them their freedom. He represents the kind of character kept almost completely offstage in *Uncle Tom's Cabin*. He even approaches Cassy, his daughter, with the intention of making her his mistress. Cassy tells Archy, who is also an illegitimate slave offspring of Colonel Moore and who will later become Cassy's husband, about her father's attempt to seduce her. Archy, who is the narrator of the novel, gives this account of the incident:

But she—poor child—heard him with shame and dread; and was ready, she told me, to sink into the earth with terror and dismay. In relating it, she blushed—she hesitated—she shuddered—her breathing became short and quick—she clung to me as if some visible image of horror were present before her, and bringing her lips close to my ear, she exclaimed in a trembling and scarcely audible whisper—"O Archy,—and he my father!"

Harsh critics of *Uncle Tom's Cabin* would often accuse Stowe of an obscene imagination in her assumption of the existence of sexual relationships between white masters and black slave women, but they were nearly always thinking of what she had mentioned as probable rather than what she actually described. Hildreth included in his novel what Stowe assumed but did not actually portray.[19]

In *Uncle Tom's Cabin*, Eliza has "a rich, full dark eye" with "long lashes" and "ripples of silky black hair." When Haley the slave trader looks at her with undisguised admiration, "the brown of her complexion gave way on the cheek to a perceptible flush. . . ." Yet Stowe did not offend the pious by including in the story scenes of seduction or even attempted seduction. Such liaisons as exist in the novel are placed in the past. Eliza fits the type of the slave paramour but not the actual role. She has "reached maturity without those temptations which make beauty so fatal an inheritance to a slave."[20]

Eliza represents another of the evils of slavery. She has no rights as a wife or mother. Stowe knew how to heighten the irony of the "marriage" of George and Eliza. She briefly included a flashback to the "wedding" ceremony. Eliza had worn orange blossoms in her hair, had a white wedding dress and white gloves. Cake and wine had been served at a reception and there had been many "admiring guests to praise the bride's beauty and her mistress' indulgence and liberality." And yet it all served no purpose. When the financial pinch comes, Shelby sells Harry, the son of Eliza and George Harris, to a slave trader. He also separates Tom from his wife, Chloe, and therefore the reader realizes he is equally willing to separate a slave husband from his wife.[21]

Even though her marriage is not legal, Eliza has attempted to fulfill the traditional role of woman as wife and mother. She has a calming and stabilizing influence on her impetuous and potentially violent husband. When his white master goes out of his way to make his lot hard and humiliating, George reacts bitterly:

"My master! and who made him my master? That's what I think of— what right has he to me? I'm a man as much as he is. I'm a better man than he is. I know more about the business than he does; I'm a better manager than he is. I can read better than he can; I can write a better hand;—and I've learned it in spite of him; and now what right has he to make a dray-horse of me?—to take me from the things I can do, and do better than he can, and put me to work that any horse can do? He tries to do it, he says he'll bring me down and humble me, and he puts me to just the hardest, meanest, and dirtiest work, on purpose!"[22]

Stowe had probably anticipated that women would be more likely than men to read *Uncle Tom's Cabin*, and she presented them generally in the novel as people whose major role is to serve as moral beacons for men. Eliza tries to calm George. "I'm afraid you'll do something dreadful," she says. "I don't wonder at your feelings at all; but oh, do be careful—do, do—for my sake—for Harry's!" In addition to counseling her husband, Eliza is important as a mother. Even before Shelby has decided to sell her son Harry away from her, we discover that she has already borne two infant children who died, "children to whom she was passionately attached." George wholly accepts the moral superiority of Eliza and of women generally. "Pray for me, Eliza," he says; "perhaps the good Lord will hear you."[23]

Like George Harris with regard to Eliza, Shelby assumes the moral superiority of his wife as a matter of course. "In fact, if not exactly a believer in the doctrine of the efficiency of the extra good works of saints," the narrator tells us, "he really seemed somehow or other to fancy that his wife had piety and benevolence for two—to indulge a shadowy expectation of getting into heaven through her superabundance of qualities to which he made no particular pretension." In her portrait of Mrs. Shelby, Stowe is apparently attempting to show that many white southerners, and particularly white southern women, are involved in the sordid aspects of slavery against their will. Mrs. Shelby has "a natural magnanimity and generosity of mind which one often marks as characteristic of the women of Kentucky. . . ." In addition, "she added high moral and religious sensibility and principle, carried out with great energy and ability into practical results."[24]

Yet none of her virtues weigh in the slightest when it comes to the matter of whether a slave should be sold. When her husband tells her that he has sold Tom, she pleads with him:

"What! our Tom?—that good, faithful creature:—who has been your faithful servant from a boy! O, Mr. Shelby!—and you have promised him his freedom, too—you and I have spoken to him a hundred times of it. Well, I can believe anything now,—I can believe *now* that you could sell little Harry, poor Eliza's only child!" said Mrs. Shelby, in a tone between grief and indignation.

"Well, since you must know all, it is so. I have agreed to sell Tom and Harry both; and I don't know why I am to be rated as if I were a monster, for doing what every one does everyday."[25]

Shelby probably thinks of himself as a kindly master. He does not physically maltreat his slaves, and his manner to them is that of a benevolent patriarch. In his farewell to young George Shelby, Tom pays tribute to Mr. Shelby as a "good Mas'r" but he describes Mrs. Shelby as a "Christian." Shelby derives his morality from what is usually done in society rather than from any real examination of issues. When he suggests to Mrs. Shelby that Tom will find another wife down the river, Mrs. Shelby says she has tried to teach the slaves that their marriage vows are sacred. "It's a pity, wife," Shelby replies, "that you have burdened them with a morality above their condition and prospects." With regard to an argument like this one, David Levin, a modern critic, makes the perceptive observation, "Mrs. Stowe shows us a situation in which logic has gone wild. Like the creator of Jason Compson, she has an astonishingly fine ear for the language of racism and the fundamental contradictions embraced by men who must defend slavery."[26]

It was a shrewd stroke on Stowe's part in *Uncle Tom's Cabin* to make the involvement of the North in slavery evident almost at the beginning of the novel. In most antislavery fiction, the North was seen as the home of freedom and the possible refuge of slaves. On reading such novels, the northerner might feel a disapproval of slavery, but he was unlikely to feel any responsibility for it. In *Uncle Tom's Cabin*, northerners were forced to recognize their complicity in slavery and to decide clearly for or against it. Many years later, in the preface to the 1879 edition of the novel, Stowe made the strange comment that when she wrote the novel she had expected it to be more favorably received in the South than in the North:

She had painted slave-holders as amiable, generous, and just. She had shown examples among them of the noblest and most beautiful traits of character; had admitted fully their temptations, their perplexities, and their difficulties, so that a friend of hers who had many relatives in the South wrote to her in exultation. "Your book is going to be the great pacificator; it will unite both north and south." Her expectation was that the professed abolitionists would denounce it as altogether too mild in its dealings with slaveholders. To her astonishment, it was the extreme abolitionists who received it and the entire South who rose up against it.[27]

The conviction that *Uncle Tom's Cabin* would be well received in the South seems incredibly naïve. "There is something almost amusing in Mrs. Stowe's honest expectations that the deadliest blow the system ever suffered," wrote Charles Dudley Warner in 1896, "should have been received thankfully by those whose traditions, education, and interests were all bound up in it." Was this merely the convenient and slippery argument of a self-righteous reformer, exhibiting the duplicity with which her opponents frequently charged her? It is quite unlikely. To understand her conviction on this point, we need to turn to evangelical Christianity. Stowe believed that a person could be convinced of his sin, repent, and resolve to live a new life. Conversion was not, moreover, limited to one person. It could affect a whole community, and even a nation was not necessarily to be excluded from it. Stowe seems to have thought that once the southerners had a vivid portrait before them of what slavery actually was, great numbers of them and eventually a majority would concede that it was an evil institution and would work toward its abolition.[28]

The conviction that slavery might be ended by a great act of national repentance was not new to the abolition movement. When Theodore Weld left Lane Seminary in 1834 and began to organize opinion against slavery, James G. Birney had written in his diary, "I give him one year to abolitionize Ohio." Lewis Tappan also thought that Weld's campaign would meet with enormous success. Weld himself had told Tappan that within five years half a million slaves would be free and within ten years a million and a half would be free. Thus, there was some precedent for the effect which Stowe hoped *Uncle Tom's Cabin* might have upon the South.[29]

On the other hand, her conviction that the novel might not be well received among antislavery leaders in the North is easy to understand. In her explanation of expected opposition, she mentioned not the North generally but the "professed abolitionists" in the North. Stowe was more willing to make concessions to the dilemmas of southern slaveholders than the abolitionists generally were. In addition, she probably knew that many abolitionists would object to one of the ideas presented in the last pages of the novel, when George Harris urges American blacks to follow his example and emigrate to Liberia. The abolitionists, especially the Garrisonian abolitionists, had traditionally been opposed to colonization. Though there was no hint in the novel that the blacks would not return voluntarily to Africa, Stowe might have foreseen that even a suggestion that they should emigrate would not be well received by abolitionists. And then there was the fact that the scenes of the novel take place in the South and in the western states and not in the East. Wholly absent in the novel are abolitionists like William Lloyd Garrison and Wendell Phillips or, for that matter, like Arthur or Lewis Tappan. Instead, we find the abolitionists represented by peaceful Quakers of Ohio who shelter George, Eliza, and Harry Harris and help them escape to Canada. It would not be surprising if Stowe wondered whether the abolitionists of the East would be satisfied to be thus excluded. While she was writing *Uncle Tom's Cabin,* she did not know that the novel would be sensationally successful and that its success would blunt any opposition which abolitionists in the East might have felt. The fact that it was a powerful indictment of slavery would prove to be more important to abolitionists generally than the fact that the contribution to antislavery made by abolitionists of the East went largely unrecorded in the novel.[30]

Eliza flees across the Ohio River, carrying Harry in her arms, jumping from ice floe to ice floe, and takes refuge in the home of Mr. and Mrs. Bird of Ohio. Mr. Bird is a state senator in the legislature and bears some points of resemblance to Mr. Shelby. Both men accommodate their principles to self-interest and public opinion. They are not so much wicked as morally limp. "Both Shelby and the Ohio senator leave moral and religious questions to their wives," comments David Levin, "and thus declare that in the real world moral and religious questions are unimportant."[31]

Though the two men, Mr. Shelby and Mr. Bird, are rather similar to one another, the same is not true of their wives. Where Mrs. Shelby merely pleads with her husband, Mrs. Bird, a northern woman, is more rebellious. Mr. Bird had voted in the state legislature to make it illegal to assist fugitive slaves. At first sight Mrs. Bird hardly seems to be capable of any effective resistance. She is "a timid, blushing little woman of about four feet in height, and with mild blue eyes, and a peach-glow complexion, and the gentlest, sweetest voice in the world;—as for courage, a moderate-sized cock-turkey had been known to put her to rout at the very first gobble . . . !" Yet, Mrs. Bird is a powerful figure. She represents the virtues associated with women as the conservers of family life. When Mr. Bird suggests that Eliza and Harry will have to be turned over to the slave catchers because the law says they must be, the combative instincts of Mrs. Bird are aroused:

"Now, John, I want to know if you think such a law as that is right and Christian?"

"You won't shoot me, now, Mary, if I say I do?"

"I never could have thought it of you, John; you didn't vote for it?"

"Even so, my fair politician."

"You ought to be ashamed, John. Poor, homeless, houseless creatures! It's a shameful, wicked, abominable law, and I'll break it, for one, the first time I get a chance; and I hope I shall have a chance. I do! . . ."

Catharine Beecher had said that it should be the role of woman to persuade the men of her family or among her friends to do the right thing. Mrs. Bird has moved to a more daring position—persuade them if you can, she believes, but rebel if you can't.[32]

On the other hand, Mrs. Bird is not quite as rebellious as her speech to her husband might indicate. She is portrayed in such a way that the reader will not think of her as violating the genteel code for women. On everything but the moral threat to the family implied in slavery, she fulfills the role generally allotted to women in the thought of the time. The omniscient narrator points out that, in general, Mrs. Bird knew little and cared less about political issues. "Now, it was a very unusual thing for gentle little Mrs. Bird ever to trouble her head with what was going on in the house of the state," the narrator says, "very wisely considering that she had enough to do to mind her own." Another way in which possible criticism against Mrs. Bird is anticipated is through humor. Realizing her arguments have convinced her husband that he ought to aid Eliza, Mrs. Bird does not insist that he admit he has changed his mind:

Now, little Mrs. Bird was a discreet woman,—a woman who never in her life said, "I told you so!" and, on the present occasion, though pretty well aware of the shape her husband's meditations were taking, she very prudently forbore to meddle with them, only sat very quietly in her chair, and looked to her liege Lord's intentions, when he should think proper to utter them.[33]

SLAVE TRADERS AND SLAVE CATCHERS

Mr. Haley, the slave trader, appears in the first scene of *Uncle Tom's Cabin*, but the full implications of his role become apparent only when he unsuccessfully pursues Eliza and Harry from Kentucky to Ohio and when he takes Tom and other slaves he has bought from Mr. Shelby down the river to New Orleans. Haley is flanked by two other slave catchers who are a good deal worse than he is, probably the better to persuade the reader to accept the genuineness of his portrait. Haley has a good opinion of himself. He thinks he is both kindly and adroit in the methods he has developed for separating slave mothers from their children. He sends the slave mother away for a day or two, not telling her that her child will be sold away. Thus there is no distressing scene of parting. Tom Loker, another slave dealer, spurns Haley's indirect methods:

"[W]hy, I buys a gal, and if she's got a young un to be sold, I jest walks up and puts my fist to her face, and says, 'Look here, now, if you give me one word out of your head, I'll smash yer face in. I won't hear one word— not the beginning of a word,' I says to 'em. 'This yer young un's mine, and not yourn, and you've no kind of business with it. I'm going to sell it, first chance; mind you don't cut up none o' yer shines about it, or I'll make ye wish ye'd never been born.' I makes 'em as whist as fishes, and if one on 'em begins and gives a yelp, why,—" and Mr. Loker brought down his fist with a thump that fully explained the hiatus.

Mr. Marks, another slave catcher, is a shrewdly circumspect lawyer, "short and slender, lithe and cat-like in his motions," with "a peering mousing expression about his keen black eyes. . . ." He is concerned only with what is legal or, failing that, with what is not likely to be prosecuted. He is at least as cruel as Loker. Reflecting that rewards are often paid whether the slaves are dead or alive, Mark says, "[A]ll you've got to do is shoot 'em, or swear they is shot. . . ."[34]

Haley may not be any more humane than Loker or Marks, but he is better able to conceal the nature of his activities behind a cloud of euphemisms. All his comments reflect his economic interest. He assumes that everyone else must be as self-interested as he is, and thus he states his opinions with an artless simplicity. In the first scene, when Shelby tells him that the religious faith of Uncle Tom is genuine, Haley says he is impressed; but it soon becomes apparent that he merely thinks religion will make it possible to sell Uncle Tom for a higher price:

"Some folks don't believe there is pious niggers, Shelby," said Haley, with a candid flourish of his hand, "but I *do*. I had a fellow, now, in this yer last lot I took to *Orleans*—'twas as good as a meetin, now, really, to hear that critter pray; and he was quite gentle, and quiet like. He fetched me a good sum, too, for I bought him cheap of a man that was 'bliged to sell out; so I realized six hundred on him. Yes, I consider religion a valeyable thing in a nigger, when it's the genuine article, and no mistake."[35]

Every conviction of Haley's is eventually disclosed as a matter of his own financial interest. When someone mentions to him the rumor that slaves do not live long in the Deep South, he answers complacently, "Wal, yes, tol'able fast, ther dying is; what with the 'climating and one thing and another, they dies so as to keep the market up pretty brisk." He does not complain when he discovers that the slave catchers he hires to pursue Eliza have no dogs. The difficulty with dogs, from his point of view, is that they might "damage the gal." If she were to lose her beauty, he would have to accept a lower price for her in the slave market. Haley represents slavery at one of its most morally vulnerable points, and it is important that he is portrayed not as a great villain but rather as a shrewd businessman. He buys a slave woman who has been tricked by her master to get aboard the river steamer with her child, not knowing that she has been sold and will be separated from her husband. Then he proceeds to sell the child away from its mother. He handles the matter with his usual dexterity. When the boat stops at Louisville, the woman goes to the railing in hopes of seeing her husband on the wharf, leaving her child for a few minutes. Haley takes the opportunity to spirit the child away, and when the mother comes back he tells her what has happened. "Lucy," he says, "your child's gone; you may as well know it first as last. You see, I know'd you couldn't take him down south; and I got a chance to sell him to a first-rate family, that'll raise him better than you can." Haley prides himself on how well he managed the affair, but the slave mother despairs and, in the middle of the night, throws herself overboard and is drowned. Though Haley is sorry for this turn of events, his sorrow is the result of his concern for himself. "The trader . . . sat discontentedly down, with his little account-book," we are told by the narrator, "and put down the missing body and soul under the head of *losses*!"[36]

Southern proslavery critics of *Uncle Tom's Cabin* objected to the portrayal of Haley in the novel, but frequently on a curious point. "Into what society can Mrs. Stowe have been admitted to see slave-traders so much at ease in gentlemen's houses?" asks Louisa S. McCord in the *Southern Quarterly Review.* "We have lived at the South, in the very heart of the slave country, for thirty seven years, out of the forty of our lives, and have never seen a slave-trader set forth in a gentleman's house." The reviewer is not sophisticated enough to realize that the absence of slave traders from gentlemen's houses may partly be explained by the willingness of white southern gentlemen and ladies to close their eyes to the real meaning of slavery. Mrs. McCord also missed the fact that Stowe had anticipated her objection. Not for nothing had Stowe as a child listened to those arguments conducted by her father at the dinner table. In the novel she hectored the reader, it is true, but her point was a valid one. The omniscient narrator imagines a dialogue with a proslavery person:

"He's a shocking creature, isn't he,—this trader? so unfeeling! It's dreadful, really!"

"O, but nobody thinks anything of these traders! They are universally despised,—never received into any decent society."

"But who, sir, makes the trader? Who is most to blame? The enlightened, cultivated, intelligent man, who supports the system of which the trader is the inevitable result, or the poor trader himself? You make the public sentiment that calls for his trade, that debauches and depraves him, till he feels no shame in it; and in what are you better than he?"

Haley himself makes a similar point in the novel, and more effectively than the omniscient narrator does. "I'm as good as they is," he says to himself; "tan't any meaner sellin' on 'em than 't is buyin'."[37]

CLERGYMEN

Two clergymen appear briefly in a scene on the riverboat in which Haley takes Tom to New Orleans. One of them, "a grave-looking gentleman in black," who is proslavery, voices the "Cursed be Canaan" argument—that Noah's curse of his son Ham in the Bible had, in fact, condemned blacks to perpetual slavery. He is answered by an antislavery clergyman, a "tall, slender young man, with a face expressive of great feeling and intelligence." He quotes the biblical verse, "All things whatsoever ye would that men should do unto you, do ye even so unto them." He says, "I suppose . . . *that* is scripture, as much as 'Cursed be Canaan.'" This is the only time in *Uncle Tom's Cabin* when clergymen are actually introduced as characters. There are, however, references to proslavery sermons. In one of the early scenes of the novel, when Mrs. Shelby has discovered that Uncle Tom and Harry are to be sold, she exclaims despairingly that she has always known slavery to be wrong. "Well, therein you differ from many wise and pious men," says Mr. Shelby. "You remember Mr. B's sermon, the other Sunday." Later in the novel, the proslavery Marie St. Clare recounts to her husband, Augustine, how a "Dr. G." has "preached a splendid sermon." Mrs. St. Clare paraphrases the clergyman's argument:

"The text was, 'He hath made everything beautiful in its season'; and he showed how all the orders and distinctions in society came from God; and that it was so appropriate, you know, and beautiful that some should be high and some low, and that some were born to rule and some to serve, and all that, you know; and he applied it so well to all this ridiculous fuss that is made about slavery, and he proved distinctly that the Bible was on our side, and supported all our institutions so convincingly. . . ."

Mrs. St. Clare says to her husband—who is both a critic of slavery and a religious skeptic—that she wishes he could have heard the sermon. Augustine St. Clare replies irreverently that he doesn't need to go to church to hear such arguments, that he can read them all in the *New Orleans Picayune* and smoke his cigar at the same time.[38]

How to handle biblical arguments concerning slavery had long been a problem for abolitionists. They could emphasize the example of the Golden Rule, as the antislavery clergyman on the riverboat in *Uncle Tom's Cabin* does. On the other hand, for a people who read their Bibles literally and often narrowly, as orthodox Protestants frequently did, it was difficult to find sources in the Bible for antislavery. Did not the patriarchs in the Old Testament have slaves? If slavery had been evil, why had Moses prescribed extensive regulations for it? The New Testament as a source for antislavery seemed scarcely better. If slavery was evil, why had Jesus said nothing against it? And did not St. Paul counsel

the slave Onesimus to return to his master? Anyone who reads much
of the proslavery literature written before the Civil War will have difficulty in suppressing a groan every time the name Onesimus appears.[39]

Some of the abolitionists despaired of finding support for their views
in the Bible and decided to ignore the subject. William Lloyd Garrison
apparently avoided a direct discussion of biblical arguments with regard
to slavery. Oliver Johnson, who was closely associated with him and was
one of his biographers, declared that Garrison rejected those sections
of the Bible which justified, or might seem to justify, slavery. Garrison
decided, said Johnson, "that the revelation of God in man was older and
more authoritative than that inscribed upon any parchment, however
ancient, or by whatever miracles authenticated; and if . . . professors of
theology affirmed . . . [that] the Bible sanctioned slavery, then the passages containing such sanction could not be from God, but must be
from the devil." Lydia Maria Child had answered the argument that
Christ had never forbidden Christians to own slaves by declaring that
neither had he ever forbidden counterfeiting. On the other hand, it was
illogical to assume that his silence implied approval of it. Stowe generally avoided legalistic chapter-and-verse arguments. In *Uncle Tom's
Cabin*, she was chiefly content to show the ironic contrast between proslavery appeals to the Bible and the actual operations of the slavery
system.[40]

In "The Minister's Housekeeper," one of her New England short
stories published in 1872, Stowe satirized those ministers who use the
Bible to prove whatever they want it to prove. Sam Lawson, the narrator
of the story, is somewhere between the village handyman and the village
loafer. He possesses a witty detachment from the ideas of his fellow
villagers. He comments on how the local minister handles inconvenient
texts in the Bible:

"He was great on texts, the doctor was. When he hed a p'int to prove, he'd
jest go through the Bible, and drive all the texts ahead o' him like a
flock o' sheep; and then, if there was a text that seemed agin him, why,
he'd come out with his Greek and Hebrew, and kind o' chase it 'round a
spell, jest as ye see a feller chase a contrary bell-wether, and make him jump
the fence arter the rest. I tell you, there wasn't no text in the Bible that
could stand agin the doctor when his blood was up."[41]

In *The Key to Uncle Tom's Cabin* (1853), Stowe would with some
nervousness take on the task of justifying antislavery from the Bible.
She described slavery in the Old Testament with the euphemistic term,

"patriarchal state of servitude which existed in the time of Abraham. . . ."
As we might have guessed, patriarchal servitude was "very different
from American slavery. . . ." The chief difference was that the slaves
were really more like subordinate workmen than they were like slaves.
When the angels appeared to Abraham, for example, he did not command his servants to prepare food for them. Instead he killed the calf
himself and bade Sarah, his wife, to knead meal into cakes. Stowe assumed
from this account that it was apparently as much the custom for
Abraham and Sarah to do the work of their household as it was for
their servants to do so. The relationship of the "servants" to Abraham
was "more the relation of the members of a Scotch clan to their feudal
lord than that of an American slave to his master." Old Testament
slavery was, she argued, in some respects a mere extension of the family,
and thus if the patriarch died childless the "head steward" who was a
slave might inherit the property. Abraham had said in the book of
Genesis, she pointed out, that since he was "childless," the "steward of
my house" would be his "heir." It is an interesting argument. We cannot help wondering whether the head stewards ever reflected that since
the patriarchs often lived several hundred years and had a prodigious
number of children their own chances of inheriting the patriarchy were
bleak.[42]

Stowe drew another comparison between biblical and modern American slavery which would seem to be inconsistent with the previous one.
The heathen had to be enslaved during the time of the Old Testament
patriarchs, she argued, because of their paganism and the low state of
their morals. "We are taught thus to regard the Hebrew system," she
said, again avoiding the word *slavery,* "as an educational system, by
which a debased, half-civilized race, which had been degraded by slavery
in its worst form among the Egyptians, was gradually elevated to refinement and humanity." The bond servants had "the most disgusting
personal habits, the most unheard of and unnatural impurities . . . so
that it was necessary to make laws with relations of things of which
Christianity has banished the very name from the earth." She apparently
meant sodomy. It seems strange that she did not recognize how easily
this argument could be turned into a justification of American slavery.
In this country, apologists for slavery had frequently argued that the
blacks when they came to America were wholly destitute of a moral
sense, and therefore they had to undergo a period of generations under

the tutelage of slavery. People who argued in this way seldom had any specific date as to how long this period of tutelage must last.[43]

Another of Stowe's arguments concerning the Bible and slavery was that the early Christians had found many institutions and practices which they knew to be evil. The child was the slave of his parents. The wife was the slave of her husband. Instead of combating institutions, she said, the early Christians had attempted to save the souls of individual people. They did not attack slavery, she believed, for a similar reason. Unable to abolish slavery, they had tried to mitigate its effects upon individual slaves. One of the southern apologists for slavery, Rev. E. J. Stearns, challenged Stowe on this point, saying that the Christians had found institutions, like polygamy, which they could not abolish but which they forbade their disciples to practice. There was no obligation under Roman law to hold slaves, and therefore the Christians could easily have forbidden slavery among their own members. The fact that they did not do so implied, he concluded, that the early Christians found nothing wrong with slavery.[44]

Though Stowe rejected the "cursed be Canaan" argument which justified slavery, she herself derived from the Bible a curious theory which, if valid, might result in slavery or something very close to it. "The African race appear as yet to have been companions only of the sufferings of Christ," she wrote in 1858:

> In the melancholy scene of his death—while Europe in the person of the Roman delivered him unto death and Asia in the person of the Jew clamored for his execution—Africa was represented in the person of Simon the Cyrenean, who came patiently bearing after him the load of the cross; and ever since then poor Africa has been toiling on, bearing the weary cross of contempt and oppression after Jesus. But they who suffer with him shall also reign; and when the unwritten annals of slavery shall appear in the judgment, many Simons who have gone meekly bearing their cross after Jesus to unknown graves, shall rise to thrones and crowns! Verily a day shall come when he shall appear for these his hidden ones, and then "many that are last shall be first, and the first shall be last."

How did one know that Simon of Cyrene was a black? The Cyrene he came from was a town in what is now Libya. It was then a Greek city and the racial origins of Simon are unknown.[45]

Stowe was vague as to the time when the labor and suffering of the blacks is to end on this earth. She did not say clearly, in fact, that they would end. She did not seem to be aware, moreover, that the story of Simon of Cyrene could easily be turned into a proslavery argument. In 1852, Mrs. Mary H. Eastman in *Aunt Phillis's Cabin*, one of the many proslavery fictional replies to *Uncle Tom's Cabin*, presented Simon as a figure who indirectly represented a Christian endorsement of slavery. It was not one of "the wealthy or learned Jews," the narrator of her novel says, who "bore the Savior's cross, when . . . he trod the hill of Calvary." Instead, "it was a black man who relieved him of his heavy burden. . . ." While it is not explicitly stated that the story is a proof that black slavery is a Christian institution, it is strongly implied.[46]

The fact that Stowe's arguments with regard to the Bible and slavery will not bear much scrutiny is probably related to a difficulty of her position at the time. She would never dream of rejecting biblical arguments about slavery on their face. Instead she explained away, she interpreted, she even juggled a bit. She drove the texts before her as the clergyman in her story had driven them, as if they were a flock of sheep. What she was apparently attempting to do was to avoid the charge of religious skepticism. Though her critics often charged her with irreligion, they could not point to passages in her writings which clearly demonstrated the truth of their indictments. Part of the power of the antislavery message in *Uncle Tom's Cabin* was that it did not ask the religiously orthodox to forsake belief in the infallibility of the Bible.

VIII

Uncle Tom's Cabin Part II

MOST OF THE LATTER HALF of *Uncle Tom's Cabin* is devoted to two portraits of slavery in the South—the first at its best in the home of Augustine St. Clare in New Orleans, the second at its worst in the isolated plantation of Simon Legree in the upper Red River section of Louisiana. Neither St. Clare nor Legree is wholly southern in background. St. Clare was born in Louisiana, but as a boy he was in delicate health and was sent to live for several years with relatives in Vermont, which presumably had a healthier climate. As a result, he is thoroughly familiar with the differing ideas and attitudes of South and North. He owns slaves, but he admits that it is wrong to do so. He is co-owner with his brother of a plantation which has many slaves, but he has nothing to do with its management. The only slaves he has any close association with are house slaves in his New Orleans home. He owns them, he says, for no better reason than that they make his life comfortable; but this is probably not the only explanation. He may hesitate to free his slaves because he honestly believes they may find it difficult to survive in freedom in either the South or the North. He is the first to admit that he lacks the will to act upon principle. He is a kindly master and indulges his slaves. On the other hand, he is the most astute and unsparing critic of slavery in the novel.

Simon Legree was born and reared in Vermont. He is now a middle-aged man and has been living in the South during most of his years of maturity. He represents the worst aspects of the economic and social systems of both the North and the South. He has Yankee efficiency and no tolerance for the generally slipshod methods of southern slavery. He makes no concessions to the supposedly kindly patriarchal theories of slavery espoused by southern apologists. The effect of involving the North in the characters of both St. Clare and Legree is to make the debate over slavery in the novel national rather than merely sectional.

Augustine St. Clare has charm and force. He may hark back to Stowe's schoolgirl crush on Byron. He has "a noble cast of head," "golden-brown hair," and "large blue eyes." He has other characteristics which remind us of Byron—insight, wit, eloquence, humor, and indignation at the wrongs of society. Less moody than Byron, he suggests a Byronic hero made over for Victorian taste. Irreverent and sarcastic he sometimes is, but there is no faint hint of sexual transgressions. He is a good family man, and his regard for women and children leaves nothing to be desired.[1]

A major theme in *Uncle Tom's Cabin* is, of course, the evil of the separation of families. This section of the novel continues the theme, but from a different point of view. Augustine St. Clare is a free man and is not physically separated from his wife. Because of her coldness and selfishness, however, a separation might be better than the unhappiness which he endures because of her. He would never have married her if it had not been for a disaster in his life which had occurred before he met her. He had been in love with a charming, high-minded, and beautiful woman. She had an evil guardian who opposed Augustine's suit and intercepted his letters to her. Then the guardian wrote to Augustine, telling him that the woman he loved was engaged to marry someone else. In despair, Augustine had hurriedly courted and married the languid and selfish Marie, the heiress of a southern plantation worth a hundred thousand dollars. Only after he was married did he learn that he had been deceived by the guardian. In the tradition of the sentimental novel, Augustine had read a letter from his beloved telling him of the deception and had turned "deadly pale." This is a dangerous moment in *Uncle Tom's Cabin*; it runs the risk of becoming a melodramatic tearjerker. The event does serve, however, as a part of the novel's attack on slavery. Since his wife cares nothing for him, Augustine is of course unhappy. Later in the novel, he is separated from Eva, his daughter whom he deeply loves, by her death. Thus the attention of the reader is directed to the dreariness of the life of even a white slaveholder which is not protected by the warmth and protection of a loving family. In this sense, at least, the situation of Augustine is similar to that of a slave who has been separated from his family by being sold away from them.[2]

Though Augustine is married to a whining and selfish wife, he does not have to forego the influence of a noble woman. (No hero in Stowe's fiction ever does.) The noble woman in his life is his mother. His father had managed a large plantation with five hundred slaves. As slave masters go, he had been kindly and just, or at least he might have been if he had been left to himself. He had, however, listened to the opinions of his overseer, a big brutal man who, like the evil slave owner Simon Legree, was born and bred in New England. A cleavage had developed within the family. Alfred, Augustine's twin brother, had followed the lead of his father in taking for granted the idea that in this world some are born to command and others to obey. He came to assume as a matter of course that the slaves would have to be flogged if they did not do their work. Augustine, on the other hand, followed the example of his gentle mother. When his father "looked sternly" at him, he went off to his mother's room and sat beside her. "I remember just how she used to look, with her pale cheeks, her deep, soft serious eyes, her white dress,—she always wore white," he tells his cousin, Ophelia, "and I used to think of her whenever I read in *Revelations* about the saints that were arrayed in fine linen, clean and white." Constantly, his mother had read the Bible to him and had discussed with him the evils of slavery. She had no real influence with her husband. He argued that if he did not follow the advice of his overseer, he would lose his valuable services. Augustine might have been so much influenced by his mother that he would be unable to manage his slaves when he grew up, but this did not happen. The narrator of the novel says that in spite of all his fineness of temperament he has "the rough bark of manhood." Marie, his wife, who has no high opinion of him and complains that he is too indulgent with his slaves, nonetheless concedes that he is able to control them. "If you ever looked full in his eye, it's peculiar,—that eye," she says to Ophelia, "and if he speaks decidedly, there's a kind of flash. I'm afraid of it myself; and the servants know they must mind." On the other hand, moral scruples prevent Augustine from sharing the management of the plantation with Alfred. It is his brother who takes charge. Augustine lives in wealth and idleness in New Orleans. He is the beneficiary of slavery, but also its critic.[3]

Evangeline, or Eva, is, of course, one of the famous children of literature. With her "long golden-brown hair that floated like a cloud" and "the deep spiritual gravity of her violet blue eyes," she more than any other child figure in American literature would become the symbol of the perfection of innocence. At first glance, she may seem to be like some of the angelic children of Dickens's fiction. In 1843, Stowe had criticized Dickens's portrayal of children. She had complained of his "young ladies, like Rose Maylie, who talk sentimentally of angels and heaven; and children, like little Nell, who talk delightfully of dying, and who die in the sweetest and most poetic manner possible." Was not speaking sentimentally of angels and heaven, speaking delightfully of dying, and dying in a poetic manner exactly what little Eva herself would later do in *Uncle Tom's Cabin*?[4]

Eva falls off the steamboat on its way down the Mississippi to New Orleans, and Uncle Tom jumps overboard and rescues her. She persuades her father to buy Tom, and he becomes a coachman in the St. Clare home in New Orleans. Yet Eva turns out to be different from the child heroines of Dickens. The chief difference is that she shows a perception of evil and a willingness to grapple with it which they lack. These aspects of her character first become apparent to us in her response to what happens to Old Prue, the slave of a neighboring family. Old Prue has had her children sold away from her and, in despair, has become an alcoholic. She steals in order to obtain money for liquor and as a result receives increasingly savage whippings from her owner, whippings which have no real effect in changing her. When Eva sees Uncle Tom earnestly talking to Old Prue, she insists on knowing what the trouble is. Tom tells her, though reluctantly. In her response, Eva "did not exclaim, or wonder, or weep, as other children do. Her cheeks grew pale, and a deep earnest shadow passed over her eyes." Later, Old Prue dies from a whipping and Eva overhears another slave woman telling of the death. Aunt Dinah, the slave cook, tries to prevent Eva from hearing the story, but again she insists on knowing what has happened. "I shan't faint, Dinah," says the child, "and why shouldn't I hear it? It an't so much for me to hear it, as for poor Prue to suffer it." When she says this, Eva is probably ten or eleven years old. It may stretch matters to imagine so adult an attitude in a child. On the other hand, it is evident that Eva is far from the angelic children of the popular literature of the time and equally far from the sugary little simpleton which she frequently became in *Uncle Tom's Cabin* as a play.[5]

By the time she wrote *Uncle Tom's Cabin*, Stowe had achieved a religious faith whose essence was love. She had achieved it by absorbing, accepting, and eventually rejecting many of the Calvinist ideas she had been taught. Eva, on the other hand, had come simply and naturally to espouse a religion of love. Near the end of her life, St. Clare asks Eva about her religion:

"What is being a Christian, Eva?"
"Loving Christ most of all," said Eva.
"Do you, Eva?"
"Certainly I do."
"You never saw him," said St. Clare.
"That makes no difference," said Eva. "I believe him and in a few days I shall *see* him," and the young face grew fervent, radiant with joy.

A belief such as this may seem to the modern reader sentimental in the extreme. In itself, there is nothing wrong with it. Christian mystics have frequently believed something like this. Howard Mumford Jones, with honesty and insight, confessed in 1962 that with all his reservations about Eva, he was nonetheless impressed by her. She was, he thought, "a child out of William Blake or Wordsworth, a symbol of a lost and powerful influence whose mere existence is a cutting commentary on what Christianity is and we will not let it be."[6]

Eva's opposite is her selfish mother, Marie St. Clare, a woman who seems to be in some respects a literary ancestor of Mrs. Compson in Faulkner's *The Sound and the Fury*. The cult of the noble woman in nineteenth-century literature sometimes has a curious corollary. When a woman is bad, she is horrid. Marie says of one of the disobedient slaves that if she had her way she would have her whipped "till she couldn't stand." Concerning this comment, Augustine says to Ophelia, "Tell me of the lovely rule of woman! I never saw above a dozen that wouldn't half kill a horse, or a servant, either, if they had their own way with them!—let alone a man." In her cold, obtuse, and aggressive way, Marie is almost as evil as Simon Legree himself. Although the white South reacted to her as a slander of southern womanhood, she is a convincing character. It is from human nature in general that she is drawn, not specifically as a southerner. In 1921, Bliss Perry said of her that she "might have been one of Balzac's indolent, sensuous women."[7]

Ophelia, Augustine's middle-aged cousin who has been brought from

Vermont to manage the household in New Orleans, as the hypochon-
driac Marie says ill health prevents her from doing, is both a serious
and a comic character. With the exception of Simon Legree, she is the
novel's only major character from New England. Knowing her type and
her milieu perfectly, Stowe is especially imaginative and in control
when she portrays her in the novel. E. Bruce Kirkham, a modern critic,
makes the important point that a character like Ophelia would probably
be familiar to many readers in the North as the more exotic southern
characters would not be. Thus, the care with which the portrait of
Ophelia is drawn made it more likely that northern readers would believe in the reality of other characters in the novel who were largely
outside their own experience. We see in Ophelia a representative of
Puritanism without its intellectualism but with its rigid ideals of personal conduct. She does not realize, however, that her ideas do not transfer easily to a quite different society. Her discovery of their inadequacy
is sometimes comic, as when she tries to instruct Aunt Dinah, the slave
cook, in the complexities of housekeeping and cooking as practiced in
New England. She discovers that, with all of her slipshod methods,
Aunt Dinah is a better cook than she is. The true inadequacy of Ophelia's
ideas in terms of their application to the South, however, shows up when
they take the form of moral principles.[8]

It is not until Ophelia has replaced her inflexible sense of duty with
the virtue of love, a love which she learns from Eva and Uncle Tom,
that she is regenerated and able to function morally within society.
Stowe may have had her in mind when she said she thought *Uncle Tom's
Cabin* would be more favorably received in the South than in the North.
She is not the kind of representative of the North, it is true, which the
white South most feared and hated; she is quite unlike William Lloyd
Garrison or Wendell Phillips. Neither is she an example of the transcendental New Englander sometimes derided in southern magazines and
newspapers. In Ophelia, Stowe seemed to be making a concession to
the South. Ophelia has a religion of abstract benevolence, but it does
not prevent her from feeling an antipathy to blacks. Since white southerners apparently have this antipathy to a lesser degree, Stowe seems to
be saying, they are in this respect better than white northerners. Southern
readers of *Uncle Tom's Cabin* were seldom able to recognize the implied
compliment. They wrote angrily about the inconsistencies of Ophelia's
attitudes as if they had somehow escaped Stowe's attention.[9]

Of the black characters introduced in the New Orleans section of

Uncle Tom's Cabin, the child Topsy is by far the most important. Stowe probably recognized that the goodness of Uncle Tom needed still more balance—more balance, that is, than it had received from some of the minor characters like Sam and Andy in the early sections of the novel. The fact that Topsy is a child and that she is generally a comic character may obscure her function of saving the novel from the charge of portraying all the blacks as inherently good. Augustine gives Topsy as an ironic present to Ophelia. He recognizes that Topsy is a challenge to the whole moral system of his Yankee cousin. For reasons of self-protection, probably, Topsy has abandoned any ideal of goodness for herself. She steals and lies as naturally as she breathes, and the perceptive reader will grasp the truth that slavery produces many Topsys.

When she first appears, Topsy is almost wholly destitute of any perception of right or wrong. She is less well realized as a character than the little Pearl of Hawthorne's *The Scarlet Letter*, but she suggests comparison with her. Neither Hawthorne nor Stowe was convinced that children are inherently innocent. If they are not born evil, they at least pick up a shrewdness with regard to it much more quickly than the philosophers of the Enlightenment or such transcendentalists as Emerson might be willing to admit. When the Puritan elders ask little Pearl who made her, she ignores the expected answer and replies—with unconscious accuracy—that her mother picked her off a rose bush. When Ophelia asks Topsy who made her, the child gives a similar answer. The idea of being "made" by anyone amuses her, her eyes twinkle, and she replies, "Nobody, as I knows on," and then she adds, "I spect I grow'd."[10]

The principles of child-rearing which Ophelia has learned in New England are a failure when applied to Topsy. It is not that Topsy is stupid. Ophelia begins by attempting to teach her to make up beds. Topsy proves herself to be adept at the task, but while Ophelia's back is turned she steals a ribbon and a pair of gloves and hides them in her sleeve. Ophelia sees the ribbon protruding from the sleeve and pounces upon it. "What's this?" she demands. "You naughty, wicked child,—you've been stealing this!" Topsy is not at all disconcerted. "Laws," she replies, "that ar's Miss Freely's ribbon, an't it? How could it a got caught in my sleeve?" When Topsy persists in denying the theft, Ophelia loses her temper and shakes her, making the gloves fall from her sleeve. She thinks now that she has caught Topsy and that she will be forced to admit her wrongdoing. Topsy admits the theft of the gloves but persists in denying that she took the ribbon.[11]

For a time Ophelia relentlessly pursues her method of moral instruction. She is brought to the extreme, unnatural to her kindly heart, of whipping Topsy. At first, it seems an effective device. Topsy "invariably made a terrible commotion, screaming, groaning, and imploring," but her response was wholly pretended. After one of her whippings, Topsy describes the punishment to the other slave children of the household out of Ophelia's hearing. "Law, Miss Feely whip!—wouldn't kill a skeeter, her whipping. Oughter see how old Mas'r made the flesh fly; old Mas'r know'd how!" Ophelia herself comes to recognize that any method of instruction which relies ultimately on force will have no moral effect.[12]

As Topsy sensibly sees the issue, evil may be a better means for her protection than good. It may enable her, at the least, to maintain a sense of herself which she would lose if she accepted the conceptions of goodness taught by slavery. "Law, you niggers," she says to the other slave children, "does you know you's all sinners? Well, you is—everybody is. White folks is sinners too,—Miss Feely says so; but I spects niggers is the biggest ones." As Huck Finn would reject the religious moralizings of Miss Watson without perceiving the reasons why they are wrong, so Topsy sees through to the essential truth that the moral system of Ophelia has no relevance for her. "[L]or!" she tells the other slave children, "ye an't any of ye up to me. I's so awful wicked there can't nobody do nothin with me. I used to keep old Missis a swarin' at me half de time. I spects I's the wickedest critter in the world." And then she proceeds to "cut a summerset and come up brisk and shining on to a higher perch, and evidently plume herself on the distinction."[13]

The center of Ophelia's failure to teach Topsy is found in her racial prejudice. This prejudice is apparent when she first arrives in the St. Clare household in New Orleans. On entering, Eva runs to kiss the slaves:

"Well!" said Miss Ophelia, "you southern children can do something that I couldn't"

"What, now, pray?" said St. Clare.

"Well, I want to be kind to everybody, and I wouldn't have anything hurt; but as to kissing—"

"Niggers," said St. Clare, "that you're not up to—hey?"

"Yes, that's it. How can she?"

Later in the novel, Ophelia protests to Augustine against his allowing Eva to sit on Uncle Tom's knee:

"How can you let her?" said Miss Ophelia.

"Why not?" said St. Clare.

"Why, I don't know. It seems so dreadful."

"You would think no harm in a child's caressing a large dog, even if he was black; but a creature that can think, and reason, and feel, and is immortal, you shudder at; confess it, cousin. I knew the feeling among some of your northerners well enough. Not that there is a particle of virtue in our not having it; but custom with us does what Christianity ought to do,—obliterates the feeling of personal prejudice. I have often noticed, in my travels north, how much stronger this was with you than with us. You loathe them as you would a snake or a toad, yet you are indignant at their wrongs. You would not have them abused; but you don't want to have anything to do with them yourselves. You would send them to Africa, out of your sight and smell, and then send a missionary or two to do all the self-denial of elevating them compendiously. Isn't that it?"

"Well, cousin," said Miss Ophelia, thoughtfully, "there may be some truth in this."

"What would the poor and lowly do, without children?" said St. Clare, leaning on the railing, and watching Eva, as she tripped off, leading Tom with her. "Your little child is your only true democrat. Tom, now, is a hero to Eva; his stories are wonders in her eyes, his songs and Methodist hymns are better than an opera, and the traps and little bits of trash in his pocket a mine of jewels, and he the most wonderful Tom that ever wore a black skin. This is one of the roses of Eden that the Lord has dropped down expressly for the poor and lowly, who get few enough of any other kind."

Later in the novel, Eva tells Topsy that Ophelia would love her if only she were good. On this point, Topsy is wiser than Eva. "No," she replies, "she can't bar me, 'cause I'm a nigger—she'd's soon have a toad touch her! There can't nobody love niggers, and niggers can't do nothin'! I don't care," she says and begins to whistle.[14]

At this point Stowe introduces a problem in *Uncle Tom's Cabin* which was almost as difficult of solution as that of slavery, and one which has by no means been solved up to the present time—the matter of social relationships among members of different races. Partly because she is a child, Eva can solve the problem easily in her relationship with Uncle Tom. If she had been several years older, complications would inevitably have developed. Then the idea of her sitting upon Uncle Tom's knee would necessarily involve the issue of sex. It is true that neither could she sit on the knee of a white man with whom she had no close family relationship. On the other hand, the horror felt by society would have been greatly compounded if she had sat on the knee of a black man. Perhaps because slavery was the most obvious and pressing problem of the time, Stowe did not often face the companion problem of social relationships among races. When she did face it, she nearly always confined her observations to the relationships of white children to blacks.

Eva does suggest a way in which racial prejudice can be overcome. She tells Topsy that she loves her. We may feel a slight letdown when she gives her reason. "I love you, because you haven't had any father, or mother, or friends;—because you've been a poor, abused child!" Then Eva tells Topsy that she will die soon. "I am very unwell, Topsy, and I think I shan't live a great while; and it really grieves me, to have you be so naughty," she says. "I wish you would try to be good, for my sake;—it's only a little while I shall be with you." And Topsy strongly responds. "O, dear Miss Eva, dear Miss Eva!" she says, "I will try, I will try; I never did care nothin' about it before." Augustine overhears this interchange between Eva and Topsy and says to Ophelia, "It puts me in mind of mother. . . . It is true what she told me; if we want to give sight to the blind, we must be willing to do as Christ did—call them to us, and *put our hands on them*." After Eva's death, Ophelia does tell Topsy that she loves her. She "raises her gently" from the floor where she lies weeping, but she does not embrace her. It may be that Stowe could not imagine a revolution of character which would go that far.[15]

At one point in *Uncle Tom's Cabin*, Eva and Topsy are placed side by side and the omniscient narrator of the novel comments upon the differences between them:

> There stood the two children, representatives of the two extremes of society. The fair, high-bred child, with her golden head, her deep eyes, her spiritual, noble brow, and prince-like movements; and her black, keen, subtle, cringing, yet acute neighbor. They stood the representatives of their races. The Saxon, born of ages of cultivation, command, education, physical and moral eminence; the Afric born of ages of oppression, submission, ignorance, toil, and vice!

Neither child fits the character of the two races as Stowe usually described them. Elsewhere in her writings, Saxons are generally seen as coldly logical and domineering, especially so in their relationships with other races. Eva is not like this. In addition, Topsy hardly fits the stereotype of the blacks found in the above passage. If she was "born of ages . . . of submission," she is anything but submissive herself. The submission to little Eva is so clearly a special instance that it can hardly be classified as a racial trait. Topsy is even further from those conceptions of blacks found elsewhere in the writings of Stowe when she was convinced that they were inherently simple, loving, childlike, and docile.[16]

It is not wholly clear why Stowe asks the reader to reflect on the racial differences between Eva and Topsy. St. Paul had advised the early Christians that some members of the church would have different functions corresponding to those of individual organs of the human body—such as eyes, arms, and legs. These different organs would presumably work together to perform tasks which could not be accomplished by any of them alone. In the comparison of the two children, Stowe apparently meant to suggest something of the same solution to the problems of race. The Saxons, when they became truly Christian, would no longer be coldly logical, nor would they dominate other races. On the other hand, their "ages of cultivation, command, education, physical and moral eminence" would seem to give them a major role in the development of civilization, especially in the task of uplifting other races. It would be the parable of the talents all over again. To whom much was given much would be expected. The role of the blacks, on the other hand, was apparently to be more humble in the divine scheme. Removed from the evils of slavery and given kindly and loving treatment, perhaps Topsy would cultivate the same virtues as those to be found in Uncle Tom. If this happened, slavery would be replaced by a system in which different races would be politically equal but still have quite different missions in life. The picture may have been persuasive then, but it does not take much insight to foresee that a system of values like this one would not be attractive to the blacks once they had attained their freedom.[17]

The most important indictment of slavery in *Uncle Tom's Cabin* is found in the ideas of Augustine St. Clare. As a polemicist he has great advantages. He has traveled widely and has lived in New England long enough to understand the ideas and attitudes of the region thoroughly. From his mother, he has learned that slavery is an evil institution. He reflects on his own experience and expresses his ideas with clarity and force. He does not express them, however, to those people who might get him into trouble because of his antislavery opinions. If he had publicly become an abolitionist, northern readers might have admired him more, but he would have lost his chief purpose in the novel. Unlike nearly all the opponents of slavery in the North, he is not denouncing evils he knows merely by secondhand report. Also unlike northern antislavery leaders, he is not embattled in constant debates with fiery opponents.

Augustine does not recount tales of horror of slavery. He probably knows that such stories can easily be dismissed by the advocates of slavery as exceptions. In addition, they can be countered with tales of the kindness and fair treatment of other slaveholders. He concentrates, as Thomas Jefferson did before him, on the question of whether a power which is almost absolute can ever be truly benevolent. His nephew, Henrique, the teen-age son of his proslavery brother, demonstrates how a high-spirited young white southerner might react when confronted with what would seem to be the mildest form of opposition from a slave:

> "What's this, Dodo, you little lazy dog! you haven't rubbed my horse down, this morning."
> "Yes, Mas'r," said Dodo, submissively; "he got that dust on his own self."
> "You rascal, shut your mouth!" said Henrique, violently raising his riding-whip. "How dare you speak?"
> The boy was a handsome, bright-eyed mulatto, of just Henrique's size, and his curling hair hung round a high, bold forehead. He had white blood in his veins, as could be seen by the quick flush in his cheek, and the sparkle of his eye, as he eagerly tried to speak.
> "Mas'r Henrique!—" he began.
> Henrique struck him across the face with his riding-whip, and, seizing one of his arms, forced him on to his knees, and beat him till he was out of breath.
> "There, you impudent dog! Now will you learn not to answer back when I speak to you? Take the horse back, and clean him properly. I'll teach you your place!"[18]

The attribution of Dodo's high spirit to his white intermixture is, of course, a racist idea. This defect on Stowe's part does not, however, invalidate an equally important point—that she clearly has depicted a major evil of slavery. Henrique is given a power over another human being which no one should have and which he is especially incapable of using wisely. Augustine and Alfred St. Clare witness the incident. Augustine argues that more and more slaves will have white intermixture and thus it will become more and more difficult for masters to control them. Blacks with white intermixture will be more likely to have "haughty feelings," and thus a bloody revolution of slaves is inevitable. The modern reader is hardly likely to agree with Augustine that slaves with white intermixture are inherently more freedom-loving than those without it, but he may agree that such a revolution would be probable. Alfred complacently argues that the whites will indefinitely have the power to keep the blacks and mixed bloods down. "We have energy enough," he says, "to manage our own powder." Pointing to Henrique's lack of self-control, Augustine observes, "Some trained like your Henrique will be grand guardians of your powder magazines—so cool and self-possessed! The proverb says, 'They that cannot govern themselves cannot govern others!'" Even Alfred admits, "There is a trouble there. . . ." He adds that "our system is a difficult one to train children under," and he wonders whether Henrique should be sent to the North for his education where he will be forced to consider the opinions of his "equals."[19]

Augustine dismisses as humbug all the arguments for slavery founded upon the Bible, as well as those based upon the assumption that civilization can exist only if there is a permanent lower class in society which will do all the dirty work. He boldly asserts that the real argument for slavery is that it is of economic value to the whites, and especially to the masters of plantations. The analysis suggests Marx himself. Of slavery, Augustine says to Ophelia:

"Strip it of all its ornament, run it down to the root and nucleus of the whole, and what is it? Why, because my brother Quashy is ignorant and weak, and I am intelligent and strong,—because I know how, and *can* do it, —therefore, I may steal all he has, keep it, and give him only such and so much as suits my fancy. Whatever is too hard, too dirty, too disagreeable, for me, I may set Quashy to doing. Because I don't like work, Quashy shall work. Because the sun burns me, Quashy shall stay in the sun. Quashy shall earn the money, and I will spend it. Quashy shall lie down in every puddle, that I may walk over dryshod. Quashy shall do my will, and not his all the days of his mortal life, and have such chance of getting to heaven, at last, as I find convenient. This I take to be about what slavery *is*. I defy anybody on earth to read our slave-code, as it stands in our law-books, and make anything else of it. Talk of the *abuses* of slavery; Humbug! The *thing itself* is the essence of all abuse. And the only reason why the land don't sink under it like Sodom and Gomorrah, is because it is *used* in a way infinitely better than it is. For pity's sake, for shame's sake, because we are men born of women, and not savage beasts, many of us do not, and dare not,—we would *scorn* to use the full power which our savage laws put into our hands. And he who goes the furthest, and does the worst, only uses within limits the power that the law gives him."[20]

Most of the abolitionists defended capitalism as the best of all economic systems. Augustine admits that, in different ways, the northern wage system and the slave system both exploit workers. He is willing to concede the point to his brother Alfred that in the North and in

Great Britain the threat of starvation compels the labor of the poor and that in some instances they may be materially less well off than the slaves. To Ophelia, Augustine mentions Alfred's argument that there "must . . . be a lower class, given up to physical toil and confined to an animal nature." From the work of this lower class, "a higher one thereby acquires leisure and wealth for a more expanded intelligence and improvement, and becomes the directing soul of the lower." Augustine admits that it is a consistent argument but says that he cannot accept it because he is not an aristocrat but a democrat. Ophelia protests that the two systems, slavery and capitalism, are not really the same. The free laborer, even in England, she argues, "is not sold, traded, parted from his family, whipped." "He is as much at the will of his employer," Augustine replies, "as if he were sold to him. The slave-owner can whip his refractory slave to death,—the capitalist can starve him to death. As to family security, it is hard to say which is worst,—to have one's children sold, or see them starve to death at home." At this point we are far beyond the middle-class views of William Lloyd Garrison, to whom it had scarcely occurred that the northern wage system might also have serious evils.[21]

Augustine is also close to Marx in his conviction that political, social, and religious ideas may be mere rationalizations of the interests of dominant economic classes. The real reason for the passionate defense of slavery in the South, he maintains, is economic. "Planters, who have money to make by it,—clergymen, who have planters to please,—politicians, who want to rule by it,—may warp and bend language and ethics to a degree that shall astonish the world at their ingenuity," he says; "they can press nature and the Bible, and nobody knows what else, into the service; but, after all, neither they nor the world believe in it one particle the more." He is also willing to apply the same logic to his refusal to free his own slaves. "My servants were my father's, and what is more, my mother's; and now they are mine, they and their increase, which bids fair to be a considerable item." On the other hand, he knows that this argument is morally indefensible.[22]

White northerners are not morally superior to white southerners, Augustine maintains; the difference is that slavery is less important economically to them. He and Ophelia are cousins. Her father had remained in New England and his had settled in Louisiana. "My father, you know," he says to her, "came first from New England; and he was just such another man as your father,—a regular old Roman,—upright, energetic, noble-minded, with an iron will. Your father settled down in New England, to rule over rocks and stones, and to force an existence out of Nature; and mine settled in Louisiana, to rule over men and women, and force existence out of them." Nothing was different about the two men, he says, except their environment. "Your father, for example, settles in Vermont," he says to Ophelia, "in a town where all are, in fact, free and equal; becomes a regular church member and deacon, and in due time joins an Abolition society, and thinks us all little better than heathens. Yet he is, for all the world, in constitution and habit, a duplicate of my father. I can see it leaking out in fifty different ways. . . ." Ophelia's father, Augustine argues, owes his democratic convictions not to himself but to his society. Augustine argues that if both his and her father had owned plantations in Louisiana, "they would have been as like as two old bullets cast in the same mould." Augustine has another comment which is similar to one of the ideas of Marx. He forecasts revolution. "One thing is certain," he tells Ophelia, "that there is a mustering among the masses, the world over; and there is a *dies irae* coming, sooner or later. The same thing is working in Europe, in England, and in this country."[23]

In the New Orleans episodes of *Uncle Tom's Cabin*, Tom is being prepared for the role of martyr. A good deal is said in this part of the novel about his racial traits. The climate of Louisiana is compared to that of Africa, and the voice of the omniscient narrator reflects on Tom's ancestors. "The negro, it must be remembered," explains the narrator, "is an exotic of the most gorgeous and superb countries of the world, and he has deep in his heart, a passion for all that is splendid, rich, and fanciful; a passion which, rudely indulged by an untrained taste, which draws on them [*sic*] the ridicule of the colder and more correct white race." Stowe is nearly always ecstatic when she mentions Africa. It is probable that she did not know that western Africa, the part of the continent from which most American blacks had come, was not the tropical paradise she envisioned but largely a rugged and barren land. She saw the African homeland of the American slaves as "that far-off mystic land of gold, and gems, and spices, and waving palms, and wondrous flowers, and miraculous fertility. . . ." Almost unconsciously she may have been attempting to make it an attractive place because later in the novel she would advocate colonization of American blacks in Africa. Even at this point, she prepares the mind of the reader for this later development. In Africa, "the negro race, no longer despised and trodden down, will, perhaps, show forth some of the latest and most magnificent revelations of human life."[24]

Uncle Tom's religious ideas are broadened and deepened in the New Orleans section of the novel. Eva recognizes at once his capacity for depth of religious reflection. So does Augustine. Tom becomes Augustine's confidant and spiritual adviser. When Augustine asks Tom whether it does not disturb his faith to know that his master is a skeptic and is also a man who knows a great deal more than he does, Tom earnestly shakes his head. Submissive on other points, Tom is unyielding on this one. "O, Mas'r," he exclaims, "haven't you jest read how he hides from the wise and prudent, and reveals unto babes?"[25]

In addition, Tom shows that he has the desire for freedom which Stowe sometimes seems to have reserved for blacks with white intermixture. After the death of Eva, Augustine decides to give Tom his freedom and begins the legal proceedings. He is a little nettled, however, by the light which comes into Tom's eyes at the prospect of freedom. At this point, Augustine temporarily loses his usual perceptiveness concerning the nature of slavery:

"You haven't had such very bad times here, that you need to be in such a rapture, Tom," he said dryly.

"No, no, Mas'r! 'tan't that, it's bein' a *free man*! That's why I'm joyin' for."

"Why, Tom, don't you think for your own part, you've been better off than to be free?"

"*No, indeed*, Mas'r St. Clare," said Tom, with a flash of energy. "No, indeed!"

"Why, Tom, you couldn't possibly have earned by your work, such clothes and such living as I have given you."

"Knows all that, Mas'r St. Clare; Mas'r's been too good; but Mas'r, I'd rather have poor clothes, poor house, poor everything, and have 'em *mine*, than have the best and have 'em any man's else. I had so, Mas'r; I think it's natur, Mas'r."

When Stowe was theorizing about race, she was by no means certain that all races have an innate desire for freedom. On the other hand, when she was confronted by a situation in which exactly this issue arose, she had a deeper insight. She realized that the desire for freedom is not a matter of race but of being human.[26]

The New Orleans episodes of *Uncle Tom's Cabin* show some of the kindlier aspects of slavery, but they also show that—even at its best—

the institution makes the slaves wholly dependent on their masters and mistresses for their well-being. The St. Clare family begins to break up. First, little Eva dies. This is, of course, one of the longest death scenes in literature. Nineteenth-century Protestant Christians frequently believed that just before a Christian dies he is likely to catch a glimpse of heaven, and if the people by his bedside observe carefully they too might catch at least a reflected glow of this ecstatic moment. The idea was satirized in Emily Dickinson's poem, "I heard a Fly buzz when I died," but Stowe took it with complete seriousness. In her description of Eva's death, she may owe something to family accounts of her own mother's death. Lyman Beecher had seen the moment of Roxana's dying as her grand entrance into heaven. Something similar happens when Eva dies. "O! love,—joy,—peace!" she murmurs at the moment of her death, and the implication seems to be that she is describing the heavenly beauties she sees before her.[27]

In the drama which *Uncle Tom's Cabin* would become, Eva's death is close to mere melodrama. In the novel it has a function in advancing an important theme. Like Uncle Tom, Eva represents the religion of Christian love. After the death of Eva, Ophelia comes to recognize the deficiencies of a logical but cold religion. She tries to comfort Topsy who, prostrate with grief, says she wishes she had never been born. "Topsy, you poor child," says Ophelia, "don't give up. I can love you, though I am not like that dear little child. I hope I've learnt something of the love of Christ from her. I can love you. . . ." This declaration helps to turn Ophelia's past failures with Topsy to success. "From that hour," the narrator tells us, "she acquired an influence over the mind of the destitute child that she never lost."[28]

The death of Augustine closely follows that of Eva. It is associated with evils which the Beecher family had long combated. He is in a public dining room when two "gentlemen" who are intoxicated begin to argue and then proceed to blows. When Augustine attempts to intervene, one of the men stabs him with a bowie knife. He is taken to his home mortally wounded. The incident might well have come out of one of Lyman Beecher's antiwhiskey or antidueling sermons. The reader may suspect that he is in for another death scene as long as that of little Eva, but this one is brief. Up until this point neither the ministrations of little Eva nor those of Tom have been able to bring Augustine to a belief in God and Christ, but on his deathbed he rids himself of his skepticism. He asks Uncle Tom to pray for him, and in his last moments he opens his eyes "with a sudden light as of joy and recognition," to exclaim, "*Mother!*" before dying.[29]

With the death of Augustine comes the end of our view in the novel of slavery at its best. So excellent as a theorist of slavery's evils, Augustine had foolishly not thought of what would happen to his slaves if he should die. Topsy is saved because he had transferred ownership of her to Ophelia, who had overcome her repugnance to slavery in order to be certain that she could rescue Topsy and later free her. All the other slaves of the St. Clare household, including Uncle Tom, are now owned by Marie St. Clare. It does not take them long to learn that her methods of handling them are different from those of her husband. Soon after his death, Marie sends the slave Rosa, who has committed a trivial offense, to the "calaboose" or public whipping place in New Orleans, where she receives fifteen lashes. At this point, *Uncle Tom's Cabin* comes close to an issue which Stowe had carefully avoided—the sectional issue between the North and the South. Ophelia had gone to Marie to plead for Rosa but had been refused. When Ophelia realized that she could not prevent Rosa from being whipped, "All the honest blood of womanhood, the strong New England blood of liberty, flushed to her cheeks, and throbbed bitterly in her indignant heart. . . ."[30]

Soon afterward Marie decides to sell nearly all of her slaves and to return to her father's plantation. Tom is among those who are sold. Augustine had not completed the legal papers necessary to manumit him. Just as she had no influence with Marie on the issue of flogging Rosa, Ophelia cannot move Marie on the issue of respecting Augustine's wishes with regard to Tom's freedom. For a second time, Uncle Tom comes close to freedom only to have it snatched from him. From this point, he moves steadily toward his final destruction.

IX

Uncle Tom's Cabin
Part III

THE LAST SECTIONS of *Uncle Tom's Cabin* contain some of its weakest writing, but they are also the clearest source of its meaning. In creating Simon Legree and his isolated Red River plantation in Louisiana, Stowe apparently had in mind the presentation of slavery, as she phrased it, "at something approaching its worst." It is not that we can be certain whether she exaggerated its evil. The argument of how bad the conditions of the slaves were is still with us, and it is as difficult as it ever was to describe what was "typical." In addition, the exposure of horrors always puts a strain upon the talent of a writer and the credulity of a reader. There are not many convincing portraits of human monsters in literature and fewer still of monsters whose evil is also meant to demonstrate the evils of an institution. In the twentieth century, the Nazi concentration camps made an enormous impact upon history but, so far, a comparatively minor one in literature. In attempting to portray human monsters, a writer is likely to lose himself in a catalog of ghastly details, and what emerges is not convincing.

Most of the villains of nineteenth-century literature possessed evils which were personal rather than institutional. Fagin in *Oliver Twist* is a leader in the institution of organized crime, and yet he probably appeared to most of his readers as evil principally in himself. Stowe did her best to create an authentic villain in the slaveholder, Simon Legree. The chief trouble the modern reader is likely to have with him is that he is something of a bugaboo. He rants and raves, he foams at the mouth, and he even does cruel things. Nevertheless, the reader gradually becomes aware that his creator has him under wraps. There are horrors which, because of the genteel public taste of the time, could only be hinted. One of the villainies of Legree is to force young women to become his mistresses, but this evil in the novel is either placed in the past or merely suggested as a possibility. It never happens "on stage." That Stowe is restrained in her portrait of Legree is suggested by the reaction of a southern woman to him. Mary Boykin Chesnut, the southern diarist, did not like *Uncle Tom's Cabin*. She recognized in Simon Legree, however, a character who represented troubling evils of slavery. In portraying him, she thought, Stowe had insufficiently realized the potential for the evil of such men. "You see, Mrs. Stowe did not hit the sorest spot," Mrs. Chesnut wrote in her diary. "She makes Legree a bachelor." She meant that if Legree had had a wife and children, Stowe would have been obliged to describe the damage to his family which resulted from his sexual relations with slave women. On the other hand, it is not surprising that Stowe did not provide Legree with a wife and children. One reason why *Uncle Tom's Cabin* was so much more popular than those antislavery novels which made sexual immorality an explicit theme may have been just this point. Pious people did not like to read directly about such things, and in *Uncle Tom's Cabin* they were not obliged to do so.[1]

Simon Legree first appears in the novel when he attends a slave auction in New Orleans, the one at which the slaves of the St. Clare household have been put up for sale:

A little before the sale commenced, a short broad muscular man, in a checked shirt considerably open at the bosom, and pantaloons much the worse for dirt and wear, elbowed his way through the crowd, like one who is going actively into a business; and, coming up to the group, began to examine them systematically. From the moment that Tom saw him approaching, he felt an immediate and revolting horror at him, that increased as he came near. He was evidently, though short, of gigantic strength. His round bullet head, large slight-gray eyes, with their shaggy sandy eye-brows, and stiff, wiry, sun-burned hair, were rather unprepossessing items, it is to be confessed; his large, coarse mouth was distended with tobacco, the juice of which, from time to time, he ejected from him with great decision and explosive force; his hands were immensely large, hairy, sun-burned, freckled, and very dirty, and garnished with long nails, in a very foul condition.

Legree seizes Tom's head in order to make him open his mouth so that he can examine his teeth, has him roll up his sleeves so as to display his muscles, and puts him through a series of jumping exercises in order to test his agility. After he has bought Tom and several other slaves, he doubles up his fist which resembles a blacksmith's hammer and says to them, "Now, . . . d'ye see this fist? Heft it! . . . Look at these yer bones. Well, I tell ye this yer fist has got hard as iron *knocking down niggers.* I never see the nigger, yet, I couldn't bring down with one crack." He tells Tom that he doesn't keep an overseer but handles his slaves directly, and he adds the superfluous comment, "I don't show no mercy!" The fact that Legree has no overseer saves Stowe from the task of describing the complex relationship between master and overseer on a southern plantation.[2]

Simon Legree, like the cruel overseer on the plantation of Augustine St. Clare's father, is from New England, specifically from Vermont. Making the principal villain in the novel a New Englander was a shrewd device. Stowe apparently meant to suggest that it was slavery as a system which was evil and that white northerners might make even worse slave masters than white southerners. Legree is a monster, but he has a pious and devoted mother. She had the traits of saintly women Stowe celebrated elsewhere in her fiction. She had led Simon, as a boy, "at the sound of Sabbath bell, to worship and to pray" and had "trained her only son, with long, unwearied love, and patient prayers." It is not clear what went wrong. Simon may suggest that Calvinism, like any other religion, has its failures. The system was so rigorous that perhaps its failures might be all the more spectacular. Principally to blame for Simon's going to the bad was his "hard-tempered sire, on whom the gentle woman had wasted a world of unvalued love. . . ." For a time Simon tried to follow the religious example of his mother. The "good angels called him," and he was "almost persuaded. . . ." Evil proved to be the stronger force, however, and when his mother remonstrated with him, he struck her to the ground. He ran away, first to the sea and then to Louisiana. When he appears in the novel, he is wholly given over to evil.[3]

In addition to buying Tom, Legree buys Emmeline, a beautiful fifteen-year-old quadroon. Her former mistress had been "an amiable and pious lady of New Orleans" who had given her religious instruction so that she had become a Christian. She had never been required to do hard work, and thus she had delicate hands. The son of her former mistress had mismanaged his mother's investments, and she had become bankrupt. At this point, a New York firm which owned the mortgage of the estate advised its New Orleans representative "to dispose of the business in the way that seemed to him the most suitable, and remit the proceeds." Again in the novel the hand of northern complicity in slavery is made evident. Both Emmeline and her mulatto mother are put up for sale. Her mother has Emmeline brush her hair back severely in order to keep her from the notice of libidinous slave buyers, but the auctioneer insists that the curls be restored. "Them curls," he observes, "may make a hundred dollars difference in the sale of her." In the most explicitly sexual passage of the novel, Simon Legree closely examines Emmeline at the auction. "He put out his heavy, dirty hand," says the narrator, "and drew the girl towards him; passed it over her neck and bust, felt her arms, looked at her teeth, and then pushed her back against her mother, whose patient face showed the suffering she had been going through at every motion of the hideous stranger." Legree buys Emmeline but not her mother, refusing the tearful pleas of both. "[T]he hammer falls," says the narrator melodramatically; "he has got the girl, body and soul, unless God help her!"[4]

It is instructive to compare the scene of the sale of Emmeline in *Uncle Tom's Cabin* with Richard Hildreth's treatment of a similar subject. In *The White Slave*, published in 1852 as a revision of his earlier antislavery novel, *Archy Moore*, Hildreth described the auction of a black woman slave. He includes the indecorous humor of the bidders. The auctioneer says of her that she is "warranted . . . healthy, sound, and honest." "But no virgin," calls out one of the men in the crowd, a comment which provokes "a violent explosion of laughter." The first version of Hildreth's novel, the one entitled *Archy Moore*, was regarded as so shocking in 1836 that no firm would take it. Hildreth had been obliged to pay the printing costs himself. The name of the printer, John Eastham, did appear on the title page of the 1836 edition; but even this proved to be a rash act, because as a result Eastham had lost his contract as official printer for the city of Boston. The newspapers and periodicals would not review the novel. The New York Anti-Slavery Society refused to allow copies of it to be sold in its offices because the "obscenities" of slavery were too graphically represented. Lydia Maria Child wrote a defense of the novel, but its frankness troubled even her. She excused the explicitness of the sexual scenes in the novel by saying that the slave narrator, Archy Moore himself, had not been reared in a truly moral society. It would be hopeless in "the degrading influence of slavery" to expect "elevated purity of sentiment, or unimpaired moral strength, either in the slaves or their masters." From all this, the reader can surmise that what may seem to be a shrinking from reality on Stowe's part may actually be a necessary resort to euphemism because of the genteel taste of the age.[5]

The Legree plantation is the only one in *Uncle Tom's Cabin* which is actually shown in operation. Even so, the details of its workings are given sparsely. Whether they are accurate it is difficult to say. Southern critics of the novel concentrated on the unfairness of depicting so evil a character as Simon Legree as if he were representative of a whole class of slaveholders. They had little to say about errors in details of Stowe's account of plantation life. That this was a difficult section of the novel for her is certain. In July, 1851, nearly a month after the serial version of the novel had begun to be published in the *National Era*, she wrote to Frederick Douglass to ask whether he knew anyone who could answer some questions she had prepared concerning the operation of a southern plantation. She told him that she had an account written from the point of view of a "Southern planter" but she was "anxious to have something more from another standpoint," by which she probably meant from the point of view of a slave. "I wish to be able to make a picture," she said, "that shall be graphic and true to nature in its details." Since the part of the novel dealing with the Shelby plantation in Kentucky had already been published, she must have been thinking of the Legree plantation in Louisiana. Douglass himself had been a slave in Maryland, where plantations were substantially different from those in Louisiana. It is not known whether he suggested anyone to advise her or did so himself. More than a hundred years later, Avery O. Craven, the southern historian, cited this letter as evidence that Stowe knew little about slavery. What she "knew," he said, was "what the abolitionists thought slavery was like. . . ." Other critics and historians have expressed this idea, but they are rarely specific as to what it was, exactly, that she did not know. In the main, critics have brought up only matters of comparatively minor detail, and not many of those, with which to fault *Uncle Tom's Cabin*. Perhaps the critics in the South in the 1850s thought that the errors of the novel were too numerous to list or that other matters were more important. It is possible, however, that Stowe had studied the subject in some detail, and that she knew a good deal about it.[6]

The loneliness and gloominess of the Louisiana rural landscape are emphasized to suggest the isolation of Simon Legree's plantation on the Red River. The travelers go first on a river boat significantly named "Pirate" and the rest of the way by wagon. "It was a wild, forsaken road," says the narrator,

now winding through dreary pine barrens, where the wind whispered mournfully, and now over log causeways, through long cypress swamps, the doleful trees rising out of the slimy, spongy ground, hung with long wreaths of funereal black moss, while ever and anon the loathsome form of the moccasin snake might be seen sliding among broken stumps and shattered branches that lay here and there, rotting in the water.[7]

While traveling on the boat, Legree obligingly explains to a stranger his methods of managing his slaves. "I don't go for savin' niggers. Use up, and buy more, 's my way;—makes you less trouble, and I'm quite sure it comes cheaper in the end. . . ." To the question of how long slaves generally last under this treatment, Legree replies, "Stout fellers last six or seven years; trashy ones gets worked up in two or three." Previously he had tried to take care of his slaves, but he had lost money. "Now, you see," he explains, "I just put 'em straight through, sick or well. When one nigger's dead, I buy another." Stowe did not attempt to show Legree as a representative slaveholder. A southern apologist for slavery aboard the boat explains to a northerner dismayed by the cruelty of Legree, "You must not take that fellow to be any specimen of Southern planters." Nor did Stowe charge southern slaveholders with being wholly indifferent to how their neighbor slaveholders treated their slaves. Legree's plantation is in a remote section of Louisiana, and he has no neighbors.[8]

Emmeline is a comparatively mild example of "the beautiful quadroon" figure in antislavery fiction. She does not, for example, become Legree's mistress. In other antislavery novels of the period there were women like Emmeline, but it was their sexual degradation which was the major theme. The quadroons of most antislavery novels were shown merely as the unresisting victims of white men's lusts. Stowe's quadroon slaves, both men and women, are victims of slavery but not silent victims. They often realize that they are not fully accepted by either whites or blacks and feel correspondingly resentful. Aunt Dinah, a wholly black slave in the St. Clare household, had taunted the quadroon Rosa with the dilemma of being a slave of a mixed race. "You seem to tink your-self white folks," Dinah had said. "You an't nerry one, black *nor* white. I'd like to be one or turrer." It may be significant that it was Rosa who, after the death of Augustine, apparently said something impudent to Marie, her white mistress. Rosa was the slave Marie selected to be sent to the calaboose for a public whipping.[9]

It is Cassy, the former slave mistress of Simon Legree, who most clearly represents the alienation and rebellion of quadroons in *Uncle Tom's Cabin.* Her age is not given, but she is probably about forty. Legree's apparent intention is to replace her with the younger Emmeline. Cassy is not jealous. She hates Legree and does what she can to protect Emmeline from him. When she first appears in the novel, Cassy is a woman characterized equally by dignity and despair. Legree, to punish her for some unnamed offense, probably a refusal to have sexual inter-course with him, makes Cassy pick cotton as an ordinary slave field hand. She performs these duties quickly and well, making no effort to placate Legree and depriving him of any possibility of complaining of her work. In the fields, she encounters Uncle Tom. She sees him slipping part of the cotton he has picked into the sacks of slaves unused to the task so that they will not be whipped for falling short of their quotas. Cassy and Tom become friends, and she tells him the story of her life.

Her father had been a white man who owned both her and her almost white mother. He had Cassy educated in graceful accomplish-ments at a French convent school in Louisiana. Like Augustine St. Clare, her father had neglected to provide for the freedom of his slaves. When he suddenly died of cholera, both mother and daughter were sold to satisfy creditors of the estate. Cassy had been bought by a handsome scoundrel who had assured her that he loved her and had fathered two children by her. When he got into financial difficulty, however, he be-trayed Cassy and her children. He went away for a few days so that he would not be present when creditors, armed with papers signed by him, sold her and the children. Her new master had threatened to sell the chil-dren away from her if she did not submit to him. Eventually, he sold them anyway. While Cassy was walking on a street in New Orleans, she had a glimpse of the fate of her little boy. He had been taken to the cala-boose to be whipped. She saw him as he burst free momentarily from his tormentors and clung to his mother. Her pleas were ignored. The child had been snatched from her and a whole section of her dress had been torn away. When she rushed home to get her new master to

intervene, he laughed at her and told her the boy was getting his
"desserts" and was just being "broken in." When Cassy bore another
son by this man, she killed the child by giving him an overdose of
laudanum. Cassy hurriedly relates these events to Uncle Tom, and the
reader has few means of assessing their reality.[10]

Her master then sold Cassy to Legree. The last section of the novel
includes horrors, but the manner of telling them teeters between the
eighteenth-century Gothic novel and Victorian melodrama. Cassy has
a mysterious power over Legree. Most of the women characters in
Stowe's fiction derive their power from gentleness and love. When these
qualities are unavailing, however, women apparently have other powers
in reserve. In explaining the relation of Cassy to Legree, the narrator
of the novel says that

the most brutal man cannot live in constant association with a strong
female influence, and not be greatly controlled by it. When he first bought
her, she was . . . a woman delicately bred; and then he crushed her, without
scruple, beneath the foot of his brutality. But, as time, and debasing influences, and despair, hardened womanhood within her, and waked the fires
of fiercer passions, she had become in a measure his mistress, and he alternately tyrannized over and dreaded her.

The precise reason for Cassy's power over Legree is not explained.
The use of the word *mistress* here is not explicitly sexual, but the
implication is probably part of Stowe's meaning. Whatever the nature
of her relationship with Legree, she is capable of defying him. When
Legree on one occasion grabs her by the wrist, she says, "Simon Legree,
take care! . . . You're afraid of me, Simon, . . . and you've reason to be!
But be careful, for I've got the devil in me!"[11]

Cassy realizes that her influence over Legree is not strong enough
to protect Emmeline from him, and she decides that the two of them
must run away, though their chances of avoiding capture in the swamps
are small. They also risk serious injury or even death from the attacks
of fierce dogs or from the gunfire of their pursuers. When the two
women disappear, Legree thinks they are somewhere in the swamps and
takes horses, slaves, and dogs in a party of pursuit. To Sambo, one of the
cruelest of his slaves, he says, "You may fire on Cass, if you like; it's
time she was gone to the devil, where she belongs," but he cautions him
not to hurt Emmeline. Actually the two women have hidden in the
attic of the plantation house. It is at this point that *Uncle Tom's Cabin*
takes on most obviously the characteristics of a Gothic novel. Legree

had once killed a black woman in the attic, and the house slaves say that sometimes the sound of blows and wailings can be heard coming from there. Legree, for all his bravado, is afraid of ghosts and dares not go to the attic. Since the house servants are equally afraid to go there, it is a good hiding place. The dramatic devices may be embarrassing to the modern reader. There is a "heavy old Dutch clock" that slowly strikes twelve midnight. Cassy has installed a broken bottle in a window of the attic to magnify the sound of the wind. Downstairs, Legree hears a "wild shriek . . . pealing down the stairway" which makes his knees knock together. When he works up his courage to go up and investigate, a "gust of wind swept down, extinguishing the candle he held in his hand," and he hears "fearful, unearthly screams." He backs away.[12]

Cassy represents the desperate acts to which a mulatto may be forced in the South, a theme which was to continue in the fiction of the region long after the slaves had been freed. She has been so maddened by cruelty that she is capable of killing Legree. In 1966, Severn Duvall commented on the tradition of which Cassy is a part:

Over the years . . . have come Southern writers like Cable and Faulkner willing to face imaginatively the contradictions of their [the mulattoes'] peculiar heritage. Certainly no modern reader of *The Grandissimes* and *Madame Delphine*, of *Light in August, Absalom, Absalom!*, and *Go Down, Moses* can escape the conclusion that miscegenation is still a crucial theme, or that the patriarchal legend still establishes its ironic patterns through the collateral genealogy of black and white. . . . Other writers, far more talented and much closer to the scene, have taken up the themes of Mrs. Stowe. But however lurid and glaring it may seem to the sophisticate of today, however crude its appeal, *Uncle Tom's Cabin* still knifes to the heart of the matter.[13]

Unable to find Cassy and Emmeline, Legree wreaks his vengeance on Uncle Tom. Ever truthful, Tom admits that he knows where Cassy and Emmeline are hiding, but of course he refuses to betray them. Legree has already had trouble with Tom. Though he works hard and fulfills every other command of his master, Tom will not flog the other slaves as Legree commands him to do. What Legree regards as stubbornness comes to a climax in Tom's refusal to help him find the escaped women. Legree resolves, once and for all, to break Tom's spirit or to kill him. This is the scene to which the whole novel has been moving, and it would not be surprising if Stowe had thought of it before she had planned any of the other characters or events. Artistically the scene is marred by the intrusion of the voice of the narrator. Before Tom is flogged, the narrator takes on some imaginary proslavery spokesman. "Ye say that the *interest* of the master is a sufficient safeguard for the slave," the narrator says. "In the fury of man's mad will, he will wittingly, and with open eye, sell his own soul to the devil to gain his ends; and will he be more careful of his neighbor's body?"[14]

Since the religion of Uncle Tom has caused such widespread skepticism and rejection in modern times, it is instructive to compare him with a character in Richard Hildreth's *Archy Moore*, the antislavery novel first published in 1836. There is a character in *Archy Moore* similar to Uncle Tom, so similar that there has been a good deal of conjecture that Stowe might have read the earlier novel. The slave Thomas of *Archy Moore*, like Uncle Tom, is "of unmixed African blood," has "a stout, muscular frame," "bodily strength," and "a capacity for enduring privation and fatigue." Both Thomas and Uncle Tom are devout Christians. Thomas was converted by "certain Methodists" and Uncle Tom, though his denomination is not specified, drives Ophelia's carriage to a Methodist church in New Orleans and may have attended services there himself. Thomas of *Archy Moore* is "gentle as a lamb." "It seemed as if several of the most powerful principles of human nature had been eradicated from his bosom," Archy Moore, the narrator of the novel, tells us. Thomas "believed that God had made him a servant, and that it was his duty to obey his master and be contented with his lot. Whatever cruelties or indignities the unprovoked insolence of unlimited authority might inflict upon him, it was his duty to submit in humble silence and if his master smote him on one cheek, he was to turn the other also." Both Thomas and Uncle Tom are completely honest. Thomas would "rather starve than steal" and "preferred being whipped to telling a lie." Both characters are teetotalers.[15]

The difference in the novels, however, is soon apparent. Stowe was a Christian, while Hildreth was openly skeptical. Where Stowe saw the patient virtues of Uncle Tom as almost sublime, Hildreth saw the piety and submission of his character Thomas as qualities he has only before he has been educated to the true meaning of slavery. Thomas must divest himself of these traits, Hildreth believed, before he can truly become a man. And Thomas does divest himself of them. When his wife is flogged by a cruel overseer for a trivial offense and dies, Thomas becomes a rebel and a killer. He loses his respect not only for all slaveholders but also for Christianity. He returns to the magical rites of the

old African religion which some of the older slaves have kept alive on
the plantation. He flees to the swamps and makes forays on plantations
in the neighborhood, stealing stock in order to survive. Tracked by the
overseer who has killed his wife, Thomas captures him and—coldly and
methodically—shoots and kills him. At the ending of the early version
of the novel, Thomas is still at large. In the later and revised version,
The White Slave; or, Negro Life in the Slave States, published in 1852
after the great success of *Uncle Tom's Cabin*, Thomas is captured by a
posse and is burned at the stake. Uncle Tom is portrayed as a Christian
martyr, but Thomas is a rebel who breathes defiance against slavery
and against American institutions generally.[16]

Though Thomas's defiance and Hildreth's religious skepticism still
find admirers among readers, the religion of Uncle Tom should also
command our respect. Uncle Tom's religion is necessarily less intellectual
than that of the Calvinists, but it impresses us more. He has none of
that niggling concern for his soul which is often an unpleasant feature
of Calvinism. His chief resolve is not to deny his God under torture, as
Legree is attempting to force him to do. Another resolve is not to betray
the hiding place of Cassy and Emmeline. One of Charles Finney's ideas
of Christian perfectionism was that of the "second conversion." The first
conversion of a Christian, though a dramatic event, is less important
than the second. In the first conversion, the Christian gives chiefly intellectual assent to his faith. In the second conversion, one which comes
nearly always after a period of great suffering and doubt, the Christian
commits himself to God with his whole being. If he is not perfect, he at
least knows the way he should go and does not doubt that with God's
help he can come near attaining his goal. Uncle Tom is religious from
the beginning, but under torture he obviously experiences doubt. "O
Jesus! Lord Jesus!" he prays, "have you quite forgot us poor critturs?"
After this outburst, however, it may be that he reaches the stage of
the second conversion. He steels himself to endure the death which he
has every reason to believe is in store for him.[17]

After the first flogging of Tom, Cassy secretly slips down from the
attic where she is hiding to visit him. She tells him he must not resist
Legree. He must even fulfill Legree's command to flog women. "But it
can't be that the Lord will lay sin to our account . . . ," she says to Tom;
"he won't charge it to us, when we're forced to it; he'll charge it to
them that drove us to it." Tom rejects this argument. The fact that
Simon Legree is wicked, he says, "won't keep us from going wicked. If I

get to be as hard-hearted as that ar Sambo, and as wicked, it won't make much odds to me how I come so; it's the bein' so,—that ar's what I'm a dreadin'." Having rejected temptation, Tom later shows that he is not a Calvinist. When asked, "But why . . . does [God] . . . put us where we can't help but sin?" Tom replies, " I think we *can* help it."[18]

Even before the events which have led to the death of Uncle Tom occur, he has been a faithful Christian on the Legree plantation. Some of the slaves had known scarcely anything of religion before his arrival; a few of them had never even heard the name of Jesus. The cruelties they have suffered have caused them, in turn, to be cruel to one another. Tom acts as an example of patience and love to the other slaves and comes "to have a strange power over them." On those Sundays on which they are not forced to work in the fields, they gather to hear Uncle Tom talk of Jesus and heaven and love, although Legree will not permit them to pray or sing. Cassy changes the name of Uncle Tom to Father Tom. Perhaps this change in title helps to explain the fact that many readers have thought of him as an old man. He was a fairly young man at the beginning of the novel. About five years have elapsed by the time of his death, although he has undergone much suffering.[19]

The most obvious examples of Uncle Tom's success in converting evil men to Christianity occur not long before his death. Sambo and Quimbo are two brutal blacks whom Legree uses to flog the other slaves. Their names might later suggest stereotypes of idiotically happy and thoughtless blacks, but these men are quite different. They are "an apt illustration of the fact that brutal men are lower even than animals." They are large and powerful. "Their coarse, dark heavy features; their great eyes, rolling enviously on each other; their barbarous, guttural, half-brute intonation; their dilapidated garments fluttering in the wind, —were all in admirable keeping with the vile and unwholesome character of everything about the place." One way in which Stowe suggests an unusual depth of evil in a male character is to show him as cruel to women. Sambo kicks a black woman slave because she will not "marry" him or prepare food for him. She tells him she cannot marry him because she already has a husband in New Orleans. Quimbo is also cruel to women. He drives away "the weary women who are waiting at the end of a day of labor in the fields to grind their corn for supper." Gleefully, both men recall a time when they helped catch a slave in the swamps, the slave "stickin' in de mud,—chasin' and tarin' through de bushes, dogs a holdin' on to him!" Sambo remembers particularly one slave woman mauled by dogs. "Lord, I laughed fit to split, dat ar time we cotched Molly," he says. "I thought . . . [the dogs] a had her all stripped up afore I could get 'em off. She car's de marks o' dat ar' spree yet." In reading about Sambo and Quimbo, the reader may wonder what to make of all the comments which Stowe had made elsewhere in the novel on the inherent meekness and goodness of the blacks.[20]

The conversion of Sambo and Quimbo has the completeness and suddenness of that of the thief on the cross. When Legree withdraws after the last whipping of Tom, Sambo and Quimbo reflect on the patient fortitude of this man. They "took him down," perhaps suggesting the descent from the cross of Christ. "Sartin, we's been doin' a drefful wicked thing!" says Sambo; "hopes Mas'r have to 'count for it, and not we." They "washed his wounds." When Tom recovers consciousness, Sambo says, "O Tom! do tell us who is *Jesus*, anyhow? . . . Jesus, that's been a standin' by you so, all this night!—Who is he?" When Tom tells him about Jesus, Sambo replies, "Why didn't I never hear this before? but I do believe. I can't help it." Tom prays, "O, Lord! give me these two more souls, I pray!" At this point in the novel the truly omniscient narrator replies, "That prayer was answered."[21]

There are a good many strange coincidences at the end of *Uncle Tom's Cabin*. George Shelby, the son of the Mr. Shelby who sold Uncle Tom at the beginning of the novel, shows up two days after the last flogging but while Tom is still alive. The elder Shelby has died and young George, as the first act upon inheriting his estate, has resolved to trace the whereabouts of Tom, buy him back, and free him. As Leslie Fiedler says, Stowe cannot help telling the truth that white rescue when it comes at all is likely to be too late. In his dying moments, Tom recognizes the son of his old master. "Bless the Lord . . .," he exclaims. "They haven't forgot me. It warms my soul; it does my old heart good!" Like the aged Jacob in the Bible who hears that his son Joseph is not dead, Tom says, "Now I shall die content! Bless the Lord, oh my soul!" Tom dies forgiving all of his persecutors, even Legree. "He an't done me no real harm," he tells George Shelby, "only opened the gate of the kingdom for me; that's all."[22]

Though George Shelby may admire the pacifism of Uncle Tom, he does not emulate it. When Tom dies, George contemptuously asks Legree whether he can buy Uncle Tom's body. Legree replies, "I don't sell dead niggers," and he allows Shelby to take the body away. Just before he leaves, Shelby charges Legree with murder. "But, sir," he says, "this innocent blood shall have justice. I will proclaim this murder. I will go to the very first magistrate, and expose you." "Do!" replies Legree scornfully; "I'd like to see you doing it. Where are you going to get witnesses? how are you going to prove it?—Come now!" George is forced to recognize that under the state slave code no slave can testify against a free man and, other than Legree, there is no free man or woman on the plantation. Frustrated, George Shelby flares up and knocks Simon Legree down. The narrator says that he is "blazing with wrath and defiance" and "would have formed no bad personification of his great namesake triumphing over the dragon." The reader can scarcely miss how different is the role of Uncle Tom from that of George Shelby. Tom is admired because he patiently submits to the wrongs done him. George Shelby knocks Simon Legree down. One wonders whether the contrast in the two men is the culmination of all that Stowe has said about the racial character of the "submissive" blacks and the "aggressive" Anglo-Saxons.[23]

George Shelby sorrowfully returns to Kentucky. Tom has asked him not to tell Aunt Chloe the circumstances of his death, but she perceptively grasps the truth. "Just as I knew 't would be," she says, "sold, and murdered on dem ar' old plantations!" George does not reply, and Mrs. Shelby tells Chloe that though no human agency can heal her wounded spirit, Jesus can do so. George decides to free all his slaves. At first they do not want their freedom because they think they will be obliged to leave the plantation. When they discover that Shelby means for them to stay on as hired workers, they accept freedom enthusiastically.[24]

Toward the end of the novel, the scene shifts to the Harrises. Eliza had fled to Ohio shortly before Uncle Tom left with Haley on his way to Louisiana, and soon afterward Eliza had been joined by George Harris. Perhaps five years have gone by since George and Eliza fled from Kentucky, but nothing is said about what they have been doing all this time. They have gotten only as far as Sandusky, Ohio, and are waiting for a boat which is to take them to Canada.

The narrator in *Uncle Tom's Cabin* compares the freedom which George and Eliza Harris experienced when they arrived in Canada with that which the white colonists had won in the American Revolution:

Is there anything in it [freedom] glorious and dear for a nation, that is not also glorious and dear for a man? What is freedom to a nation, but freedom to the individuals in it? What is freedom to that young man, who sits there, with his arms folded over his broad chest, the tint of African blood in his cheek, its dark fires in his eye,—what is freedom to George Harris? To your fathers, freedom was the right of a nation to be a nation. To him, it is the right of a man to be a man, and not a brute; the right to call the wife of his bosom his wife, and to protect her from lawless violence; the right to protect and educate his child; the right to have a home of his own, a religion of his own, a character of his own, unsubject to the will of another.[25]

Even critics who have praised *Uncle Tom's Cabin* have sometimes objected to the large number of coincidences at the end of it. We have already seen that George Shelby finds Uncle Tom only shortly before his death. Cassy and Emmeline escape from Legree's plantation. They disguise themselves, Cassy as a Spanish Creole lady and Emmeline as her attendant. They take passage on the same boat in which George Shelby travels on his way back to Kentucky. Encouraged by his sympathetic manner, Cassy becomes acquainted with Shelby and subsequently tells him the whole story of her life. Stowe invents on the spot a new character, a Madame Thoux, who is also a passenger on the boat, and she too confides the story of her life to Shelby. She had been a quadroon slave who was bought by a kindly man who took her to Jamaica. He freed her from slavery and married her. Now her husband is dead and she has inherited his fortune. Shelby perceptively realizes that the stories of Cassy and Madame Thoux fit in with what he already knows of George and Eliza Harris. He tells Cassy that her daughter, now Eliza Harris, is still alive. He tells Madame Thoux that her brother, George Harris, also is still alive.[26]

With the exception of Cassy, none of the slaves who escape to the North or to Canada in *Uncle Tom's Cabin* remain in either place; all of them go to Africa. Ophelia takes Topsy with her to Vermont and rears her there. The people in the community do not entirely approve of Ophelia's bringing a black to live among them. Some of them think that Topsy is "an odd and unnecessary addition to their well-trained domestic establishment. . . ." In spite of the prejudice of the community, Ophelia perseveres, treating Topsy with the love she has learned from Eva and Tom. Topsy, in turn, is baptized into the Christian faith and comes to show "intelligence, activity, and zeal." When she grows up, she becomes a missionary in Africa.[27]

The Harrises also go to Africa. With the aid of money given to him by his wealthy sister, Madame Thoux, George takes his family at first to France, but he is not satisfied there. In the last pages of the novel, he writes an impassioned letter to a friend on the best place for American blacks and his ideas of how he would like to spend the remainder of his life. The blacks have every right to live as free and equal in the United States, he says, but he does not wish to do so, not even if there were no danger of his being reclaimed as a fugitive slave. "I want a country, a nation of my own," he says. "I think that the African race has peculiarities, yet to be unfolded in the light of civilization and Christianity, which if not the same with those of the Anglo-Saxon, may prove to be, morally, of even a higher type." In an earlier era, he declares, the virtues of the Anglo-Saxons had led them to a preeminent position in the history of the world:

To the Anglo-Saxon race has been intrusted the destinies of the world, during its pioneer period of struggle and conflict. To that mission its stern, inflexible, energetic elements, were well adapted; but, as a Christian, I look for another era to arise. On its borders I trust we stand; and the throes that now convulse the nations are, to my hope, but the birth-pangs of an hour of universal peace and brotherhood.[28]

Are the blacks capable of a higher religious development than the Anglo-Saxons? It would seem so. "I trust that the development of Africa is to be essentially a Christian one," says George.

If not a dominant and commanding race, they [the blacks] are, at least, an affectionate, magnanimous, and forgiving one. Having been called in the furnace of injustice and oppression, they have need to bind closer to their hearts that sublime doctrine of love and forgiveness, through which alone they are to conquer, which it is to be their mission to spread over the continent of Africa.[29]

George Harris takes not merely his wife and child but also Emmeline and Madam Thoux with him to Liberia. Though Cassy does not accompany the group, she searches for, finds, and buys her lost slave son in New Orleans, and he eventually departs for Liberia. Since all the escaped slaves except Cassy go to Africa, one wonders why she stays. The reason may have been that Stowe was reluctant to send absolutely all of the former slaves out of the country. Even so, the fact that all of them but one go must have had an odd effect on a contemporary reader of the novel. He was encouraged to think that if the slaves were freed they would not settle in the North or in Canada. Neither would they remain in the South. They would go to Africa. Thus, the reader was not asked to contemplate the possibility that free blacks would be a substantial minority in any part of the United States. It is an ironic fact that, at the time she wrote *Uncle Tom's Cabin*, though Stowe could present blacks more convincingly and more humanly than any other American writer of the period, she could not, apparently, imagine them as permanent citizens of the United States.

Since the blacks are not to stay in this country when they are freed, little is said about what their role will be here. If northern whites are to be given the task of helping to take care of the blacks, it is apparently only to prepare them for their great civilizing mission in Africa. Though Stowe does not directly say that the people of the North as well as the South will no longer have blacks in their midst if the blacks are freed, the novel certainly does encourage the reader to believe that this is what will happen—if not immediately, at least eventually.

Uncle Tom is depicted as the perfect Christian. His piety and religious faith would seem to make him equal to the apostles, and he is superior to some of them. On nearly all issues he is submissive to his white masters. Stowe apparently means to take the ideal of the perfect Christian and to turn it against slavery. Here is a man who fulfills every requirement which slavery can possibly legitimately require of him, but nonetheless he is whipped to death. Stowe takes the "unimportant" virtues which both northern and southern whites had been willing, at least in a backhanded way, to accord to blacks and builds an argument for abolition around them. Uncle Tom may not have enough self-assertiveness to be entirely credible, but his virtues are at least impeccable. He is loyal, trusting, and enduring to the end. If he had been freed, the novel seems to say, he would not be a source of disruption in society. For readers who might not be able to accept the idea that most blacks would be like Uncle Tom, Stowe apparently has in reserve the idea of colonization. If the blacks are troublesome in society, the reader might legitimately conclude, they would be troublesome in Africa and not in the United States. The novel does not say this, of course, but readers would be justified in inferring something like this result.

If all the blacks in the novel were as saintly as Uncle Tom, its force would have been seriously compromised. Even as it was, many reviewers —southern and northern—sarcastically satirized Uncle Tom's impossible perfections. Stowe anticipated this objection, apparently, by creating a whole group of other black characters in the novel who are not free from defects. Frequently these are defects which whites commonly attributed to blacks. No other novel up until that time had anything like the range of black characters which *Uncle Tom's Cabin* had. In addition to Uncle Tom, there are George and Eliza Harris, Sam, Andy, Aunt Chloe, Topsy, Aunt Dinah, Old Prue, Cassy, Emmeline, Sambo, Quimbo, and others. Among these characters are faults enough to satisfy almost any skeptic who might object to the idealized Uncle Tom. As different as these other blacks are from one another, however, they frequently share a trait with one another. They are extremely susceptible to religious conversion, much more so than are the white characters in the novel. Topsy, Sambo, and Quimbo demonstrate this quality in an extreme form, but presumably the others are also subject to it.

More important than colonization in the novel, obviously, is the abolition of slavery. Stowe has no specific plans about how this aim is to be achieved. There is no suggestion that the South is to be coerced. The implication seems to be that once the horrors of slavery are properly shown to the southerners, they will themselves see the necessity for abolishing it. Reared in a household of preachers, Stowe had in all likelihood absorbed early the idea that the aim of exhortation should be to convince the sinner of his evil but wisely to leave to him the means he should use to express his repentance and reparation. In dealing with individual sinners, this doctrine might be more likely to work than when it was applied to a whole society.

It is an interesting question what ardent natures will do when it becomes clear that their solution to a problem meets implacable resistance. Uncle Tom's Cabin would have an enormous and largely favorable response everywhere except in the place where it most mattered—in the South. What would Stowe do if the South strongly rejected her conviction that slavery must be abolished? There is no clear answer to this question in the novel, but there are hints. When George and Eliza Harris are fleeing across Indiana, they are aided by Phineas Fletcher, a Quaker. Actually Phineas is a recent Quaker convert and has adopted the faith because he has fallen in love with a beautiful Quaker girl. In order to save the fleeing slaves, Phineas pushes Tom Loker, a slave catcher, off a thirty-foot cliff and seriously injures him. Yet the reader of the novel was unlikely to think that Phineas had done anything wrong. George Shelby, as we have seen, knocks down the unrepentant Simon Legree. From instances like these, the reader of the time might justifiably conclude that it was not the proper role of the Anglo-Saxon to acquiesce in the evils of slavery. He should attempt to persuade if he could, but if he could not it might be justifiable for him to use force. The narrator of Uncle Tom's Cabin says of Simon Legree after he has been struck by

George Shelby, "Some men . . . are decidedly better by being knocked down." If great numbers of the people of the South should be adamant in the defense of slavery, Stowe might become willing for them to be knocked down too.[30]

Thus *Uncle Tom's Cabin* ends in an ambivalent way. It contains a plea to the South to abolish slavery, but it holds in reserve other methods of achieving that end, if the South refuses. John William Ward argues that the fact that Eliza Harris makes her escape to Canada disguised as a man has significance for Stowe's attitude toward slavery. It was women whom Stowe saw as most strongly representing the forces of love and persuasion in society. Eliza's disguise as a man may indicate, Ward thinks, that womanly persuasion is not enough. "The patient, submissive character, ennobled by feeling and symbolized most by the good woman," he says, "is simply ineffective."[31]

This is a perceptive suggestion, but the reader may wonder whether the "patient, submissive character, ennobled by feeling" in the novel is not chiefly Uncle Tom. Though he is a man, he is also a black, and Stowe presents him in such a way as to suggest that his meekness and love are qualities which he is more likely to have because he is black. Those critics who fault Tom's religion because they think it demonstrates the errors of Christianity may be on the wrong course. There may be errors in his religion, but the willingness to endure cruelty and injustice for the sake of his faith may be as sensible a reaction to the world's evil as any other. Tom is presented as a character with great fortitude and consistency. What troubles us is that the faith of Tom is tied so strongly to the supposed traits of his race. No white person in the novel feels called upon to emulate his rejection of force or his uncomplaining submission to evil. In addition, there is no suggestion that the white characters are obligated to do so. Some of them are presented as all the more admirable, in fact, because they do bitterly complain and are willing to use force. With Tom's virtues attributed to the fact that he is black, it is not wholly clear how he can claim credit for them. After slavery was abolished, Uncle Tom would remain for a long time as hero for whites but not for blacks. For the blacks, patience and submission as exemplified in Uncle Tom would increasingly come to mean a useless acquiescence to his position of helplessness in society.

X

The Reception of Uncle Tom's Cabin in the North

UNCLE TOM'S CABIN was published as a book in March, 1852, and within a few days it had sold 10,000 copies. Within a year, the number had risen to 300,000 copies in the United States, then an unprecedented number for any book, except the Bible, in so short a period of time. In its first printing, the price of the novel was $1.50 for its two volumes, $1.00 for the paperback edition. Several months later there was a cheap single-volume paperback edition which sold for 37½ cents. Even though leading libraries were sometimes obliged to keep several dozen volumes on hand, they often could not keep up with the demand. The novel inspired a whole new industry of souvenirs of its leading characters. Enterprising manufacturers hurriedly produced candles, toys, figurines, and games based upon it. One of the games had players compete with one another in reuniting members of slave families. By the time a year had passed, three hundred infants in Boston alone had been christened with the name Eva. There was a movement in northern churches to make the novel a textbook for Sunday School classes.[1]

A reviewer in the *Literary World*, a New York magazine, did not like *Uncle Tom's Cabin*, but he conceded that it was extremely popular. "No age or sex is spared, men and women and children all confess its power," he said. "No condition is exempt; lords and ladies, flunkies and kitchen-maids are equally infected with the rage. The prevailing affection is universal, and all have Uncle Tom, whether at rest or in motion, at leisure or at work, on the rail or in the idle repose of the parlor, or in the busy bustle of the kitchen." Even the large number of copies sold, the reviewer said, was not a true indication of its popularity because it probably had "ten readers to every purchaser." Richard Henry Dana, Jr., noticed that four of the passengers in a railway car in which he was traveling had copies of it. Ralph Waldo Emerson would later say that *Uncle Tom's Cabin* "encircled the globe, and was the only book that found readers in the parlor, the nursery, and the kitchen in every household."[2]

Since antislavery novels had never before been received with much favor, the success of *Uncle Tom's Cabin* came all the more as a surprise to many people. There had been hints before its publication as a book, however, that it might be popular. These hints came in the large number of enthusiastic letters received by the *National Era* while it was publishing the novel as a serial. Nevertheless, the evidence was not sufficient to induce much eagerness among the book publishers. Sampson and Lowe, a Boston firm, refused to publish it, and there is indirect evidence that other publishing firms also rejected it. John P. Jewett, a minor publisher in Boston of books on practical subjects, accepted *Uncle Tom's Cabin* because his wife had read it in the *National Era* and had been much impressed. He made the offer that the Stowes should put up half the money and share half the profits, but they were far too poor to risk money on what seemed an uncertain financial venture. Accordingly, they were happy to accept Jewett's terms of a 10 percent royalty. Jewett later quoted Calvin Stowe's naïve comment, "I tell wife that if she can get a good black silk dress or fifty dollars in money for the story she had better take it." Jewett was also quoted as saying that had he wished, he could have bought the publication rights of *Uncle Tom's Cabin* as a novel for $25.00, with no payment of royalty.[3]

Several eminent American writers gave *Uncle Tom's Cabin* at least a qualified endorsement. Ralph Waldo Emerson said that it appealed "to the universal heart." Whittier offered "[t]hanks for the Fugitive Slave Law! . . . for it gave occasion for 'Uncle Tom's Cabin!' " When he began to read the novel, Longfellow had apparently not expected much. "Began 'Uncle Tom'—a pathetic and droll book on slavery," he wrote in his journal. Nearly two weeks later, however, he had obviously caught some excitement from reading it. "Every evening we read ourselves into despair in that tragic book, 'Uncle Tom's Cabin.' It is too melancholy, and makes one's blood boil too hotly." A year later, he was saying, "How she is shaking the world with her 'Uncle Tom's Cabin!' At one step she has reached the top of the staircase up which the rest of us climb on our knees year after year. Never was there such a literary *coup-de-main* as this."[4]

Several years later, James Russell Lowell wrote that the sensational popular success of *Uncle Tom's Cabin* had obscured its literary merit for many critical readers. Writing in 1859, Lowell said that he had read the book in Europe "long after the whirl of excitement produced by its publication had subsided, in the seclusion of distance, and with a judgment undisturbed by those political sympathies which it is impossible, perhaps unwise, to avoid at home." He concluded that "the secret of Mrs. Stowe's power lay in that creative genius, by which the great successes in creative literature have always been achieved—the genius that instinctively goes right to the organic elements of human nature, whether under a white skin or a black, and which disregards as trivial and conventional and factitious notions which make so large a part of our thinking and feeling." He wrote to Stowe, "You are one of the few persons lucky enough to be born with eyes in your head."[5]

The literary defects of *Uncle Tom's Cabin* made some of the American intellectuals of the time uneasy. William Hickling Prescott said that "in a twinkling," it had "shot up into a celebrity equal to that reached by the best of Scott's novels, while in point of literary execution merely, it is not equal to the worst." Julia Ward Howe confessed many years later that she had not been much taken with the novel when it first appeared. "I began to read it in the *National Era*," she said in 1905,

but it did not greatly attract me. The faults of style did not appear to indicate in the writer a first-class literary ability. The sort of religion exemplified, especially in the character of little Eva, could hardly have been congenial in those days to one who read Emerson and attended the preaching of Theodore Parker.

Later, Howe came to regard the novel more favorably, but even then it was chiefly its antislavery influence which impressed her. Many American writers of the time apparently cared little for it. Hawthorne, Thoreau, Melville, Whitman, and Dickinson never mentioned it. Washington Irving said nothing about it directly, but there are indications that he did not like it. In addition to its literary defects, he may have disliked the fact that it espoused the cause of antislavery, since he had no interest

in the subject himself. What might have repelled the other writers most
of all was the perfervid religion espoused by the author and by some of
the novel's characters.[6]

Some of the intellectuals among the clergy reacted strongly in favor
of *Uncle Tom's Cabin*. "O Heaven!" wrote William Henry Channing
after reading it. "How patient are God and nature with human diabolism!
It seems to me that I have never begun to do anything for antislavery
yet. And now, with one's whole heart bleeding, what can we do? . . .
How this book must cut a true-hearted Southerner to the quick!—cut us
all, for we verily are all guilty together." This tone was more emotional
than that of most northern clergymen, even those who greatly admired
the novel. On the other hand, it was a tone common to ordinary readers
who reacted with great force to its depiction of the evils of slavery.
Stowe herself quoted a letter which some anonymous person, probably
a woman, had written to her:

I sat up last night long after one o'clock, reading and finishing "Uncle Tom's
Cabin." I *could not* leave it any more than I could have left a dying child;
nor could I restrain an almost hysterical sobbing for an hour after I laid
my head upon my pillow. I thought I was a thorough-going Abolitionist
before, but your book has awakened so strong a feeling of indignation and
compassion, that I seem never to have had *any* feeling on this subject till
now. But what can we do? Alas! alas! what *can* we do? This storm of feeling
has been raging, burning like a very fire in my bones, all the livelong night,
and all through my duties this morning it haunts me,—I *cannot* do away with
it. Gladly would I have gone out in the midnight storm last night, and, like
the martyr of old, have been stoned to death, if that could have rescued
these oppressed and afflicted ones.[7]

That it was principally women who were most deeply moved by
Uncle Tom's Cabin is suggested by George Templeton Strong, a prominent New York lawyer. He recorded in his journal that it was a "sentimental romance . . . that set all Northern women crying and sobbing
over the sorrows of Sambo." And yet, Strong himself became an admirer
of the book and of Stowe herself. That it was not women alone who
were susceptible to emotions aroused by the novel is suggested in a
story by John Dix, an immigrant from England. Dix told of a man
who had been "sleeping one night in a strange house." He was "annoyed
by hearing somebody in the adjoining chamber alternately groaning and
laughing." He "knocked upon the wall and said, 'Hallo, there! What's
the matter? Are you sick or reading 'Uncle Tom's Cabin'?" The stranger
replied that he was reading the novel.[8]

Emotional responses to *Uncle Tom's Cabin* tended to weaken its antislavery message. Undoubtedly some—possibly a good many—readers of the time were more impressed by the scenes in which little Eva appeared than they were by the novel's opposition to slavery. Eva had an enormous appeal. Poems to her proliferated. One of them, written by John Greenleaf Whittier, is not a great deal better than the others. Even the readers of the *Liberator*, in their letters to the editor on the subject of *Uncle Tom's Cabin*, reacted more strongly to the death of Eva than to the antislavery parts of the novel. A flood of poems about Eva appeared in magazines and newspapers, particularly in the abolition journals. More or less typical was one which spoke of the "winning warmth of holy love" which "beamed in the sweetness of her smile." The modern reader of such poems can scarcely help wondering whether their authors thought that slavery was the lesser evil in the novel and that its greatest tragedy was the death of Eva.[9]

Even those reviewers who otherwise approved of *Uncle Tom's Cabin* sometimes complained of the excessive sentimentality of the portrayal of Eva. "The little Nells, little Pauls, little Henrys, and little Evas," said one critic, "are a class of people for which we care but little. Dickens has much to answer for in popularizing the brood of little impossibilities, who are as destitute of the true qualities of childhood as the crying babies which are hung up in the windows of toy-shops." The possibility that *Uncle Tom's Cabin* might excite emotions in readers without increasing their enthusiasm for abolition was real enough that Wendell Phillips, in one of his speeches, warned against it. Many readers had admired the novel, he said, without abandoning their proslavery principles. "There is many a man who weeps over Uncle Tom," he complained, "and swears by the [New York] *Herald*" (a proslavery newspaper). This reaction to the novel may have been fairly common. In 1877, there was a novel published for children about life in a New England village. The narrator of the novel described the time in 1852 when *Uncle Tom's Cabin* first appeared as a book. Nearly everyone in the village read it. Much thumbed copies circulated from house to house and it was greatly admired. On the other hand, when a teacher in the local school organized a project to make clothes for a black girl student, some of the villagers opposed it. Objections to the project spread to students in the school, and it was openly derided by some of the boy students who called it a "Nigger Sewing Bee."[10]

It required an unusual measure of generosity for William Lloyd

Garrison to praise *Uncle Tom's Cabin.* There was the fact that his opposition to slavery went unrecorded in the novel, the emphasis being on the antislavery attitudes of ordinary people in Ohio, especially the Quakers there. Other than Simon Legree, the one New Englander of importance in the novel was Ophelia. She was not the kind of New Englander whom Garrison would be likely to admire. For one thing, her religious denomination, though not specified, was obviously one of the orthodox denominations, none of which had taken a stand against slavery. In addition, the novel contained specific ideas which Garrison would have certainly opposed—for example, the conviction that American blacks should return to Africa. And then there was the fact that Stowe was the daughter of his old antagonist, Lyman Beecher. Also, if Garrison had praised *Uncle Tom's Cabin,* he would have been obliged to overlook the fact that the novel had originally been published in the *National Era,* a journal which he had frequently denounced for its "milk and water" abolitionism. Garrison apparently realized from the first that the novel might have an important influence, and he made a serious effort to cultivate the good opinion of Stowe. He wrote her a humorous letter, for example, saying, "I estimate the value of anti-slavery writing by the abuse it brings. Now all the defenders of slavery have let me alone and are abusing you."[11]

In his review of *Uncle Tom's Cabin* in the *Liberator,* Garrison began with high praise. He singled out Stowe's "rare descriptive powers," her "uncommon moral and philosophical acumen, great facility of thought and expression, feelings and emotions of the strongest character." Long familiar as he had been with the evidence of oppression of slaves, Garrison said that he was impressed anew. He mentioned the "frequent moistening of our eyes, and the making of our heart grow liquid as water, and the trembling of every nerve within us, in the perusal of the incidents and scenes so vividly depicted in her pages." He admired the character Uncle Tom. Like Jesus himself, Tom was "willing to be 'led as a lamb to the slaughter,' returning blessing for cursing, and anxious only for the salvation of his enemies. His character is sketched with great power and rare religious perception. It triumphantly exemplified the nature, tendency and results of CHRISTIAN NON-RESISTANCE."[12]

Or did it? Garrison was a nonresister himself, though a fiery one, but he objected to a tendency in the novel to have the blacks carry the full burden of the nonresistance argument:

We are curious to know whether Mrs. Stowe is a believer in the duty of non-resistance for the white man, under all possible outrage and peril, as well as for the black man; whether she is for self-defense on her own part, of that of her husband or friends or country, in case of malignant assault, or whether she impartially disarms all mankind in the name of Christ, be the danger of suffering what it may.

If Stowe did not believe that the blacks were more called to nonresistance than the whites, she should say so, because that was what the novel would seem to imply. To many white people, said Garrison, "They [the blacks] cannot be animated by a Christian spirit, and yet return blow for blow, or conspire for the destruction of their oppressors. *They* are required to put away all wrath, to submit to every conceivable outrage without resistance, to suffer with Christ if they would reign with him." On the other hand, many whites had a quite different standard of conduct for themselves:

[For] those whose skin is of a different complexion, the case is materially altered. . . . When they are spit upon and buffeted, outraged and oppressed, talk not then of a non-resisting Saviour—it is fanaticism! talk not of overcoming evil with good—it is madness! Talk not of peacefully submitting to chains and stripes—it is base servility! Talk not of servants being obedient to their masters—let the blood of the tyrants flow.

By the time he came to the end of his review, Garrison almost seemed to dislike *Uncle Tom's Cabin* more than he liked it. On the other hand, his objections to the colonization proposals introduced toward the end of the novel were surprisingly mild. Perhaps because he thought he had gone far enough by satirizing the passive role given to blacks in the novel concerning the theme of nonresistance, he mentioned his objection to colonization only briefly. He observed merely, "The work toward its conclusion, contains some objectionable sentiments respecting African colonization, which we regret to see."[13]

It was the colonization arguments of *Uncle Tom's Cabin* which came closest to causing some abolitionists, especially the Garrisonian abolitionists, to reject the novel altogether. For the Reverend Henry Clarke Wright, the endorsement of colonization in the novel canceled out any virtues which it might have had. In a letter to Garrison, Wright said, "It has fascinated and repulsed me at the same time, as a reptile that enchants you, while it excites your loathing and abhorrence. I have heard so much said in its favor, I tried to like it but could not." Its colonization opinions were "but the echoes of the arguments by which the negro haters of this republic have for thirty years been seeking to drive the free colored people from this land. I could not but weep tears of mingled pity and indignation over one, who, after moving and melting and swaying my heart and sympathies . . . should wind up identifying herself with . . . men of such cruel stony hearts and bloody hands."[14]

The reviewer for the New York *National Anti-Slavery Standard*, published by Garrison supporters, was decidedly cool to *Uncle Tom's Cabin*. Like other Garrisonians, he objected to the suggestion that the blacks should return to an African homeland. If the "personal knowledge" of Stowe had been "more extended," he said, she never would have had George Harris emigrate to Liberia at the end of the novel. Quite aside from this issue, he thought the book had little "merit as a novel." It had "faults of style, and sometimes baldness of plot, and want of skill in delineating character," especially the character of the whites. Yet he was willing to admit that the novel was important because it would help to spread the abolition message. It had a "charm" which gave it a "strong hold upon the popular feeling. . . ." That the reviewer saw the novel as nothing extraordinary is suggested by his final comment: he would recommend it "with much the same feeling" that he would recommend "an Anti-Slavery tract."[15]

Lydia Maria Child, a friend and ally of Garrison and a Unitarian, had had a distinguished career as an opponent of slavery. She tried to be fair to *Uncle Tom's Cabin*, describing it in a letter as "a story . . . with great pathos and power." She found it difficult, however, to feel any sustained enthusiasm for a novel which came out of the orthodox religious tradition of New England. She admitted that it had only "a moderate sprinkling of Calvinism" in it but added that she did not like Calvinism "even in homeopathic doses." Like the reviewer in the *National Anti-Slavery Standard*, she recognized that the novel would probably have a wide appeal. Its Calvinism would, for example, "make it acceptable to a much larger class of readers, who are not in the habit of taking in much humanity, unless stirred up with a portion of theology, like brimstone and molasses." Actually there is virtually no specifically Calvinist doctrine in the novel. Child's reservations about it may come from the fact that Stowe was one of the Beechers, rather than from the novel itself. She mentioned it only in personal letters. As a writer she had every opportunity to praise or condemn it publicly, but she chose not to do so.[16]

Black abolitionists also were much disturbed by the colonization theme of *Uncle Tom's Cabin* and by the excessive meekness of Uncle Tom. Like some of the white abolitionists, they probably hesitated to criticize it as much as they would have liked because of its power to convert people to antislavery. Frederick Douglass gave it great praise. "The word of Mrs. Stowe is addressed to the soul of universal humanity," he said. In later years, after the Civil War, he said, "It was a flash to light a million camp fires in front of the embattled hosts of slavery." It was "plainly marked by the finger of God." At the time of its publication, however, there were clear signs that he had trouble accepting parts of it. He wrote her a letter in which he apparently tried to avoid offending her while still disagreeing with her. On other issues and with other people he had been quite capable of disagreeing with friend as well as foe. At one time, for example, he had caused dismay among abolitionists who generally admired him by calling for slave insurrections in the South. Charles H. Foster, in his study of Stowe published in 1954, has suggested that Douglass may have been the model for the fiery character of George Harris in the novel. What is surprising in the letter of Douglass to Stowe is the concessions which he was willing to make to her ideas concerning the supposed racial traits of the blacks. One hardly knows whether to conclude that his reaction was an example of how powerful racist dogma was at the time, even among its black victims, or to assume that Douglass was playing a role which foreshadowed what would be called "Uncle Tomism" in the twentieth century. He told Stowe that it was unlikely that many blacks would wish to leave the United States and emigrate to Liberia. One reason he gave for their reluctance was their apparent racial trait of inherent timorousness:

The black man (*un*like the Indian) loves civilization. He does not make very great progress in civilization himself, but he likes to be in the midst of it, and prefers to share its most galling evils, to encountering barbarism. Then the love of country, the fear of isolation, the lack of adventurous spirit, and the thought of seeming to desert their "brethren in bonds," are a powerful check upon all schemes of colonization, which look to the removal of the colored people. . . . The truth is, dear madame, we are *here*, and here we are likely to remain. . . .[17]

Other black abolitionists objected more strongly than Douglass to the colonization theme of *Uncle Tom's Cabin*. For some of them it was enough to make them reject the novel entirely. "Uncle Tom must be killed, George Harris exiled! Heaven for dead Negroes! Liberia for living mulattoes. Neither one can live on the American continent," said the *Provincial Freeman,* a black antislavery journal published in Canada. "Death or banishment is our doom," the editor objected, "say the Slaveocrats, the Colonizationists and Mrs. Stowe!!" Black delegates to the American and Foreign Anti-Slavery Society convention in 1853 introduced a resolution condemning the colonization views of *Uncle Tom's Cabin.* The resolution mentioned that the novel had been praised at a meeting of the American Colonization Society and expressed the hope that something might be done to counteract that part of its influence. The resolution was passed by the Society.[18]

Some black critics recognized that it was the submissive character of Uncle Tom which constituted the chief long-range dangerous effects of the novel's influence. Precursors of much twentieth-century criticism of blacks, these critics found Tom a disturbing model for a black hero. William C. Nell, a black abolitionist, argued that "resistance to tyranny was obedience to God. . . . [H]ence . . . the only drawback to the matchless Uncle Tom of Mrs. Stowe was his virtue of submission to tyranny— an exhibition of grace which . . . [Nell did] not covet." William G. Allen, another black abolitionist, said, "Uncle Tom was a good old soul, thoroughly and perfectly pious." He had, in fact, "too much piety." Allen confessed that he himself was, by comparison, an example of "total depravity," but he could not be sorry. He was convinced "that it is not light the slaveholder wants, but fire, and he ought to have it. I do not advocate revenge, but simply resistance to tyrants, if it need be, to the death."[19]

George T. Downing, another black critic of the novel, admired George Harris far more than he did Uncle Tom. Of all the black characters in the novel, Downing said, Harris was "the only one that really portrays any other than the subservient, submissive Uncle Tom spirit, which has been the cause of so much disrespect for the colored man." In 1853, William J. Watkins, a black, made a speech before a committee of the Massachusetts State Legislature appealing for the right of blacks to be members of the state militia. He accused white people of caste consciousness and racial prejudice, complaining that their "*beau-ideal* of Heaven" was "a place of unfading joy, and resplendant magnificence, where you shall play forever upon golden harps, and the colored people, if they, like Uncle Tom, submit to your indignities with Christian meekness with becoming resignation, shall be permitted, from the Negro pew, to peep into the glory of your . . . heaven to all eternity." C. L. Redmond, a black delegate at the convention of the Colored Citi-

zens of Massachusetts, made a speech in 1858, saying (his words paraphrased by the secretary of the convention) he "regretted that he was
obliged to ask for rights which every pale-face vagabond from across
the water could almost at once enjoy. He did not go so far as Uncle
Tom, and kiss the hand that smote him."[20]

Martin R. Delany, a fiery black abolitionist, came closest to a total
rejection of Uncle Tom's Cabin. He attacked its colonizationist arguments and, as a black, declared, "Mrs. Stowe knows nothing about us."
For him, the chief value of the novel was to be found in its use of slave
narratives. In a letter to Frederick Douglass' Paper, Delany censured
Stowe for having criticized the black government of Haiti while praising
that of Liberia. Mrs. Stowe, he maintained, "had no real sympathy for
the slaves," for the "thrice-morally crucified, semi-free [black] brethren
anywhere, or of [sic] the African race at all."[21]

White abolitionists more conservative than Garrison had difficulties
different from his in accepting Uncle Tom's Cabin. Lewis Tappan was
one of the men who in 1840 had rebelled against Garrison's leadership.
Tappan was opposed to the women's rights crusade and to the doctrine of
nonresistance, both of which causes were espoused by Garrison. Aside
from believing that these causes were irrelevant to the more important
antislavery crusade, Tappan was opposed to them on principle. He had
been one of the founding members of the new anti-Garrison group, the
American and Foreign Antislavery Society. One of the rules of this
society was to exclude women as voting members. As a pious Presbyterian, Tappan also had been opposed to the reading of novels. Changing his mind and making an exception of Uncle Tom's Cabin may have
been a decision which came only after a struggle. Yet he did endorse it.
Of Stowe he said that "the citadel of Human slavery, is at length in-
vested by a woman, whose missiles are doing execution on an unprecedented scale." There is evidence, however, that he approved more
of Stowe's nonfictional A Key to Uncle Tom's Cabin, published in 1853,
than he did of the novel itself. Of the Key, he wrote, "It may prove that
facts are stronger than fiction, or rather that unadorned facts do more
execution than fictional facts." His preference for a factual study may
represent a pale reflection of his old objection to the reading of novels as
sinful in itself.[22]

James G. Birney, the 1844 presidential candidate of the Liberty
Party, shared many of Lewis Tappan's conservative views. He too had
shunned novels and was opposed to women's taking an active role in

politics or in abolition agitation. Garrison had argued that the abolitionists ought not to form political parties or support candidates who advocated abolition. He believed that such activities would inevitably lead to
compromises in which the abolition emphasis would be diluted. Thus,
he strongly opposed Birney. When *Uncle Tom's Cabin* was published
in 1852, Birney had already retired from the more active forms of
antislavery agitation. In 1845 he had been seriously injured in a fall
from a horse and was prevented from making speeches. On the other
hand, he continued to follow the issues of slavery closely and wrote
widely about them. Like Tappan, Birney did not allow the fact that
he had opposed women as active participants in the antislavery struggle
to cause him to reject *Uncle Tom's Cabin*. Also like Tappan, Birney did
not allow his former religious objections to the reading of fiction to
lead him to reject it because it was a novel. He wrote Stowe a warm
letter of endorsement. Because he had been reared in a slaveholding
family, he could testify to the accuracy of her portrayal of southern life.
He recalled that when he was six or seven years old, his grandfather
had given him a slave boy of about the same age. "While the whole
world testifies to the felicitous and touching manner in which you have
interested them in a kind of life about which they cared so little and
consequently knew so little," he said, "I wish to add my testimony . . .
to the trueness with which you have held up to them a state of society
which 'Uncle Tom's Cabin' was intended to represent. If there is any
error at all, it is in writing things too much of the *couleur de rose*."
Though Birney rejected the idea of forcible colonization of American
blacks in Africa, he agreed with Stowe that it might be wise for them
to choose to go there. In 1852 he developed the idea in a pamphlet that
American blacks, because of the great prejudice against them in this
country, might sensibly decide that the best course for them would be
to leave this country. Since his position was similar to that of Stowe,
it is not surprising that he did not chide her for her attitude to the
emigration of blacks.[23]

There are enough favorable comments from abolition leaders concerning *Uncle Tom's Cabin* that the modern reader may easily misjudge
their real opinions of it. Most of these leaders, and especially the Garrisonians, said little or nothing about it, and what they did say was in
most cases expressed soon after its publication. After the Civil War,
many of them would write their memoirs of the days of antislavery
agitation, and it is generally difficult to find in their accounts any men-

tion at all of Stowe or *Uncle Tom's Cabin.* A novel as an abolition document may not have been wholly to their taste. In addition, Stowe was not their kind of person. Her lack of interest in organizations may have repelled them. For some of them, her close association with orthodox Protestant religion—the kind of religion which they frequently condemned for its indifference to slavery—may have led them to be grudging in their acknowledgments of her contribution. Elizabeth Hitchcock Jones, a Garrisonian abolitionist, expressed an unfavorable opinion about *Dred*, Stowe's second antislavery novel which was published in 1856. She wrote to Abby Kelley Foster, another Garrisonian, and advised her not to waste her time reading *Dred*. "I do not know," she said, "how a woman who ever knew anything about the divine passion could have made such a surface work of such a matter. Nothing very deep has ever been awakened in her own heart, I am sure." She admitted that *Dred* might do some good, and therefore she would "say nothing against it except among ourselves." In 1872 Stowe would give a public reading of sections of *Uncle Tom's Cabin* in Boston. Several other antislavery leaders were on the platform with her, and two of them agreed that *Uncle Tom's Cabin* had been the single most powerful force in ending slavery. When William Lloyd Garrison, who was also on the platform, was asked whether he agreed with this opinion, he balked. He was quoted in a local newspaper as saying that "it was of little moment to undertake to determine what human instrumentality was the most effective, under God, in bringing about that result."[24]

Proslavery sentiment, even in the North, was strong enough to prevent church bodies from endorsing *Uncle Tom's Cabin*. Individual clergymen, however, often spoke in favor of it. Theodore Parker said that "such a triumph . . . was never known before." Its success was "not due alone to the intellectual genius and culture of the writer; it is due to a quality far higher and nobler than her intellect." The author had "won" her readers because she had "appealed to their consciences, . . . touched their Hearts, . . . awakened their souls." Speaking as a Unitarian, he acknowledged that Stowe had come out of the conservative Protestant tradition. "New England Orthodoxy," he said, "never did a better thing." Similar approval was expressed by other clergymen. Though he was not himself religious, Richard Hildreth, the author of *Archy Moore*, the abolitionist novel of 1836, argued that *Uncle Tom's Cabin* strongly appealed to the public not principally because it was antislavery but because it was Christian. It owed its popularity "to its character as a religious novel . . . and to Uncle Tom not as a slave, but as a Christian hero." He went so far as to argue that the "anti-slavery" of the novel "so far from helping it rather hurt it . . . and but for its admirable realization of the Christian hero, saint and martyr, it would scarcely have been known out of the small circle of anti-slavery readers."[25]

It is true that some hostile reviewers of *Uncle Tom's Cabin* in the North saw it as a covert attack on ministers and churches, sometimes on the Christian religion itself. "She has quite a peculiar spite against the clergy," said a reviewer in the *New York Courier and Enquirer*, "and of the many she introduces at different times into the scenes, all save an insignificant exception, are Pharisees or hypocrites. One who could know nothing of the United States and its people, except by what he might gather from this book, would judge that it was some region on the confines of the infernal world." (Actually, there were only two clergymen characters in the novel and one of these was anti-slavery.) An editor of the *New York Observer*, a conservative Presbyterian journal, wrote that the novel was "anti-Christian" and "decidedly anti-ministerial." "We have marked numerous passages," he said, "in which religion is spoken of in terms of contempt, and in no case is religion represented as making a *master* more humane, while Mrs. Stowe is careful to present the indulgent and amiable masters as men without religion. . . . Mrs. Stowe labors through all her book to render ministers odious and contemptible by attributing to them sentiments unworthy of men or Christians." Lewis Tappan remarked that some of the proslavery religious journals were attacking Stowe's commitment to the Christian religion, but he added that such attempts had been met with "indignant censure."[26]

Unlike those critics of *Uncle Tom's Cabin* in the South who frequently appealed to the Bible as justifying slavery, northern proslavery clergymen only rarely raised this particular issue. One who did was the Reverend Mr. Nehemiah Adams, a Congregational minister in Cambridge, Massachusetts, who wrote a lengthy piece attacking *Uncle Tom's Cabin*. He argued that slavery had been endorsed by God himself, as expressed in the Bible. Though he did not directly charge Stowe with irreligion, he did issue a general warning. "Zeal against American slavery has . . . been one of the chief foes to the Bible," he said. "Let him who would not become an infidel and atheist beware and not follow his sensibilities, as affected by cases of distress, in preference to the word of

God, which the unhappy fate of some who have made shipwreck of
their faith in their zeal against slavery shows to be the best guide."
Adams had traveled in the South and had written a book on the subject.
Everywhere he had found benevolent masters and contented slaves. A
parody of his book appeared in an article in the *Liberator*. Its title was,
"A South-Side View of Prostitution; or, Three Months in the Brothels
of Boston, in 1854. By Rev. Nehemiah Eves, D.D." In the parody, Dr.
Eves confessed that he had been "misled by the publications of Moral
Reform Societies, especially by the writings of Mrs. Harriet Beachmore."
He had "expected to be shocked on his visits to Boston brothels; instead
he was pleasantly surprised and gratified by what he saw there."[27]

Some of the conservative clergymen in the North who praised
Uncle Tom's Cabin were especially pleased by the colonization ideas expressed in it. Slavery was wrong, they were prepared to admit, but it did
not follow that the blacks should remain in the United States. One article
to that effect was written by a minister, probably Dr. Leonard Bacon, who
had long been a friend of the Beechers. There is strong evidence that it
was he who wrote the review which appeared in the *New Englander*.
"Mrs. Stowe has done what multitudes would much rather she had not
done," said the reviewer. "She has made the public realize, to a most
alarming extent, the unspeakable wickedness of American slavery. She
has told, in general, nothing more than what all intelligent persons knew
well enough before. . . . But Mrs. Stowe has brought the dreadful meaning of facts into contact with millions of minds." It was necessary, the
reviewer said, to rescue the ideas of the novel from "the distinctive
doctrines and obnoxious measures of the Anti-Slavery Societies." One
way in which Stowe was different from most antislavery people was,
he thought, that she recognized the importance of the idea of the blacks
having a country of their own. In the novel she had demonstrated that
"though *among* the American people . . . [the blacks] are not *of* the
American people." She had shown that "the tie which connects the
injured mulatto or quadroon with his dark mother's kindred is far
stronger than that which connects him with the proud and domineering
race of his white father." Though the reviewer did not say that this
feeling of black kinship with their black ancestors should lead them
to return to Africa, this seemed to be his implication. *Uncle Tom's
Cabin* demonstrated, he said, that "a distinct *nationality* is the object of
a natural yearning with the free and enlightened Africo-American, whatever the shade of his complexion."[28]

One idea in *Uncle Tom's Cabin* which gave its defenders a good deal of trouble was its advocacy of defiance of the Fugitive Slave Law. Hostile reviewers of the novel in the North and the South emphasized this issue. In the North, Richard R. Mason had serious misgivings about whether it was wise for Stowe to have taken this particular position. What was "most to be feared" from defiance of the Fugitive Slave Law, he said, was that it would form "a dangerous public sentiment on the subject of resistance to a law of Congress." The nation should "proceed very cautiously in the adoption of a remedy which is in itself liable to the most momentous objections." The Reverend Mr. Richard Salter Storrs, Jr., editor of the *Independent*, a religious newspaper in New York which was sometimes said to be second in influence only to Horace Greeley's *New York Tribune*, tried to minimize the dangers of defying the Fugitive Slave Law. He argued that to refuse to obey so iniquitous a law did not imply an attack on the principle of law itself. As an analogy, he proposed that the public authorities in the state of New York might refuse to return a runaway apprentice from New Jersey. Such a refusal might be wrong, Storrs maintained, but it was no threat to the principle that the laws should not be openly defied. The analogy did not really fit. To refuse to return an apprentice would be merely to refuse to honor the law of another state. To refuse to obey the Fugitive Slave Law would be, on the other hand, to defy an act of Congress and ultimately a provision of the Constitution. Stowe had been willing to face the fact that her stand in *Uncle Tom's Cabin* involved a defiance of law. Most of the northern reviewers, even those who praised the novel, were not prepared to go this far.[29]

Perhaps the major point of hostile reviewers of *Uncle Tom's Cabin* in the North was that while slavery would be an indefensible institution if whites were slaves, it was the only suitable one for blacks because of their inherently inferior traits. "We are not disposed to deny to the author . . . the possession of skill as a writer," said the reviewer in the New York *Literary World*. "Her narrative is fluent, fervid, and emphatic; in her minute and literal descriptions, she shows herself a shrewd observer and an exact painter. Her domestic interiors, Chloe's well-ordered cottage, for instance, and Dinah's ill-ordered kitchen, are painted with a wonderful fidelity and truth, and are evidently copies of what the keen woman's eye and perception of the authoress have seen in reality." What the reviewer objected to was that Stowe did not understand the basic issue—that it would be no favor to give the blacks their freedom because they were incapable of using it wisely. She had allowed her heart to overrule her head. Reformers were often subject to this kind of weakness. They were "indefatigable in their efforts to clothe the infant Hottentot, that he may simmer in warm flannel," but "they have not a rag to spare for the pale nakedness shivering at home." Stowe's "negro sympathy" was characterized by "unnatural and unwholesome excitement." Slavery was not nearly the evil that she supposed. A black did not often mind being separated from his family. "[T]he negro, as he passes through a succession of wives," said the reviewer, "contemplates a divorce with as much coolness as a conclave of Connecticut legislators." In the latter sections of his essay on the novel, the reviewer became more and more annoyed. He ended his review by saying that a reader could hardly be expected to react with pleasure to a novel like *Uncle Tom's Cabin* "when warm weather is coming rapidly in." Uncle Tom himself was "too potent and decidedly odorous for our—perhaps fastidious—taste." He thought that the novel would cause only temporary bad feeling between the North and the South. Its worst effect might be that it might cause an occasional respectable white man in the North to marry a fully black or mulatto woman, "thereby setting a laudable example to the rising generation of amalgamationists." The reviewer in *Graham's Magazine* was also annoyed and deplored abolition as a subject for novels. "The shelves of booksellers groan under the weight of Sambo's woes, done up in covers! What a dose we have had and are having! . . . A plague of all black faces! We hate this niggerism, and hope it may be done away with."[30]

Even reviewers who praised *Uncle Tom's Cabin* were often doubtful whether it would have any effect upon the debate on slavery. This conclusion would seem to have been borne out in the election of 1852. From the time of its publication in March until the November elections, the novel continued its great success as a best seller, but the antislavery vote declined. The major reason for the decline was that the radical Barnburner group, which in 1848 had defected from the Democratic Party and thrown its lot in with the antislavery Liberty Party, had now returned to the Democratic fold and thus the Liberty Party vote declined. The losses of the Liberty Party encouraged some political observers to argue that *Uncle Tom's Cabin* would not lead to any enlargement of the antislavery vote. One of these observers was George Ticknor, the Boston scholar and historian. After the election of 1852 he wrote a letter in which he said that the novel was "a book of much talent, especially dramatic talent." On the other hand, Stowe had taken the wrong method of criticizing slavery. The novel "exasperates the slave-holders, and perhaps most seriously offends those among them who most feel the evils of slavery, and who most conscientiously endeavor to fulfill the hard duties it imposes on them, the very class whom Mrs. Stowe should, both as a Christian woman and a politician, have sus-tained and conciliated." Outside the South, Ticknor said, the novel would "produce an effect exactly in proportion to the distance of its readers from the scenes it describes. . . . Thus, in New England, where we have learned to distinguish between our political relations to the South and our moral relations to slavery, it deepens the horror of servitude, but it does not affect a single vote. . . . But of one thing you may be sure. It will neither benefit the slaves nor advance the slave question one iota toward its solution." An editorial in the *New York Times* made essen-tially the same point even before the November election. The effect of the novel was, it said, "to render slavery more difficult than ever of abolishment. It will keep ill blood at the boiling point, and irritate in-stead of pacifying those whose proceedings Mrs. Stowe is anxious to influence on behalf of humanity."[31]

Uncle Tom's Cabin continued to have a very large sale, but a year after its publication a writer in *Putnam's Monthly Magazine* in New York argued that it had made no real change in northerners' attitudes toward slavery. Uncle Tom need not have been a slave to have called forth so much sympathy; he could have been any unfortunate person. It was Stowe's "consummate art" as a "story teller" that had allowed her to invest the cause of abolition with more merit than it deserved. "The antislavery sentiment obtruded by the author in her own person, upon the notice of the reader," said the anonymous writer, "must be felt by everyone to be the great blemish of the book." If a judicious editor had excised the "excrescences" of special pleading in the novel, it "would deserve to be placed by the side of the greatest romances the world has known." Though it lacked the "delicacies of language" of Irving and Hawthorne, the descriptive power of Cooper, and the "bewildering sensu-ousness" of Melville, it had "broader, deeper, higher and holier sym-pathies than can be found in our other romances; finer delineations of character, a wider scope of observation, a more purely American spirit, and a more vigorous narrative faculty." All this did not obscure the fact that its political effect had been and would continue to be negligible. Southern opponents of the novel, the writer thought, should calm down.

It had given "a much more agreeable picture of Southern slavery" than had any other antislavery novel. If southerners were doubtful about whether *Uncle Tom's Cabin* had been harmless, they should look at the returns of the last election. These "certainly did not afford any reason to believe that the minds of our countrymen had been at all influenced by Mrs. Stowe's enchantment."[32]

From 1852 to the beginning of the Civil War in 1861, political leaders rarely commented on *Uncle Tom's Cabin*, publicly or privately. It was not usual for political leaders or commentators to discuss the ideas of the time in terms of novels, and the fact that this novel had been written by a woman made it even less likely that it would be discussed by them. The way the novel figured politically was chiefly in the comments of newspapers attached to the causes of the major political parties which were either proslavery or at least opposed to abolition. The *Lincoln* [Maine] *Democrat* said that it was "a mischievous dangerous work, got up on purpose for evil. . . . It is really lamentable that where great evil is being concocted, you will always hear the rustling of petticoats." The *Cleveland Daily Plain Dealer*, another Democratic newspaper, wrote about *Uncle Tom's Cabin* in terms almost as hostile as anything in the South. "A pure blooded African when let alone has no aspirations for liberty as we understand it," said an editorial. "He never had any at home. He knows nothing about it and cares less. He is content with plenty of 'hog and hominy,' something he could never get in Africa and which he is glad to get here. He looks to his master as his provider and protector, a sort of patriarch who in the hour of danger will defend him with his life. We know this is not the picture found in 'Uncle Tom's Cabin,' nor in the New York *Tribune*, but it is the truth nevertheless."[33]

Even antislavery political parties found little use for *Uncle Tom's Cabin* in their appeals to voters before the Civil War. By 1852, the Liberty Party was virtually dead. Though its leaders were certain to have been aware of the influence of the novel, they apparently made no direct mention of it themselves. The Free Soil Party emphasized the glories of freedom, but they meant freedom for whites. The leaders of the party were attempting to prevent the expansion of slavery into the territories, but many of them were notoriously antiblack and had little interest specifically in abolition. When the Republican Party began to attract attention, it showed scarcely more concern than that of the Free Soil Party for the evils of slavery, as long as those evils were confined to the South. The leaders of the party discovered, however, that as they were already prominently identified with antislavery, they need not— and in terms of attracting voters probably should not—say much on the topic. Even in 1860, *Uncle Tom's Cabin* was too radical for the Republican Party. The defiance of the Fugitive Slave Law expressed in the novel was enough in itself to make it useless to the party. Though he objected to some of its provisions, Abraham Lincoln argued that Congress was within its rights in passing the Fugitive Slave Law and pledged his willingness to enforce it. In the first year or so of his administration, he did enforce it.[34]

Lincoln probably never read *Uncle Tom's Cabin*. William H. Herndon, law partner and close personal friend of Lincoln, wrote to Wendell Phillips in 1857 that as late as the year 1853 he himself had still "hated the very name of anti-slavery." David Davis, who would become Lincoln's campaign manager in Illinois in 1860 and who was sometimes said to have been the closest friend that Lincoln ever had during his entire life, the man who was chiefly responsible for Lincoln's securing the Republican Party's nomination for president in 1860, did not react favorably to *Uncle Tom's Cabin*. Sarah Davis, his wife, read it, admired it, and attempted to interest her husband in it. She had been a student at Catharine Beecher's school in Hartford. She had known Stowe there and for a number of years had kept up a correspondence with her. Davis told his wife that the novel did not give a true picture of slavery and urged her to read the anti-Uncle Tom novel by W. L. G. Smith, *Life at the South; or "Uncle Tom's Cabin" as It Is* (1852). Sarah Davis did read Smith's novel, but she insisted to her husband that it did not compare "with the other Uncle Tom." There is no evidence that Davis came around to his wife's point of view. Of course, the opinions of his close friends and associates were not necessarily those of Lincoln. Such little evidence as we have suggests, however, that Lincoln's changes in attitude toward slavery came largely from sources other than *Uncle Tom's Cabin*.[35]

Yet it is probable that the novel had a profound effect on opinion with regard to slavery in the North in the 1850s. Not long after it was published, Rufus Choate, the prominent proslavery lawyer and formerly a senator from Massachusetts, was quoted as saying that *Uncle Tom's Cabin* would make "two millions of abolitionists." In 1872 a biographer of Horace Greeley would argue that the chief force in developing support for the Republican Party in the 1850s had been *Uncle Tom's Cabin*.

After the Civil War a number of both northern and southern historians would argue that the novel had been the most important source for opposition to slavery in the North. In 1893, James Ford Rhodes paid tribute to *Uncle Tom's Cabin* because it had led people who had been previously ignorant of or indifferent to the evils of slavery to become concerned about them:

The great influence of Mrs. Stowe's book . . . was shown in bringing home to the hearts of the people the conviction that slavery is an injustice; and, indeed, the impression it made upon bearded men was not so powerful as its appeal to women and boys. The mother's opinion was a potent educator in politics between 1852 and 1860, and boys in their teens in the one year were voters in the other. It is often remarked that previous to the war the Republican party attracted the great majority of the schoolboys [in the North], and that the first voters were an important factor in its final success.[36]

XI

The Reaction to Uncle Tom's Cabin In the South

THE RESPONSE IN THE SOUTH to *Uncle Tom's Cabin* was nearly all out-rage and invective. Most of the few people who praised the novel took care to remain anonymous. Virtually all the favorable public comments came from areas of the South close to the North, or from southerners who no longer lived in the South. The reviewer in the *Wellsburg* [Virginia—now West Virginia] *Herald* said that *Uncle Tom's Cabin* "is really a very well-conceived and very interesting performance, such as no liberal minded slaveholder would object to." The reviewer in the *Georgetown* [Kentucky] *Herald* said that the usual antislavery novel was filled with "lacerating descriptions of floggings and burnings to death," but that *Uncle Tom's Cabin* "contains no such dreadful details. It is at once an impartial statement of the case as regards slavery, and a gracefully told tale of human life and human hearts, glowing with heavenly colours, and full of the force and power which nature and truth impart." The reviewer in the *Jefferson* [Missouri] *Inquirer* said that he had expected before reading the novel that it would be "all that fanaticism and heresy could invent" and was therefore "greatly prejudiced against it." On reading it, however, he had found "that it is a work of more than ordinary moral worth and is entitled to considera-tion." Though "in some particulars, the scenes are too highly colored and too strongly drawn from the imagination," the novel was "a mirror of several classes of people we have in our mind's eye, who are not free from all the ills flesh is heir to." The reviewer hastened to explain the groundlessness of the fear "that the book would result in injury to the slave-holding interests of the country." He hoped "before our friends form any harsh opinions of the merits of *Uncle Tom's Cabin*, and make up any judgment against us for pronouncing in its favor (barring some objections to it), that they will give it a careful perusal." He ended his review, perhaps a little nervously, by saying, "We yield to no man in his devotion to southern rights and interests."[1]

The most favorable southern opinion of *Uncle Tom's Cabin* was expressed by Daniel R. Goodloe. A North Carolinian, Goodloe had been apprenticed to a printer in Oxford, North Carolina. Though he had only a modest status, he had published some antislavery pamphlets in North Carolina, arguing that it was slavery which was chiefly responsible for weaknesses in the southern economy. Apparently no one had paid much attention to his opinions, perhaps because the pamphlets did not circulate widely. Goodloe left North Carolina and secured a government clerkship in Washington. In a published letter, he praised *Uncle Tom's Cabin* and endorsed its antislavery position. He emphasized that Stowe evidently had no intention of slandering the South. Mr. Shelby, Uncle Tom's Kentucky master, Goodloe said, is "by no means a bad character," and "his wife and son are whatever honour and humanity could wish." The worst villains in the novel were both northerners. Haley, the slave trader, "has the accent of a Northerner," and Simon Legree is from Vermont. "It is, therefore, evident that Mrs. Stowe's object in writing 'Uncle Tom's Cabin' has not been to disparage Southern character," he said. "A careful analysis of the book would authorise the opposite inference—that she has studied to shield the Southern people from opprobrium, and even to convey an elevated idea of Southern society, at the moment of exposing the evils of the system of slavery. She directs her batteries against the institution, not against individuals."[2]

As far as is known, the editors of the Wellsburg, Virginia, and the Georgetown, Kentucky, newspapers suffered no adverse criticism for their favorable comments on *Uncle Tom's Cabin*. The reviewer of the *Jefferson* [Missouri] *Inquirer* was, however, the object of something like a threat from the *St. Louis* [Missouri] *Republic*. "You may think to save yourself by your parenthesis, or afterthought, of 'banning some objections to it [*Uncle Tom's Cabin*].' But you shall not," said the editor.

"Does this not place you in the position of an open and avowed approver of abolition doctrine? Most unquestionably it does; and you now fight under the banner which Mrs. Stowe has unfurled, side by side with Fred Douglass, in whose honourable company your name is honourably mentioned." After the letter of Daniel R. Goodloe was published in *The Key to Uncle Tom's Cabin* in 1853, he was discharged from his government clerkship in Washington.[3]

Other favorable comments from southerners regarding *Uncle Tom's Cabin* were made anonymously. John Dix, an Englishman who emigrated to the United States, reported in a travel book that an unnamed southern senator and slaveholder had been persuaded to read the novel and, "on being asked what he thought of it, he merely replied that he should be very sorry for his wife to read it." In 1882, one observer would recall that he remembered something which Francis Lieber, an immigrant from Germany and a professor at South Carolina College, had told him. At the time *Uncle Tom's Cabin* was first published, Lieber was said to have had a conversation with a South Carolina senator [William C. Preston?] who had warmly praised the novel. "I can match every incident in it," the senator was quoted as saying, "out of my own experience." In a letter, Lydia Maria Child cited "Senator Pierce" [Senator James A. Pearce?] of Maryland as having praised *Uncle Tom's Cabin*, apparently in a conversation with someone. When he came to the part of the novel in which Mr. Shelby is obliged to sell Tom to pay a creditor, Child quoted him as saying, "Here's a writer who knows how to sympathize with the South. I could fall down at the feet of that woman. She knows how to feel for a man when he is obliged to sell a good honest slave."[4]

A New Englander, Charles Holbrook, a young man who had recently graduated from Williams College, came to the South to tutor the children of a planter in Rockingham County, North Carolina, and recorded the reactions of his employer and his employer's wife and children to *Uncle Tom's Cabin*. A neighbor had brought a copy of the novel with him when he returned from a visit to New York and had lent it to Holbrook's employer. Holbrook read it and was much impressed. He recorded in his diary, "I believe it to be the most interesting book I ever read." He also read the novel aloud to the children of his employer, who were sympathetic to it and could fill in details of cruelties to slaves from their own experience or from those told to them by others. His employer, far from being angry with Holbrook for having read the novel to his children, read it himself and was also favorably impressed—at least at first. On the other hand, the planter's wife read it and was "bitter against it." "Mr. G. likes *Uncle Tom's Cabin,*" wrote Holbrook in his diary, because of its "true character." He confided to Holbrook that he had met a slave trader transporting a "drove" of blacks which had included about twenty children. After reading the novel, he had decided not to carry out his previous intention to sell one of his men slaves away from his wife and children. A few days later, however, he decided that the novel was a bad book. "Mr. Galloway says he will burn 'Uncle Tom's Cabin,'" Holbrook wrote in his diary. "He has changed his mind on it. Mrs. G. thinks Mrs. Stowe is worse than Legree!" And there the matter apparently ended.[5]

In a letter to Stowe, John Greenleaf Whittier mentioned hearing of a northern woman living in the South who had read *Uncle Tom's Cabin* "to some twenty young ladies, daughters of Louisiana slave-holders, near New Orleans, and amidst the scenes described in it." The young ladies had "with one accord pronounced it true." Dr. Charles G. Parsons, a northern physician, told of hearing of a semipublic reading of the novel while he was visiting in Georgia. The book was read before a group of nearly sixty lower class whites in a "mule stable." His informant told Parsons that the members of the audience listened to the tale with great interest and were generally able to match the characters and incidents of the novel from their own experience. "There was no intimation from any one present," Parsons quoted his informant as saying, "that the tale was overwrought." In a visit to the South in 1854, Frederick Law Olmsted met a white mountaineer in Tennessee who had a copy of *Uncle Tom's Cabin*. The man told Olmsted he had "been down in the nigger counties a good deal" and that he had seen the bad effects of slavery as they "worked on the white people." Olmsted asked the man what the opinion of his mountaineer neighbors was concerning slavery, and he replied, "Well, there are some thinks one way and some another, but there's hardly any one here that don't think slavery's a curse to our country, or who wouldn't be glad to get rid of it."[6]

A few southern reviewers rejected the antislavery arguments of *Uncle Tom's Cabin* calmly and without any implication that Stowe was intent on the monstrous aim of vilifying the South. In the anti-Uncle Tom novel, *The Slaveholder Abroad; or, Billy Buck's Visit, with his Master, to England* (1860), Ebenezer Starnes had his narrator say that *Uncle Tom's Cabin* was "a clever book, written by a woman of genius" and that it "abounded in ingenious appeals to the best sympathies of human nature against oppression." Nonetheless it was "an exaggerated and distorted view of slavery—a view which presented the exception for the rule." Much more common among white southerners was a tone of outraged protest. John R. Thompson, the editor of the *Southern Literary Messenger*, was willing to concede that Stowe had talent as a writer. "Possessed of a happy faculty of description, an easy and natural style, an uncommon command of pathos and considerable dramatic skill," he said, "she might have done much to enrich the literature of America, and to gladden and elevate her fellow beings." Instead, she had "volunteered officiously to intermeddle with things which concern her not—to libel . . . a people from among whom have gone forth some of the noblest men that have adorned the race—to foment heartburnings and unappeasable hatred between brethren of a common country."[7]

The emotional tone of the review by Thompson was surprising because previously he had attempted to keep the *Southern Literary Messenger* moderate in tone and to avoid heated discussions of sectional issues. He had originally intended for George Frederick Holmes to write the review. He had written to Holmes asking him to review it and had indicated what manner of approach he would prefer. "I would have the review as hot as hell-fire," he said, "blasting the vile wretch in petticoats who could write such a volume." Since Holmes's review did not arrive in time for the current issue of the magazine, Thompson wrote his own. When Holmes's review arrived, it was published in the December 1852 issue of the magazine. It was a strong castigation of the novel, but in general it was expressed in a judicious manner. Several months later, Holmes reviewed *The Key to Uncle Tom's Cabin*, which was published in 1853. In this review he may have reflected the rising anger among white southerners which occurred in reaction to the widespread and continuing praise *Uncle Tom's Cabin* received in the North and abroad. In his review of *The Key*, Holmes came near losing all control. When she wrote *Uncle Tom's Cabin*, he said, Stowe had been "an obscure Yankee school mistress, eaten up with fanaticism, festering with the malignant virtues of abolitionism, self-sanctified by the virtues of a Pharisaic religion, devoted to the assertion of women's rights, and an enthusiastic believer in many neoteric heresies." Now, a year after the publication of the novel, she was famous. "Is she not venerated as the ancient Sibyl who points the way to realms of Saturnian bliss, if she can only unite the fanaticism and blind delusion of the world for the achievement of a vicarious sacrifice at the expense of the South?" Holmes proceeded to damn Stowe in almost the strongest way in which a woman with any pretense to being a lady could be damned. He accused her of having a morbid interest in sex. "It is a horrible thought that a woman should write or a lady read such productions as those by which her celebrity has been acquired," he said.

Are scenes of license and impurity, and ideas of loathsome depravity and habitual prostitution to be made the cherished topics of the female pen, and the familiar staple of domestic consideration or promiscuous conversation? Is the mind of woman to be tainted, seduced, contaminated, and her heart disenchanted of all its native purity of sentiment, by the unblushing perusal . . . of such thinly veiled pictures of corruption? Can a lady of stainless mind read such works without a blush of confusion, or a man think of their being habitually read by ladies without shame and repugnance?

William Gilmore Simms, writing in the *Southern Quarterly Review*, was even more excited. "Mrs. Stowe betrays a malignity so remarkable," he said, "that the petticoat lifts of itself, and we see the hoof of the beast under the table."[8]

Louisa S. McCord, thought to be the outstanding woman of letters in the South, reviewed *Uncle Tom's Cabin* in the *Southern Quarterly Review*. Choosing her was apparently a device to have a respectable woman cast out another woman from all decent society. She congratulated Stowe for the money she had made from the sale of her novel but, as for herself, she would be "loath to take it with the foul imagination which could invent such scenes, and the malignant bitterness (we had almost said ferocity) which, under the veil of Christian charity, could find the conscience to publish them." *Uncle Tom's Cabin* represented "the loathsome rakings of a foul fancy." The *New Orleans Crescent* said Stowe was

part quack and part cut-throat. There never before was anything so detestable or so monstrous among women as this. Men, often barbarous and bloody, have sometimes been known to preach like this, but never until now did a female so far forget all the sweet and social instincts of her sex, as to do what Mrs. Stowe has done—endeavor to whet the knife of domestic murder and shake over the innocent head of every matron, maid and babe in the South, the blazing torch of midnight conflagration, the brutal and merciless instruments of death, that are struck to the heart or dash out the brains of the sleeping or the helpless, in the bursting out of a slave insurrection.[9]

A common charge against Stowe was that it was inappropriate for a woman publicly to discuss sexual evils. "Grant that every accusation brought by Mrs. Stowe is perfectly true, that every vice alleged occurs as she has represented," George Frederick Holmes said,

the pollution of such literature to the heart and mind of woman is not less —but perhaps even more to be apprehended. It may accord with the gross fancies and coarse nature of a Cincinnati schoolmistress to revel over the imagination or the reality of corruption, with which she is much more conversant than the majority of Southern gentlemen, but the license of a ribald tongue must be excluded from the sanctity of the domestic hearth. If Mrs. Stowe will chronicle or imagine the incidents of debauchery, let us hope that women—and especially Southern women—will not be found poring over her pages.

The reviewer was fearful that the foundations of society were crumbling. Such heresies as the theories of Fanny Wright and George Sand, the multiplication of novels, and the woman's rights movement had "unsexed in great measure the female mind, and shattered the temple of feminine delicacy and moral graces; and the result is before us in these dirty insinuations of Mrs. Stowe." Another critic, David Brown, said that Uncle Tom's Cabin was "shamelessly profligate," so much so that it could be used as "a guide-book to the market-place of abomination, for the use of travelling roués of the north."[10]

Some of the strongest condemnations of the discussion of the sexual issues of slavery in Uncle Tom's Cabin came from women in the South. An anonymous letter from a woman appeared in the New Orleans Picayune. The writer said that Stowe had "proved herself false to her womanly mission." She was "deficient in the delicacy and purity of a woman" and had "painted from her own libidinous imagination scenes which no modest woman could conceive of." The writer thanked Stowe for "one good effect" of reading Uncle Tom's Cabin. Before reading it she had been "somewhat inclined to sympathize with some of the supposed wrongs of women—to advocate for a little more freedom for them." Now, however, she had told her husband that she "would promise to 'obey' now more loudly, were we to be married over again." She had become more "a true woman" because of the novel of "the man Harriet." In Maria J. McIntosh's The Lofty and the Lowly, an anti-Uncle Tom's Cabin novel, the omniscient narrator comments on a wicked abolitionist at a meeting in the North: "On either side of him sat—start not reader —a woman." And in Mary H. Eastman's Aunt Phillis's Cabin, the omniscient narrator invents a new organization, the "F.S.F.S.T.W.T.R.—The Female Society for Setting the World to Rights."[11]

Sometimes even clergymen in the South denounced Stowe almost in street language. After seeing a portrait of Stowe, the Reverend Mr. William G. Brownlow of Knoxville, Tennessee, said that she was "as ugly as Original sin—an abomination in the eyes of civilized people." She was a "tall, coarse, vulgar-looking woman—stoop-shouldered with a long yellow neck, and a long peaked nose—through which she speaks." On another occasion, he said that *Uncle Tom's Cabin* was "a filthy, lying book" which had actually been written by Stowe's "hypocritical brother and husband." Later it would turn out that Brownlow would oppose secession and favor the Union during the Civil War. The violence of his opinions against Stowe and *Uncle Tom's Cabin* may partially explain the general absence of moderate opinion with regard to the novel in the South. Even people who would turn out to be opposed to secession would strongly condemn the attack on slavery by an outsider.[12]

A major defense of slavery in the reviews of *Uncle Tom's Cabin* in the South was that the Bible had sanctioned it. There was much solemn quotation of scripture. It was a pious age and many reviewers cited both the Old and New Testaments to show that slavery had been approved in the Bible, or at least had nowhere been proscribed by it. The reviewers were nearly all strict constructionists in interpreting the Bible just as they were of the Constitution. They explained how God had cursed the sons of Ham. Without question, they thought—though without any evidence—that the descendants of Ham were blacks. Approvingly they quoted the statements in the Bible that the sons of Ham would always be "servants of servants." Some of the reviewers, perhaps those uneasy with the sons-of-Ham argument, preferred verses of scripture found in the New Testament—the fact that Saint Paul had returned a runaway slave to his master implied that he had no objection to the institution of slavery.[13]

Southern reviewers of *Uncle Tom's Cabin* made virtually no attempt to prove that slaves were protected by law from excessive punishment or other cruelties. On the other hand, they had a great deal to say about the defiance of law in the novel. Dr. James A. Waddell, a North Carolina physician, was shocked because Senator Bird of Ohio had helped Eliza to escape her pursuers from Kentucky. "When we defeat the execution of the law, Constitutionally and regularly administered," said Waddell, "we may *benefit* an individual, but we certainly *wrong* society itself, the welfare and stability of which depend upon the stability of law. We have no right to do a positive good to the *few*, when our act involves a positive injury to the many." In portraying the Quakers as helping George and Eliza Harris to escape from slavery, said A. Beatty, a slaveholder in Missouri, and especially in having George Harris say without censure that he would resist capture to the death, Stowe had raised grave issues. She "certainly knows that when white men—whether Quakers or no—help fugitive slaves, they are accessories in a murder, when an owner or his agent is killed." She also "assumes a heavy responsibility" when she "advises the fugitive slave to take the life of his owner to avoid recapture." Beatty thought that the advocacy of such criminal acts was shocking. He was also convinced that she would "find very few readers to applaud her object, when nakedly stated."[14]

The chief defense of slavery in anti-*Uncle Tom's Cabin* reviews in the South was the supposed inherent inferiority of the blacks. The fundamental weakness of the novel, said George Frederick Holmes in the *Southern Literary Messenger*, was the assumption in it that black people are like white people. "[T]he whole tenor of this pathetic tale derives most of its significance and colouring from a distorted representation or a false conception of the sentiments and feelings of the slaves," he maintained. What would be "grievous misery to the white man is . . . none to the differently tempered black" and thus slavery "constitutes no portion of his wretchedness." Stowe did not realize, Louisa S. McCord argued in the *Southern Quarterly Review*, that the runaway slave would soon regret his rash act and would long for his master's "well filled corn crib." The "negro, left to himself," she added, "does not dream of liberty. He cannot indeed grasp a conception which belongs so naturally to the brain of the white man. In his natural condition, he is, by turns, tyrant and slave, but never the free man." Slavery was not merely justifiable for him, McCord thought, but a great blessing and "it is a cruel task to disturb him in the enjoyment of that life to which God has destined him. He basks in the sunshine, and is happy. Christian slavery, in its full development, free from fretting annoyance and galling bitterness of abolition interference, is the brightest sunbeam which Omniscience has destined for his existence."[15]

The separations of families which were described in *Uncle Tom's Cabin* were the occasion of comment among many southern reviewers. They did not deny that separations sometimes happened, though they often said that they were much rarer than northern people supposed. They frequently argued that family separations were nearly always the result of the evil conduct of the slaves themselves. William Gilmore Simms argued, in addition, that blacks thought so little of the institution of marriage that they were not often much troubled if they were obliged to part from members of their families. Simms ascribed the supposed indifference of blacks to these partings to their inherent "moral obtuseness." An attitude of indifference was particularly characteristic, he thought, of the black male. "The negro, in fact, is proverbially a Lothario," said Simms. "He is seldom faithful to his vows. He loves to rove. . . . He does not relish that his wife's eyes shall be too frequently upon him." Such a man would not be unhappy if he was sold away from his wife and children because then he could enjoy new attachments. The Reverend Mr. E. J. Stearns defended separation of slave families as the lesser of two evils. If a master were not allowed to separate families among his slaves, he said, he would forbid them to marry anyone not belonging to himself. He would fear the legal complications if the husbands or wives of his slaves should be sold to a distant owner. It was a well-established "physiological law," said Stearns, that "where families and petty clans marry 'in and in,' for several generations, they are deteriorated, sinking rapidly into imbecility."[16]

Some southerners showed an uneasy awareness that such arguments as those of Simms and Stearns were not wholly satisfactory. John R. Thompson in the *Southern Literary Messenger* admitted that the separation of families was an evil of slavery but one which he believed had been exaggerated by critics of the institution. "Evils are inseparable from all forms of society," he said, "and this giant evil (if you will call it so) is more than counter-balanced by the advantages the negro enjoys." John Candler, an English Quaker, traveled in the South and discussed his antislavery ideas with prominent people there. In 1853, Candler called upon the governor of Mississippi, who courteously received him. General Henry Stuart Foote, the governor, said Candler, "is the most determined pro-slavery advocate I ever saw; but notwithstanding his prejudices, he has been so far worked upon by Harriet Beecher Stowe, or some other agency that he would be willing, he said, to see a bill passed to prevent the separation of husband and wife, and of young children from their parents." The statement by Foote which Candler proceeds to quote does not, however, quite substantiate this conviction. Foote told Candler that he had intended to introduce a bill to the state legislature which would make family separations of slaves illegal, "but my friends told me I must not do so, as it would give rise to great excitement in the state, and afford a triumph for the Abolitionists."[17]

One objection to *Uncle Tom's Cabin* frequently found among southern reviewers was that it was unscrupulous to attack an institution by means of a novel. There are indications in some of the reviews that southern critics had not really expected a major attack upon slavery in this particular form. They were familiar with abolition pamphlets and had learned the techniques of parrying their arguments. A novel was less easy to refute and southern reviewers often complained that it was unjust to expect them to be able to comment on incidents which had not really happened. A novelist could choose his examples in such a way, said A. Woodward, that he could prove almost anything. By the use of fiction, one could "prove the sinfulness of every institution beneath the sun, social, civil, and religious."[18]

It was William Gilmore Simms, himself a novelist, who most extensively developed the argument that it was unfair to use a novel as a vehicle of social criticism. "The attempt to establish a moral argument through the medium of fictitious narrative is, *per se*," he said, "a vicious abuse of art and argument. The thing cannot be done conscientiously. Art has its laws, and, in such a work, art is paramount. The novel is made to yield, and must yield, where the fiction demands it." Simms himself did not write novels to correct some great wrong, but it would be difficult to argue that his own novels are wholly free from the moralizing over social and political evils which he maintained was one of the evils of *Uncle Tom's Cabin*. In a biography of Simms, Edd Winfield Parks conceded that Simms's "concern with strict artistry was limited" in his fiction. The "omniscient author," said Parks, did not "hesitate to tell what is or is not true, what must or must not be supposed." Though Simms roundly damned *Uncle Tom's Cabin*, he would in time come to have a grudging admiration for it. In 1854, he wrote, "The dramatic faculty of *Uncle Tom's Cabin* is somewhat remarkable." Stowe was "a woman of great inventive faculty, and 'Uncle Tom,' considering wholly aside from the slavery question, is a story of great and striking, though coarse attraction." Stowe had unfairly emphasized the evils of slavery, he thought, but she had "done it with rare ability and audacity" and thus it was not surprising that the novel had been "so successful."[19]

The fact that *Uncle Tom's Cabin* really did have literary merit may help to explain an oddity among its southern reviewers. Though many of them protested against Stowe's misreadings of the meaning of American slavery it seems to have occurred to only one of them that her actual experience of slavery might have been very slight. They did not know—and Stowe did not tell them—that her only visit to the South was one of a few days to Kentucky in 1834. How they would have pounced on the fact had they known of it. Only one of the reviewers suspected the truth. Louisa S. McCord in the *Southern Quarterly Review* at one point boldly conjectured that Stowe's errors about the South and about slavery probably came from her lack of direct experience. "We doubt if Mrs. Stowe has ever crossed the line of a slave state at all," said McCord. "If she has, it has evidently not been further south than the mere crossing of the Kentucky border." McCord had hit upon the exact truth. She was probably incapable of exploiting her one big insight and it is significant that she mentioned it, almost incidentally, in the middle of a paragraph. For her, southern society was so inherently noble that she could scarcely imagine slavery as having the slightest flaw. The slave codes did not matter to her because the people enforcing them, she was convinced, were Christian gentlemen. All examples of the cruelty of slavery she saw merely as the result of the faults of human nature in general and—as she and other southern reviewers never tired of saying—"exceptional cases." It is interesting to conjecture what might have happened if such a person as William Gilmore Simms had made the major theme of a review of *Uncle Tom's Cabin* the idea that Stowe had no direct experience with southern society and thus only a second-hand knowledge of slavery. At that time, a conviction that a novelist might have sufficient imaginative talent to make a personal knowledge of slavery largely unnecessary would have struck readers everywhere as wholly absurd.[20]

Southern reviewers seldom liked any of the white characters in *Uncle Tom's Cabin*. They may have disliked the white southern characters more than the northern ones. They were generally convinced that the southern characters, aside from little Eva, had the single aim of defaming the South. They regarded the defects of the northern white characters, on the other hand, as faithful portrayals of the faults of Yankee civilization. The possibility that Stowe might have made Simon Legree a New Englander to direct the force of her criticism against slavery as an institution rather than against the white South almost never occurred to southern critics. Some of them triumphantly pointed out Legree's New England origin as if this were a fact which Stowe had somehow overlooked. Slave owners were cruel, they argued, only when they came from the North.

William Gilmore Simms said:

He [Legree] is a Yankee by birth and education and is representative of New England,—not of the South. He belongs to the same race which butchered the Indians, burnt the witches, tortured the Quakers, persecuted the Manhattenese Dutchmen, and sold negroes and redmen, princes of the land, into captivity, pocketed the spoils, swore their seals from the bill of sale, and then cried upon the Lord to vouchsafe his blessings on the good day's work! Yes, we do not doubt that Legree is true to the parish from which he came. He inherits all its virtues.

Even so, Simms also accused Stowe of subtly insulting the Legaré family, which was prominent in the South. *Legree*, he pointed out, was pronounced the same as *Legaré*. Stowe's choosing such a name for her chief villain was an "exhibition of wantonness."[21]

Though they disclaimed responsibility for Legree, some southern critics were nonetheless troubled by him because in the novel nothing can be done to him under the law for his murder of Uncle Tom. When Shelby threatens to charge Legree with murder, Legree scornfully points out that under the slave codes no black can testify in court. The Reverend Mr. E. J. Stearns replied that Legree could easily have been prosecuted for murder because he had said to George Shelby, "I gave him [Tom] the cussedest flogging I ever gave a nigger yet. I believe he's trying to die; but I don't know as he'll make out." All that Shelby would have had to do, said Stearns, was to testify to these words of Legree and "any Southern jury would have brought in a verdict of *Guilty* . . . almost without leaving the jury-box; for Southern juries . . . bring in a verdict according to the law and evidence. . . . I wish I could say as much for *all* Northern juries." George Frederick Holmes in the *Southern Literary Messenger* said that the murder of Uncle Tom was "an outrage which every Southern man would reprobate with indignant scorn—and punish by the summary application of Lynch law, which may be sometimes profitably applied."[22]

One southern view of Simon Legree, that of Mary Boykin Chesnut, was unlike that of nearly all the others. Writing privately in her diary, Chesnut objected to some of the scenes of cruelty in *Uncle Tom's Cabin* because she thought they were unconvincing. For example, she found the scene wholly implausible in which the master of George Harris ties him to a tree and allows his adolescent son to whip him with switches. On the other hand, she thought Simon Legree was a disturbingly credible character not because of his murder of Uncle Tom but because of his slave mistresses. She thought that relationships between white masters and slave women were more common than was usually supposed. She spoke of the gossip in which everybody could tell you who was the white father of a mulatto child on another plantation but was strangely silent about similar situations on the home plantation. She sketched a brief portrait of an imaginary plantation owner with a double standard of morality. "A magnate who runs a hideous black harem with its consequences under the same roof with his lovely white wife, and his beautiful and accomplished daughters. Is there such a being?" she asked and then proceeded to describe him.

He holds his head as high and poses as the model of all human virtues to those poor women whom God and the laws have given him. From the height of his awful majesty, he scolds and thunders at them, as if he never did wrong in his life. Fancy such a man finding his daughter reading "Don Juan." "You with that immoral book!" And he orders her out of his sight.[23]

Southern reviewers were seldom impressed by Stowe's attempts in *Uncle Tom's Cabin* to present good slaveowners as well as bad. Shelby and Augustine St. Clare were certainly better than Legree, they were willing to concede, but in one sense they were worse. They were presented as if they were representative southern gentlemen. That Mr. Shelby was not a gentleman was evident enough, said Louisa S. McCord. If he had been he never would have entertained a slave trader in his home. McCord was also shocked at the conversation of the two men. Mr. Haley, the slave trader, says to Mr. Shelby in the novel that Eliza Harris can be sold on the New Orleans slave market for a high price because of her beauty, a remark with the apparent implication that someone would buy her to serve as his mistress. "I've seen over a thousand, in my day, paid down for gals," says Haley, "not a bit handsomer." If Mr. Shelby had been a gentleman, said McCord, he would have objected strongly to such a comment. In the *Southern Literary Messenger*, John R. Thompson said that a real Kentucky gentleman would have responded to Haley by kicking him down the stairs.[24]

Some southern reviewers objected to the sale of Uncle Tom and Harry Harris as implausible. Shelby, it was argued, could have sold other slaves and achieved the same end. If by any chance he had been forced to sell these particular two, he would have sold them locally so they would not have been separated from their families. "No master could be brutish enough to sell the man who had nursed him and his children, who loved him like a son, *even for urgent debt,* had he another article of property in the wide world," said Mary H. Eastman. Mr. Shelby was generally offensive to the southern reader, said William Gilmore Simms, because he was "made to represent the planter, in a region where planters have given the first statesman [*sic*], lawyers and warriors to the nation."[25]

Augustine St. Clare, the other slaveowner drawn with some good characteristics, was received by southern reviewers even more unfavorably. They generally ridiculed both his status as a gentleman and his arguments against slavery. Louisa S. McCord said she was shocked that the *Westminster Review* in England considered St. Clare to be "a humane and cultivated gentleman." All he did was "lie upon sofas, read newspapers, and indulge himself in occasional abuse of a system by which he holds a property, the possession of which he considers as iniquitous in the extreme, and yet never takes one step to correct this iniquity." By his own admission, said the Reverend Mr. E. J. Stearns, St. Clare was "a piece of driftwood . . . floating and eddying about," "a contemptible *non-sequitur,*" and "a graceless dog." Worse still he was a "sneering sceptic." Stearns said he did not object to such a person appearing as a character in a novel but he did object "most emphatically" against his being represented as "the fairest picture of our Southern brother." An anonymous letter to the *Memphis* [Tennessee] *Daily Eagle and Enquirer* sarcastically thanked Stowe for creating a new type of southerner in St. Clare—a man who would lower himself to argue the question of slavery.[26]

Mrs. Shelby, the kindly slavemistress in *Uncle Tom's Cabin,* fared as badly among the southern reviewers as Shelby and St. Clare. Louisa S. McCord said it was impossible for the reader to believe that Mrs. Shelby felt any real concern over the sale of Harry or Uncle Tom. McCord pointed out that soon after her husband tells her of the sales, Mrs. Shelby goes quietly off to bed. The next morning she does not seem to be at all upset. After ringing the bell for breakfast without any effect, Mrs. Shelby says, "I wonder what *keeps* Eliza?" This statement provoked McCord to respond satirically, "Oh! blessed composure amidst life's whirl!" Mrs. Shelby "has apparently no sins upon her mind, nor cares either, dear virtuous lady!" William Gilmore Simms derided Mrs. Shelby's "milk and water humanity" and thought it shocking that such a woman was thought to be "representative" of women of the South, a region which had contributed "one of the noblest chapters in our history."[27]

Southern reviewers usually only disliked Mrs. Shelby, but they were outraged by Marie St. Clare. It was a slander, one reviewer argued, to portray in the novel a southern lady who could not manage her own household, thus making it necessary for a New England woman to be imported to set things to rights. St. Clare's bringing in Miss Ophelia to manage his New Orleans household, thought Mrs. Mary H. Eastman, was merely an attempt on Stowe's part to defame southern women. "According to Mrs. Stowe, mothers do not love their beautiful children in the South," said Eastman. "The husbands have to go to New England and bring back old maids to take care of them, and to see to their houses, which are going to rack and ruin under their wives' surveillance." Louisa S. McCord could only wonder in "what Southern society Mrs. Stowe" could "have associated." Mrs. St. Clare might be selfish, McCord said, but she would have manners. Stowe did not know that "a Southern lady, even in her faults—aye, term them if you will, her vices—retains still the shadow of that delicacy which is inherent in her education, if not in her nature."[28]

McCord said that no southern lady would use the word "sweat" to describe little Eva's fever. Neither would she keep a cowhide and "lay it on" the slaves. Almost any southern reader, she added, would "gasp for breath" when he read of Mrs. St. Clare slapping a slave and sending her, "a delicate and beautiful quadroon girl," to the calaboose to be given fifteen lashes. She appealed to the gentlemen of the South to resent the insult to southern womanhood in this caricature. "Will you acknowledge," she asked, "this as a picture of your wife?" John R. Thompson said that not one southern woman in a thousand would disregard the wishes of her husband as Mrs. St. Clare did in refusing to give Uncle Tom his freedom after St. Clare's death. One southern reviewer could account for Mrs. St. Clare's cruelty only under the assumption that she was more like a northern than a southern woman.[29]

As unfair as she thought parts of Uncle Tom's Cabin were, Mary Boykin Chesnut could not avoid the reflection that there might be women in the South like Marie St. Clare. In 1864, she would record in her diary her impressions of a southern woman in Virginia:

I met our lovely relative, the woman who might have sat for Eva's mother in Uncle Tom's Cabin. Beautifully dressed, graceful, languid, making eyes at all comers. Softly and in dulcet accents regretting the necessity she labored under, to send out a sable Topsy who looked shining and happy—quand même—to her sabler parent, to be switched for some misdemeanor—which I declined to hear as I fled in my haste.[30]

Ophelia fared better than Marie St. Clare among southern readers of *Uncle Tom's Cabin*. Being a New Englander, Ophelia could not be interpreted as an embodiment of the faults of southern women. The faults or supposed faults of Ophelia were sometimes exaggerated by southern readers of the novel, with the implication that they represented faults of northerners generally. In a personal letter written in the 1850s, Margaret Johnson Erwin, a southern woman slaveholder, wrote to a friend and mentioned having met some northern woman who reminded her of Ophelia. "I met a relative of that Mrs. Stowe's, a Miss Ophelia," Erwin said, "who seems to be scouting like an Indian with her ear to the ground, just to uncover trouble." Some of the southern reviewers were willing to admit that if Ophelia was not an admirable character, at least she was a well-drawn one. The Reverend Mr. Stearns said that Stowe could "paint a New England old maid to the life." On the other hand, he thought Ophelia was not representative of northern women who came to the South. For one thing, she refused to allow slaves to wait on her. "The general experience in such cases," he said, "is that they fear being confounded with negroes. . . . Hence they require far more of the time and attention of the slaves than the southern matrons." He was also shocked at the reluctance of Ophelia to touch Topsy. He thought it "hardly in the nature of any woman to shrink from the very touch of a poor neglected child, whether white or black." Yet later in the same review, Stearns apparently changed his mind and expressed a very different view. He said that Ophelia was right to be reluctant to touch Topsy and accused Stowe of advocating a dangerous intimacy between the white and black races. "The direct inference to be drawn from Mrs. Stowe's support of this disgusting doctrine is this," he said, "that she is willing to occupy the position of proposing to her country to submit themselves to the embraces of negroes, thus becoming the mother of a degraded race of mulattoes. Can she be the advocate of prostitution like this?"[31]

Little Eva was the only character in *Uncle Tom's Cabin* who received much praise from southern reviewers. Even she was occasionally rejected —and with some justice—as a sentimental and unbelievable character. Louisa S. McCord said that Eva was meant to be "a kind of ministering, guiding angel to the whole family," but as such she was "a terrible piece of precocity." A. Beatty thought Eva was not a credible character because "we miss the simplicity we are entitled to expect . . . she is too wise for her years, as well as too good for human nature." Mary Boykin Chesnut said, "Topsys I have known," but she thought that an Eva must be "mostly in the heaven of Mrs. Stowe's imagination."[32]

While the white characters in *Uncle Tom's Cabin* seemed openly offensive to southern reviewers, the black characters seemed merely unreal. William J. Grayson, in his anti-Uncle Tom poem, *The Hireling and the Slave*, was probably thinking chiefly of Uncle Tom when he described the blacks in the novel as "saints of sable hue,/Martyrs, than zealous Paul more tried and true." Mary H. Eastman said that Uncle Tom's master should have "kept him until he died, and then sold him bone after bone to the Roman Catholics. Why, every tooth in his head would have brought his price. St. Paul was nothing but a common man compared with him." Louisa S. McCord objected to Stowe's comparison of Uncle Tom to one of the bishops of ancient Carthage, deriding her because she did not know that "all men of colour are not negroes." Edward A. Pollard said that Stowe had entirely misunderstood the nature of the religious zeal of blacks. "There are no Uncle Toms in the South," he maintained. "The negro, in his religion, is not a solemn old gentleman, reading his Bible in corners and praying in his closet; his piety is one of fits and starts, and lives on prayer-meetings, with its round of 'zortations [exhortations], shoutings, and stolen sweets of baked pig." Black slaves themselves would, said Pollard, instantly have spotted Uncle Tom as an impostor because he had no place for Satan in his religion. "The negro who has 'got de 'ligion' and has never been favored in the process with a peep at 'ole Sa-ten' or is unable to give a full description of his person," Pollard explained, "is considered by his brethren a doubtful case—a mere trifler, if not a hypocrite."[33]

Since southern reviewers could not accept Uncle Tom as a credible black character, they rarely argued that his goodness was the result of the beneficent influence of slavery. After the Civil War, this particular argument would be fairly widespread in the South. When *Uncle Tom's Cabin* first appeared, southern reviewers may not have been willing to accept the idea that a black might be genuinely religious. Thus they had difficulty in accepting Uncle Tom as an example of true Christianity. One southern reviewer told a story of a pious black slave who had been given his freedom. Soon afterward he seduced the daughter of a re-

spectable white family and she gave birth to a mulatto child. The implication of the story seemed to be that it was impossible for a black to
be a genuine Christian or a person who would not be sexually
promiscuous.[34]

William Gilmore Simms was the southern critic who came nearest
arguing that the religion of Uncle Tom was a direct result of the fact
that he was a slave. Uncle Tom "is perhaps sufficiently conclusive in
behalf of the institution of [slavery]. The North has no such character.
We shall not deny Uncle Tom. He is a Southron all over. . . . We have
many Uncle Tom's." Later in the same review, however, Simms expressed
the idea that the religion of a black was likely to be genuine only when
he was old. "Mrs. Stowe, as you perceive," said Simms, "makes Uncle
Tom an old fellow. Ah! She should have known him when he was
young. He was no such saint then, we fancy, as he subsequently showed
himself."[35]

Southern critics did not often deny the credibility of Topsy as a
character, but they rarely mentioned her. A. Beatty thought Topsy
demonstrated one of the problems of slavery for which the abolitionists
had no answer. He did not believe that Topsy's moral regeneration in
the novel was at all convincing. Even if it were, the problem would
have been almost impossible of solution. Augustine St. Clare owns seven
hundred slaves jointly with his brother Alfred, said Beatty. "But where
can we find seven hundred Ophelias to educate the other slaves of the
two brothers? And where will we find suitable teachers for the other
slaves of the slaveholding states, amounting to more than three million,
even supposing their masters would give their consent to have them
educated?" The problem was such a vast one, Beatty apparently meant
to imply, that it should not be undertaken at all.[36]

The mulatto characters were more objectionable to southern reviewers than such wholly black characters as Uncle Tom or Topsy.
George and Eliza Harris, said George Frederick Holmes, are "a tawny
Apollo and Venus," and their son Harry is "an interesting yellow cupid."
Dante's Beatrice, said Louisa S. McCord, "is but a common-place damsel
by the side of Eliza." William Gilmore Simms was equally incredulous
of the idea that George Harris could possibly have been a handsome
man. Stowe has described Harris, said Simms, as having a "personal
beauty." Simms himself would like, he said, to condemn Stowe to "perpetual bedfellowship" with Harris.[37]

Another objection to George Harris expressed by southern reviewers was that it was unlikely that he would have unusual intelligence or ability. John R. Thompson said that Harris "unites the genius of an Awkwright to the person of an Antinous." There was merriment among southern reviewers over the idea that Harris or any other mulatto would be capable of inventing a machine for cleaning hemp. If such a slave ever existed, said Louisa S. McCord, his master certainly would not have set him to doing ordinary menial work. "Did ever a man in his senses," asked McCord, "ruin his property, because he is jealous of it!" A. Beatty was shocked that any man could be depraved enough to blame God, as Harris does in the novel, for the fact that he had been born a slave. There was much shaking of heads among southern reviewers over the rebelliousness of Harris, especially of his saying he will shoot the slave-catchers who are pursuing him if they press him too closely.[38]

The mulatto who excited the most indignation among the southern reviewers was Cassy. Eliza was less objectionable because she had not been portrayed as having had illicit sexual relationships. Even Cassy gave southern reviewers some difficulty in their censure of her. She was no longer young and beautiful. She had no real choice in submitting to sexual relations with white men, and she felt only shame and aversion because of them. Choosing an older woman for the role of unwilling mistress to white men has the effect in the novel of diverting the reader's attention away from the prurient aspects of sexuality. Reviewers could complain that Cassy represented the "libidinous" aspects of Stowe's imagination, but they found it difficult to make their indictment more specific.

Mary H. Eastman said that Cassy was "a most infamous creature from her own accounts, and we are [supposed?] to sympathize with her vileness, for she has no other traits of character described." Eastman thought the religious conversion of Cassy was wholly unconvincing. As evidence that it was not genuine, she cited the fact that Cassy later stole money from the strongbox of Simon Legree when she was planning with Emmeline to run away. Not only does Cassy steal, said Eastman, but she "fibs tremendously afterwards." She mentioned no specific lie and apparently meant that it was dishonest for Cassy to pass herself off as a white in her flight to freedom from slavery. Louisa S. McCord avoided the whole question of Cassy's supposed sexual depravity. She merely said that nothing could be more ridiculously improbable than the scene in which Cassy, on her flight to the North, is shown as "passing for a lady, in the cabin of a Southern steamboat."[39]

Perhaps surprisingly, a few southern reviewers were willing to concede that illicit sexual relations between white men and black women might be common under the conditions of slavery. Dr. A. M. Woodward, a Kentucky physician, said in extenuation of the practice that among whites "the evil falls mostly on the male population; females not being exposed to the same temptations." Woodward admitted that promiscuity under slavery was almost inevitable. "The [white] boy is let loose at an early age and runs into all manner of excesses; not so with the girl; for from childhood to adult age, she is under the eye of her mother; and I do not suppose, that for intelligence, beauty and refinement, the world can produce a set of females superior to the southern ladies." As in other times and other places, female chastity was somehow supposed to compensate partially for the lack of it in the male. Northerners ought not to blame southern white men, said Woodward, for allowing their half-white children to remain in slavery. "Men are everywhere (with a few exceptions,) the world over," he said, "utterly devoid of all parental affection for their illegitimate children." And then what could the white southern father of mulatto children do? "Suppose he liberates them," said Woodward; "their condition is but little improved thereby, unless he sends them out of the country."[40]

The Reverend Mr. E. J. Stearns argued that interracial sexual relations were illegal in the South, but he admitted it was rarely possible to enforce the law. He thought that the "proper question" was not whether slavery produced many mulattoes but whether a free society might not produce even more of them, and he pointed to the example of Jamaica. Louisa S. McCord believed that the status of the mulatto under slavery, though different from Stowe's "horrible imaginings," was nonetheless "a painful one." McCord shared a belief prevalent at the time that mulattoes are frequently infertile, representing nature's attempt to compensate for the supposed wrongness of their having been created. Since the mulatto was a "monstrous formation" which nature "disowns," said McCord, he would not be likely to propagate his kind for more than two or three generations. The position of the mulatto would necessarily be anomalous in any society, she argued, but he was probably "happiest" under slavery in the South, "where he quietly passes over a life, which, we thank God, seems like all other monstrous creations, not capable of continuous transmission." Edmund Ruffin, the southern agriculturalist, publisher, and writer on political issues, admitted that there was some truth to the charges of interracial sexual relations in *Uncle Tom's Cabin.* There were "revolting cases of vice in high position (in connexion with our institution of slavery) which give color to the general libels of such writers as Mrs. Stowe—& it is the too great toleration of such criminals in society, even by many who abhor their vices, & despise the actors, that give any force to these general libellers & denouncers of slavery." William Gilmore Simms pooh-poohed the whole matter of the sexual exploitation of black women under slavery. He said that Stowe had paid too much attention to such sources as "some silly white woman of the South, who has doubts of her husband's good behaviour when he goes abroad o' nights."[41]

A frequent charge against *Uncle Tom's Cabin* among southern critics was that it subtly advocated racial intermarriage and amalgamation. Louisa S. McCord said that she looked "shudderingly forward to *her* [Stowe's] results. Amalgamation is evidently no bugbear to this lady." A character in Mary H. Eastman's anti-Uncle Tom novel, *Aunt Phillis's Cabin,* satirically describes Uncle Bacchus, an elderly slave, as a potentially good husband for an abolitionist woman in the novel who is probably modeled upon Stowe. He would "just suit her, with his airs and graces; but I do not think she is stylish enough for him." In her own voice, Eastman said that some people might think it was commendable for Stowe to educate her own children with blacks but she herself "would rather *my* children and negroes were educated at different schools, being utterly opposed to amalgamation, root and branch."[42]

Toward excessive whippings and other maltreatments of slaves, the southern critics of *Uncle Tom's Cabin* reacted generally as they did to charges of separations of slave families. Such cruelties, they said, were extremely unusual. Only rarely did they argue that the slaves were protected by law against excessive punishment. Occasionally there is a comment such as that in James M. Smythe's *Ethel Somers; or, The Fate of the Union* (1857), an anti-Uncle Tom novel. The narrator of the novel explains that they are "benignant statutes for the protection of the slaves" in the South. He does not show them in operation in the novel, however, or even mention any specific one of them. Dr. A. M. Woodward also argued that the laws in the South generally protected slaves against excessive punishment but—like Smythe—he gave no details. In the course of his defense, he made a revealing admission. "The right to punish being vested in the master," he said, "he inflicts the punishment in his own way, and to some extent, at his own discretion. The master is judge, juror, and executioner. Whipping is the ordinary punishment inflicted on slaves for crime. Whether it is the punishment most likely to deter them from the commission of it, I know not; but they [the masters] can find no punishment better adapted to the proposed object."[43]

A few southern critics of the novel were willing to admit that laws regulating excessive punishment of slaves were defective and sometimes cruel in themselves. It was sometimes argued that they were descended from an earlier and less civilized age. Though such laws were still in the law books, apologists for slavery contended that they were widely regarded as dead letters and no longer enforced. Others argued that admittedly cruel provisions of the slave codes had to be retained because they would be needed in the event of a slave insurrection. Still others argued that the worst provisions of the slave codes would long ago have been repealed had it not been for abolition agitation. Some of the reviewers argued, however, that the provisions were not unjust and that some of them had a Biblical sanction. One of the provisions in some states was that if a slave was flogged and later died, the master could not be indicted for homicide unless the slave died on the same day in which the flogging took place. The Reverend Mr. E. J. Stearns said that God himself had laid down a similar law for the ancient Israelites. Did not the book of Exodus say that a slavemaster could not be charged for the death of his slave if the slave should "continue a day or two" after receiving the punishment? Had not holy scripture gone on to justify this proviso with the explanation that "he [the slave] is his [the master's] money"? Stearns issued an awful warning to the abolitionists, saying:

Recollect that the Mosaic law is from God, I know this is denied by some, but I am speaking to Christians. . . . [I]ts provisions . . . [are] the very best that the nature of such a code will admit of; in other words, perfect adaptations of means to ends, and, as such, applicable not only to the Jewish people, but to every people. Here we have the vindication of the slave code in a nutshell.

William Gilmore Simms conceded that the slave codes did not protect the slaves from cruel treatment. On the other hand, he was not much troubled by the fact that they did not. Those slavemasters who were guilty of mistreating their slaves might escape earthly punishment, he said, but they would surely be punished by God. Such cases, he said, we must leave to a "higher tribunal."[44]

A few of the southern reviewers showed an uneasy recognition that the slave codes were unjust, even barbarous. A. Beatty thought that it was a reproach to the South that state legislatures had "not made *excessive* or *unreasonable* punishment of slave or slaves, an indictable offence." The law "should protect slaves as far as possible, against the exercise of tyrannical authority by their masters." On the other hand, he thought that the examples of cruelty to slaves in *Uncle Tom's Cabin* were "highly coloured, and often much exaggerated."[45]

Even a comment like this one of Beatty, one which admits that there was at least something to the charge that the slave codes did not give the slaves more than minimal protection against mistreatment, was rare among the southern reviewers. They generally avoided discussion of slave codes altogether. Instead, they emphasized the "patriarchal" aspects of slavery. In their view, the master of a plantation was seen as having a relationship to his slaves like that of a father to his children. Just as governments had wisely chosen not, in general, to interfere with the treatment a father might mete out to his children, law in the southern states had given a similar broad range of authority to the master over his slaves. No precise regulations were needed, it was argued, to set the limits of the master's authority. The argument that the slavemasters were "patriarchs" might have seemed a little risky to some. After all, had not the abolitionists charged that the slaveowners were frequently the fathers of their own slaves? Of course, a word like "patriarch" did not suggest any such thing. It had a Biblical ring. It seemed to portray slavemasters as benevolent men who could nearly always be trusted to be just and fair. Therefore, there need be no laws set up to regulate their conduct with regard to their slaves.

When the kindliness of a master could not be depended upon to insure fair treatment of a slave, the fact that the slave was valuable property was brought forward as a deterrent to cruelty. In those few instances in which neither the benevolence of the master nor his property interest protected the slave, there was still another restraint upon the master which worked in the slave's favor. The outraged contempt which his white neighbors would express to a cruel master would force him to treat his slaves fairly. Like every institution, some southern pro-slavery spokesmen argued, slavery was capable of being abused but it was not inherently evil. The South was not ready to abandon slavery, said Edward J. Pringle, simply because it was not a perfect institution. There is "no Divine institution that man has not defaced, no human institution without its errors." Stowe had been "unjust." "In dwelling with great skill and dramatic power upon the abuses of the system, and upon nothing beyond, she has given a most false and wrong impression of what slavery is. She has filled her Northern readers with a delusion."[46]

One southern critic argued that *Uncle Tom's Cabin* had helped to foster a sentimental humanitarianism among slaveowners. In 1860, A. T. Goodloe, an Arkansas slaveowner, wrote a letter to the *Southern Cultivator*, an agricultural magazine published in Augusta, Georgia. He complained that *Uncle Tom's Cabin* and "other vile publications" of the abolitionists had had a pernicious effect in the South. "The general published opinion seems to be," he said, "that negroes should be managed with great lenity and encouraged to labor by kind words." He was himself convinced that it was a fallacious argument. "Now, I speak what I know when I say it is like 'casting pearls before swine' to try to *persuade* a negro to work. He must be *made* to work, should always be given to understand if he fails to perform his duty he will be punished for it." What kind of punishment he gave his own slaves is indicated later in his letter. It "has always been a rule with me to whip any negro that tries to tell me anything about the overseer," he said. "I think I can find out without their assistance whether he is a gentleman or not."[47]

Southern reviewers of *Uncle Tom's Cabin* sometimes said that they despaired of convincing outsiders that it was a libel upon the South and upon slavery. Such efforts, said George Frederick Holmes in the *Southern Literary Messenger*, "are useless, for our adversaries are as deaf and as poisonous too, as the blind adder. . . . We have not the ear of the court; our witnesses are distrusted and discredited, and in most cases, they are not even granted a hearing." Thus, southern reviewers seemed often to be talking neither to the North nor to the outside world generally but merely to other white southerners. If they could not convince northerners that slavery was a beneficent institution, they could at least warn them of the dangers of interference with it. "We are too strong to be legislated out of existence by any power in the world," said William Gilmore Simms. "The argument of truth having failed us, we have still the means of protecting ourselves against falsehood. . . . We have numbers, and arms, and the courage which can wield them with success, and there is but one power of which it needs that we be watchful—our own government." Simms made this comment in 1853 at a time when the federal government was not hostile to slavery, but he realized that the time

might come when it would be. The South's "enemies" had gone too far
to stop:

Nothing but a convulsion which shall shake the country to its center, can
now arrest them. We must be prepared for this—prepared to engage in
the final issue whenever the Federal Government falls into the hands of our
assailants. Pride, prejudice, hate, vanity, the love of power, the phrensies
of fanaticism, are all combined against us.

A southern character in the anti-Uncle Tom novel, *Ethel Somers; or, the
Fate of the Union* (1857), warns northerners that in spite of all the
prating about slavery in Great Britain that country will prove an unreliable ally for them. England "is your natural enemy," he says, "the South's
natural friend. In a state of disunity, she will side with the South. Her
existence depends on our cotton." Other southern critics of *Uncle Tom's
Cabin* warned the North of armed resistance if it interfered with
slavery.[48]

    There is only indirect information about how widely *Uncle Tom's
Cabin* was read in the South. Some southern newspapers indignantly
rejected advertisements for the book, but others accepted them. Local
booksellers sometimes openly sold copies. Francis Lieber, who was
professor of history and political economy at the College of South Carolina in Columbia, but who was born and reared in Prussia, wrote a
letter to a friend in which he said that the book was selling rapidly
and that the local book dealer had told him he had a hard time keeping
enough copies in stock. When traveling in the South, Frederick Law
Olmsted mentioned seeing peddlers aboard southern steamboats selling
copies. They did not "cry it out as they did the other books they had, but
held it forth among others, so its title could be seen." On one boat trip
on the Mississippi River in Louisiana, he saw three copies sold to different passengers. An anonymous northern writer in an article in the
Independent (New York City) said that he saw Mary H. Eastman's
Aunt Phillis's Cabin, an anti-Uncle Tom novel, on sale at a book stand
in the lobby of a hotel in Charleston, South Carolina. He asked the
vendor if he had a copy of *Uncle Tom's Cabin* and he replied, "I can
get it for you; don't sell it openly."[49]

    There were appeals in southern newspapers that people of the
region should not buy *Uncle Tom's Cabin*. Sometimes there were forcible
attempts to keep it from being sold. In Mobile, Alabama, a bookseller
was run out of town by vigilantes when he displayed the work in his

store. Dr. Charles G. Parsons, a northerner traveling in the South, said "several boxes" of copies of the novel were burned in Athens, Georgia. There was a public burning of the novel by the students of the University of Virginia in Charlottesville. Many years later, Lyman Beecher Stowe, Stowe's grandson, told of having heard a story of a young Englishman who was in South Carolina in 1854. A southern girl at a party told him that she had heard of *Uncle Tom's Cabin* but had not been able to obtain a copy to read. He supplied her with one. Some southern white men discovered what he had done. Soon afterward, his friends told him he must leave the state immediately because a "committee of planters were about to wait upon him." Some of these men, he was told, were ready to challenge him to a duel. The Englishman took this advice and left the state. In 1857, a court in Maryland sentenced Samuel Green, a free black, to ten years in prison for having in his possession a copy of *Uncle Tom's Cabin*, along with other abolition documents. In 1862 the governor of Maryland pardoned Green with the proviso that he would leave the United States; Green immediately departed for Canada. The most dramatic rejection of the novel came in a package addressed to Stowe from somewhere in the South. It contained the severed ear of a black with an accompanying card deriding her defense of the "D--n niggers." Calvin Stowe opened the package, discovered the ear, and disposed of it without letting his wife see it.[50]

Though the South became more and more angry with the North from 1852 to 1861, it began to ignore Stowe and *Uncle Tom's Cabin* about two years after its publication. There was a round of outrage in 1852 when the novel first appeared in book form and another round when *The Key to Uncle Tom's Cabin* was published the following year. After that it is difficult to find any references in southern periodicals and newspapers of the South to either of these books or to Stowe herself. In July, 1853, the *Newberry* [South Carolina] *Sentinel* asked publishers in the South to "sedulously exclude in future from their columns, every article that makes the remotest allusion to *Uncle Tom's Cabin*." Stowe's second antislavery novel, *Dred*, published in 1856, would go virtually unnoticed in the South. The southerners reacted at first with anger to *Uncle Tom's Cabin* and to its *Key*, rejecting them as unjust and malicious. Then, wounded and outraged, they resorted to what they apparently meant to be a dignified silence.[51]

XII

Anti-Uncle Tom Literature

IN TERMS OF LITERARY MERIT, none of the literary works which were, or which probably were, written as answers to *Uncle Tom's Cabin* are of much importance. The four best ones are Thomas Bangs Thorpe's *The Master's House*, William Gilmore Simms's *Woodcraft*, Sarah Josepha Hale's *Liberia*, and William J. Grayson's *The Hireling and the Slave*.* Most of the works have sketchy plots and pasteboard characters. Sometimes they are, in fact, scarcely distinguishable from many of the proslavery pamphlets published during the years before the Civil War. They abandon narrative for long stretches and argue much like publicists and politicians of the time.

Though it is not possible wholly to distinguish opinion from "literature," one can concentrate on characters and situations, rather than on arguments. How did proslavery writers see slaves and masters? How did they portray the opponents of slavery? How did their black slave characters differ from their free black characters? How did they view plantation society and the South generally? How did they view the North? It must be said at once that, in nearly all instances, the motives of the authors show through at every point. Better writers would have recognized how difficult it is to answer one imaginative work with an-

---

* A list of the literary works treated in chapter XII appears under note 1.

The Beecher Family, ca. 1850. Standing, left to right: Thomas, William, Edward, Charles, Henry Ward. Seated, left to right: Isabella, Catharine, Lyman, Mary, Harriet. Insert: James. Probable photographer is Matthew Brady.

Frederick Douglass. Engraving by J. C. Battre in *Narrative of the Life of Frederick Douglass*, 1845. *Courtesy National Museum of History and Technology.*

Five generations of slaves on J. J. Smith's plantation, Beaufort, South Carolina, 1862. Photograph by Timothy O'Sullivan. *Courtesy Library of Congress.*

An abandoned slave market in Atlanta, Georgia. Photograph by George M. Barnard, ca. 1864. *Courtesy Library of Congress.*

UNCLE TOM'S CABIN;

OR,

LIFE AMONG THE LOWLY.

BY

HARRIET BEECHER STOWE.

VOL. I.

BOSTON:
JOHN P. JEWETT & COMPANY.
CLEVELAND, OHIO:
JEWETT, PROCTOR & WORTHINGTON.
1852.

Title page from the first edition of *Uncle Tom's Cabin. Courtesy Rare Books Department, Wake Forest University Library, Winston-Salem, North Carolina.*

"Uncle Tom and Little Eva."
The big eye and gentle demeanor of
Uncle Tom may suggest Stowe's idea
that blacks are inherently religious.
In this scene in the novel, Little
Eva is sitting on Uncle Tom's knee.
A Currier and Ives lithograph.

"I Am Going There; or, The Death of Little Eva." This illustration served as the cover
for the sheet music *Uncle Tom's Cabin*, composed by John S. Adams. (Boston:
Oliver Ditson, 1852.) *Courtesy Library of Congress.*

At Right: Miss Ophelia and Topsy.
Illustration from the new edition of
Uncle Tom's Cabin published by
Houghton Mifflin Co., 1895–1896.
Courtesy New York Public Library.
Below: "Tom Reading His Bible."
In this George Cruikshank
illustration, the cabins in the
background apparently have thatched
roofs. From a British edition of
Uncle Tom's Cabin. (London:
John Cassell, 1852.)

EMMELINE ABOUT TO BE SOLD TO THE HIGHEST BIDDER.

"Emmeline About to be Sold to the Highest Bidder." The illustrations in many books show octoroons or mulattoes with no suggestion that they may have black intermixture. Illustration by George Cruikshank from the Cassell edition of 1852.

THE POOR BLEEDING HEART.

"The Poor Bleeding Heart." Lucy drowns herself when her baby is sold away from her. George Cruikshank illustration from the Cassell edition of *Uncle Tom's Cabin*.

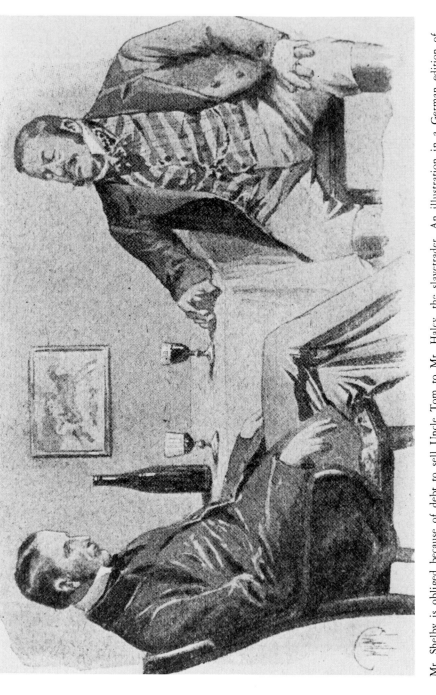

Mr. Shelby is obliged because of debt to sell Uncle Tom to Mr. Haley, the slavetrader. An illustration in a German edition of *Uncle Tom's Cabin. Onkel Toms Hutte. Fur die Jugend und das Volk.* Hrsg. von Robert Munchgesang. Mit Bildern von F. Muller-Munster. (Reutlingen, Enzzlin & Laiblins, n.d.)

СУДЬБЫ КНИГ · СУДЬБЫ КНИГ · СУДЬБЫ КНИГ

Р. Д. Орлова

ХИЖИНА,
УСТОЯВШАЯ СТОЛЕТИЕ

Cover from the Russian book written by Raisa Davydovna Orlova.
Khizhina, Ustoiavshaïa Stoletie [*Withstanding More than a Century,
Harriet Beecher Stowe's Uncle Tom's Cabin*]. (Moscow: Kniga, 1975.)

Eliza Crossing the Ice. From the French series "Héroïsme de l'amour maternel." Lithography and editing by Chez Miné. (Paris, n.d.) *Courtesy Stowe-Day Foundation. Hartford, Connecticut.*

Eliza Crossing the Ice. Possibly a cigar box liner or shiny book illustration; no other information available. *Courtesy Stowe-Day Foundation, Hartford, Connecticut.*

An advertisement for a dramatic production of *Uncle Tom's Cabin*. In the novel, no dogs pursue Eliza. Dogs were added in the play, and as productions became more elaborate, the dogs became larger, fiercer, and more numerous. The caption beneath this picture describes the dogs as "blood-hounds," but they are obviously some other breed, probably Great Danes.

Uncle Tom's Cabin;

OR,
LIFE AMONG THE LOWLY.

The cover of a 12-page pamphlet advertising a production of the play by
the Davis Company, probably in the 1890s. By this time the final scene—previously
showing Uncle Tom's ascension into heaven—now frequently portrayed the arrival of
the Union armies in the South to abolish slavery. *Courtesy Harold W. Tedford
Collection, Wake Forest University, Winston-Salem, North Carolina.*

James B. Lowe as Uncle Tom in the
1927 Universal Pictures version of
Uncle Tom's Cabin.

Uncle Tom's Cabin: A History. Ricardo Pitts-Wiley as Uncle Tom (center, facing
audience); David Kennett (behind and to the right of Uncle Tom) as Simon Legree.
From the dramatic adaptation by Adrian Hall and Richard Cumming, Trinity Square
Repertory Company, Providence, Rhode Island, 1978.

other. In addition, it is more difficult to defend an institution than to attack it. Some proslavery reviewers recognized that writing anti-Uncle Tom novels would probably be a useless endeavor. "It can be doubted," said George Frederick Holmes in the *Southern Literary Messenger,* "whether an assault on a solemn interest, moral or social, conveyed under the garb of fiction can ever be satisfactorily answered in a similar form. If it could be, it would be too trivial to be worthy of such an elaborate defense." At best, a fictional reply would be "a mere counter-irritant." It would place "the replicant in a secondary position," exhibit him "in the false light of a mere imitator and plagiarist . . . . thus obviously yielding the vantage ground to the offender."[2]

Just as Stowe had done in *Uncle Tom's Cabin,* nearly all the authors of anti-Uncle Tom literary works adopted the convention of direct address to the reader, a device which may sometimes turn the modern reader away from both sides of the argument. *Uncle Tom's Cabin* has virtues which compensate for the defects of direct address, but the anti-Uncle Tom literary works rarely do. The deficiencies of most of them are almost immediately seen in the inability of the authors to imagine convincing characters and incidents, but ultimately the matter of tone is more important. They are generally emotional. They frequently approach the question of slavery as if it could be adequately defended chiefly by a close reading of the Bible and of the Constitution. They generally ignore the cruelties of the institution and, when such evils do appear in their works, they are often justified by appeals to a crudely racist theory which condemns the blacks to a hopelessly inferior status.

The most obvious differences among the anti-Uncle Tom writers were sectional. The northerners were a little less vehement than the southern ones. They knew more about the North and were less likely to see the region quite simply as the locus of evil. They were less concerned with expressing their outrage than with persuading their readers in the North that slavery was a better institution than its critics said it was. They usually saw almost all northerners as neutral or indifferent on the issue of slavery and concentrated their invective on the abolitionists. On the other hand, the anger of the southern writers of anti-Uncle Tom literature often prevented them from making much effort to examine differences of opinion among northerners or to attempt to persuade them. Sometimes their anger spilled over into a detestation of "Yankee civilization" generally.

In nearly all anti-Uncle Tom literature, the major figure is the benign and patriarchal slavemaster. Always he is a plantation owner. Nearly always he is financially well off, if not wealthy, though sometimes he suffers reverses apparently in order to allow the slaves an opportunity to demonstrate their loyalty to him. Colonel Montrose in Maria J. McIntosh's *The Lofty and the Lowly* returns early in the novel to his plantation in Virginia after a trip to town. He assembles his slaves together before a pitchpine bonfire. "Each had a kind clasp of the hand, a word of pleasant greeting, and a testimonial of remembrance—a bright bandana handkerchief, and calico dress to the women—a jacket and muffler to the men," the narrator says. To Old Cato, his slave and right-hand man, Montrose brings a special gift of a coat with "cloth of a finer quality than that usually worn by the negroes," a muffler, and a fur cap. Cato thanks his master, saying, "I 'fraid you make me proud, sir, when I get all dese on." A kindly white neighbor of Colonel Montrose gives the slaves their cue. "We have a great deal to be thankful for to-night, my friends—have we not?" And the meeting ends with the singing of a hymn, "Come Thou Fount of Every Blessing." In Caroline Lee Hentz's novel, *Marcus Warland*, the narrator says of some of the slave characters, "It is true, they were *slaves*, but their chains never clanked. Each separate link was kept moist and bright with the oil of kindness."[3]

The slaveowners in most of the novels are so benign that one can hardly help wondering how they handle the discipline problems which at times must inevitably come up. In Mary H. Eastman's *Aunt Phillis's Cabin*, the master mildly rebukes the slave Aunt Phillis because she has allowed a runaway slave to hide in her cabin. He tells her it would never do for him to get the reputation of allowing his "servants" to abet the crimes of those of his neighbors. Instantly contrite, Aunt Phillis promises never to repeat her offense. Sometimes the proslavery writers profess themselves to be bewildered by accounts in the North that slaves are cruelly punished. In McIntosh's *The Lofty and the Lowly*, the daughter of a slaveowner is puzzled and saddened to read in northern newspapers of the supposed mistreatment of slaves. She "searched in vain the tablets of her memory for the sounds of rattling chain or the lash; or the sight of scar or brand, or mutilation, or any of those thousand acts of tyrannical power which it sickens the very soul to recall, and of which every northern paper she perused was full." When punishments do take place in these proslavery literary works, they are not often examples of physical chastisement. In W. L. G. Smith's *Life at the South*, a slave

named Tom is mildly punished for failing to do his work. Another slave
has bested him in a cotton chopping contest and he sullenly refuses to
work at all. His master, after several gentle reprimands, imprisons Tom
in a cabin for twenty-four hours without food. As a result, Tom changes
his attitude. When asked whether the punishment has been sufficient, he
replies, "Massa, I have now no oder than good thoughts; the bad ones
I have parted with."[4]

Whippings are rare for the slaves in anti-Uncle Tom literature, but
they do take place sometimes. In Caroline E. Rush's *The North and
South* a slave boy named Jim steals a silver dollar from the pocketbook
of his mistress. Jim is "a bright mulatto boy, about fourteen years old."
The evidence of his guilt is not wholly conclusive; he has been seen
coming out of the room in which the purse had been left. Under ques-
tioning, he steadfastly denies that he took the money. He "stood before
his master and mistress, very pale, even beneath his brown skin," says
the narrator, "but anyone could plainly see that he was guilty." His
master calls him a "black dog" and orders the overseer to give him ten
lashes every hour until he confesses. After the first whipping, Jim confesses to having stolen the dollar but says that he has lost it. Another
whipping is administered and he admits that he has hidden the dollar
in the woodpile. The narrator explains that Jim was, "like the most of
his race, a great thief; and he added to this crime its usual attendant disregard for truth."[5]

Most slavemasters in anti-Uncle Tom literature are more kindly than
this man. When they are obliged to whip their slaves, they do so reluctantly and only when other methods of reformation have failed. Mr.
Wardloe, the benevolent slaveowner of Baynard R. Hall's *Frank Freeman's Barber Shop*, serves as a member of a patrol of white men organized to catch slaves away from their quarters without a pass. They
catch Sambo, one of Wardloe's slaves, who says he has only "bin down
to meetin'" and begs for mercy. The other members of the patrol think
Sambo should be given two dozen lashes in order to "teach him to pray
a little faster" next time. Mr. Wardloe asks to be allowed to take Sambo
aside and to administer the punishment himself. He whispers to Sambo
to yell loudly as he flogs a near-by gatepost, and Sam naturally com-
plies. Wardloe gives his last two blows to Sambo himself as an indication
that he is not wholly to be trifled with. "Reader! I well know that
there are many Uncle Wardloes in the South," says the narrator of the
novel. The benevolent slaveholder described in Smith's *Life at the South*

is a man with "a kind heart and a scrupulously honest disposition. If he ever plied the lash to the stubbornly disobedient slave, he used it, as nearly as we can recollect, precisely as a father does in the wholesome correction of his children. He did not punish with wantonness." Sometimes the anti-Uncle Tom novelists used the device of having a faithful slave reply to critics of slavery. In the anonymous *Yankee Slave-Dealer*; *or, an Abolitionist Down South*, a skulking abolitionist tries to get Uncle Moses, a slave, to admit that he is often flogged. Uncle Moses denies the charge and adds, "I don't b'leve any servant who does right's ever whipped like a brute as you say."[6]

Other anti-Uncle Tom novelists leave vague the matter of how frequently and how severely slaves are whipped, but they emphasize the point that such punishments are necessary. "Africans hate civilization," explains the narrator of Mrs. Henry B. Schoolcraft's *The Black Gauntlet*, "and are never happier . . . than when allowed to live in the abandonment, nakedness, and filth, their instincts crave." There is no reason to worry that they will be permanently injured by mistreatment. "[A]ll the calumnies about the planters knocking the slaves senseless to the earth is [sic] the purest fiction," says the narrator; "for their skulls are so thick that it is doubtful whether any white man's strength could consummate such a feat, even if he was indiscreet enough to make the attempt." Billy Buck, a slave character in Ebenezer Starnes's *The Slaveholder Abroad*, argues that slaves are necessary in the South because only they can work in the fields in a hot climate. Supposedly, because of their inherent character traits, the masters will have to punish them. He replies to Englishmen skeptical of the virtues of slavery as follows: "Wa da been gwin git [where are they going to get] anybody able to work in cottonfield in brilin hot sun, but black nigger? I want know dat! An wa de debbil da gwine find nigger wid head to work widout buckra [white] man to show um? or dat gwine be willin, cepin he druv?" Billy Buck does not go on to explain how a slave is "druv," but he probably means by whippings.[7]

A number of the anti-Uncle Tom novels express the familiar proslavery argument that slaveholders are not likely to mistreat their slaves because of their value as property. The narrator of James M. Smythe's *Ethel Somers*; *or, the Fate of the Union* says that property itself is almost enough to insure the kindly treatment of slaves. He knows of "slaveholders who are kind to their slaves when they are kind to nobody else." Hall's *Frank Freeman's Barber Shop* expresses a similar idea. He admits that an occasional slaveowner is cruel to his slaves, but he says that other slaveowners in the community will refuse to sell to such a man. Yet the speaker also seems to think that a few cruel slaveowners in a community have a useful function. Sometimes, he says, a "wicked negro would be turned over to severe and cruel owners that served the community as a public whipping post." Even so, he adds, these cruel owners were "never esteemed" by respectable people. He does not speculate on the question of whether a mistreated slave was likely to derive much benefit from the fact that his owner was not esteemed by his white neighbors. When cruelties to slaves are shown in anti-Uncle Tom literature, they are the result of the personal defects of particular masters or, in rare instances, of mistresses. They are obviously not meant to be an indictment of the institution of slavery itself. In Eastman's *Aunt Phillis's Cabin*, there is a cruel slaveowner character, Mr. Lee, who sells seven of the children of one of his women slaves away from her, one after another. The narrator explains Lee's evil as the result of "money, drink, and the devil."[8]

In Robert Criswell's anti-Uncle Tom novel, *"Uncle Tom's Cabin" Contrasted with Buckingham Hall*, a kindly slaveowner gently disputes the charge of an idealistic young northern man that slaves are frequently mistreated. When the young man asks skeptically whether all the masters are kindly, the southern slaveowner replies that of course they are not. He himself could point to some masters who are "hard and cruel," but he adds that "as a general thing, the slaves have reason to be, and are, contented with their condition." Mr. Harding, one of the cruel slaveowners described in Criswell's novel, was an abolitionist when he lived in Ohio, but because a southern plantation was left to him by one of his wife's relatives, he had come to the South "in spite of his prejudices." After nine years of operating the plantation, Harding "abuses his slaves worse than any Southerner I ever heard of." It is true that he is "naturally despotic," but his chief fault is that as a northerner he does not understand the inherent nature of the blacks in the way that southern slaveowners do. He expects his slaves "to do as much in a day as white men; and because they do not he beats and half starves them." The wife is "as barbarous as her husband." When her riding horse is brought to her in the morning, she takes a white handkerchief and rubs it over him. If it is in the least "soiled or dusty," she immediately orders her groom to be whipped.[9]

Though they generally describe southern characters as kindly, the anti-Uncle Tom writers sometimes argue that violence is justifiable, or at least excusable, against abolitionists. A slaveowner in Eastman's *Aunt Phillis's Cabin* says,

Mobs of any kind are rare in the Southern country. We are not (in spite of the bad qualities ascribed to us by the Abolitionists) a fussy people. Sometimes when an Abolitionist comes along, we have a little fun with him, the negroes enjoying it exceedingly. Slaveholders, as a general thing, desire to live a peaceful, quiet life; yet they are not willing to have their rights wrested from them.

Uncle Bacchus, a slave, tells his white masters that he wishes the Lord would see fit to bring all the abolitionists to Virginia so that they could be tarred and feathered. He himself would be willing, he says, "to spread de tar on neat, and to stick de feathers close and thick." In Hall's *Frank Freeman's Barber Shop*, the narrator describes the destruction of an abolitionist editor's printing press. Lynch law is sometimes justifiable, he argues, because "the most atrocious of all crimes may be committed under cover of law, when the law itself instead of preventing is compelled to aid them." Nobody would argue, he said, that a mailman should be compelled to deliver packages with dangerous explosives in them. He would be justified in throwing them in the water. "Of course, the powder packers and massacre-mongers would be very angry, and give pages of constitutional law and other legal flummydiddle," he said, "but such would never convince an unsophisticated citizen that he ought to sit still and be killed."[10]

In anti-Uncle Tom literature, the wives of the slaveowners are even more kindly than their husbands, as we might expect. In Schoolcraft's *The Black Gauntlet*, the narrator contrasts the beautiful southern belle with the mature matron she will become after she has married and has had years of experience as mistress of a plantation. As a young girl she has had no responsibilities "except in her flower-garden, in reading, or perfecting her education, and doing amateur fine needlework." Her life changes dramatically when "she becomes a planter's wife." No longer is she "a laughing, thoughtless flirt, seeking only to make herself beautiful and admired." Instead she develops into "a responsible, conscientious 'sister of charity' to her husband's numerous dependants [*sic*]. Northern ladies never saw a day in all their lives that could comprise all the responsibilities of a Southern planter's wife." Anthony Trollope visited the United States in 1861 and noted that this particular argument was still often heard in defense of slavery. He mentioned the complaint of a slavemistress who said that Stowe had no idea how much trouble it was to look after "our people." Trollope remarked that politeness forbade him to answer this argument with "the plain truth." Nonetheless, he admitted that he had an almost uncontrollable urge to reply, "Madam —dear madam, your sorrow is great; but that sorrow is the necessary result of your position."[11]

Where cruelty exists on a slave plantation as depicted in anti-Uncle Tom literature, it is nearly always the fault of the overseer, not of the slavemaster. Mr. Hecky, the overseer in Hall's *Frank Freeman's Barber Shop*, is one of these. He is "a tall, gaunt, white man. Across his shoulders hung, like a belt, a carter's whip—its horrid lash like a snake with a long thin tail." To visitors on the plantation, Mr. Hecky says, "If you think I don't do my duty, look at their backs!"[12]

Mr. Hecky gets a chance to demonstrate his methods in handling slaves. He finds a young pregnant black woman slave who is surreptitiously using "rods" to pick specks and briars from the cotton, a practice which is forbidden because it damages the fibre. Mr. Hecky, in a fury, flogs the woman. Even though she is pregnant, he "ferociously" kicks her in the side. Some white southerners witness this brutal treatment and strongly censure Mr. Hecky to his face, but they apparently do not dream of interfering with him. "Man! If I were a negro, and my brother cut your throat," says one of them, "I would *never* lay the lash upon him!" The man who says this, as angry as he is, apparently feels no responsibility for stopping Hecky from beating the woman. It is difficult to assess the motives of Baynard R. Hall for including such a scene in his novel. It would seem not to differ from the scenes of cruelty in antislavery novels. It does not lead Hall to the conclusion, however, that slavery is an evil institution. All it seems to mean is that some slaves in the South do undoubtedly suffer from cruelties, especially at the hands of overseers.[13]

By far the best of the anti-Uncle Tom novels is *The Master's House* by Thomas Bangs Thorpe. There are so many objections to slavery in it that sometimes critics have described it as an antislavery novel. The argument of Thorpe is not, however, that slavery should be abolished. The novel is a plea, principally to upperclass white southerners, that men of good will should unite to prevent or mitigate the cruelties of slavery. Of the abolition of slavery itself, he says nothing and apparently has no hope. Thorpe was born in Massachusetts and emigrated as a young man to Louisiana, where he lived for fifteen years. While there he became a writer of southwestern humor, his best known work being "The Big Bear of Arkansas." In addition, he had great talent as a landscape painter. In *The Master's House*, he depicted the cruelties of slavery in detail. He was willing to concede that many slavemasters had a genuine regard for their slaves, looked after their welfare, and treated them in a kindly manner. Nonetheless, he also thought that the argument of good treatment of slaves as a justification for slavery was a convenient rationalization.[14]

Gerald Mildmay, the hero of *The Master's House*, is a white southerner with New England ancestors on one side of his family. He marries a New England woman who detests slavery at first but who gradually modifies her opinion of it when she sees how conscientiously her husband attempts to care for their slaves. Mildmay moves his family and slaves from the worn-out soil of North Carolina to Louisiana, and there he sets up a new plantation. In Louisiana, his neighboring planter acquaintance, Colonel Moreton, is a man who is more of a defender of southern institutions than Mildmay himself. The two men conduct debates over what the position of the South should be with regard to slavery. They often disagree with one another, but they accept each other's sincerity—for a time, at least—and do not openly quarrel. Mildmay urges Colonel Moreton to look at "the burnings and lynchings of negroes, which have disgraced the fair fame of the South, and it will be found that the planters, the men of wealth and education, have seldom been participators." On the other hand, the poor whites who have frequently engaged in violence against the blacks have not been held in check by a more responsible class of white men. The lower class whites have been allowed to adopt "the corrupt idea, that their excessive zeal gave evidence of devotion to Southern interests."[15]

In addition to restraining the violence of the poor whites, Mildmay argues, the planter class should recognize that as strongly established as slavery is in the South, its defenders cannot hope to preserve it indefinitely by forbidding discussion of it. "We cannot stop freedom of speech," says Mildmay. The North agrees "that there is no power in Congress to interfere with the States in the matter [of slavery]." He sees "all Southern members in Congress, who bring slavery before that body for the purpose of sustaining abstract rights, as injuring the institution; and though their intentions may be good, they are none the less practical enemies to the South." In addition, though he recognizes the

Fugitive Slave Law as the law of the land, he believes it is a great mistake for the South to insist upon its enforcement in the North. This law, says Mildmay, is "a source of the greatest evil to our good name, and the popular support of our institution. Suppose we lose negroes," he argues. "[L]et us look upon those [slaves] that escape as if it [*sic*] were the same amount of value destroyed by the elements, and if we cannot manage to be insured, let us brave our losses with philosophy."[16]

Mildmay also takes the Whig view that the South should encourage industries and free labor. He attempts to convince Colonel Moreton, who looks with suspicion on white mechanics and trained white workmen generally, that only by encouraging free industry can the South be made independent of northern manufactures. A thoughtful tone pervades *The Master's House*. "The peculiar character of our institutions requires that the master should necessarily delegate a great deal of power to his confidential agent—the overseer," says Mildmay to a group of other slavemasters, "but that authority is to be exerted wisely, and, except in extreme cases, violence is not to be used. . . . Unless, gentlemen, we protect our slaves . . . from the death-dealing influences of irresponsible white men, society among us will rapidly degenerate into barbarism." From the events which occur in the novel, however, it is difficult for the reader to believe that the patriarchal slavemasters, even when they wish to do so, can restrain other white men, especially their overseers, from the cruel treatment of slaves. At least Thorpe shows clearly that Mildmay is not able to protect his slaves against injustice at the hands of his overseer, Mr. Toadvine.[17]

A savage and vengeful man, Toadvine restrains himself in the presence of Mildmay but often punishes the slaves brutally when he is alone with them; and once, in a fit of passion, he kills one of them. Mildmay does what he can to bring Toadvine to justice. We get a picture in the novel of what such a trial might have actually been like. The defense counsel for Toadvine tells the jury composed of lower class white men that "while the master is treading, with dainty steps, his marble halls, the faithful overseer is winding his devious way through interminable swamps. . . . While the master sees his negroes fat, sleek, happy, and idle, the overseer beholds them as the necessary objects of strict discipline, and is forced to make them do their work." The jury acquits Toadvine of all charges.[18]

In other respects, however, Thorpe sometimes has a tendency to descend from a serious treatment of slavery's injustices to a comic view of them. He comes near suggesting that the wrongs done to the blacks are less serious than they might seem because of the innate traits of the blacks. This idea is developed as one of the themes of "southwestern" humor, a tradition which could sometimes be insensitive to human suffering, to put it mildly. A slave trader in the novel tells the story of a Mr. Pinckney, a southern slavemaster who indulges his slaves to an extreme degree. Benson, Pinckney's slave, has so little black intermixture that he can pass for a white. He accompanies his master to the North and picks up a fair approximation of the manners of cultivated white people. On returning to the South, Pinckney loses Benson, after betting on a horse race, to a man who has no fine conscience in dealing with his slaves. Even the slave trader who tells the story thinks Benson's new owner treats him cruelly. This nameless man lives in a log cabin, eats corned pork, and amuses himself by

drinking whiskey, running horses, and hunting niggers. He was a real spirited gentleman, but rather imprudent in whipping, for he used to lay it on when he got mad, so that the nigger never got over it, and that is a foolish wasting of property, for you see . . . there is no feeling in a nigger's hide below the skin, and if you will take time, you can get it all out of his body without touching a vital [part].[19]

At the time Benson is acquired by his new master, he is wearing clothes brought from France and has a gold watch in his pocket. His new owner says to him:

"Benson, my boy, that half neck ahead of my horse as they came out at the stand, made me your master; now I have a prejudice agin dandy niggers, agin learned niggers and agin white niggers; and as I don't fancy the airs Mr. Pinckney put on, I think I'll commence your education by whipping out of your hide all the gyrations he's larned you; and if you live through it, maybe you'll make a good cotton picker at last."

The slavemaster flogs Benson and in the process cuts his broadcloth suit "into flinders." Probably in order to remove the sting from this story, Thorpe has Benson escape to Canada. There the former slave passes as a white man and resumes his upper-class affectations. He "sets up a perfumery" and marries an unsuspecting white woman from England.[20]

The slave trader's story is the only point in the novel at which Thorpe is insensitive to the cruelties practiced against the slaves. As the novel progresses, its theme becomes more and more serious and less humorous. Thorpe apparently could not bring himself to believe that Mildmay, or anyone else, would be able to prevent slaves from being maltreated. Mildmay encounters trouble with his neighbors because of his advanced opinions. Colonel Moreton is eventually so enraged by them that he challenges Mildmay to a duel. Although Mildmay kills Moreton, he takes no pleasure in his victory. Moreton's wife goes mad with grief, and Mildmay's own wife, sympathizing with her neighbor, wastes away and finally dies. At the end of the novel, Mildmay is sitting in darkness beside his wife's grave, all of his dreams of personal happiness shattered and his hopes for reforms of slavery blasted. An ending like this one virtually destroys the effect of the discussions of possible alleviations of the cruelties of slavery. Thorpe left the South permanently in 1853 and, in 1854 *The Master's House* was published, the author using the pseudonym *Logan*. In 1855 the third edition of the novel appeared, this time under Thorpe's real name. Some of the ambivalence of *The Master's House* may be reflected in the subsequent events of the life of Thorpe himself. He was briefly associated with the Know Nothing Party, though he soon detached himself from it. Later still, he was attached to the Union Army during the Civil War, serving as the chief staff officer of General Benjamin Butler, who would become notorious in the South as "the Beast of New Orleans." Unlike Butler, however, Thorpe won the praise of even some of the white southerners. He made a determined effort to rid New Orleans of epidemics by rigorous sanitation measures.[21]

The greatest failures in anti-Uncle Tom literature are the slave characters, who are all too obviously patterned to fit the proslavery argument. The slaves are either contented in their condition and loyal to their masters or they are foolish rebels who do not understand their own best interests. Stephen A. Hirsch, a modern critic, has perceptively pointed out that in virtually all the anti-Uncle Tom novels, the slaves themselves play only a minor role. "Despite the uncles, aunts, and cabins populating the titles," he says, "only one novel, Smith's *Life at the South*, has a black as its main character." In one respect, however, nearly all the black characters are unlike those in the nostalgic fiction of the old plantation, written by white southern writers in the 1880s and 1890s. The slaves in the anti-Uncle Tom literature of the 1850s seldom exhibit a profound and mystical attachment to their white masters and mistresses. Their loyalty has a strongly matter-of-fact character. Friendly familial associations are mentioned, but the major point is that the blacks in these novels see slavery as a system which prevents them from falling into want and deprivation. The slaves may praise "massa" or "missis," but freedom from worry over their material needs is their usual reason for speaking favorably of slavery. Old Rufus, a slave in Martha Haines Butt's *Antifanaticism: A Tale of the South*, serves as a representative of many other slave characters of this sort. "Dis nigger never leab his massa to go wid nobody," he says, " 'caze he know dat nobody ain't gwine to treat him good no how like massa does."[22]

One of the anti-Uncle Tom novels does, it is true, attempt to portray an exalted relationship between master and slave. In *Old Toney and His Master* by Theodore Dehone Mathews, Colonel Shelton is portrayed as an aristocrat of truly grand proportions. As host to the guests at his plantation mansion, he is shown "bowing as a courtier at the palace of the Tuilleries [*sic*] in the days of Louis XV." Old Toney, Colonel Shelton's slave, is scarcely less magnificent. Though the hair on his "venerable head" is as white as "freshly ginned cotton," there is nothing else old and feeble about him. One of his differences from Stowe's Uncle Tom is that he is his master's overseer of the slaves and that he "flogged the boys [slaves] by way of exercise, if they neglected their duties."[23]

Colonel Shelton and Old Toney have a sublime attachment for each other, which fully matches anything that the white southern romancers of the late nineteenth century would be able to imagine between master and slave. When his son is killed, Colonel Shelton falls "weeping like a child on the breast of his slave." Yet Old Toney is quite unlike the faithful slaves of post-Civil War white southern fiction. The principal difference is that he is not meek and gentle. Slave characters in later fiction sometimes accompany their masters as servants when they go to war, but they take no part in the fighting. Old Toney, on the other hand, is a formidable soldier. Many years before he had fought alongside his master against the Indians of Florida. Old Toney had "scalped many a Seminole." Their "scalps he still retained and exhibited with pride to the 'rest of the niggers,' as trophies of his . . . prowess." It is probably the fact that Old Toney is so dashing a warrior and so flamboyant a character that explains why other proslavery novelists did not attempt to create characters like him in their fiction. He is so aggressive a hero that one cannot imagine him as a slave.[24]

Slaves in anti-Uncle Tom literature are usually shown as happy, often singing at their work. In J. Thornton Randolph's *The Cabin and Parlor*, however, the narrator of the novel is momentarily puzzled when he notices that the minor key of many of the songs of the slaves is "almost mournful." He soon thinks of an explanation which will preclude the possibility that they might be unhappy. The music of native Africans is also seemingly sad, he says, but the likelihood is that this is merely the impression white listeners receive. The reader can easily determine for himself, he observes, that the music of American blacks does not indicate they are unhappy as slaves. On the contrary, they think of their music as an occasion for "mirthful enjoyment." In only one of the anti-Uncle Tom novels is there a suggestion that blacks might have great talent in music. In Mathews's *Uncle Toney and His Master*, the narrator praises the singing of a black church choir on a South Carolina plantation. He speaks of "the deep bass tones, like the swell of an organ, in perfect unison with the flute-like tones of the women—the tenor, the alto, the treble, and the bass often heard upon different octaves, but all in perfect accord." The narrator says that he has often heard trained singers in Charleston, but none of them was equal to the black singers in this choir. The comment stands alone in the proslavery fiction of this period in its willingness to concede that blacks might have a higher talent of any kind.[25]

The most idyllic picture of slavery in anti-Uncle Tom literature is to be found in the poem, *The Hireling and the Slave*, by William J. Grayson, the South Carolina author. It has similarities to Oliver Goldsmith's "The Deserted Village" and suggests the dependence of the South upon eighteenth-century English literature:

> So blessed with moderate work, with ample fare,
> With all the good the starving pauper needs,
> The happier slave on each plantation leads;
> Safe from harassing doubts and annual fears,
> He fears no famine in unfruitful years;
> If harvest fail from inauspicious skies,
> The master's providence his food supplies;
>
> . . . .
>
> And Christian slaves may challenge as their own,
> The blessings claimed in fabled states alone—
> The cabin home, not comfortless, though rude,
> Light daily labor, and abundant food,
> The sturdy health that temperate habits yield,
> The cheerful song that rings in every field,
> The long, loud laugh, that freemen seldom share,
> Heaven's boon to bosoms unapproached by care.
>
> . . . .
>
> While, nestling near, to bless their humble lot,

Warm social joys surround the Negro's cot,
The evening dance its merriment imparts,
Love, with his rapture, fills their youthful hearts,
And placid age, the task of labor done,
Enjoys the summer shade, the winter sun,
And, as through life no pauper want he knows;
Laments no poor-house penance at its close.[26]

One of the contented black slave characters in an anti-Uncle Tom novel also bears the name of Tom. This is William Gilmore Simms's *Woodcraft*, published in 1852. Naming his own chief black character Tom might suggest that Simms had *Uncle Tom's Cabin* in mind when he was writing his own novel. *Woodcraft* was published only a few months after the appearance of *Uncle Tom's Cabin* as a book, but it is possible that Simms might have read it, or at least have heard of it, when it was appearing as a serial in the *National Era*. There are similarities between *Woodcraft* and *Uncle Tom's Cabin* but nothing definite enough to prove a relationship between them. Simms himself said in a letter to a friend that he thought *Woodcraft* was "probably as good an answer to Mrs. Stowe as has been published," but this is not the same as saying he wrote his novel specifically with this purpose.[27]

In *Woodcraft*, Captain Porgy, the picaresque hero of some of Simms's earlier novels of South Carolina life, is cast as a benevolent and patriarchal slavemaster. In previous novels, Porgy had been a comic character whose escapades and faults, especially his indulgence in overeating, had made him an unlikely example of the highest type of southern gentleman. Now his character has to undergo some refurbishing to qualify him for his new role. The time of the novel is immediately after the American Revolution. Porgy has returned from service in the American army to find his plantation in South Carolina has become a weed patch. In addition, it has been mortgaged to those "patriots" who had sat out the war and bought land cheaply for future speculation. In the fact of these difficulties, Porgy resolves to rebuild his plantation, pay off his debts, provide a home for his slaves, and incidentally to reform his own character. He has the opportunity to marry a neighboring wealthy widow, but he is too honorable to do so because it would seem obvious, perhaps even to himself, that it was a device for getting out of his own financial difficulties.[28]

Tom, Porgy's slave, has none of the religious qualities of Stowe's Uncle Tom. He is "a native African," "a fellow of flat head and tried fidelity." He has a nose "that scarcely pretended to elevate itself on the otherwise plain surface of an acre of face." He is good humored and an excellent cook, especially when the dish is terrapin soup, of which his master is most fond. It other ways, this Tom has all the defects generally attributed to blacks in anti-Uncle Tom literature. During Captain Porgy's financial troubles, Tom never worries about where the food for his cooking is to come from. "Sambo seldom troubles himself to look out for the morrow," the narrator of the novel explains. "His doctrine somewhat tallies with that of Scripture . . . sufficient for the day the evil thereof. . . . He never houses a harvest in anticipation of the storm."[29]

Captain Porgy sometimes speaks roughly to Tom and on occasion even threatens to whip him. Yet their relationship is shown as friendly, almost affectionate. The narrator says that any reader familiar with a "Carolina plantation" will understand that "successive generations have grown up" in which the interests of master and slave have "indissolubly mingled." When it appears that Porgy may have to sell Tom because of debt, we find out just how strong his attachment to his slave is. "No! no! old fellow!" he exclaims, "I will neither give you nor sell you, nor suffer you to be taken from me in any way, by Saint Shadrach! . . . Nothing but death shall ever part us, and even death shall not if I can help it. When I die, you shall be buried with me. We have fought and fed too long together, and I trust we love each other quite too well, to admit to separation." Tom fails to comprehend the meaning of this outpouring. Porgy apparently is suggesting that rather than separate from Tom, he would kill him and then commit suicide. Tom did not, the narrator says, "conceive the tenor of his master's speech." We do not discover whether Tom is devoted enough to his master to acquiesce to his own death. Since Porgy's financial status improves, his determination to kill the slave rather than part with him is never put to a test.[30]

A succession of black characters in the anti-Uncle Tom novels proclaim their devotion to old massa and missis and pay tribute to the benefits of slavery. Many of these are aged and infirm, and the reader may wonder what the young and healthy slaves think of the institution. Aunt Peggy, in Eastman's *Aunt Phillis's Cabin*, is one of a number of dying slaves who expire blessing the kindness of their owners. Old Bacchus, a slave, explains to his master that Aunt Peggy is obviously near the end of her life. "She's failin', sir," says Bacchus, "you can see by de way she sets in de sun all day, wid a long switch in her hand, trying to hit de little niggers as dey go by. Sure sign she's gwine home. . . . She sarved her time cookin and bakin, and she's gwin to a country whar there's no 'casion to cook any more." A standard device in the novels is to have a northern woman, opposed to slavery, marry a southern man and gradually learn the beneficence of the institution. Sometimes the change in the northern woman's attitude takes place at the bedside of a dying slave or at a slave funeral. In John W. Page's *Uncle Robin in His Cabin in Virginia,* the Pennsylvania-born wife of the southern master visits the cabin of the dying Aunt Juno, an aged black woman who was born in Africa. "My dear husband," says the wife, "what a beautiful thought it is that a poor African, once condemned to be eaten by cannibals, should now be on her death-bed in a Christian country, surrounded by Christian friends, and rejoicing in the assurance of eternal salvation, procured by the death of her Saviour." "Yes, my dear," her husband replies, "it might carry consolation to the bosom of a Wilber-force, mourning over the horrors of the African slave-trade." Caroline Lee Hentz and W. L. G. Smith also included death-bed scenes of slaves in their novels. In Butt's *Antifanaticism: A Tale of the South,* the formula is slightly varied. Her dying slave is a little girl. The death of this child suggests, at least to some degree, a black version of the death of little Eva. To her white mistress, the little black slave girl says, "Don't grieve for Hannah, Miss Dora. I am going home to heaven. I dreamed last night that I saw a little angel beckoning to me. I love you, Miss Dora, but must leave you soon. I hope to meet you in heaven."[31]

Sometimes, the anti-Uncle Tom writers apparently felt the need to have slaves who would philosophize on the subject of slavery, justifying it in principle. Since wholly black slaves are generally intellectually unequal to this sort of endeavor in these novels, the task is usually left to slaves who are partly white. One such character is Aunt Phillis in Eastman's *Aunt Phillis's Cabin.* "The blood of the freeman [a white freeman] and the slave mingled in her veins," and thus she has "a well regulated mind." She does not argue that she is content to be a slave. The narrator tells us that she "would have been truly happy to have obtained her own freedom, and that of her children, but she scorned the idea of . . . obtaining it otherwise than as a gift from her owner." Her ideas about slavery are a mixture of a pious belief in scripture and in the sanctity of laws regarding property. In reading the Bible, she "often pondered on the words of the angel [to Hagar], 'Return and sub-

mit thyself to thy mistress.'" Aunt Phillis accompanies her owners on
a visit to the North, and, while there, some wicked abolitionists endeavor
to persuade her to attempt to escape. "I want none of your help," says
Aunt Phillis. "My husband and children are at home [down South]; but
if they wasn't I am an honest woman, and am not in the habit of *taking*
anything. . . . I am not going to begin stealing, and I fifty years of age."
Having said this, Aunt Phillis straightens her tall figure and her eyes
flash. The abolitionists, discomfited, slink away. In James M. Smythe's
Ethel Somers; or, The Fate of the Union, a slave character philosophizes
that principles of freedom are not applicable to blacks. "The Declaration of 'Dependence may do . . . for white folks, an not all of them,"
he says, "but it isn't worth a chaw of backer to a nigger. . . . I don't
b'leeve it was ever 'tended for them."[32]

The opposite of the loyal black slave in anti-Uncle Tom literature
is the rebellious slave who runs away. It is never cruel treatment which
causes him to flee. Either he is sullen or unruly by nature or he is too
foolish to know when he is well off and is thus vulnerable to the wiles
of abolitionists who whisper the delights of freedom in his ear. The
slave Charles in Randolph's *The Cabin and Parlor* is portrayed as one
of these foolish persons. "His light and graceful figure, as he walked,
had that swaying motion, which seems peculiar to races of tropical
blood," says the narrator of the novel. "His eyes were large and bright
and intelligent. Yet his face, expressive as it was, gave the idea of weakness. His attire was somewhat dandyfied. Having always lived at the
mansion, where he heard only the most refined conversation, he had a
vocabulary almost as correct as that of his late master." When he runs
away to Philadelphia with his wife Cora, also a slave, he loses his self-
confidence immediately. "Not every one of the harder and sterner race
to which we belong," says the narrator, "can realize, to its full extent
at least, the prostration of spirits which overcame both Charles and Cora.
Self-reliance is the peculiar characteristic of the Anglo-Saxon."[33]

The subject of runaway slaves naturally leads Randolph to a graphic
description of a slum in the North. One of the themes of anti-Uncle
Tom literature is that the evil of cities is characteristic of northern and
British civilizations, but that the South is an agrarian utopia. Sometimes
these novels suggest the slum fiction of such writers as Stephen Crane,
which would be written about forty years later. In *The Cabin and Parlor*,
Philadelphia is "a vast sink of filth, destitution, vice, crime, disease, and
ungodliness of every description." A black "urchin" is seen picking up

a rotten peach from the street and eating it. There are black women in the slums who are described as "generally large and filthily dirty, with sleeveless dresses, torn and greasy . . . , bosoms lewdly exposed, hair uncombed and matted, and legs and feet naked. . . . They pass the time calling to each other across the street, bandying vulgar jests, or swearing oaths of horribly blasphemy." In Grayson's *The Hireling and the Slave*, the free black in northern cities lives a miserable life:

> There in suburban dens and human sties,
> In foul excesses sunk, the Negro lies.
>
> . . . .
>   [W]ith each successive year,
> In drunken want his numbers disappear.

Sometimes the North is yoked with England or with Europe generally as having a callous aristocracy which mistreats the poor. A southern character in James M. Smythe's *Ethel Somers; or, The Fate of the Union*, says to a northerner, "The lords of the loom and your merchant princes in northern cities have begun already to ape the manners of the titled gentry of Europe. How often do you see them already dashing through the streets in their splendid carriages, with liveried drivers and servants."[34]

The slaveowner in the anonymous anti-Uncle Tom novel, *The Olive-Branch; or, White Oak Farm*, goes so far as to tell his slaves they can have their freedom any time they want it. "He had on more than one occasion intimated to his servants," says the narrator, "that, if any of them believed their condition would be improved by a removal to a free State, he was ready to give them the most liberal opportunities of securing their discharge by due process of law." On the other hand, once having given his slaves their freedom, he will not take them back when they discover how wretchedly they must live as free men and women. In Eastman's *Aunt Phillis's Cabin*, a runaway slave named Susan petitions to be taken back into slavery and is refused. In her despair, she throws herself into the fire and is seriously burned, though she is prevented from killing herself. Some slavemasters, it is true, magnanimously allow their runaway slaves to return to them. Tom, a slave in Smith's *Life at the South*, runs away from the plantation of his benevolent master. In the North, Tom had adopted a ridiculously inflated style of speech. "Can I add ignominy to perjury?" he asks himself in reflecting on whether to ask his old master to take him back. He does ask him, and his master consents to receive him again as a slave. At this point Tom reverts to southern black dialect. "As for dis nigger," he says, "he's gwine to old Virginny." When he arrives back at the plantation, he runs to find his cabin "with the little yard and veranda, just as he left it four years before." He embraces his wife and children. "Thankfulness gushed up from the deep fountain of his soul," the narrator says, "and he closed his eyes in gratitude."[35]

The free black, at least if he lives in the North, is frequently depicted in anti-Uncle Tom literature as a "dandified nigger." There is one in Eastman's *Aunt Phillis's Cabin*. A black man comes down a street in Philadelphia wearing a top hat, carrying a cane, and smoking a cigar. He refuses to give way on the sidewalk to a white man. The white man, a northerner, takes offense at his lack of deference. He knocks the black man down, saying, "Now . . . you've had a lesson; the next time you see a gentleman coming along, turn out of the way for him, and you'll save your new clothes." There are no southern "uppity" black characters portrayed in anti-Uncle Tom literature, but the reader occasionally receives the impression that such people exist even among the slaves. "I must admit to you that I have the most repulsive feelings toward negro gentlemen," said Edward A. Pollard in *Black Diamonds Gathered in the Darkey Homes of the South*.

When I see a slave above his condition, or hear him talk insultingly of even the lowest white man in the land, I am strongly tempted to knock him down. When Mrs. Lively [an imaginary slavemistress] tells her very gentlemanly dining room servant that he carries his head too high, I make it a point to agree with her; and whenever she threatens to have him "taken down a button-hole lower," I secretly wish I had that somewhat mysteriously expressed task to perform.[36]

In anti-Uncle Tom literature there are generally two quite different kinds of abolitionists. In a few instances, they are well intentioned but foolish and misguided. Usually, however, they are mean, narrow, and hypocritical. Their meanness to the people with whom they associate contrasts with the philanthropy they frequently feel for slaves who are a long way off. Nearly all the abolitionists are men. In Hall's *Frank Freeman's Barber Shop*, the president of the abolition society in Boston is the Reverend Ananias Sharpington, D.D. He has an "ultra-bilious complexion," a nose like the bill of a hawk, and two "gray-green"eyes which are crossed. His theological creed is unorthodox. He believes in the "higher law," and if it should lead to "theft, murder, anarchy, all was *fiat justia*!" Black is his "all absorbing color." His clothes are black, including his stockings. He loves funerals because of their black crepe.

He has a black horse, keeps a "black boy" to "black" his boots, drinks a "black tea," and "in short, was black inside as well as out." The level of hatred of abolitionists by some of the anti-Uncle Tom writers is suggested by the fact that in Mathews's *Old Toney and His Master* there is an abolitionist who dies and goes to hell. Abolition is not specifically mentioned as the reason for his damnation, but it is probably meant to figure as part of the indictment against him. Alfred Orton, the abolitionist, confronts after his death "an infinite ocean of fire, whose waves, hot and burning, would ever roll, and surge, and hiss and roar, above his guilty head and his damned-forever spirit."[37]

Sometimes the abolitionists in anti-Uncle Tom literature are the victims of their own duplicity. In Hall's *Frank Freeman's Barber Shop*, an abolitionist is fairly caught when he attends a black wedding and is asked to kiss the bride. He shows his hypocrisy by refusing and slinking off. In Criswell's *"Uncle Tom's Cabin" Contrasted with Buckingham Hall*, there is a foolish abolitionist who comes to the South. He is unable to distinguish pure whites from those mulattoes who have a small amount of black intermixture. When southern white men introduce him to a woman who is partly black, he woos and marries her, ignorant of the trick which has been played upon him. Criswell has another abolitionist in the novel, a man with the revealing name of S. S. Doubleface. He leaves his home in Boston to visit for several months in the South. He buys a woman slave who can pass as a white and takes her to stay with him at a fashionable hotel in New Orleans. He writes to his wife back in Boston, telling her that he is "daily instilling *moral precepts* into the minds of all." Unluckily for him, one of his Boston acquaintances who is also visiting in New Orleans sees him in the hotel with his paramour, and threatens to expose Doubleface unless he leaves her. Doubleface is obliged to sell her at a "half price" discount.[33]

The sexual motive as an explanation for abolitionism is prominent in anti-Uncle Tom literature. In her *Ellen; or the Fanatic's Daughter*, Mrs. V. G. Cowdin has a profligate abolitionist character. He "professed to be a minister of the Gospel, but in reality, used religion as a mere cloak beneath which, for a time, his vices were effectively hid." Sometimes abolitionist characters come to the South in disguise. They foment rebellion among the slaves and seduce the slave women. Cassie, one of the slave women in W. L. G. Smith's *Life at the South*, tells her master that Mr. Bates, the northern tutor of the white children on the plantation, has "been gallant" with her and has coaxed her "to go ober de hill" with him. The abolitionist is thus discovered and is obliged to flee to the North. In the anonymous *Mr. Frank, the Underground Mail Agent*, a novel written under the pseudonym *Vidi*, the narrator describes an abolition convention. Several "rakish-looking old Quakers" are careful to seat themselves beside "buxom-looking negro-wenches." They engage in "sly ogling, and secret pressure of the waist," and are rewarded with "a corresponding rolling of the eye, with an unlimited display of ivory." Also at the convention are "huge, amorous-looking negro gallants" who have come to flirt with white "country girls." They begin with "sly and sheepish glances." As they grow bolder, they cause "some very deep blushes to mantle over fair faces, except in those cases in which all traces of female modesty . . . [have] disappeared." A different kind of evil afflicts other abolitionists at the convention. Wealthy people, they grieve over the wrongs done to slaves in the South, but not to their own servants. Not far away their white coachmen are patiently awaiting them atop their carriages in freezing weather.[39]

Sometimes the abolitionists in anti-Uncle Tom fiction are not evil but merely silly. In these instances abolitionism is shown just as another fad and is associated with women's rights, Unitarianism, transcendentalism, atheism, Fourierism, and spirit rapping. In *Mr. Frank, the Underground Mail Agent*, a disturbance erupts on the floor of an abolition convention when the advocates of homeopathic medicine revile those who favor alleopathic medicine. Someone introduces a resolution denouncing Christianity. A woman addresses the convention and argues that women ought to have the rights of men "without their cares and responsibilities." The narrator of the novel says at this convention that the black and white people are seated alternately with one another and that the sight of them reminds him of strips of bacon.[40]

Abolitionists who are honest in their antislavery are extremely rare in anti-Uncle Tom literature, but they do exist. In *Ellen; or, the Fanatic's Daughter*, Mrs. V. G. Cowdin has an abolitionist character who comes from the North to Georgia with the intent of arousing revolt among the slaves. A kindly southern white Christian minister who is a slaveowner, converts him to the belief that slavery is a beneficent institution. "He frequently conversed with me upon the slavery question," the former abolitionist explains, "and his honest, common-sense views, acted like a charm in dispelling the fanatical opinions that had led me, like some demented creature, seeking amid comfort and content for horrors, that existed only in the depraved imagination of the mischief maker." In

some of the anti-Uncle Tom novels, abolitionists learn from experience
what proslavery writers regard as the folly of imagining that a black
might be capable of using his freedom wisely. In Hentz's *The Planter's
Northern Bride*, an abolitionist in New England adopts a runaway slave
as virtually his own son. The black man is "repulsive," "gigantic in
stature, black as ebony, with coarse and brutal features." The abolitionist
takes him into his home, seats him between his wife and daughter at
the dining table, and assigns to him the best bedroom in the house.
Horrified by the proximity of the black man, the daughter of the abolitionist falls ill. Loyalty to her father forbids her to tell him the reason
for her illness, and the abolitionist is too stupid to see it for himself.
In time, the black man becomes "insolent and overbearing," and thus
the abolitionist is "compelled to turn him out of the house." Having
learned what the narrator says the whites in the South have known from
long experience, the abolitionist puts a double lock on his door. His
dreams are "haunted by black spectres, armed and equipped for murder
and robbery."[41]

A similar story is told by Mrs. G. M. Flanders. Her novel, *The Ebony
Idol*, tells of a quiet little New England town caught up in the abolitionist movement. The Curean African Aid Society of the town finds a runaway slave named Caesar and invites him to come and settle with them.
A kindly minister invites him to live in his house but is dismayed when
he sleeps on the dining room table, frightening the minister's daughter
almost into hysteria. Another married couple of the town try to persuade their adopted daughter to marry Caesar; she indignantly refuses.
He accepts every kindness which he receives as no more than his due.
Finally he arouses the ire of Miss Dickey, the elderly town heiress, by
killing her favorite cat, Euphemia, which has scratched him. This outrage and a general disgust for Caesar lead the people to the point that
they cease all association with him.[42]

Nearly all the anti-Uncle Tom novels stressing the evils of close
association with blacks were written by northerners. It is true that this
theme is not wholly absent in southern proslavery fiction. In *The Slaveholder Abroad*, Ebenezer Starnes, himself a southerner, tells of a white
southerner traveling in England and seeing a white working-class girl
in London who has been living as the mistress of a black man. He is
her pimp, and the two have been "living luxuriously" on her earnings
as a prostitute. She has been "cohabiting with this monstrous loathsome
being for two months." When she is brought to court and charged with

prostitution, she stands before the judge affectionately holding "the tatterdemalion's greasy black paw." Nearly all of the proslavery white novelists from the South, however, avoided the theme of racial contamination between black and white. The reason might have been that they wished to develop another idea which was inconsistent with the notion that close association with blacks inevitably led to the degradation of whites. They sometimes argued that it was only the kindly white southerners who did not feel repelled by the presence of blacks. On the other hand, hypocritical northerners, and especially abolitionist northerners, prated about the evils of slavery but refused to have any physical association with blacks. Thomas Dehone Mathews in his *Old Toney and His Master* developed this theme. "Yes, hear it," says the white southern narrator of the novel, "ye so-called philanthropists, who would shrink from the touch of the black man and think it pollution!—ye who would refuse to sit down by his side and give him wholesome advice and friendly counsel, but who will stand off at a distance, and poke into his hand a pitiful dime or a six-pence stuck into the end of a 'ten-foot pole!' "[43]

Some of the novels are difficult to classify as pro- or anti-slavery. Sarah Josepha Hale's *Liberia, or, Mr. Peyton's Experiments* is one of these. It is not explicitly anti-Uncle Tom; in fact, it comes to a conclusion somewhat similar to that of Stowe's novel, proposing that the blacks should return to Africa. On the other hand, it is much more sympathetic to southern slaveowners than is *Uncle Tom's Cabin.* Slavery's wrongs, as Hale saw them, were wrongs almost exclusively to the white people of the South. There are no accounts in her novel of beatings, separations of families, or other cruelties to slaves. The point of the novel is that nothing can be made of the blacks because of their inherent racial inferiority; therefore, the only solution to the problem of slavery is for the blacks to leave the country.[44]

Mr. Peyton, a kindly slaveholder, frees his slaves, but he also takes pains to insure that they will make the transition to freedom as easily as possible. He builds cabins for them on his property and supplies them with tools and seeds. In addition, he counsels them when they encounter problems. Even so, they do not prosper. A trusted former slave explains to Peyton what the trouble is. "Laws! Mas'r Charles," the former slave says, "a nigger can't be any thing but a nigger." Only a few of the blacks succeed as farmers on the plantation. Others fail to cut their own firewood; they become a nuisance to their white neighbors by stealing livestock and chickens; they quickly fall into want and deprivation.[45]

Casting about for another solution, Peyton sends some of his former slaves north to live in Philadelphia. There they find that the white population is violently prejudiced against them. Again only a few of them succeed. If they are not threatened by rioting whites, they are impeded by their own lack of ability, especially their laziness. Always patient and resourceful, Peyton then thinks that the blacks might be happier if they lived in Canada. He visits a colony of free blacks there but finds that few of them are happy. They complain that they cannot find work, that the whites are unfriendly to them, and that the climate is too cold. Eventually, Peyton hits upon the idea of sending his former slaves to Liberia. The scheme is a complete success. Though we do not learn the details of their life in Africa, the former slaves write back enthusiastic letters to their old master about how happy they are there. Hale seems to sigh with relief once she has got her shiftless black characters out of the United States and into Africa where she apparently thinks they belong.[46]

Other anti-Uncle Tom writers discuss colonization as a possible answer to the problem of slavery. The narrator of Hall's *Frank Freeman's Barber Shop* advises free blacks to go to Africa, where they can hold up their heads. The narrator of Page's *Uncle Robin in His Cabin in Virginia* says that if slaves could by some extraordinary means be freed, they should be returned to Africa. The narrator of Randolph's *The Cabin and Parlor* says that colonization of blacks in Africa may be "God's will." The narrator of *Mr. Frank, the Underground Mail Agent*, thinks colonization would be a blessing for the United States but that it would be too expensive to reimburse the slaveholders for their property and to transport the former slaves to Africa.[47]

With the exception of Thomas Bangs Thorpe in *The Master's House*, the authors of anti-Uncle Tom literature have few suggestions to make concerning possible reforms of slavery. Maria J. McIntosh in *The Lofty and the Lowly* has her narrator say that southerners need to consider some changes in their treatment of slaves. "[W]e have sinned against them not by cruelty, but by neglect," the narrator observes. "To acknowledge the truth, we Southerners have a great deal of 'Laissez faire' about us in all things. . . . But we are waking up, and if we can only shut our ears to the crude speculations of those who seek to teach where they ought to be contented to learn—we may yet make amends to our people and the world for our long sleep." The narrator does not go on to list what changes in slavery should be made. In a backhanded way, other anti-Uncle Tom writers sometimes admit that slavery may have serious faults as an institution. "I have no wish to uphold slavery," says the narrator of Eastman's *Aunt Phillis's Cabin*. "I would that every human being that God has made were free, were it in accordance with His will. . . . Neither do I desire to deny the evils of slavery. . . . I only assert the necessity of the existence of slavery at present in our Southern states, and that, as a general thing, the slaves are comfortable and contented, and their owners humane and kind." Sometimes the defenders of slavery came near throwing up their hands in despair at the stubbornness of abolitionists. "[S]how us any fair, open, practical system for universal emancipation," says the narrator of Hall's *Frank Freeman's Barber Shop*, "and the South will erect you a monument, and call you *Pater Patriae*." The narrator of Rush's *The North and South* says she would "rejoice to see the bondsman go free, and every slave walk forth in the light of liberty." Whether and when the slaves should be free, she adds, should be left wholly to the discretion of white southerners, and abolitionists were only making things worse. The narrator of *Mr. Frank, the Underground Mail Agent* tells of a slaveowner who is at the point of emancipating his slaves. Irritated past endurance by the fanaticism of abolitionists, he changes his mind at the last moment and keeps them in slavery.[48]

It is not the South which should change its ways, the anti-Uncle Tom writers generally say. The North is the region which needs most to examine its conscience and pursue a new course. The narrator of Hentz's *The Planter's Northern Bride* sorrowfully contemplates the evils which lie ahead. "[T]he stars of the Union may be quenched in the smoking, and the American eagle flap its wings in blood," she says. She bitterly reflects that the children of abolitionists of the North may emigrate to the South only to be killed in a slave insurrection. "[Y]our daughter, clasping her innocent babes to her bosom," she says, "may lift her dying eyes to heaven, feeling the conviction, keener than her last death pang, that a father's hand guided the blow of which she is the victim." Even worse is the possibility of civil war. "Can you sever the interests of the North and the South, she asks the people of the North, "without lifting a fratricidal hand?" Most of the other anti-Uncle Tom writers were not as pessimistic as Caroline Lee Hentz on this point. On the other hand, they express the conviction that if serious trouble were to come, it would be the fault of the North. The South, in their view, was almost wholly blameless in the disaster which seemed to be approaching.[49]

XIII

The Reception Abroad
Of Uncle Tom's Cabin

THE LARGE NUMBER of copies of *Uncle Tom's Cabin*, about 300,000, which sold in this country the first year after publication was greatly outdistanced by the approximately one million copies sold in Great Britain during the same period. Because so many editions were published in that country, an accurate count of the total number of copies can only be roughly estimated. One reviewer in England said, "There has been nothing like it in the history of book-making." An Englishman wrote to a friend in New York, "Everybody is reading it. . . . My daughter saw a baker's boy sitting on his bread cart in the street reading it. Masters and mistresses read it in the parlour, and their servants at the same time in the kitchen." So many housemaids were reading it, said another reviewer, that thousands of beds were going unmade. According to a third reviewer, a village in England had been so isolated in 1848 that three weeks passed before anyone there had heard of the revolution in France. The same village, however, had "scarcely a cottage" where the inhabitants had "not wept over the death of Eva, and laughed till their sides ached at the absurdities of Topsy."[1]

Uncle Tom's Cabin was widely read in Great Britain, but it was not merely a popular success. Lord Shaftesbury called it "that marvelous book, that singular and unprecedented compound of angelic genius and infantine simplicity." The Earl of Carlisle wrote a preface to a British edition—pirated, it is true—comparing it to Niagara Falls in its "overwhelming, irresistible, eternal Truth." William Ewart Gladstone used the novel as part of a strange humanitarian project—the reformation of prostitutes. Over a period of much of his mature life, whenever he saw a prostitute on the street he would stop her and give her a kindly lecture. Sometimes he would also give her a copy of *Uncle Tom's Cabin*, a book whose moral tone would encourage her, he apparently thought, to abandon her sinful ways. "It is a *great* book," he would say.[2]

One of the most thoughtful of the reviews of *Uncle Tom's Cabin* was that of Nassau William Senior, a professor of political economy at Oxford. Senior was widely known not only for his conservative economic and political theories but also for his interest in social questions. He served as a member of royal commissions investigating the conditions of the poor. He was aware that not all the responses of his countrymen to *Uncle Tom's Cabin* were disinterested:

The evil passions which "Uncle Tom" gratified in England were not hatred or vengeance, but national jealousy and national vanity. We have long been smarting under the conceit of America—we are tired of hearing her boast that she is the freest and most enlightened country that the world has ever seen. Our clergy hate her voluntary system—our Tories hate her democrats—our Whigs hate her parvenus—our Radicals hate her litigiousness, her insolence, and her ambition. All parties hailed Mrs. Stowe as a revolter from the enemy. She came to us knowing all the weak points in the camp, all the gaps in his line. She taught us how to prove that democrats may be tyrants, that an aristocracy of caste is more oppressive than an aristocracy of station; and, above all, that a clergy supported by their flocks is ready to pervert the fundamental principles of Christianity to suit the interests or the prejudices of their paymasters.[3]

Stowe, Senior thought, could hardly have managed by calculation to write a novel which would appeal to such a variety of opinion in Great Britain. Pious people did not, for example, hold against it—as they ordinarily might have—the fact that it was a novel. If it had contained a romantic love story, it might have been less popular among religious people, especially among the Dissenting sects, since there was a strong conviction among many of them that such a topic was inherently wicked. In addition, he thought that the religion espoused by the novel was unlike that of many other orthodox Protestants. The fact that it was different prevented it from offending and turning off people who were either not religious at all or not as conventionally religious as Stowe. "New Englander as she is," said Senior,

> there is nothing austere or ascetic, or menacing in her religion. It is a religion of hope, of love, not of fear or of denunciation. Present assistance and future reward are constantly promised; temptation and punishment are kept out of sight. Our Saviour appears in every page; the existence of Satan is almost ignored, except, indeed, when she makes the negroes assign to him the duty of taking the slave traders who tear children from their parents. "For if the devil don't get them, what he good for?" No sectarian doctrine, no sectarian feeling intrudes.[4]

Though the doctrines of Calvinist orthodoxy are not emphasized in *Uncle Tom's Cabin*, Senior pointed out, neither are they denied. In addition, he noted that Stowe had managed to appeal to another group besides the religious one, a group which was not numerically large but which was nonetheless important—the skeptical humanitarians. In drawing Augustine St. Clare—for most of the novel, at least—as a religious skeptic but as one who was nonetheless concerned over the injustices of slavery, Stowe had appealed to the sympathies of people who were not likely to be attracted to the religion of the author, but who might be impressed by the humanitarian arguments of St. Clare against slavery.[5]

In the United States, chiefly in the South, many of the reviewers of *Uncle Tom's Cabin* discussed the question of whether the Bible did, in fact, endorse slavery. In Great Britain, this issue was only rarely mentioned. This approach to slavery might have aroused a considerable interest among the Dissenting sects, but their spokesmen had little to say about it. They, like other British reviewers, saw appeals to the Bible in defense of slavery as perversions of Christianity. Senior thought, for example, that such arguments had no importance except as an American curiosity. In Puritan times, he explained to the presumably puzzled readers in Great Britain, the Bible was "considered by all, as it is now by many, as a single book, every word of which had been dictated by God." The Puritans, both English and American, espoused this belief. They made no distinctions between "what Moses was forced by the hardness of his countrymen's hearts to tolerate, and what was a moral rule of general and eternal obligation." Since the seventeenth century, Englishmen had come to recognize that many of the rules of the Bible had been "temporarily laid down for the guidance of semibarbarians living under a theocracy." On the other hand, many Americans, even those who had been educated, had not made this intellectual shift. Early New England communities had extracted from the Bible "their municipal code" and had "fancied that they had thus obtained institutions wiser than any that man could invent." In the United States, there was still a widespread belief in the Bible as the ultimate source of human government and law. Any Englishman could discover this tendency in America for himself by examining the American debates over slavery, whether the disputants were pro- or antislavery.[6]

Senior thought that *Uncle Tom's Cabin* would make a powerful impression wherever it was read, but he also thought that there was a special reason for its making a sensational impact in Great Britain. Since American writers of fiction had infrequently written about blacks, Englishmen—even those who had read American novels—were relatively unfamiliar with the subject. They had known, of course, that slavery was a system which easily lent itself to abuses. If the slave codes permitted separations of families, for example, and if it was more profitable in one part of the South to raise slaves for the market and to sell them in other parts of the South, then thousands of families would be separated. On the other hand, "until we were roused by 'Uncle Tom,'" said Senior, "we had not, to use a conventional Americanism, 'realised' their results." Stowe had brought to the British reader the meaning of these family separations and other evils of slavery in human terms. "The great authoress has put into our hands a telescope," he said, "through which the coloured races are brought so near to us, that we can see them in their labour and in their sports, in their sufferings, and in their enjoyments, in their insecure happiness—if any state that is insecure deserves to be called happiness—in their terrors, and in their despair." Thus the success of *Uncle Tom's Cabin* in Great Britain might have been foreseen by an astute observer. The novel portrayed "a spectacle . . . strange without being surprising . . . unlike anything that ever was seen before and yet . . . obviously real."[7]

Senior believed that *Uncle Tom's Cabin* was important because it enabled the British reader to form some conception not only of what slavery was like but also of what blacks were like. Even the cultivated Englishman, said Senior, was likely to have received most of his ideas of blacks from "ethiopian minstrel shows." Other British reviewers praised the novel for the range and variety of its black characters. Defending Stowe against the charge of idealizing them, the reviewer in the *Prospective Review* said, "By the side of Uncle Tom, George

Harris, and Eliza, she has set Black Sam, a compound of selfishness and cunning, who regarded with complacency the sale of Uncle Tom as making way for his own advancement." The reviewer also pointed out that Andy, another slave on the Shelby plantation, helps Eliza escape not because he sympathizes with her but because he realizes that Mrs. Shelby does not want her caught; and, as he sensibly reflects, it is "allers best to stand on Missis' side the fence, now I tell yer." The reviewer concluded that there "was shrewdness in this, but no generosity." The brutal Sambo and Quimbo on Legree's plantation led the same reviewer almost to "loathe" the black race, but he understood on reflection that blacks, like whites, had examples of evil as well as of good among them.[8]

Many of the British reviewers praised Uncle Tom as a character, but often they did not have much to say about him. Perhaps the reason was that he was so noble that he could easily be written off as an exceptional case. Other black characters seem to have impressed them more. Frequently the reviewers discussed the other characters in terms of their methods of coping with the injustices of slavery. The reviewer in the *Prospective Review* developed this theme in his analysis of the character Topsy. "The idea attached to the American negro [in Great Britain]," said the reviewer, "is that of mingled drudge and buffoon. . . . We laughed at, and not with him." He expressed his surprise at Topsy's keen comprehension of her lack of status in a predominantly white society. "When Miss Ophelia teaches her perverse pupil to make a bed and recite her catechism, or cross questions her as to her birth and former history," he observes, "the New England virgin is altogether floored by the sharp little negro." Thus Topsy was not merely "pitiable."[9]

As much as British reviewers generally praised *Uncle Tom's Cabin*, many of them objected strongly to one of the ideas in the book. Augustine St. Clare in his discussions of slavery with Ophelia had been willing to concede that common laborers in free societies, and especially in Great Britain, were scarcely more in control of their own destinies than were American slaves. "The slaveowner can whip his refractory slave to death," said St. Clare; "the capitalist can starve him to death." British reviewers generally found this comparison offensive. In addition, they objected to St. Clare's prophecy of revolution not only in England but in other countries as well. "One thing is certain," St. Clare had said to Ophelia, "there is a mustering among the masses, the world over, and there is a *dies irae* coming on, sooner or later. The same thing is work-ing in Europe, in England, and in this country."[10]

Stowe, it would turn out later, was not prepared to maintain as her own opinion the conviction that the condition of the worker in Great Britain was almost as bad as that of the slave. In a preface she wrote for a British edition of *Uncle Tom's Cabin*, the only edition which paid her a royalty and thus was not pirated, Stowe attempted to lessen the damage she had done to her cause by having St. Clare criticize Great Britain so severely. "It must be borne in mind that these ideas [those critical of the British treatment of working people]," she said,

occur in the dramatic part of the book and are placed in the mouth of an honourable and highminded slaveholder. It was impossible to give a dra-matic representation of such a character without the introduction of this parallel. Every Southern print, every Southern politician, makes a stereotyped apology for slavery, that the slave is better off than the labouring class of any other part of the world, with the exception, perhaps, of the Free States of America.

These apologists for slavery, she said, especially singled out British mis-treatment of laborers because England's abolition of slavery in the West Indies "would otherwise be a weight too intolerable to be borne." She acknowledged that she had drawn her own ideas of the British poor from the novels of Dickens, Kingsley, and Charlotte Elizabeth. She argued that efforts to improve the lot of the poor in England were "inextricably" linked to "the interests of freedom in America."[11]

These comments of Stowe came too late for British reviewers to take account of them in reviewing *Uncle Tom's Cabin*. Thus they were obliged to make what they might of the opinions of Augustine St. Clare. Though some acknowledged that there might be some truth in his criticisms, most reviewers strongly objected to them. The Earl of Carlisle liked everything about the book except St. Clare's criticism of the status of British laborers. He thought these views showed "a singular want of knowledge" of actual conditions. The harm done in Great Britain itself would be slight, he said, because people there knew the charges to be untrue. He could only regret, however, that a weapon had been handed to slavery's defenders in America. "The proprietors of slaves should not be encouraged to lay the unction to their souls," he said, "that the com-mon run of mechanics and labourers of England are on a level of degra-dation with slaves in a rice-swamp in Carolina."[12]

The reviewer in the *North British Review* agreed with St. Clare that the condition of working people in Great Britain was bad, but he was convinced it was their own fault. If one could only teach them "to lay by when they have good wages, not to marry improvidently, not to bring up their children in ignorance, not to join trade-unions, (a horrible slavery, but self-imposed)," and not to do other things, their "condition" would "indefinitely improve." There was no barrier to the success of a willing worker in Great Britain. A man of the "lowest grade" could "attain any position, not hereditary." Another reviewer argued that, contrary to the opinion expressed by St. Clare in the novel, many British workmen were not required to work unreasonably long hours. The Lancashire cotton spinners were, for example, "limited to only $68\frac{1}{2}$ hours per week."[13]

The criticisms of British treatment of laborers in *Uncle Tom's Cabin* presented no problem for N. W. Senior. He brushed off St. Clare's strictures as "some socialist nonsense about capitalists starving their workmen to death." Other reviewers were less confident that St. Clare's views on this subject were wholly false. From Virginia, where he was visiting at the time, William Makepeace Thackeray wrote to a friend in England that "the sum of unhappiness is as great among our wretched poor as it can be here. . . . Perhaps one of the good effects of *Uncle Tom's Cabin*," he said, might be that it would "pique black & white manowners into generosity & I dare say better the labourer's condition in Dorsetshire as in Virginia." Some of the British reviewers agreed with Thackeray that the novel might lead to a closer examination of the conditions of British laborers with a view toward improvement.[14]

It may have been partly because of his critical views of the British labor system that Augustine St. Clare was often regarded unfavorably for other reasons by the British reviewers. Louisa S. McCord, in the *Southern Quarterly Review*, was on the wrong track when she expressed her amazement as a southerner that anyone in England could imagine St. Clare as a cultivated gentleman. The reviewers in Great Britain sometimes denied him any such status. The reviewer in the *Dublin University Magazine* admired, for example, the ability of Stowe to create black characters—"Oh! what niggers she does sketch!" On the other hand, he did not care for St. Clare. He is "intended to be a polished, easy gentleman; but gentleman he is not, at least by the standard of the English. His ease is vulgarity—his nonchalance, effrontery—and his general demeanour too full of swagger." The reviewer in *Blackwood's Edin-*

burgh Magazine was dismayed to find St. Clare "sitting on the floor, and laying his head back on Miss Ophelia's lap—who lays her 'hand on his forehead'—he saying to her, "Don't *take on* so awfully serious!'" This reviewer was also puzzled that Stowe could conceive of St. Clare as a hero when it is obvious that he is a *"sceptic* on religious subjects." The reviewer concluded that an intelligent man living in the southern regions of the United States and witnessing the cruelty and hypocrisy of his society could hardly manage to be a Christian. Perhaps Stowe had meant "to intimate that . . . [religious skepticism] is a dark and grievous characteristic of the whole class which he represents."[15]

As in the North in the United States, the emphasis among the reviewers of *Uncle Tom's Cabin* in Great Britain was on its antislavery theme rather than on its literary merit. Charles Kingsley had a great admiration both for Stowe and for the novel. There may have been some caution, however, in his letter to her. He put the most extravagant admiration for the novel in the mouth of his mother, rather than in his own. His mother had lived in the West Indies, he told Stowe, and had experienced slavery there. She had "read your book with delighted tears. What struck her was the way in which you had . . . dived down into the depths of the negro heart, & brought out his common humanity without losing hold for a moment of his race-peculiarities." Kingsley did not identify these "race-peculiarities."[16]

British reviewers sometimes mentioned the literary defects of *Uncle Tom's Cabin.* They objected to the emotional tone of the narrator and especially to Stowe's direct addresses to the reader in which she lectured passionately on the evils of slavery. In France, George Sand would mention these defects of the novel, but she thought that they should not be allowed to obscure its virtues. "Mrs. Stowe is all instinct," wrote Sand, and for that

very reason . . . she appears to some not to have talent. Has she not talent? What is talent? Nothing, doubtless, compared to genius; but has she genius? I cannot say that she has talent as one understands it in the world of letters, but she has genius, as humanity feels the need of genius,—the genius of goodness, not of the man of letters, but of the saint. Yes,—a saint! Thrice holy the soul which thus loves, blesses, and consoles the martyrs. Pure, penetrating, and profound the spirit which thus fathoms the recesses of the human soul. Noble, generous, and great the heart which embraces in her pity, in her love, an entire race, trodden down in blood under the whips of ruffians and the maledictions of the impious.[17]

Gustave Flaubert was less willing to make allowances for *Uncle Tom's Cabin*. Though he liked some of the characterizations and found some *"jolies choses"* and certain *"qualités de sentiment"* in the novel, he generally disapproved of it. "I am going to read *Uncle Tom* in English," he wrote to a friend; "I have, I admit, a prejudice against it even before I start. Literary merit has not given this book the success it has enjoyed." Reading it confirmed his disapproval. It

is done from a moral and religious point of view; it should be done from a *human* point of view. I don't find it necessary, in order to sympathize with a slave who is being tortured, to have that slave be a brave man, a good husband and father, a singer of hymns, and a reader of the Bible. I don't insist that he must pardon his tormenters or that he should be sublime and exceptional. When there are no longer slaves in America, this novel will have no more value than all those histories which represent Mohammedans as monsters. One thing only has made this book so successful—it is *timely*. Truth for truth's sake and the eternal beauty of pure art do not arouse the masses to the same degree.

He was annoyed by the intrusion of Stowe's opinions in the novel. "Does one have to moralize on slavery?" he asked. "To show its existence is enough."[18]

In England too, there were people well known in literature who disliked *Uncle Tom's Cabin*. It is not surprising that Thomas Carlyle would not care for it. For one thing, slavery was in his view the inevitable and right condition for blacks because of their supposed racial defects of intelligence and will. Carlyle wrote to Emerson in 1853 that true enlightenment would come to the world only when "the strenuous effort and most solemn heart-purpose of every good citizen in every country of the world" would work to that end. In the meantime, mankind was suffering "this malodorous melancholy 'Uncle Tommery'." To his sister Jean, Carlyle wrote about the same time, "*Uncle Tom's Cabin* is the mania of *this* season; what will that of the *next* be? . . . [T]o me for one, it seemed a pretty perfect sample of Yankee-Governess Romance, & I fairly could not and would not read beyond the first 100 pages of it."[19]

Like Flaubert, Matthew Arnold found the religion of Stowe offensive. He also thought that the picture of her as reproduced in the public prints an indication of her limitations. In a letter to Arthur Hugh Clough in 1853, he wrote, "The woman Stowe by her picture must be a Gorgon. I can quite believe all you tell me of her—a Strong Dissenter—religious middleclass person—she will never go far, I think." What Clough said about Stowe to Arnold is unknown, but this reply of Arnold would suggest that it was unfavorable. At the time, Clough was visiting in the United States and apparently after writing to Arnold he met Stowe at a dinner given by the Longfellows in Cambridge and was favorably impressed by her. "She is small and quiet, unobtrusive, but quick and ready-witted enough. . . . I liked her very well," he wrote. He also thought that her portrait had been misleading. "She has none of the stiffness of the picture I have seen of her," he said. Three years later, Clough would write a mildly favorable critical comment about Stowe's novel *Dred* in a letter to James Russell Lowell. He thought it "very good in its strong satire against the religious." He also liked the portraits of slaves and slavery—which after the fashion of the time he called "its nigger parts." He disliked "the sentimental chapters" and thought that "the whole thing perhaps has been rather done in a hurry."[20]

Many of the objections to *Uncle Tom's Cabin* among the British reviewers reflected a disbelief in the extreme goodness of Uncle Tom. The reviewer in the *London Times* was hostile to the novel generally, but his chief complaint was that he could not accept Uncle Tom. Adam before the fall "could not possibly have been more thoroughly without flaw," the reviewer said. Tom is

the only well-authenticated instance we know, in modern times, of that laudable principle, in virtue of which a man presents his left cheek to be smitten after his first has been slapped. The more you "larrup" Uncle Tom the more he blesses you; the greater his bodily agony the more intense his spiritual delight. The more he ought to complain, the more he doesn't; the less he has cause for taking a pleasant view of life and human dealings, the less he finds reason to repine; and his particular sentiments are all to match.[21]

Some of the hostile critics had so much fun in deriding the improbable virtues of Uncle Tom that the reader can hardly help wondering whether they do not distort the meaning of his goodness. What seems to have amazed some of them was not so much whether any person could be as noble as Uncle Tom as whether any black could be noble at all. That slavery itself was an evil institution they were generally willing to concede. On the other hand, they seemed to think its evils operated much more lightly upon blacks than they would upon whites because of the supposed racial traits of the blacks. One of the persons who sympathized with slaveowners, if not exactly with slavery, was William Makepeace Thackeray. Visiting in the United States at the time of the great popularity of *Uncle Tom's Cabin*, Thackeray wrote a letter from Washington to a friend in England and expressed his low opinion of the blacks, based upon what he had seen of them in the South:

I feel as if my travels had only just begun—There was scarce any sensation of novelty until now when the slaves came on the scene; and straightway the country assumes an aspect of the queerest interest; I don't know whether it is terror, pity or laughter that is predominant. They are not my men & brethren, these strange people with retreating foreheads, with great obtruding lips & jaws; with capacities for thought, pleasure, endurance quite different to mine. They are not suffering as you are impassioning yourself for their wrongs as you read Mrs. Stowe . . . ; they are grinning & joking in the sun; roaring with laughter as they stand about the street in squads; very civil, kind & gentle, even winning in their manner when you accost them at gentleman's houses, where they do all service. But they don't seem to me to be the same as white men, more than asses are the same animals as horses; difference of colour, habits, conformations of brains, that we must acknowledge it, & can't by any rhetorical phrase get it over; Sam is not my man & my brother . . . ; the very aspect of his face is grotesque & inferior. I can't help seeing & owning this; at the same time of course denying any white man's right to hold his fellow-creature in bondage & make goods & chattels of him & his issue; but where the two races meet this weaker one must knock under; if it is to improve it must be on its own soil, away from the domineering whites; & who knows whether out of Liberia there mayn't go forth civilisers & improvers of the black race, in which case the sufferings of a small portion of their brethren during a few centuries under European taskmasters, on this continent, will have worked for the ultimate good of the native community.

In 1854, there appeared a note in the *Westminster Review* which told a story going the rounds in London. Thackeray was said to have explained why his own novel, *Henry Esmond*, had not been as popular as *Uncle Tom's Cabin*. "I forgot," he was reported as saying, "to put a nigger in my novel."[22]

Charles Dickens was more critical of slavery than was Thackeray, but there was in him the same ambivalence about the inherent fitness of blacks for freedom, especially when they were a minority in a predominantly white society. Slavery is wrong, he said, but he seemed also to think that because of the racial defects of the blacks, it was not as wrong as it was usually made out to be. He was willing to give some of the blame to slavery itself for having influenced the character of the blacks for the worse. On the other hand, he clearly thought that the difficulties of blacks in the United States came partly through their own inherent weaknesses. After the publication of *Uncle Tom's Cabin* in England, Dickens wrote a letter of congratulation to Stowe. The letter itself has not survived, and our knowledge of it is limited to its publication in abridged form after the death of Dickens, in Stowe's new preface to the 1879 edition of *Uncle Tom's Cabin*. Unfortunately, in this rendition of the letter there is an omission just at the point at which Dickens might well have made a significant comment with regard to his own opinion of the inherent traits of blacks. Dickens praised the novel. He said he had read it "with deepest interest and sympathy" and had the highest regard for "the generous feelings which inspired it, and the admirable power with which it is executed." Then he expressed an important reservation:

If I might suggest a fault in what has so charmed me, it would be that you go too far and seek to prove too much. The wrongs and atrocities of slavery are, God knows! case enough. . . . I doubt there being any warrant for making out the African race to be a great race, or for supposing the future destinies of the world to lie in that direction; and I think this extreme championship likely to repel some useful sympathy and support.[23]

Dickens was probably referring to the sections of *Uncle Tom's Cabin* which contain Stowe's vision of a future black civilization of splendor and humanity in Africa. In addition to this letter, there is further evidence of Dickens's opinion of the novel in a review he composed jointly with his associate, Henry Morley, for publication in the magazine they edited, *Household Words*. Unfortunately, it is not possible to distinguish which sections of the review were written by Dickens. The two men praised the novel as an "admirable book with all its faults (and it is not free from the fault of over-strained conclusions and violent extremes)." They said it was "a noble work; full of high power, lofty humanity; the gentlest, sweetest, and yet boldest, writings. The authoress, Harriet Beecher Stowe, is an honour to the time which has produced her, and will take her place among the best writers of fiction." On the other hand, the two reviewers were convinced that American slavery was not as bad as she had portrayed it. For a really cruel system of slavery, they argued, she would have had to go to South America. There savage dogs were trained to pursue fleeing slaves, holding them if they did not resist and killing them if they did. The reviewers acknowledged that families were separated under slavery in the United States, but they thought this was not the injustice that Englishmen might commonly suppose. *Uncle Tom's Cabin* was not, therefore, an accurate portrait of American black slaves. "Uncle Tom, Aunt Chloe, and their friends are," said the reviewers, "perhaps rare specimens of negro characters." The concern these characters felt over separation from members of their families was, for example, quite unrepresentative of the concern of slaves generally. It was true that blacks had "been depressed so far toward the state of simple beasts of burden, that they have acquired the hearts and brains of horses and oxen." The reviewers thus did give slavery some of the blame for having dulled family feeling among the blacks, but they also seemed to believe that it was the innate traits of the blacks which helped to account for their faults. Thousands of blacks, they said, "are content to be well fed and housed, occasionally patted on the head or played with, and, when their master finds it needful to reduce his stock, part with a mere transitory brutish pang from a contented wife in Maryland, perhaps, to lie down with a new wife in a new stall in Tennessee." As a proof of the contentment of blacks under slavery, Dickens and Morley cited the rarity of runaways. Out of three millions of slaves in 1850, they said, only a thousand had attempted to escape. Blacks for the most part, the two men argued, "look up to the white man who rules them with the same affection that a dog feels for the master to whose hand it has become accustomed."[24]

Without indicating what made them think so, Dickens and Morley said that the slaveholders in the United States would be glad to divest themselves of their slaves if only there were some convenient way of doing so. "There is spread widely in America a strong desire to do what is right," they said, "and we believe that a large majority of the proprietors in the slave states" would free their slaves if they could "see their way clearly to the employment of free labour" and could also make "due provision for the future life of the emancipated slaves." People in the United States distressed over the cruelties of slavery should, the reviewers believed, concentrate their attention not on abolishing the institution but on mitigating its abuses. Why not have a campaign, they suggested, against the whipping of slaves? "[T]hough there *may* be little of lashing and wailing in the slave system, as it is commonly administered in North America," they said, "yet men are degraded by being set to work by a coarse action on their fears." Happily, they said, the submissive racial traits of the blacks were such that physical punishment was not necessary to make them work. "The negro has what the phrenologists would call love of approbation very strongly marked," they explained. "Set him to work for the hope of distinction, instead of the fear of blows." In addition, the slaveholders should be encouraged to educate their slaves. "[E]ducate the negroes on plantations," the reviewers urged; "make them intelligent men and women, let them imbibe in their full freedom the doctrines of Christianity."[25]

Dickens and Morley did not believe that antislavery was a cause of the first magnitude, because slavery was an inefficient labor system which was doomed to failure. It could not compete with free labor. In addition, they doubted that any system of labor would make the blacks good workmen. If the blacks were freed in the United States, they prophesied, a new and serious problem would arise. The chief threat to slavery was not the abolitionists but the swelling tide of thousands of Irishmen coming into the United States. "Negro labor will become every year less in demand as the number of Irish and other emigrants increase in America," they said. "The time is not far distant when the demand for negroes will be confined wholly to those districts in which the climate appears to be unsuited for field labour by whites." As this change took place, the colonization of blacks in Africa would become more and more an attractive idea to white Americans. There was no doubt that the blacks would be returned to Africa. The only question was whether they would go of their own free will or whether they would be forced to go. If the white people of the United States were sensible, the blacks when they returned to Africa would be "educated into love of freedom." They would "pass over to Liberia, and form a nation . . . whereof Americans might boast forever." When the modern reader gets to this part of the review, he may recognize that the antislavery theme of *Uncle Tom's Cabin* has been neatly bypassed. Dickens and Morley seemed to be saying that though Stowe had a great humanitarian purpose in writing the novel, she could have spared herself the trouble. Slavery would soon disappear, they were convinced, whether it was attacked or not.[26]

Lord Denman, who had formerly been the Lord Chief Justice of England, found Dickens's and Morley's review of *Uncle Tom's Cabin* offensive. At the time, Denman was an old man and ill, in fact very near the end of his life. One point which annoyed him in the review was the idea that *Uncle Tom's Cabin* was guilty of "over-strained conclusions and violent extremes." He also thought that the reviewers had an inadequate appreciation of Stowe's powers as a writer. He himself was convinced that the novel exhibited "a graphic skill and pathetic power" and that in these qualities Stowe "far surpassed all [other?] living writers," including, presumably, Dickens himself. Denman also emo-

tionally charged that Dickens had "taken pains to discourage the efforts
. . . to put down slavery and the Slave Trade, thus having done his best
to replunge the world into barbarism." Dickens did not continue the
debate, perhaps out of respect for the age and the physical feebleness
of his opponent. When Lord Denman died his daughter wrote to Dickens
apologizing for the attack her father had made upon him. She excused
her father on the basis of his unsettled mind in the weeks before his
death.[27]

Dickens replied to the letter of Lord Denman's daughter and explained his ideas on slavery in further detail. He said he had written
that part of the review which contained the greatest praise of *Uncle
Tom's Cabin*, but he was willing to be held responsible for the less
favorable opinions in it. He thought it would have been a mistake for
him to attack the slaveholders in the review. "I have been in America,
and know the Americans very well," he wrote. "American slave owners
are an extremely proud and obstinate race—I suppose the most obstinate
race on the face of the Earth." If he had written "a fiery declamation"
against slavery, it would have been "wafted by the Anti-Slavery Societies
. . . all over the civilised world." He had decided that the slaveholders
should be given some respite:

> The way to save . . . [the slave] is to step in with persuasion and argu-
> ment and endeavour to reason with the holders and show them that it is
> best, even for themselves, to consider their duty of abolishing the system.
> I can imagine nothing more hopeless than the idea, while they are smarting
> under attack, of bullying or shaming them. You might as well fire pistols
> at the Alps.

Dickens here was making a point different from that of his and Morley's
review. The chief idea in the review had been to persuade American
slaveholders to reform the worst evils of slavery. They had said nothing
about abolishing it.[28]

Dickens also suggested in his letter to Denman's daughter a *real-
politik* motive for his failure to attack slavery. "I apprehend there will
soon be a war in Europe," he said. Doubting that the British could depend upon their European allies, he concluded that it was not diplomatic
to annoy the Americans. "The only natural alliance for England . . . is
with America," he said. "If the slavery issue should then be full of green
wounds as to hold America aloof, I think I plainly see that the great
man of our people will say, 'we have thrown this great and powerful

friend away for the sake of the Blacks'—and that the Blacks will for a long time afterwards have a very small share of popular sympathy."[29]

To other people, Dickens expressed his reservations about Stowe and about *Uncle Tom's Cabin*. In a letter to the Duke of Devonshire, he confessed that he found Uncle Tom to be "too celestial." Sara Jane Clark, a young American who visited Dickens in England, reported him as saying in a published interview that Uncle Tom was "an impossible piece of ebony perfection." He added, " 'Mrs. Stowe hardly gives the Anglo-Saxons fair play. I liked what I saw of the colored people in the States. I found them singularly polite and amiable, and in some instances decidedly clever: but then,' he added with a comical arching of his eyebrows, 'I have no prejudice against White people.' " Also in one of his letters he accused Stowe of plagiarism:

She . . . is a leetle unscrupulous in the appropriatin' way. I seem to see a writer with whom I am very intimate [Dickens himself?] (and whom nobody can possibly admire more than myself) peeping very often through the thinness of the paper. Further I descry the ghost of Mary Barton and the very palpable mirage of a scene in The Children of the Mist.[30]

Though many reviewers in Great Britain found faults, especially literary faults, in *Uncle Tom's Cabin*, they were generally willing to acknowledge that it also had merit. They were even more in agreement that it was by far the most potent weapon against slavery which had yet been devised. On this point they were joined by many of the eminent people of Great Britain, and especially by members of the aristocracy, who did not necessarily write reviews. The combination of the great popular success of the novel and its endorsement by distinguished men and women enhanced its antislavery power. As N. W. Senior frankly said, it is probable that the enthusiasm for the book in Great Britain was partly caused by the fact that it was an effective and detailed portrait of the ugly side of America. People might have thought that it seriously modified or even canceled the claims of the United States to be a civilized nation. The tone of the support would suggest, however, that national pride in Great Britain was a relatively minor reason for the success of *Uncle Tom's Cabin* there.

From all indications, Stowe herself had little idea of just how widespread and fervent the foreign—and especially the British—acclaim would be. One of the first signs of the groundswell of opinion was a mammoth petition formulated as an antislavery document by British women. A group of women, including the Duchess of Sutherland, the Duchess of Bedford, the Duchess of Argyll, the Countess of Shaftesbury, the Lord Mayor's lady, Viscountess Palmerston, Mrs. Milman, Mrs. Tennyson, Mrs. Dickens, and many other prominent women convened a meeting at Stafford House, the London home of the Duke and Duchess of Sutherland, and drew up the petition. It was entitled "An Affectionate and Christian Address of Many Thousands of Women of Great Britain and Ireland to Their Sisters, the Women of the United States of America":

[W]e cannot be silent on those laws of your country, which, in direct contravention of God's own law . . . deny in effect to the slave sanctity of marriage, with all its joys, rights, and obligations; which separate, at the will of the master, the wife from the husband, and the children from the parents. Nor can we be silent on that awful system which, either by statute or by custom, interdicts to any race of men, or any portion of the human family, education in the truths of the Gospel and the ordinances of Christianity. . . . We appeal to you, then, as sisters, as wives, and as mothers, to raise your voices to your fellow-citizens, and your prayers to God, for the removal of this affliction and disgrace from the Christian world.

The writers of the petition added a comment which served to improve its tone. They maintained that they did not "say these things in a spirit of self-complacency, as though our nation were free from the guilt which it perceives in others." Women all over Great Britain were asked to sign the petition. In all there were twenty-six massive folio volumes bound in black leather containing more than 500,000 signatures. The committee decided that Stowe was the most appropriate person to whom the petition could be presented.[31]

From the first there was great interest in Great Britain and in other countries concerning the character and background of Stowe. Eliza Lee Cabot Follen, an American who was in England at the time, wrote a letter of inquiry to Stowe asking for some personal information about the author of *Uncle Tom's Cabin*. Stowe, who had admired Follen's children's books, replied, "So you want to know something about what sort of woman I am! Well, if this is any object, you shall have statistics free of charge. To begin, then, I am a little bit of a woman,—somewhat more than forty, about as thin and dry as a pinch of snuff; never very much to look at in my best days, and looking like a used-up article now." Mrs. Follen showed the letter to George Eliot and she, in turn, wrote to two of her friends, "The whole letter is most fascinating and makes one love her." Later Eliot would become one of Stowe's friends and the two would correspond with one another over a period of years.[32]

The Stowe party sailed from Boston in March, 1853. When the ship docked in Liverpool, a young man who was the brother-in-law of Matthew Arnold came out in a tender to invite the Stowes to stay at the home of his uncle, John Cropper, one of the wealthy and influential merchants of the city. As the carriage went along the streets, Stowe was astonished to see people nodding and bowing to her. The Croppers, who were prominent in the antislavery movement in England, had a breakfast for her the next morning with about forty important people as other guests. There was speechmaking. Since standards of the time would not permit a woman to make a speech, Calvin responded to the addresses of congratulation—as he was to do more and more on similar occasions in many parts of the nation. When the Stowes went to Glasgow, the Lord Provost called for them in his "luxurious equipage" to take them to see the cathedral. The Lord Provost of Edinburgh, when she went there, met the Stowe party at the railway station. Again there was a tour with crowds of people waving and smiling. From there she went to Aberdeen and then to Stratford and at last to London, where the Lord Mayor held a great dinner for her at the Mansion House. On this occasion, she sat opposite Charles Dickens. A week after arriving in London, Stowe was the honored guest at a party given by the Duchess of Sutherland at Stafford House, which faces St. James Park and is opposite Buckingham Palace. Before her tour was over she had met Lord John Russell, Viscount Palmerston, Lord Shaftesbury, the Duchess of Argyll, Dean Milman of St. Paul's, Archbishop Whately of Ireland—who told her he would have the fact that he had met her carved on his tomb—Thomas Babington Macaulay, Charles Kingsley, and Lady Byron. On a later trip she would meet the Brownings in Italy. The British government apparently decided that it would be impolitic for Queen Victoria to take any notice of Stowe's visit. In 1856, however, Queen Victoria and Prince Albert "accidentally" met the Stowes and exchanged greetings with them in a railway station where they had stopped on their way to Scotland.[33]

The American government maintained an official silence regarding the enthusiastic reception Stowe received abroad, but there are some indications of private opinions among members of the administration of President Franklin T. Pierce. In 1856, George Mifflin Dallas, formerly vice-president in the Polk administration and at the time the United States ambassador to Great Britain, complained in a private letter:

Is she a citizen of the United States? Judging from the pertinacity with which she applies her talents to undermine the Constitution and degrade the character of her country, she is far worthier of repudiation and banishment than ever was Arnold or Burr. Genius does not always choose patriotism for a companion.

Proslavery newspapers in the United States warned the leaders of Great Britain and of European countries generally that their adulation of *Uncle Tom's Cabin* might have consequences they had not counted on. In 1853, the *Richmond* [Va.] *Examiner* argued that the underlying reason for the immense popularity of *Uncle Tom's Cabin* abroad had nothing to do with the issue of American slavery. The more probable explanation, said an editorial in the paper, was

that the people of Europe see themselves and their rulers in the slaves and their masters, and give the book a political significance which feeds the flame that smoulders in the breasts of oppressed millions. The press is not free there and that fact gives spice to the allegory which they make of *Uncle Tom's Cabin.*

The proslavery *New York Herald* warned that the novel might set off revolutions in foreign countries. An editorial said that

Planters at the south may continue to employ slave labor, and happiness and contentment may still pervade the negro population, in spite of the insidious attempts of abolitionist incendiaries. But she [Stowe] will have contributed largely to accomplish a work of far greater importance. The aristocrats of England and Europe, who fancy they are dealing a desperate blow at our institutions by their patronage of Uncle Tom, will discover when it is too late that they themselves are the Legrees and Haleys upon whom retribution must fall.

The editors who wrote these opinions may not have been aware that *Uncle Tom's Cabin* was not regarded with approval by all the authorities in Europe. Catholic officials in Rome, for example, forbade the circulation of the novel in the papal states in 1853. One can only conjecture the reasons for their objections to it. It may have been that they were troubled by Augustine St. Clare's prophecies of revolution in many countries. Perhaps the Protestant emphasis of the novel was offensive to them. It seems unlikely that they would condemn the book merely because it was antislavery.[34]

Despite the enthusiastic reception of Stowe and *Uncle Tom's Cabin* in Great Britain, their admirers had little to say about how slavery was to be abolished in the United States. Lord Palmerston was quoted as having said to Stowe when he met her that *Uncle Tom's Cabin* was the first novel he had read in thirty years. He had been so impressed with her novel that he had read it through three times. He congratulated her on its "statesmanship." What precisely he meant by the word he did not, as far as is known, explain. He apparently meant that she had taken a fair and objective view of the slavery issue and not a narrowly partisan one. If this is what he meant, he would have found few people in the American South who agreed with him. His silence on how slavery was to be ended was followed by a similar silence on the part of almost everyone else in Great Britain.[35]

In a few instances, British reviewers of *Uncle Tom's Cabin* seemed to take equal pleasure in reacting with horror to the evils of slavery and with something like satisfaction to the fact that the American Constitution made the abolition of slavery virtually impossible. N. W. Senior showed this divided tendency clearly. He recited in detail the provisions of the Fugitive Slave Law under which he thought there was a real possibility that free citizens, black or white, might be forced into slavery. Senior pointed out that if a person was suspected of being a runaway, all the federal marshal would have to do would be to certify such a status as fact and turn him over to those people who claimed him. The victim would have no right to appeal to the courts. Senior criticized the law in these words:

America calls herself free, but such oppression is not to be found in Naples or in Russia. What security has any coloured person, what security indeed has any white person, under such a law as this?—under a law by which he can be declared a slave is his absence, or an *ex parte* application, and receive the first notice that his freedom has been questioned from those who handcuff him as a slave?

Senior contended that American slavery was not merely worse than other tyrannies of the modern world; it was worse than the slavery of ancient Greece or Rome. Then, at least, there was no question that a kindly master could free his slaves if he chose. In some of the southern states even this right was denied: "Republican America has elaborated a tyranny such as no democracy, no aristocracy, no monarchy, no despotism, ever perpetrated, or, so far as known, ever imagined."[36]

On the other hand, Senior did not believe that the combined agitation against slavery in the northern states and in other countries of the world would have the slightest effect in changing proslavery opinion in the southern states. No amendment abolishing slavery had any chance of passage because of the peculiarities of the American Constitution. The North might be able to prevent the admission of future slave states and it might be able to secure the repeal of the Fugitive Slave Law, but when Senior asked the rhetorical question of whether there was anything else the North could do, he answered with a single word, "Nothing." The North "may indulge the hope that the meliorating influence of knowledge and religion will induce the inhabitants of the Southern States themselves to amend gradually their atrocious slave codes." Senior himself saw almost no chance that this would happen, saying:

Public opinion in the Slave States instead of improving is deteriorating. There are no instruments by which it can be enlightened or shamed. The press, the pulpit, the legislative bodies are silenced. Any man "tainted," to use the language of a Southern Presbyterian clergyman, "with the bloodhound principles of abolition," or even suspected of being so tainted, is ruined, outraged, and exiled if he is allowed to live.[37]

On the one hand, Senior saw American slavery as one of the cruelest institutions which had ever existed; on the other hand, he did not believe there was any possibility in the foreseeable future of abolishing it or even of mitigating its worst evils. He did not foresee a Civil War, and yet it is possible to suspect that he felt some degree of satisfaction in the impossible dilemma facing the Americans. They could neither resign themselves to slavery, he seemed to say, nor abolish it.

Many of the British reviewers of *Uncle Tom's Cabin* made an effort to examine the issues of American slavery fairly and honestly. Though they sometimes brought with them biases of their own, they often strove to overcome them. They were rarely willing to admit that the British laborers were as badly off as Augustine St. Clare in the novel had said they were, but they often did concede the point that their condition constituted a national scandal. Probably the most important bias of the British reviewers was not even dimly visible to them. It was the same bias held by a great many northern reviewers in the United States. They could easily see that slavery usually led to great cruelties and injustices. What they failed to see was that the blacks could have been much like white people had they been reared in a different culture and environment. Because they believed the blacks to be inferior, the British and the American reviewers had a seriously limited view of the evils of slavery.

XIV

Uncle Tom's Cabin
As a Play
In the 1850s

PERHAPS AS MANY AS FIFTY people would eventually see *Uncle Tom's Cabin*, the play, for every one person who would read the novel. As a play it was successful almost from the start, and it would eventually become the greatest popular hit in American dramatic history. Even if she had thought of doing so, Stowe could not have secured a copyright for a stage adaptation. It was not until 1856 that a Congress passed a law enabling a novelist to retain control of or gain financial benefit from a stage production of his fictional work. If she had been able to secure a copyright, it is doubtful whether she would have permitted the novel to be adapted for the stage. She had not yet abandoned her earlier prejudices against the theater. There is another reason, however, that she might not have applied for a copyright, even if it had been legally possible for her to do so. It had been chancy to publish *Uncle Tom's Cabin* as a novel. It was even more of a risk to produce it as a play. Abolition was virtually unknown as a subject for drama. In addition, there had been few black characters in American plays aside from the malign stereotypes of the minstrel shows. A black hero would probably have struck almost any stage manager as an absurdity. If she had been able to secure a copyright and if she had been willing to allow companies to produce *Uncle Tom's Cabin*, Stowe might have become wealthy instead of comfortably well off. On the other hand, the play itself would have been less interesting as social history. The fact that in their adaptations of the novel for the stage writers were allowed to make whatever changes they liked is part of the significance of the history of *Uncle Tom's Cabin* as a play. If Stowe had been able to control the changes which were made, it is unlikely that she would have permitted many of them.[1]

Soon after the publication of *Uncle Tom's Cabin* the novel, Asa Hutchinson, a "temperance singer" who had a slight acquaintance with Stowe, asked her for permission to make a stage adaptation of the novel. By this time, Stowe had come a considerable distance in freeing herself from the narrow conventions of her religion. She had overcome her suspicion of painting and sculpture portraying the naked human body. No more did she fault Dickens for not giving his good characters a firmly orthodox Christian faith. She no longer wrote articles condemning dancing. She still drew the line, however, with regard to plays. What orthodox Protestants thought of the theater is indicated by the fact that not until 1862 was it legal to present a play of any kind in the city of Hartford.[2]

It is not surprising that Stowe shared the convictions of many pious people concerning the theater. She believed that drama itself was, if not in itself suspect, at least so likely to be abused that Christians should not give it any encouragement. She expressed these objections in a letter to Asa Hutchinson, refusing him permission to make a play of *Uncle Tom's Cabin*. She was willing to admit that his adaptation of the novel would, in all likelihood be harmless, but it would set a bad precedent:

If the barrier which now keeps young people of Christian families from theatrical entertainments is once broken down by the introduction of respectable and moral plays, they will then be open to all the temptations of those who [*sic*] are not such, as there will be, as the world now is, five bad plays to one good.

It was "impracticable," she said—as if anticipating an objection Hutchinson might make—to hope that the drama would be reformed. "[A]s a friend to you . . . ," she said, "[I] hope that you would not run the risk of so dangerous an experiment." Hutchinson accepted Stowe's refusal and abandoned his efforts. Other people, however, soon took advantage of the fact that she did not have a legal right to forbid dramatic adaptations.[3]

Eventually Stowe changed her mind and withdrew her objections to turning *Uncle Tom's Cabin* into a play. On at least three occasions she attended performances of it herself. In addition, she wrote an adaptation for a dramatic reading which was performed in 1855. Entitled *The Christian Slave*, this version was read by Mrs. Mary E. Webb, a black woman. While it received favorable notices, it did not become popular; in fact, it was apparently never performed by anyone else.[4]

Quite aside from the controversial nature of *Uncle Tom's Cabin* as an abolition play, the book presented other kinds of difficulties for the dramatist, since it had several subplots and a great many characters. If it was clearly to include the major events of the novel, the play would have to be much longer than plays usually were at that time. Even so, great sections of the novel would have to be omitted. In the novel, Augustine St. Clare and Ophelia discuss the institution of slavery at considerable length. Stowe too, as the omniscient narrator, had a good deal to say on that subject in the novel. For dramatic reasons, virtually all of these ideas would have to be omitted. Aside from the complexity of the novel, the audiences witnessing the play also had to be considered. What would people think of an antislavery play? What would they think of a black hero? The result of all these considerations was that stage adaptations of *Uncle Tom's Cabin* were substantially different from the novel. The most important difference was that adapters often softened and attenuated the antislavery of the novel.[5]

The most important version of *Uncle Tom's Cabin* as a play, though not the first one, was written by George L. Aiken. A young Bostonian of twenty-two years, he was an adapter of plays and in some instances an original playwright who worked in the company of George C. Howard, his cousin. Howard was then the manager of the Troy Museum (of Troy, New York). Theaters sometimes were called "museums" partly because they often contained exhibitions of one kind or another, but chiefly because the word *museum* was a euphemism intended to soften the opposition of the pious to the drama. He was on the lookout for a new play. He had performed the leading role in William Henry Smith's highly successful temperance play, *The Drunkard*, but now he was principally interested in finding a play which would have an important role for his four-year-old daughter, Cordelia. She had already been a success as little Dick in a dramatic version of Dickens's *Oliver Twist*. Cordelia would have an almost legendary success in the role of little Eva. Many years later when she was an old woman, Cordelia Howard

McDonald would remember that her father had first been interested in *Uncle Tom's Cabin* because it might be a means of popularizing antislavery opinion. Little is known directly of his opinions on slavery, however, and scarcely more about the opinions of Aiken. One of the plays Aiken had previously written was *Helos, the Helot, or the Revolt of Messene*, a work which dealt with the subject of slavery in ancient Sparta. It is obvious from a reading of his version of *Uncle Tom's Cabin* that he was antislavery. There are, it is true, evidences of caution in his adaptation. Some of the changes he made were probably the result of nothing more than the need to simplify the complexities of the novel's plot and to reduce the number of its scenes and characters. Other changes, however, suggest that he was consciously attempting to present to viewers of the play a different impression from that received by readers of the novel.[6]

In the American theater of the 1850s, most plays were very short, necessarily so because between the acts there were performances by singers, dancers, acrobats, and ventriloquists. In addition, after a play the audience was usually treated to a farcical skit. Certainly anyone adapting *Uncle Tom's Cabin* for the stage would be obliged to omit many scenes and characters. In his first version of the play, Aiken included only the events of the first two-thirds of the novel, concluding with the death of Eva. Later, Aiken wrote a sequel—a second play which carried the action of the novel from the death of Eva to that of Uncle Tom. Then he wrote the stage version of *Uncle Tom's Cabin* essentially as it would remain thereafter, a version which incorporated the events of the two earlier adaptations. It was a very long play, consisting of six acts and thirty scenes. Later it was made still longer, with seven acts and thirty-four scenes. All between-the-acts performances and the short comedy after the play were omitted, a change which represents a turning point in the tradition of the American theater. More and more plays were presented as the only feature of an evening's entertainment.[7]

It is a tribute to Aiken that he was able to retain much that was controversial in *Uncle Tom's Cabin* without sacrificing its popular appeal. George Harris was allowed to say that he would rather die than be taken back into slavery, and he was even permitted to fire upon and wound one of his pursuers, a man who was engaged in the lawful occupation of slave-catching. In addition, Aiken included the speech in which Tom tells St. Clare that even though he is well treated and better off materially as a slave, he would prefer to be a free man. Aiken also dealt with the touchy subject of northern white prejudice against blacks. He retained the scene in the novel in which Topsy says that Ophelia has a horror of touching her because she is black. In the play, as in the novel, Ophelia later acknowledges her fault and expresses contrition for it.[8]

Both in the novel and in the play the religion of Uncle Tom is a compound of genuine faith and superstition. Stowe had not hesitated to give Uncle Tom a religion which many people might have thought of as in part superstitious. On the other hand, it does not really suffer from the admixture. Because Aiken was obliged to present the religion of Uncle Tom more briefly than Stowe had done in the novel, it inevitably lost some of its depth and sincerity. Even so, Aiken did manage— given the brief amount of time he had to explore the issue in the play— to indicate the genuineness of Uncle Tom's religious faith. At one point, Stowe had Uncle Tom explain an important point to Augustine St. Clare: "We does for the Lord," says Tom, "when we does for his critters." In addition, he tells St. Clare that the Lord has "work" for him to do. Comments like these suggest a religion which has meaning in terms of one's actions. In including them, Aiken showed that he recognized Tom's faith as being something more than the clichés of piety.[9]

In at least one respect, Aiken was more willing than Stowe to deal directly with one of the issues of racial prejudice in *Uncle Tom's Cabin.* In the novel, Stowe put more limits on the relationship between Eva and Uncle Tom than that between Eva and Mammy. In the novel, Eva kisses Mammy but not Tom, while in the play, Aiken has Eva kiss Uncle Tom. One reason for this was that Aiken had omitted Mammy as a character in the play. It was necessary for Eva to kiss one of the black characters in order for Ophelia to object. In other respects, Aiken's handling of the intimate relationship between Eva and Uncle Tom may be more conventional than that of Stowe in terms of the etiquette of racial caste of the time. In the novel, Eva places a wreath of roses around Tom's neck and sits on his knee. When St. Clare and Ophelia come upon this scene, Tom is embarrassed and reacts with "a self-deprecating and apologetic air," but he says nothing. In the play, Aiken presents the same scene but he has Tom make his apology explicit. "I begs pardon, mas'r," Tom says to St. Clare, "but the young missis would do it. Look yer, I'm like the ox mentioned in the good book, dressed for the sacrifice." Though a change is clearly necessary in the play to make Tom's reluctance to have Eva sit on his lap appear obvious to an audience, the comparison of Tom to an ox might have been Aiken's concession to white prejudice.[10]

In the play, Topsy suffers even more than Tom in Aiken's adaptation of the novel. It is true that in the play, Topsy is not a completely comic character. To some extent, Aiken made a social critic of Topsy when he transferred to her the comments about the arrogance of mulattoes, voiced by Aunt Dinah in the novel. "I despise dem what sets up for fine ladies," Topsy complains in the play, "when dey ain't nothing but cream-colored negroes." In most respects, however, Topsy comes off badly in the play. Aiken must have recognized that she was the character in the novel who might most easily be transformed into the stereotype of blacks nearly always found in the popular theater, especially in the minstrel shows. He himself yielded to the impulse to make her little more than the butt of ridicule in the play. In the novel, Stowe had shown Topsy as having both comic and serious traits. Aiken touched only lightly on the serious traits and accentuated the crudely comic ones. In the novel, for example, Topsy undergoes a regeneration of character. After the death of Eva and Augustine St. Clare, Topsy is taken to Vermont by Ophelia to be brought up. When she is grown, she becomes a missionary.[11]

In the play the regeneration of Topsy was handled much more casually. She merely says, "I ain't half so wicked as I used to was." Since her declaration is not accompanied by any obvious change of character, the audience probably received it with skepticism and thought of it as comic. Nothing is said about her Christian faith, or about her becoming a missionary. Aiken added a humorous Yankee character, Gumption Cute, to his version of the play. Cute follows Ophelia to Vermont and becomes her suitor because he hopes to acquire her considerable property. Ophelia is already in love with another comic Yankee character who had been added by Aiken to the play—Deacon Perry. When she rejects Cute's offer of marriage, he refuses to leave until she changes her mind. At this point Topsy comes on stage and goes into action. The stage directions read as follows:

TOPSY *enters with a broom and beats* CUTE *around the stage.* OPHELIA *faints in the* DEACON'S *arms.*—CUTE *falls, and* TOPSY *butts him, kneeling over him.*—*Quick drop.*

This is the last of Topsy we see in the play.[12]

Though Topsy was a lesser character in Aiken's play than she was in Stowe's novel, the defect might not have been fully apparent even to those members of the audience who had read the novel—at least it probably was not apparent in the performances of *Uncle Tom's Cabin* given by the George C. Howard Company. The reason was that the part was taken by Mrs. George C. Howard, and she was a superb actress. Her rendition of Topsy was "wilder, and more tangle-haired, and moping and grinning than in the original," said one reviewer, "and with a touch —showing an artist's hand—of additional bitterness, *'cos she's a nigger!'* She seems, as the play goes on, the very Pariah of our society."[13]

Later, Stowe herself would be favorably impressed by Mrs. Howard's portrayal of Topsy. Stowe saw the Aiken version of the play when the George C. Howard troupe came to Boston. Francis H. Underwood, one of the founders of the *Atlantic Monthly*, told of taking her to see it:

I asked Mrs. Stowe to go with me to see the play. She had some natural reluctance, considering the position her father had taken against the theatre and considering the position of her husband as a preacher; but she also had some curiosity as a woman and as an author to see in flesh and blood the creations of her imagination. I think she told me she had never been in a theatre in her life. I procured the manager's box and we entered privately, she being well muffled. She sat in the shade of the curtains of our box, and watched the play attentively. I never saw such delight upon a human face as she displayed when she first comprehended the full power of Mrs. Howard's *Topsy*. She scarcely spoke during the evening; but her expression was eloquent—smiles and tears succeeding each other through the whole.

It must have been for her a thrilling experience to see her thought bodied upon the stage, at a time when any dramatic representation must have been to her so vivid. Drawn along by the threads of her own romance, and inexperienced in the deceptions of the theatre, she could not have been keenly sensible of the faults of the piece or the shortcomings of the actors.

I remember that in one scene *Topsy* came quite close to our box, with her speaking eyes full upon Mrs. Stowe's. Mrs. Stowe's face showed all her vivid and changing emotions, and the actress must surely have divined them. The glances when they met and crossed reminded me of the supreme look of Rachel when she repeated that indescribable *Helas!* There was but a slight wooden barrier between the novelist and the actress—but it was enough! I think it a matter of regret that they never met.

Calvin Stowe was a professor at Andover Seminary until 1864, and as long as he remained there it might have been inconvenient for Stowe to admit any liking for the theater. Elizabeth Stuart (Phelps) Ward, whose father was a professor at the Seminary, recalled in 1896 how censoriously the school regarded such matters. "A tradition that she [Stowe] visited the theatre in Boston when she felt like it sometimes passed solemnly from lip to lip," wrote Mrs. Ward, "but this is the most serious criticism upon her which I can remember."[14]

It is understandable that Aiken, for dramatic reasons, omitted nearly all the debates over slavery which occurred in the novel. On the other hand, their omission meant that much that was explained to the readers of the novel was not explained to the play's audience. The discussion of Shelby and his wife over the sale of Uncle Tom was important in the novel, since it demonstrated that even a kindly master might find it necessary to separate members of a slave family. In the play it was omitted. It is especially unfortunate that the audiences of the play were allowed to learn little about northern complicity in slavery, a major idea in the novel. Omitted was the conversation between Senator Bird and Mrs. Bird, the northerners who debated with each other the question of whether they were morally obligated to obey the law and return Eliza and her child to their lawful owners. More serious was the omission of the conversations on slavery which Augustine St. Clare and Ophelia had with one another. It was in these conversations that the evils of slavery were most clearly discussed and the matter of northern complicity most thoroughly explored. In addition, these two characters compared the southern and northern labor systems and agreed with one another that the evils of slavery were no proof that laborers in the North and in Great Britain did not suffer from gross abuses. In the play, Augustine St. Clare was scarcely a critic of slavery. Instead, he was portrayed almost solely as Eva's doting father who wore lavender trousers.[15]

The character of Ophelia suffered more of a loss than that of St. Clare in being transferred from the novel to the play. In the novel, she had been portrayed with faults, but she developed into a remarkably intelligent and compassionate person. More than any other character, she had conveyed indignation to the readers of the novel when she encountered the cruelties of slavery. In the play, on the other hand, she was a stock figure, a comically ridiculous New England old maid. Her standard line was "How shiftless!" At one point she said to another New England character after she had returned from the South to Vermont: "I liked the country [the South], but the people are so dreadful shiftless." Deacon Perry, the character to whom she made this remark, replied that this trait was the "result, I presume, of living in a warm climate." This was the kind of comment which Stowe had either avoided altogether or, if some character had said something which reflected on the South generally, she would usually have had some other character challenge it. There is another statement by Ophelia in the play which is not found in the novel. In the play, when she took Topsy back to Vermont with her, she introduced her to Deacon Perry as her "daughter," meaning, of course, her adopted daughter. Stowe would probably not have objected to Ophelia's doing this if the purpose had been to illustrate the change in her character. In the play, however, it was merely a comic device. Deacon Perry's response was to express his horror, in an aside to the audience, that Ophelia might have been married to a "colored man" while she was in the South.[16]

Relatively unimportant scenes in the novel became paramount in the play. The scene in which Eliza crosses the Ohio River by jumping from ice floe to ice floe, holding little Harry in her arms, was described in two short paragraphs in the novel. In the play it was one of the most important scenes. There had been no dogs chasing Eliza across the ice in the novel, and Aiken himself did not add any. In time, dogs—sometimes great packs of them—were added to dramatic productions, first as harmless bloodhounds and later as English mastiffs or Great Danes. The dogs became an essential part of the play, probably causing stage managers endless anxiety. The actress portraying Eliza would frequently carry meat hidden in her clothing to encourage the dogs to chase her.[17]

Other than being knocked down by George Shelby, Simon Legree in the novel had not suffered any penalties for his crimes. Stowe might have thought that if he had received worse punishment, the reader might have shifted his attention from the evils of slavery to a satisfaction over the retribution given to an evil man. Aiken, on the other hand, followed the conventional formula of melodrama, having Legree murder St. Clare. When the officers come to arrest Legree, he flees and is shot to death.[18]

The death of Uncle Tom was considerably less melodramatic in the novel than it was in the play. In the play, he makes his last speech to George Shelby, as he does in the novel, forgiving Simon Legree and exultantly proclaiming, "Heaven has come!" What happens next, however, is startling. Eva—now an angel—appears high above the other characters on stage. "*Gorgeous clouds, tinted with sunlight*," say the stage directions. "EVA, *robed in white, is discovered on the back of a milk-white dove, with expanded wings, as if just soaring upwards. Her hands are extended in benediction over* ST. CLARE [also resurrected for the occasion], *and* UNCLE TOM, *who are kneeling and gazing up to her. Impressive music.—Slow curtain.*"[19]

Aiken's ending of the play with the death of Uncle Tom has important implications for the treatment of the antislavery theme. All the arguments of George Harris for colonization of the blacks in Africa are omitted. Solely from a dramatic point of view, the omission is effective. In addition, it saved the play from censure by those many abolitionists who were opposed to colonization. Yet it is unfortunate that the play ends with justice for the slaves being found in heaven rather than on earth. Whatever wrongs Uncle Tom had suffered in this world would seem to be more than redressed, since he was shown on his way to future glory. Stowe herself, in *The Christian Slave*—her own adaptation of the novel for a public reading—ended with the death of Uncle Tom.[20]

The "complete" *Uncle Tom's Cabin* was first performed in Troy, New York, on November 15, 1852. It was a great success, especially with those people who had previously shunned the theater. The play, said the reviewer in the *Troy Budget*, "has drawn a class of auditors . . . who heretofore have rarely witnessed dramatic performances. They have been amply repaid—and many who have heretofore opposed the stage, after seeing *Uncle Tom's Cabin*, have gone to their homes with better impressions of it." The *Troy Daily Times* said that "the most respectable" and "best people" were seen in the audience. While there is a tradition that the play ran for a hundred performances in Troy, then a city of 30,000 people, one scholar has counted the performances and has set the number at fifty-seven, but even so it was a tremendous run. No play had ever had so many performances in so short a time in so small a place.[21]

With these successful productions behind it, the George C. Howard troupe moved to New York City, where the play opened on July 18, 1853, at the National Theatre, which was near the notorious Five Points section of the city. This theater was known for the kinds of offensive plays respectable people had most deplored. Here, as in other theaters of New York, prostitutes were said to solicit customers in the balcony. On the lower floor a woman was forbidden admittance unless she was accompanied by a "gentleman." The manager recognized from the beginning that *Uncle Tom's Cabin* was different from the plays previously presented at the National and would require different rules for the audience. He extended the ban on "ladies unaccompanied by gentlemen"

—the euphemism for prostitutes—to the entire theater. Also, he introduced the then almost unknown feature of the matinée. Women and children could attend the theater during the day with much less risk of becoming involved in a disagreeable incident when passing through the low section of the city.[22]

Previously known as a gathering place for the sinful, the National Theatre now became "The Temple of the Moral Drama," a title bestowed without irony. People who ordinarily avoided theaters, especially the National, flocked in to see *Uncle Tom's Cabin*. Large groups of church people would often attend led by their pastors. Adolphus M. Hart, a newspaperman, commented on how the play was able to attract widely diverse groups to the theater:

There was an air of sanctity in the upper tiers [the more expensive seats], which betokened that the work had a powerful influence in awakening the religious feelings of certain classes of the people, whilst in the balconies and pit, there was another class intent on every scene in the drama that could gratify their morbid love of cruelty and make them gloat over pictures of human wretchedness and misery. [Occasionally, one might see in the boxes] some demure looking gentleman, who had never been at a theatre before . . . who drew out his white pocket handkerchief and applied it to his eyes, as the black apostle of liberty, Uncle Tom, was reading the Bible, or Little Cordelia Howard was suffering perhaps her hundredth martyrdom.

Though Hart believed the lower class members of the audience in the galleries were enjoying the cruelties practiced against the slaves in the play, he did go on to describe these people as "shouting and hallooing as Eliza was crossing the Ohio, or George Harris was shooting his pursuers." The reviewer for the *New York Atlas* made a more careful observation: "The gallery was filled with a heroic class of people, many of them in red woollen shirts, with countenances as hardy and rugged as the implements of industry employed by them in the pursuit of their vocations." He was puzzled by the silence of the audience at the dramatic moment when Eliza escaped from her pursuers and reached the northern bank of the Ohio River. When he turned to look at them, he was astonished to discover that the whole audience, including the rough men in the gallery, were in tears.[23]

Some of the newspaper reviewers sensed that something important for society was happening because of the play. The reviewer in the antislavery *New York Tribune* wrote:

No mob would have dared to disturb the Abolition party at the National Theatre. It was composed largely of the stuff which demagogues acting under oligarchs have used for the purpose of burning down halls, destroying printing presses, assaulting public speakers, intimidating, striking, killing. Now that is changed, at least in Chatham street [the location of the National Theatre].

The reviewer recalled a time, thirteen years before, when the Freeman's Hall in Philadelphia had been burned down by a mob composed of people like many of the men and boys who were now seeing *Uncle Tom's Cabin*. Now, the "'b'hoys' were on the side of the fugitive," said the reviewer. "The pro-slavery feeling had departed from among them. They did not wish to save the Union. They believed in the higher law." Thus, the play had helped to convert a new group in the North to abolition—that group of rough men and boys who before had had the most contempt for blacks and who were most likely to disrupt the meetings of the abolition societies.[24]

In addition to having a matinée, the manager of the National Theatre made another significant change during the run of *Uncle Tom's Cabin*. Blacks had nearly always been excluded from theaters in New York. Now the manager of the National Theatre decided to admit them, though on a segregated basis. He installed "a neat and comfortable parquette" near the pit for black patrons. This change in policy was the subject of a cartoon in *Yankee Notions*, a local publication. In the picture, a placard reading "This Bench is Taken" has been changed to read "This Wench is Taken," and has been attached to the back of the skirt of a black woman attending the play. Unaware of the placard and puzzled by the laughter which follows her as she walks down the aisle, she is saying to her escort that she cannot imagine what "de nasty white trash was laffin at." The review in the *National Anti-Slavery Standard* commended the National Theatre for admitting blacks but censured it for segregating them. Even though the blacks were segregated in the theater, the editorial added, at least they were placed in a section where they could plainly see and hear the play. In this respect, they were better off than they would have been had they attended churches in New York, where, if blacks were admitted at all, the ushers would show them to a pew "least favourable for sight and hearing."[25]

An unknown correspondent for Garrison's *Liberator* wrote an enthusiastic review, more enthusiastic in fact than Garrison's review of the novel. Garrison probably would have been pleased that the play omitted all references to colonization, since his chief objection to the novel was that it advocated colonization. The idea emphasized by the reviewer for the *Liberator* was that the play had a power to convert to antislavery classes of people who before had never shown any enthusiasm for the cause:

If the shrewdest abolitionist among us had prepared the drama with a view to make the strongest anti-slavery impression, he could scarcely have done the work better. O, it was a sight worth seeing those ragged, coatless men and boys in the pit (the very *material* of which mobs are made) cheering the strongest and sublimest antislavery sentiments! The whole audience was at times melted to tears, and I own that I was no exception. It was noticeable that the people, after witnessing the death of Uncle Tom, went out of the house as gravely and seriously as people retire from a religious meeting! I wish every abolitionist in the land could see the play as I saw it, and exult as I did that, when haughty pharisees will not testify against slavery, the very *stones* are crying out!

Some of the "pharisees" were, of course, northern clergymen. Of them, Theodore Parker declared in one of his sermons that since the theater had begun to preach antislavery there might be some hope that "humanity will get even to the churches."[26]

Henry James saw a performance of *Uncle Tom's Cabin* at the National Theatre when he was about ten years old. Even as a man of seventy, he remembered the event clearly. "I must have partaken thoroughly of the feast," he wrote in 1913, "to have left the various after-tastes so separate and so strong." Eliza, he recalled, had a "swelling bust encased in a neat cotton gown." He remembered her, "infant in arms, balanced for a leap from one [ice floe] to the other." The stage set had "the audible creak of carpentry about it" and retrospectively he could only wonder at "the simple faith of an age beguiled by arts so rude." And yet the play, at least "for one small spectator," was "a great initiation; he got his first glimpse of that possibility of a 'free play of mind' over a subject." He especially remembered the "tragi-comical Topsy, the slave-girl clad in a pinafore of sackcloth and destined to become for Anglo-Saxon millions the type of the absolute in the artless."[27]

One of the most virulent and lengthy of the anti-*Uncle Tom's Cabin* dramatic reviews was written for an earlier production of the play, also at the National Theatre, an inferior adaptation which appeared nearly a year before the George C. Howard version opened there. In this adaptation, Uncle Tom was not killed but was returned to Kentucky where he was freed by George Shelby. The first performance of this version was on August 23, 1852, but it was unsuccessful and closed on September 10. Even though this version made concessions to proslavery thought, James Gordon Bennett of the *New York Herald* severely condemned it, saying it was

an insult to the South. [It contained] the most extravagant exhibitions of the imaginary horrors of . . . slavery. The negro traders, with their long whips, cut and slash their poor slaves about the stage for mere pastime, and a gang of poor wretches, handcuffed to a chain which holds them all in marching order, two by two, are thrashed like cattle to quicken their pace.

Though he thought the play poorly done, Bennett chiefly criticized it because it was a threat to the peace of the nation:

The institution of Southern slavery is recognized and protected by the federal constitution, upon which this Union was established and which holds it together. But for the compromises on the slavery question, we have no constitution and no Union—and would, perhaps, have been at this day, in the condition of the South American republics, divided into several military despotisms, constantly warring with each other, and each within itself. The Fugitive Slave Law only carries out one of the plain provisions of the constitution. When a Southern slave escapes to us, we are in honor bound to return him to his master. And yet, here in this city—which owes its wealth, population, power, and prosperity to the Union and the constitution, and this same institution of slavery, to a greater degree than any other city in the Union—here we have nightly represented at a popular theatre, the most exaggerated enormities of Southern slavery, playing directly into the hands of the abolitionists and abolition kidnappers of slaves, and doing their work for them. What will our Southern friends think of our professions of respect for their delicate social institution of slavery, when they find that even our amusements are overdrawn caricatures exhibiting our hatred against it and against them? . . .

We would, from all these considerations, advise all concerned to drop the play of *Uncle Tom's Cabin* at once and forever. The thing is in bad taste—is not according to the good faith of the constitution, or consistent with either of the two Baltimore platforms; and is calculated, if persisted in, to become a firebrand of the most dangerous character to the peace of the whole country.[28]

It is hardly necessary to say that serious versions of *Uncle Tom's Cabin* were not performed in the South. Partly because relatively few southerners saw the play, there was only an occasional outburst against dramatic productions in the North found in southern newspapers and periodicals. Even if white southerners had found it easy to attend the play, they probably would not have done so. By the time dramatic versions were beginning to be produced, in fact, the white South had already generally decided that a dignified silence was the best response to *Uncle Tom's Cabin* in whatever form it might be presented. One critic in the South did recognize fairly early, however, that a dramatic version might be a more dangerous threat than the novel. It was "an abuse of the stage" to dramatize the novel, said an article in the *New Orleans Weekly Picayune*. A stage production was merely an attempt to give the novel

a more effective form . . . fixing it with all the arts of scenery, on the memory of thousands who do not read as a true picture of life and morals at the South; bringing up a new generation with the ineradicable idea that there is one-half of the territory of the United States, a people to whom the monstrous inhumanities and shameless corruptions described with so much deplorable art by this authoress, are familiar and welcome as their daily food. The success of the attempt must be a dreadful calamity, the course of innumerable horrors to both sections and both races; and even if it should not prove to be successful, the attempt itself is a great crime, meriting universal abhorrence.[29]

Some productions of *Uncle Tom's Cabin* as a play in New York were obviously designed to retain the drama and pathos of the novel but to soften greatly, or in some instances even to eradicate altogether, the antislavery theme. One of these was the version written by Henry J. Conroy. Since the adaptation was never printed, what can be learned of this version must be deduced from the advertisements, the reviewers, and the statements of rival producers. Conroy said he had tried to preserve the fidelity of the novel but had attenuated what he termed "the many crude points," and thus he found himself obliged to remove "the objectionable features which meet the eye of the reader while perusing the book." In this version, Uncle Tom does not die but is rescued by George Shelby from the clutches of Simon Legree and returns happily as a slave to the old plantation in Kentucky. Eva recovers from her illness. Charles Dudley Warner once wrote that Stowe herself had gone to see the Conroy version of the play when it came to Hartford. Bewildered by the many changes of the plot, she had to have them explained to her. She was also offended by the strong language of one of the characters who had been added by Conroy—a Mr. Penetrate Partyside—and left the theater in disgust.[30]

P. T. Barnum became interested in the Conroy version of the play and had it produced at his American Museum theater in New York. He saw the play, not for its antislavery appeal, but merely as a commercial opportunity. His advertisement frankly admitted that Conroy's version of the play had a thesis different from that of the novel:

It represents Southern Negro

SLAVERY AS IT IS

embracing all its abhorrent deformities, its cruelties, and barbarities.

It does "nothing extenuate nor set down aught in malice," while it does not foolishly and unjustly elevate the negro above the white man in intellect or morals.

It exhibits a true picture of negro life in the South, instead of absurdly representing the ignorant slave as possessed of all the polish of the drawing room, and the refinement of the educated whites.

It appeals to reason instead of the passions; and so far as truth is more powerful than error, will the impressions of the drama be more salutary than those of any piece based upon fanaticism without reason, and zeal without knowledge.

The advertisement concluded wth a reference to the "remarkably diverting and comical performances" in the play.[31]

Barnum also added a greater element of spectacle than that found in the National Theatre version. One of the scenes in his production had a panoramic view of the Mississippi River which was advertised as being "alone . . . worth the price of admission." There was a blue haze over the river and a steamboat in the distance in the moonlight. Puffs of smoke emerged from the stacks of the steamer and there was the sound of rotating wheels.[32]

The Conroy version of *Uncle Tom's Cabin* was a popular success, but the abolitionists disowned it. "The effect of the dramatist has evidently been to destroy the point and moral of the story of Uncle Tom, and to make a play to which no apologist for slavery could object," said the reviewer in the *New York Tribune*. "He has succeeded; and in doing so, has made a drama which has nothing to recommend it but its name." At the rival National Theatre, Aiken—or perhaps someone else—inserted a section designed to deride the Barnum production, a short dialogue between the characters Gumption Cute and Topsy:

Cute: I'm a man of genius. Did you ever hear of Barnum?
Topsy: Barnum! Barnum! Does he live out South?

Cute: No, he lives in New York. . . . Well, as I was saying, Barnum made
 his money by exhibiting a woolly horse; now wouldn't it be an all-
 fired speculation to show you as the woolly gal?

Topsy: You want to make a sight of me?

Cute: I'll give half the receipts, by chowder!

Topsy: Should I have to leave Miss Feely?

Cute: To be sure you would.

Topsy: Den you hab to get a woolly gal somewhere else, Mas'r Cute.
 Runs off.

Cute: There's another speculation gone to smash, by chowder![33]

It was the minstrel shows which most obviously exploited the anti-
Uncle Tom theme. The Conroy stage version could be seen, it is true,
as an implied defense of slavery, but the minstrel shows often made
the defense explicit. Christy and Wood's Minstrels began in 1853 by
devoting one act of their show to a burlesque of the Aiken version of
Uncle Tom's Cabin. They entitled this section of their show "Life among
the Happy." This was so successful that in the spring of 1854 the company developed a full-length "opera" on the subject. In this version,
both Augustine St. Clare and Simon Legree are omitted. Uncle Tom is
not sold away from his kindly master. In the first scene he has just returned from a revival camp meeting and he criticizes the dandified pretensions of "free Darkies" and expresses his love for "Old Kentuck." In
another scene George Harris serenades Eliza. In the last act, George and
Eliza are joined in a slave ceremony by "jumping the broom," the slave
equivalent of a wedding.[34]

The "happy" Uncle Tom content with slavery and faithful to "ole
massa" became a staple of the minstrel shows. Sam Sanford, one of
the minstrel show producers, later recalled how he developed a minstrel
version satirizing *Uncle Tom's Cabin*. When he was in Philadelphia in
1853, he recalled, "I did a piece called 'Rebuke to Uncle Tom' in which
I tried to depict slave life as I knew it, and as it actually existed at the
time. I took in $11,000 in nine weeks." One of the songs from this show
has survived:

> Oh, white folks, we'll have you to know
> Dis am not de version of Mrs. Stowe;
> Wid her de Darks am all unlucky
> But we am de boys from Old Kentucky.
>
> Den hand de Banjo down to play.
> We'll make it ring both night and day

> And we care not what de white folks say,
> Dey can't get us to run away.

One way in which minstrel shows attempted to answer the charge that slavery was cruel because it separated families was to ridicule the idea of love between man and woman or between parents and children among blacks. As the modern scholar Alexander Saxton has pointed out, the minstrel show ridiculed "the very notion of love, or any other human or humane emotion, among the blacks. . . . Indeed all that was needed to render a serious theme ludicrous in blackface minstrelsy was to permit its dehumanizing form to overbalance the content." Parodies of *Uncle Tom's Cabin* emphasized the idea that it was not cruel to separate black families because the blacks had nothing corresponding to true family feelings. These parodies were popular for many years. They continued to be produced in the North, for example, throughout the period of the Civil War.[35]

Even the best of the productions of *Uncle Tom's Cabin*, the Aiken version, could sometimes make degrading concessions to proslavery sentiment. John E. Owens, a theater manager in Baltimore, wrote to G. C. Howard:

Can the *Uncle Tom* you play be so adapted and softened in its style without losing much of its interest, as to be made not only acceptable but telling to a Baltimore audience? If it is susceptible of being so altered. . . , I would not hesitate, if you conclude to play here, to announce the piece as *The Great New York Uncle Tom*, and I feel confident it would create as favourable a sensation here as it has done elsewhere whenever properly put on the stage?[36]

The offer was accepted. What changes were made we know only in a general way. The actors playing George Harris and Simon Legree were instructed to "tone down" their roles and the actress portraying Marie St. Clare was told to make her "more sympathetic." The actress portraying Eliza was also asked to make changes in her interpretation of the role. In a rehearsal, a member of the Howard cast is said to have complained, "Isn't it all rather on the comedy side?" Owens frankly admitted that turning the play into a comedy had been his whole intention. "I've taken up all sorts of situations from old farces, and so on," he was quoted as saying, "anything to cover up the real drift of the play." Owens himself played the role of Uncle Tom and vulgarized the part into a blackface stereotype characteristic of minstrel shows. At one point in the play, Tom appears on the stage with the toes of his shoes polished but with mud on the heels and insteps. After the performance of the play was over, G. C. Howard is said to have asked Owens what the purpose of the partly polished shoes of Uncle Tom had been. Owens is reported as replying, "Howard, a Nigger never polishes more than the toes!" Cordelia Howard, the little girl who had made a great success of the role of Eva, is said to have heard her father tell this story. Her response was gently to ask her father to change the word "Nigger" to "colored gentleman," then considered to be the polite term. Though not explicitly proslavery, the changes in the Aiken performances in Baltimore amounted to depriving the play of virtually all of its antislavery thesis. The audiences in Baltimore were expected to laugh at a series of farcical situations and not to ponder the question of slavery at all.[37]

Another change made by the George C. Howard troupe turned out to have long-range importance. Aiken himself was probably not responsible for adding many years to the age of Uncle Tom as he was played on the stage. Uncle Tom in the novel, as we have seen, was a muscular, healthy, and fairly young man. Aunt Chloe calls him her "ole man," it is true, but the term seems to be simply an affectionate substitute for the word *husband* and probably was not meant to indicate his age. In one of the later chapters of the novel, after some years have passed, the narrator speaks of Uncle Tom as having "brawny arms," an unlikely description if he had been an old man. That he was not at first portrayed in the G. C. Howard version of the play as an old man is suggested by a review in the *New York Daily Times*, which described him as "a strong, black, labouring man." The reviewer said that when Uncle Tom appeared on the stage for the first time in Howard's adaptation of the play, the audience thought he would be a humorous character and was prepared to laugh. He had "the accent which, in the theatre, is associated always with the comic." There was a difficult moment when it looked as if it would be impossible for the audience to take him seriously. They could easily have thought of him, the reviewer said, as "a camp-meeting preacher" who would "overdo the matter, or would be so ignorant as to make his religious sentiments ridiculous." The actor playing the part, however, was able to overcome this handicap. The reviewer observed:

His very first words . . . showed that a good hand had the part. The accent, a broad and natural accent, but the voice deep and earnest—so earnest that the first laugh at his nigger words from the pit, died away. . . . "No," said he, "I can't run away. Let her [Eliza] go—it's her right! If I must be sold, le'b me be sold—Mass'r allers found me on the spot. I nebber hab broke my trust, and nebber will."[38]

G. Germon, the actor who played the part of Uncle Tom described in this review, was a white actor. All the black characters in the cast were, in fact, played by whites. As a white actor and as a leading man of the Howard troupe, Germon had at first objected to playing a "Jim Crow darkey." He thought it would be impossible to portray any black character on the stage as to have him taken seriously. "My very make-up as a Negro means burlesque," he is reported to have protested, "and Uncle Tom will make everybody laugh. I want to be a straight actor." George C. Howard was apparently obliged to exert all his powers of persuasion to get Germon to take the part. One of Howard's arguments was said to be that Uncle Tom was a new type of character on the stage. If he should catch the fancy of the public, Germon would be able to advertise himself as the original actor who had portrayed Uncle Tom. Whatever his reasons, Germon did take the part. It is surprising that with his early prejudices against portraying a black character seriously, he was nonetheless able to play Uncle Tom in an intelligent and sympathetic way.[39]

Germon played the part of Uncle Tom during the run of the play in Troy, New York. When the company moved to New York City, he played the role from July 18 to August 22, 1853. At that time, he left the G. C. Howard company and was replaced by J. Lingard, another white actor, who must have had a quite different conception of the part. No longer was Uncle Tom "a strong, black, labouring man." "The character of the meek, pious, and subdued old negro . . . was ably delineated," said the reviewer in the *New York Atlas*, "and Mr. Lingard was entitled to the respect and good will of all who witnessed the effort." Later in the review, Lingard's Uncle Tom was described as a "pathetic" man.[40]

The question of Uncle Tom's age, both in the novel and in the play, is a puzzling one. Though Stowe obviously made him a fairly young man, the reviewers of the novel were sometimes determined to ignore the evidence and describe him as an "old man." Part of the reason for this opinion may have been that at a time when people lived fewer years than now, the standards for being considered a young person were more arbitrary. In his review of the novel, A. M. Woodward described Uncle Tom as "an old man, not less than forty-five, and probably fifty years of age." Another reason might have been that readers found it difficult to associate Uncle Tom's qualities of meekness, patience, and calm fortitude with virtues a young man might be expected to have. In the play, there were even more compelling reasons for making Uncle Tom old, since in minstrel shows the only black characters with any dignity at all were portrayed as those "old folks at home" who remembered days long past on the plantation. Thus, it might have seemed wholly natural to make Uncle Tom an old man. In addition, had he been portrayed as a young man he might conceivably have been seen as a sexual threat—a threat, for example, to the absolute purity of little Eva. What is incontestable is that he appeared as an old man in almost all productions of the play from then on. There is a photograph of David Belasco in the role of Uncle Tom as he played it in San Francisco in 1873. Though Belasco was only twenty years old at the time, he is made up to be a bald, elderly man with a fringe of white hair at the base of his skull. This is how most people who saw the play were likely to remember the character. It is also the conception of him that many modern blacks have. "Mrs. Stowe's hero," says Alex Haley, "is a white-haired, pious, loyal slave-foreman."[41]

In the South, just as there were anti-Uncle Tom novels, there were also anti-Uncle Tom plays. None of the scripts of the plays has survived. What we know about these versions we can learn only from what reviewers said about them. In New Orleans, there were at least three anti-Uncle Tom plays performed in the 1850s. One of them was written by Joseph M. Field and was entitled *Uncle Tom's Cabin: or Life in the South as It Is.* The play was advertised as having been written by Harriet Screecher Blow. This was also a character in the play, although there are no direct indications of how she was portrayed. One scene from the play has survived because it was reproduced, probably verbatim, in a newspaper review. There is a "Canadian snow scene, where amid old pines bending under waves of snow and glittering with ice, the [slave] fugitives long to get home and sing the popular song: 'Carry me back to old Virginny, To Old Virginny's Shore.'" A "philanthropist" approaches the cold and miserable Uncle Tom:

Phi[lanthropist].—Well, Uncle Tom, you seem to be in trouble. What do
you want?
Uncle Tom.   —Donno, Massa.
Phi.   —Do you want a house?
Uncle Tom.   —No, Massa.
Phi.   —Do you want clothes?
Uncle Tom.   —No, Massa.
Phi.   —Well, what do you want?

(In the distance, the strains of "Old Folks at Home" are indistinctly heard, and Uncle Tom, listening with tears in his eyes, breaks out, saying—
  "Massa, *that's what I want*!"

"This point in the drama . . . ," said the reviewer, "brought tears to the eyes of about every one present, in the same manner as other points produced irresistible laughter." Though the scene was "quite melo-dramatic," said the reviewer, it was "also exceedingly correct." In the last act of the play Uncle Tom returns happily to a life of slavery in the South. The finale consists of "a gang of plantation negroes, dancing 'Juba' and singing 'Old Jawbone' as the curtain fell."[42]

Thomas D. Rice's *Southern "Uncle Tom's Cabin,"* first produced in New York, came to New Orleans in 1854. In the course of the play, Rice as Uncle Tom sang a song, "Wait for the Wagon," in which he told of his "strange adventure among the Northern States" as a runaway slave. Unable to find work, he had been obliged to go to jail so that he would have something to eat. In the song, he says:

> I travel'd round de country an' felt dat I was free,
> For I was cold and starvin' from de elbow to de knee,
> But Massa has forgib me, an' I know dat all am right
> Tho' if [to the audience] it gives you pleasure, I'll
>   run off eb'ry night.

This minstrel show was a great success in New Orleans. The *Daily Picayune* said that it was "the most popular piece ever produced" in the city. George Kunkel's Nightingale Ethiopian Opera Troupe began a tour of the South with another minstrel parody of the play. In an an-nouncement, the *Charleston* [S.C.] *Standard* predicted that "Aunt Harriet Beecher's *toe* will, we anticipate, be entirely dislocated." Parts of the South were too inflamed about *Uncle Tom's Cabin*, however, to permit the performances of even a burlesque version of it. The Charleston city council passed a resolution that no blacks should be allowed in the theater to see the show. The criticism in Savannah, Georgia, was even stronger, so much so that the troupe did not perform the play; in fact, the tour was abandoned altogether.[43]

Uncle Tom's Cabin as a play was almost as great a popular success in many foreign countries as it had been as a novel. In December of 1852, several months before the Aiken version came to the National Theatre in New York, there were six versions of the play being pre-sented in London. In some of these, the changes from the novel were drastic, more so than in the American productions. In one of the London productions, Tom is not the meek, Christian man of the novel but a dashing hero who performs acrobatic feats and daredevil horseback rides. At the end of the play, he escapes from the Legree plantation on a race horse. In one version, both Tom and Eva speak in Cockney accents. In another, Tom dies but his death has no religious meaning. Sometimes Tom is decidedly a subordinate character, the major roles being those of George and Eliza Harris. In one version, Simon Legree appears wearing a bearskin coat with a matching fur cap—in Louisiana. In the same play, St. Clare is unsympathetically portrayed. He is described in the cast of characters of the play as "Mr. Yahoo, a Young American Exquisite." In the same version, plantation owners readily admit among themselves that they are fathers of some of their slaves. Haley the slavetrader apparently thinks that Shelby may be the father of little Harry Harris, the slave child, and that the relationship may explain the reluctance of Shelby to sell him. "Taint none of your own, is he?" Haley frankly asks. Shelby denies being Harry's father, but he is not insulted nor seemingly even surprised by the question. He merely replies, "Why, no; not the boy."[44]

As a play, *Uncle Tom's Cabin* was almost as popular in France as it was in England. One periodical, *La Charivari*, published a cartoon showing Uncle Tom being almost pulled apart by two rival theater managers—one frantically hanging on to his arm, the other to his leg. The French took more liberties than the English in adapting events of the novel for the stage. In one version, Uncle Tom, Eliza Harris, Topsy, and Cassy escape from Simon Legree's plantation. The plantation is in Kentucky, not in Louisiana. The fugitives float down the Ohio River on a raft accompanied by George Harris in a canoe and pursued by Tom Loker, the slave-catcher, in a boat. In one of the last scenes, they are all shown approaching the "rapids" of the Ohio River. On the backdrop of the stage, there is a large picture of Niagara Falls, a suggestion that this is the direction in which the fugitives are heading. In a later scene farther down the river, raft, canoe, and boat are seen again, the implication being that they had all gone over Niagara Falls. The boat of Tom Loker, however, is empty and he apparently has drowned, but the others have all made the descent over the falls without mishap. There is another surprise in the play for anyone familiar with North American geography. The fleeing slaves, still on the raft and in the canoe, float farther down the Ohio River and finally arrive in Canada! A placard is placed on the stage announcing "*Canada—Terre Libre.*"[45]

Wherever it was performed, *Uncle Tom's Cabin* the play gave a different impression from that of the novel, even though in most of the productions it retained the antislavery theme. The strength of dramatic productions lay largely in the fact that they appealed to a portion of society which had hitherto been almost impervious to abolitionist arguments. People who were unlikely to read a book or even a newspaper, people who belonged, in fact, to the class which had been recruited for riots against abolitionists, now began to show a great shift in opinion. They no longer believed in slavery.

On the other hand, it is probable that many of the people who saw the play came away from it with a more ambivalent impression of blacks than had the readers of the novel. Slavery was an evil institution, a point the various productions of the play nearly always made quite clear, but it did not always necessarily follow that blacks were wholly fit for freedom. From the beginning, *Uncle Tom's Cabin* as a novel but even more as a play had a strangely dual character. Both were antislavery, and both—the play much more than the novel—perpetuated stereotypes of blacks which would cause trouble later when the blacks were emancipated. In the play, at least in the Aiken version, people were encouraged to think about blacks in a new and better way than they had in the past. Yet the blacks were portrayed in such a way as to suggest that they had far less inherent intelligence and ability than whites. A changed stereotype was being fashioned for the blacks which was all the more powerful because it was conceived in idealism. To blame Stowe for this development is beside the point, particularly since she had virtually no control over what was done in adapting the novel for the stage. On the other hand, it is important to recognize that *Uncle Tom's Cabin* as a play was largely responsible for major changes in the way blacks were perceived.

XV

Stowe and Antislavery

1853 - 1856

THE FAME OF UNCLE TOM'S CABIN, as both a novel and a play, obviously served to increase the fame of Stowe herself. Now that she was a celebrity, anything she said about slavery was certain to receive careful attention, friendly or unfriendly. She herself tended to discount the literary importance of the novel. Apparently the chief reason she did so was to persuade those readers prejudiced against fiction because of their religious training to make an exception in the instance of this particular novel. She wrote to a clergyman saying that she hoped Christians would not allow "conscientious scruples" against fiction to prevent them from reading it. The novel was, she explained, "fiction truer than fact." She distinguished between the fictional motive and a presumably more important motive. "*Uncle Tom's Cabin* had a purpose entirely transcending the artistic one," she wrote, "and accordingly encounters at the hands of the public demands not usually made on fictitious works." She did not say what these demands were, but it is logical to assume that she believed it was more important for a reader to espouse antislavery than to admire *Uncle Tom's Cabin* as a literary work.[1]

One effect of Stowe's taking this position was that her own role changed substantially. If abolition was the more important issue, then writing fiction would necessarily have to become the less important one.

Though her career as a novelist did not end, she was now faced with issues rather similar to those of other antislavery leaders. Thus for the next few years, on an almost day-to-day basis, she became involved in the slavery controversy, which became increasingly turbulent. The reformist novelist runs the risk of becoming just another dissident voice. He almost inevitably develops a second career in which the most important fact about him is not that he is a novelist but that he is a person with a cause, and he finds himself at a disadvantage, working much of the time outside the field in which he chiefly excels.

The most immediate problem Stowe encountered was how to respond to the passionate attacks of her opponents. At first, she reacted to these sensibly and calmly. In *Uncle Tom's Cabin*, she had made an attempt to portray slaveholders justly. Some of the characters in the novel, at least, were caught in a system which they themselves knew to be wrong and one which they would like to abolish. As she moved toward direct controversy with proslavery spokesmen, however, her methods gradually changed. Instead of attempting to convince the South that slavery was evil, she concentrated more and more on mobilizing opinion against it in the North and abroad. The change in her approach may have been inevitable as the battle between the pro- and antislavery factions became more intense. While it would be several years before she decided to take a more aggressive stand, she eventually did engage in the harsh methods of attack which increasingly characterized both sides in the controversy.

The difference in Stowe's role as a novelist and her role as a publicist for abolition is shown clearly in a comparison of *Uncle Tom's Cabin* with *A Key to Uncle Tom's Cabin*, the book she published the following year. The latter work was intended to answer the charge that she had depicted American slavery unfairly. *A Key* consists of 260 large double-columned pages of small print. She attempted to show first, that the characters and incidents of the novel were sometimes modeled upon actual persons and actual events; second, that when actual people or incidents were not portrayed, they might logically be assumed to exist under slavery; and third, that public opinion in the South and also in the North had shut its eyes to the cruelties and injustices of slavery.

The first section of *A Key*, the one in which Stowe attempted to identify models for the characters and events of *Uncle Tom's Cabin*, is likely to seem tedious to the modern reader. He learns with a jolt just how low a status fiction had with the ordinary nineteenth-century reader. A writer who did not say that he had actual models for his novel had a good deal of explaining to do. Stowe, like many of her readers, sometimes seemed to assume naïvely that to be taken seriously the characters and events of *Uncle Tom's Cabin* ought to have real people and events as their prototypes. She did not often identify the models, but nearly always they were people she had met or incidents she had witnessed, though a few of them she admitted hearing about secondhand. Luckily, she was less interested in identifying them than in arguing that the characters and events of the novel were not improbable under slavery. For many readers, however, it was the particular people, places, and events which mattered. There was a great deal of speculation on such questions as: Who was the real Uncle Tom? Who was the real Eliza? At what exact point did she cross the Ohio River? For fifty years after the publication of *Uncle Tom's Cabin* there was a considerable literature about persons who claimed to be the prototypes for this or that character. At the Chicago Exposition of 1893, the "true and only" cabin of Uncle Tom was one of the exhibits.[2]

The last sections of *A Key* are the best and contain an effective presentation of the case against slavery. The book has sometimes been compared, to its disadvantage, with Theodore Weld's *American Slavery As It Is* (1839). Weld had collected numerous accounts of slavery, some of which came from newspaper clippings and advertisements. Others were excerpts from books and articles of people—both pro- and antislavery—who had observed slavery at first hand. The intention of the book was to present extensive evidence of slavery's cruelties and injustices. There is a good deal of the same kind of evidence in *A Key to Uncle Tom's Cabin*, some of it quoted directly from the Weld volume. But there is something more. *A Key* contains a more comprehensive analysis of the institution of slavery than that found in Weld's book, as well as a more searching criticism of the arguments— social, political, legal, and religious—which were brought forward in its support.[3]

At that time it was not easy to collect specific evidence against slavery. Statistics were sparse. Proslavery advocates in the South, where much of the evidence existed, were not generally willing to make damning information public. Stowe's method in assembling data might seem primitive to the modern researcher. To the argument that slave families were rarely separated, she quoted from slave auction handbills which listed individual members of families for sale, with no indication that a buyer must purchase entire families. Some of the handbills said frankly that the slaves could be bought either individually or in "lots." As an additional argument that slave families were frequently separated, she examined the census statistics. These showed that the number of slaves in Virginia and North Carolina was increasing very slowly, and in some areas it was declining. On the other hand, the number of slaves was rapidly accelerating in Mississippi and Louisiana. Her interpretation of the statistics was that slaves in Virginia and North Carolina were being sold farther south and that there was almost no evidence that there was much effort to prevent the separation of families.[4]

It was not possible, of course, for Stowe to prove through statistics how many slaveholders were kindly and how many were cruel. She did, however, point to evidence that cruel owners existed, evidence which could be found in a lengthy collection of handbills and newspaper advertisements for runaway slaves. These sometimes would indicate the brand marks or the stripes of whips which identified slaves. In a few instances the advertisements offered a reward for a slave, "alive or dead." Also, there was the matter of court cases. For example, Stowe quoted from the *Alexandria* [Va.] *Gazette*. A slave, identified only as "the negro Henry," had attacked a white man "with intent to kill." He was tried in the town of Charleston, Virginia (now West Virginia). "The evidence of the prisoner's guilt was conclusive," said the account in the Alexandria paper. "A majority of the Court thought that he ought to suffer the extreme penalty of the law." Such a sentence would have required a "unanimous agreement," however, and there had been at least one juror opposed. Therefore, as a substitute for the death penalty, Henry was sentenced to receive a whipping of five hundred lashes, no more than thirty-nine at any one time. The newspaper account went on to say that "the physician of the gaol was instructed that they [the whippings] should not be administered too frequently and only when, in his opinion he [Henry] could bear them. Stowe quoted a soothing rationalization of the sentence, written by the editor of the *Charleston Free Press*: "This may seem to be a harsh and inhuman punishment, but when we take into consideration that it is in accordance with the law of the land, and the further fact that the insubordination among Slaves of this State has become truly alarming, we cannot question the righteousness of the judgment."[5]

George Frederick Holmes, editor of the *Southern Literary Messenger*, maintained that in *A Key* there was a basic inconsistency in the charges against slavery, pointing out that sometimes Stowe argued "that even the best dispositions on the part of the slaveholders . . . are ineffectual to redress or alleviate the miseries incident to slavery." Elsewhere in the book, however, she developed a thesis inconsistent with this idea. She argued that "even good laws are entirely nugatory in consequence of the fraud, the villainy, and the evasions" of individual slaveholders, lawyers, and judges. There is indeed an inconsistency, at least a theoretical one, between the two lines of argument which Stowe pursued in *A Key*. If the apologists for slavery had been willing to attempt to show that southern laws really did generally protect the slaves against cruel and unjust treatment and had cited instances in which they had done so, they might have exploited what could have been an inconsistency on her part. If they had pursued this line of argument, however, they would have had to admit that many of the provisions of the slave codes ought to be repealed or amended. Apologists for slavery almost never argued in this way. Under attack, slavery became more, rather than less, resistant to change. Having undertaken a defense of slavery, its apologists frequently swallowed it whole and ignored the cruelty of the statutes which dealt with it. Instead of admitting the cruelty of the slave codes, they emphasized the kindliness of the masters which prevented them from using the powers the law gave them.[6]

Stowe was undoubtedly right when she maintained that kindly slaveholders were prevented by law from doing certain things which could have been beneficial for their slaves. In some states, masters could not free their slaves, they could not allow them to go into business for themselves, they could not teach them to read and write. On the other hand, it did not necessarily follow that the so-called "protective statutes," those laws which in theory were supposed to shield slaves from cruel treatment, actually had this effect. Many of them had loopholes which favored the master's interests. There was again the troubled matter of court cases, which somehow nearly always seemed to go against the slaves. Southern apologists for slavery who referred to court cases had extremely slim pickings in finding examples indicating that slaves enjoyed meaningful legal protection against abuses. This difficulty probably explains why so few of them undertook this line of argument. Theoretically, there might have been an inconsistency in Stowe's two methods of attacking slavery. Practically, however, both of her objections were valid.

One example of a "good" law which might be evaded by an evil slaveowner was the one in Louisiana which forbade the sale of a slave child away from its mother if it was under ten years of age. In *Uncle*

Tom's Cabin, the daughter of Cassy is only nine years old when she is sold away from her mother. Stowe probably did not know about the Louisiana law when she wrote the novel. It was the only slave state which had such a law, but southern critics of the novel triumphantly pounced upon Stowe's error and pointed out that such a sale would have been illegal. In *A Key*, Stowe replied as follows:

Suppose Butler [Cassy's master] wants to sell Cassy's child of nine years. There is a statute forbidding to sell under ten years; what is Cassy to do? She cannot bring suit. Will the State prosecute? Suppose it does; what then? Butler says the child is ten years old. . . . What is Cassy to do? She cannot testify; besides she is utterly in Butler's power. He may tell her that if she offers to stir in the affair, he will whip the child within an inch of its life; and she knows he can do it, and that there is no help for it; he may lock her up in a dungeon, sell her on to a distant plantation, or do any other despotic thing he chooses, and there is nobody to say—Nay.

How much does the protective statute amount to for Cassy? It may be very well as a piece of advice to the public, or as a decorous expression of opinion; but one might as well try to stop the current of the Mississippi with a bulrush as the tide of trade in human beings with such a regulation.[7]

Stowe was especially concerned over the fact that many clergymen, south and north, justified slavery and blindly overlooked its horrors. Many other clergymen, probably a considerable majority, had nothing to say about it. Here the legacy of Calvinism in the upbringing of Stowe was important. She did not assume that the nature of man is inherently good or that such evil as exists comes wholly from a corrupt society. In addition, though she was deeply committed to the Christian religion, she had no particular awe of clergymen. The fact that her father, her husband, and all seven of her brothers were or would become clergymen meant that she had had a good deal of experience with the profession. She knew that the frailties of human nature were liberally distributed among its members. Therefore, she did not hesitate to criticize clergymen, sometimes harshly, for their opinions about slavery. Clergymen, south and north, would sometimes rail at her for her lack of "respect for the cloth." It was a mere evasion of the issue of slavery.[8]

In *A Key to Uncle Tom's Cabin*, Stowe quoted excerpts from some of the sermons of proslavery clergymen, one of which was preached to slaves in New Orleans by the Reverend Mr. Theophilus Clapp:

You should realize that a wise, kind, and merciful Providence has appointed you your condition in life; and, all things considered, you could not be more eligibly situated. The burden of your care, toils and responsibilities is much lighter than that which God has imposed on your master. . . . You have your troubles; so have all. Remember how evanescent are the pleasures and joys of human life.[9]

Even more oleaginous was the Reverend Mr. William Meade, the Episcopal Bishop of Virginia, who preached a sermon to slaves in which he discussed the question of what their attitude should be toward the punishments they received from their masters and mistresses:

Suppose that you deserve correction, you cannot but say that it is just and right you should meet with it. Suppose you do not, or at least you do not deserve so much, or so severe a correction, for the fault you have committed, you perhaps have escaped a great many more, and at last paid for all. Or, suppose, you are quite innocent of what is laid to your charge, and suffer wrongfully in the particular thing; is it not possible you may have done some other bad thing which was never discovered, and that Almighty God, who saw you doing it, would not let you escape without punishment one time or another?

To this argument Stowe merely replied, "The reader must admit that he [Bishop Meade] takes a very philosophical view of the subject." She also had an eye for religious hypocrisy on the subject of slave "marriages." She quoted from the report of a committee which was given a question to consider by a Baptist association in Georgia. It was whether a slave, separated by sale from his wife or her husband, should be allowed to remarry. The committee in its report resorted to euphemism, saying, "That, in view of the circumstances in which servants [slaves] in this country are placed, the committee are unanimous in the opinion that it is better to permit a servant thus circumstanced to take another husband or wife."[10]

Occasionally Stowe would be much disturbed by some particularly cruel mistreatment of a slave. At one point she came close to advocating the same lynch law against which she had previously protested. In the *Souther vs. Commonwealth* [Virginia] case, a master had been accused of killing a slave by torture—administering whippings and burnings over a period of several days. On learning that the jury found the offense to be nothing worse than "murder in the second degree," Stowe was outraged. "One would think that the community would have risen up by an universal sentiment," she said, "to shake out the man, as Paul shook the viper from his hand."[11]

Generally in *A Key* Stowe was successful in her attempts to keep argument from descending into invective. She described the debate over slavery as a "holy controversy," but she insisted that it should

be one of principle, and not of sectional bitterness. We must not suffer it to degenerate, in our hands, into a violent prejudice against the South; and, to this end, we must keep continually before our minds the more amiable features and attractive qualities of those with whose principles we are obliged to conflict.

Also, she realized that the North was not guiltless of discrimination against blacks. In many northern states there were laws and social practices which were unfair to them. She asked her northern readers, since they could not do anything immediately about slavery, at least to become concerned about the status of blacks in their own communities:

The writer will say to every individual Christian, who wishes to do something for the abolition of slavery: Begin by doing what lies in your power for the coloured people in your vicinity. Are there children excluded from schools by unchristian prejudice? Seek to combat the prejudice by fair arguments, presented in the right spirit. If you cannot succeed, then endeavor to secure for them, in every walk of life, the ordinary privileges of American citizens. If they are excluded from the omnibus and railroad-car in the place where you reside, endeavor to persuade those who have the control of these matters to pursue a more just and reasonable course. Those Christians who are heads of mechanical establishments can do much for the cause by receiving colored apprentices. Many masters excuse themselves for excluding the colored apprentice by saying that, if they receive him, all their other hands will desert them. To this it is replied, that if they do the thing in a Christian temper and for a Christian purpose, the probability is that, if their hands desert at first, they will return to them—all of them, at least, whom they would care to retain.[12]

A Key to Uncle Tom's Cabin was a useful compendium of the arguments—political, legal, and religious—which were formulated to attack slavery. It had a defect, however, when it was compared with the novel itself. Southern critics of the novel could argue that its events were improbable, its characters unreal, and its arguments false. What they could not do, however, was deny that it presented a portrait of slavery which was convincing to a great many people. On the other hand, southerners and proslavery critics generally had considerable experience in answering the kinds of arguments against slavery which were found in *A Key to Uncle Tom's Cabin*. They were, in fact, a mere continuation of the national debate on the subject.[13]

Hostile critics of *A Key* were generally inclined to see as an exceptional case every instance cited in it of the cruelty and injustice of slavery. Handbills offering rewards for runaway slaves "dead or alive" were discounted. "These are pieces of bravado on the part of masters," said a review in *De Bow's Review*, "and if the negroes had been killed, would have been murder according to the laws of the states in which they were advertised." Admittedly there were laws which decreed cruel punishments for slaves, but they were rarely enforced. What the law permitted was no necessary indication of what was actually done. Such laws belonged to a different era when human relationships themselves were frequently cruel, but the laws had become dead letters, kept on the books through apathy or perhaps in order to provide a way for society in the South to deal with some possible emergency, such as a slave rebellion. Sometimes it was argued that the abolitionist agitation in the North was to blame for the unwillingness of southerners to change their slave codes. The Reverend Mr. E. J. Stearns defended the Louisiana law which permitted a free man to clear himself of a murder charge simply by his own oath of denial when the victim was a slave, if there were no white witnesses present at the time the alleged crime was committed. Did Mrs. Stowe imagine, asked Stearns, that the guilty white master would wholly escape the justice he deserved? She should remember that a false oath would send such a man "into eternity with the awful guilt of perjury on his soul, to receive a double punishment hereafter."[14]

In addition to attacking slavery in the South, Stowe endeavored to heal the misunderstandings and hostility among various abolition groups in the North. She made a special attempt to lessen the distance between herself and the Garrisonian abolitionists. In a letter to Wendell Phillips, she said, "Because you gentlemen [abolitionists of the Garrison school] differ from me in religious faith, is to my mind no reason why I should not sympathize with you in charity." She could not wholly accept William Lloyd Garrison himself, however, without expressing to him some reservations. Among the orthodox church members, Garrison had a reputation for religious skepticism. This came partly from his unwillingness to state his religious convictions unequivocally and partly from his attacks both upon church bodies and upon individual clergymen because of their hostility to abolition, or at least their indifference to it. Stowe went to call on Garrison and asked him pointedly though in a friendly spirit, "Mr. Garrison, are you a Christian?" Garrison is said to have smiled and to have parried her question with another, "And who is my neighbor?"[15]

On essentially the same question, Stowe wrote a letter to Garrison discussing her differences with opinions expressed in the *Liberator*, opinions which she did not clearly identify:

> I am a constant reader of your paper, and an admirer of much that is in it. I like its frankness, fearlessness, truthfulness, and independence. At the same time I regard with apprehension and sorrow much that is in it. Were it circulated only among intelligent, well-balanced minds, able to discriminate between good and evil, I should not feel so much apprehension. To *me* the paper is decidedly valuable as a fresh and able exposé [exposition?] of the ultra progressive element in our times. What I fear is, that it will take from poor Uncle Tom his Bible, and give him nothing in its place. You understand me—do you not?
>
> In this view I cannot conscientiously do anything which might endorse your party and your paper, without at the same time entering protest against what I consider erroneous and hurtful. With this view I . . . give you the greatest possible proof of esteem and regard by thus frankly telling you my whole mind, and expecting you to be well pleased with my sincerity.

Garrison was too wily an antagonist to be pushed into the position of being obliged to explain his own religious views. "That you occasionally find in the paper [*The Liberator*] sentiments distasteful to you, at variance with your ideas of right," he replied, "is not at all surprising. *So do* I. But what then? Is not this inseparable from free discussion? And may not 'error of opinion be safely tolerated where truth is left free to combat it'?" To her argument that she would not object to the *Liberator* if it were "circulated only among intelligent, well-balanced minds," he replied, "So says the Romish Church in regard to the indiscriminate circulation of the Bible among the laity. So says Absolutism, respecting the diffusion of intelligence among the masses. I am surprised at the narrowness of your limitation. Are the people not to be trusted?"[16]

Of religion itself, Garrison would only say that he knew of no one who wrote for the *Liberator* who wished "to rob 'Uncle Tom' of his Bible." The writers who wrote for the paper were willing

for him to place whatever estimate he can upon it; and for you and me to do the same; but for neither of us to accept any more of it than we sincerely believe to be in accordance with reason, truth, eternal right. How much of it is true and obligatory, each one can determine only for himself; for on Protestant ground, there is no room for papal infallibility.

It is unlikely that Stowe found this position with regard to religion satisfactory. In time she did become reconciled if not to his religious views at least to Garrison himself. After the Civil War, she would give him very high praise. "We have written the name of a man," she said of Garrison in a magazine article in 1866, "who has had a more marked influence on our late national history than any other one person who could be mentioned."[17]

Stowe also made an effort to placate the opposition of abolitionists—black and white—who objected to the colonization views expressed by George Harris in the last pages of *Uncle Tom's Cabin*. Evidence on this point is indirect and not wholly clear. At the meeting of the American and Foreign Anti-Slavery Society in New York in May of 1853, one of the delegates arose to object to the colonization ideas of *Uncle Tom's Cabin*. In the words of the minutes of the corresponding secretary of the convention, the delegates "hoped something would be done to counteract the Colonization influence of that book." Then the secretary read a note from Stowe which has not survived. In the minutes, the note was paraphrased and her retraction is expressed in a garbled fashion:

[S]he [Stowe] had no sympathy with the coercive policy of the Colonization Society, but she thought Liberia now a "fixed fact," and that the opportunity there afforded of sustaining a republican government of free people
of color ought not to be disregarded by them or their friends; concluding
with an assurance that she was "not a Colonizationist."

The letter did not satisfy some of the delegates at the meeting. Some unnamed person arose and criticized what in the corresponding secretary's notes is described as "the evil influence of the last chapter of 'Uncle Tom's Cabin' in the matter of Colonization." At this point, Dr. Leonard Bacon—a close friend of the Beecher family—arose and attempted to put the matter more clearly. Again, our knowledge of what was said is limited to the report of the convention's secretary. "Mrs. Stowe had told him [Bacon] that if she were to write 'Uncle Tom' again, she would not send George Harris to Liberia."[18]

A year later in 1854, Stowe was still reflecting on a plan which would involve the departure of at least some of the blacks from the United States. In *Sunny Memories of Foreign Lands*, an account of her travels in Europe, she reported a conversation she had had with the Duke of Argyll in England. He had suggested founding a black college in Antigua and had asked Stowe what she thought of the idea of encouraging blacks to settle there. She thought it would be a bad plan:

I told him my impression was, that Canada would be a much better place to develop the energies of the race. First, on the account of its cold and bracing climate; second, because having never been a slave state, the white population there are more thrifty and industrious [than that of Antigua?], and of course the influence of such a community was better adapted to form thrift and industry in the negro.

There was something both of the benevolent racist and of the naïve humanitarian in this suggestion. Apparently the American blacks were to have their inherent laziness gradually bred out of them by exposure to a cold climate over a period of generations. It is not known what the Duke of Argyll thought of this proposal. It seems unlikely that the Canadians would have welcomed millions of blacks, most of whom had formerly been slaves.[19]

Elsewhere in *Sunny Memories of Foreign Lands* there is another reference to colonization. One of Stowe's warmest friends as well as a staunch advocate of abolition was the Duchess of Sutherland. The Duchess encountered much criticism among the proslavery faction because her name was associated, though unfairly, with the expulsion of 15,000 tenants from the Sutherland estates in Scotland in the second decade of the nineteenth century. Actually, the Duchess had had nothing to do with the matter, since the expulsion had happened many years before she had married into the Sutherland family. The circumstances of the tenant removal were complex and Scottish historians are still divided in their opinions on the subject. Stowe rushed into the battle to defend her friend, a battle she probably should have avoided.[20]

In her defense, Stowe briskly recounted in one paragraph the history of the enclosure movement in Great Britain since early in the eighteenth century. In Scotland, she said, the "border chiefs found it profitable to adopt the agriculture to which their hills were adapted." She apparently meant that they shifted from growing crops to raising sheep, an occupation which required fewer laborers. The chiefs "decided to keep only as many [of the laborers] as could profitably cultivate the land." The effect of this decision was that it "threw many people out of employ, and forced them to seek for a home elsewhere." Stowe's judgment of this expulsion was a mixture of *laissez-faire* and highmindedness. "Like many other movements which, in their final results, are beneficial to society," she said, "this was at first vehemently resisted, and had to be carried into effect in some cases by force." Farther south in England, there had usually been other employment to which the displaced tenants could turn:

To a certain extent as . . . [the enclosure movement] progressed northward, the demand for labor in the great towns absorbed the surplus population; but when it came into the extreme Highlands, this refuge was wanting. Emigration to America now became the only resource; and the surplus population was induced to this by means such as the Colonization Society now recommends and approves for promoting emigration to Liberia.

"Induced" was considerably too mild a word for what actually happened to the Scottish tenants. There is no other evidence that she advocated forced expatriation of American blacks, but one can hardly help wondering what methods she might have advocated if colonization had actually come about in the United States and many blacks had refused to leave the country.[21]

In 1856, Stowe published her second novel, *Dred: A Tale of the Swamps.* Though historians and literary critics have paid much less attention to *Dred* than to *Uncle Tom's Cabin,* it treats slavery in more detail. Perhaps the fullness of treatment of the subject partly explains why a variety of readers, such as Harriet Martineau, George Eliot, and Queen Victoria—the last by secondhand account—thought it was the better novel. Public debaters over slavery are usually kept offstage in *Uncle Tom's Cabin.* In *Dred,* the reader may sometimes have the odd feeling that he is attending a joint meeting of the legislature of a southern state and of a Boston antislavery society. There is a great deal of rhetoric on both sides. In addition, both sides appeal largely to their own supporters, not to their opponents.[22]

Uncle Tom's Cabin is a novel of hope but *Dred* is one of something close to despair. The earlier novel, it is true, had—in some of the speeches of Augustine St. Clare—come near to prophesying revolution, but it was clear that such a disaster was conditional upon nothing being done to end slavery. By the time she came to write *Dred,* Stowe had lost much of her conviction that the South could be shown the evils of slavery and induced to abolish it. In *Dred,* proslavery opinion is accelerating rather than declining. In *Uncle Tom's Cabin,* Uncle Tom dies a martyr but the reader is allowed to hope that eventually the system of slavery which killed him would be abolished. The martyrs in *Dred,* on the other hand, simply die. Other characters in the novel express sorrow for their deaths, but there is no implication that they will lead to the abolition of slavery or even to a mitigation of its cruelties.

The faults of *Dred* are more serious than those of *Uncle Tom's Cabin*. The reader receives virtually no preparation in the first half of the novel for what happens in the last half. It begins on a light-hearted note. Stowe attempted to do something for which she had little talent— to write a love story. Nina Gordon, the heroine, is a southern belle. At the beginning of the novel she is a heartless flirt, engaged to marry three different suitors at the same time. She is meant to be delightfully saucy and roguish but she is merely tiresome. Her feet are compared to little mice, she is always cocking her pretty head and saying something arch, and she dismisses her suitors with a wave of her hand. One British reviewer said bluntly that she had the mind and manners of a "Yankee factory girl." Her increasing knowledge of the evils of slavery broadens her views and deepens her sympathies for other people, but the change occurs too quickly and too patly in the novel to be convincing.[23]

The white protagonist of the novel is Edward Clayton, the suitor whom Nina eventually chooses. Like Augustine St. Clare in *Uncle Tom's Cabin*, Clayton knows slavery from the inside, having been born and reared as an aristocrat in the South. St. Clare is an attractive character because of his wit and skepticism, but Clayton is much more earnestly Victorian. The early parts of *Dred* sympathetically portray the problems of those slaveholders in the South who genuinely wish to better the lot of their slaves. Apparently something happened while Stowe was writing the novel to make the last sections entirely different. In 1884, James C. Derby recounted a story told by M. D. Phillips, the publisher of *Dred*. Phillips said that Stowe was deeply shocked by the physical assault of Preston Brooks of South Carolina on Charles Sumner on the floor of the United States Senate in 1856. She was so angered by the attack, said Derby, that "instead of carrying some of her characters and making them like little Eva, charming and tender, she introduced the spirit of revenge under the name of the negro Dred." The indignation of Stowe apparently took an extreme form. She killed off her heroine Nina in the middle of the book. By doing so she was enabled to utilize a device which is found in some of her other works. The hero, an earnest young reformer, confides his deepest thoughts not to his sweetheart or wife but to his sister. Perhaps Stowe may have been thinking of her own relationship with Henry Ward Beecher. The radical change that takes place in *Dred* was probably one of the faults which led William Styron, in 1970, to say that it has "ghastly shortcomings as a work of fiction," though he also expressed the opinion that it was a "neglected work." Toward the end of *Dred*, Stowe described a physical attack against her idealistic hero, Edward Clayton, which was similar to that of Brooks against Sumner. Somewhere in the middle the novel loses its calm and thoughtful approach and becomes a tale of horrors. No longer is there hope of conciliation with the South. No longer is there hope that slavery may be ended. All that can be done is to rescue a few of its victims.[24]

It was the humor and skepticism of Augustine St. Clare which saved him from being a priggish hero. In addition to denying these qualities to Edward Clayton, Stowe loads a heavy liability upon him. One of her ideas was that women are the primary source of love and concern for others in society. If she could not imagine a woman leading anti-slavery forces in the South, she may have reasoned that she could at least imagine a man with some feminine qualities who would do so. Edward has a mouth which is "even feminine in the delicacy and beauty of its line, and the smile which sometimes played around it had a peculiar fascination." Stowe may have been fascinated by Edward, but the reviewers of *Dred* were not. The reviewer in *Blackwood's* said that Edward might be "a model American" but he was also "a conscientious blockhead." The reviewer in the *Irish Quarterly* said, "We don't care a button what happens to him." The reviewer in the *London Times* wondered how "so fastidious a young man" could bring himself to attend a revival camp meeting. Even the reviewer in the *New Englander*, who generally praised the novel, could not admire Edward and dismissed him as a poor imitation of Augustine St. Clare.[25]

In 1939, Shields McIlwaine would make the legitimate point that Stowe in choosing North Carolina for the setting of *Dred* had shown her lack of knowledge of the South. She did not recognize that in this particular state there was not a sharp distinction between the great planters, on the one hand, and the poor whites on the other. Of all the southern states, North Carolina had the largest percentage of small farmers who owned their own land. In the novel, Stowe shows no perception of the fact that substantial numbers of the white people of the state are neither great planters nor poor whites. For her, the "aristocratic firebrands" effectively control both the politics and the economics of the state. To enlist the emotional support of the poor whites, all the aristocratic leaders have to do is to hold up to them the specter of black supremacy.[26]

Like the white characters of *Dred*, the black characters did not obtain a favorable reception from the reviewers. Tiff, for example, was far below Uncle Tom in popularity. Like Tom, Tiff is a slave who becomes the property of a bad master. He is a good man but much less impressive than Tom. For one thing, Tiff snobbishly brags about the family tree of his original owners, the Peyton family, who were decidedly F.F.V.s. He was once part of the marriage dowry of one of the Peyton daughters. She had married beneath herself to a poor white, the drunken and dissolute Mr. Cripps, and he rapidly ran through her fortune until almost nothing was left but old Tiff himself. His mistress had died and Tiff is now left to the mercies of Mr. Cripps and his slatternly new poor-white wife, Polly.[27]

The religion of Tiff, unlike that of Uncle Tom, is wholly of the conventional sort and consists chiefly of blessing God and putting himself wholly in His care. As his religion affects other people, it is directed mainly to trying to save the Peyton children from the irresponsibility of their father and stepmother. The way that Tiff states his religious aims is to say that he hopes to "bring dem yer chil'en to de kingdom." It is difficult to imagine Tiff carrying on a dialogue with any white person on the meaning of religion, as Uncle Tom does with Augustine St. Clare and even with Simon Legree. Tom is a handsome and muscular man, but Tiff is ugly:

His countenance presented, physically, one of the most uncomely specimens of negro features; and would have been positively frightful, had it not been redeemed by an expression of cheerful kindliness which beamed from it. His face was of ebony blackness, with a wide, upturned nose, a mouth of portentous size, guarded by clumsy lips, revealing teeth which a shark might have envied. The only fine feature was his large black eyes.[28]

Possibly more important than his religion is the fact that Tiff has primitive powers associated with the world of nature. At first these mysterious attributes seem impressive. Fish will bite at his hook when they avoid the hooks of everyone else. Hens are eager to lay eggs for him and cackle "confidentially" to him. Turkeys gobble and strut for him and show him their "downy offspring":

All sorts of wild game, squirrels, rabbits, coons, and possums, appeared to come with pleasure and put themselves into his traps and springs, so that, where another man might starve, Tiff would look around him with unctuous satisfaction, contemplating all nature as his larder, where his provisions were wearing fur coats, and walking about on four legs, only for safe keeping till he got ready to eat them.[29]

In Tiff, Stowe may have been attempting to meet the objections of those readers who had found Uncle Tom to be too noble, too idealized. Tiff is an example of what is sometimes called "romantic racialism." He is given qualities superior to those of members of the white race, but apparently these are meant to serve as partial compensation for his less favorable traits. Tiff is a child of nature, but the reader would be justified in wondering whether he is much else. For one thing, Tiff apparently finds it impossible, even though he has had a good deal of instruction, to learn to read. When someone asks him about his progress in learning, he replies, "Why, no, honey, I dunno as I can rightly say dat I's larn'd to read, 'cause I's 'mazing slow at dar ar; but den, I's larn'd all de best words, like Christ, Lord, and God, and dem ar; and whar dey's pretty thick, I makes out quite comfortable." Since Tiff is one of the most important black characters in *Dred*, the reader may wonder whether his inability to learn is a suggestion of the inherent defects of the blacks as a race.[30]

On first examination, the character Dred might be seen as a much more impressive black than Tiff. He has none of the meekness of Tiff. Instead he thinks seriously of leading a slave rebellion, and there is every reason to believe that if he did so he would be both a courageous and competent leader. Common report had it that his father had been Denmark Vesey, the South Carolina black who had—in terms of historical fact—led the slave revolt in Charleston, South Carolina, in 1822. In some respects, Dred is closer to that other revolutionary of real life, Nat Turner, the man who led the slave revolt in Virginia in 1831. Dred has Turner's knowledge of the Bible and he himself is rather like an Old Testament prophet. Because he is a Mandingo, Dred is less impressive as a black hero than he might otherwise be. Stowe believed that the Mandingoes were a princely tribe in Africa which at some distant time in the past had had associations with whites. These had presumably been European explorers from whom the blacks had received a substantial white intermixture. Thus the possibility exists that Dred has received his qualities of intelligence and his gift for leadership from his white ancestors.[31]

In one respect, however, Dred is more nearly black than white. Like Tiff, Dred possesses powers which belong to the world of nature rather than to that of human intelligence. He speaks to wild animals and they understand him. They will feed from his hand and allow him to pick them up. He answers a bird in the forest with an "exact imitation" of its call and the bird immediately recognizes a kindred spirit and begins a conversation with him. Dred can read "the language of the leaves," a gift which is not described but which is one of the indications that he is among "the elect." In addition, he has the gift of "second sight." This enables him to elude his pursuers in the swamp; by some mysterious sense he knows where they are and in which direction they will go. The first time he meets Nina Gordon, the white heroine of the novel, she has not as yet experienced any symptoms of illness, but Dred immediately recognizes that she is marked for an early death. Both Tiff and Dred sometimes seem like forerunners of some of the nonwhite characters of literary naturalist writers of forty years later. Then such novelists as Frank Norris and Jack London would give the "primitive" races unusual powers. Like Tiff and Dred, they would sometimes be able to relate easily to the world of animals. In addition, they had mysterious senses which enabled them to know things which were beyond the range of rational explanation. On the other hand, Norris's and London's characters would lack the qualities of will and intelligence. These would be qualities which the two authors almost wholly associated with whites.[32]

There are other ways in which Dred is not wholly satisfactory as a hero. He makes fiery speeches but that is about all. If he did more, Stowe may have reflected, he might become a positive handicap to the antislavery theme of the novel. He might arouse, for example, the fears of white readers who would suspect that if the blacks were not kept in check by slavery they would become ungovernable, especially in those sections of the United States in which they constituted a majority or a large minority. The result is that throughout the last half of the novel Dred does little more than suddenly appear like Robin Hood at moments of crisis, saving the persecuted slaves from disaster by leading them to his hideaway deep in the Dismal Swamp. He talks about leading a slave revolt, but he never does so. For all his handicaps, Dred is still in some ways an impressive character. Probably because Stowe herself did not know what else to do with him, he is shot by one of his white pursuers in the swamp. He escapes but only to drag himself to his hiding place and die. Dred could be a foreshadowing of Bras Coupé, the rebellious slave character in George Washington Cable's *The Grandissimes* (1880).[33]

Contemporary reviewers did not, however, think much of Dred. It was to be expected that reviewers in southern periodicals would not like him. The reviewer in the *Southern Literary Messenger* said that he was "the most uninteresting and unnatural character in the book." Reviewers in the North were scarcely more impressed with him. The reviewer in the *New Englander* said that he "excites for himself no profound feeling." One northern antislavery reviewer, a clergyman, said that Dred "fails to excite our sympathies. He is an unreal presence,—a dark, gloomy, ghostly being . . . at whose sufferings we are not very much moved, and over whose fate it is impossible to fetch a tear, hardly a sigh, and that of relief." In England, the reviewer in the *Quarterly Review* objected to the faulty Old Testament rhetoric of Dred. He "crosses the narrow line which separates the sublime from the ridiculous," he said, and also "the broad one which distinguishes sense from nonsense. What is the meaning of 'the line of confusion and the stones of emptiness'?" The reviewer in *Tait's Edinburgh Magazine* made the naïve and revealing comment that Dred was less popular with readers than Uncle Tom had been because he "wanted the grace of suffering patiently whatever should befall him." The opinion suggests that even readers in the North and abroad may not have been willing to accept a rebellious black hero.[34]

In both the South and the North, Stowe had appealed to whites in *Uncle Tom's Cabin* to help end slavery. In *Dred*, she is speaking only to white northerners. It is true that Edward Clayton attempts to persuade his fellow white southerners that they must reform the evils of slavery and even prepare for its eventual abolition. His efforts come to nothing. Edward has a sympathetic friend, Frank Russel, who attempts to explain to him the fanciful nature of all his hopes of persuading the white South to change its mind. Edward tells Frank Russel that he believes that at some future time the people of the South will come to recognize the economic wastefulness of slavery even if they fail to see its cruelty. Russel replies that the economic argument will be as ineffective as the moral one. "What do you suppose these men [the plantation owners] care about the poor whites, and the ruin of the State, and all that?" he asks. Disaster "won't come in their day, and 'after us the deluge,' you know. That's the talk!"[35]

There is another kind of pessimism in *Dred* which is more difficult to analyze or account for, but it is nonetheless important. Stowe was apparently losing confidence—at least for the time being—in her previous answers to the question of whether blacks have sufficient intelligence and will to enable them to live as equal citizens in a free society. As a writer of fiction, she had the habit of turning ideas over in her mind without necessarily coming to a definite conclusion. In *Dred* the reader encounters questions which are never satisfactorily answered and which he is forced to interpret in his own way. The more Stowe reflected on the issue of the racial traits of blacks, the more she apparently wondered whether their defects were wholly due to their education and environment. The attempt in the novel to give the characters of Tiff and Dred the traits of primitive men close to the world of animals is one aspect of this doubt. Another example is found in the failures the Claytons experience in attempting to educate their slaves for freedom. In *Dred* the reader encounters an idea wholly absent in *Uncle Tom's Cabin*. A considerable doubt is cast on the belief that the blacks have innate traits which need only cultivation to enable them to make their places in American society.

Edward and Anne Clayton attempt to educate their slaves, both children and adults. In defiance of a state law forbidding such a practice, Anne teaches the slave children to read and write. There is no doubt of the children's willingness to learn. The narrator of *Dred* employs the language of phrenology to explain their eagerness. "The African race have large ideality and veneration," he says. Though they have "the faults of children," they "unite many of their most amiable qualities, in the simplicity and confidingness with which they yield themselves up in admiration to a superior friend." The reader may wonder at this point whether in Stowe's view the blacks as a race will ever become responsible adults in their own right.[36]

Anne Clayton becomes deeply discouraged by the failure of her attempts to teach black children. At first, she reacts to her difficulties by redoubling her efforts. "I come from the old Virginia Cavalier blood," she says to one of her friends, "and am not afraid of anything." To Nina Gordon, however, Anne begins to express doubts about whether blacks can ever be successfully taught. Dulcimer is a little black boy who makes almost no progress in reading, writing, or arithmetic. More seriously, it seems to be impossible to teach him to be honest or responsible. "He is as wholly destitute of any moral organs as a jackdaw," says Anne. "One sometimes questions whether these creatures have any more than a reflected mimicry of a human soul—such as the German stories imagine in kobolds and water-spirits. All I can see in Dulcimer is a kind of fun-loving animal." Thus, Anne becomes a pessimist concerning the ability of the blacks to develop either intellectually or morally. She criticizes her brother Edward for his excessive idealism. "His faith in human nature is unbounded," Anne tells Nina; "I think it is one of his foibles, for my part." Unlike the Topsy of *Uncle Tom's Cabin*, Dulcimer does not respond to the efforts made to educate him. Between the time that she wrote the earlier novel and *Dred*, Stowe shows signs of having lost some of her belief in the capability of blacks for mental or moral improvement.[37]

Edward Clayton retains his faith in the possibilities for improvement of blacks, but his reasons are hardly ones to inspire confidence. "Oh, I think," he says, "the African race evidently are made to excel in that department which lies between the sensuous and the intellectual—what we call elegant arts. These require rich and abundant animal nature, such as they possess; and if ever they become highly civilized, they will excel in music, dancing, and elocution." Significantly, he suggests that the time must be extended indefinitely before they can reach their full potential. "The Ethiopian race is a slow-growing plant, like the aloe," he explains, "but I hope, some of these days, they'll come into flower; and I think if they ever do, the blossoming will be gorgeous." In *Uncle Tom's Cabin*, there had been no mention of a possibility that the process of civilization might take an indefinitely long time. In addition, the future flowering of the blacks had not been qualified by an *if*. In *Dred*, the reader is not told directly of the continuing disillusionment of Anne over the possibility of educating the black children, but he is allowed to infer it from the changes which she makes in the course of study. When an exhibition is held at the plantation to show the progress of the pupils, nothing is said about their proficiency in reading, writing, and arithmetic. Instead, the exhibition is wholly given over to demonstrating their ability to play the banjo, to sing, and to dance.[38]

Edward Clayton also has difficulties in educating the adult slaves on the plantation to become responsible and moral people as well as industrious and efficient workers. He has some success in trying to inculcate a system of morality among them. He first attempts to teach them to be honest. He sets up a committee among them to judge and punish such crimes as theft. He is frequently obliged to overrule the committee, however, because the slaves generally favor harsh punishments. Whether the slaves eventually do become comparatively honest the reader is never clearly told. Though the evidence is indirect, there is doubt that they become good workmen. After some time has passed, Anne tells one of her friends that the experiment "is not a money-making operation" and "barely pays for itself." The implication seems to be that if philanthropic slaveowners in the South should decide to educate their slaves for freedom they must be content—for an indefinite period—with making little money on their plantations.[39]

Both the school for slave children taught by Anne Clayton and the Edward's experiment in teaching adult slaves to farm come to an abrupt end. Edward is threatened by his neighbors with prosecution for violating the state law which forbids teaching slaves to read. In the ensuing controversy, Tom Gordon—Nina's villainous brother—organizes a band of vigilantes which makes a cowardly attack upon Edward in a remote area of the plantation. Gordon strikes Edward from behind with a gutta-percha cane, the same weapon which Preston Brooks had used in his attack upon Charles Sumner in the United States Senate. Edward falls to the ground and Tom Gordon cointinues beating him until he loses consciousness. The narrator of *Dred* says that Gordon "proved his eligibility for Congress by beating his defenseless acquaintance on the head, after the fashion of chivalry of South Carolina." The comment shows the direction in which Stowe was moving. In *Uncle Tom's Cabin*, she had taken pains to avoid comments which implied a general condemnation of the South or of a southern state.[40]

Three pages from the end of *Dred*, Edward Clayton takes all his slaves with him to Canada and sets them free. He buys a large tract of land and establishes a township, "one of the richest and finest in the region." He builds himself "a beautiful residence, where he and his sister live happily together, finding their enjoyment in the improvement of those by whom they are surrounded." At first the "neighboring white settlers" in Canada "looked coldly upon Edward, fearing that he would be the means of introducing a thriftless population among them." Soon, however, they are "entirely won over," because "the improvements which Clayton and his tenants have made has [*sic*] nearly doubled the price of real estate in the vicinity." Edward had apparently failed in North Carolina in his task of making good workmen of the blacks, but in Canada he succeeds. Of course, the difference may be that in North Carolina the blacks were enslaved and now they are free, but the novel does not specifically make this point. Nothing is said about the blacks in Canada buying land for themselves. So far as we are allowed to find out, they will remain as tenants on land Edward owns. The reader will naturally wonder how they might have fared if he had not been there to supervise matters. In any event, the success of Edward's experiment is described too briefly for it to be convincing to the reader.[41]

Aside from having Edward Clayton make the enigmatic comment that God might intervene somehow in the dispute over slavery, Stowe avoided in *Dred* any definite conclusions with regard to the question of how the institution might be abolished. She herself was probably not aware that her despair over the possibility of convincing the South of the evils of slavery might mean that the issue would be settled by war. The reviewer of *Dred* in *Blackwood's Magazine* in Edinburgh, Scotland, however, drew the conclusion after reading the novel that a civil war in the United States was probable. He noted Stowe's pessimism concerning the chances of reforming even the worst abuses of slavery, much less of abolishing it. Since no changes in slavery could be effected by persuasion, the reviewer said, abolition must "therefore . . . be decreed," and the result would be "to summon the furies of civil war."[42]

Why did Stowe change from the hopefulness of *Uncle Tom's Cabin* to the near despair of *Dred*? On this point, it is possible to offer only conjectures. The modern reader knows that *Uncle Tom's Cabin* had a great influence in convincing the North of the evils of slavery. He may not recognize, however, that the novel probably fell short of Stowe's hopes for it. In addition to convincing the North, she apparently hoped to convince the South as well. Such expectations may now seem so visionary as to be quixotic, but they probably did not seem so to her. Her belief in the power of God to change men and nations gave her great hopes at first that slavery might indeed be abolished. By the time *Dred* was published, four years after the appearance of *Uncle Tom's Cabin*, she no longer had any illusions about changing the mind of the South. Thus her change from optimism to pessimism, from persuasion to harsh criticism, is understandable.

Calvinism is not the best of traditions for those who wish to engage in reform. One can scarcely avoid the suspicion that Stowe was effective as an opponent of slavery to the extent that she had liberated herself from Calvinist theology. It is true that she *had* liberated herself to a considerable extent. In future years, she would liberate herself still more. In such novels as *The Minister's Wooing* (1859), she would take on the question of whether the doctrine that a person could do nothing to bring about his own salvation might not be an indictment of God's justice and mercy. On the other hand, the strain of Calvinism in her may have induced her to believe that slavery could not be abolished unless God willed it to be. If He had decided the time had not come, then all the anguish in the world could not change the fact. Seeing how firmly slavery was entrenched and how adamantly the South resisted any attempts to change it, much less abolish it, Stowe might well have been pessimistic. Though she did not say so, she could hardly avoid recognizing the possibility that slavery might endure for generations, perhaps centuries.

More difficult to understand are the indications that when she wrote *Dred*, Stowe was losing some of her optimism about whether the blacks might have enough inherent ability and intelligence to survive in a free society, especially one in which they were in a minority in a society where whites were the majority. In *Uncle Tom's Cabin*, this problem had not been faced because the novel had ended with the idea that the true home of the American blacks was to be in Africa. By the time she wrote *Dred*, Stowe no longer believed that American blacks would return to Africa. The opposition to this "solution" to the American race problem by both black and white abolitionists had been overwhelming.

Was there a link between Stowe's praise of the traits of the blacks in *Uncle Tom's Cabin*—their supposedly inherent spirit of love and kindliness—and the colonization theme of its last pages? Was the hopefulness of the book related to the fact that the northern white reader was encouraged to believe that most of the free blacks would not settle in the North, would not, in fact, remain in this country at all? It had been one thing to have a faith in inherent black potential if the American blacks were going to return to Africa. It might be a more difficult faith to maintain if nearly all the American blacks were going to stay in this country. The reader can only wonder whether the pessimism which characterizes *Dred* is related to Stowe's changed views on colonization.

There is another possible explanation for Stowe's change of attitude in *Dred*. Many of the reviewers of *Uncle Tom's Cabin*, even some of those who had admired the novel, had expressed skepticism concerning the nobility of several of its black characters, especially that of Uncle Tom. He was, in fact, too noble in the opinion of many to be wholly credible. In writing *Dred*, Stowe may well have taken account of these objections. The novel rightly emphasizes the cruelties of slavery, but it says less about the innate traits of blacks, and what it says is not encouraging. This is an important change. If the reader of *Dred* had little reason to believe that the blacks might become responsible citizens, he might regretfully conclude that evil as it was, slavery might be the only institution which could keep in check the defects of the blacks. Those few black characters in the novel who have unusual qualities of character all have some white intermixture. In making this shift, Stowe may have gone further than she realized. She may have unconsciously allowed herself to express doubts about the abilities of blacks, doubts which she may have had before but which she had repressed. Whatever the causes, *Dred* portrays blacks in a most disappointing way. It is not surprising that it is now so little read. It comes close—at least now and then—to implying that blacks will never be more than second-class citizens in this country.

XVI

The Civil War

THE CIVIL WAR exposed qualities of mind and temperament which Stowe
had probably had all along but which heretofore had rarely shown
themselves. It would never have occurred to her to argue, as Abraham
Lincoln did, that whether the North was on God's side might be a more
important question than whether God was on theirs. The Beechers had
never been reluctant to maintain that the reforms which they advocated
clearly represented the will of the Almighty. They had appealed to God
in their warfare against dueling, against demon rum, and against the
Catholics. In the enthusiasm of battle they had sometimes thrown the
cloak of true religion over their causes. With this background, Stowe
saw the War essentially as a religious war. To question any particular
act of the Union forces as it related to the South was for her almost
unthinkable. Part of the reason for the inflexibility of her opinions may
have been her necessary role as a noncombatant. Pushed to the extremes
of moral imperative, a noncombatant may have even stronger temptations than a dedicated soldier to see a war in terms of absolute good and
evil.

By the time the Civil War had begun, Stowe had already lost some
of the sense of balance and fairness in her attitude toward both the
South and the North which had been one of the sources of strength of

Uncle Tom's Cabin. In the novel, she had not concentrated on the defects of the South, though naturally her task had obliged her to enumerate the defects of slavery. Neither was there any attempt in the novel to absolve the North of the guilt of complicity for the institution. In addition, humor in the novel had served an important function. The antics of Topsy had the effect of showing, for example, that however evil slavery might be, white southerners were faced with difficult problems which white northerners were not. In addition, no problem depicted with humor would seem to be so serious as to be wholly beyond solution.

As the battle over slavery intensified, Stowe's humor largely disappeared. It is true that it would have been difficult for anyone to keep a sense of humor under the steady barrage of abuse to which she was subjected. If she had been of a more philosophic turn of mind, she might have reflected that the intensity of the opposition was more the result of her success than of her own qualities as a person. As criticism of her became more bitter, she addressed herself less and less to the South and more to the North and to opinion abroad. Even to those people to whom she appealed, her message became progressively more harsh. The North, in her view, was so sunk in sloth and indifference that only the strongest language could arouse it to the crimes of the South. At a certain point, pessimism becomes a call to violence if for no other reason than that a society cannot live indefinitely with an evil it regards both as intolerable and as beyond any means of rational solution.

When John Brown raided the federal arsenal at Harper's Ferry in 1859, Stowe saw him as a pure hero. From an attitude of defiance to the Fugitive Slave Law she had moved to a point in which insurrection was justifiable as an antislavery tactic. At the time of the raid she was in Italy, following with intense interest the attempts of that country to free itself of Austrian domination and to unify itself as a nation. She made John Brown a martyr not essentially different from any other battler for freedom against a despotic government. Brown was hanged on December 2, 1859, and Stowe's reactions to this event were published a few weeks later:

Thus do all signs gather round this new year; and when we hear from home we find that in America the same demons of slavery are trembling and quailing before some advancing power. We hear here in Italy of a brave good man [John Brown] who calmly gave his life up to a noble effort for human freedom, and died in a way that is better than the most

successful selfish life. We read of troops of soldiers to guard that calm man—
a whole country under martial law, and yet not able to subdue the tremor
caused by his great quiet spirit. John Brown is a witness slain in the cause
which is shaking Hungary, Austria, Italy, France; and his death will be
mightier for that cause than even his success. The cross is the way to the
throne.[1]

Stowe did not raise the issue of whether the methods of Brown in
combating slavery had been legitimate. A few months later, she might
have been thinking of him when she wrote, "Lord Bacon says that
'revenge is a species of wild justice'; and when true justice cannot be
had, it will spring up." In time she would come to see Brown quite
simply as a great and noble martyr. In 1863, she would write of his
earlier battles in the Kansas-Nebraska dispute of the mid-1850s. "Then
came the battle for Kansas-Nebraska," she said, "fought with fire and
sword and blood, where a race of men, of whom John Brown was the
immortal type, acted over again the courage, the perseverance, and the
military religious ardor of the old Covenanters of Scotland, and like
them, redeemed the Ark of Liberty at the price of their own blood."[2]

In the election of 1860, Stowe supported the Republican Party but
she had reservations about it. "We are aware that the Republican Party
are far from being up to the full measure of what *ought* to be thought
and felt on the slavery question," she said. "But they are for *stopping
the evil*—and in this case to arrest is to cure. . . . Meanwhile, the friends
of anti-slavery principle should not relax labor." When Lincoln was
elected, she did not foresee the possibility of war. Instead, she saw
the Republican victory as providing an encouragement for abolition.
It would come first, she was convinced, in the border states, but it might
not be long delayed in the others. "The poor oppressed white voters—
the patriots and Christians shocked and alarmed at the barbarism of
slavery—the political economists sick of its waste—the cowed and over-
ridden free laborers—the foreign non-slaveholding emigrants [immi-
grants?]—," she said, "will now all fuse together, and show in every
slave state a strong front against this tremendous evil, and they will have
for their background the support of the national executive."[3]

When the southern states began to secede under the lame-duck administration of President James Buchanan, he attempted to conciliate
them and Stowe was outraged. She complained of the "cool, decisive
manner with which the President . . . identifies himself with the Southern
states, and speaks with perfect naïveté from their point of view." On the

other hand, he "turns upon the Northern states, and charges upon *them* the whole guilt and responsibility of the extravaganzas now going on in the South." She proceeded to her most crushing indictment of all; the vacillation of Buchanan was due to his irreligion. "[H]e ignores the existence of any moral and religious sense as forming any component element in regulating national movements." Such callousness, she thought, could spring only from atheism:

"The fool hath said in his heart there is no God." David had not seen the bottom of atheism. The fool he speaks of had, it seems, raised the question. It had occurred to him as a possibility. It was left for the XIXth century to show a specimen of a state-paper proposing to a Christian nation to become more formally than ever they had been before robbers, kidnappers, and pirates—without betraying through a line that God had ever been heard of in America—unless it be in certain customary rhetorical phrases at the close.[4]

When Fort Sumter fell and Lincoln called for volunteers, Stowe accepted the war as a holy crusade. In "Getting Ready for a Gale," an article published in the *Independent*, she was obviously ready for war. The title might suggest that she thought the struggle would be a brief one since a "gale" is not a hurricane, but she did examine the possibility that victory might not come easily. "No transient enthusiasm is going to settle this matter," she said. "We have before us a long, grave period of severe self-denial and enterprise which will *task* the resources, physical, mental and moral, of our Northern states." The probability of great bloodshed, however, she masked in euphemisms. As has been said of other wars, the Civil War was to be the last:

We are married to this cause; we have taken it for better or worse, for richer or poorer, till death do us part. It is one part of the last struggle for liberty—the American share of the great overturning which shall precede the coming of Him whose right it is—who shall save the poor and needy, and precious shall their blood be in his sight.

If it was everyone in the North who was wedded to the cause, she at least recognized that it would be the young men of the North who would die for it. "Our sons and brothers whom we are sending to take their lives in their hands, and may never return [*sic*]," she said; "but this is a cause to die for—and, thanks be to God our young men embrace it as a bride, and are ready to die."[5]

Once the war had begun, the great issue for Stowe—as for the abolitionists generally—was the end of slavery. To deny it, even to delay it, was almost to show oneself not merely to be blind and deaf to all pleas for justice but almost to be enrolled in the forces of the Anti-Christ. The extreme rhetoric which she had previously directed against Buchanan she now employed against Lincoln. In 1862, Lincoln issued his famous reply to Horace Greeley that his aim in the War was to save the Union and not to end slavery, and Stowe responded by imagining how Christ himself might have replied to such a declaration:

My paramount aim in this struggle is to set at liberty them that are bruised, and *not* either to save or destroy the Union. What I do in favor of the Union, I do because it helps to free the oppressed; what I forbear, I forbear because it does not help to free the oppressed. I shall do less for the Union whenever it would hurt the cause of the slave, and more when I believe it would help the cause of the slave.

Just as she had previously come near accusing Buchanan of atheism, now she openly wondered about the religious faith of Lincoln:

If he [Lincoln] loves the Union, does he believe in Christ? Does he not believe that Christ has power and will to do what he said?—and when his [Christ's] swift arrows are sent out against oppression and cruelty, shall our armies be held right in the way of them? If they be, there will be many mothers who will weep themselves to stone, like Niobe, whose sons were slain by the arrows of the All-beautiful [Apollo].[6]

Probably the bitterest fact about the Civil War which Stowe was obliged to face was that many of the British, including some of those persons who had enthusiastically hailed *Uncle Tom's Cabin*, were lukewarm, indifferent, or positively hostile to the cause of the North in the Civil War. She attributed the first statements in Great Britain critical of the North's cause as merely a few voices, composed chiefly of spokesmen for British industry and business who were pleased to see their commercial rival suffer a defeat. Soon, she was confident, there would be an uprising of sentiment for the Union cause in Great Britain. The North could count on those "millions of brave Christian English hearts, who are our brethren, our kinsmen, according to the flesh." When this tide of opinion failed to materialize, Stowe melodramatically berated British spokesmen. "O England! England!," she said, paraphrasing the words of Jesus at Gethsemane, "What! could ye not watch with us in one hour?" A little later she was moved to sarcasm. "Place two facts in juxtaposition and let the world look at them," she said. "The Confederate States, the first political union built on negro slavery—England the first state to raise the question of recognition." And then she proclaimed an indifference to foreign opinion. "Well, as for us," she wrote, "we do not *need* sympathy and can very well afford to dispense with it." No matter what happened, she said, the North would never abandon the cause: "[W]e of the free states of the North will fight this battle through to the end. While there is a brick in our chimneys, a tile on our roofs, a drop of blood in our hearts, every man, woman, and child of us are of one mind to give it all to this cause—for it is the cause of God and liberty—the cause of human rights and human equality."[7]

In time, Stowe came to moderate her tone toward Great Britain. Opinion there was too important for her to risk alienating it. Another reason for caution was that Lincoln had specifically disowned abolition of slavery as a war aim. If she said to the British that the purpose of the war was to free the slaves, her opponents could say, logically enough, that Lincoln did not agree. Her major effort was an article published in January of 1863 in the *Atlantic Monthly* with a simultaneous publication in a British magazine. It is probable that when she wrote the article, she knew that Lincoln planned soon to issue the Emancipation Proclamation. On November 13, 1862, she wrote to James T. Fields that she was going to Washington:

I am going to . . . see the heads of departments myself and to satisfy myself that I may refer to the Emancipation Proclamation as a reality and a substance not to fizzle out at the little end of the horn[,] as I should be sorry to call the attention of my sisters in Europe to any such impotent conclusion. . . . I mean to have a talk with 'Father Abraham' himself among others.[8]

This was the occasion of the only meeting which took place between Stowe and Lincoln. There is no direct account of it. What is known of it apparently came from an account by someone in the family, probably one of her children. Her daughter, Harriet, twenty-six years old at the time, accompanied her mother to Washington. Charles Edward Stowe, her son who was then a boy of twelve, also went with her. Unlike his sister, he was actually taken with his mother into the presence of Lincoln. It was probably an instance of what was regarded at the time as fitting in terms of a male prerogative. The account of the meeting, however, apparently came from the daughter, not the son, and she was probably repeating what her mother said to her. Lincoln was supposed to have said to Stowe, "So this is the little lady who made this great war." There is no evidence that Lincoln had ever read *Uncle Tom's Cabin* or that he had seen the play. In a later historical sketch of Lincoln, Stowe provided indirect evidence that he had not read it. She said that he had never read but one novel in his life, Scott's *Ivanhoe*, and even it he had not finished. Lincoln's humorously charging Stowe with responsibility for the Civil War would be taken up many years later by hostile critics of Stowe when the story became publicly known. They would argue that she had indeed been the chief cause of the war. Since she saw the war as God's means of ending slavery, there is no reason to suppose that she would have shrunk from the charge. If she had objected, the reason might well have been her recognition of the importance of the roles of many other people who had opposed slavery.[9]

Lincoln might have told Stowe in his meeting with her of his plans to issue an emancipation proclamation. If he did tell her, it is not surprising that she did not mention it in her article in the *Atlantic*. Almost certainly, Lincoln would not have wanted such important information to come from someone else. Stowe's article was written in the form of a reply to a mass petition which had been addressed to the women of the United States in 1853, enlisting their aid in ending slavery and signed by more than a half million British women. Stowe gave her own article the ironic title, "A Reply to the Affectionate and Christian Address of Many Thoustands of Women of Great Britain and Ireland. . . ." She knew that virtually all of those who were instrumental in getting people to sign the petition were now indifferent or even hostile to the Union cause. On the other hand, she could not exploit this inconsistency by resorting to sarcasm. Therefore, the tone she took in her article was one of dignified sadness and regret.[10]

Part of Stowe's task was easy. She could show that the leaders of the Confederacy did not merely view slavery as an unfortunate necessity of the time, but that they proclaimed it as the best of all possible systems for the circumstances in which they were placed. In one of his speeches, Alexander Stephens, the vice-president of the Confederacy, said that the southern people had recognized "the great truth that the negro is not equal to the white man; that slavery, subordination to the superior race, is his natural and moral condition." And Stephens had not hesitated to ascribe slavery ultimately to God, saying, "It is not safe for us to inquire into the wisdom of His Ordinances, or to question them."[11]

It was more difficult for Stowe to try to convince British readers that the direction, if not the announced policy, of the Republican administration in Washington was antislavery. When Republicans spoke of restoring the Union as it was," she explained, they did not mean to restore it to its status immediately before the election of 1860. Instead, they "meant the Union in the sense contemplated by the original framers of it." Since the Founding Fathers had been nearly all "from principle opposed to slavery," she argued, to reinstate the Union to the meaning which it had in 1787 would mean "restoring a *status* in which, by the inevitable operation of natural laws, peaceful emancipation would become a certainty." British readers might well have wondered why "natural laws" apparently had led the nation no closer to the abolition of slavery in the nearly seventy-five years which had passed since the adoption of the Constitution. She developed a whole series of arguments for supposing that the triumph of the Union armies would mean the abolition of slavery, but she must have known that few people in Great Britain would believe them if abolition did not soon become one of the war aims of the Republican administration.[12]

Stowe attempted to avoid in her article the angry tone of recrimination she had sometimes taken earlier in the war, but she was not entirely successful. She did say frankly that "the cause of freedom . . . [had] found little or no support from the British." There had been only "a few and scattering . . . voices for Liberty." "We loved England," she said; "we respected, revered her, we were bound to her by ties of blood and race. Alas! must all these declarations be written in the past tense?" Much louder in England than the voices of those who had supported the Union, she observed, were those who supported the Confederacy, and louder still had been an action of the British government:

Yes, we have heard on the high seas, the voice of a war-steamer [the *Alabama*], built for a man-stealing Confederacy with English gold in an English dockyard, going out of an English harbor, manned by English sailors, with the full knowledge of English Government-officers, in defiance of the Queen's proclamation of neutrality. So far has English sympathy overflowed.[13]

In her private letters, Stowe sometimes expressed herself even more strongly. In 1862, the Duchess of Argyll wrote to her to express her regret that her country had not supported the cause of the North. She and her husband were almost alone in England, she said, in their pro-Union stand. In her letter of reply, Stowe castigated the perfidy of those people in England who were antislavery only when it cost them nothing. "The utter failure of Christian anti-slavery England, in those *instincts* of a right heart which always can see where the cause of liberty lies has been as bitter a grief to me as was the similar prostration of all our American religious people in the day of the Fugitive Slave Law."

The British antislavery societies were "a humbug, a pious humbug, like the rest. . . . [I]t is our agony; we tread the winepress alone & they whose cheap rhetoric has been for years pushing us into it now desert 'en masse'." The letter was different in tone, of course, from the noble sadness of her published appeal to Great Britain. When the war was over, she expressed her anger more openly, writing in a published article:

We have been hurt at what seemed to us the want of sympathy, the direct antagonism, of England. We might have been less hurt if we had properly understood that Providence has placed us in a position so far ahead of her ideas or power of comprehension, that just judgment or sympathy was not to be expected from her. [The United States had gone] through our great war with no help but that of God, obliged to disregard the misconceptions and impertinences which the foreign press rained down upon us, so, if we are wise, we shall continue to do so.[14]

As the Civil War developed into mass carnage, the rhetoric of both sides escalated. As happens in wars, the advocates of both sides developed different standards in interpreting truth according to which side's interests were involved. Stowe was willing to believe virtually all the tales of atrocities of southern soldiers and to see northern soldiers as "a noble army of martyrs." There was much criticism in Great Britain when General Benjamin F. Butler, commander of the Union forces in New Orleans, ordered his soldiers to treat southern white women who were disrespectful to them as if they were prostitutes. On this point, Stowe complained in her letter of 1862 to the Duchess of Argyll:

Why do the horrible barbarities of *southern* soldiers cause no comment? Why is the sympathy of the British parliament reserved for the poor women of New Orleans deprived of their elegant amusement of throwing vitriol into soldiers' faces & practising indecencies inconceivable in any other state of society[?] Why is *all* expression of sympathy on the southern side[?]

In her public statements during the War, Stowe was less emotional than she was in this letter, but even in the "Affectionate Appeal," she did say that the "oppression and robbery . . . [of the Confederacy] as sure as there is a God that ruleth in the armies of heaven . . . [would] bring down a day of wrath and doom."[15]

In addition to her fulminations against the South and against Great Britain, Stowe also sometimes turned her wrath against those people in the North who disagreed with her. She had been on friendly terms with Hawthorne. When she was in Europe, she had written that his stories had reminded her of the pictures of Rembrandt. Hawthorne, she said, "chooses simple and everyday objects, and so arranges light and shadow as to give them a sombre richness and a mysterious gloom." *The House of Seven Gables* could best be interpreted, she thought, as "a succession of Rembrandt pictures." During the Civil War, however, Stowe criticized Hawthorne severely. In 1863, Hawthorne published *Our Old Home*, his reminiscences of his years in England. When James T. Fields, his publisher, warned Hawthorne that it might not be advisable for him to dedicate his book to his old friend, ex-President Franklin Pierce, Hawthorne replied that it was Pierce who had sent him to England as a consul; that is, had "put me into the position where I made all these profound observations of English scenery, life, and character," and thus he could see no reason for not dedicating his book to him. Stowe detested Pierce, believing him to be proslavery. "Do tell me," she wrote to Fields, "if our friend Hawthorne praises that arch-traitor Pierce in his preface [to *Our Old Home*], and your loyal firm publishes it. I never read the preface and have not yet seen the book; but they say so here, and I can scarcely believe it of you, if I can of him. I regret that I went to see him [Hawthorne] last summer. What! patronize such a traitor to our faces?"[16]

The most faulty of Stowe's pronouncements about the war are probably those dealing with aspects of military life about which she knew little. She was convinced the Army would instill character into young American men. These men may have previously "lived effeminate lives" or, on the other hand, they may have been potentially violent criminals. "Many a poor Battery bully of New York, many a street rowdy," she said, "felt uplifted by the discovery that he too had hid under the dirt and dust of his former life this divine and precious jewel. Many an idler or ruffian leaped for joy to find that he too could be a hero." The nation itself was "being educated into faith in God by a terrible discipline."[17]

On the other hand, Stowe did not forget that human liberty ought to be the chief war aim of the North and she did not hesitate to criticize those northern leaders who expressed hatred of the blacks or infringed upon their rights. In 1862, she mentioned a "celebrated General in the Western states" who "harangues a crowded and cheering audience." She quoted the unnamed general as advocating a good cause but for a wrong reason. He thought that blacks should be enlisted in the Union armies, saying in a speech:

Mind you now, don't misunderstand me, I *hate* the negro—nobody could hate him more. I never see one walking the street that I don't think, "There goes the cause of all our trouble." I hate the negro . . . and it is not because I have the least favor to him that I say we must call upon him, but because I see it as an absolute necessity to the safety of the white race!

Stowe confessed her disappointment that the General could envision the war aims of the Union merely as the "lowest form of brute self interest." "Now, a nation on the very eve of righting the greatest of modern wrongs. . . ," she said, "ought by some means to be lifted up to a higher and more honorable point of view." The northern people should "remember the great doctrine of universal brotherhood, and the sins of our nation against those equal rights which are asserted, to our shame, in the constitution of every state."[18]

Stowe supported the harsh war measures of the Union armies. She praised the decision of General William T. Sherman to withdraw rations from southern white civilians made destitute in eastern Tennessee in 1864 by battlefield operations. "At first my order operated very hardly," she quoted Sherman as saying, "but no actual suffering resulted, and I trust that those who clamored at the cruelty and hardships of the day have already seen in the result a perfect justification of my course." Stowe commented almost flippantly. "Seeing it himself," she said, "it is . . . clear that if they did not, it would not particularly distress him." She also quoted Sherman's statement concerning his proposed plan for securing supplies for his army as it marched through Georgia:

Georgia has a million of inhabitants. If they can live, we should not starve. If the enemy interrupt my communications, I shall be absolved from all obligations to subsist on my own resources but [shall?] feel perfectly justified in taking whatever and wherever I can find. I will inspire my command, if successful, with my feelings, and that [*sic*] beef and salt are all that are absolutely necessary to life, and parched corn fed General Jackson's army once, on that very ground.

Stowe said that this statement was "rigidly just."[19]

Just as she saw the hand of God in the victories of the North, so Stowe saw it in the punishment which was being inflicted upon the South. "Verily his inquisition for blood has been strict and awful," she said, and "for every stricken household of the poor and lowly [of the North] hundreds of households of the oppressor have been scattered." Virginia had apparently been especially singled out for the vengeance of the Lord:

[T]hat land, with its fair name, Virginia, has been made a desolation so signal, so wonderful that the blindest passer-by cannot but ask for what sin so awful a doom has been meted out. The prophetic visions of Nat Turner, who saw the leaves drop blood and the land darkened, have been fulfilled. The work of justice which he predicted is being executed to the uttermost.[20]

This is the kind of rhetoric, of course, which wars inspire. Words like Stowe's might have helped to win the war, though one wonders whether they had this result. It is less doubtful that rhetoric can become so impassioned that it will impede the peace which will follow. This is especially true of a civil war in which the rival factions remain united politically. On this point, Lincoln was wiser than Stowe. He knew the North should not lose the sense that a time would come when North and South would be obliged to change their attitudes toward one another. They would have to learn to live together in a spirit of tolerance if not of agreement. Stowe lost the distrust she had had of Lincoln in the early years of the war and wrote a moving tribute to him. When he was assassinated, however, he was for her the martyrd President who should be avenged, rather than the conciliator between North and South. The wounds of the war and especially the wound of his death to the nation were too deep to allow her to serve, at least in the first months and years after the war, as a healer between North and South. She would come to a more kindly and forgiving attitude toward the South in future years, but it would take a struggle on her part to achieve it.[21]

XVII

Reconstruction and Beyond

AFTER THE CIVIL WAR, Harriet Beecher Stowe had two different and perhaps in some ways mutually contradictory attitudes toward the South. On the one hand, she thought that the leaders of the Confederacy ought to be punished; on the other hand, she thought that there should be a delay, perhaps an indefinite delay, in according the newly freed blacks the full rights of citizenship. Her conviction that Confederate leaders should be punished lasted, in its full intensity at least, only a few months after the war, but her reluctance to give blacks full rights of citizenship was a more deep-seated conviction and lasted a longer time. She thought that the blacks, deprived of any experience in self-government, would inevitably fall under the control of demagogues if their freedom, particularly their right to vote, came too quickly. On the other hand, she had little idea that delay in giving the blacks citizenship rights might easily be converted into a plan for denying such rights indefinitely. What later would be called "gradualism" became, in effect, a means of making second-class citizens of many of the blacks for at least a hundred years.

The Reconstruction period exposed another of Stowe's weaknesses. She had never been much interested in politics, but her indifference had been only a slight handicap for her. In the battle for the abolition of slavery, she had not been obliged to consider political solutions because none had any real chance of passage in Congress or of being implemented in the slave states if they had been passed. After the Civil War, her lack of interest in politics would mean that she would be handicapped as a friend of the blacks and as one of the leaders of their cause. The issue was no longer the great one of abolishing slavery. It was a complex matter of how to insure as nearly as possible that the blacks would enter into American life as citizens with the rights and privileges other people took for granted. Moral fervor would no longer be nearly enough. It would have to be accompanied by an intelligent interest in a large number of questions, some of them seemingly unrelated. In time, Stowe came to recognize the nature of at least some of these problems, but the process for her—as for many northern well-wishers of the blacks—was a slow and painful one.

There was a third reason for Stowe's weakness as a leader of opinion with regard to the civil rights of the newly freed blacks. Her interests as a writer of fiction shifted to other issues. Her New England stories, to which she chiefly confined herself after the war, sometimes charmed readers, partly because she was writing about a society which she understood better than she did the South. There were black characters in some of these stories, but none of them was likely to cause readers to reflect on the question of what should be the political and social status of blacks in the South. In addition, she took up a cause which had nothing to do with the rights of blacks and which proved to be a singularly barren one. After the death of Lady Byron, Stowe wrote an emotional defense of her relationship with Lord Byron based upon confidences Lady Byron had given her. One reason for what seems now to have been an unfortunate diversion of energy may well have been that Stowe was not much interested in the complex issues of Reconstruction and, therefore, had relatively little to say about it.[1]

When the war ended, Stowe thought the primary task of that time was to punish the Confederate leaders. The North should waste no time in "deploring the woes of the assassins," she said. Nor should they limit themselves to seizing and hanging "the poor, ignorant, stupid, imbruted, semi-barbarians who were set as jailers to keep these hells of torment [Confederate prisons for northern soldiers]." Rather, the nation should "punish the educated, intelligent chiefs who were the head and brains of the iniquity." "O ye who have pity to spare," she said, spare it for the broken-hearted friends, who, to life's end, will suffer over and over all that their dear ones endured. Pity the mothers who hear their sons' faint calls in dreams, who in many a weary nightwatch see them pining and yearn with a life-long unappeasable yearning to have been able to soothe these forsaken, lonely death-beds. Oh, man or woman, if you have pity to spare, spend it on their victims, on the thousands of living hearts which these men of sin have doomed to an anguish that will end only with life! [The northern prisoners have been] slowly tortured and starved and done to death, by the fiendish policy of Jefferson Davis and Robert Edmund Lee.[2]

Davis was singled out with a special bitterness. During the war, had he not been "living in ease and luxury in Richmond," knowing well that "men were dying by inches in filth and squalor and privation in the Libby Prison, within bowshot of his door?" As late as 1868, Stowe was still speculating on the question of whether Davis and other southern leaders had not been conspirators in the assassination of Lincoln. "Whether or no Jefferson Davis and his fellows in the rebel government were actually aiding and abetting in this particular crime," she said, "it has not been unjust nor unnatural to suspect them of it." And she proceeded to examine a tangle of hearsay and innuendo which might indicate that Davis had conspired in the assassination. She did not suspect that Lee was also guilty of this crime, but she did think he was as guilty as Davis of failing to prevent the mistreatment of Union army prisoners. "If General Lee had been determined *not* to have prisoners starved or abused," she asked, "does any one doubt that he could have prevented these things? Nobody doubts it. His raiment is red with the blood of his helpless captives."[3]

Before the war, Stowe had argued that the North must share the blame with the South for the wrongs of slavery. Now after the war they were both guilty, but in significantly different ways and to different degrees. The sins of the North were chiefly those of omission; it had been the South which had actually committed nearly all of the sinful deeds. "It was God's will," she said, "that this nation—the North as well as the South—should deeply and terribly suffer for the sin of consenting to and encouraging the great oppressions of the South." The weeping of wives, mothers, and sisters of soldiers in both the Confederate and Union armies was divine retribution for the earlier weeping of "slave mothers, whose tears nobody regarded." The North had been unwilling to heed the cries of the slaves and, as a result, the South had been able to inflict on northern soldiers the same kinds of cruelties they had inflicted on the slaves. These northern soldiers had suffered "at the hands of these slave masters, with whose sins our nation has connived."[4]

These outbursts served chiefly to relieve Stowe's feelings and had little to do with the policies she would soon be advocating. She began to look eagerly to the South for signs of moderation and compromise. This would have been a commendable approach if it had been accompanied by a clear awareness that the rights of the blacks in the South should not be put off indefinitely. To her readers, most of whom were white northerners, she spoke of the dangers of moving too quickly in insisting that the former slaves be given their rights. She also felt it would be necessary to carry white opinion in the South with them in their efforts to bring about change. At about this time, Henry Ward Beecher was coming to have quite a different attitude toward the South from the one he had while the Civil War was still in progress. Earlier he had argued that the North should have among its war aims the punishment of Confederate leaders and the denial of citizenship to all who had fought against the Union. After the war, he took the position of advocating conciliation with the white South. His attitude involved him in much ambiguity about the time when blacks would receive suffrage and other rights. Stowe joined her brother in this particular stand. The only real difference between the two was that Beecher spoke publicly of his change in attitude; Stowe was generally content to express her rather similar views in private letters.[5]

In 1866, the Duchess of Argyll wrote to Stowe and apparently expressed some concern about whether the former slaves would secure their political rights, including the right to vote. Stowe wrote to her a justification for the delay, beginning with an emphasis on the fact that slavery had been abolished:

Oh, my friend, when I think of what has been done these past few years & of what is now doing I am lost in amazement. I have just, by way of realizing it to myself[,] been reading Uncle Tom's Cabin again—& when I read that book scarred with the memories of an anguish & horror that can never be forgotten I think it is all over now!—all past! & that now the questions debated are simply of more or less time before granting legal suffrage to those who so lately were held only as articles of [illegible word] merchandise. When this comes over me, I think no private or individual sorrow can ever make me wholly without comfort. If my faith in God's presence & real living power in the affairs of men ever grew dim—this makes it impossible to doubt.

Thus, Stowe could not support the measures of the Radical Republicans. "Charles Sumner is looking simply at the abstract right of the thing," she said to the Duchess, while on the other hand, Henry Ward Beecher was looking

at actual probabilities. We all know that the state of society at the South is such that laws are a very inadequate protection even to white men. Southern elections always have been scenes of mob violence when only white men voted. Multitudes of lives have been lost at the poles [sic] in this way—& if against their will negro suffrage is forced upon them, I do not see how any one in their senses can expect any thing less than an immediate war of races.

If the southern states were required to grant suffrage to the blacks as a condition of being readmitted to the Union, they would "grant it— grant it nominally because they would know that this grant never could or would become an actual realization. And what would then be gained for the negro?" The North should have faith in President Johnson. He was "honestly seeking to do right," but she added ambiguously that "if he fails in knowing just what right is, it is because he is a man born and reared in a slave state and acted on by many influences which we cannot rightly estimate." Whatever his failings, Johnson had an excellent adviser in Henry Ward Beecher. "My brother has talked with . . . [Johnson] earnestly and confidentially," she said, "and has faith in him as an earnest good man seeking to do right." Stowe possibly did not then realize that Henry would come to see granting political rights to blacks in the South as a matter for the increasingly distant future.[6]

The emotional tone of her letter to the Duchess of Argyll and her appeal to the mysterious purposes of God make the reader suspect that Stowe was unconsciously evading an important issue. Of course, we have the benefit of hindsight. We know that the delay in granting suffrage to the blacks in the South would last, in many areas, for a hundred years. The Duchess might sensibly have replied that if the North turned its attention chiefly to the gains of the past, even those gains might be lost. The same year Stowe wrote this letter she also wrote a letter to her brother Charles. In it she mentioned a fear she had not expressed to the Duchess. "Corrupt politicians are already beginning to speculate on . . . [the blacks] as possible capital for their schemes," she said, "and to fill their head with all sorts of vagaries." Here her concern was not with whether a law granting suffrage to the blacks in the South might be impossible to enforce. She was worried over what the blacks would do with political rights if they had them. It might have been a legitimate reservation if it had been accompaned by a strong conviction that the delay in granting rights to the blacks in the South ought not to be indefinitely prolonged. The absence of any guarantees meant that Stowe was, in effect, letting the rights of blacks go by default.[7]

Stowe's faltering on the subject of civil rights for the blacks was obviously a retreat from her earlier positions. There had never been a suggestion in her writings that the end of slavery would not mean the beginning of citizenship for blacks. In addition, she had argued that the rights granted by a government might become meaningless if they were not accompanied by the right to vote. When Italy was unified in 1860, she had said that the major achievement was obtaining suffrage for the Italians. "There is nothing develops a man like a vote," she said. "It changes him from an animal to a reasonable creature and this voting business in Italy has done the work of years in awakening dormant minds and making men out of clods." The reader must necessarily ask why after the Civil War was over she felt differently about granting suffrage to southern blacks?[8]

One reason for the shift in Stowe's attitude is impossible to document but may well be the most important of all. She might have wished to discard the image of a reformer so zealously dedicated to a cause that she had little knowledge of the process by which it might be achieved. She had long been castigated as a fanatical abolitionist and after the North's victory she might have wished to show moderation in advocating immediate change. Since she did not oppose civil rights for blacks in the free states, there is no reason to suppose that she was theoretically opposed to those rights in the South. To her, as for others in the North, it was a matter of timing. If the white South could be convinced that the northerners were not motivated by vengeance, if something could be done to expand the economic opportunities of the newly freed blacks, she probably hoped against hope that the right to vote would follow. That it might be nearly a hundred years before blacks were granted suffrage in some parts of the South probably never occurred to her.

In 1866, Stowe published an essay on Reconstruction in which she wrote of an imaginary group of northern white people seated around a table expressing different views. One of the characters is Theophilus, who has little hope. Having freed the slave, he says, the North now will "turn him out defenseless to shift for himself in a community every member of which is embittered against him." The people in the North were scarcely in a position, he says, to argue that southern states should give blacks the right to vote. Had not the Connecticut voters only recently turned down an amendment to the state constitution which would have given suffrage to blacks? Even northerners who were not antiblack were not much interested in the issues of Reconstruction. Instead, says Theophilus, "all I can see in the North at present is a raging, tearing headlong chase after money." Under the circumstances it is not surprising that the condition of the former slaves in the South is about as bad as it could be. They are "suffering the vindictive wrath of former masters." Laws are being passed, "hunting them out of this State and out of that; the animosity of race—at all times the most bitter and unreasonable of animosities—is being aroused all over the land." The results can be easily predicted. National leaders in the North will for a time support, at least in theory, the rights of the former slaves, "but the moment that political combinations begin to be formed, all the rights and interests of this helpless people will be bandied about as so many make-weights in the political scale." The blacks will probably not get the vote, he predicts, but if they do get it they will not keep it.[9]

Mrs. Crowfield, another imaginary character in the essay, takes a more optimistic view. The "dangers" which Theophilus has listed are "real and great," she says, but he has omitted other things which he ought to consider:

There never has been a time in our history when so many honest and just men held power in our land as now—never a government before in which the public councils recognized with more respect the just and the right. There never was an instance of a powerful government showing more tenderness in the protection of a weak and defenseless race than ours has shown in the care of the freedmen hitherto. There never was a case in which the people of the country were more willing to give money and time and disinterested labor to raise and educate those who have thus been thrown on their care.

She thinks Theophilus might be wrong in supposing that the North is about to abandon the blacks in the South. "Let us wait, at least," she says, "and see." She notes the success of the Freedmen's Bureau in settling a number of blacks on land in the South. She thinks that an improvement in the economic condition of blacks in southern communities will lead logically to their being granted political rights. If this does not happen, she has an alternative plan for them. They can emigrate to the North. "No laws hold them," she says; "active, industrious laborers will soon find openings in any part of the Union."[10]

In 1868, Stowe began to live in Florida during the winter months of the year. Frederick Stowe, her son, had been wounded in the Civil War and, in addition, his fondness for liquor had deepened into an addiction. It was hoped that Frederick would improve if he lived in the open air and got more exercise. Therefore, Stowe bought the land principally for him. It was near Mandarin, Florida, a village on the St. Johns River, a few miles from Jacksonville. Although for a good many years she lived in the South for a part of the year, she was not closely in touch with many southern people. Most of her neighbors in Florida were northerners who had come there for the climate or for the cheap land. In addition, she was a busy woman with a living to earn, especially since Calvin had retired in 1863. Accordingly, she had only a limited acquaintance among her southern neighbors. Though she said on more than one occasion that she never had any unpleasant encounters with southerners in Florida, it is possible that many of them were not eager to know her.[11]

Stowe wrote a good deal about the newly freed blacks in the South but not often in terms of their civil rights. She was chiefly concerned with what might be done to improve their economic opportunities. Her articles were printed in northern magazines, and it is unlikely they were read much in the South. In these articles she developed the theme that white people who employed blacks might well be able to make a substantial profit. One of her major ideas for black employment rested upon a racist idea. The whites could not labor in the fields in the hot climate of the South, she argued, and therefore the blacks were the only ones who could perform this labor.

As early as 1862, Stowe had attempted to answer those critics in the North who had wondered what would happen to the freed blacks in the South if the North should win. Would not the relationships between the races be so embittered in the South, these critics asked, that the whites would take out their resentments on the blacks? As an answer, Stowe had argued that the question to be addressed to white southerners after the war would be, "What will you do without *them*? [the blacks]?" The hard fact was, she said, that the whites could not labor in the fields. The South

has a climate where a generation of white men must perish of malaria and fevers before they can become acclimated; and here on the soil is a race of hardy peasantry, who appear to have been purposely made and contributed by the Almighty to resist malaria and to delight in the heats that wither the whites—and yet our legislators are gravely pondering the question where they shall ship these laborers, in case they are reduced by God's providence to give them the birthright of liberty!

The government need not spend any money at all for the freed slaves, she argued. After all, it had not spent any for the thousands and thousands of immigrants who had been coming into the country from Europe. "Do just what you have done with the oppressed and the poor of all nations," she said; "give them equal rights, a fair start, and the restraint and protection of just laws, and God and human nature will answer for the rest."[12]

After the war, Stowe changed her mind and became much less confident that the slaves could shift for themselves if they were given their freedom. She retained the idea, however, that the whites should employ the blacks in the South as hired agricultural laborers. Her chief argument was that they had no real choice. Somewhere along the line she dropped the idea that after a generation or two the whites might become acclimated to work in the fields in the South. Instead, she envisioned a labor system in which virtually all outdoor physical labor would be done, for the foreseeable future, by the blacks. In Florida, she said, she had noted that in the really hot weather the white men would leave the fields by ten o'clock in the morning and for the rest of the day confine themselves either to indoor jobs or to those which would permit them to work in the shade. On the other hand, the hot sun had no effect on the black workers. "The sun awakes all their vigor and all their boundless jollity," she said. "When their nooning time comes, they sit down, not in the shade, but in some good hot place in the sand, and eat their lunch, and then stretch out, hot and comfortable, to take their noon siesta with the full glare of the sun upon them." She was especially impressed by one such man who worked on the Stowe plantation. She watched "old Simon" working with his wheelbarrow in the hottest weather:

"Why, Simon!" we say: "how *can* you work so this hot weather?"
The question provokes an explosion of laughter. "Ha, hah, ho, ho, ho, misse! It be hot; dat so; ho, ho, ho!"
"How *can* you work so? I can't even think how you can do such hard work under such a sun."
"Dat so; ho, ho! Ladies can't; no, dey can't, bless you, ma'am!" And

Simon trundles off with his barrow, throws it down, and chuckles again.
A little laugh goes a great way with Simon; for a boiling spring of animal
content is ever welling up within.[13]

Simon's reaction to Stowe's surprise at his being able to work in
the hot sun is somewhat ambiguous. He says that "ladies" cannot do it
—not that white men cannot. Simon may have been a male chauvinist
but not necessarily a racist. Stowe apparently assumed, on the other
hand, that the lesson to be learned from his statement was that whites
of both sexes cannot stand to work any considerable time in the hot sun.
Because the blacks could presumably do this, she believed that they
should be trained in the South to become efficient agricultural workers.
She wrote:

All that is wanted to supply the South with a set of the most desirable
skilled laborers is simply education. The negro children are bright; they
can be taught any thing; and if the whites, who cannot bear tropical suns
and fierce extremes, neglect to educate a docile race who both can and will
bear it for them, they throw away their best chance of success in a most
foolish manner. No community that properly and carefully educates the
negro children now growing up need complain of having an idle, thriftless,
dishonest population among them. Common schools ought to prevent that.

Stowe did not speculate on what might happen if it should turn out
that some of the blacks might not be content with a permanent status
as hired agricultural laborers.[14]

In the North, the theory was that while an energetic person might
start as the employee of other people, he need not remain in that position. In time, he might acquire property and work for himself. Was
this the process Stowe envisioned for black workers in the South? In
theory it was. "The negroes, so far as we have observed in our experience [in Florida]," she wrote, "are as determined to *save* money and
careful of it as any Yankee. Their ambition is to buy land and own
little pieces of their own; and certainly this is a very wholesome one."
And yet there was a formidable obstacle. "Landowners, as a general
thing, are not willing to sell to them," she admitted, "and all sorts of
difficulties are thrown in the way of their acquiring real estate." She
was uneasily aware that nearly all of the blacks might retain their
status as landless laborers for the indefinite future.[15]

The kinds of "difficulties" Stowe meant are illustrated by her story
of a local black known as Old Cudjo, a man whom she knew herself.
When she met him, he was "an aged negro, misshapen, and almost

deformed. He was thin and bony and his head and beard were grizzled with age. He was black as night itself; and but for a glittering, intellectual eye, he might have been taken for a big baboon,—the missing link of Darwin." Old Cudjo had saved his money until he could buy a small tract of land. By heavy and sustained labor he had cleared his land of scrub palmettos and had planted a field of cotton. In addition, he had built some outbuildings and a fence consisting of three thousand split rails. He worked four years only to discover that the man who had sold the land to him had not possessed legal title to it. Thus the farm with all the improvements passed from his hands. Luckily for him, the injustice done to him came to the attention of some of his white neighbors—Stowe did not say whether they were northern or southern. They went to the county courthouse and discovered that the new owner had not yet filed the necessary papers to insure ownership. They filed papers for Old Cudjo—the legal problem here is not entirely clear from Stowe's account—and thus he was able to repossess the farm. It was a great success story. One may wonder, however, how many Old Cudjos there were in the South of that time and how often they fared as well as this one did.[16]

Stowe was convinced that the white South would soon see the necessity for educating the blacks in order to prepare them for citizenship. In 1877, she quoted a statement from the governor of Florida on the subject:

Now that a very large element of our population is released from bondage and entrusted with the power of the ballot, a system of free schools has become a means of self-preservation. To educate the colored race and fit them to exercise the privilege of voting intelligently—to perform all the sacred rights of freedom, to enjoy their liberty and become wise and good citizens—imposes on us a task to perform, a responsibility from which we cannot escape.

Stowe was encouraged by the fact that the man who made this statement was a Democrat. She praised his "good statesmanship," and added, "Who cares whether a man calls his party this or that, if he will carry out principles like these?"[17]

Stowe and members of her family were themselves involved in efforts to teach blacks in Florida to read, but these efforts were accompanied by serious handicaps. "A quantity of spelling-books brought by us was received among them with enthusiasm," she said, "and every Sunday our veranda was thronged with learners. Many poor, stupid-looking women,

after ploughing all day in the field, would come up at night with their
spelling-books and beg us to teach them in the evenings." She recognized
the fact that people of any race might find it difficult to learn to read
if they had started when they were adults and had time only at night
for instruction, time which also came after a long and hard day of work:

Alas! we never felt so truly what the loss and wrong is of being deprived
of early education as when we saw how hard, how almost hopeless, is the
task of acquisition in mature life. When we saw the sweat start upon these
black faces, as our pupils puzzled and blundered over the strange cabalistic
forms of the letters, we felt a discouraged pity.

She wondered whether any person, white or black, might not find it
almost impossible to learn to read if he was "beginning the alphabet at
forty."[18]

The comment is sympathetic to the plight of the older blacks, but
its implication seems to be that all but the most rudimentary education
may be impossible for them. Some of her reservations suggest comparison with those of the character Anne Clayton in *Dred* when she attempts
to teach the slave children of a plantation. Like Anne Clayton, Stowe
herself suggested that if education was impossible for the blacks they
at least need not be denied the comforts of religion. "Like all the
negroes, they had an uninstructed but very strong religious proclivity,"
she wrote. She described their religious services in which they "pray, and
shout, and move in a weird sort of religious dance to the music of
what they call a 'spiritual,' till a late hour." She admitted that there
was "no clear idea of instruction in this." She went on to argue that the
religion of the blacks gave them advantage over poor southern whites;
the black laborer was certainly better off than the white laborer "who
spends his leisure hours in the grog-shop in the hearing and singing of
drunken songs." The comparison between white and black laborers may
have been Stowe's unconscious effort to hide something from herself.
She was close to suggesting that religion might be a fit substitute for
education. Charles Stowe, her son, apparently did not share his mother's
optimism about blacks. He described the Stowe home in Florida as "a
free boarding house for lazy negroes."[19]

Stowe apparently thought that a public school system for all children, both black and white, would soon be a reality in all the southern
states. Sometimes she came close to saying that such a system was already
in operation, an assumption far from true. "The common-school system

has been established throughout the Southern States," she wrote in 1879, "and recognized in theory by the wisest Southern men as to be applied impartially to whites and blacks." There was circular reasoning, of course, in this way of putting it. Who were the wisest southern men? The apparent answer was that they were the ones who recognized the need for the education of both blacks and whites. She did not say whether such people were the majority in the South or whether their counsels were likely to prevail. Sometimes she conceded that many southern people were not enthusiastic supporters of public schools even for the whites, much less for the blacks. She noted that the movement for public schools in the South, even for the whites, had met "active and powerful resistance." She was quite aware that the opposition to education for blacks was even stronger. Even though the blacks had "an earnest desire . . . for education," she wrote, there was "in many sections [of the South] a blind prejudice against any efforts to give it to them." In these circumstances, the "work of building schoolhouses for the colored people and of supporting teachers was divided between the Freedmen's Bureau and various religious bodies [of the North] whose missionaries were in the field." Thus, the reader discovers that the battle for public education in the South, and especially for the blacks, was far from being won.[20]

Stowe had nothing to say about the desirability of establishing colleges and universities for blacks in the South. The chief reason for her silence may have been that she thought that any suggestion of the kind might imperil the success of the movement there for elementary and high school education. Perhaps there was another reason, however, for her apparent lack of enthusiasm for southern black colleges. Before the war she had assumed that the higher education of the time, with its emphasis on classical languages, was as suitable for blacks as it was for whites. At the end of her novel *Dred*, published in 1856, Harry Gordon (a slave character, light-skinned enough to pass as a white, who escapes to Canada) takes great pride in the fact that his young son "is construing *Caesar's Commentaries* at school, and often reads his lesson of an evening to his delighted father, who willingly resigns the palm of scholarship into his hands." In 1872, Stowe praised the establishment of Howard University in Washington, D.C., describing it as a place "where the colored race may have all the advantages of a thoroughly classical education." She may have doubted, however, whether many southern blacks at that stage of their history needed to study Latin and Greek.

There is no suggestion in her writings that black institutions like Howard University should be established in the South, nor did she advocate the founding there of any other black colleges or universities.[21]

Stowe limited her recommendations for the education of blacks in the South to elementary schools. They should learn reading, writing, and arithmetic. Whatever additional subjects there might be would be confined to "practical" subjects like carpentry and agriculture for the boys, and cooking and sewing for the girls. The effect of such education would enable the black students to perform menial work more efficiently. In 1869, she said that the Freedmen's Bureau might be able to "make emancipation . . . popular" by training black girls and young women for household service. "A set of well-trained cooks and chambermaids turned out into the various families of the South," she said, "would not only get good situations and good wages, but would go farther towards making clear the propriety of emancipation and making the new order of things popular than any other one thing we could mention." She added, "On the whole, the negro is a pleasant creature to deal with. There is a degree of jollity and joyousness, a quaint humor and ceaseless good nature, that makes them [sic] agreeable."[22]

Stowe herself, partly with her own money, partly with the aid of British donors, and partly with the aid of the Freedmen's Bureau, established in 1869 a school for both white and black children in Mandarin, Florida. The building was used as a church on Sundays and as a school on weekdays. To one of the British donors, Stowe wrote:

You have no idea what it is to start such a school amid the prejudices of such a community. In the first place, tho' they are pleasant and kind enough, —the old white settlers regard us Yankees with some suspicion. They also despise the negroes and hate them. The negroes naturally are wary and do not give their confidence at once. They are *very* ignorant and untaught.

Originally, Stowe had not meant to include whites in the school, but— as she explained in her letter to the donor—it was necessary that the opportunity for education be extended to both races in the school. She said she had discovered that "the school house will have to be open to both white and black children or we could not keep it going. Teaching the whites is the only way of protecting the blacks."[23]

Stowe also discovered that there were equally strong pressures in the community to keep the whites and blacks of the new school segregated. There were folding doors in the middle of the one-room building;

therefore, classes for blacks could be held on one side of the building
and classes for whites on the other. Another of the British donors apparently wrote a protest against segregation in the school, to which Stowe
responded with the following explanation:

> In relation to the subject that you mentioned—it has been found ex-
> pedient as yet, in the South to teach the white and black in separate schools.
> The white children will *not* come to the same school with the black ones.
> Although the school should be of the very best kind and freely offered,
> no inducement would ever persuade parents to let their children come to
> them—they would greatly prefer that they would grow up without any
> education at all. But it is very essential that they should be educated—not
> only on their own account—but as a protection to the blacks. It has been
> found in Richmond, that the only way to protect black schools from mobs,
> was to set up schools for the white children, and civilize that class, of whom
> mobs are generally composed. And so far the thing has worked very well.
> My little school-house will have to serve for both classes, and this thing
> must be managed with great care at first. If we are going to soften and
> modify the prejudices of the whites, we must pursue such a course as will
> induce them to our schools, and get them under our influence. You would
> yourself see the necessity of pursuing such a course, if you were on the
> ground.

The faint hope Stowe held out to the British donor—that eventually
the school would be racially integrated—was not realized. In fact, she
never did publicly discuss the issue of racially integrated education in
the South. The subject of her own relationship to the school was too
sore for her even to admit that she was receiving funds from outside the
South—both from Great Britain and from the North. She warned a
British correspondent that she was unwilling "to take the responsibility
of any public appeal" for the school. She urged that the British donors
not disclose the fact that they had made contributions, saying "it would
be sure to get over here and set the country all in a flame. It is astonish-
ing how everything I say and do gets in the papers, often in the most
absurd and untrue ways."[24]

When the blacks received the right to vote in Florida, Stowe said
nothing publicly, though it is apparent in her private letters that she
approved of the legislation. In 1876, she wrote a letter from Florida
to Mrs. Lucy Perkins, a friend in Hartford. She told a story of "our
Aunt Caty," a black woman who wore a white turban and had a
"peculiar Ethiopian wit & sense of drollery." Aunt Caty had described
the efforts to keep blacks from voting in a local election:

"Good Lord, dey was goin to get all the white folks far & near to come & crowd the poles so as to keep de colored folks off from votin—But Sam Bowdin [a white?] he got drunk & let it out to My William. . . . Then William he sent all around for ten miles & warn all de colored folks & they comes into Mandarin night afore & camps under de great oaks—every mothers son—. . . & de minute poles open *dere dey was*! & got all through votin afore de 'crackers' got dere"—Then she laughs & shook her sides—& took off how the crackers came shambling along about eleven & twelve when all de darkies had voted—it was as good as a play—to hear her tell of it.

It is possible that the Aunt Caty in the above account may have been the same as the Aunt Katy who was the subject of an article Stowe had published in 1870, six years previously. In this article, Stowe proposed that the vote be extended to black women as well as to black men. She mentioned Aunt Katy, a black woman of her acquaintance in Florida. "I pay seven dollars school tax," Stowe quoted Aunt Katy as saying, "and the school is in part mine." And Stowe quite agreed. "What should be the qualification of a voter?" she asked.

Is it intelligence? She [Aunt Katy] is this day more intelligent and quite as strong and quite as able to discharge service for the State as any male land-owner in her neighborhood. . . . As to moral qualifications the case is even stronger. There is a good motherly judgment, a fine moral nature about many of these old colored women that is a grade above the men of the same race. Of the two they are the more intelligent and fitted to vote intelligently, so far as our observation extends.[25]

Stowe did not publicly argue the question of civil rights for southern blacks. She might have thought that these would inevitably come and that she ought not to irritate white sensibilities any more than she absolutely had to. She showed herself eager to do what she could to lessen sectional bitterness. In 1875, she visited Savannah and wrote an article praising the Confederate memorial which had recently been erected there. "What strikes us most is the solemn brevity—the absence of verbiage—the noble calmness which characterizes the whole [of the inscription]. It reads, 'And I will make them one nation in the land upon the mountains of Israel, and they shall no more be two nations neither shall they be divided into two kingdoms any more.' "[26]

In 1879, Stowe wrote an essay reviewing the progress of the blacks in the South, emphasizing their increasing material prosperity and their greater opportunities for education. She had only one ambiguous statement with regard to their political rights: "The legal state of the negro

is universally conceded as a *finality* by the leading minds of the South."
This statement would prove to be considerably less than a complete
guarantee of black civil rights.[27]

The last public comment, and almost the last private one, Stowe
made about blacks was at her birthday party in 1882. She was seventy-
one years old. A number of literary and intellectual leaders were there—
including Oliver Wendell Holmes, John Greenleaf Whittier, Bronson
Alcott, and William Dean Howells. In addition, there were appreciative
letters from Mark Twain, Henry James, Julia Ward Howe, Francis
Parkman, Thomas Wentworth Higginson, Wendell Phillips, and James
Russell Lowell. Stowe was now almost wholly in retirement. Her speech
to the assembled group on the occasion was gentle and conciliatory:

> And one thing more—and that is, if any of you have doubt, or sorrow,
> or pain—if you doubt about this world—just remember what God has done.
> Just remember that this great sorrow of slavery has gone—gone by, forever.
> I see it every day at the South. I see these people growing richer and richer.
> I see men very happy in their lowly lot; but, to be sure, you must have
> patience with them. They are not perfect, but have their faults, and they
> are serious faults in the view of white people. But they are very happy,
> that is evident; and they do know how to enjoy themselves—a great deal
> more than you do. An old Negro friend in our neighborhood has got a
> new, nice two-story house, and an orange grove, and a sugar mill. He has
> got a lot of money, besides. Mr. Stowe met him one day, and he said, "I
> have got twenty head of cattle, four head of hoss, forty head of hen, and
> I have got ten children—*all mine, every one mine.*" Well, that is a thing
> a black man could not say once; and this man was sixty years old before he
> could say it. With all the faults of the coloured people, take a man and put
> him down with nothing but his hands, and how many could say as much
> as that? I think they have done well.[28]

It may be unfair to examine too carefully a statement like this one.
Stowe was speaking extemporaneously and was responding emotionally
to the tributes to her. In addition, she was elderly and the mental de-
terioration which would soon become obvious may already have begun.
Yet the statement does suggest why her ideas which had been powerful
in helping to abolish slavery might have been quite inadequate as an
expression of the role of blacks in a free society. The reader may rejoice
with her in the achievement of the black man who had acquired the
ownership of property and had the satisfaction of knowing that his
children were his and were not slaves. More difficult is it to know how
to respond to the statement, "But they [the blacks] are very happy, and
that is evident; and they do know how to enjoy themselves—a great

deal more than you do." Her comment is uncomfortably close to what advocates of slavery had said earlier. One of the chief defenses of slavery had been that the blacks are constitutionally a happy, jolly race and therefore the rights which white people would find necessary to their happiness were neither necessary nor even important to the blacks. When she went on to speak of "the faults of the coloured people," she did not enumerate them. She did not have to, since there was a vast folklore on that subject.

When the Civil War was over, Stowe did not have much that was significant to say concerning the new status of blacks. By the time the new civil rights won by the blacks during Reconstruction began to be destroyed in the South in the 1890s, Stowe had lapsed into senility. In the last years of her life—she died in 1896—she became like a little child, except for occasional intervals of lucidity. Quite aside from her physical and mental decline, however, there was something else which indicates the defects of Stowe's attitudes toward the blacks. In the 1850s she had accepted some of the racist ideas of the time, but she had nonetheless forged a powerful weapon in *Uncle Tom's Cabin* against slavery. Wrong and inadequate as many of her ideas of race now seem to us, they were at least superior to those of nearly all the other white people of the time. These ideas of race could not be changed sufficiently, however, to serve as a basis for the idea of full equality for all blacks. Her objections to giving the right to vote to the newly freed blacks after the war was essentially a matter of timing. She was uneasily aware, as more insistent reformers were not, that there was only so much "reform" the white South could absorb all at once. She would soon come to the conclusion that blacks should receive the right to vote as well as equality in all other civil relationships. The weakness of Stowe's campaign for the rights of blacks is not to be found in any particular declaration she made on the subject. The trouble was that she was trapped in the racial and racist theories of the nineteenth century. While she modified these theories a good deal, she did not renounce them, but then scarcely anyone at the time did. She did the best she could, but it was not good enough. She saw blacks as being so innately different from whites that her campaign to make them legally and socially equal had an almost quixotic character. Her ideas of the inherent traits of the blacks would present many difficulties for emerging black intellectuals. It would not be long before they would reject them, though a much longer time would pass before they would reject her as well.

XVIII

The Reputation of Uncle Tom's Cabin The Novel 1865-1940

FOR A LONG TIME after the Civil War, *Uncle Tom's Cabin* remained popular among readers in the North. One indication that it was widely read is that as late as 1899 it was still the volume most frequently checked out of the New York Public Library. Historians and literary critics often mentioned it, but the emphasis was more often on its status as a great humanitarian document rather than strictly as a novel. On the other hand, there were some critics—most of them novelists themselves—who recognized that with all its faults, *Uncle Tom's Cabin* also had merit as a work of literature. In addition, they sometimes thought that it was at least a promising beginning of a body of literature which would explore the relationships between blacks and whites in the United States as well as relationships between the North and the South.[1]

One of the enthusiastic admirers of the book was John W. De Forest. A Union officer during the Civil War and a novelist who had himself treated the theme of the contrast between the North and South, De Forest admired Stowe, especially for her ability to portray aspects of life in this country which he thought nearly all the other writers had neglected. He recognized that *Uncle Tom's Cabin* had weaknesses, some of them serious. He went so far as to say that parts of the novel were no more than "village twaddle." He disliked the sentimentality of the portrayal of little Eva and he had serious reservations about the "impeccable Uncle Tom." In spite of the faults of the novel, however, he wrote in 1868 that it was impressive in its "picture of American life, drawn with a few strong and passionate strokes, not filled in thoroughly, but still a portrait." No other novel in American literature, he said, had portrayed the nation's "life so broadly, truly and sympathetically." He thought that Stowe had depicted American life in a way which could be compared with what Dickens, Thackeray, and Anthony Trollope had done for England and Victor Hugo had done for France. Fourteen years later, in 1882, De Forest had even higher praise for her: "I put Mrs. Stowe at the head of all living novelists [he probably meant all living *American* novelists], especially in the characteristics of power and sincerity, both of feeling and style."[2]

De Forest expressed his dissatisfaction with the character Uncle Tom when he created a similar character in one of his own novels. "Major" Scott is a former black slave in *Miss Ravenel's Conversion from Secession to Loyalty* (1867). He is employed by the Union Army of occupation in Louisiana during the Civil War as the overseer of a work crew composed of other recently freed slaves. The omniscient narrator of the novel specifically compares Scott to Uncle Tom. "In pious conversation, venerable air, grand physique, superb bass voice, musical ear, perfection of teeth, and shining white of the eye," the narrator says, Scott "was a counterpart of Mrs. Stowe's immortal idealism, Uncle Tom." Scott does have virtues—he is, for example, a courageous and able soldier, as he proves later in his participation with the Union army in a battle against the Confederates. On the other hand, he is also considerably different from Uncle Tom. Like "some white Christians," the narrator says, "this tolerably exemplary black had not yet arrived at the ability to keep the whole Decalogue. He sometimes got a fall in his wrestlings with the sin of lying, and in regard to the Seventh Commandment he was even more liable to be overthrown than King David." What De Forest was apparently attempting to do was to portray a black with some heroic qualities but not with what he regarded as impossible ones.[3]

Henry James might seem, perhaps, an unlikely writer to have admired Stowe, but he did. Toward the end of his life he remembered the great impression that *Uncle Tom's Cabin* had made upon the nation when he himself was only a child of nine. Though he recognized the power of the novel, he was rather uncertain about the source of it. He said that in 1852 *Uncle Tom's Cabin* knew the large felicity of gathering in alike the small and the simple and the big and the wise, and had above all the extraordinary fortune of finding itself, for an immense number of people, much less a book than a state of vision, of feeling and of consciousness, in which they didn't sit and read and appraise and pass the time, but walked and talked and laughed and cried and, in a manner of which Mrs. Stowe was the irresistible cause, generally.

It was probably not a calculated work of fiction but it nonetheless made a great impression. "Letters, here, languished unconscious," he said, "and Uncle Tom, instead of making even one of the cheap short cuts through the medium in which books breathe, even as fishes in the water, went gaily roundabout it altogether, as if a fish, a wonderful 'leaping' fish, had simply flown through the air." James might have done the reputation of Stowe a greater favor if he had speculated more boldly on the question of why the novel had drawn forth the admiration of such a wide range of readers. He may have come closer to observing her best qualities as a writer when as a young man he had met her and observed what he called "her extraordinary little vague observant, slightly wool-gathering, letting her eyes wander all over the place kind of little way."[4]

William Dean Howells also praised Uncle Tom's Cabin but said more than James did about its bad qualities. "As one reads the book now," he wrote in 1879, "it seems less a work of art than of spirit. The art is most admirable; it is very true and very high,—the highest that can be known to fiction; but it has fearful lapses, in which the jarring and grating of the bare facts set the teeth on edge; there are false colors in characters; there are errors in taste." In spite of its faults, Howells was prepared in 1898 to describe it as "the great American novel." Like many other critics of his time, Howells did not give Uncle Tom's Cabin sufficiently detailed criticism to enable a reader to understand clearly what it was that he did and did not like. We may sometimes even wonder whether he was praising Stowe in an obligatory and ritualistic way. His manner of expression does not always express a strong conviction.[5]

Equally fervent but equally unsatisfactory as criticism are some of the comments of other writers of the late nineteenth century. At Stowe's seventy-first birthday party in 1882, George Washington Cable sent her a message "rejoicing over the continuance on earth of one who has earned the gratitude of two races of humanity. . . . Blessings on the day when Harriet Beecher Stowe was born." Five years later, Mark Twain, on another public occasion, praised her by saying, "Mrs. Stowe, you have

made a book, and here given to the stage a drama which will live as long
as the English tongue shall live." And yet Twain had almost nothing to
say—either at this occasion or at any other time—about *Uncle Tom's
Cabin* except that it was a great book. The only character in Stowe's
fiction which Twain mentioned was Sam Lawson, the village philosopher
in some of her New England novels and stories. The narrator of Twain's
story, "The Man Who Corrupted Hadleyburg," praised Lawson as an
effectively drawn character.[6]

Though they were more cautious than some of the famous literary
names of the period, some of the writers of American literary histories
for a long time frequently found merit in Stowe's writings, and especially
in *Uncle Tom's Cabin*. In his *A Literary History of America* (1900),
Barrett Wendell, professor of English at Harvard, acknowledged that
parts of *Uncle Tom's Cabin* had been "written carelessly" and that the
novel contained many "crudities," but even with these defects it was "a
remarkable piece of fiction." He did not care for its "conventional and
rambling" plot. On the other hand, he was impressed with its delineation
of characters, finding them "though little studied in detail," nevertheless
with "a pervasive vitality which no study can achieve; you unhesitatingly
accept them as real." He also thought that Stowe was able to make
"convincing the backgrounds in which her action and her characters
move." She had sufficient talent, he thought, that "if circumstances had
permitted its development, might have given her a distinguished place
in English fiction."[7]

Among literary historians, especially among those writing before
the strong black rejection of *Uncle Tom's Cabin*, a movement which
occurred in great force only after World War II, opinions similar to
those of Wendell were fairly common. One of the most enthusiastic of
the favorable accounts was that of Constance Rourke in her *Trumpets
of Jubilee* (1927). In *Uncle Tom's Cabin*, said Rourke, Stowe had
"command of structure—for carelessly combined as it seems, the book has
a structure, with a free flow of narrative, and a wealth of invention."
Unlike those critics who criticized Stowe for her lack of direct knowledge of slavery, Rourke commended her for using the knowledge which
she had in such a way as to present a convincing portrait. Rourke
thought that Stowe "used every touch" of experience, "acquiring the
basic gift of the creative artist, that of deriving the essential from the
fragmentary, of judging the whole piece by the small bit of pattern."
Rourke disagreed with those critics who "belittle *Uncle Tom's Cabin* as

a work which was always over-colored, which never had a place outside
the turbid sphere of propaganda." It was not propaganda, she said, or
at least it was not "propaganda soul and simple." Though it "lacks the
hardiness and purity of view which belong to great writings," still the
"unbroken force" of its "emotion produced breadth . . . ; the story at
least brings to mind what is meant by the epical scale; it has above all
that affecting movement toward unknown goals over long distances
which becomes the irresistible theme of the greater narrative." With all
its faults, *Uncle Tom's Cabin* "presents an elementary human condition
with all its stark humiliations and compulsions the straits of mind and
body and feeling to which man can reduce man." Thus, the book was
"something of a miracle, a greater miracle than was realized by an enormous public."[8]

Unlike literary critics and literary historians in the years following
the Civil War, most of the historians had little to say about *Uncle Tom's
Cabin*. Probably the major reason they neglected it was that the discussion of effects of works of literature upon the events of history, or even
the discussion of social history at all, was rare among historians of the
time. Those historians who did mention the novel usually contented
themselves by saying that it had a strong influence in mobilizing northern
opinion against slavery. In his *History of the United States from the
Compromise of 1850* (1893), James Ford Rhodes broke with this tradition. He discussed in detail the political and social effects of the novel
from the time of its publication in 1851-52 to the Civil War. *Uncle
Tom's Cabin* was, he said, "an outburst of passion against the wrong
done to a race, and it was written with an intensity of feeling that left
no room for care in the artistic construction of the story. The style is
commonplace, the language is often trite and inelegant, sometimes de-
generating into slang, and the humor is strained." Rhodes may have
been making concessions to some of his literary friends, but he had high
praise for the novel as an accurate portrayal of slavery. "While she had
not the facts which a critical historian would have collected," he said,
"she used with the intuition of genius the materials gained through
personal observation." Rhodes gave a full account, more so than any other
historian until the present time, of the political and social effects of
Uncle Tom's Cabin in the years immediately following its publication.[9]

Opinions of *Uncle Tom's Cabin* in the South after the Civil War
were less ambivalent, of course, than they were in the North. In the
minds and hearts of many white southerners, Stowe herself became one

of the chief symbols of the perfidy of the North. The comment which Lincoln had apparently made to her, "So you are the little lady who made this great war," did not become publicly known until 1897 when Annie Fields edited *The Life and Letters of Harriet Beecher Stowe* and included an account of it in her notes. Long before then, however, many white southerners had decided that Stowe was one of the chief causes of the defeat of the Confederacy and that she had acted out of a calculated malice. In 1870, William Hand Browne, the editor of *Southern Magazine*, published in Baltimore, wrote to Paul Hamilton Hayne in South Carolina expressing his disgust with northern pretensions: "I look forward to the threatening *Yankeeisation* of the South with unspeakable dread and abhorrence. It would not matter so much if the prospect were of being Anglicized, Gallicized, Teutonised or Freejeeised. But to be infected with the Yankee soul—the Yankee spirit—great heavens!" In another letter to Hayne, Browne said, "I rage internally when I see our Southern people—my brothers and yours—meekly admitting the Yankees' claim to have all the culture, all the talent, all the genius of the country. . . . And I rage tenfold when I see our people, aye, our women and maidens—taught to hanker after the works of Mrs. Stowe, that Pythoness of foulness."[10]

In 1885, Paul Hamilton Hayne wrote a letter to Charles Gayarré expressing his anger on reading of a birthday party arranged for Stowe by her publisher. The affair had been gotten up, he said, "to burn incense upon the altar of her enormous vanity!" He was particularly outraged that his fellow southerner George Washington Cable had written a letter to Stowe, to be read at the party. Cable had "absolutely *gushed* over her 'Uncle Tom,'" said Hayne, "drivelled about his love, reverence, and admiration for New England." Hayne wrote a highly emotional poem directed at some unnamed person. Entitled "A Character," the poem spoke of the "bluff manners" of a certain woman. She had "the Devil's own art in veiling . . . infinite gulfs of guile." It was she who was chiefly responsible for the fact that many a southern soldier "rots, festering, vile, loathsome, in burial shrouds of shame." Such evil could only be adequately punished by God himself:

> Beware! by the God above us, who parteth the false from the true.
> There's a Curse in the Future, *somewhere*, an ambushed Curse for you.
> It will break from the way-side fiercely, when least you dream of a blow;
> A tigerish fate in its fury, to rend and lay you low:
> And 'ere it hath sucked your heart's blood, & stifled your latest breath,
> The thought of your victims, Woman! will sharpen the sting of death![11]

About the year 1888, Grace King, the Louisiana writer, visited for several days in the home of Charles Dudley Warner in Hartford. Very early in the morning she saw from her bedroom window a woman out in the garden walking quickly about and talking to herself. Later at breakfast, she asked Mrs. Warner about the strange visitor. "Oh, that was Mrs. Harriet Beecher Stowe," Mrs. Warner said. "She is always running around the neighborhood of a morning. You will see her often. No one pays any attention to her!" Mrs. Warner went on to explain that Stowe was now senile and in a second childhood. Of her reaction to this announcement, Grace King wrote in her autobiography, published in 1932, "A cannon ball could not have astounded me more. Harriet Beecher Stowe! She who had brought the war upon us, as I had been taught, and all our misfortunes! That was Harriet Beecher Stowe! The full realization of where I was came upon me."

"You have read her book?" asked Mrs. Warner.

"No, indeed! It was not allowed to be even spoken of in our house!" Some sympathy for the mental condition of Stowe is implied in the account of King, but she could only insist that whatever sympathy she felt was "in spite of her [Stowe's] hideous, black, dragonlike book that hovered on the horizon of every Southern child."[12]

In the 1890s, William Lyon Phelps assigned *Uncle Tom's Cabin* to his literature classes at Yale and asked his students to write a "critical theme" on it. Among his students there were several southerners and in their themes he found some "vigorous denunciations." As late as 1924, he still remembered the theme of "one warm-hearted young gentleman from a Southern State." "After I had finished this book," the student wrote, "I kicked it out of the room, kicked it down stairs, kicked it out of the dormitory, and shall never read it again." A rather similar event happened about 1905 at Harvard. In his *Lanterns on the Levee* (1941), William Alexander Percy remembered how as a student from Mississippi he was teased by his Harvard classmates: "It would cross someone's mind that I had been less than appreciative of . . . *Uncle Tom's Cabin*." Percy was "pinned to the floor and sat on by rowdy well-wishers while others would read aloud Mrs. Stowe's more sadistic and blood-boiling passages, with Simon Legree gestures." Percy was amused by these incidents in retrospect, but he might have felt differently about them when they happened.[13]

For about fifty years after the Civil War, examples of hatred expressed in the South toward Stowe and *Uncle Tom's Cabin* are not difficult to find. Perhaps the strongest example of hatred was that of Thomas Dixon, the North Carolina novelist, who was unwilling to admit any merit in the novel or any kindly motive on Stowe's part. In his early manhood he had been a clergyman as well as a state legislator. His career as a writer began, he said, when he attended a performance of *Uncle Tom's Cabin*. Outraged by what he regarded as its injustice to the white South and its misconception of the racial traits of the blacks, Dixon left the theater vowing to tell the South's "true story." The true story was, apparently, that because of the innate defects of the blacks as a race, the white southerners had been obliged to enslave them. His novels are appallingly crude. Usually what happens in them is that the white southern characters endure pillage and rape by the blacks during the Reconstruction period. Eventually the whites rebel and wrest control of local and state governments from carpetbaggers, scalawags, and black politicians. The novels sold millions of copies. It was Dixon's *The Clansman* (1905) that was made into the famous movie *Birth of a Nation* (1915), directed by D. W. Griffith.[14]

"One drop of Negro blood makes a Negro," declares the narrator of Dixon's novel, *The Leopard's Spots: A Romance of the White Man's Burden, 1865-1900* (1902). "It kinks the hair, flattens the nose, thickens the lips, puts out the light of the intellect, and lights the fire of brutal passions. The beginning of Negro equality as a vital fact is the beginning of the end of this nation's life." Dixon explored the theme of the inherent evil of the blacks over and over again in his novels. No black is trustworthy, he argued. To be a black is to be a thief, a rapist, or a murderer—sometimes all three. If a black has white intermixture, he is especially dangerous. White intermixture, Dixon thought, improved the intellect of blacks without changing their morals. In order to demonstrate this particular point, Dixon took some of the characters in *Uncle Tom's Cabin* and changed them to fit in with his theories of race. Tim Shelby, one of Dixon's characters, had formerly been a black slave on the plantation of Mr. Shelby of *Uncle Tom's Cabin*. Now he has been freed and has become an official in the Freedmen's Bureau in the South. A southern white girl, driven by necessity, applies for a teaching position in one of the Bureau's black schools. Tim Shelby tells her that she can have the position if she will kiss him. She tells white men of the community what he has said and he is lynched. When he is found, "His neck was broken and his body was hanging low—scarcely three feet from the ground. His thick lips had been split with a sharp knife and from his teeth hung this placard: 'The answer of the Anglo-Saxon race to Negro lips that dare pollute with words the womanhood of the South. K.K.K.' "[15]

Although Dixon had no use whatever for blacks, he subscribed to some of the reformist ideas of the muckrakers in the early years of the twentieth century. He was aware of widespread financial and political corruption and championed the cause of the poor white if not that of the poor black. In *The Leopard's Spots*, he introduced the character Simon Legree. This man was meant to be the same character in *Uncle Tom's Cabin*, but his career has been brought up to date. Dixon's Simon Legree had avoided military service during the war by disguising himself as a German immigrant woman, working on an obscure farm in Louisiana tending cows. After the war he abandoned his disguise and moved to North Carolina where he was unknown. Now he is a scalawag, helping the northern carpetbaggers to fleece the whites of the South. Since only a few southern whites can vote, Simon Legree in this novel spends much of his time stirring up the black voters. "It was a spectacle for gods and men," says the narrator of the novel, "to see him harangue that Union League [the northern political party] in the platitudes of loyalty to the Union, and to watch the crowd of negroes hang on his every word as the inspired Gospel of God." "You are to rule this land," Legree says in one speech to the blacks. "Your old masters are to dig in the fields and you are to sit under the shade and be gentlemen." In reply, an "old negro" shouts, "Glory to God!" Eventually the white southerners regain political control of the state. Toward the end of the novel, Legree is obliged to flee to the North. In New York City, he buys a seat on the stock exchange with the money he has stolen as a corrupt politician in the South, and he makes additional millions by issuing watered stock and by crushing the unions in northern factories. Thus, in some respects, the novels of Dixon were similar to the northern muckraking novels of the time.[16]

Though many southerners continued for a long time to react with hatred to *Uncle Tom's Cabin*, others would have a better opinion of it. They would see the novel not as a deliberately false portrait of the South and of slavery. Because of her lack of knowledge, Stowe had simply misunderstood the actual workings of slavery. Uncle Tom, for example, was no longer necessarily seen in the South as an unreal character. His virtues were admitted but their meaning came, these white southerners thought, from the virtues of slavery itself. In 1887, James Lane Allen, the Kentucky novelist, wrote an article in which he argued that Uncle Tom owed his integrity and kindliness to the fact that he had been reared as a slave. Nearly every small white boy in the South, even after the war, said Allen, was likely to have known at some time an aged black man who was his particular friend and who was more or less like Uncle Tom. This elderly black was "the greatest of all the Negroes, greater even than the cook." Perhaps he had given the white boy a squirrel to tame. Often the boy would slip out of his own home to have a meal in a Negro cabin. There he would hear folk stories which would leave him with "a wondering look in his eyes and a vague hush of spirit." The chief error which Stowe had made in her novel, thought Allen, was her failure to recognize that Uncle Tom's virtues were virtues which slavery had given him.[17]

"For of all races," said Allen, "the African—superstitious, indolent, singing and dancing, most impressionable creature—depended upon others for enlightenment, training, and happiness." There was no question about the source of Uncle Tom's virtues in the novel:

If, therefore, you find him so intelligent that he may be sent on important business commissions, so honest that he may be trusted with money, house, and home, so loyal that he will not seize opportunity to become free: if you find him endowed with the manly virtues of dignity and self-respect united to the Christian virtues of humility, long-suffering, and forgiveness, then do not, in marveling at him on these accounts, quite forget his master and his mistress,—they made him what he was, and it is something to be said on their behalf, that in their household was developed a type of slave that could be set upon a sublime moral pinnacle to attract the admiration of the world.

In an argument like this, one can see an almost complete reversal of southern white opinion of Uncle Tom since the time the novel was first published. In the 1850s, southern white readers had generally agreed that Uncle Tom was an impossibility, a mere figment of Stowe's imagination; now he is wholly real but his virtues are to be explained by the fact that he was owned by moral, conscientious slaveholders.[18]

Joel Chandler Harris carried the new southern revisionist version of *Uncle Tom's Cabin* even further than Allen. In 1904, Harris declared that while Stowe had believed herself to be writing an indictment of slavery, any reader who actually understood the institution in the South would recognize that she had unconsciously shown it to be beneficent. Unknown to herself, Stowe had written "a defense of the system that she intended to attack." She had had the "genius" to see the characters and situations of slavery truly and

to that genius she surrendered herself against her moral purpose. . . . She was impelled by the demands of her art, to set forth the facts as she found them. And so, as it turns out, all the worthy and beautiful characters in her book—Uncle Tom, little Eva, and the beloved Master, and the rest—are the products of the system the text of the book, is all the time condemning.

Stowe had shown slavery as a truly evil system only when it was a northerner who had come south and bought slaves. She had demonstrated this truth in *Uncle Tom's Cabin*, said Harris, when she made the cruel Simon Legree a native of Vermont.[19]

A defense of slavery similar to that of Allen and Harris is found in the writings of Thomas Nelson Page, especially in his plantation fiction. *Red Rock* (1898) was accurately described by Jay B. Hubbell, a historian and critic of southern literature, as a novel which was "in effect a belated reply to *Uncle Tom's Cabin*." Page attempted to show the master-slave, and especially the mistress-slave, relationship as one of deep feeling and attachment on both sides. The roles of slaveowner and slave, as Page saw them, were rooted in tradition but more importantly they were a matter of the two races—the white and the black—having worked out a relationship in which the supposedly more intelligent whites would take care of the supposedly less intelligent blacks. In return, the blacks offered their labor and their unswerving loyalty. It had taken the South nearly 250 years to work out this ideal relationship, but the southern Eden had been destroyed by the Yankee serpent in the Civil War. Page recognized the cruelties of slavery more clearly than Allen and Harris; at least, on the surface, he seemed to be more aware of them. On the other hand, his explanation for these cruelties was too ingenious, for he attributed them mainly to the overseers. For some reason that Page never adequately explained, the overseers were able to mistreat the slaves in spite of the best efforts of the slaveholders to prevent them from doing so.[20]

Page did not advocate a return to slavery even though he thought that it had been the ideal relationship between whites and blacks. He was even willing to concede that abolition was probably a good thing. On the subject of the abstract wrong of slavery, he said, the nation "was indebted to a work of genius produced by a woman, a romance which touched the heart of Christendom. 'Uncle Tom's Cabin' overruled the Supreme Court of the United States, and abrogated the Constitution."

On the other hand, it contained "the general sentiment of the world against slavery" and had "contributed more than any other one thing to its abolition in that generation." For Page, however, the end of slavery did not mean that blacks should enjoy equal rights. He was particularly opposed to their being granted the right to vote.[21]

The idea that slavery was a much better institution than white northerners or blacks generally thought is scattered through the writings of white southern writers down to the time of World War II. In 1933, Stark Young, the southern novelist and drama critic, read the novel. At the time, he was fifty-two years old. Growing up in Mississippi, he said, he had had no earlier inclination to read the novel, and none of the people he had known at the time had ever mentioned to him that they had read it. "It was anathema; it had affected the question of slavery and helped the abolitionists," he said; "it was lies, or so we should think." Nor had he ever seen the play. In 1933, the play was produced in New York. In preparation for his review in the *New Republic*, Young read the novel. He did not like it. Its effect was a "complete poverty of the execution. The scenes are poor, the characters are clumsily done. There are heavy underscorings and typifications that get along with the theme; but the book scene by scene is appalling, very." It was "mere period trash."[22]

It was not merely its literary deficiencies, however, which caused Stark Young to reject *Uncle Tom's Cabin*. He thought that Stowe did not understand, for example, the "African past" of the blacks, and thus she had failed to realize that separation of black families under slavery was not the evil she thought it was. In the novel, he said, she "appears to picture African families as living hearths of devotion to their families, despite the fact that [in Africa] many slaves were sold to the traders by their own kin and tribesmen." In addition, he thought that Stowe had not understood the racial traits of even the "good" blacks. "The special goodness characteristic of his kind," Young said of Uncle Tom, "with its own spontaneity, simplicity, innocence, animality and beauty, eludes her. All she can do with her material is to superimpose her own ideas." Uncle Tom is not a "true" black. She had succeeded better, Young thought, in creating the character George Harris, because Harris had white intermixture and she understood whites better than she did blacks. She understood that "through miscegenation a man with the characteristics and nervous system of the white man might find himself enslaved." A statement like this one is an example of how long the old stereotypes of racism could persist among otherwise cultivated and intelligent people. Young sometimes tried to express a different idea about *Uncle Tom's Cabin*, one which he dimly felt but could not clearly formulate. In 1936, he viewed a musical version of it in New York. Though he still thought that Stowe "was not an artist," he added the enigmatic comment that she was "a good deal of a genius." Unfortunately, he did not explain what he meant by the distinction.[23]

In general, the political leaders and historians of the South after the Civil War denounced *Uncle Tom's Cabin* at least as strongly as its writers and literary historians. In 1885, Jefferson Davis condemned it, repeating some of the southern arguments which had been expressed at the time of its first publication. "Among the less-informed persons at the North," he said, "there exists an opinion that the negro slave at the South was a mere chattel, having neither rights nor immunities protected by law or public opinion." This was the mistake, he thought, upon which "the lauded story of 'Uncle Tom's Cabin' was founded." He found it "strange that a utilitarian and shrewd people did not ask why a slave, especially valuable, was the object of privation and abuse." If the novel had had as its subject a horse instead of a slave, said Davis, northern readers "would have been better able to judge, and would most probably have rejected the story for its improbability."[24]

Even many years later, southerners—sometimes those who were sensitive to other social issues—were likely to dismiss *Uncle Tom's Cabin* as an unfair portrait of slavery. In his histories of the United States written in the last years of the nineteenth century and in the early years of the twentieth, Woodrow Wilson admitted that slavery was sometimes a cruel institution. "Domestic slaves were almost uniformly dealt with indulgently and affectionately by their masters," he wrote, but field slaves were frequently not so well treated. "They had to be driven, they could not be individually directed," he explained. "The rigorous drill of an army had to be preserved." Yet *Uncle Tom's Cabin* "was not a true picture of slavery. It was a romance sprung out of the sympathetic imagination of a refined and sensitive woman, whose pity kindled at every thought of the blacks at the South." Stowe had been right in believing that slavery had "terrible possibilities" and sometimes even "terrible realities" because "of the master's power and the slave's subjection," said Wilson, but instances of cruelty were not typical. "No one could read in it [*Uncle Tom's Cabin*] the real life of the negro or take from it any just conception of southern masters. Those who read it, nevertheless, knew no other picture than this, and were filled with pity and deep horror. Politicians had presently good reason to know what this new engine of agitation meant." Elsewhere, Wilson put the matter more definitely. *Uncle Tom's Cabin*, he said, "played no small part in creating the anti-slavery party."[25]

In 1893, Francis A. Shoup, who had been a brigadier general in the Confederate Army, wrote an extended critique of *Uncle Tom's Cabin* in the *Sewanee Review*. His place of birth was Indiana and he had grown up there, but as a young man he came to the South, and when the Civil War began he joined the Confederate army. In his article, he argued that having lived in both the North and the South he understood better than most people how both regions felt about slavery. Stowe, in his opinion, had "genius" as a writer; he was particularly impressed by the accuracy and fairness of her description in her novel of the Shelby plantation in Kentucky. On the other hand, he thought much less of her depiction of Simon Legree's plantation in Louisiana. Like Woodrow Wilson, Shoup believed that the fact of her being a woman had caused Stowe to have a distorted judgment on the subject of slavery:

She did what most women are wont to do—she took counsel of her emotions—she translated herself in fancy to the cottonfields of the South as a slave, and then interrogated herself as to how she felt. . . . In her transmigration she carried with her all her intellectual vigor—all of her refined sensibilities and rugged New England love of freedom; the supposititious personality of the cotton-field was no longer poor Sambo, but the high-strung highly cultured Mrs. Stowe. It is not wonderful that she did not like her hypothetical situation, nor that she should feel an intense desire to tear into shreds any instrument which kept her there. Thus it was that her war . . . was upon the Constitution from the beginning.[26]

Even more strongly than Stowe identified with Uncle Tom in the novel, she—Shoup was convinced—shared the outlook of one of the other characters, that of Ophelia. "A spinster and a typical native of Vermont," who spoke "for the author throughout the book," Ophelia so strongly suggested the character of Stowe herself that "one cannot but think of . . . [her] as Mrs. Stowe's sister." Both Stowe and Ophelia, he believed, theoretically had a high regard for the welfare of blacks but also a personal distaste for them. More serious, however, he regarded as "fact" that neither the author nor the character in the novel had any comprehension of the innate traits of blacks. It is impossible to reason with blacks, Shoup thought. You have to punish them physically, he said, because punishment is all they understand. He argued that Topsy obviously recognized the nature of her own racial traits better than Ophelia. When Ophelia tells Topsy that she doesn't know what to do with her because of her badness, Topsy replies, "Law, Missis, you must whip me; my old Missis allers whipped me. I an't used to workin' unless I gits whipped." Southerners had understood from long experience the truth of Topsy's observation, Shoup said. He made no reference to Ophelia's later experience with Topsy, of her discovery that force was an ineffective means of dealing with the child and that only love and understanding could accomplish any permanent change in her conduct.[27]

Shoup was willing to concede that Stowe had not meant to do any harm when she wrote *Uncle Tom's Cabin*. The trouble was that she did not understand what it would lead to. Whatever the evils of slavery, he thought, the price of righting such wrongs as had existed was wholly out of proportion to the benefits gained:

Shades of the sweet and peaceful Southern home of older days! Gone from the face of the earth forever! The price of progress is at the cost of bleeding hearts. Bleeding hearts!—has Mrs. Stowe ever tried to think what her book has been a chief factor of bringing upon the world? Has she ever tried to weigh the occasional and rare horrors of the old slave days, hard as they were, against the agonies of the million of brave men mutilated and done to death in the ranks of the blue and gray? Has she ever reflected upon the ten—the twenty millions of wives and mothers, sweethearts and daughters, whose hearts have been torn up by the roots of the wild slaughter between brothers? Truly the indulgence of sentiment is costly.

In addition, Stowe had done great harm to the blacks themselves. Nearly thirty years after the end of the war, their situation was worse than it had ever been before:

That free and open cheerfulness, ready to burst into peals of laughter, the prompt and respectful bow, the song and dance, the jollity at Christmas, and the expressions of love and loyalty to the white people are in large measure gone. Surliness and reserve have taken their place. Crimes have become ten-fold more numerous, and some never heard of in the old times, have become common.

Shoup thought that freedom might in time confer at least some benefits on the blacks, but he added that "it may well be questioned if the new state will ever match the Christian fidelity of Uncle Tom, the faithful tenderness of Aunt Chloe, and the patience and love of Eva's mammy."[28]

In 1914, Thomas Pearce Bailey, a southerner, also wrote an extended analysis of *Uncle Tom's Cabin.* Bailey was Dean of the Department of Education and Professor of Psychology at the University of Mississippi. At one time he had been superintendent of the public schools in Memphis, Tennessee. In addition, he had formerly been a visiting professor at the University of Chicago and again at the University of California. Bailey had been influenced by the Social Darwinists' ideas of race and saw blacks as members of a race which had reached a less advanced stage of evolution than had the whites. Those who espoused this kind of racism were frequently confident that they could recognize a racial trait in almost any idiosyncrasy of an individual character. Early in *Uncle Tom's Cabin,* Uncle Tom jokingly says that his children are so "full of tickle" that they cannot always behave themselves properly. Bailey solemnly concluded that Uncle Tom had unconsciously pointed out a racial trait in his children. The expression, "full of tickle," said Bailey, "is most true to life. The organic sensations of the negro, including the sexual sensations, seem to be greatly developed. His imaginative, 'sensual concretism,' love of pleasure, eagerness for excitement, quick emotion . . . all seem connected with this inside 'ticklishness.'" Bailey also thought that the omniscient narrator in the novel had unconsciously hit upon another racial trait in a description of the disorderly kitchen of Aunt Dinah, the slave cook in the St. Clare household in New Orleans. Ophelia is dismayed to find that Dinah has no sense of order or system in cooking or housekeeping. Dinah's lack of system was "most significant," Bailey said, and was "possibly . . . connected with weakness of development of the associative system in the brain." He did not mention the narrator's other point that Dinah turned out to be a much better cook than Ophelia.[29]

Stowe had made a serious error, Bailey thought, when she described mulatto characters in the novel as beautiful or handsome. She had not recognized the dangers to which she was subjecting the whites. "Sad experience shows there are types of white men and women," said Bailey, "that are strongly attracted by what is unusual in physical attractiveness." Thus the description of the beauty of the mulattoes might have "a subtle influence that can lead to no good." He did not believe that Stowe was indirectly advocating racial amalgamation. She simply had not had the experience with blacks which most white southerners acquired as a matter of course. White southerners had come to recognize, for example, the necessity for racial segregation. The northern whites would recognize this need also as soon as a substantial number of blacks had immigrated to the region. "Kinship by race," he said, "is a trait imbedded in the very genes of all of us." He was willing to admit that segregation had an ugly side. "It is humiliation for some of us [white southerners] to have negroes get clear off the sidewalk in order to give us a superfluity of room," he said, "and sad for us to see that our children seem to take this action as a matter of course, or even to demand it as a right." On the other hand, he thought that segregation was necessary.[30]

Ulrich B. Phillips, a southern white historian, said in 1930 that Stowe had greatly exaggerated the evils of slavery. He was particularly disturbed by the portraits of slave traders in *Uncle Tom's Cabin*. He used the familiar arguments that both slaveowners and slave traders could "not have been fiends in human form," as they were depicted in the novel. If they had been, they "would speedily have become bankrupt." He thought that Stowe had unconsciously recognized the truth of this observation when she had allowed Haley, a slave trader, to say that he thought "humanity was the best policy" in dealing with slaves. In making this point, Phillips showed himself as blind to the irony in the novel. Haley shows only a pretense of humanitarianism as a slave trader. Phillips sometimes seemed to be uneasily aware that determining how many slaveholders were kindly might be an impossible task. He admitted, for example, that on some plantations "the whip was as regularly in evidence as the spur on a horseman's heel. That cruelties occurred is never to be denied." Nonetheless, he thought that Stowe had "exploited them in *Uncle Tom's Cabin* and had validated her implications to her own satisfaction in its *Key*."[31]

At least one southern white historian of the 1930s had words of praise for *Uncle Tom's Cabin*. Dumas Malone wrote:

As a Southerner who did not read it until after he was grown may I say . . . that it proved to be a far more sympathetic treatment than I had anticipated. Its author . . . was far more warm-hearted than the great body of the Abolitionists. No mere moralist but a born storyteller, she worked in a richer medium. She stands as an example of the Puritan spirit, inveterate in its reforming tendencies, but liberated and humanized in the West, and with a distinctive fire and warmth that was inborn.

As if he thought he might have gone too far, Malone expressed some reservations: "There was about her an endearing lack of practicality and a certain rich luxuriance." Perhaps a bit loftily he added that "almost all the feminine reformers have had recourse to the written word."[32]

In the South after the Civil War, most of the people who expressed opinions of *Uncle Tom's Cabin* strongly censured it. Literary historians, writers, historians, and political leaders often argued that Stowe's major purpose in writing the book had been to defame the South. As the years passed, however, they often changed the basis of their objections. They became more willing to concede that Stowe had been motivated by good intentions. She was no longer dismissed as an evil woman, but she was still seen as a badly mistaken one. What she did not understand, many southerner observers of the period maintained, was that the laws regulating slavery were one thing but the institution itself was another. According to this view, slavemasters and whites were generally much kinder to the slaves than she had given them credit for being.

In the North during the same period, there was a shift of opinion going on which was in some respects similar to that in the white South. By the year 1900, a good many northern critics and scholars were expressing something like embarrassment with regard to the novel. There was, first of all, the question of its sentimentality. Perhaps more importantly, there was a falling away in the North from the old abolitionist faith that the blacks are inherently capable of taking on full citizenship in a free society. Though white northern and white southern critics still had different opinions of *Uncle Tom's Cabin*, they had moved closer to one another. What the white southern writers increasingly had come to say was that Stowe had had good intentions but she had been wrong about the nature of slavery. On the other hand, white northern writers were saying more frequently that Stowe was probably right about the evils of slavery, but she was wrong in having too high an opinion of the innate character of the blacks. They thought she had idealized a number of her black characters. Uncle Tom in particular was seen as far too noble to be a credible character, and especially a credible black.

Among influential critics, Stowe's literary reputation suffered a decline in 1869 when she decided to publish what she said Lady Byron had told her of the sexual relationship between Lord Byron and his half-sister, Augusta Leigh. Stowe had met Lady Byron in England in 1853 and the two had become close friends. In telling Stowe about Byron's sexual transgressions, Lady Byron had given them as her reason for leaving him. Nine years after the death of Lady Byron, Stowe published charges against Byron in an article in the *Atlantic Monthly*. The resulting shock and denunciation was said to have caused the magazine to lose 15,000 subscribers. What horrified many people was not whether the charges were true; it was the fact that a subject like this should be brought up at all. In 1905, nine years after Stowe's death, Byron's incestuous relationship with his half-sister was confirmed by one of his descendants who had access to the family papers. What the modern reader is likely to wonder is whether the reasons Stowe gave for writing the article adequately explain her motives. Stowe wrote a passionate defense ostensibly to defend the character of Lady Byron from detractors who held her responsible for the break with her husband. Since the principals were dead, it is the passion which might be questioned. Was it an attempt on her part to produce a new sensation which would rival that caused by *Uncle Tom's Cabin?*[33]

Even George Eliot, a friendly critic of Stowe, thought that the article on Byron was a serious mistake. Charles Dickens was frankly hostile, writing to James T. Fields, his American publisher, that he wished "Mrs. Stowe in the pillory." Algernon Charles Swinburne in a letter to Paul Hamilton Hayne referred to Stowe as "Mrs. Bitcher Spew" and dismissed *Uncle Tom's Cabin* as a novel about "a nigger of the clerical order." After the widespread criticism of Stowe because of her indictment of Byron, a number of critics began to wonder publicly whether the great success of *Uncle Tom's Cabin* might have had less to do with its literary merit than with the excitement of public feeling over slavery.[34]

In a history of American literature published in 1891, Julian Hawthorne, the son of Nathaniel Hawthorne, dismissed *Uncle Tom's Cabin* both as a bad novel and as an unreliable portrait of slavery. "From the literary point of view," he said, "its merit is small, both as to style and characterization." The "girlish imagination" of Stowe, "already attuned to a key of transcendental morality, was influenced by the cruelties and injustices of which she had heard many sensational reports, and some of which, perhaps, she saw." The result was that "[a] more emotional, impassioned, one-sided book was never written. . . . There was enough truth in the details . . . of the story to render it plausible." To most of the readers of the time, "it seemed a confirmation, in telling and readable form, of the most reckless charges of the Abolitionists." In 1892, Agnes Repplier said that she had read it as a girl "from cover to cover with the innocent credulity of youth." Now she was skeptical of it. She was especially critical of its "noble" black characters. She said archly that the blacks she herself had known in actual life were not like the black characters of *Uncle Tom's Cabin.* They were, in fact, "very little better than white people." Slavery must have been a beneficent institution, she concluded, if its result "was to produce a race so infinitely superior to common humanity."[35]

Beginning in the 1890s, both northern and southern critics sometimes applied the principles of Social Darwinism and literary naturalism to *Uncle Tom's Cabin*. The racism implicit in these movements led to a revival and sometimes even an intensification of all the old pre-Civil War arguments over the supposed inherent differences of races. Based upon biology rather than upon the Bible, the new racism frequently condemned nonwhite races, and especially the blacks, to a position of inferiority. In 1910, John Erskine examined *Uncle Tom's Cabin* in the light of the new racism and thought he could detect in it a portrayal of black racial traits of which Stowe herself had been unconscious. "To her mind slavery was responsible for practically everything except color that distinguished the black man from the white," said Erskine; "yet, her accuracy of observation resulted in a portrait easily recognized as true, though it might be explained by other causes than slavery."[36]

In portraying Simon Legree's slaves, Sambo and Quimbo, men who took an obvious delight in tracking down their fellow slaves with fierce dogs, Stowe was unwittingly describing "the volatile childishness of the race, for which slavery perhaps is not wholly responsible." Uncle Tom's willingness to suffer uncomplainingly might be a racial rather than strictly a personal trait. "It is significant that the slave who does not run away, but submits even to torture with a quixotic patience," said Erskine, "is the full-blooded negro, Uncle Tom." It was Topsy, however, who Erskine thought most clearly represented Stowe's unconscious insight into the inherent traits of the blacks. The contrast of Topsy and Ophelia was "one of the best of the story." It was "typical of the paralyzing astonishment that overtakes the Anglo-Saxon nature on its first experience of negro ways." Stowe had attempted to convince the reader that Topsy was capable of reformation, but Erskine could not share her optimism. "There is little in . . . [Topsy's] nature but perversity, and the depth of her affection for Eva does not convince the reader as it does Mrs. Stowe that she ever became a useful member of society."[37]

One result of the unfavorable criticism of *Uncle Tom's Cabin* in the North was a movement in New York City in 1903 to restrict the circulation of the novel in public school libraries. The debate was not precisely on the issue of censorship. A committee of the board of education had prepared a list of sixty outstanding books which it required for purchase in every school library, and *Uncle Tom's Cabin* was one of these books. A good many white southerners had moved into New York and it was they, apparently, who most objected to the novel's presence in the school libraries. Their protests in turn activated defenders of the novel, and the board of education affirmed the decision of its subcommittee to include the book on the list.[38]

After World War I, northern literary critics often dismissed *Uncle Tom's Cabin* as a bad novel, but they were less likely than earlier critics to complain that it had too favorable a view of blacks. Though he admired the social purpose of the novel, Vernon L. Parrington, in his *Main Currents in American Thought* (1927), said that it was "noble propaganda" rather than a work of art. Stowe had had a "New England conscience" and an "ardent nature." On the other hand, she had "never trained herself in craftsmanship, never learned restraints, but suffered her pen to range freely as her emotions directed." The "creative instinct was strong in her but the critical was wholly lacking." Thus, her work had suffered "the fate that pursues those who forget that beauty alone survives after emotion subsides." In 1934, Norman Foerster said that the novel had caused great controversy when it was first published and was greeted as an important literary work, but now "we can see that . . . [it] was merely another expression of romantic revolt and humanitarianism—the struggle for freedom and the blind desire to better the lot of mankind." Occasionally a northern critic in the 1920s and 1930s would agree with some of the earlier southern objections to the novel. In 1935, Fred Lewis Pattee said the notion that

Mrs. Stowe wrote *Uncle Tom's Cabin* to placate the South, that she made Simon Legree a Northern Yankee to forestall their objections, that she had no thought of any purpose save that of bringing North and South into harmony on the question that was bringing them to the brink of war is disproved by the novel.

To argue that its purpose had been to conciliate the South, Pattee thought, was "to confess to not having read the book." Stowe had flung "a stone from a sling." The novel was "a war document," written "when the nation, North and South, was boiling with passion." In 1927, Sinclair Lewis said that *Uncle Tom's Cabin* was "the first evidence to America that no hurricane can be as disastrous to a country as a ruthlessly humanitarian woman."[39]

Like the northern literary critics, northern white historians after World War I often found *Uncle Tom's Cabin* bad as a novel and even worse in its effect on the debate over slavery. In 1934, James Truslow Adams said:

Painting the evils [of slavery] in the most lurid colors, there was no single incident in it which could not have been duplicated in real life, but sweeping all the possible horrors into one gripping story the impression was profoundly misleading. The effect was to indict an entire people for the crimes and cruelty of a small minority, and the South went up in a flame of passion. In the North the recital was taken as a true picture of slavery as it existed in daily life in all the slave States. Thus the novel unquestionably contributed to the state of mind which brought about the Civil War.

In *The Civil War and Reconstruction* (1937), J. G. Randall said that *Uncle Tom's Cabin* showed "the potency of literature in the governance of men's minds." It was "a work of popular fiction which set up a Christian martyr in a black skin as a hero, idealized the Negro, exaggerated his unhappiness in the South, and presented a harrowing picture of brutality." Soon many historians would become less confident than Randall that they could distinguish between the "real" and the "idealized" black. In addition, they were less certain about the degree of unhappiness which blacks had experienced under slavery.[40]

The absent party in the opinions so far discussed in this chapter has been that of the blacks. What did they think of *Uncle Tom's Cabin* in the period after the Civil War? There is almost no evidence of what former slaves thought of the novel, but there is some. Examples of the opinions of ex-slaves are found in an article written by Albion W. Tourgée and published soon after Stowe's death in 1896. Tourgée was a native of Ohio and a Union officer in the Civil War who came to live in North Carolina after the war. During the time of Reconstruction, Tourgée campaigned for the rights of blacks and wrote novels which dealt with the South both before and after the war. The most famous of these novels are *A Fool's Errand* (1879) and *Bricks without Straw* (1880), dealing with the status of the blacks in North Carolina during and after Reconstruction. Tourgée greatly admired Stowe, but he thought she had misinterpreted both her black and white characters in *Uncle Tom's Cabin*. Her principal error, he thought, had been to transfer the New England tradition of logical debate to the South where it was almost wholly unknown. Because the white southern characters in the novel so insistently debated the moral issues of slavery, Tourgée believed them to be "essentially New Englanders."[41]

More surprisingly, Tourgée thought that the black characters in the novel were also New Englanders or, as he put it, "blacked Yankees." It was Uncle Tom himself who chiefly represented this trait, especially in his willingness to engage in debate with his masters, even the cruel Simon Legree. Uncle Tom's "predilection for casuistry," said Tourgée, was wholly uncharacteristic of the southern slave:

As a matter of fact the slave was not given to subtle theorizing. His past had effectually repressed any tendency he might otherwise have developed to discuss his hopes and fears, rights and wrongs—and men do not argue with those who have the power of life and death over them. Through all the book there is a freedom of expression, an effusive interchange of ideas between master and servant which is quite foreign to the conditions of slavery and which, no doubt, goes far to account for the fact that the man who has been a slave and comes afterward to read it, is rarely impressed, as the one who has been a free man all his life is sure to be. Perhaps the most striking characteristic of slavery was the secretiveness it imposed upon the slave nature with regard to himself, his thoughts, desires and purposes. To the slave, language became in very truth an instrument for the concealment of thought, rather than its expression. Only in moments of rapt religious excitement did he fully unbosom himself and then only in figures but half intelligible to those not kindred in experience. Uncle Tom was not only a Yankee in his love of speculation but a Quaker in meek self-surrender. It is doubtful slavery ever produced exactly this type of religious enthusiast. Those it did bring forth were not cool casuists, but either silent, self-absorbed dreamers, or flaming zealots; but Uncle Tom, like Eva, was potential rather than actual.[42]

In the article, Tourgée told of an experiment he had conducted over a period of fifteen years while he was living in North Carolina after the Civil War. He either read *Uncle Tom's Cabin* to a number of ex-slaves himself or he had it read to them for the purpose of determining to what extent they thought it was an accurate portrait of southern slavery. He made an effort to choose "the most intelligent, colored people" he could find. None of them thought the portrait of slavery in the novel was accurate, he said, and their objections centered on the character of Uncle Tom:

Almost every one of them noted the freedom of speech between master and servant. Said one of the shrewdest and most thoughtful:

"Seems like that Uncle Tom must have been raised up North."

"Mrs. Stowe didn't know much about niggers, that's shore," said another.

A blind man, whose daughter read the book to him, gave as his comment:

"She didn't know what slavery was, and so left out the worst of it."

Tourgée did not quote the words of this ex-slave as to what the "worst" of slavery was. Instead, he gave his own version of what the slave was probably trying to say. "He meant," Tourgée said, "that it destroyed hope, aspiration, desire for betterment of individual or collective conditions." The evidence of what former slaves might have thought of Uncle Tom is slight, but it is nonetheless instructive. They did not think of Uncle Tom as too meek, as later generations of black activists would. Instead they thought of him as unrealistically critical of his masters. Tom spoke out more frankly, the ex-slaves thought, than a real slave would have dared to do.[43]

Black intellectuals said little after the Civil War about Stowe or about *Uncle Tom's Cabin*. They were confronted with a dilemma. On the one hand, they were obliged to recognize that Stowe had been greatly influential in ending slavery. They also probably knew that white critics, even those who professed to admire her, nonetheless sometimes thought that her opinion of the innate character and ability of blacks was too high. In addition, most of the attacks upon her were accompanied by the assumption, expressed or implied, that blacks are inherently inferior to whites. It is not surprising, then, that blacks were seldom critical of Stowe or of *Uncle Tom's Cabin*. What reservations they may have had about the novel they understandably kept to themselves.

The blacks who did mention Stowe nearly always spoke of the power of *Uncle Tom's Cabin* in enlisting popular opinion against slavery. Frederick Douglass attended the party for Stowe's seventy-first birthday in 1882. He was glad to be present, he said, "for to no one person had it been given to move so many minds and hearts in behalf of the lately enslaved as to Mrs. Stowe. Hers was the word for the hour, and it was given with skill, force, and effect."[44]

Booker T. Washington praised Stowe in his biography of Frederick Douglass which was published in 1907. She had "so stirred the hearts of the Northern people that a large part of them were ready either to vote, or, in the last extremity, to fight for the suppression of slavery. The value of *Uncle Tom's Cabin* to the cause of Abolition can never be justly estimated." In 1898, Paul Laurence Dunbar published a poem entitled "Harriet Beecher Stowe":

> She told the story and the whole world wept
> At wrongs and cruelties it had not known
> But for this fearless woman's voice alone.
> She spoke to consciences that long had slept;

Her message, Freedom's clear reveille, swept;
    From heedless hovel to complacent throne.
    Command and prophecy were in the tone,
    And from its sheath the sword of justice leapt.
Around two peoples swelled a fiery wave,
    But both came forth transfigured from the flame.
    Blest be the hand that dared by strong to save,
And blest be she who in our weakness came—
    Prophet and priestess! At one stroke she gave
    A race to freedom, and herself to fame.[45]

It is not surprising that nonmilitant blacks like Booker T. Washington and Paul Laurence Dunbar praised Stowe. It may be more significant, however, that other blacks more critical of racism and discrimination in the United States than these two men also praised her. In addition to Frederick Douglass, Charles W. Chesnutt, the black novelist, referred briefly to Stowe in his own biography of Douglass published in 1899, as the author of "that wonderful book" which "set the world on fire over the wrongs of the slave." In 1911, W. E. B. DuBois wrote a review of Charles E. and Lyman Beecher Stowe's *Life of Harriet Beecher Stowe*. Like other blacks of the period, DuBois emphasized chiefly the influence of *Uncle Tom's Cabin* as a work which had helped end slavery; he said relatively little about the black characters in the novel. "Those of us who as children wept over 'Uncle Tom's Cabin' and wondered if it could be 'really true,'" he said, "are both pleased and saddened to learn the stories of the real Legree, Eliza and Topsy." He was also interested in the life of Stowe herself and especially in those events which "aroused in her the burning indignation against 'man's inhumanity to man' which could not rest until it had written itself down in an epoch-making protest against the institution of chattel slavery." At the end of his review, he said, "Thus to a frail overburdened Yankee woman with a steadfast moral purpose we Americans, both black and white, owe our gratitude for the freedom and union that exist to-day in these United States."[46]

Perhaps the comment of a black which most clearly indicated some of the criticisms which *Uncle Tom's Cabin* would later encounter was that of George W. Williams. In his *History of the Negro Race in America from 1619 to 1880* (1883), Williams gave high praise to the novel as a landmark in the progress of blacks in this country. He even shared, to some extent, Stowe's beliefs with regard to the innate racial traits of the blacks. He said that the novel "illustrated the power of the Gospel of Love, the gentleness of Negro character, and the powers and possibilities of the race." He thought that Stowe had "written more and written better about the American Negro than any other person during the present century." And yet, as he reflected on her conceptions of black character, he wondered if she had not made a serious error in her assessment of Uncle Tom. He "is too goodish, too lamb-like, too obsequious. He is a child of full growth, yet lacks the elements of an enlarged manhood. His mind is feeble, body strong—too strong for the conspicuous absence of spirit and passion." It had been a mistake for Stowe to ascribe "to the Negro a peculiarly religious character and disposition," Williams thought. "The Negro is not, as she supposes, the most religious being in the world. He has more religion and less religion than any other of the races, in one sense. And yet, divorced from the circumstances by which he has been surrounded in this country, he is not so very religious. Mrs. Stowe seizes upon a characteristic that belongs to mankind wherever mankind is enslaved and gently binds it about the neck of the Negro. All races of men become religious when oppressed."[47]

In 1912, James Weldon Johnson, the black writer, published a novel, *The Autobiography of an Ex-Colored Man*. Its unnamed protagonist has enough white intermixture to enable him to "pass" as a white. He has been reared in Connecticut but his mother was originally from the South. She had had a liaison with a white man there and he had sent her to Connecticut along with their child when he decided to marry a white woman. The narrator/protagonist only gradually becomes aware of his mixed racial heritage. In his early years his mother had not spoken to him about it. One day when he was about twelve years old he "drew from the circulating library a book that cleared the whole mystery, a book that I read with the same feverish intensity with which I had read the old Bible stories, a book that gave me my first perspective of the life I was entering; that book was *Uncle Tom's Cabin*." Writing as an adult, the narrator says that he has never lost the conviction that Stowe's novel was "a fair and truthful panorama of slavery." He feels greatly indebted to it because "it opened my eyes as to who and what I was and what my country considered me; in fact, it gave me my bearing." On the other hand, his enthusiasm for the novel has nothing to do with Uncle Tom. "For my part, I was never an admirer of Uncle Tom," he says, "nor of his type of goodness."[48]

Between World War I and World War II black intellectuals made very few comments on *Uncle Tom's Cabin*. The idea that it was important because it had helped to end slavery was no longer expressed. On the other hand, the novel was not really attacked by the blacks; there was nothing like the widespread criticism and rejection which would come at the end of World War II. It is probably not possible to indicate at all precisely when Uncle Tom became for many blacks the stereotype of the subservient, "handkerchief head" black who was too cowardly to stand up for his own rights or for those of other blacks. In fact, sometimes the stereotype of Uncle Tom would come to mean a black who actively worked against the welfare of black people generally. It is almost certain that the stereotyped Uncle Tom of this new conception circulated privately among blacks a good many years before it surfaced in print. The first modern reference I have found to the term "Uncle Tom" as a description of a class of blacks who lack self-respect and courage was printed in 1920. At a convention of the Universal Negro Improvement Association, an organization which was led by Marcus Garvey, one of the unnamed delegates made a militant speech. He said, "It takes 1,000 white men to lick one Negro," and he called for a new brand of aggressive leadership among the blacks. "The Uncle Tom Nigger has got to go," he said, "and his place must be taken by the new leader of the Negro race. That man will not be a white man with a black heart." Though the speaker did not specifically indicate the Uncle Tom of the novel and may possibly not even have had him in mind, it was this association which would determine the opinion a great many blacks would have of Stowe and of *Uncle Tom's Cabin* for a long time.[49]

From 1865 to 1940, the opinions of Stowe and of *Uncle Tom's Cabin* had varied widely. By the year 1940, white readers in the United States were often not very far apart in their opinions of it. In the North, white critics and historians had, for the most part, rejected *Uncle Tom's Cabin* both for its literary defects and for its supposed weaknesses in its portrayal of slavery. The novel was condemned as sentimental, and one of the signs of its sentimentality was thought to be its portrayal of black characters. It showed them as better than blacks "really" were. Among historians there was a rather similar criticism. White historians frequently expressed the idea that Stowe had had an inadequate knowledge of slavery and that her portrait of it in the novel was thus defective. Chiefly what they meant by this criticism was that she had seen slavery as more cruel than it "really" was. Virtually none of the people who made this charge made any very searching attempt to show in what ways her views of slavery were faulty. White southern critics frequently agreed with the criticisms of white northern critics of *Uncle Tom's Cabin*. The main difference was that white southern critics frequently felt that northern white critics did not criticize *Uncle Tom's Cabin* with sufficient severity. Black critics, by the year 1940, had generally fallen silent. The earlier praise of the novel and of Stowe herself by black intellectuals had come to an end, but as yet there was little to replace it. There were few signs that lively skirmishes between her partisans and opponents would occur after World War II. There would be savage attacks upon the novel, especially by black intellectuals, but it would also gain shrewd defenders among literary critics and historians.

XIX

Uncle Tom's Cabin
The Play
1865 - 1940

AFTER THE CIVIL WAR, serious critics of *Uncle Tom's Cabin* had much more to say about the novel than they did the play. As a play, it so frequently pandered to popular taste that its antislavery theme was weakened and its black characters became increasingly stereotyped. Uncle Tom himself often became a mere figure of pathos and not a man of dignity who spoke out against oppression. The antics of Topsy and of other black characters were exaggerated to the point that they could scarcely be distinguished from those of the blacks of minstrel shows.

A comment by Mark Twain in 1867 when he was visiting in New York City suggests that *Uncle Tom's Cabin* as a play was beginning to have, after the Civil War, audiences different from those of the period of the 1850s. Twain remembered that before the war, "Everybody went [to the play] in elegant toilettes and cried over Tom's griefs. But now, things are changed. . . . Uncle Tom draws critical, self-possessed groups of negroes and children at Barnum's Museum." It is too bad that Twain did not tell us what the "critical, self-possessed . . . negroes" said. (It is unlikely he meant that the children were also critical.)[1]

It is significant that Twain mentioned the children as an important part of the audience, because the play would increasingly be designed in order to appeal to them. Advertisements sometimes urged parents to bring their children to see *Uncle Tom's Cabin* because of the educational benefits they would receive. An old show bill for a production of the play in Longbottom, Ohio, in 1866 has survived. It says, "Take the children and give them an ideal and lasting lesson in American history. It is delightful, wonderful, instructive and moral." As children became a substantial part of the audiences for the play, it is probable that changes were made to accommodate it for youthful viewers. " 'Uncle Tom's Cabin,' which is at least as harmless a spectacle as 'Hickory, Dickory, Dock,' " said a reviewer in the *New York Times* in 1869, "will be represented . . . [at the Olympic Theatre] until further notice. The original drama, we learn, has been rewritten, but the story and the characters of course will be recognized."[2]

During the Civil War, there were already traveling companies which had no other play but *Uncle Tom's Cabin* in their repertoire. Some of the companies were so poor that their members would walk from one town to another. Their plays would be given in such places as town halls, court houses, or sometimes even barns. They gave "comps" (complimentary tickets) to local people who lent them furniture and other articles to be used as stage props. They were sometimes called "turkey actors" because they were willing to accept barter instead of money for the price of admission. Some of them traveled in wagons and took tents with them in which they staged their performances. One such wagon is described as having a crude portrait on its side of Abraham Lincoln signing the Emancipation Proclamation. Each actor nearly always played several parts. The actress playing Eliza might later appear in the play as Marie St. Clare and later still as Cassy. An actor might be Mr. Shelby early in the play, Augustine St. Clare in the middle sections, and Simon Legree in the last act. Little Harry Harris of the first act would later become little Eva or Topsy. There existed one acting script which required only three actors, and another required only five. Small acting companies traveled all over the North and West, though it was some time before they ventured South. Hard-bitten miners in Colorado and Nevada were likely to weep over the death of little Eva, to laugh over the antics of Topsy, and to hiss Simon Legree. In 1888, a drunken cowboy who attended the play in Tombstone, Arizona, became so excited during the performance that he shot and killed one of the dogs pursuing Eliza.[3]

Some of the traveling *Uncle Tom's Cabin* companies staged elaborate and expensive productions but usually limited their appearances to the larger cities. They had bands for a town parade which preceded the performance, choruses, "cake walk" dancers, and even menageries of animals. There was a pony to draw little Eva's phaeton, a mule for Lawyer Marks, and dogs, of course, to chase Eliza across the ice floes of the Ohio River. Stage managers would add larger and fiercer dogs. Instead of harmless bloodhounds there began to appear Great Danes, English mastiffs, or Russian wolfhounds. Stage settings included scenes of mountains, an old-time slave market, a great plantation festival, a steamboat race on the Mississippi, and the apotheosis of little Eva—all of which were, of course, "masterpieces of stage painting." One production had a real cascade of water on stage and another had an orange grove with "real fruit." One traveling show of the 1880s had fifty actors, twelve dogs, a mule, and an elephant. A production in 1891 had alligators to snap at Eliza and little Harry when they crossed over the Ohio River. There was machinery to allow little Eva to ascend from earth to heaven, dangling at the end of piano wire. In addition to its band, this company had an orchestra, and there would be a dramatic tremolo of musical instruments while little Eva was dying.[4]

In some of the stage productions of the period, Uncle Tom's death scene was much more dramatic than that called for in the earlier Aiken versions of the play. One of the prompt books describes the final scene of the play as follows:

Dark cloud drop rises slowly and discovers very large fan center. Fan separates from the center and falls slowly right and left, discovering Tom on car, with back to audience, and hands outstretched upwards. Two large silver and gold gates about second groove closed. On either side angels with large palms. Lights full up. Car with Tom ascends slantingly up stage. The two angels swing around, gates open slowly, discover two more angels right and left on top of gate posts as car with Tom passes through the gates. Black cloud drop rises and discovers Eva and St. Clare with angels extending hands to Uncle Tom.—Chorus of negroes all through.[5]

The enthusiasm for productions of *Uncle Tom's Cabin* also continued abroad. In 1878, Augustin Daly reported that in London there were five different productions of the play being presented, "but no one place is hurting the other." In one of these productions, neither Uncle Tom nor little Eva was allowed to die. In another, the producer had "created a mate for Topsy in the character of the 'fancy darkey' named Julius. . . . The two dance breakdowns together, and sing comic duets and talk comic trash in a mixture of Cockney, Irish and Scotch, which the innocent (or rather guilty) actors imagine is a good imitation of the genuine canebrake lingo." In 1897, Harry Peck wrote his impressions of a production of the play in Liverpool. The Shelby mansion in Kentucky was of "white marble with Italian pillars, and it was embowered in palm trees and other tropical foliage while far away in the background stretched the blue waters of an inland sea, not usually recorded on the maps, and upon which were to be descried a few stray gondolas." Mrs. Shelby in this production of the play was wearing a diamond-studded tiara and a low-necked dress. Augustine St. Clare's mansion in New Orleans "had snow-capped mountains behind it." When George Harris eluded the slave-catchers and arrived in Canada, "he took out of one of his coat-tails a large cotton pocket handkerchief which displayed the British emblem, and spread it under his chin like porous-plaster. This was the cue for the orchestra, which struck up 'God Save the Queen.' "[6]

In the United States, productions of *Uncle Tom's Cabin* became so numerous that they were a common butt of humor. In Lancaster, Pennsylvania, a newspaper reported in 1880 that the tenth Uncle Tom company had visited the town that year "and no more are wanted." A Detroit paper of 1881 spoke of being "tortured with an invasion of Uncle Toms!!!!!" Concerning the common practice of doubling of parts by actors, one reviewer in Pennsylvania said:

The little Eva, I guess, was really Uncle Tom's grandmother, and the Topsy was old enough to be her sister. The only scenery they had was a house that fell apart every few minutes and a curtain with the Brooklyn Bridge by moonlight on it. The "real ice" was a couple of soap boxes whitewashed, an' the skinny purps they call Siberian bloodhounds forgot to chase Eliza and fought over a bone that somebody chucked at 'em.

A reviewer in Cincinnati in 1881 thought that the time would come when "a long-suffering public may arise in its might and extinguish the meekly prayerful Uncle Toms, the talkative Markses and the angelic Evas. They *do* say that the interior inhabitants of Ohio, upon the announcements of a party performing this drama, immediately betook themselves to the woods."[7]

The cynics who derided the play probably had no idea what was coming. Instead of subsiding, the Uncle Tom mania grew. In 1879, the *New York Dramatic Mirror* listed the routes of forty-nine of what had already begun to be called "Tommer shows," that is, acting companies wholly given over to productions of this single play. By the 1890s, there were, according to one estimate, approximately five hundred companies producing Tommer shows. Both simple and elaborate productions proliferated. In 1895, one production had "20 drops and 28 set pieces." It featured a steamboat race between the *Natchez* and the *Robert E. Lee*. For little Eva in the parade there was a gold chariot which the advertisements said had cost $1,500. Another show had a hundred ponies. One had twenty-four hounds to chase Eliza across the Ohio. In 1902-1903 one company advertised itself as a "$30,000 production, the biggest traveling opera house attraction in the world." It traveled on the railroad in "three specially constructed palace cars with eighty people, thirty ponies, horses, donkeys, mules and oxen, fifteen ferocious man-eating bloodhounds, and three musical groups—a twenty-piece silver cornet band and orchestra, a fourteen-man genuine African male drum and fife corps, and a twelve-girl creole drum and bugle corps." Another company had a "seventeen-year-old colored giant drum major and wing-and-buck dancer, eight feet tall." Sometimes Uncle Tom himself had to be refurbished so as to fit in more easily with all this grandeur. In an 1889 adaptation of the play, as a servant in the St. Clare household, he wore "a Prince Albert of a full-dress suit with gloves, cravat, etc.," as well as "a gray wig."[8]

In the 1890s, Chicago was the center for the mounting of Tommer shows. One promoter was so overwhelmed by the great number of companies and productions that he humorously advertised for available actors as follows: "Uncle Toms, prime, $60 [a week?]; fair, $50; culls, $35." The ratings did not refer chiefly to acting ability. A "prime" was someone who could "double in brass" (play a musical instrument) in the parade and "take care of the live stock," a "fair" could only play an instrument, and "culls" could do nothing but act. To his surprise, the producer found that his humorous sally was answered by a great many letters from prospective actors and actresses asking to be listed in the proposed exchange.[9]

Year after year the critics wrote off Tommer shows as artistic failures, but the public enthusiasm for them grew. One reviewer in 1902 estimated that in that year alone a million and a half people in the United States, one in every thirty-five inhabitants of the total population, would see a production of the play. In 1912, Charles E. Stowe, the son of Harriet Beecher Stowe, estimated that there had been 250,000 productions of the play in this country. In 1947, Harry Birdoff, who wrote a history of productions of the play, used a different method of calculation from that of Charles E. Stowe. He did not indicate a precise figure, but he did say that Charles Stowe's estimate was much too low. In 1952, another historian of the play estimated that as many as a million performances of the play had been given in the nearly one hundred years since it had first appeared. It had "not merely out-drawn every other play; it had drawn more people into the theatre than the combined efforts of any other dozen plays."[10]

Although it was much more popular than the novel, *Uncle Tom's Cabin* the play was nearly always guilty of such lapses of taste that thoughtful people who saw it seldom commented upon its portrayal of slavery. Perhaps the fact that it apparently had so little to say on this subject may have been part of its appeal. There was a widespread tendency in the North to forget the Civil War as the culmination of a great national movement which had brought freedom to the slaves. These productions of *Uncle Tom's Cabin* enabled northern audiences to exult in the victory of the Union forces without being made uncomfortably aware of what freedom for the blacks had actually turned out to mean. On one issue, however, northern audiences for the play may have been sensitive. In the novel and in the earlier Aiken version of the play, Simon Legree had been clearly identified as a Yankee. In the 1920s, one writer recalled that he had seen at least as many as twenty-five productions of the play as a boy in a northern state in the 1880s and 1890s. In none of them, however, had there ever been the slightest intimation that Simon Legree had come from anywhere but the South.[11]

As an old woman, Cordelia Howard—the actress who had played the role of little Eva in the 1850s and whose acting career had lasted many years after the Civil War—wrote her reminiscences and said that performances of the play over the years had suffered a serious artistic decline:

I think there never was a play with quite such a varied career as *Uncle Tom's Cabin*. It began with something of dignity and even grandure [*sic*], in pleading an unpopular cause, both North and South. It kept its own for many years, and then gradually became so degraded, with its bloodhounds, donkeys, and double casts, that it has become really a burlesque and is the butt of all the critics' ridicule. But it has a wonderful vitality, and I think it will rise from its ashes and probably regale one or two more generations. One reason, of course, is that it represents a phase of society entirely passed away. Like the novel, it will become a classic.[12]

Even though *Uncle Tom's Cabin* lost a good deal of its emphasis upon the evils of slavery in the years following the Civil War, it was

still unacceptable in most regions of the South. Reverend Mr. Henry
Clay Trumbull, formerly a Union army chaplain, wrote a book of his
memoirs in 1898 and reported on the reactions of two young men from
the South who visited New York City soon after the end of the Civil
War. Eager to experience the amusements of the place, they went to
see a production of *Uncle Tom's Cabin.* Leaving the theater, the two men
walked together in profound silence, lost in thought. Then one man said
to the other, "Well, *that's* what licked us!"[13]

In the years immediately following the Civil War, it was a daring
Tommer company which attempted a production of the play in the
South. Soon after the war, a company played *Uncle Tom's Cabin* in
Louisville, Kentucky. While it encountered much hostility, it was still
moderately successful. In 1872 a company performed it in New Orleans.
In this production, some of the antislavery lines of the play were omitted.
Years later, a son of two of the actors in this production said that it
was played "not as a political document but as a rattling old melodrama
of the South with all the varieties of appeal necessary to success—
violent action, tragedy and retribution, sticky sentimentality and frequently low comedy relief." On the first night of its run, the play encountered a "few jeers" from the audience, but "the majority of those
who came to carp went away well satisfied with their evening's entertainment." In 1877, another company brought a production of the play
to New Orleans. This one also heavily emphasized comedy and melodrama. One of the billboards for the play proclaimed that it contained
"Morsels of Ethiopian Mirth, Fun and Frolic description of the different
phases of SLAVE LIFE ON THE OLD PLANTATION!" This time the play
met with no opposition. In 1881, an "idealized" version of the play was
performed in Macon, Georgia, without objection from the community.
"Idealized" probably meant that the antislavery theme had diminished
to the vanishing point.[14]

In 1881, a Tommer company attempted to tour Virginia and Georgia, but the actors discovered that the wounds of the past were still too
fresh for them to succeed. The newspapers of Richmond and Norfolk
campaigned against the play being performed in the South. Some of
the company's posters in these two cities were ripped off by protesters.
The troupe got as far as Lynchburg and then gave up, canceling further
engagements and returning to the North. In Georgia in the same year,
an audience in the town of Griffin pelted a troupe with rotten eggs and
damaged the stage scenery. When this company played in Atlanta, only

two small boys showed up as members of the audience. In Savannah, the troupe made only enough to pay for the rental of the theater, not enough to enable it to leave the city. The baggage of the actors was confiscated by the railroad company in exchange for tickets back to the North. Even so, the troupe's agent later bravely ran an advertisement, "We are the first company ever thru the South with *Uncle Tom's Cabin*."[15]

In Bonham, Texas, a small town north of Dallas, a performance was announced in 1890. Jefferson Davis had just died and his funeral was scheduled for the day on which the play was to open. About 2,000 people gathered outside the theater to express their indignation at the performance. The town band played "Dixie" continuously to drown out the actors' lines. Other groups of people shouted and generally created a disturbance, some of them setting off giant firecrackers and ringing bells. The manager of the theater summoned the town's mayor for police protection, but he said he could do nothing. The actors huddled together in the darkened building, hoping that the crowd would give up and go away. They left only when it was too late for the play to be presented. In 1894, billboards announcing a production of a Tommer show in Charlottesville, Virginia, were defaced with the letters, S. C. V. (Sons of Confederate Veterans). On one of the billboards, a picture of Abraham Lincoln was entirely blacked out, and underneath a picture of Eliza fleeing across the Ohio River there was written the word "Lie." In spite of these difficulties, the play had at least a modest success in Charlottesville and the troupe was requested to return with another performance of the play the following year. The same company encountered more opposition, however, when it attempted to stage the play in Culpepper, Virginia. It tried to mollify the protesters by omitting the scene in which Uncle Tom is whipped, but it was not a sufficient concession. A mob broke up the performance and pelted the actors with stale vegetables.[16]

In time the prejudice against performances of the play in the South died down. In 1883, *Uncle Tom's Cabin* was again produced in New Orleans. The Tommer company advertised it as "the success of both hemispheres . . . direct from London, England." The *New Orleans Daily Picayune* was not enthusiastic about the play, but neither was it hostile. "No one can seriously oppose the performance of *Uncle Tom's Cabin*," an editor wrote. "It is not worth objecting to." He thought that the public had a "moral right" to see the play. "It is well understood," he added, "that *Uncle Tom's Cabin* is an exaggeration of events imagined by Mrs. Stowe many years ago. That which is good in it, the picture of the faithful, old servant, the refinement of the St. Clares, and the ludicrous side, will live."[17]

In 1897, a troupe gave a production of *Uncle Tom's Cabin* in Alexandria, Virginia, without incident, and in the same year a production ran for three weeks in Louisville, Kentucky. In 1901, the local chapter of the United Daughters of the Confederacy in Lexington, Kentucky, presented a petition to a theater manager there objecting to plans for a performance. He replied as follows: "Ladies, a copy of your resolution in reference to *Uncle Tom's Cabin* has been received. Replying to the same, I have only to say, the war has been over about thirty-six years." A year later, another Kentuckian advised his compatriots in the South not to be agitated about dramatic productions of *Uncle Tom's Cabin*. The play had become, said Joseph M. Rogers, "one of the crudest pieces of stage composition which any audience is likely to see." It "lacks literary and dramatic merit," but more importantly it was "ethically as little related to the book from which it is derived as to 'MacBeth.'" Its impact was small and its effect upon the ideas of people with regard to slavery was negligible. "Politically speaking," he said, "'Uncle Tom's Cabin' is as dead as Hector, who never had a ghost at all, as far as we know."[18]

Oddly, it was in Kentucky—and not in the North—that a black actor first played the role of Uncle Tom in the play. This event occurred, moreover, before the play became generally acceptable in the South. Gustave Frohman in 1876 had a theatrical troupe in Richmond, Kentucky. The company was about to go broke and as a measure of desperation Frohman decided to stage a production of *Uncle Tom's Cabin*. Frohman, then a young man, conceived the idea of producing the play with a black in the title role. In making this change, he was far ahead of his time. Even in New York City, it was not until about the year 1910 that blacks began to play black characters alongside white actors. So far as is known, the Kentuckians offered no objection to Frohman's having a black play this part. On the other hand, the Kentucky State Legislature thirty years later, in 1906, solemnly passed a law which made it illegal to present "any play that is based upon antagonism between master and slave, or that excites racial prejudice." Violators were to be punished with a fine of not less than $100 nor more than $500 and a prison sentence of not less than one month nor more than three months.

The law was aimed at preventing productions of *Uncle Tom's Cabin*. It stayed on the books until it was repealed in 1974. It apparently was never enforced but it may have prevented Tommer companies from staging productions of the play within the state.[19]

Even in the North, Uncle Tom shows occasionally encountered hostility. George Jean Nathan described how, about the year 1900, a performance of the play in Trenton, New Jersey, was attended by some obstreperous Princeton undergraduates. Probably by a prearranged plan, one of the students leaped to his feet while viewing the play and protested that there was a "colored" performer in the cast. The actor portraying Uncle Tom stepped up to the footlights and explained that he was a white, not a black. The play again proceeded. Then another college student stood up in the audience and shouted, "I think he is deceiving us. I think he really is colored, and I object to a Negro acting in a company of white actors." The students refused to allow the play to continue until the actor had proved that he was white. "The actor obliged," said Nathan, "and exposed a white swath where shellac wig and burnt cork had met." Only then did the students cease their objections to the performance.[20]

To what extent did the dramatic productions of *Uncle Tom's Cabin*, which multiplied in the years after the Civil War, have anything significant to say about slavery, the Civil War, or the post-Civil War role of blacks in American society? There is not much contemporary opinion which addresses itself to this question, but there is a world of indirect evidence that the play did not cause audiences to reflect on the meaning of slavery or on the role of the free black in society. Some of the critics of the play have attempted to answer the question of the serious import of the play during the period of its greatest popularity, but few of them have had much to say that was encouraging. In 1956, J. C. Furnas, a hostile observer, wrote of an old woman who recalled a performance of the play she had seen as a child. "An old Negro with white hair," she remembered, "and a big man in a black coat with a whip. It was sad." This brief account probably comes near summing up what many audiences carried away with them in terms of the meaning of the play. In 1956, F. W. Boreham recalled productions of the play he saw in the 1890s. "How many times I watched Eliza, her little boy in her arms, leaping frantically from one huge block of ice to another, as she made her desperate bid for freedom," Boreham said, "I can now hazard no conjecture. We knew it all by heart, yet never for a moment tired of it."

He did wonder whether the antislavery theme of the play had made much of an impression upon the minds of the audience: "Did we, I wonder, recognize the ethical and spiritual issues involved in it? I have my doubts." He was speaking principally of the reactions of children to the play, but it is probable that the adults who saw it thought scarcely more about the "ethical and spiritual" issues of the play than the children did.[21]

Charles H. Foster, a sympathetic critic of Stowe, thinks that a subconscious cruelty lurked behind the motives of the great crowds of people who flocked to see Uncle Tom shows. By the 1890s, Foster notes, Tom shows "approximated a homemade gladiatorial contest. There was a parade with a Negro band and a white one, and in leash the bloodhounds (really mastiffs or Great Danes)." The parade was a suggestion to the onlookers that if they attended the play they would witness

the darkest passions. Only wait and a black man would be whipped to death beneath the long curling bull whip of a white giant. For the vicious, here was the wished-for moment like the slaughter of the victim before the howling Roman mob. For all, the spectacle meant immediately that the Negro had been defeated at the hands of the white man.

It made no difference that after death Uncle Tom was welcomed into heaven, for "this was anticlimax to the vulgar imagination. Like showing the flag in fireworks on the fourth of July, it was simply a justification for the preceding excitement." This reading of the effect of the play might be unfair to some people, Foster says, because there were those who "pitied Uncle Tom, vibrated to the piety of Eva, and innocently enjoyed the humor of Topsy and other characters." On the other hand, he finds it significant that the peak of popularity of the Tom shows "coincided with the cynicism and the immorality of the Gilded Age. In the show there was a ruthless exploitation of American sensibility matching the more obvious exploitation of the American continent."[22]

It is true that many of the devices of melodrama were used to make the scene of the whipping of Uncle Tom a chilling event on stage. It became a tradition for Simon Legree, "foaming with rage," to strike "his victim to the ground." Then he would beat Uncle Tom on the head with the handle of his whip. In some productions, the actor playing Uncle Tom, to enhance this moment, would have a container of red fluid resembling blood spread over his head and chest at the moment of the blow. In some performances, Legree had long, black, snaky locks with a "jet chin piece and drooping moustaches." Theodore Roberts, one of the best known of the actors who portrayed Simon Legree, was red-headed and baldish with a broken nose and "a glowering savage face." When he had killed Uncle Tom, he would shout to Sambo and Quimbo, his evil slaves, "Take him out, and throw him in the hog-pen."[23]

Whether seeing a black flogged to death was a major reason people went to see the play is, of course, impossible to ascertain with any real confidence. It would seem that some of the critics, as unsophisticated as many of them were, would have mentioned this as a reason for the popularity of the play, but apparently none of them ever did. There cannot be an absolutely certain judgment, of course, with regard to an unconscious motivation. If the audience came to the play to exult in the death of Uncle Tom by torture, however, one would think it would have been more satisfactory to portray him as the strong and fairly young man he had been in the novel. Yet in the plays he was virtually always shown as a man long past his prime and sometimes as an aged man with scanty white hair and a quavering voice. It is difficult to see a figure like this as a suitable object for the audience's enjoyment of the spectacle of his being whipped to death. It is true that in 1892 Krafft-Ebing recorded that one of his neurotic patients had confessed to a feeling of a sexual arousal when he saw Uncle Tom being whipped on the stage.[24]

On the other hand, it is not difficult to suspect that the suffering and death of Uncle Tom in the play were not always taken with much seriousness. In a London production in 1878, Uncle Tom had just been whipped by Legree and was lying on the stage, presumably dying. The actors in the play were not ready for the next scene. To stall for time, the actor playing Tom sang a song, "Good Ol' Jeff Hab Gwine t'Rest." Even when he had finished his song, the actors were still unprepared for the next scene, so he arose and performed "a good ol' plantation dance" before lying down to die. John L. Sullivan, the Boston heavy-weight boxer, played the part of Simon Legree in one of the touring companies of the play. Apparently one of the attractions of these per-formances was seeing Sullivan knock about the actors portraying blacks, especially the actor who played Uncle Tom. Sullivan was said to have treated the actors playing Uncle Tom so brutally that within a few weeks he had used up a half-dozen of them. One of the Uncle Tom actors attempted to withstand the punishments of Sullivan by wearing cotton padding within his clothes, but even he suffered considerably. As a pro-fessional boxer, Sullivan had no high opinion of blacks. He would not, for example, accept a challenge from a black contender for the championship because he thought to do so would be beneath his dignity.[25]

In one production of the play, a black boxer, Peter Jackson from Australia, played the part of Uncle Tom. At the point in the play when Uncle Tom is sold to Simon Legree and sighs, "May de Lawd ha' mercy on my soul," the action would come to a temporary halt. The curtain would go down and the fighter's manager would step up to the footlights to make a brief speech. "Now, ladies and gentlemen," he would say, "Peter Jackson will box three friendly and scientific rounds to show how he will wrest the pugilistic crown from 'Gentleman Jim' Corbett!" When the curtain rose again, there would be a roped arena on stage. Uncle Tom would have shed his white wig and would now be dancing about in boxing trunks. He would then have a spirited workout with his sparring partner who had played the part of Mr. Shelby earlier in the play. There is no record that anyone thought all this might have thrown a curious light on the antislavery theme of *Uncle Tom's Cabin.*[26]

If there is no certainty about whether audiences came to see *Uncle Tom's Cabin* in order to indulge their sadistic hatred of blacks, it is not difficult to demonstrate that the blacks which audiences usually saw in productions of the play were not portrayed sympathetically. Degrading racial stereotypes were common. One performance had "18 Georgia Plantation shouters." Another had the "Original Whangdoodle Pickaninny Band ON THE OLD PLANTATION!"[27]

Some of the most obvious and offensive black stereotypes in the play were conveyed through the portrayals of Topsy. If other actresses had performed the part as well as Mrs. George C. Howard, Topsy might have fared much better. Mrs. Howard, who had played the role successfully in the 1850s and continued to do so after the Civil War, managed to portray the exuberance of the child without making her into a caricature. When the Howards took their production of *Uncle Tom's Cabin* to England after the Civil War, a London reviewer singled out Mrs. Howard for special praise, saying she was "such a perfect embodiment of Mrs. Harriet Beecher Stowe's Topsy that one would imagine both ladies had studied from one model." The critic recognized that most actresses had vulgarized the part. Mrs. Howard's Topsy was "not the Topsy we have been familiar with on the stage." In her portrayal Topsy was "a child for whom nobody cares, that in a figurative sense may be said with perfect truth 'never to have been born.' . . . At one moment she is stubborn, insensate and unimpressionable—in another, she flies into an ungovernable, almost demoniac rage." Yet, as portrayed by Mrs. Howard, the extreme reactions of Topsy never belied her humanity. Instead, "her cunning and revenge exhibit in a wonderful degree the effects of bad passions, allowed to grow up unchecked, like weeds in the fair garden of the breast. Her elf-like figure, and the strange, wild screaming chant in which she sang the song, 'I'se So Wicked,' was something quite *sui generis*."[28]

Such sensitive portrayals of Topsy must have been rare, even in the best days of *Uncle Tom's Cabin* as a play. After the Civil War they became rarer still. In most of the productions, the sole function of Topsy was to supply low comedy. She became famous for her song:

> Oh! der is one will come an' say:
>   Be good, Topsy, learn to pray;
> An' raise her buful hands dat way—
>   Ching-a-ring a ricked!
> 'Tis Little Eva, kind an' fair,
>   Says: if I's good, I'll go dere;
> But den I tells her: I don't care!
>   Oh, aint I very wicked?
> Eat de cake, an' hoe de corn.
>   I'se de gal dat ne'er was born,
> But 'spect I grow'd up one dark morn:
>   Ching-a-ringa smash goes de break-down!

In 1947, Harry Birdoff described one of the Topsys who played in the mining camps of the West in the 1870s, saying she had a "raucous voice, like that of a cricket with laryngitis." Instead of being "the wild waif of Mrs. Stowe's imagination," she became "the living embodiment of the 'wickedest nigger on earth.'" Little Eva was often, although not always, played by a child, female or male, but Topsy was much more often played by an adult woman or an adult man. Sometimes she was portrayed in such a way as to bring an element into the play which had been wholly absent in her character in the novel—the suggestion of sexual "wickedness." After Little Egypt made sex titillation a sensation at the Chicago Exposition of 1893, the Topsys of Uncle Tom plays sometimes substituted for their previous "breakdown" dances take-offs on a dance by Little Egypt.[29]

In some versions of the play, Topsy would express her dislike of mulattoes. In the novel, somewhat similar objections had been expressed by Dinah, one of the slaves in the St. Clare household in New Orleans. Stowe's apparent purpose had been merely to show that racial prejudice flourished among blacks as well as among whites. In the original Aiken version of the play, the comments of Topsy on mulattoes probably had the same purpose that Dinah's comments had in the novel. In later versions, however, Topsy's disparaging comments about mulattoes sometimes seemed to have the purpose of suggesting that mulattoes were even worse than blacks without white intermixture. "You tink youse white folks," Topsy says to a mulatto character in a 1912 adaptation of the play. "You aint nuffin but yaller niggers, neither black nor white. Golly, I's glad I'se one ting or tother. I's black, and I's glad of it." She sings a song:

> I wouldn't if I could.
> I wouldn't be a yaller nigger.
> 'Cause dey ain't no good.[30]

In the fifty years following the Civil War, the Tom shows flourished. What did blacks think about them? As we have already seen, relatively few blacks mentioned *Uncle Tom's Cabin* the novel and none discussed it in any detail. The silence was even more characteristic of the black reaction to *Uncle Tom's Cabin* the play. There are so few references to it among black writers that the silence itself must be significant. That the blacks did not invariably dislike the play is suggested by the fact that one white observer mentioned going to one of its productions given by a black acting group in Davenport, Iowa, in 1902. Robert Bosworth, who was one of Minnie Maddern Fiske's leading men, told about a group of white actors going "to a funny little theater . . . to see a performance [of *Uncle Tom's Cabin*] by colored troupers. We went to laugh but remained to pray, for we saw an exquisitely beautiful, dignified and marvelously pathetic and sweet performance given of Uncle Tom by Charles Albins, who afterwards came to New York and played Othello."[31]

An account of black reactions to the parade of an *Uncle Tom's Cabin* troupe in a southern town is found in a book by William Lyon Phelps published in 1924. He wrote of a "northern tourist"—possibly himself—who had visited a town in the South "a few years ago." He discovered that the appearance of the play there generally meant a holiday for the blacks. He had registered at a local hotel on the day the play was to be performed. After ringing in vain for the bellboy, he went downstairs to ask the white hotel clerk at the desk what was the matter. The clerk replied that *Uncle Tom's Cabin* was being played in town and the fact "was sufficient explanation as to the whereabouts of every colored man, woman and child for ten miles around. They are all packed out on Main Street to see the big parade, and you couldn't get one of them to work until it passes if you gave them a dollar for each piece of luggage." If the parade was not over soon, the clerk said, it would be impossible to get anything to eat in the hotel restaurant. "Order them to work?" he said. "Well, I guess not. It would start a riot, and everyone from the dishwasher to the head waiter would walk out on us and we'd be boycotted." The visitor "found the streets jammed and the trees and telegraph posts crowded with pickaninnies." He said nothing specifically about the reactions of blacks to the play. It is not even certain that they were allowed to attend a performance of it. All we are told is what some of them thought of little Eva when she appeared in the parade. "The mammies cried, 'Dar now! Ah could kiss dat child to deff.'" He also noted that little Eva was chewing gum.[32]

In 1926, a white writer recalled a performance of the play she had seen many years before in an old soldiers' home for Union veterans. It was badly done and the former soldiers were generally critical of it, but a black veteran of the Union Army had a quite different reaction. For him the play recalled the injustices of slavery and it apparently was nothing less than a transcript of life:

Halfway back in the auditorium we presently spied a coal black negro in the familiar blue uniform. He himself had been a slave, and had later fought to free the slaves. He watched the stage in absorption that was almost bewilderment, and down his poor old black cheeks the tears were running, and drying white against the black as he winked them away, not to miss a word of the play. To him this was no troupe of poorly trained actors who went through a tiresome routine because they knew no other way to make a living. Acting itself before his eyes was the drama of his race's long enslavement.[33]

Why do we know so little of what blacks thought of *Uncle Tom's Cabin* the play? Many of them probably saw it, but their silence is the one overwhelming fact of their reaction. They probably realized that the play, like the novel, had been influential in ending slavery. On the other hand, it is unlikely that they could bring themselves to praise the play which had so many degrading stereotypes of blacks in it. They may have thought that their only recourse was to remain silent.

Beginning in the 1890s some of the productions of *Uncle Tom's Cabin* in the North ended not with Uncle Tom approaching the gates of heaven but with the Union armies triumphing over the Confederates.

There would be a tableau showing Lincoln signing the Emancipation Proclamation. Sometimes in the grand finale, the men in blue would carry the American flag while they sang a patriotic song. During the Spanish-American War, a version of the play was presented with the military uniforms modernized to correspond with the times. Now northerners and southerners were triumphing together over Spain, not engaging in fratricidal war. How far most of the productions of the play were from any advocacy of a change in the status of blacks generally is suggested by a comment in the 1890s by a reviewer who saw a production of the play in Paris. Puzzled, he noted that in the French performance of the play there had been a curious ending. The blacks had achieved "social equality" with the whites.[34]

These intrusions of history in the last scenes of *Uncle Tom's Cabin* may seem casual, even trivial, but they represent an improvement over many of the earlier productions. The play had become a set piece, and audiences had not been encouraged to take seriously the issues of slavery. The producers of the play may have felt that to dwell on the historical theme might have caused audiences to think about what had happened to the blacks after the war, a subject which they probably wished to avoid. However *deus ex machina* the appearance of the Union Army in the last scene might be, it did put the events of the play into a definite historical context. Freedom for the blacks had been, after all, one of the aims of the North in the Civil War. This was a theme which before had rarely been implied. Whether audiences went to see *Uncle Tom's Cabin* to observe an old black man being whipped to death is a question which may never have a clear answer. On the other hand, there is no doubt that most of the people who saw it in the year after the Civil War show very little evidence that the play caused them to reflect seriously on the issues of slavery.

In the twentieth century, it was almost inevitable that *Uncle Tom's Cabin* would be adapted for the movies. Most of the movie versions were no better than those of the stage. Edwin S. Porter produced the first film version in 1909. Porter was one of the early innovators among film directors. His "The Great Train Robbery" (1903) is said to be the first film which definitely told a story. *Uncle Tom's Cabin* was the first novel to be turned into a screen play and the first movie with subtitles, which apparently perpetuated some of the worst of the black stereotypes of many of the stage productions. One historian of films describes it as "sentimental" and "mostly concerned with the faithful, dog-like devotion of Uncle Tom for little Eva." Uncle Tom was played by a white actor. In 1914, there was another movie version of the play, this time with black actors playing the black parts. In other respects, however, this version was scarcely an improvement over the earlier one. In 1918, there was a third version. The director reverted to the old pattern of having a white actor play Uncle Tom, and his version was little if any better than the earlier two.[35]

In 1927, there was a major Hollywood production of *Uncle Tom's Cabin*, one costing $2,000,000, then considered a tremendous sum for a movie. Charles Gilpin, a black actor who had played the leading role in Eugene O'Neill's *The Emperor Jones* on the stage in New York, was first chosen to play the part of Uncle Tom. Harry Pollard, the white director, insisted that Gilpin be meek and submissive in the rôle of Uncle Tom. He said that Gilpin was too "aggressive" in his interpretation of the part, though there was also studio gossip that Gilpin drank too much. After heated arguments, Gilpin, described by a film historian as "an intelligent, proud, and sensitive person," gave up the part and returned to New York. Since there were no acting roles open to him, he was obliged to "go back to his old job as liftman rather than play a well-paid screen role, the treatment of which, in his opinion, helped to malign his people." His salary for the screen role was said to have been $1,000 a week. Soon he was operating a chicken farm in New Jersey, and not long afterward he died.[36]

James B. Lowe was the black actor who took the place of Charles Gilpin in the film. A historian of blacks in films has described Lowe as an actor who had played an "athletic vagabond" in a series of films "as a black sidekick of the white cowboy hero." Apparently he was allowed some concessions by Pollard in his interpretation of the role of Uncle Tom. One white reviewer of the film said that in this version, "Uncle Tom . . . wears his ball and chain with a difference." Even so, the film studio felt obliged to make some concessions to Confederate organizations in the South. There were cuts in those scenes which emphasized the "cruelty of slavery." The New England origin of Simon Legree was strongly apparent. One black reviewer said that so many concessions had been made to white southerners that an unsophisticated viewer might draw the conclusion that slavery had been a northern and not a southern phenomenon. He would assume that the appearance of troops at the film meant that slavery was at last abolished in the North. After listing the faults of the film, another black reviewer said that even though it was generally "humiliating" to blacks, there was some consolation in the fact that Lowe had been able to get a substantial sum of money from white producers. A few of the black reviewers of the film were enthusiastic. "If a Negro ever felt like doing something to try to elevate his people," said one of them, "he ought to feel like it when he sees the eternal hope in the old slave's eyes in his darkest hours."[37]

In the 1920s and 1930s there continued to be stage versions of *Uncle Tom's Cabin*, most of them performed by small traveling companies. In 1927, there were a dozen Tommer companies on tour. A magazine article asserted in 1931 that after seventy-eight years of "continuous performance, here, there, and everywhere," the play had breathed its last in a final performance. The report of its death was premature. The editor of *Billboard* wrote in 1935, "At the present time, *Uncle Tom's Cabin* is produced mainly in one-night stands. Stock companies take it out every spring and summer." Also in 1935, a manager of a small traveling theatrical group was quoted as saying that his company still presented the play quite often because "it invariably brought more money to the box office than any Broadway show."[38]

In 1933, there was a revival of the play in New York with Otis Skinner playing the part of Uncle Tom. Skinner, then seventy-five years old, had played the role fifty-seven years before when he was only eighteen. A reviewer mentioned some of the defects of the play, but nonetheless expressed the opinion that it still had great power. "It is only in scattered lines here and there," he said, "that the over-simple motivations that satisfied playgoers of the early Victorian era seem ridiculous." Even Simon Legree turned out to be a generally credible character though he had trouble making one of his lines in the play appear convincing. "I, too," he said to the considerable amusement of audiences, "was nursed at the bosom of a mother." In other respects, one reviewer said, the actor portraying Legree made him "a villain of royal parts." He was not merely a stage villain. Instead he was shown "as much a 'victim of environment' as the most skillfully drawn gangster of modern melodrama." It was Otis Skinner, however, who the reviewer thought gave the best performance of the play:

He plays the part [of Uncle Tom] for utter sincerity and achieves his goal. There is no laugh, for example, when he comes to his famous lines, "You may own my body, but my soul belongs to God." Mr. Skinner makes it a simple declaration of faith, and the audience subdued by his consummate art, accepts it as just that.[39]

In 1936, George Abbott produced a musical version of the play in New York. Stark Young, who reviewed it, seemed to modify his previous objections to Stowe. He found himself impressed, at least, with "the touches of affection" which Abbott had given it. One of the changes Abbott made was in the ending. He did not, as some of the earlier producers of the play had done, end it with the arrival of the Union army in the South and the freeing of the slaves. In Abbott's production, the emphasis was on what freedom had specifically meant for the blacks. There was a parade of modern blacks across the stage at the end of the play. Some of them had menial occupations, but others were representative of such professions as law, medicine, and teaching.[40]

In 1935, there was a ballet version of *Uncle Tom's Cabin* with the choreography written by E. E. Cummings. The directions for the dance of Mr. and Mrs. Shelby say that they "constipate the frontstage with platitudes of terpsichore." Some of the blacks of the Shelby plantation are shown as ecstatically religious. They are "yearngrovelling" and "frantically fallrising" and they "squirmspurt whirl surgingly outward and at the footlight high together leaping stand." Topsy dances "a dance of instinct unsubdued." Eva is an angel "with fluttery faintly softly shining wings." Simon Legree tears up Uncle Tom's Bible. During the ballet, huge golden doors of heaven open up for Uncle Tom. After his death, however, a "monstergoddess" appears and dances the "dance of Avenging Africa." Cummings apparently recognized that a defect in previous adaptations of the play had been that blacks were shown as if they were almost wholly unresentful of the wrongs which had been done to them.[41]

In some foreign countries, *Uncle Tom's Cabin* was adapted for anti-American propaganda. In 1907, a group of Chinese actors in Tokyo staged a production of this kind. No copy of the script remains, but the description of the play implies that it portrayed the mistreatment of blacks before the Civil War as a foreshadowing of American imperialism in the Far East. There were specific references to the mistreatment of the Chinese. Americans had helped to suppress the Boxer Rebellion and had discriminated against Chinese immigrants in their own country. One historian of Chinese literature has said that in 1917 a nationalist renaissance of the drama began in major cities in the country. Of foreign plays, two were favorites. One was *La Dame aux Camelias* by Alexandre Dumas *fils*. It was popular because it reminded the Chinese of similar "bonds of narrow matrimonial conventions" in their own past. The other popular foreign play was *Uncle Tom's Cabin*. The Chinese were fond of it because they "knew by bitter experiences the sufferings and humiliations of an oppressed race." Both plays received from Chinese audiences "passionate, ear-deafening applause."[42]

In 1932, the Moscow Second Art Theatre produced an adaptation of the play. All the religion was omitted. Uncle Tom was killed but nothing was said of his going to heaven. Little Eva was not delicate and spiritual, as described by an American reviewer in the *New York Herald-Tribune*, but was "almost tomboyish." Her name was changed to Dora and the reviewer thought she was apparently intended to represent "something of an American forerunner to a vigorous present-day Komosol (Young Communist) championing the cause of the downtrodden proletarian Negro." The cabin of Uncle Tom was "a tropical affair of bamboo stalks and loosely woven matting." The slaves sang Russian folksongs.[43]

Even in its earlier productions before the Civil War, *Uncle Tom's Cabin* had often been vulgarized and had carried a message substantially different from that of the novel. After the war the process of vulgarization was both more widespread and more thorough. Earlier audiences knew that though the black characters in the play were not always to be taken seriously, the fact of slavery was very real indeed. After the war, this restraint was removed. Audiences could abandon themselves both to the pathos of Uncle Tom's plight and to the humor of such characters as Topsy without asking themselves whether either of these things had any serious meaning. What chiefly happened was that the theme of the evils of slavery was drowned out in the crudely comic characterization of most of the black characters. Sometimes, it is true, there were productions of the play which reflected the spirit of the novel. More often, however, the play did more to hamper than to help the cause of the blacks in the United States.

XX

Critical Reception of Uncle Tom's Cabin 1941 to the Present

IN RECENT YEARS *Uncle Tom's Cabin* has attracted some spirited enthusiasts and defenders. After World War II, however, the novel was forced to endure one last barrage of unfavorable criticism. The earlier criticism of Stowe had usually been that she had portrayed black characters, and especially Uncle Tom, too favorably; after World War II she was censured for not having portrayed them favorably enough. No longer was Uncle Tom seen as a Christian-martyr hero. Instead he was frequently condemned as a servile, obsequious black who had been unwilling to take his own part or that of other blacks. Frequently detached from both the novel and the play, Uncle Tom became a symbol of the black who commands no respect from others and demands no rights. In fact, often enough he was thought to be a "handkerchief head" black who was capable of betraying the rights of other blacks in order to curry favor with the whites.

In 1949, James Baldwin wrote an impassioned denunciation of *Uncle Tom's Cabin.* Perhaps one reason he disliked it so much was that as a child he had been strongly influenced by it. His mother has said that it was the first complete book he ever read. "There was something about that book," she is quoted as saying. "I couldn't understand it. He just read it over and over again." One of Baldwin's biographers has speculated that it may have been Topsy who chiefly attracted him to the novel. She was ugly, and James Baldwin thought himself to be ugly. Being intelligent, she rejected the role of the slave by burlesquing it. Also, Topsy's life had a "happy ending," and for a child who had an "awful" childhood, this was an aspect of her history which would not have escaped his notice.[1]

In his indictment, Baldwin rightly chooses the conversations between Ophelia and Augustine St. Clare as central to the meaning of *Uncle Tom's Cabin*. Yet he probably misunderstands Stowe's attitudes toward both characters. In one of these conversations, St. Clare ironically says that, so far as he can tell, the blacks have been turned over to the devil in this world, however they may turn out in the next. Understandably, Baldwin objects to what he calls the "vehemently right-minded" response of Ophelia. "This is perfectly horrible," she says to St. Clare. "You [southern slaveowners] ought to be ashamed of yourselves!" Of this statement, Baldwin says, "Miss Ophelia's exclamation, like Mrs. Stowe's novel, achieves a bright, almost a lurid significance, like the light from a fire which consumes a witch." This is a misreading both of Ophelia's statement and of the novel. Stowe undoubtedly admired Ophelia for her integrity but not as an analyst and interpreter of slavery. Ophelia's outburst must have seemed as foolish and mistaken to Stowe as it does to Baldwin. In addition, Baldwin charges Stowe with threatening the slaveholders with the "theological terror" of damnation. There is nothing in the novel to suggest that she did this, and Baldwin cites no direct evidence. By the time she wrote *Uncle Tom's Cabin*, Stowe had moved beyond the paralysis of Calvinism. At the time of the first appearance of the novel, reviewers noted the absence of threatening language in it, especially threatening religious language. It is true that St. Clare does prophesy a *Dies Irae*. What he means, however, is essentially what Baldwin himself was to mean when he wrote *The Fire Next Time*. St. Clare means quite simply that if nothing is done to better the condition of the poor there will be a whole series of revolutions.[2]

Baldwin may have made a better point in his objections to the character of Uncle Tom, but his rejection is too sweeping. He says that Tom "has been robbed of his humanity and divested of his sex. It is the price for that darkness with which he has been branded." If there is some truth in this indictment, it is a historical rather than an absolute truth. How many characters of any race in nineteenth-century American literature are adequately portrayed in terms of their sexual natures?

In addition, it is difficult to see in what sense Tom has been robbed of his humanity. He brings a moral stamina to his ordeal which enables him to undergo death by torture rather than to betray other blacks. As faulty as her view of blacks was, Stowe could see them more clearly than any of the other American writers of the time. The only possible exception was Melville. Even he was not wholly satisfactory on this point because he only occasionally dealt with the theme of the evils of prejudice against blacks, and then in a highly ambivalent way. In condemning Stowe without reservation, Baldwin brings the same absoluteness of vision to history which Ophelia—before her character is regenerated—brings to morality.[3]

Lyle Glazier, a black scholar, has expanded some of Baldwin's arguments. He praises *Uncle Tom's Cabin* more than Baldwin does. Its chief merit, he thinks, is that its "dialogue often rings with the exact note of truth." As an example he quotes a passage early in the novel when Aunt Chloe attempts to do justice to the cooking of a black woman at another plantation but demolishes all her claims with regard to the "higher branches" of the art. "Some one with a good ear," says Glazier, "listened in on the kitchen talk for Aunt Chloe's tone of voice." More importantly, Glazier thinks that Stowe is an excellent writer when she exposes the evasions and rationalizations of proslavery thought, as she does, for example, in the speeches of the slave-trader Haley. Also in spite of himself, Glazier is attracted to parts of *Uncle Tom's Cabin*. "You can ridicule . . . the speeches, but no matter how little sympathy you have for the piety," he says, "you can't stop reading, for you've been hooked by a most adroit story teller."[4]

Like Baldwin, Glazier identifies religion as one of the great evils of *Uncle Tom's Cabin*. He recognizes, as Baldwin does not, that there is no attempt in the novel to threaten anyone with hell. He believes instead that the emphasis on immortality in the novel has the implication that earthly life does not matter except as a preparation for salvation. Stowe does not deeply care what happens to Uncle Tom on earth, Glazier thinks, since he is obviously bound for heaven. This emphasis on the "pearly gates," argues Glazier, "nearly cancels out the anti-slavery propaganda." It does not quite do this, he adds, because Stowe retains the "conviction" that "slavery is dreadful and must be done away with." The argument here is whether religion necessarily prevents a person from being interested in questions of earthly justice. This is true of some people's religion but it was not true of Stowe's.[5]

Like Baldwin, Glazier thinks that Stowe was guilty of racial prejudice. For Glazier, the fact that Ophelia admits that she has a dislike for blacks which makes her reluctant to touch them somehow translates into the idea that Stowe herself must have felt the same way. "Mrs. Stowe cannot fully rid her mind of the suspicion that blackness is an evidence of sin," he says. How do we discover that she has this suspicion? She "quite candidly projects her own misgivings through Miss Ophelia. 'I've always had a prejudice against Negroes,' says Miss Ophelia, 'and it's a fact. I never could bear to have that child [Topsy] touch me.'" Ophelia receives no credit from Glazier for having acknowledged her fault or for having attempted—apparently with success—to rid herself of it. Stowe comes off even more unfairly. Many an author must reflect wryly that when he tries to expose an error or frailty in human beings he is likely to be accused of being guilty of it himself.[6]

The most sustained indictment of Stowe for being guilty of racial prejudice is that of J. C. Furnas, a white scholar. His *Goodbye to Uncle Tom* (1956) argues that she is the most important single source of the prejudice against blacks which afflicts modern society. "The devil could have forged no shrewder weapon for the Negro's worst enemy," Furnas says of *Uncle Tom's Cabin*. "Mrs. Stowe's book was obviously decent and Christian, obviously warm with the hopes of helping poor people with dark skins." Yet its effect had been catastrophically different from the intentions of its author:

As her work soaked into the common mind, fostering cheap sagacity about alleged racial traits down to our own day and affecting millions who have never read Uncle Tom or seen a Tom-show, it has sadly clogged the efforts of modern good will, acting on sounder information, to persuade people that this kind of racist idea does not hold water.

That Stowe was attempting to liberate the blacks from slavery, Furnas is willing to concede. On the other hand, he is convinced that she unconsciously fastened upon them a degrading racial stereotype which was a burden comparable to that of slavery itself:

Slaves themselves [in *Uncle Tom's Cabin*], when markedly of African race, are either gentle and pellucidly Christian or diabolically brutalized. When markedly tinged with "white blood," they are far more intelligent, enterprising and sensitive and show it by running away in great numbers. . . . [White] Northerners are much to blame for un-Christian repugnance toward Negroes, for black skins contain souls of which heaven is solicitous. But one must not expect full intelligence and refinement from any member of this innately handicapped "African race," a term that can dispense with definition since everybody knows more or less what is meant. The fact is that "Africans" are genetically endowed with natures nearer the "animal" than ours.[7]

Furnas's indictment is not wholly untrue, since Stowe was following the lead of the thought of her time in ascribing traits of intelligence and character to blacks. What she was apparently attempting to do was to change the much more virulent racism espoused by intellectuals, as well as by ordinary people, and to make it flexible enough to admit the idea that the blacks as a people are innately capable of both civilization and citizenship. Her ideas concerning the racial character of blacks were strongly resisted, and not merely by apologists for slavery. What has perhaps been demonstrated in this study has been the truth that Stowe's racism before and after the Civil War was much milder than that of even northern intellectuals generally. For sixty or seventy years after its publication, *Uncle Tom's Cabin* would frequently encounter the charge that it showed blacks as more capable and, above all, as more noble than the facts about the race warranted. To turn on the person who attempted to modify the racism of her time and charge her with the great tide of racism which was characteristic of the nineteenth century is—to put it mildly—unjust.

Furnas censures white southerners for complaining of the supposed genetic defects of blacks because, he thinks, they themselves suffer from a debased heredity. In early colonial times, he explains, "Dixie-to-be . . . got most of the less promising human material." The reasons were economic:

The main flow [from Great Britain] of paupers, debtors, orphans, whores and minor felons landed from Maryland southward, because that region was chronically hungry for mass labor for the large-scale production of indigo, naval stores and the tobacco that, says [Thomas J.] Wertenbaker, was to the south of 1750 what cotton was in 1850.

Thus the faults of the modern South are not, in Furnas's view, primarily the product of social and economic forces. They come rather from the inferior genetic endowment of the whites of the region.[8]

Apparently, this biological explanation for the faults of the white South sometimes troubles Furnas, for it leads him to reflect on the question that if white southerners were genetically inferior, how did it happen that they fought so ably and courageously during the Civil War? He explains that it was the hardships of the frontier which compensated for their bad heredity. "The underfed men in gray or butternut who fought their hearts out at Shiloh and Franklin and made such dashing marches for Old Jack [Stonewall Jackson] had many forebears among these ruthlessly screened misfits," he says. Frontier hardship could improve their bravery and physical prowess but it could not improve their minds. Thus the South of the 1950s had become the natural home of "crack-jawed fundamentalism" and "jackleg fascism." At this point in Furnas's argument the reader may feel that he is approaching a kind of *cul de sac*. The theory that the whites of the South are genetically inferior to whites of the North is not technically an example of racism, but it leads to similar conclusions. Just as many white southerners developed a powerful theory of race in the nineteenth century which consigned the blacks to an eternal barbarism, Furnas comes close to doing the same thing to white southerners of his time.[9]

Furnas does not argue, of course, that Stowe thought up racial prejudice all by herself and thus unleashed a poisonous theory upon an unsuspecting world. He thinks, however, that through the agency of *Uncle Tom's Cabin* a substantially new and in some respects more dangerous racism was formulated. It was more dangerous because it was not based upon power alone. Rather, it was dependent upon rationalizations which gave it the imprimatur of advanced ideas of religion and morality. *Uncle Tom's Cabin* was

cataclysmic and catalytic too precisely because of this smallish person, small personally as well as physically, glib, lazy-minded, a common denomination of millions of the brains and consciences of her time. [She] was a character created by Louisa M. Alcott: the ugly duckling gradually evincing talent in a Yankee context, committed to a world where women make do because men are shiftless, though pretentious and important, gamely scribbling hack work to eke out the family purse. Call her Jo March, with a small-boned skeleton, curly hair, many children, and a touch of megalomania.

Among the signs of her deficiencies was the fact that her brother, sister, husband, and children were also deficient. She had a "white sepulcher of a brother [Henry Ward Beecher], a psychopathic half-sister [Isabella Beecher Hooker], an alcoholic son [Frederick Stowe], and a drug addicted daughter [Georgina]." Her husband was a "potent but flabby bedfellow." What can one expect, Furnas seems to wonder, from a woman with such a background as hers? It is an old technique, of course, to demolish a person's character and ideas by pairing him with his faulty relatives and associates. Not many people would prove invulnerable to this line of attack if one accepted its premises.[10]

Goodbye to Uncle Tom is not wholly a bad book. Published two years after the decision of the Supreme Court outlawing segregation of blacks, the book displayed the anger of Furnas about the tide of resistance to integration in the South. Much of his book is concerned with showing how pervasive racial prejudice has been in our society and how it has been based upon the most suspect kinds of evidence. The error in the book is to pile up the charge of racism against one of the few people in this country who truly grappled with the problems of racism in the nineteenth century. In blaming Stowe for not knowing what only a study of modern biology and anthropology could have told her, Furnas is unfair to her. He gives her no credit for having created black characters in her fiction who have a fullness of humanity beyond that of the black characters of other writers of her time. Stowe did not believe that blacks and whites are equal in endowment. She did try to put the best interpretation she could on the conceptions of the inherent traits of blacks which were the received opinion of her time.[11]

Furnas shows his unfairness to Stowe especially when he discusses her ideas on black intelligence. He mentions the widely accepted idea of the mid-nineteenth century that blacks develop as whites do until the age of puberty, but then, because of their supposed inherent inferiority, they increasingly lag behind. Furnas says that Stowe "glibly chimed in" with this theory, but the example he gives shows her doing just the opposite. He quotes her statement in *The Key to Uncle Tom's Cabin* that "the writer has often observed this fact—that, for a certain time, and up to a certain age, they [the blacks] kept equal pace with, and were often superior to, the white children with whom they were associated." As a reason for their later failures to keep up with whites, Stowe said of the blacks: "[T]here came a time when they became indifferent to learning, and made no further progress. This was invariably at the age when they were old enough to reflect upon life, and to perceive that society had no place to offer them for which anything more would be requisite than the rudest and most elementary knowledge." Surprisingly, though Furnas paraphrases briefly this reason Stowe gave for the lack of progress of blacks in schools, he gives her no credit for her perception of a social fact. It is not lack of native black intelligence which Stowe sees as the reason for the failures of black students to match the progress of white students. Rather, she censures the society of her time, in the North as well as in the South, for its unwillingness to give black children the same encouragement it gave white children. Having decided that her ideas are wrong, Furnas is unwilling to praise her even when she was arguing sensibly.[12]

Some modern black scholars have argued that Stowe was as bad as if not worse than the out-and-out proponents of slavery. "As a result of Mrs. Stowe's halfhearted attack upon the institution of slavery," says Addison Gayle, Jr., "the southern propagandists carried their verbal warfare against Blacks to new heights." Stowe had portrayed Uncle Tom as a "feeble-minded child." From this image of blacks, it was only a step for such white southern propagandists as Albert Taylor Bledsoe and George Fitzhugh to portray blacks scarcely, if at all, different from beasts. "To cast aspersion upon Uncle Tom, the meek-mannered, mild, brainless man-child," says Gayle, "southern writers concocted the portrait of the 'brute Negro,' born not of woman but of animal, whose capacity for murder, rapine, and destruction was mitigated by the stern tutelage of benevolent masters." Aman Baraka (Leroi Jones) has written a short story entitled "*Uncle Tom's Cabin*: Alternate Ending." One of the characters in the story is an elderly white teacher who tries to impose on the minds of students in a northern high school largely composed of blacks the stodgy and restrictive ideas of white middle class society. Apparently, this woman is supposed to be the modern equivalent of Stowe.[13]

Sometimes modern black scholars have indicted Uncle Tom because they believe that a Christian acquiescence to one's fate is the same thing as a philosophy of hopelessness or of cowardice. In 1964, Donald Chaput complained of the spinelessness of Uncle Tom. He cited the passage in which Tom says, "I'm in the Lord's hands, nothin' can go furder than he lets it—and that's one thing I can thank him for. It's me that's sold and going down, and not you [his wife] nur the chil'en. Here you're safe—what comes will come only on me; and the Lord, he'll help me—I know he will." Chaput thought that Stowe had done "irreparable harm" in portraying slaves as "servile, bootlicking blacks, who willingly accepted their place because they knew they were predestined for it." He placed his hope for a better understanding of blacks and slavery in those historians who would be free from this "ridiculously transplanted New England Calvinism." Arlene A. Elder, in 1978, expressed a slightly higher view of *Uncle Tom's Cabin*. She conceded that Augustine St. Clare and George Harris are characters not wholly without interest to modern readers. They are "the most complex characters in the book," but they "take second place . . . to Simon Legree's brutal flogging of saintly Uncle Tom or to Little Eva's tear-shrouded apotheosis as an angel." Elder thought that Stowe's sentimental images of blacks had affected not merely the views of white readers but had even had a bad influence on black writers who had reflected some of their racial stereotypes.[14]

Some recent white critics have rejected *Uncle Tom's Cabin* as strongly as have any of the black critics. They usually have complained more of its sentimentality than specifically of its portrayal of blacks. Unable to take the novel seriously, these critics have often found it scarcely discussable. That it may have done harm to the blacks they are often willing to concede, but this is not their principal objection to it. If they mention the novel at all, they quickly dismiss it as a work which has historical but not literary importance. In 1982, Hugh Kenner was probably reflecting a widespread attitude among critics when he said that "Mrs. Stowe's famous eleven-Kleenex tract, sanctified by a testimonial of Lincoln's, soars aloft into the Disneyfied sunset of Literature."[15]

Beginning with the year 1941, a number of scholars have published detailed studies of Stowe, and thus it is now possible for the modern reader to see her life and work in a broad perspective. In 1941, Forrest Wilson published his massive and well-researched biography of Stowe, *Crusader in Crinoline.* He greatly admired her, calling her "one of the most consistently Christ-minded women America ever produced." His book has the merit of being based upon a careful examination of the extensive papers of the Stowe and Beecher families. He was not much interested, however, in exploring the social and intellectual background of her thought nor in showing in detail the variety of responses to *Uncle Tom's Cabin.* There is little in the book concerning the ways in which it affected the course of the national debate over slavery and even less about the history of critical attitudes toward it. His study is largely a study of Stowe herself, emphasizing her relations with relatives and friends. In 1954, Charles H. Foster published *The Rungless Ladder: Harriet Beecher Stowe and New England Puritanism,* and in it he clarified some of the complexities of religious thought which had influenced Stowe. In 1977, E. Bruce Kirkham published *The Building of Uncle Tom's Cabin.* This is a careful and detailed study of the writing of the novel.[16]

Among the historians, Allan Nevins in 1947 restored Stowe and *Uncle Tom's Cabin* to something like the high evaluation given by the earlier historian, James Ford Rhodes, in 1893. Nevins praised the novel for both its historical and its literary value:

A lesser novelist than Mrs. Stowe would have indicted the slaveholder, as [Richard] Hildreth did in *The White Slave*; but with a sure instinct she indicted the institution. Her condemnation was not for the Southerners, unfortunate in inheriting slavery, but for the system. Some of her finest characters such as the brilliant St. Clare and the splendid Mrs. Shelby, are Southerners, while her basest villain, Simon Legree, is a Yankee by birth. Nor is the indictment crudely drawn. It is given us by implication in an intensely human story; a story animated by a feeling not in the least political or sectional, but humanitarian and Christian. It is the feeling of John Woolman, not that of Garrison. The book attuned itself to the strong philanthropic impulse of the age—the impulse that was opening schools, wiping away slums, passing factory acts, ameliorating the hard lot of the poor and oppressed. It attuned itself no less to the essential spirit of Christianity— the spirit of Him who had died for all who were weary and heavy laden. It was a rebuke to callous materialism, whether Southern or Northern, and to that text-chopping type of Christianity, both Northern and Southern, which justified servitude by Biblical citations.

On the other hand, Nevins argued, Stowe "did not fall into the error of writing a mere tract." Such characters as Uncle Tom, little Eva, Topsy, Ophelia, George and Eliza Harris, and Marie St. Clare "were genuine creatures of the imagination, who impressed themselves permanently upon the folk-consciousness of the nation." Proof that the influence of the novel had not been "narrow" and "transitory" was suggested by the fact that it was still read in many countries all over the world. "In far-off lands, where men and women cared little whether slavery remained part of the American system or was rent from it," said Nevins, "the sufferings and successes of this vivid knot of human beings had an instant appeal."[17]

After saying much that was perceptive, Allan Nevins came close to making the same error which some of the historians who had strongly condemned the novel had made. The "chief defect" of the novel, he thought, "lay in its idealization of the Negro." It did not exaggerate the possible evils of slavery, but

it did overstate the contemporaneous case for the slave. Countless northern readers who had never seen a plantation pictured all Negroes thenceforth in terms of the saintly Uncle Tom, whose soul belongs to God alone, the sturdy George Harris, hugging the free soil of Ohio to his bosom, the devoted Eliza, his wife, and the irresponsible but delightful Topsy.

Nevins believed that the trouble with the novel was that it had too many admirable black characters. These blacks

are not the Negroes we see in the pages of [Frederick Law] Olmsted or of the scientific modern students of antebellum Southern life; black folk struggling with many a slip out of barbarism into civilization, with the faults, passions, and limitations of Africa clinging to them as mud clings to a man springing from a slough.

Such men as Uncle Tom and George Harris might have "actually lived," said Nevins, "but Mrs. Stowe seemed to teach that all the slaves of 1850 were of that rare fibre." One can only wonder why Nevins thought that Stowe believed all blacks to be like Uncle Tom or George Harris, since there are many other blacks in the novel who are not merely un-heroic but unprincipled as well.[18]

Some modern critics of *Uncle Tom's Cabin* have recognized that Stowe presented slavery in such a way as to do rough justice to both its defenders and its opponents. More than anyone else, it was probably Edmund Wilson who led other critics to take another look at the novel, one that was more favorable than traditional views of the past. In 1948, Wilson noted that relatively few people in modern times had read the book. If a person did read it, he would undergo "a startling experience":

It is a much more remarkable book than one had ever been allowed to suspect. Out of a background of undistinguished narrative, carelessly written and not even quite literate, the characters spring to life with a vitality that is all the more striking for the dullness of the prose that presents them. These characters, as in Dickens, express themselves a great deal better than the author expresses herself. Mrs. Stowe had something like a conviction that her book was written by God, that some power beyond herself had laid hold of her as a medium for its message; and this is actually more or less the impression that the novel produces on the reader. The Shelbys and George and Eliza and Aunt Chloe and Uncle Tom seem to project themselves out of a void. They come before us, arguing and struggling, like real people that cannot be quiet.[19]

Wilson recognized that *Uncle Tom's Cabin* had been written with "generous emotion" and "lively imagination," but he emphasized that there was something more. The novel is important, he said, because Stowe had been able to grasp the essence of the ways in which people—white and black, northern and southern—differed with regard to slavery and to their perceptions of one another. "As we read on," Wilson said, we become aware that the author has a critical mind which has seized the complex situation which is ruling and coordinating her characters, no matter how vehement they are. Though there is much that is exciting in "Uncle Tom's Cabin," it is never cheap melodrama of the kind that we get in the play; and though there is a good deal of old-fashioned religion and a couple of Dickensian death scenes, there is very much less sentimentality than the stage version might lead us to expect. We come to recognize, at work in the book, a first-rate modern social intelligence, not unworthy to be compared with that of Bernard Shaw in "Major Barbara" or E. M. Forster in "A Passage to India."[20]

Unlike the modern black critics of *Uncle Tom's Cabin*, Edmund Wilson was wholly unconcerned with the issue of whether Uncle Tom might project too meekly submissive an image of black character. Instead, he shifted the argument to a different issue. The pacifism of Uncle Tom, he argued, had the merit of showing the hypocrisy of the religion of both the white South and the white North. Except for the Quakers in the novel, he observed, none of the "white groups that figure in *Uncle Tom's Cabin* is living in accordance with the principles of the religion they all profess." It is Uncle Tom, almost alone, who takes

the white man's religion seriously and who—standing up bravely, in the final scenes, for the dignity of his soul but at the same time pardoning Simon Legree—attempts to live up to it literally. The sharp irony as well as the pathos is that the recompense he wins from the Christians, as he is gradually put through their mill, is to be separated from his family and exiled, tormented, imprisoned and done to death.[21]

Another prominent modern American critic who wrote a largely favorable account of *Uncle Tom's Cabin* was Lionel Trilling, who in 1957 briefly analyzed the novel. Like many other critics, he thought that the primary importance of the novel was that it helped to persuade people that slavery was evil. He said of it that "perhaps no other single book has ever so directly influenced the course of history. . . . It overrode considerations of national policy and brought the issue of morality and humaneness squarely to the fore." He thought it was regrettable that the work was chiefly remembered as a play, "for actually the novel is by no means bad. Mrs. Stowe was no genius, but she had a very competent talent and could tell a good straightforward story." He commended her efforts to be fair to the South and observed that she was "at pains to say that the cruelty lies in the system [of slavery] and not in the plantation owners. She was an intelligent woman and there is intelligence in her novel." Another reason for its importance, he argued, was that

no other work has contributed so many legendary figures to American life, even though some of them are referred to with irony: Eliza crossing the ice to escape the bloodhounds is the type of persecuted innocence, as little Eva is the type of saccharine self-conscious childish virtue; whatever has no ascertainable origins can be counted on to bring a reference to Topsy, who "never was born" and just "growed"; Simon Legree is the name for any cruel superior; and among Negroes Uncle Tom is—rather unfairly—the name for a Negro who ingratiates himself with the whites by his pious sentiments.

Even more enthusiastic than Trilling has been Professor Kenneth S. Lynn of Harvard, who said:

Those critics who label *Uncle Tom's Cabin* good propaganda but bad art simply cannot have given sufficient time to the novel to meet its inhabitants. If they should ever linger over it long enough to take in the shrewdness, the energy, the truly Balzacian variousness of Mrs. Stowe's characterizations, they would surely cease to perpetuate one of the most unjust clichés in all of American criticism.[22]

Another of the admirers of *Uncle Tom's Cabin* is David Levin, a professor of American literature at the University of Virginia. He admits that his "most difficult problem as a teacher" has been to teach this novel, "which many students [in 1972] now reject as James Baldwin rejected it, for combining sentimentality and racial condenscension with vindictive stereotypes in a way that deserves the scornful title [of James Baldwin] Everybody's Protest Novel." Some of the students in his classes have declared, said Levin, "that Mrs. Stowe 'knows nothing about black people,' and that for knowledge of conventional characters we might as well read instead a few of the original radio scripts for Amos 'n Andy."[23]

Levin thinks his students are wrong in their rejection of *Uncle Tom's Cabin*:

As we read . . . [it] retrospectively, aware of subsequent history and literature, we see not only Mrs. Stowe's anticipation of other authors' themes, character types, and issues, but also her remarkable understanding of them. If God did write the book for her, as she is said to have claimed years afterward, He made more use of her social intelligence than her emphasis on His inspiration would seem to allow.[24]

Levin has understood, as Edmund Wilson apparently did not, that some kind of interpretation of Uncle Tom himself is necessary if he is to be rescued from the charge of being merely servile. He defends Uncle Tom not principally as a black but as a human being placed in a particular society and in a particular situation in that society. Levin thinks that Tom reacts quite sensibly to the choices which are offered to him. Tom's submission to being sold by Mr. Shelby is not, Levin argues, the decision of a man who has no sense of his own worth or rights, Tom, says Levin, "offers as his explicit reason the given condition by which the plot originally moves; that if he doesn't go with Haley the entire plantation and all the slaves will go to Haley by default." Tom's decision, Levin admits, comes from a "misplaced faith in Shelby," but he thinks it also comes from his "practical good sense of the common danger." "If I must be sold, or all the people on the place, and everything go to rack," Tom says in the novel, "why let me be sold. I suppose I can b'ar it as well as any on 'em." One may wonder at this point why Uncle Tom does not suspect that his sale will protect the other slaves on the plantation only until the next time Mr. Shelby gets into financial trouble. It is true that Levin does show an awareness, however, of one of the ways in which Stowe had apparently tried to protect Tom from the charge of being too submissive.[25]

Levin is on firmer ground in his defense of Tom for his refusal to kill Legree when he has the chance. Tom will not heed Cassy's plea that Legree, in a drunken stupor, deserves to die and that Tom should kill him with an ax. "The Lord hasn't *called* us to wrath," Tom declares to Cassy. "We must suffer and wait his time." In defending Tom's decision, Levin points out that Stowe had anticipated the objections of "our outraged contemporaries." In the novel, Cassy replies to Tom:

"Wait! . . . Haven't I waited?—waited till my head is dizzy and my heart sick? What has he made me suffer? What has he made hundreds of poor creatures suffer? Isn't he wringing the life-blood out of *you*? I'm called on; they call me! His time's come, and I'll have his heart's blood."

"Tom, of course, wins that argument," says Levin, "but we must remember that Mrs. Stowe wrote both speeches." Levin makes the point by implication that Stowe has attempted to show Tom's nonresistance not as a weak submissiveness to tyranny but as a matter of principle.[26]

The best part of Levin's defense of Stowe and of *Uncle Tom's Cabin* is not to be found, however, in an examination of particular acts of her characters or of the arguments which they express. Neither is it to be found in defenses of the statements and the general attitudes of Stowe herself. Levin recognizes that one need not agree with all of Stowe's ideas or with her own assessment of the moral worth of her characters in order to recognize the importance of her achievement. "To see the richness of the historical evidence. . . ," Levin says, "we must study the complex reality of the whole book." To examine meaning in this broad sense is essentially what he does in his essay. The result is that he has written one of the most perceptive assessments of Stowe to be found anywhere.[27]

In the 1960s, a number of white critics attempted to reinstate Uncle Tom as a hero with the argument that in his passive resistance to Simon Legree, he convinced white Americans of the evils of slavery as he could not have done in any other way. Some of the critics who developed this argument compared Uncle Tom with the black civil rights leader, Martin Luther King, Jr. In 1962, Howard Mumford Jones described Uncle Tom as a "splendid black Christian Prometheus, epic in his grandeur and simplicity, whose attitude toward injustice anticipates . . . the Christianity of Dr. Martin Luther King, Jr." Jones thought that Uncle Tom was to be ranked with Jean Valjean, "each a transcendent incarnation of a profound belief in the Christian commandment that governs Dr. King's philosophy of non-violence: 'Love your enemies, and pray for them which despitefully use you, and persecute you.' "[28]

In 1969, Kenneth Rexroth's argument in defense of Uncle Tom was similar to that of Jones. Tom is not a portrait of "the humble and obedient slave," he said. "He is by far the strongest person in the book. Although he is whipped to death by the psychotic Simon Legree, his end is not only a tragedy in Aristotle's sense, the doom of a great man brought low by a kind of holy *hubris*, but like Samson, he destroys his destroyer." Other than having been knocked down by George Shelby, Legree suffers no penalties at all; therefore Rexroth must have meant that someone or something else had been destroyed by Uncle Tom. He probably meant that slavery had been given a fatal blow by the death of Uncle Tom. That he was not wholly satisfied with this conclusion is suggested by some of his other observations. He praised Stowe for having made "the full humanity of the Negro visible to all, black or white, all over the world." He was willing to admit that it is "possible to disagree with her idea of what a full human being should be," but he insisted that "she did the best according to her lights." Then, perhaps defensively, he added that her lights were "just as illuminating as any that have been lit in a more cynical and rationalistic age, by writers with a different kind of sentimentality." Rexroth did not give us his own ideas of what "a full human being" should be. His praise of Uncle Tom leaves the reader puzzled and unsure. He was convinced that it is the moral leader and not the advocate of violence who truly regenerates a society. He saw the death of Martin Luther King, Jr., in 1968 as comparable to the martyrdom of Tom. "As for Uncle Tom," said Rexroth, "he was assassinated in Memphis, and has been before, and will be again, until something like Mrs. Stowe's secular, evangelical humanism, or Whittier's or Whitman's wins out at last, or the Republic perishes."[29]

There is something in these comments by both Jones and Rexroth which suggests that they would have liked to see Tom become a secular rather than a religious hero. In a rationalistic age, they may have thought that it was no longer possible to imagine a religious hero. Jones described Tom as a "Christian Prometheus." If Stowe has thought of this particular metaphor, she might well have turned it around, calling him a "Promethean Christian." Rexroth attributed "secular, evangelical humanism" to Stowe rather than to Tom, but Tom would seem to be the principal exemplar of this "humanism." If Jones and Rexroth intended to shift the interpretation of Tom from religious to secular, they were probably involved in an enterprise which would fail. Tom's religion is an essential part of the man. If he is to be a secular hero who has the mission of showing American society that it has not lived up to its ideals, neither he nor his cause will gain much. A secular society often comes near discarding the whole notion of blame. A religious society can sometimes be equally indifferent to its crimes, but it may at least have more of the capacity for blaming itself for them and thus regenerating itself.

In 1962, the last year of his life, William Faulkner was a visiting writer in residence at West Point. In a question-and-answer session with an audience of students there, he made the point that the primary aim of a writer ought to be "to tell a story," not to develop a theme or to prove a moral point. Someone in the audience asked Faulkner whether he thought that most authors wrote for the pure pleasure of telling a story or whether they were more likely to "have some motives such as teaching a lesson." Faulkner replied that he could imagine a writer "who has been so harried and so outraged by a social condition that he can't keep that social condition out of history. But he is primarily telling a story." At this point, a second member of the audience asked Faulkner, "Sir, along this same line, would you say that books such as *Uncle Tom's*

Cabin would be written because of sociological conditions?" Faulkner replied as follows:

"I would say that *Uncle Tom's Cabin* was written out of violent and misdirected compassion and ignorance of the author toward a situation which she knew only by hearsay. But it was not an intellectual process, it was hotter than that; it was out of her heart. It just happened that she was telling a story of Uncle Tom and the little girl, not of slavery, because everybody knows that slaves have always had a hard time of it, not just Negro slaves in America, but writing a story which moved her, seemed so terrible and so hot to her that it had to be told. But I think she was writing about Uncle Tom as a human being—and Legree and Eliza as human beings, not as puppets."[30]

In 1982, Robert Penn Warren read aloud sections of *Uncle Tom's Cabin* in what a newspaper reporter described as "a Deep South accent" at the Pierpont Morgan Library in New York. Warren commented on Stowe and on the novel. "She didn't need a Ph.D.," he was quoted as saying. "She read all the books she was supposed to as a young lady. . . . 'Uncle Tom's Cabin' is not a sectional book, not just North and South, but about human relations. Mrs. Stowe played fair; she made Simon Legree a Yankee. She was against racism as well as against slavery."[31]

By the 1940s, productions of *Uncle Tom's Cabin* as a play had almost completely ceased. In 1943 the play *Harriet*, by Florence Ryerson and Colin Clements, was produced on Broadway with Helen Hayes as the actress portraying Stowe. The play had a good many inaccuracies but had a considerable power in its depiction of Stowe. In 1944, Metro-Goldwyn-Mayer considered making a new movie version. Lena Horne was suggested for the role of Eliza, Margaret O'Brien for Eva, and Lewis Stone for Augustine St. Clare. There was so much objection among black organizations and liberal groups generally that the plans were canceled. Almost the only way the play could be produced in this country was by parodying it. In 1951 the Rodgers and Hammerstein musical, *The King and I*, had a comic ballet sequence, "The Little House of Uncle Thomas," which showed the reception of the novel at the royal court of Siam in the 1860s.[32]

Some modern productions of *Uncle Tom's Cabin* have called forth protests. In 1954 an adaptation of the novel was staged in Bridgeport and New Haven, Connecticut. The local units of the National Association for the Advancement of Colored People (NAACP) and of labor unions were aided by pastors of churches in the area in objecting to a revival of the play. One of the objectors censured the play for depicting "incidents that tend to portray only the weaknesses of a racial minority and continue to hold up for ridicule people who in their earlier days of settlement were unfortunately subjected to conditions which would now be considered atrocious." John Mason Brown, the dramatic critic, wrote an article protesting the denial of free expression. He said it was ironic that the move to censor should come from groups of people who themselves had often been the victims of censorship. The protests may have been part of the reason that the troupe decided to cancel its plans for taking the play to New York. In 1958 there was a new release of the 1927 version of *Uncle Tom's Cabin* with sound effects added. In this version, there was a new scene at the end in which Raymond Massey portrayed Abraham Lincoln in the act of signing the Emancipation Proclamation. There were protests against the showing of this film, which may have helped to shorten its brief run. In 1965 there was a German movie version (*Onkel Tom's Hutte*) filmed in Yugoslavia with Ertha Kitt as one of the players. At the end of this version of the movie, there was a slave revolt which apparently represented the attempt of the director to avoid the charge that the film portrayed blacks as excessively meek.[33]

In 1975, the Workshop of the Players' Art in the Bowery, a dramatic group in New York, produced a new version of the play directed by Lionel H. Mitchell. In the *New York Times*, Mel Gussow praised it: "Tom is not a fool" in this version, "but a stoic and a martyr, a concept that is accentuated by the performance of Robert Stocking. His Tom is a dignified, self-educated man, who walks slowly and carries a big Bible." Like other modern productions of the play, this version attempted to present the black characters as more rebellious than they had been in earlier productions. "The blacks laugh behind their masters' backs," said Gussow, "and occasionally sass them to their faces. . . . Topsy tells the audience, 'You kin never tell white folks d'troof; they're unprepared for it.'" Gussow thought that the play had a number of faults. For one thing, it was still "wearing the mark of George L. Aiken's antique play." The white characters in it were especially recognizable as old-fashioned stereotypes, none more so than the villains. "The play could use judicious cutting," he added, "less exposition and more interpretation, so that we can see with greater clarity the black point of view towards *Uncle Tom's Cabin*."[34]

A more ambitious modern production of *Uncle Tom's Cabin* was that of the Trinity Square Repertory Company of Providence, Rhode Island, in 1978. Entitled *Uncle Tom's Cabin: A History*, the play was adapted by Adrian Hall and Richard Cumming from the novel and from the George Aiken version of the play. Some parts of the Hall/Cumming version did not differ a great deal from the novel or from Aiken's dramatic production. The adapters attempted to show, however, what the play had frequently become in its long history of performance—drama which patronized its stereotyped black characters. For the great part of the play, Uncle Tom is presented as dignified in his oppression and willing to suffer martyrdom. In a fantasy scene, however, Tom departs radically from his usual meek role and shoots Augustine St. Clare. He proclaims that he does this because St. Clare is the father of Little Eva. Her crime when she had been alive was that she wanted "to change mah skin an pull de racial kink from out mah hair. She gone to Heben talkin' mighty big 'bout woolly pates an' pigments an' designs." In the next scene, however, Uncle Tom is wholly back in character as an unresisting slave of saintly forbearance.[35]

Hall and Cumming also attempted a companion theme to the evils of slavery—the banning and censorship the drama has suffered in its long history in America. The two themes, according to most of the critics who reviewed the play, did not mix well. In addition, not all the critics were happy with the attempt of the playwrights to include both serious drama and burlesque in a single scene. On the other hand, the critics generally had high praise for the actors and actresses who took the major parts. Their criticisms centered on the conviction that this version of the play attempted too much. One of them said that it was "good history" but "bad theater." Another said that the idea of parodying some of the scenes in *Uncle Tom's Cabin* might have been good in theory, but he admitted that he liked best those sections of the play which were closest to the original novel: "When the play settles down to a straight-forward retelling of the story of Uncle Tom, Little Eva, Eliza, Topsy, Simon Legree, Aunt Ophelia, and the many other, famous and infamous, characters in the novel it is most effective. The inherent melodrama and sentimentality is unobtrusive and inoffensive." It may be that both the 1975 version of the play in New York and the 1978 version in Providence are foreshadowings of better productions of *Uncle Tom's Cabin* in the future. Perhaps the play can be adapted in ways that will retain some of its former power.[36]

Uncle Tom's Cabin is still often translated and reprinted. In the 1983-84 *Books in Print* catalogue there were twelve editions in print in this country. From a similar book in France, one can find six editions in print. One observer has pointed out that in the single year of 1953 there were six different editions published in Italy. In the *National Union Catalogue* there are listed editions of *Uncle Tom's Cabin* printed within the last twenty years in France, Germany, Italy, Spain, the Netherlands, the Soviet Union, Greece, Yugoslavia, Hungary, Poland, Lithuania, Estonia, Czechoslovakia, Roumania, Norway, Turkey, Mexico, and Argentina. There has also been a translation of the novel into Yiddish.[37]

In 1976, a North Carolina family, neighbors of mine, participated in an international exchange program for children. They invited a girl of eleven from Mexico to live with them for several months. When she arrived she brought with her a copy of *Uncle Tom's Cabin* only to find that the adults in the family had not read it and their children had never heard of it.

Dramatic productions abroad of *Uncle Tom's Cabin* are still sometimes to be found. Often their purpose is anti-American propaganda. In 1953, there was a children's production of the play in Budapest. Uncle Tom in this version—unlike that of the 1932 Russian adaptation in Moscow—was allowed to retain his religious faith, but he was a minor character in the play. Simon Legree was portrayed as a conniving financial speculator from Wall Street. "Do you, children," one character was quoted as asking the audience, "wish to side with Simon Legree or with the camp of peace led by the Soviet Union?"[38]

In 1957, *Uncle Tom's Cabin* was dramatized in China. Its name was changed to *Sorrows of the Negro Slave*. (The word *uncle* sometimes causes trouble for translators; in some languages, the meaning of the word is apparently restricted to a person who is actually related by blood or marriage.) In this adaptation, Uncle Tom is portrayed in such a way as to suggest the class struggle. Tien Han, a reviewer of the play in China, compared the fictional death of Tom with a real event in American history, the execution of John Brown in 1859. The reviewer referred to Brown as "another negro," apparently not knowing that Brown was white. He regretted the fact that Uncle Tom was not more like John Brown. It was obvious that Brown knew "a good washing with fresh blood and not tolerance, vengeance-wreaking hatred and not love" were necessary if slavery was to be abolished. Thus, Tien Han thought, it was not illogical for the Chinese adapter of the play to sub-stitute the ideas of John Brown for those of Uncle Tom. Brown's ideas were "already a big step toward revolution." "Why can we not allow Tom," he asked, "to have John Brown's type of awakening?"[39]

The Chinese dramatic adaptation of *Uncle Tom's Cabin* had other differences from either the novel or the play. Uncle Tom had said to Simon Legree, "My body belongs to you but my soul belongs to God." The Chinese reviewer of the play quoted Uncle Tom as saying, "Some one sold my body to you by force. But my soul will always be mine." At the end of the Chinese version of the play, Uncle Tom is burned at the stake. The Chinese reviewer admitted that to have Tom killed in this way was a departure from the novel. He justified the change by arguing that burning blacks at the stake in lynchings was not uncommon in the United States. He had read about the practice in one of the histories of the United States written by William Z. Foster, a man who had been a candidate for the American presidency of the Communist Party of America.[40]

In his review, Tien Han cautioned his Chinese readers not to assume that the horrors of slavery belonged only to the past history of the United States. In important respects, he thought, American blacks of 1957 were even worse off than they had been in 1852 when *Uncle Tom's Cabin* was first published. "Before the Civil War," he explained,

certain contradictions existed between the northern and southern parts of that country. Negroes passing days of frightful wretchedness in southern plantations could take the so-called "underground train" and, with compara-tive ease, flee to the North or Canada. But today, under the watchful eyes of the American imperialist rulers, the negro—escape being out of the question—finds it extremely difficult even to go abroad to take part in progressive conferences. [Thus] the fact of American imperialist reaction [had] remained unchanged throughout the last hundred years.[41]

Epilogue

TO READ THE OPINIONS of *Uncle Tom's Cabin* which have been expressed over the past 130 years is something like examining a history of racism in America for this period, at least racism as it has been applied to blacks. J. C. Furnas was right when he said that *Uncle Tom's Cabin* was like a three-stage rocket—it was first powerful as a novel, then as a play, and eventually in the twentieth century as a film. It is doubtful that any work of American literature has received such a variety of interpretations, both in the reviews and criticisms it has generated and in the many ways in which it has been adapted as a play. When the novel was published in 1852, even northern reviewers in surprisingly large numbers criticized it for what they felt were exaggerated accounts of the evils of slavery. Nevertheless, it is obvious that Stowe's book was a powerful force in changing the minds of white northerners and in alerting opinion abroad to the evils of American slavery.*

For a long time the almost universal detestation of *Uncle Tom's Cabin* prevented all but a few readers in the South from examining it from any point of view except that of its alleged unfairness to the South and to slavery. When the Civil War was over and the white South had time to calm down, readers and critics there discovered that the novel

---

* Furnas, *Goodbye to Uncle Tom*, p. 254.

contained ideas about blacks which might be used to suggest a more sympathetic interpretation of their own view of history. With a little judicious manipulation, many of these white southern interpreters convinced themselves that they could find in *Uncle Tom's Cabin* itself sufficient evidence to justify their own conviction that blacks ought not to have a status in society equal to that of whites. They did not wish to return to slavery, but neither did they wish to give the blacks full rights as citizens. The white South eventually came to admit, at least by implication, that slavery had been wrong, disunion had been wrong, and therefore the South's decision to initiate the Civil War had been wrong. On the other hand, they reasoned, it did not follow that the antebellum white South had been wrong in its belief in the inherent inferiority of blacks.

In the late nineteenth and early twentieth centuries, a substantial number of white northern critics of *Uncle Tom's Cabin* had also changed their opinions and had moved closer to those held by white southerners. A view frequently expressed, especially after northern disillusion with the Reconstruction of the South, was that slavery had been an evil institution and Stowe had been right to indict it. On the other hand, a surprisingly large number of white northern critics came to think Stowe had been wrong in making the black characters in her novel too noble, amiable, and intelligent to be credible. If these critics had said that her black characters generally had better qualities than people of any race, they might have had a point. Usually, however, they merely said that her black characters were presented as being better than real blacks.

In the last forty years, the current of opinion toward Stowe and *Uncle Tom's Cabin* falls chiefly into three categories. Black critics and scholars strongly reject the novel, deploring the frequent recourse to racist explanations of the traits of the characters, especially those of the blacks. A great many white critics—probably a majority—also reject the novel but principally because they find it almost wholly lacking in literary merit. There is a third group, however, who have something like the enthusiasm of earlier critics for both the author and her book. Nearly all of these critics are white, and to those who reject the novel on literary grounds, these critics say that Stowe's faults are a matter of style rather than of substance. They argue that while she used the form of the sentimental and domestic novel, she was able to transcend that form because she had a broad grasp of human nature and was able to analyze both institutions and individual characters with great insight. To the black critics who deplore the novel, the white critics who admire it generally concede that it contains serious faults in its interpretation of the black characters. They argue, however, that Stowe's racism belongs to her time and place. They see her as struggling, and with considerable success, to free herself from it. Properly understood, they argue, the racism is not sufficient to invalidate the novel, and they conclude that Stowe was able not merely to analyze slavery perceptively but to present credible characters, black and white, reacting to a monstrous institution.

Notes

In citing works in the notes, short titles have generally been used. Works frequently cited have been identified by the following abbreviations:

Autobiography   Lyman Beecher, *Autobiography, Correspondence, etc., of Lyman Beecher, D.D.*, ed. Charles Beecher, 2 vols. (New York: Harper Bros., 1864).

Crusader in Crinoline [Robert] Forrest Wilson, *Crusader in Crinoline: The Life of Harriet Beecher Stowe* (Philadelphia: J. B. Lippincott Co., 1941).

Dred   Harriet Beecher Stowe, *Dred: A Tale of the Great Dismal Swamp*, 2 vols. (Boston: Phillips, Sampson & Co., 1856).

HBS   Harriet Beecher Stowe.

Life and Letters   Harriet Beecher Stowe, *The Life and Letters of Harriet Beecher Stowe*, ed. Annie Adams Fields (Boston: Houghton Mifflin Co., 1897).

Key to UTC   Harriet Beecher Stowe, *A Key to Uncle Tom's Cabin: Presenting the Original Facts and Documents upon Which the Story Is Founded* (Boston: J. P. Jewett, 1853).

UTC   Harriet Beecher Stowe, *Uncle Tom's Cabin; or, Life among the Lowly*, 2 vols. (Boston: J. P. Jewett & Co.; Cleveland: Jewett, Proctor & Worthington, 1852).

World's Greatest Hit   Harry Birdoff, *The World's Greatest Hit: Uncle Tom's Cabin* (New York: S. F. Vanni, 1947).

I. The Early Years: 1811–1826

1. Stuart C. Henry, *Unvanquished Puritan: A Portrait of Lyman Beecher* (Grand Rapids, Mich.: William B. Eerdmans Publishing Co., 1973), passim.

2. Lyman Beecher, *Autobiography, Correspondence, etc., of Lyman Beecher, D.D.,* ed. Charles Beecher, 2 vols. (New York: Harper Bros., 1864), 2:118-19, 1:28, 145; HBS, *The Life and Letters of Harriet Beecher Stowe,* ed. Annie Adams Fields (Boston: Houghton Mifflin Co., 1897), pp. 34-35; Henry, *Unvanquished Puritan,* p. 89.

3. *Life and Letters,* p. 36.

4. *Autobiography,* 1:18; Calvin E. Stowe, "Sketches and Recollections of Dr. Lyman Beecher," *Congregational Quarterly* 6 (1864): 234; HBS, *Oldtown Folks* (Boston: Fields, Osgood & Co., 1869), pp. 443, 223-26; *Life and Letters,* p. 40; HBS to Charles E. Stowe, 30 September 1880, in Charles Edward Stowe, *Life of Harriet Beecher Stowe Compiled from Her Letters and Journals* (Boston: Houghton Mifflin Co., 1889), p. 509.

5. *Autobiography,* 1:352-53, 1:429, 460, Lyman Beecher to Edward Beecher, 22 June 1820 and 7 April 1821; Robert Merideth, *The Politics of the Universe: Edward Beecher, Abolition, and Orthodoxy* (Nashville: Vanderbilt University Press, 1968), pp. 37-38.

6. *Autobiography,* 1:18.

7. Kathryn Kish Sklar, *Catharine Beecher: A Study in American Domesticity* (New Haven: Yale University Press, 1973), p. 147, n. 21, p. 305; Lyman Beecher Stowe, *Saints, Sinners and Beechers* (Indianapolis: Bobbs-Merrill Co., 1934), p. 336.

8. There are brief biographies of all of Lyman Beecher's children in Henry, *Unvanquished Puritan,* pp. 289-94; seven of them—Catharine, Charles, Edward, Harriet (Beecher Stowe), Henry Ward, Isabella (Beecher Hooker), and Thomas—were considered important enough to be included in the *Dictionary of American Biography*; Marie Caskey, *Chariot of Fire: Religion and the Beecher Family* (New Haven: Yale University Press, 1978), p. 323.

9. *Autobiography,* 1:303-4, 56, 232, 307; [Robert] Forrest Wilson, *Crusader in Crinoline: The Life of Harriet Beecher Stowe* (Philadelphia: J. B. Lippincott Co., 1941), pp. 32-34, 38-39; Henry, *Unvanquished Puritan,* p. 54.

10. *Life and Letters,* pp. 36-37.

11. HBS, *The Lives and Deeds of Our Self-Made Men* (Hartford, Conn.: Worthington, Dustin & Co., 1872), pp. 507-8.

12. Henry F. May, "Introduction," HBS, *Oldtown Folks* (Cambridge: Harvard University Press, Belknap Press, 1966), pp. 8-9; Charles H. Foster, *The Rungless Ladder: Harriet Beecher Stowe and New England Puritanism* (Durham: Duke University Press, 1954), p. 6; Edmund Wilson, *Patriotic Gore: Studies in the Literature of the American Civil War* (New York: Oxford University Press, 1962), p. 10; John William Ward, "Afterword," HBS, *Uncle Tom's Cabin* (New York: New American Library, 1966), p. 485.

13. *Life and Letters,* p. 40.

14. Ibid.

15. HBS, *Poganuc People: Their Loves and Lives* (New York: Fords, Howard & Hulbert, 1878), p. 175.

16. *Autobiography,* 1:528-29; *Life and Letters,* pp. 38-39.

17. Sklar, *Catharine Beecher,* p. 59; Thomas Woody, *A History of Woman's Education in the United States,* 2 vols. (New York: Science Press, 1929), 1:320-22; *Crusader in Crinoline,* p. 69.

18. The manuscript of HBS's *Cleon,* a play, has been lost. Part or all of it is printed in *Life and Letters,* pp. 44-49; *Crusader in Crinoline,* pp. 69-70.

19. *Crusader in Crinoline,* p. 71; *Life and Letters,* pp. 49-50.

20. C. E. Stowe, *Life of Harriet Beecher Stowe,* pp. 34-36.

21. [John Dix], *Transatlantic Tracings; or, Sketches of Persons and Scenes in America* (London: W. Tweedie, 1853), pp. 49-50.

22. Merideth, *Politics of the Universe*, pp. 13-14; Henry, *Unvanquished Puritan*, pp. 251-53.

23. Henry, *Unvanquished Puritan*, pp. 105-6; Sklar, *Catharine Beecher*, pp. 28-38, 54; Franklin Bowditch Dexter, *Biographical Sketches of the Graduates of Yale College*, 6 vols. (New York: Henry Holt & Co., 1885–1912), 5:568; *Autobiography*, 1:478-79; Merideth, *Politics of the Universe*, p. 64; Robert G. Ingersoll, "A Tribute to Henry Ward Beecher," *Works of Robert G. Ingersoll*, 12 vols. (New York: Dresden Publishing Co., 1909), 12:419.

24. Harriet to Edward Beecher, 1826?, quoted in C. E. Stowe, *Life of Harriet Beecher Stowe*, pp. 36-37.

25. *Autobiography*, 1:524-25; L. B. Stowe, *Saints, Sinners and Beechers*, p. 156.

26. Quoted in Charles Edward Stowe and Lyman Beecher Stowe, *Harriet Beecher Stowe: The Story of Her Life* (Boston: Houghton Mifflin Co., 1911), p. 124. Augustine St. Clare, a character in *Uncle Tom's Cabin*, repeats almost word for word this version of Mary Hubbard's strictures on slavery. HBS, *Uncle Tom's Cabin; or, Life among the Lowly*, 2 vols. (Boston: J. P. Jewett & Co.; Cleveland: Jewett, Proctor & Worthington, 1852), 2:12.

27. HBS to Frederick Douglass, 9 July 1851, MS letter, Stowe-Day Foundation Library, Hartford, Conn.

28. Sklar, *Catharine Beecher*, p. 278, n. 10; *Life and Letters*, p. 17; *Autobiography*, 1:312.

29. HBS, *Lives and Deeds*, p. 516.

II. HARTFORD AND BOSTON: 1826–1832

1. William Ellery Channing, *Works* (Boston: American Unitarian Assoc., 1890), p. 19.

2. Lyman Beecher to Edward Beecher, 4 September 1826, Lyman Beecher to Catharine Beecher, 8 September 1826, *Autobiography*, 2:47, 49-50, 85; Sklar, *Catharine Beecher*, p. 67.

3. Henry, *Unvanquished Puritan*, pp. 181-91; Arthur W. Brown, *William Ellery Channing* (New York: Twayne Publishers, 1961), pp. 46-48.

4. Walter M. Merrill, *Against Wind and Tide: A Biography of William Lloyd Garrison* (Cambridge: Harvard University Press, 1963), pp. 33-34; *Liberator*, 1 January 1831.

5. Wendell Phillips Garrison and Francis Jackson Garrison, *William Lloyd Garrison, 1805–1879: The Story of His Life Told by His Children*, 4 vols. (New York: Century Co., 1885–1889), 1:261; W. L. Garrison, *Journal of the Times*, 30 January 1829, quoted in John L. Thomas, *The Liberator. William Lloyd Garrison: A Biography* (Boston: Little, Brown & Co., 1963), p. 59.

6. Lyman Beecher, quoted in Thomas, *The Liberator. William Lloyd Garrison*, pp. 57-59; W. L. Garrison, *Journal of the Times*, 30 January 1829.

7. Thomas, *The Liberator: William Lloyd Garrison*, pp. 125-26.

8. Catharine E. Beecher, *An Essay on Slavery and Abolition with Reference to the Duty of American Females* (Philadelphia: Henry Perkins; Boston: Perkins & Marvin, 1837), pp. 10-11, 87-88; [Richard Hildreth], *Brief Remarks on Miss Catharine E. Beecher's Essay on Slavery and Abolition: By the Author of Archy Moore* (Boston: I. Knapp, 1837), p. 6.

9. HBS, *Lives and Deeds*, pp. 160-61; L. B. Stowe, *Saints, Sinners and Beechers*, p. 60.

10. L. B. Stowe, *Saints, Sinners and Beechers*, p. 66.

11. P. J. Staudenraus, *The African Colonization Movement: 1816–1865* (New York: Columbia University Press, 1961), pp. 15, 17, 19-20, 29, 139-40, 170-71, 32, 195-96.

12. Catharine Beecher, *Educational Reminiscences and Suggestions* (New York: J. B. Ford, 1874), pp. 62-65; Grace Steele Woodward, *The Cherokees* (Norman: University of Oklahoma Press, 1962), p. 71; Thurman Wilkins, *Cherokee Tragedy: The Story of the Ridge Family and the Decimation of a People* (New York: Macmillan Co., 1970), passim; "Worcester *v.* Georgia, 6 Peters, 515 (1832)," in Henry Steele Commager, ed., *Documents of American History*, 5th ed. (New York: Appleton-Century-Crofts, 1949), pp. 258-59.

13. HBS, quoted in Catharine Beecher to Lyman Beecher, 16 February 1827, in C. E. Stowe, *Life of Harriet Beecher Stowe*, p. 37.

14. Ibid., pp. 47-48.

15. Ibid., HBS to Edward Beecher, February 1829, pp. 46-47.

16. HBS to Mary Dutton, 1830, unpublished letter, Beinecke Rare Book and Manuscript Library, Yale University, quoted in E. Bruce Kirkham, "Harriet Beecher Stowe and the Genesis, Composition, and Revision of *Uncle Tom's Cabin*" (Ph.D. diss., University of North Carolina, 1968), pp. 22-23.

III. CINCINNATI: 1832–1850

1. Edward Deering Mansfield, *Personal Memories, Social, Political and Literary with Sketches of Many Noted People, 1803–1843* (Cincinnati: R. Clarke & Co., 1879), pp. 139-279; *Trial and Acquittal of Lyman Beecher, D.D., Before the Presbytery of Cincinnati, on Charges Preferred by Joshua L. Wilson, D.D., Reported for the New-York Observer, by Mr. Stansbury, of Washington, D. C.* (Cincinnati: n.p., 1835), p. 33; Nathaniel Taylor, quoted in *Autobiography*, 2:248; Henry, *Unvanquished Puritan*, pp. 15-18.

2. *Autobiography*, 2:270-72, 1:70, 2:247, Lyman Beecher to Catharine Beecher, 8 July 1830, 2:224; Henry, *Unvanquished Puritan*, pp. 20, 25.

3. Charles Dickens, *American Notes*, in *The Nonesuch Dickens*, 23 vols. (Bloomsbury [London]: The Nonesuch Press, 1937–1938), 1:160-61; Catharine Beecher to Harriet Beecher [Stowe], 17 April and 2 May 1832, *Autobiography*, 2:267-68; Sklar, *Catharine Beecher*, pp. 107-8.

4. Ray Allen Billington, *Westward Expansion: A History of the American Frontier* (New York: Macmillan Co., 1949), pp. 339-40.

5. Henry, *Unvanquished Puritan*, pp. 170-72.

6. *Autobiography*, 2:322; Henry, *Unvanquished Puritan*, p. 191.

7. H. Lyman, "Lane Seminary Rebels," in William Gay Ballantine, ed., *Oberlin Jubilee: 1833–1883* (Oberlin, Ohio: E. J. Goodrich, 1883), p. 62; *Autobiography*, 2:324; Henry, *Unvanquished Puritan*, p. 193.

8. Theodore Weld to Arthur Tappan, 12 April 1834, *Autobiography*, 2:324-25.

9. Theodore Weld to Lewis Tappan, 9 March 1836, *Letters of Theodore Dwight Weld, Angelina Grimké Weld and Sarah Grimké: 1822–1844*, ed. Gilbert H. Barnes and Dwight L. Dumond, 2 vols. (1934; reprint, Gloucester, Mass.: Peter Smith, 1965), 1:273; *Crusader in Crinoline*, p. 137.

10. Quoted in Lewis Tappan, *The Life of Arthur Tappan* (New York: Hurd & Houghton, 1870), p. 225; Henry, *Unvanquished Puritan*, pp. 178-79.

11. Calvin E. Stowe, "Sketches and Recollections of Dr. Lyman Beecher," *Congregational Quarterly* 6 (1864): 233; [John J. Miter], *A Statement of the Reasons Which Induced the Students of Lane Seminary to Dissolve Their Connection with That Institution* (Cincinnati: n.p., 1834), p. 26; *Autobiography*, 2:234; *Liberator*, 12 January 1833, cited in Leon F. Litwack, *North of Slavery: The Negro in the Free States, 1790–1860* (Chicago: University of Chicago Press, 1961), p. 117.

12. *Autobiography*, 2:323, 325; L. B. Stowe, *Saints, Sinners and Beechers*, p. 59; [Miter], *A Statement of the Reasons*, pp. 24-25.

13. *The Statutes of Ohio and of the Northwest Territory*, ed. Salmon P. Chase, vol. 1 (Cincinnati: Corey & Fairbank, 1833–1835), pp. 393-94, 555-56; Richard

C. Wade, "The Negro in Cincinnati, 1800–1830," *Journal of Negro History* 39 (1954):50-55.

14. "Minute Book," pp. 216-21, quoted in Henry, *Unvanquished Puritan*, pp. 196-97; *Liberator*, 4 October 1834.

15. *Autobiography*, 2:329-32; James H. Fairchild, *Oberlin: The Colony and the College* (Oberlin, Ohio: E. J. Goodrich, 1883), p. 56; [Miter], *A Statement of the Reasons*, pp. 3-4.

16. *Liberator*, 17 January 1835; *Fifth Annual Report of the Trustees of the Cincinnati Lane Seminary* (Cincinnati: Corey & Fairbank, 1834), pp. 39, 41, 47, cited in Henry, *Unvanquished Puritan*, pp. 198-203; *Autobiography*, 3:322.

17. Henry, *Unvanquished Puritan*, pp. 198-99; Merideth, *Politics of the Universe*, pp. 88-89.

18. HBS to Wendell Phillips, 23 February 1853, Crawford Blagden Collection, Houghton Library, Harvard University; quoted by Phillips in "Explanation and Defense," *National Anti-Slavery Standard*, 23 March 1853. Phillips's reply is also quoted in this article.

19. Theodore Weld to Wendell Phillips, 28 February 1853, Crawford Blagden Collection; Wendell Phillips, "Explanation and Defense," p. 173.

20. Theodore Weld to Wendell Phillips, 28 February 1853, Crawford Blagden Collection; Theodore Davenport Bacon, *Leonard Bacon: A Statesman in the Church* (New Haven: Yale University Press, 1931), pp. 235-36; Garrison and Garrison, *William Lloyd Garrison*, 1:475-76; Merideth, *Politics of the Universe*, pp. 89-90; Russel B. Nye, *William Lloyd Garrison and the Humanitarian Reformers* (Boston: Little, Brown, 1955), p. 108.

21. Lyman Beecher to William Beecher, 15 July 1835, *Autobiography*, 2:345; Lyman Beecher to Thomas Brainerd, 23 May 1840, Beecher Collection, Yale University Library, quoted in Henry, *Unvanquished Puritan*, p. 238.

22. HBS to Georgina May, November 1832, quoted in C. E. Stowe, *Life of Harriet Beecher Stowe*, pp. 49-51.

23. HBS to Georgina May, May 1833, ibid., p. 67.

24. *Crusader in Crinoline*, p. 139; Edward Dwight Eaton, "Calvin Ellis Stowe," *Dictionary of American Biography*.

25. Calvin E. Stowe, "The Woman Question and the Apostle Paul," *Hearth and Home* 1 (11 September 1869): 601; *Crusader in Crinoline*, pp. 162-67.

26. *Crusader in Crinoline*, p. 231.

27. *Autobiography*, 2:351; Henry, *Unvanquished Puritan*, pp. 220-22; Robert S. Michaelsen, *The American Search for Soul* (Baton Rouge: Louisiana State University Press, 1964), p. 245; Sklar, *Catharine Beecher*, pp. 116-17.

28. Sklar, *Catharine Beecher*, pp. 116-17; *Lowell* (Mass.) *Journal*, 10 September 1834, quoted by James Hall in *Western Monthly Magazine* 2 (December 1834): 655, quoted in Randolph C. Randall, *James Hall, Spokesman of the New West* (Columbus: Ohio State University Press, 1964), p. 245.

29. Henry, *Unvanquished Puritan*, p. 239; Lyman Beecher to Nathaniel Wright, 4 January 1840, Nathaniel Wright to Lyman Beecher, 14 January 1840, Nathaniel Wright Papers, Box 24, Library of Congress, quoted in Sklar, *Catharine Beecher*, p. 123.

30. Sklar, *Catharine Beecher*, pp. 117-18.

31. An Alabama Man [William Birney?], "Some Account of Mrs. Beecher Stowe and Her Family," *Fraser's Magazine* 46 (1852): 519.

32. Richard Henry Dana, Jr., *The Journal*, ed. Robert F. Lucid, 3 vols. (Cambridge: Harvard University Press, Belknap Press, 1968), 2:518-19.

33. Julia Ward Howe, "Harriet Beecher Stowe," *Reader Magazine* 5 (March 1905): 616-17.

34. Betty Lorraine Fladeland, *James Gillespie Birney: Slaveholder to Abolitionist* (Ithaca, N. Y.: Cornell University Press, 1955), pp. 32, 38-39, 82, 129; William MacDonald, "James Gillespie Birney," *Dictionary of American Biography*.

35. Daniel Aaron, "Cincinnati, 1818–1838: A Study of Attitudes in the Urban West" (Ph.D. diss., Harvard University, 1942), p. 458; Sklar, *Catharine Beecher*, p. 124; Fladeland, *James Gillespie Birney*, pp. 139-42.

36. C. E. Stowe and L. B. Stowe, *Harriet Beecher Stowe*, p. 108.

37. C. E. Beecher, *An Essay on Slavery*, passim.

38. Ibid., pp. 100-101.

39. Ibid., pp. 87-88; [Hildreth], *Brief Remarks on Miss Catharine Beecher's Essay*, p. 8.

40. C. E. Beecher, *An Essay on Slavery*, pp. 20-21.

41. Joseph C. and Owen Lovejoy, *Memoir of the Rev. Elijah P. Lovejoy: Who Was Murdered in Defence of the Liberty of the Press, at Alton, Illinois, Nov. 7, 1837* (New York: John S. Taylor, 1838), pp. 118-21, 126, 128; Merideth, *Politics of the Universe*, pp. 92, 100-101; Jean Fagan Yellin, *The Intricate Knot: Black Figures in American Literature, 1776–1863* (New York: New York University Press, 1972), p. 124; Edward Beecher, *Narrative of Riots at Alton: In Connection with the Death of Rev. Elijah P. Lovejoy* (Alton, Ill.: George Holton, 1838), p. 88.

42. E. Beecher, *Narrative of Riots*, pp. 22-23, 6-7.

43. Baynard R. Hall, *Frank Freeman's Barber Shop: A Tale* (New York: C. Scribner, 1852), pp. 295-96.

44. Henry Howe, *Historical Collections of Ohio*, 2 vols. (Norwalk: State of Ohio, 1896), 1:825; Henry, *Unvanquished Puritan*, p. 237.

IV. HARRIET BEECHER STOWE IN CINCINNATI: 1836–1850

1. Sklar, *Catharine Beecher*, pp. 169-70.

2. *Crusader in Crinoline*, pp. 217-25.

3. HBS to Calvin E. Stowe, 4 September 1842, Beecher-Stowe Collection, Schlesinger Library, Harvard University.

4. HBS to Calvin Stowe, January 1847, in C. E. Stowe, *Life of Harriet Beecher Stowe*, pp. 117-18; HBS to Mrs. George Beecher, 17 December 1850, Beecher-Stowe Collection, Schlesinger Library, Harvard University.

5. HBS to Calvin Stowe, 16 June 1845, in C. E. Stowe, *Life of Harriet Beecher Stowe*, pp. 111-12.

6. HBS to Calvin E. Stowe, 26 July 1849, in C. E. Stowe, *Life of Harriet Beecher Stowe*, p. 124. The Stowes named a later child a similar name, Charles Edward.

7. Calvin Stowe to Lyman Beecher, 17 July 1844, Beecher-Stowe Collection, Schlesinger Library, Harvard University.

8. HBS to Calvin E. Stowe, 19 July 1844, Beecher-Stowe Collection, Schlesinger Library, Harvard University.

9. John R. Adams, *Harriet Beecher Stowe* (New York: Twayne Publishers, 1963), p. 27; HBS to Earl of Shaftesbury, 20 July 1853, Beecher-Stowe Papers, Schlesinger Library, Harvard University; another copy of the letter is in the Huntington Library.

10. HBS to Mary Dutton, 13 December 1838, Collection of American Literature: Mary Dutton-Beecher Letters, Beinecke Rare Book and Manuscript Library, Yale University, quoted in Sklar, *Catharine Beecher*, p. 141.

11. Catharine and Harriet Beecher, *Primary Geography for Children, on an Improved Plan* (Cincinnati: Corey, Webster & Fairbank, 1833), passim. Catharine's name was listed because she was then the better known author, but Harriet was the one who wrote the book. A revision appeared under the name of Harriet Beecher Stowe with the name of Catharine omitted in a later edition, *First Geography for Children* (Boston: Phillips, Sampson & Co.; New York: J. C. Derby, 1855). The quotations come from the revised edition, pp. 34, 42, 44.

12. Hall, *Frank Freeman's Barber Shop*, pp. 169-70; HBS, *First Geography for Children*, pp. 50, 54, 66-67; HBS, "A New England Sketch," *Western Monthly Magazine* 2 (April 1834): 169.

13. HBS, *Agnes of Sorrento* (Boston: J. R. Osgood, 1862), pp. 283, 186-87;

HBS, *Sunny Memories of Foreign Lands*, 2 vols. (Boston: Phillips, Sampson & Co., 1854), 2:280.

14. *UTC*, 2:18-19; HBS, "Hartford," *Hearth and Home* 1 (30 October 1869): 712; HBS, *Pink and White Tyranny: A Society Novel* (Boston: Roberts Bros., 1871), pp. 185-86.

15. HBS [Christopher Crowfield, pseud.], "The Lady Who Does Her Own Work," *House and Home Papers* (Boston: Ticknor & Fields, 1865), pp. 127-28; Catharine Beecher, "My Autobiography for the Entertainment of Family Friends," Katharine Day Collection, Stowe-Day Foundation, Hartford, Conn., p. 9, cited in Sklar, *Catharine Beecher*, p. 278, n. 10.

16. "What Will the American People Do?" *New-York Evangelist*, pt. 1, 17 (29 January 1846): 17, pt. 2, 17 (5 February 1846): 21; Lyman Beecher, *A Plea for the West*, 2nd ed. (Cincinnati: Truman & Smith, 1835), p. 142; *Autobiography*, 2:334; Henry, *Unvanquished Puritan*, pp. 156-57.

17. HBS, *Sunny Memories*, 2:416.

18. Elizabeth Barrett Browning to Mrs. David Ogilvy, 12 September 1860, *Elizabeth Barrett Browning's Letters to Mrs. David Ogilvy, 1849–1861 with Recollections by Mrs. Ogilvy*, ed. Peter N. Heydon and Philip Kelly (New York: Quadrangle/New York Times Book Co. and Browning Institute, 1973), p. 160; HBS, "Servants," *House and Home Papers*, pp. 220-21; Edward Wagenknecht, *Harriet Beecher Stowe: The Known and the Unknown* (New York: Oxford University Press, 1965), p. 208.

19. HBS, "Literary Epidemics," pt. 2, *New-York Evangelist* (13 July 1843): 109.

20. Ibid.

21. *Cincinnati Journal and Western Luminary*, quoted in *Crusader in Crinoline*, p. 185; see also note, p. 647.

22. HBS, *The Mayflower; or, Sketches of Scenes and Characters among the Descendants of the Pilgrims* (New York: Harper Bros., 1843), pp. 99-100. See also the revised edition, *The Mayflower, and Miscellaneous Writings* (Boston: Phillips, Sampson & Co., 1855). In this edition, the comment about slavery is omitted.

23. HBS, "Immediate Emancipation, a Sketch," *New-York Evangelist* 15 (2 January 1845): 1. The story is based upon a real incident. See *UTC*, 2:312-13.

24. HBS, "Immediate Emancipation," p. 1.

25. HBS to Elizabeth Foote, August 1834, in C. E. Stowe, *Life of Harriet Beecher Stowe*, pp. 74-75.

26. HBS to Calvin Stowe, July 1837, in C .E. Stowe and L. B. Stowe, *Harriet Beecher Stowe*, pp. 87-88.

27. *Crusader in Crinoline*, pp. 193-94.

28. Mary Dutton, quoted in *Life and Letters*, p. 85.

29. HBS to James Lane Allen, 30 April 1886, quoted in Allen, "Mrs. Stowe's 'Uncle Tom' at Home in Kentucky," *Century* 34 (October 1887): 857.

30. Henry James, "The Art of Fiction," *Partial Portraits* (London: Macmillan Co., 1888), p. 389.

31. HBS, *Uncle Tom's Cabin*, new ed. (Boston: Houghton Mifflin Co., 1879), p. viii.

32. Sklar, *Catharine Beecher*, p. 233; *Crusader in Crinoline*, pp. 238-42.

V. STOWE'S IDEAS OF RACE

1. HBS, "A Brilliant Success," *Independent* 10 (30 September 1858): 1.

2. HBS, *A Key to Uncle Tom's Cabin: Presenting the Original Facts and Documents upon Which the Story Is Founded* (Boston: J. P. Jewett, 1853), p. 155.

3. HBS, *Men of Our Times; or, Leading Patriots of the Day* (Hartford, Conn.: Hartford Publishing Co.; New York: J. D. Denison; Chicago: J. A. Stoddard, 1868), pp. 385-86.

4. *UTC*, 2:300.

5. HBS, "Captain Kidd's Money," *Oldtown Fireside Stories* (Boston: J. R. Osgood & Co., 1872), p. 104; HBS, *The Minister's Wooing* (New York: Derby & Jackson; Boston: Brown, Taggard & Chase, 1859), p. 111.

6. HBS, "A Panoramic Picture," *Independent* 12 (21 June 1860): 1.

7. HBS, *Palmetto Leaves* (Boston: J. R. Osgood & Co., 1873), p. 285; HBS, "The Colored Labor of the South," *Hearth and Home* 1 (3 July 1869): 440.

8. HBS, *Dred: A Tale of the Great Dismal Swamp*, 2 vols. (Boston: Phillips, Sampson & Co., 1856), 2:68.

9. HBS, "Our Florida Plantation," *Atlantic Monthly* 43 (May 1879): 648; HBS, *Palmetto Leaves*, pp. 305-6.

10. HBS, "Southern Christmas and New Year," *Christian Union*, 19 (January 1876): 44.

11. *Key to UTC*, pp. 27-28.

12. Ibid., pp. 28-29.

13. HBS, "The Colored Labor of the South," p. 440; HBS, *Minister's Wooing*, p. 111; HBS, *Poganuc People*, p. 200; HBS, "The Parson's Horse-Race," *Atlantic Monthly* 42 (October 1878): 473.

14. HBS, *Palmetto Leaves*, p. 272; *UTC*, 1:296.

15. *UTC*, 1:162, 143; HBS, "Introduction," William C. Nell, *The Colored Patriots of the American Revolution* (Boston: Robert F. Callcut, 1855), p. [5].

16. *UTC*, 1:161-62, 27; HBS, "Our Florida Plantation," p. 642; HBS, *Minister's Wooing*, p. 156.

17. HBS, *First Geography for Children*, pp. 93, 97, 95, 89, 103.

18. HBS, *Oldtown Folks*, pp. 3, 6.

19. Ezra Hoyt Byington, *The Puritan as a Colonist and Reformer* (Boston: Little, Brown & Co., 1899), p. 144; HBS, *Oldtown Folks*, p. 19.

20. HBS, *Men of Our Times*, pp. 409-10; L. B. Stowe, *Saints, Sinners and Beechers*, p. 342.

21. HBS, "The Indians at St. Augustine," pt. 1, *Christian Union* 15 (18 April 1877): 345, pt. 2, 15 (25 April 1877): 372.

22. HBS, *First Geography for Children*, pp. 145-46, 163-64.

23. HBS, "A Student's Sea Story," *Atlantic Monthly* 43 (January 1879): 102-3.

24. C. and H. Beecher, *Primary Geography for Children, on an Improved Plan*, p. 77; HBS, *Sunny Memories*, 2:308.

25. HBS, *Sunny Memories*, 2:408-9.

26. Ibid., 2:65; HBS, "Letter from Europe, no. 2," *Independent* 9 (29 January 1857): 1.

27. HBS, *Pink and White Tyranny*, p. 341; HBS, *We and Our Neighbors; or, The Records of an Unfashionable Street* (New York: J. B. Ford & Co., 1875), p. 431.

28. HBS [Christopher Crowfield, pseud.], *The Little Foxes* (Boston: Ticknor & Fields, 1866), pp. 131-32.

29. *Key to UTC*, p. 28.

30. Ibid., p. 82; William Lloyd Garrison to John S. Rarey, 20 March 1861, *The Letters of William Lloyd Garrison*, ed. Walter M. Merrill and Louis Ruchames, 6 vols. (Cambridge: Harvard University Press, Belknap Press, 1971–1981), 5:15. (Garrison's quotation is adapted from Isaiah 28:10.)

31. HBS, *Minister's Wooing*, pp. 153-54.

32. HBS, *Woman in Sacred History: A Series of Sketches Drawn from Scriptural, Historical, and Legendary Sources* (New York: J. B. Ford & Co., 1874).

33. Alexander Kinmont, *Twelve Lectures on the Natural History of Man, and the Rise and Progress of Philosophy* (Cincinnati: U. P. James, 1839), pp. ii-iv, 1-2. I am indebted to George M. Frederickson for pointing out similarities between Kinmont's ideas of race and those of Stowe. See his *The Black Image in the White Mind: The Debate on Afro-American Character and Destiny, 1817–1914* (New York: Harper & Row, 1971), p. 110.

34. Kinmont, *Twelve Lectures*, pp. 3, 6-7.

35. Ibid., pp. 316-17.

36. Ibid., p. 190.

37. Ibid., pp. 191, 188.

38. Kenneth Rexroth has answered the question of whether Stowe was sentimental in a different way. "Is Harriet Beecher Stowe sentimental? And rhetorical? Indeed she is. So is Norman Mailer, or for that matter much greater writers, Thomas Hardy or D. H. Lawrence." *The Elastic Retort: Essays in Literature and Ideas* (New York: Seabury Press, 1973), p. 104.

VI. THE WRITING OF UNCLE TOM'S CABIN

1. Stanley W. Campbell, *The Slave Catchers: Enforcement of the Fugitive Slave Law, 1850–1860* (Chapel Hill: University of North Carolina Press, 1970), pp. 3-25; Hamilton Holman, *Prologue to Conflict: Compromise of 1850* (Lexington: University of Kentucky Press, 1964), pp. 168-72.

2. HBS, "The Freeman's Dream: A Parable," *National Era* 4 (1 August 1850): 121.

3. Quoted in C. E. Stowe, *The Life of Harriet Beecher Stowe*, p. 144.

4. HBS, postscript in letter of Henry Ellis Stowe to Calvin Stowe, [December 1850], Stowe-Day Foundation Library, Hartford, Conn.

5. HBS to Calvin Stowe, 21 January [1851] and 27 January [1851], Stowe-Day Foundation Library, Hartford, Conn.

6. HBS to George Eliot, 18 March 1876, Berg Collection, New York Public Library, quoted in E. Bruce Kirkham, "Harriet Beecher Stowe and the Genesis, Composition, and Revision of *Uncle Tom's Cabin*" (Ph.D. diss., University of North Carolina, 1968), p. 118; HBS to Alexander Milton Ross, quoted in Milton Ross, *Recollections and Experiences of an Abolitionist from 1855 to 1865*, 2nd ed. (Toronto: Rowsell & Hutchison, 1872), p. 3; *Crusader in Crinoline*, p. 255.

7. HBS, "Introduction," *Uncle Tom's Cabin*, new ed., p. xi; Forrest Wilson thought that this "vision" took place in February of 1851. See *Crusader in Crinoline*, p. 256.

8. Mrs. John T. Howard, quoted in *Life and Letters*, p. 164.

9. HBS, "Introduction," *Uncle Tom's Cabin*, new ed., p. xi; *Life and Letters*, p. 164.

10. Elizabeth Barrett Browning to Mrs. Janes, 9 April [1857], *The Letters of Elizabeth Barrett Browning*, ed. Frederic G. Kenyon, 2 vols. (London: Macmillan Co., 1897), 2:258.

11. Annie Fields, *Life and Letters*, p. 377.

12. Quoted in L. B. Stowe, *Saints, Sinners and Beechers*, p. 55.

13. HBS, "Old Testament Pictures—No. 1," *New-York Evangelist* 15 (14 November 1844): 181.

14. HBS to Dr. Wardlow, 4 December 1852, reprinted as "Letter from Mrs. Stowe," *New-York Times*, 17 February 1853, p. 3; HBS to Earl of Shaftesbury, 20 January 1853. A copy is in Beecher-Stowe Papers, Schlesinger Library, Harvard University, Folder 243a; the original letter is in the Huntington Library, San Marino, Cal.

15. Howard Mumford Jones, "Introduction," in HBS, *Uncle Tom's Cabin* (Columbus: Charles E. Merrill Publishing Co., 1969), p. viii; Mrs. John T. Howard, quoted in *Life and Letters*, p. 163; Wagenknecht, *Harriet Beecher Stowe*, p. 156.

16. "A Pioneer Editor" [an obituary of Gamaliel Bailey], *Atlantic Monthly* 17 (June 1866): 748-49.

17. HBS to Gamaliel Bailey, 9 March 1851. The original letter is lost; a typewritten copy was made in 1888 and is in the Boston Public Library, quoted in *Crusader in Crinoline*, pp. 259-60.

18. Ibid.

19. HBS, "Introduction," *Uncle Tom's Cabin*, new ed., p. xv.

VII. UNCLE TOM'S CABIN: PART I

1. Review of *UTC, North British Review* 18 (November 1852): 235-36.
2. *UTC*, 1:40-41, 47.
3. Ibid., 1:141.
4. See Theodore R. Hovet, "Harriet Beecher Stowe's Holiness Crusade against Slavery" (Ph.D. diss., University of Kansas, 1970), passim.
5. Austin Warren, *New England Saints* (Ann Arbor: University of Michigan Press, 1956), pp. 60-61; HBS, *Sunny Memories*, 2:399-400; HBS, "De Rance and Fenelon—a Contrast," *New-York Evangelist* 1 (7 July 1842): 209; May, "Introduction," HBS, *Oldtown Folks*, p. 22; Kenneth S. Lynn, "*Uncle Tom's Cabin*," in *Visions of America: Eleven Literary Historical Essays* (Westport, Conn.: Greenwood Press), p. 31.
6. *UTC*, 1:173; Heb. 11:16; *UTC*, 2:250.
7. *UTC*, 1:142.
8. Ibid., 2:121; *Key to UTC*, p. 25; Matt. 1:25, Luke 10:21.
9. Josiah Henson, *The Life of Josiah Henson, Formerly a Slave, Now an Inhabitant of Canada, as Narrated by Himself* (Boston: A. D. Phelps, 1849), passim; HBS, "Preface," Josiah Henson, *Father Henson's Story of His Own Life* (Boston: J. P. Jewett & Co., 1858); *An Autobiography of the Rev. Josiah Henson, 1789–1876* (1877; reprint, London: Frank, Cass & Co., 1971), pp. 156-63; HBS to *Indianapolis* (Ind.) *Times*, 3 August 1882, p. 2.
10. Henson, *Father Henson's Story of His Own Life*, pp. 151-52, 181-86; Foster, *The Rungless Ladder*, p. 32; Kenneth Lynn, *Mark Twain and Southwestern Humor* (Boston: Little, Brown & Co., 1959), p. 110; William H. Pease and Jane H. Pease, *Black Utopias: Negro Communal Experiments in America* (Madison: State Historical Society of Wisconsin, 1963), pp. 64-81; Walter Fisher, "Introduction," Henson, *Father Henson's Story of His Own Life* (1858; reprint, New York: Corinth Books, 1962), p. [v]; HBS to Rev. William H. Tilley, 15 May 1876, quoted in Brion Gysin, *To Master—a Long Goodnight: The Story of Uncle Tom, a Historical Narrative* (New York: Creative Age Press, 1946), p. 47.
11. Henson, *The Life of Josiah Henson*, pp. 1, 10-13, 15-18, 22-25, 27-28, 44-46.
12. Henson, *Father Henson's Story of His Own Life*, pp. 70, 73-76, 151-52; Pease and Pease, *Black Utopias*, pp. 64-81.
13. HBS, "Preface to the European Edition," *Uncle Tom's Cabin* (Leipzig: Tauchnitz, 1852), 1:vi.
14. *UTC*, 1:45, 296.
15. Ibid., 1:109-10, 112.
16. Ibid., 1:70, 116; Anthony Burgess, "Making de White Boss Frown," *Encounter* 27 (July 1966): 58.
17. *UTC*, 1:162, 29.
18. Richard Hildreth, *The Slave; or, Memoirs of Archy Moore*, 2nd ed., 2 vols. in 1 (Boston: Whipple & Damrell, 1840), passim.
19. Ibid., 1:42.
20. *UTC*, 1:17.
21. Ibid., 1:30.
22. Ibid., 1:33.
23. Ibid., 1:33, 30, 37, 166.
24. Ibid., 1:26.
25. Ibid., 1:55-56.
26. Ibid., 1:151, 2:55; David Levin, "American Fiction as Historical Evidence: Reflections on *Uncle Tom's Cabin*," *Negro American Literary Forum* 5 (Winter 1971): 135.
27. HBS, "Introduction," *Uncle Tom's Cabin*, new ed., p. xviii.
28. Charles Dudley Warner, "The Story of *Uncle Tom's Cabin*," *Atlantic Monthly* 78 (1896): 315.

29. James G. Birney Diary, 23 October 1834, James G. Birney Papers, Library of Congress, quoted in Robert H. Abzug, *Passionate Liberator Theodore Dwight Weld and the Dilemma of Reform* (New York: Oxford University Press, 1980), p. 123; Lewis Tappan to George Thompson, 2 January 1835, in Garrison Papers, Boston Public Library, quoted in Abzug, *Passionate Liberator*, p. 124; Theodore Weld to Lewis Tappan, 22 February 1836, *Letters of Theodore Dwight Weld*, 1:263-64.

30. The responses of abolitionists to *Uncle Tom's Cabin* are discussed in Chapter 10, pp. 168-76.

31. Levin, "American Fiction as Historical Evidence," p. 136.

32. *UTC*, 1:120-21.

33. Ibid., 1:58, 263-64.

34. *UTC*, 1:101-2, 98, 107.

35. Ibid., 1:14-15.

36. Ibid., 1:149, 108, 189-93.

37. L. S. M[cCord], review of *UTC*, *Southern Quarterly Review* 23 (January 1853): 90; *UTC*, 1:194, 152, 14.

38. *UTC*, 1:181-82; Gen. 9:25; Matt. 7:12; Eccles. 3:11.

39. Lev. 25:44-46; Phil. 1:10.

40. Oliver Johnson, *William Lloyd Garrison and His Times: Sketches of the Anti-Slavery Movement in America, and of the Man Who Was Its Founder and Moral Leader* (Boston: B. B. Russel & Co., 1879), p. 364; Lydia Maria Child, *An Appeal in Favor of that Class of Americans Called Africans* (Boston: Allen & Ticknor, 1833), p. 29.

41. HBS, "The Minister's Housekeeper," *Oldtown Fireside Stories*, pp. 58-59.

42. *Key to UTC*, p. 116; Gen. 15:2-3.

43. *Key to UTC*, p. 116.

44. Rev. E. J. Stearns, *Notes on Uncle Tom's Cabin: Being a Logical Answer to its Allegations and Inferences against Slavery as an Institution* (Philadelphia: Lippincott, Grambo & Co., 1853), p. 63.

45. HBS, "Introduction," Henson, *Father Henson's Story of His Own Life*, p. **v**.

46. Mary H. Eastman, *Aunt Phillis's Cabin; or, Southern Life as It Is* (Philadelphia: Lippincott, Grambo & Co., 1852), p. 124.

VIII. Uncle Tom's Cabin: Part II

1. *UTC*, 1:216.

2. Ibid., 1:222.

3. Ibid., 2:14, 1:221, 153.

4. HBS, "Literary Epidemics—No. 2," *New-York Evangelist* 14 (13 July 1843): 109; see Anne Tropp Transky, "The Saintly Child in Nineteenth-Century American Fiction," *Prospects: Annual of American Cultural Studies* 1 (1975): 392-94.

5. *UTC*, 1:312, 2:6.

6. Ibid., 2:106-7; Jones, "Introduction," *Uncle Tom's Cabin*, p. xiii.

7. *UTC*, 2:91; Bliss Perry, *The American Spirit in Literature* (New Haven: Yale University Press, 1921), p. 222.

8. E. Bruce Kirkham, *The Building of Uncle Tom's Cabin* (Knoxville: University of Tennessee Press, 1977), p. 69.

9. One reviewer in the South said that Ophelia in her aversion to blacks was representative of many white northerners. "If the slave is anywhere to look for friends to improve his condition," he said, "certainly they are to be found among enlightened and liberal Southerners, in whom this prejudice is, as might naturally be imagined, mitigated, from having played with them, been nursed by them, and surrounded by them from childhood." Review of *Key to UTC*, *DeBow's Review* 15 (1853): 491-92.

10. Nathaniel Hawthorne, *The Scarlet Letter*, ed. Fredson Bowers, vol. 1 of *Centenary Edition of the Works of Nathaniel Hawthorne*, gen. ed., William Charvat (Columbus: Ohio State University Press, 1963-), 1:98, 111-12; *UTC*, 2:38.

11. *UTC*, 2:40-41.
12. Ibid., 2:49.
13. Ibid., 2:49-50.
14. Ibid., 1:238, 257-58, 2:93.
15. Ibid., 2:94, 2:116.
16. Ibid., 2:48.
17. 1 Cor. 12:14-26; Matt. 5:15-28.
18. *UTC*, 2:71.
19. Ibid., 2:76. Augustine St. Clare's argument here is similar to that of Thomas Jefferson. See *Notes on the State of Virginia* (Philadelphia: Prichard & Hall, 1788), pp. 172-74.
20. *UTC*, 2:11.
21. Ibid., 2:21. For Garrison's attitudes toward labor, see Leon F. Litwack, *North of Slavery: The Negro in the Free States, 1790–1860* (Chicago: University of Chicago Press, 1961), pp. 172-73.
22. *UTC*, 2:10, 13.
23. Ibid., 2:13, 18-19, 25.
24. Ibid., 1:236, 259.
25. Ibid., 2:123; Luke 10:21.
26. *UTC*, 2:126.
27. Emily Dickinson, *Poems: Including Variant Readings Critically Compared with All Known Manuscripts*, ed. Thomas H. Johnson, 3 vols. (Cambridge: Harvard University Press, Belknap Press, 1955), 1:358; *Autobiography*, 1:293-300; *UTC* 2:113.
28. *UTC*, 2:117.
29. Ibid., 2:145.
30. Ibid., 2:147.

IX. UNCLE TOM'S CABIN: PART III

1. Mary Boykin Chesnut, *Mary Chesnut's Civil War*, ed. C. Vann Woodward (New Haven: Yale University Press, 1981), p. 168.
2. *UTC*, 2:164-65.
3. Ibid., 2:217-18.
4. Ibid., 2:158-59, 162, 167.
5. Richard Hildreth, *The White Slave; or, Memoirs of a Fugitive* (Boston: Tappan & Whittemore; Milwaukee: Rood & Whittemore, 1852), pp. 267-68; Hildreth, "Introduction," *Archy Moore, the White Slave; or, Memoirs of a Fugitive* (New York: Miller, Orton & Co., 1857), p. ix; [Hildreth], "Uncle Tom, the White Slave, Ida May," *Boston Evening Telegraph*, 13 November 1854; *Boston Atlas*, 24 December 1836, quoted in Donald E. Emerson, *Richard Hildreth* (Baltimore: Johns Hopkins Press, 1946), pp. 78-79; Lydia Maria Child, letter published in *Liberator*, 18 March 1837. In England, Nassau William Senior had high praise for *Uncle Tom's Cabin*, but he thought that Hildreth's novel was "a disagreeable counterpart . . . in which the hero is in love with his sister, and has his father for a rival." *American Slavery: A Reprint of an Article on Uncle Tom's Cabin* (London: Longman, Brown, Green, Longmans & Roberts, 1856), pp. 50-51.
6. HBS to Frederick Douglass, 9 July 1851, Connecticut Historical Society, Hartford, Conn., quoted in C. E. Stowe, *The Life of Harriet Beecher Stowe*, pp. 149-50; Avery O. Craven, *The Growth of Southern Nationalism, 1848–1861* (Baton Rouge: Louisiana State University Press, 1953), pp. 151-52.
7. *UTC*, 2:176, 173.
8. Ibid., 2:189-93, 195.
9. Ibid., 2:35, 148.
10. Ibid., 2:198-212.
11. Ibid., 2:256-57.

12. Ibid., 2:263, 259, 260.

13. Severn Duvall, "*Uncle Tom's Cabin*: The Sinister Side of the Patriarchy," in Seymour Gross and John Hardy, eds., *Images of the Negro in American Literature* (Chicago: University of Chicago Press, 1966), p. 180.

14. *UTC*, 2:269.

15. Hildreth, *The Slave*, 2:51-52; *UTC*, 2:89, 1:293.

16. Hildreth, *The White Slave*, pp. 304-5.

17. Theodore R. Hovet, "Christian Revolution: Harriet Beecher Stowe's Response to Slavery and the Civil War," *New England Quarterly* 47 (December 1974): 537-39; *UTC*, 2:201.

18. *UTC*, 2:202-3.

19. Ibid., 2:248. For reviewers who thought Uncle Tom was an old man, see review of *UTC*, *Westminster Review* 58 (1852): 283; A. Woodward, *A Review of Uncle Tom's Cabin; or, An Essay on Slavery* (Cincinnati: Applegate, 1853), p. 81.

20. *UTC*, 2:181-82, 184, 2:246.

21. Ibid., 2:275.

22. Leslie A. Fiedler, *Love and Death in the American Novel* (Cleveland: Criterion Books, World Publishing Co., 1960), p. 263; *UTC*, 2:279-81; Gen. 46:30.

23. *UTC*, 2:282-83.

24. Ibid., 2:307-9.

25. Ibid., 2:233-34.

26. Ibid., 2:285-304.

27. Ibid., 2:304.

28. Ibid., 2:302-3.

29. Ibid., 1:286-87.

30. Ibid., 2:283.

31. Ward, "Afterword," HBS, *Uncle Tom's Cabin*, p. 491.

X. The Reception of Uncle Tom's Cabin in the North

1. *Crusader in Crinoline*, p. 341; Kirkham, *The Building of Uncle Tom's Cabin*, pp. 190-92; *Albany* (N.Y.) *Evening Journal*, 11 January 1853; Van Wyck Brooks, *The Flowering of New England, 1815–1865* (New York: E. P. Dutton & Co., 1936), p. 420; "*Uncle Tom's Cabin* as a Sabbath School Book," *Liberator*, 18 March 1853.

2. "Uncle Tom Epidemic," *Literary World* 11 (4 December 1852): 355; Dana, *The Journal*, 2:487; Ralph Waldo Emerson, "Success," *The Complete Works of Ralph Waldo Emerson*, ed. Edward Waldo Emerson, 12 vols. (Boston: Houghton Mifflin Co., 1903–1904), 7:286.

3. *Crusader in Crinoline*, pp. 269, 273, 277; John P. Jewett, quoted in anonymous article, "*Uncle Tom's Cabin*," *Manhattan* 1 (January 1883): 29-30; Donald Edward Liedel, "The Antislavery Novel, 1836–1861" (Ph.D. diss., University of Michigan, 1961), p. 66; Wagenknecht, *Harriet Beecher Stowe*, p. 242.

4. Emerson, "Success," 7:286; John Greenleaf Whittier to William Lloyd Garrison, May 1852, *The Letters of John Greenleaf Whittier*, ed. John B. Pickard, 3 vols. (Cambridge: Harvard University Press, Belknap Press, 1975), 2:191; Samuel Longfellow, ed., *Life of Henry Wadsworth Longfellow*, 3 vols. (Boston: Ticknor & Co., 1886), 2:222-23, 233.

5. James Russell Lowell, "Mrs. Stowe's New Novel," *New-York Tribune*, 13 June 1859, p. 5; Lowell to HBS, 4 February 1859, quoted in C. E. Stowe, *Life of Harriet Beecher Stowe*, p. 133.

6. William Hickling Prescott, *Papers*, ed. C. Harvey Gardiner (Urbana: University of Illinois Press, 1964), p. 317; Julia Ward Howe, "Harriet Beecher Stowe," *Reader Magazine* 5 (March 1905): 617; Stanley T. Williams, *The Life of Washington Irving*, 2 vols. (New York: Oxford University Press, 1935), 2:393.

7. William Henry Channing, quoted in Octavius Brooks Frothingham, *Memoir*

of *William Henry Channing* (Boston: Houghton Mifflin Co., 1886), p. 259; quoted in HBS, "Introduction," *Uncle Tom's Cabin,* new ed., pp. xvi-xvii.

8. George Templeton Strong, *Diary,* ed. Allan Nevins and Milton Halsey Thomas, 4 vols. (New York: Macmillan Co., 1952), 3:67-68; [Dix], *Transatlantic Tracings,* p. 79.

9. John Greenleaf Whittier, "Little Eva," *Independent* 4 (29 July 1852): 124; *Liberator,* 10 September 1852. For other poems about Eva, see *Liberator,* 6 August 1852, 29 April 1853.

10. [Dix], *Transatlantic Tracings,* p. 78; Wendell Philips, *New York Herald,* 14 May 1853, quoted in Stearns, *Notes on Uncle Tom's Cabin,* p. 213; P. Thorne [pseud. of Mary Prudence Wells Smith], *Jolly Good Times at School* (1877; reprint, Boston: Little, Brown & Co., 1903), pp. 266, 120.

11. William Lloyd Garrison, quoted in *National Era,* 22 July 1847; Garrison, quoted in C. E. Stowe, *Life of Harriet Beecher Stowe,* p. 61.

12. Garrison, review of *UTC, Liberator,* 26 March 1852.

13. Ibid.

14. Henry Clarke Wright, letter published in *Liberator,* 9 July 1852.

15. Review of *UTC, National Anti-Slavery Standard,* 6 May 1852.

16. Lydia Maria Child to Susan (Lyman) Lesley, 29 March [1852], American Philosophical Society, Philadelphia, in Milton Meltzer and Patricia G. Holland; Francine Krasno, ed., *Lydia Maria Child: Selected Letters, 1817–1880* (Amherst: University of Massachusetts Press, 1982), p. 264.

17. Frederick Douglass, quoted in Langston Hughes, "Introductory Remarks and Captions," HBS, *Uncle Tom's Cabin* (New York: Dodd, Mead & Co., 1952), frontispiece; Litwack, *North of Slavery,* p. 246; Foster, *The Rungless Ladder,* pp. 33-34; Douglass, *Life and Times of Frederick Douglass: Written by Himself* (Hartford, Conn.: Park Publishing Co., 1881), p. 293.

18. *The Provincial Freeman,* 22 July 1852, quoted in Benjamin Quarles, *Black Abolitionists* (New York: Oxford University Press, 1969), p. 220; *Thirteenth Annual Report of the American and Foreign Anti-Slavery Society,* 1852, pp. 192-93; Litwack, *North of Slavery,* p. 255.

19. William C. Nell, letter published in *Liberator,* 10 December 1852; William G. Allen, letter published in *Frederick Douglass' Paper,* 20 May 1852, quoted in Yellin, *The Intricate Knot,* p. 139.

20. George T. Downing, letter published in *Frederick Douglass' Paper,* 22 December 1852; William J. Watkins, *Our Rights as Men: An Address Delivered in Boston, before the Legislative Committee on the Militia* (Boston: Benjamin F. Roberts, 1853), p. 8; see also Henry Bibb, "American History Coming to Light," *Voice of the Fugitive* 2 (20 May 1852); C. L. Redmond, quoted in Truman Nelson, ed., *Documents of Upheaval: Selections from William Lloyd Garrison's The Liberator, 1831–1865* (New York: Hill & Wang, 1966), p. 245.

21. Martin R. Delany, letter published in *Frederick Douglass' Paper,* 6 May 1853.

22. Lewis Tappan letter published in *British and Foreign Anti-Slavery Reporter,* 1 January 1853, pp. 7-8, reprinted in Annie Heloise Abel and Frank J. Klingberg, eds., *A Side-Light on Anglo-American Relations, 1839–1858* ([Lancaster, Pa.]: Association for the Study of Negro Life and History, Inc., 1927), p. 309.

23. James G. Birney to HBS, 12 January 1853, *Letters of James Gillespie Birney, 1831–1857,* ed. Dwight L. Dumond, 2 vols. (1938; reprint, Gloucester, Mass.: Peter Smith, 1966), 2:1160-61; Birney, *Examination of the Decision of the Supreme Court of the United States, in the Case of Strader, Gorman and Armstrong vs. Christopher Graham* (Cincinnati: Truman & Spofford, 1852), passim.

24. Elizabeth Hitchcock Jones to Abby Kelley Foster, 4 November 1856, Abby Kelley Foster Papers, American Antiquarian Society, Worcester, Mass., quoted in Alma Lutz, *Crusade for Freedom: Women of the Anti-Slavery Movement* (Boston: Beacon Press, 1968), p. 253; Garrison, quoted in *Boston Daily Advertiser, Boston*

Daily News, Boston Evening Journal, and *Boston Daily Transcript,* 27 September 1872, quoted in Frederick Trautmann, "Harriet Beecher Stowe's Public Readings in New England," *New England Quarterly* 17 (June 1974): 283.

25. Theodore Parker, "Speech of Theodore Parker at the Annual Meeting of the Massachusetts Anti-Slavery Society," *National Anti-Slavery Standard,* 24 February 1853; [Richard Hildreth], "Uncle Tom, the White Slave, Ida May, and the N. Y. Evening Post," *Boston Evening Telegraph,* 13 November 1854.

26. *New York Courier and Inquirer,* quoted in *New York Observer* 30 (23 September 1852): 306; Lewis Tappan, in *British and Foreign Anti-Slavery Reporter,* 1 January 1853, pp. 7-8.

27. Nehemiah Adams, *A South-Side View of Slavery; or, Three Months at the South in 1854* (Boston: T. R. Marvin & B. B. Mussey Co., 1854), p. 201; "A South-Side View of Prostitution; or, Three Months in the Brothels of Boston," *Liberator,* reprinted in *National Anti-Slavery Standard,* 9 December 1854.

28. [Leonard Bacon?], review of *UTC, New Englander* 10 (November 1852): 588-89, 592-95.

29. [R. S. Storrs, Jr.], *Independent* 5 (9 June 1853): 90; U. S. Constitution, Article 4, Section 2.

30. "Uncle Tom Epidemic," p. 357; review of *UTC, Graham's Magazine* 42 (February 1853): 209-15.

31. George Ticknor to Sir Edmund Head, 20 December 1852, in *Life, Letters, and Journals of George Ticknor,* ed. George S. Hillard, 2 vols. (Boston: James R. Osgood & Co., 1876), 2:285; *New York Times,* 1 September 1852.

32. [Charles Briggs?], "Uncle Tomitudes," *Putnam's Monthly* 1 (January 1853): 100-102.

33. *Lincoln* (Maine) *Democrat,* quoted in *Liberator,* 3 September 1852; *Cleveland* (Ohio) *Daily Plain Dealer,* 12 January 1861, quoted in Howard Cecil Perkins, ed., *Northern Editorials on Secession,* 2 vols. (Gloucester, Mass.: Peter Smith, 1964), 1:489.

34. J. G. Randall, *Lincoln the President,* 4 vols. (New York: Dodd, Mead & Co., 1945–1955), 1:234-35.

35. William H. Herndon to Wendell Phillips, 9 March 1857, Crawford Blagden Collection, Houghton Library, Harvard University; Sarah Davis to David Davis, 10 November 1852, Davis Papers, Williams College, quoted in Willard Leroy King, *Lincoln's Manager, David Davis* (Cambridge: Harvard University Press, 1960), p. 99, see also pp. xi, 312; William L. Smith, *Life at the South; or, "Uncle Tom's Cabin" as It Is: Being Narratives, Scenes and Incidents in the Real "Life of the Lowly"* (Buffalo, N. Y.: George H. Derby & Co., 1852).

36. Rufus M. Choate, quoted in *Independent* 4 (26 August 1852): 137; Lurton Dunham Ingersoll, *The Life of Horace Greeley* (1873; reprint, New York: Beekman Publishers, 1974), pp. 292-93; James Ford Rhodes, *The History of the United States from the Compromise of 1850 to the Final Restoration of Home Rule at the South in 1877,* 8 vols. (New York: Harper & Bros., 1892), 1:284-85.

XI. THE REACTION TO UNCLE TOM'S CABIN IN THE SOUTH

1. *Wellsburg* (Va.; now W. Va.) *Herald,* quoted in *National Era* 6 (5 August 1852): 126; *Georgetown* (Ky.) *Herald,* quoted in *National Anti-Slavery Standard,* 4 November 1852; *Jefferson Inquirer* (Jefferson City, Mo.), 23 October 1852.

2. Daniel R. Goodloe to A. M. Gangewer, 8 December 1852, quoted in *Key to UTC,* p. 64. See also HBS to Daniel R. Goodloe, 9 February 1853, in *Publications of the Southern History Association* 2 (1898): 124-27.

3. Editorial in *St. Louis* (Mo.) *Republic,* quoted in *National Anti-Slavery Standard,* 12 May 1853; L. B. Stowe, *Saints, Sinners and Beechers,* pp. 185-86; Clement Eaton, *Freedom of Thought in the Old South* (Durham: Duke University Press, 1940), pp. 252-53.

4. [Dix], *Transatlantic Tracings*, p. 78; Edward Atkinson, in "The Birthday Garden Party to Harriet Beecher Stowe," *Atlantic Monthly Supplement* 50 (August 1882): 10; Lydia Maria Child, *Letters of Lydia Maria Child* (Boston: Houghton Mifflin Co., 1884), pp. 68-70.

5. Charles Holbrook, quoted in D. D. Hall, "A Yankee Tutor in the Old South," *New England Quarterly* 33 (March 1960): 89-90; William R. Taylor, *Cavalier and Yankee: The Old South and American National Character* (New York: Braziller, 1961), p. 313.

6. John Greenleaf Whittier to HBS, 8 October 1852, *Letters of John Greenleaf Whittier*, 2:202; Charles Grandison Parsons, *Inside View of Slavery; or, A Tour among the Planters* (Boston: John P. Jewett & Co., 1855), p. 292; Frederick Law Olmsted, *A Journey in the Back Country* (New York: Mason Bros., 1860), pp. 263-64.

7. [Ebenezer Starnes], *The Slaveholder Abroad; or, Billy Buck's Visit with His Master, to England* (Philadelphia: J. B. Lippincott Co., 1860), p. 21; [John R. Thompson], review of *UTC*, *Southern Literary Messenger* 18 (October 1852): 630.

8. John R. Thompson to George Frederick Holmes, 11 September 1852, George Frederick Holmes Papers, Library of Congress, quoted in Clement Eaton, *The Freedom-of-Thought Struggle in the Old South*, rev. ed. (New York: Harper & Row Torchbook, 1964), pp. 36-37; Virginius Dabney, *Virginia: The New Dominion* (Garden City, N. Y.: Doubleday, 1971), p. 268; [George Frederick Holmes], review of *Key to UTC*, *Southern Literary Messenger* 19 (June 1853): 321-22; [William Gilmore Simms], review of *Key to UTC*, *Southern Quarterly Review* n.s. 7 (July 1853): 226.

9. [Louisa S. McCord], review of *UTC*, *Southern Quarterly Review* 23 (January 1853): 81-82; *New Orleans Crescent*, 5 January 1854, quoted in Avery O. Craven, *The Growth of Southern Nationalism, 1848–1861* (Baton Rouge: Louisiana State University Press, 1953), p. 154.

10. [Holmes], review of *Key to UTC*, pp. 322-32; [David Brown], *The Planter; or, Thirteen Years in the South, By a Northern Man* (Philadelphia: H. Hooker, 1853), pp. 26-27.

11. *New Orleans Picayune*, quoted in *Liberator*, 4 March 1853; Maria J. McIntosh, *The Lofty and the Lowly; or, Good in All and None All-Good*, 2 vols. (New York: D. Appleton & Co., 1853), 2:164; Mary H. Eastman, *Aunt Phillis's Cabin; or, Southern Life as It Is* (Philadelphia: Lippincott, Grambo & Co., 1852), p. 63.

12. William G. Brownlow, *Knoxville* (Tenn.) *Whig and Independent Journal*, 12 February, 19 November 1853, quoted in Craven, *The Growth of Southern Nationalism*, pp. 154-55; Brownlow, *Knoxville* (Tenn.) *Whig*, 5 February 1853, quoted in E. Merton Coulter, *William G. Brownlow: Fighting Parson of the Southern Highlands* (Chapel Hill: University of North Carolina Press, 1937), p. 95.

13. The most extensive treatment of the Bible as a source of justification for slavery is probably that of Rev. Leander Ker, *Slavery Consistent with Christianity, with an Introduction Embracing a Notice of the "Uncle Tom's Cabin" Movement in England*, 3rd ed., rev. and enl. (Weston, Mo.: Finch & O'Gorman, 1853), passim.

14. James A. Waddell, *"Uncle Tom's Cabin" Reviewed; or, American Society Vindicated from Aspersions of Mrs. Harriet Beecher Stowe* (Raleigh, N. C.: Southern Weekly Post, 1852), p. 45; A. Beatty, review of *UTC*, *Western Journal and Civilian* 9 (November 1852): 138.

15. [Holmes], review of *UTC*, *Southern Literary Messenger* 18 (December 1852): 728-29; [McCord], review of *UTC*, pp. 119-20.

16. [Simms], review of *Key to UTC*, p. 251; Stearns, *Notes on Uncle Tom's Cabin*, p. 41.

17. [Thompson], review of *UTC*, p. 638; John Candler, *A Friendly Mission: John Candler's Letters from America, 1853–1854* (Indianapolis: Indiana Historical Society, 1951), p. 76.

18. Woodward, *Review of Uncle Tom's Cabin*, p. 58.

19. [Simms], review of *Key to UTC*, pp. 216-17; Edd Winfield Parks, *William*

Gilmore Simms as Literary Critic (Athens: University of Georgia Press, 1961), pp. 14-15; [Simms], *Southern Quarterly Review* 9 (January 1854): 235-36.

20. [McCord], review of *UTC*, p. 108. Nearly eight years later, Margaret Johnson Erwin, a wealthy southern slaveholder, also ventured the opinion that Stowe had probably been in the South for a very short time. In a private letter, Erwin said, "It took that ignoramus, know-it-all Mrs. Stowe, to really fan the fire. A few years in Cincinnati and a week in Kentucky and she writes a tiresome, inflammatory book. . . . I try to keep an open mind, but when I see mealy-mouthing . . . being taken as Gospel from a silly New Englander—it almost kills me." Erwin may have read the suggestion that Stowe probably had spent little time in the South in McCord's review. Erwin to Samuel Sloan, 1 April 1860, *Like Some Green Laurel: Letters of Margaret Johnson Erwin, 1821–1863*, ed. John Seymour Erwin (Baton Rouge: Louisiana State University Press, 1981), p. 102.

21. [Simms], review of *Key to UTC*, pp. 235, 226.

22. *UTC*, 2:278; Stearns, *Notes on Uncle Tom's Cabin*, pp. 54-55; [Holmes], review of *Key to UTC*, p. 328.

23. Chesnut, *Mary Chesnut's Civil War*, pp. 381, 168.

24. [McCord], review of *UTC*, p. 93; [Thompson], review of *UTC*, p. 633; *UTC*, 1:17-18.

25. Eastman, *Aunt Phillis's Cabin*, p. 266; [Simms], review of *Key to UTC*, p. 230.

26. [McCord], review of *UTC*, p. 101; *UTC*, 2:24, 1:264. The phrase, "the fairest picture of our Southern brother," is used by Stowe with regard to Augustine St. Clare in *Key to UTC*, p. 35. Stearns, *Notes on Uncle Tom's Cabin*, pp. 166-67; "E," letter to *Memphis* (Tenn.) *Daily Eagle and Enquirer*, 21 August 1853, quoted in Margaret A. Browne, "Southern Reactions to *Uncle Tom's Cabin*" (master's thesis, Duke University, 1941), pp. 113-14.

27. [McCord], review of *UTC*, p. 95; [Simms], review of *Key to UTC*, pp. 230-31.

28. Eastman, *Aunt Phillis's Cabin*, p. 270; [McCord], review of *UTC*, p. 97.

29. [McCord], review of *UTC*, pp. 97-98; [Thompson], review of *UTC*, p. 635; Stearns, *Notes on Uncle Tom's Cabin*, p. 167.

30. Chesnut, *Mary Chesnut's Civil War*, pp. 606-7.

31. Margaret Johnson Erwin to Carrie Wilson, December 1850 [?], *Like Some Green Laurel*, p. 58. [The date indicated for the letter is an error; *UTC* had not yet been published.]; Stearns, *Notes on Uncle Tom's Cabin*, pp. 136-39.

32. [McCord], review of *UTC*, p. 96; Beatty, review of *UTC*, p. 135; Chesnut, *Mary Chesnut's Civil War*, pp. 307-8.

33. William J. Grayson, *The Hireling and the Slave, Chicora, and Other Poems* (Charleston, S. C.: McCarter & Co., 1856), p. 41; Eastman, *Aunt Phillis's Cabin*, p. 266; [McCord], review of *UTC*, p. 116; *UTC*, 1:259. It is not clear which bishops of Carthage Stowe was referring to in the novel. Elsewhere she spoke of St. Augustine and Tertullian as if they had some black intermixture. Neither one of these men was a bishop of Carthage, but both of them lived there for a time, Tertullian having been born there. See HBS, "Sojourner Truth, the Libyan Sibyl," *Atlantic Monthly* 11 (April 1863): 480; Edward A. Pollard, *Black Diamonds Gathered in the Darkey Homes of the South* (New York: Pudney & Russell, 1859), pp. 20-21, 34-35.

34. Woodward, *Review of Uncle Tom's Cabin*, pp. 105-6.

35. [Simms], review of *Key to UTC*, pp. 235, 252.

36. A. Beatty, "The Evils of Slavery," *Western Journal and Civilian* 10 (August 1853): 323.

37. [Holmes], review of *UTC*, p. 726; [*McCord*], review of *UTC*, p. 117; [Simms], review of *Key to UTC*, pp. 223, 229; *UTC*, 1:27.

38. [Thompson], review of *UTC*, p. 632. Mary H. Eastman said, "The instance mentioned in 'Uncle Tom's Cabin,' of a young mulatto, George Harris, inventing a

machine is very solitary [*sic*]. The negroes are opposed to innovations." See *Aunt Phillis's Cabin*, p. 272; [McCord], review of *UTC*, p. 112; Beatty, review of *UTC*, p. 137; *UTC*, 1:283.

39. Eastman, *Aunt Phillis's Cabin*, p. 269; [McCord], review of *UTC*, p. 114.

40. Woodward, *Review of Uncle Tom's Cabin*, pp. 113, 60.

41. Stearns, *Notes on Uncle Tom's Cabin*, pp. 44-45; [McCord], review of *UTC*, pp. 117-18; Edmund Ruffin, entry in diary 6 November 1857, *The Diary of Edmund Ruffin*, ed. William Kauffman Scarborough (Baton Rouge: Louisiana State University Press, 1972–), 1:120; [Simms], review of *Key to UTC*, p. 233.

42. [McCord], review of *UTC*, p. 90; Eastman, *Aunt Phillis's Cabin*, pp. 229-30, 279.

43. [James M. Smythe], *Ethel Somers; or, The Fate of the Union. By a Southerner* (Augusta: H. D. Norrell, 1857), p. 162; Woodward, *Review of Uncle Tom's Cabin*, pp. 70-73.

44. Stearns, *Notes on Uncle Tom's Cabin*, pp. 30-31; Exodus 21:20-21; [Simms], review of *Key to UTC*, p. 27.

45. Beatty, "The Evils of Slavery," p. 393.

46. [Edward J. Pringle], *Slavery in the Southern States. By a Carolinian*, 2nd ed. (Cambridge, Mass.: J. Bartlett, 1852), p. 9. For a study of the theory of slavery as a benevolent patriarchy, see Duvall, "The Sinister Side of the Patriarchy," in Gross and Hardy, eds., *Images of the Negro*, pp. 163-80.

47. A. T. Goodloe, letter to editor, *Southern Cultivator* 18 (April 1860): 130-31; Matt. 7:6.

48. [Holmes], review of *UTC*, p. 723; [Simms], review of *Key to UTC*, pp. 253-54; [Smythe], *Ethel Somers*, p. 202. For other reviewers who warned that abolitionism might lead to civil war, see Ker, *Slavery Consistent with Christianity*, p. iii; Beatty, review of *UTC*, p. 138; Waddell, *"Uncle Tom's Cabin" Reviewed*, pp. 39, 50, 65.

49. Francis Lieber, *The Life and Letters of Francis Lieber*, ed. Thomas Sergeant Perry (Boston: James R. Osgood & Co., 1882), p. 257; Frederick Law Olmsted, *The Cotton Kingdom: A Traveller's Observations on Cotton and Slavery in the American Slave States*, 2 vols. (New York: Mason Bros., 1861), 1:354-56; B. P. W., "First Impressions of Slavery," *Independent* 5 (5 May 1853): 69.

50. Parsons, *Inside View of Slavery*, p. 292; L. B. Stowe, *Saints, Sinners and Beechers*, pp. 187-88; HBS, "Simon the Cyrenian," *Independent* 14 (31 July 1862): 1; Theodore Tilton, "Out of Jail. The Black Man Who Was Imprisoned for Reading *Uncle Tom's Cabin*," *Liberator*, 4 July 1862; Florine Thayer McCray, *The Life-Work of the Author of Uncle Tom's Cabin* (New York: Funk & Wagnalls, 1889), p. 106.

51. *Newberry (S. C.) Sentinel*, "Uncle Tom's Cabin or Harriet Beecher Stowe," quoted in *National Era* 7 (7 July 1853): 107. An anonymous southern reviewer apologized in 1854 for having mentioned *Uncle Tom's Cabin* and *The Key to Uncle Tom's Cabin*. "Mrs. Stowe and her books have sunk so low," the writer said, "that it is rather an act of charity to make reference to them before our readers." "Southern Slavery and Its Assailants, by a Georgia Lady," *DeBow's Review* 15 (July-December 1854): 486. An Englishwoman visiting in Savannah, Georgia, in 1858 wrote an article which was published three years later in England. She said, "Answers to Uncle Tom (which book is itself nowhere to be found) deluge the South in newspapers." Barbara Leigh Smith Bodichon, "Slavery in the South," *English Woman's Journal* 8 (December 1861): 261-66. After 1853, there were very few references to *Uncle Tom's Cabin* in southern magazines but there may have been a great many more in newspapers. A thorough search of the newspapers might turn up many comments about it.

XII. ANTI-UNCLE TOM LITERATURE

1. The following is a list of twenty-seven proslavery literary works published from 1852 to 1861. About half of their authors said frankly that they intended their

works to be answers to *Uncle Tom's Cabin*. Perhaps another quarter of them attacked the novel. All of them were probably responding to it to some degree.

Anon., *The Olive-Branch; or, White Oak Farm* (Philadelphia: J. B. Lippincott Co., 1857); [antecedents of author unknown; probably a southerner].

——————, *Yankee Slave-Dealer; or, An Abolitionist down South: A Tale for the Times. By a Texan* (Nashville, Tenn.: The Author, 1860); [southerner].

[David Brown], *The Planter; or, Thirteen Years in the South. By a Northern Man* (Philadelphia: H. Hooker, 1853); [northerner transplanted to the South].

Martha Haines Butt, *Antifanaticism: A Tale of the South* (Philadelphia: Lippincott, Grambo & Co., 1853); [southerner].

Lucien B. Chase, *English Serfdom and American Slavery; or, Ourselves—as Others See Us* (New York: H. Long & Bro., 1854); [northerner transplanted to the South].

Mrs. V. G. Cowdin, *Ellen; or, The Fanatic's Daughter* (Mobile: S. H. Goetzel & Co., 1860); [southerner].

Robert Criswell, *"Uncle Tom's Cabin" Contrasted with Buckingham Hall, the Planter's Home; or, A Fair View of the Slavery Question* (New York: D. Fanshaw, 1852); [northerner].

Mary H. Eastman, *Aunt Phillis's Cabin; or, Southern Life as It Is* (Philadelphia: Lippincott, Grambo & Co., 1852); [southerner].

[Matthew Estes], *Tit for Tat: A Novel by a Lady of New Orleans* (New York: Garret & Co., 1856); [southerner].

Mrs. G. M. Flanders, *The Ebony Idol, by a Lady of New England* (New York: Appleton & Co., 1860); [northerner].

William J. Grayson, *The Hireling and the Slave, Chicora and Other Poems* (Charleston, S. C.: McCarter & Co., 1856); [southerner].

Sarah Josepha Hale, *Liberia; or, Mr. Peyton's Experiments* (New York: Harper & Bros., 1853); [northerner].

Baynard R. Hall. *Frank Freeman's Barber Shop: A Tale* (New York: C. Scribner, 1852); [northerner].

Caroline Lee Hentz, *The Planter's Northern Bride: A Novel*, 2 vols. (Philadelphia: A. Hart, 1854); [northerner transplanted to the South].

Mary E. Herndon, *Louise Elton; or, Things Seen and Heard* (Philadelphia: Lippincott, Grambo & Co., 1853); [southerner].

Maria J. McIntosh, *The Lofty and the Lowly; or, Good in All and None All-Good*, 2 vols. (New York: D. Appleton & Co., 1853); [southerner].

[Theodore Dehone Mathews], *Old Toney and His Master; or, The Abolitionist and the Land-Pirate, Founded on Facts: A Tale of 1824–1827. By Desmos* [pseud.] (Nashville, Tenn.: Southwestern Publishing House, 1861); [southerner].

John W. Page, *Uncle Robin in his Cabin in Virginia, and Tom without One in Boston* (Richmond, Va.: J. W. Randolph, 1853); [southerner].

J. Thornton Randolph [pseud. of Charles Jacobs Peterson], *The Cabin and Parlor; or, Slaves and Masters* (Philadelphia: T. B. Peterson, 1852); [northerner].

[Caroline E. Rush], *The North and South; or, Slavery and Its Contrasts* (Philadelphia: Crissy & Markley, 1852); [northerner].

Mrs. Henry R. Schoolcraft, *The Black Gauntlet: A Tale of Plantation Life in South Carolina* (Philadelphia: J. B. Lippincott Co., 1860); [southerner].

William Gilmore Simms, *Woodcraft or Hawks about the Dovecote: A Story of the South at the Close of the Revolution*, rev. ed. (New York: J. S. Redfield, 1854); [southerner].

William L. G. Smith, *Life at the South; or, "Uncle Tom's Cabin" as It Is: Being Narratives, Scenes, and Incidents in the Real "Life of the Lowly."* (Buffalo: George H. Darby & Co., 1852); [northerner].

[James M. Smythe], *Ethel Somers; or, The Fate of the Union. By a Southerner* (Augusta: H. D. Norrell, 1857); [southerner].

[Ebenezer Starnes], *The Slaveholder Abroad; or, Billy Buck's Visit with His Master, to England* (Philadelphia: J. B. Lippincott Co., 1860); [southerner].

Thomas B. Thorpe, *The Master's House; or, Scenes Descriptive of Southern Life.* 3rd ed. (New York: J. C. Derby, 1855); [northerner transplanted to the South].

Vidi [pseud.], *Mr. Frank: the Underground Mail-Agent* (Philadelphia: Lippin-cott, Grambo & Co., 1853); [region unknown].
I am indebted to Mr. Barrie Hayne for the listing of most of these works, for his research into the sectional antecedents of their authors, and for his opinions in the essay, "Yankee in the Patriarchy: T. B. Thorpe's Reply to *Uncle Tom's Cabin,*" *American Quarterly* 20 (1968): 180-95.

2. [Holmes], review of *UTC, Southern Literary Messenger* 18 (1852): 727.

3. McIntosh, *The Lofty and the Lowly,* 1:198-99; Caroline Lee Hentz, *Marcus Warland; or, The Long Moss Spring: A Tale of the South* (Philadelphia: T. B. Peter-son & Bros., 1852), p. 59.

4. Eastman, *Aunt Phillis's Cabin,* pp. 115-16; McIntosh, *The Lofty and the Lowly,* 2:162; Smith, *Life at the South,* p. 66.

5. [Rush], *The North and South,* pp. 224-25.

6. Hall, *Frank Freeman's Barber Shop,* pp. 97-100; Smith, *Life at the South,* p. 261; anon., *The Yankee Slave-Dealer,* p. 30.

7. Schoolcraft, *The Black Gauntlet,* pp. 218-19, 61; [Starnes], *The Slaveholder Abroad,* p. 67.

8. [Smythe], *Ethel Somers,* p. 199; Hall, *Frank Freeman's Barber Shop,* p. 78; Eastman, *Aunt Phillis's Cabin,* pp. 42-44.

9. Criswell, *"Uncle Tom's Cabin" Contrasted with Buckingham Hall,* pp. 131-32.

10. Eastman, *Aunt Phillis's Cabin,* pp. 135, 218; Hall, *Frank Freeman's Barber Shop,* pp. 395-96.

11. Schoolcraft, *The Black Gauntlet,* pp. 113-15; Anthony Trollope, *North America* (New York: Harper & Bros., 1862), p. 343.

12. Hall, *Frank Freeman's Barber Shop,* pp. 80-82.

13. Ibid.

14. Thorpe, *The Master's House,* passim; Hayne, "Yankee in the Patriarchy," pp. 180-95; Milton Rickels, *Thomas Bangs Thorpe: Humorist of the Old Southwest* (Baton Rouge: Louisiana State University Press, 1962), passim.

15. Thorpe, *The Master's House,* p. 152.

16. Ibid., pp. 286-87.

17. Ibid., p. 311.

18. Ibid., pp. 315-16.

19. Ibid., p. 103.

20. Ibid., pp. 104-5.

21. Ibid., pp. 346-91; Rickels, *Thomas Bangs Thorpe,* pp. 214-19.

22. Stephen A. Hirsch, "Uncle Tom's Companions: The Literary and Popular Reaction to *Uncle Tom's Cabin*" (Ph.D. diss., State University of New York at Albany, 1975), p. 21; Butt, *Antifanaticism,* p. 16.

23. [Mathews], *Old Toney and His Master,* pp. 27, 52.

24. Ibid., pp. 94, 48.

25. Randolph, *The Cabin and Parlor,* pp. 78-79; [Mathews], *Old Toney and His Master,* p. 54.

26. Grayson, *The Hireling and the Slave,* pp. 50-51.

27. William Gilmore Simms to James H. Hammond, 15 December 1852, *Letters,* ed. Mary C. Simms Oliphant, Alfred Taylor Odell, and T. C. Duncan Eaves, 6 vols. (Columbia: University of South Carolina Press, 1952-1982), 3:222-23; see Joseph V. Ridgely, "*Woodcraft*: Simms's First Answer to *Uncle Tom's Cabin,*" *American Literature* 31 (January 1960): 421-33.

28. Simms, *Woodcraft,* passim.

29. Ibid., pp. 51, 178; Matt. 6:34.

30. Simms, *Woodcraft,* p. 325.

31. Eastman, *Aunt Phillis's Cabin,* pp. 33-34; Page, *Uncle Robin in his Cabin in Virginia,* p. 136; Butt, *Antifanaticism,* p. 85.

32. Eastman, *Aunt Phillis's Cabin*, pp. 102-3; Gen. 16:1-6; [Smythe], *Ethel Somers*, p. 118.

33. Randolph, *The Cabin and Parlor*, pp. 27, 110.

34. Ibid., pp. 120-23; Grayson, *The Hireling and the Slave*, p. 69; [Smythe], *Ethel Somers*, p. 280.

35. Anon., *The Olive-Branch*, p. 30; Eastman, *Aunt Phillis's Cabin*, p. 65; Smith, *Life at the South*, pp. 379, 518.

36. Eastman, *Aunt Phillis's Cabin*, pp. 232-33; Pollard, *Black Diamonds*, pp. 56-57.

37. Hall, *Frank Freeman's Barber Shop*, pp. 174-81; [Mathews], *Old Toney and His Master*, p. 383.

38. Hall, *Frank Freeman's Barber Shop*, pp. 281-82; Criswell, *"Uncle Tom's Cabin" Contrasted with Buckingham Hall*, pp. 60-62, 143-45.

39. Cowdin, *Ellen*, p. 5; Smith, *Life at the South*, p. 270; Vidi [pseud.], *Mr. Frank, the Underground Mail-Agent*, p. 28.

40. Vidi [pseud.], *Mr. Frank, the Underground Mail-Agent*, pp. 38, 28.

41. Cowdin, *Ellen*, p. 82; Hentz, *The Planter's Northern Bride*, 1:140-42.

42. Flanders, *The Ebony Idol*, pp. 75, 139-62, 282; see Jeannette Reid Tandy, "Pro-Slavery Propaganda in American Fiction of the Fifties," *South Atlantic Quarterly* 21 (April 1922): 174.

43. [Starnes], *The Slaveholder Abroad*, p. 358; [Mathews], *Old Toney and His Master*, p. 93.

44. Hale, *Liberia*, passim.

45. Ibid., pp. 58-67.

46. Ibid., pp. 114-78.

47. Hall, *Frank Freeman's Barber Shop*, p. 236; Page, *Uncle Robin in His Cabin in Virginia*, p. 217; Randolph, *The Cabin and Parlor*, pp. 259-60; Vidi [pseud.], *Mr. Frank, the Underground Mail-Agent*, pp. 234-35.

48. McIntosh, *The Lofty and the Lowly*, 2:318; Eastman, *Aunt Phillis's Cabin*, p. 277; Hall, *Frank Freeman's Barber Shop*, p. 76; [Rush], *The North and South*, p. 24; Vidi [pseud.], *Mr. Frank, the Underground Mail-Agent*, pp. 162-63.

49. Hentz, *The Planter's Northern Bride*, 1:237-39.

XIII. THE RECEPTION ABROAD OF UNCLE TOM'S CABIN

1. Review of *Key to UTC*, *Eclectic Review* 97 (1853): 601; Mary Howitt, quoted in "Opinions of the Press," *Uncle Tom's Cabin* (London: John Cassell, 1852), p. xxiii; review of *UTC*, *Prospective Review* 8 (1852): 490; review of *Dred*, *Eclectic Review* 104 (1856): 323.

2. Lord Shaftesbury, quoted in Georgina Battiscomb, *Shaftesbury: A Biography of the Seventh Earl, 1801–1885* (London: Constable, 1974), p. 328; Earl of Carlisle, "Introduction," HBS, *Uncle Tom's Cabin* (London: George Routledge & Co., 1852), p. iv; W. E. Gladstone, quoted in Richard Shannon, *Gladstone*, vol. 1 (London: Hamish Hamilton, 1982), p. 255.

3. [Senior], *American Slavery*, pp. 38-39.

4. Ibid., p. 34; *UTC*, 1:86.

5. [Senior], *American Slavery*, p. 37.

6. Ibid., p. 5.

7. Ibid., p. 32.

8. Ibid. One British reviewer said that prior to the appearance of *Uncle Tom's Cabin*, Englishmen had thought of blacks almost exclusively as subjects for comedy. See review of *UTC*, *Prospective Review*, p. 494; *UTC*, 1:70-71.

9. Review of *UTC*, *Prospective Review*, p. 494.

10. *UTC*, 2:21, 25. For British objections to the comparison of American slaves to British laborers, see review of *UTC*, *Illustrated London News*, 2 October 1852; [Arthur Helps], review of *UTC*, *Fraser's Magazine* 46 (August 1852): 238; review

of *UTC, Englishman's Magazine* 1 (September-November 1852): 124-25; review of *UTC, Free Church Magazine* 1 (November 1852): 501.

11. HBS, "Preface," *Uncle Tom's Cabin; or, Life among the Lowly* (London: T. Bosworth, 1852), p. vii-ix; Charlotte Elizabeth (pseud. of Charlotte Elizabeth [Browne] Tonna, 1790–1846).

12. Carlisle, "Preface," *Uncle Tom's Cabin*, pp. iv-v.

13. Review of *UTC, North British Review* 18 (November 1852): 255; review of *UTC, Prospective Review*, p. 500.

14. [Senior], *American Slavery*, p. 47; William Makepeace Thackeray to Mrs. Carmichael-Smith, 13 February 1853, *The Letters and Private Papers of William Makepeace Thackeray*, ed. Gordon N. Ray, 4 vols. (Cambridge: Harvard University Press, 1945–1946), 3:199-200.

15. [McCord], review of *UTC*, p. 95; review of *UTC, Dublin University Magazine* 40 (November 1852): 613; review of *UTC, Blackwood's Edinburgh Magazine* 74 (October 1853): 407, 409; *UTC*, 2:7-8.

16. Charles Kingsley to HBS, 12 August 1852, Folder 242, Beecher-Stowe Collection, Schlesinger Library, Harvard University, printed in HBS, "Introduction," *Uncle Tom's Cabin*, new ed., p. xxv.

17. George Sand, review of *UTC, La Presse* (Paris), 17 December 1852, reprinted in HBS, "Introduction," *Uncle Tom's Cabin*, new ed., pp. xxxi-xxxii; reprinted in French in Edith E. Lucas, *La Littérature Anti-Esclavagiste au Dix-Neuvième Siècle. Étude sur Madame Beecher Stowe et son Influence en France* (Paris: E. de Boccard, 1930), pp. 109, 113, 128-29.

18. Gustave Flaubert to Louise Colet, 22 November 1852 and 9 December 1852, *Correspondance*, Nouvelle Édition Augmente, 9 vols. (Paris: L. Conard, 1926–1933), 3:52, 60-62; partially translated in Jean Seznec, "Notes on Flaubert and the United States," *American Society Legion of Honor Magazine* 17 (Summer 1947): 394-95; see also *The Letters of Gustave Flaubert: 1830–1857*, ed. Francis Steegmuller (Cambridge: Harvard University Press, Belknap Press, 1980), pp. 172-73.

19. Thomas Carlyle to Ralph Waldo Emerson, 13 May 1853, *The Correspondence of Emerson and Carlyle*, ed. Joseph Slater (New York: Columbia University Press, 1964), p. 489; Carlyle to his sister Jean, 19 January 1853, pp. 489-90. For the proslavery ideas of Carlyle, see his "The Nigger Question" and "Shooting Niagara: and After?" *The Works of Thomas Carlyle*, 30 vols. (New York: Peter Fenelon Collier, 1897): 16:461-94, 589-633.

20. Matthew Arnold to Arthur Hugh Clough, 21 March 1853, *The Letters of Matthew Arnold to Arthur Hugh Clough*, ed. Howard Foster Lowry (New York: Oxford University Press, Humphrey Milford, 1932), p. 133; Clough to Miss Smith, 22 February [1853], Clough, *Correspondence*, ed. Frederick L. Mulhauser (Oxford: Oxford University Press, Clarendon Press, 1957), pp. 382-83; Clough to James Russell Lowell, 11 September [1856], p. 519.

21. Review of *UTC*, (London) *Times*, 3 September 1852, p. 5.

22. William Makepeace Thackeray to Mrs. Carmichael-Smith, 13 February 1853, Thackeray, *Letters and Private Papers*, 3:198-99; review of HBS, *Sunny Memories of Foreign Lands, Westminster Review* 62 (October 1854): 617.

23. Charles Dickens to HBS, 17 July 1852, quoted partially in HBS, "Introduction," *Uncle Tom's Cabin*, new ed., pp. xx-xxi.

24. [Charles Dickens and Henry Morley], "North American Slavery," *Household Words, A Weekly Journal* 6 (18 September 1852): 1-4; *UTC*, 1:236, 259-60.

25. [Dickens and Morley], "North American Slavery," pp. 5-6.

26. Ibid.

27. Lord Denman to *London Standard*, 27 September 1852, [4] October 1852. This and six other letters to this newspaper on the subject were published as a pamphlet, *Uncle Tom's Cabin, Bleak House, Slavery and Slave Trade. Seven Articles by Lord Denman* (London: Longman, Brown, Green & Longmans, 1853), pp. 27-29. For an excellent discussion of the subject, see Harry Stone, "Charles Dickens and

Harriet Beecher Stowe," *Nineteenth-Century Fiction* 12 (December 1957): 191; Sir Joseph Arnould, *Life of Thomas, First Lord Denman*, 2 vols. (Boston: Estes & Lauriat, 1874), 2:264.

28. Dickens to Mrs. Margaret Cropper (The Hon. Mrs. Edward Cropper), 20 December 1852. MS letter in Free Library of Philadelphia, quoted in Stone, "Charles Dickens and Harriet Beecher Stowe," pp. 195-96.

29. Ibid. It is not clear whom Dickens meant by "the great man of our people."

30. Dickens to the Duke of Devonshire, 29 October 1852, in *The Nonesuch Dickens*, 12:425, Dickens to the Hon. Mrs. Richard Watson, 22 November 1852, 12:430-31; Grace Greenwood [pseud. of Sara Jane Clark], undated clipping in the Massachusetts Historical Society from the *New York Tribune*, quoted in Stone, "Charles Dickens and Harriet Beecher Stowe," p. 189. Dickens is probably referring to Thomas John Didben's *Montrose; or, Children of the Mist.*

31. The petition with its more than 500,000 signatures is now in the Stowe-Day Foundation Library, Hartford, Conn.; quoted in *Crusader in Crinoline*, pp. 341-43.

32. HBS to Eliza Lee Cabot Follen (Mrs. Charles T. Follen), 16 February 1853, quoted in C. E. Stowe, *Life of Harriet Beecher Stowe*, pp. 197-98; George Eliot to Mr. and Mrs. Charles Bray, 12 March 1853, MS letter in Beinecke Rare Book and Manuscript Library, Yale University, printed in *The George Eliot Letters*, ed. Gordon S. Haight, 9 vols. (New Haven: Yale University Press, 1954–1978), 2:92.

33. *Crusader in Crinoline*, pp. 342-86, 420-23.

34. George Mifflin Dallas to William L. Marcy, 7 November 1856, Marcy Papers, Library of Congress, quoted in John M. Belohlavek, *George Mifflin Dallas: Jacksonian Patrician* (University Park: Pennsylvania State University Press, 1977), p. 174; *Richmond* (Va.) *Examiner*, 29 April 1853, quoted in Hermann Eduard von Holst, *The Constitutional and Political History of the United States*, 8 vols. (Chicago: Callaghan & Co., 1881–1892), 4:243; *New York Herald*, quoted in *Independent* 5 (5 May 1853): 69-70. An editorial in the *New York Times* said, "It is feared that in their eagerness to hold up American Slavery to the detestation of English laborers, they [British admirers of *Uncle Tom's Cabin*] may unwittingly arouse a deep dissatisfaction with their own condition." 18 September 1852, p. 1. For the banning of *Uncle Tom's Cabin* in the papal states, see *New York Herald*, 31 May 1853 and *American Almanac*, 1854, p. 348. The novel was never listed in the Catholic index of forbidden books.

35. Quoted in L. B. Stowe, *Saints, Sinners and Beechers*, p. 196.

36. [Senior], *American Slavery*, pp. 26, 65.

37. Ibid., pp. 67-68.

XIV. Uncle Tom's Cabin as a Play in the 1850s

1. "Copyright Provisions," *United States Statutes at Large*, vol. 11 (18 August 1856), pp. 138-39; Fred Lewis Pattee, *The Feminine Fifties* (New York: D. Appleton-Century Co., 1940), p. 136.

2. Barbara M. Cross, *Horace Bushnell: Minister to a Changing America* (Chicago: University of Chicago Press, 1958), p. 35.

3. Quoted in Harry Birdoff, *The World's Greatest Hit: Uncle Tom's Cabin* (New York: S. F. Vanni, 1947), pp. 23-24.

4. HBS, *The Christian Slave: A Drama Founded on a Portion of "Uncle Tom's Cabin." Dramatized by Harriet Beecher Stowe, Expressly for the Readings of Mrs. Mary E. Webb* (Boston: Phillips, Sampson & Co., 1855). In 1873, Stowe would say that many church members had come to realize that going to the theater might be an "innocent amusement." See "A Bird's-Eye View of the West," *Christian Union* 8 (12 November 1873): 387.

5. Edward G. Fletcher, "Illustrations for Uncle Tom," *Texas Quarterly* 1 (Spring 1958): 167-68; Wagenknecht, *Harriet Beecher Stowe*, pp. 132, 135-36, 235-36.

6. For information on the changes made by George L. Aiken in adapting *Uncle Tom's Cabin* from a novel to a play, I am indebted to David Grimsted, "Uncle Tom from Page to Stage: Limitations of Nineteenth-Century Drama," *Quarterly Journal of Speech* 56 (October 1970): 235-44; see also, Richard Moody, *America Takes the Stage: Romanticism in American Drama* (Bloomington: Indiana University Press, 1955), p. 60; Robert C. Toll, *Blacking Up: The Minstrel Show in Nineteenth-Century America* (New York: Oxford University Press, 1974), pp. 28-29.

7. Edgar W. Ames, "The First Presentation of *Uncle Tom's Cabin* at Troy Museum, Troy, New York, Sept. 27, 1852," *Americana* 6 (November 1911): 1045-52; *World's Greatest Hit*, pp. 44-51; Grimsted, "Uncle Tom from Page to Stage," pp. 235-36; George C. Odell, *Annals of the New York Stage* (New York: Columbia University Press, 1927–), 6:310.

8. George L. Aiken, *Uncle Tom's Cabin or Life Among the Lowly: A Domestic Drama in Six Acts* (New York: Dick and Fitzgerald, Publishers, n.d.), pp. 7, 32, 43, 17-20, 35. This undated edition has the printed note on the inside cover, "The text of this play, is correctly reprinted from the original authorized acting edition, without changes." It cannot be based wholly upon the Aiken version of the play as it was originally presented. There is a satirical section in this version directed at the rival production of *Uncle Tom's Cabin* staged by P. T. Barnum. The Barnum production did not begin until November 7, 1853—a year later than the G. C. Howard production in Troy, New York, the one for which Aiken wrote the script. Thus, this edition must have come at least a year after the first presentation of the Aiken version and perhaps was printed several years later. The likelihood is, however, that this is the first printed edition of the Aiken version of the play. *UTC*, 1:164, 238, 257, 285, 2:126.

9. Aiken, *A Domestic Drama*, p. 44; *UTC*, 2:127; Frederickson, *The Black Image in the White Mind*, pp. 111-12.

10. *UTC*, 1:238, 256-57; Aiken, *A Domestic Drama*, pp. 17-19.

11. *UTC*, 1:309, 2:304.

12. Aiken, *A Domestic Drama*, pp. 45, 50, 58.

13. *New York Daily Times*, 27 July 1853, p. 1. Mrs. Howard played Topsy in Uncle Tom shows for thirty-five years, retiring in 1888; see *World's Greatest Hit*, pp. 42-43.

14. Quoted in McCray, *The Life-Work*, p. 122; Elizabeth Stuart Phelps Ward, *Chapters from a Life* (Boston: Houghton Mifflin Co., 1896), p. 133.

15. *UTC*, 1:55-60, 118-22, 245-55, 263-66, 303-6, 2:6-25.

16. Aiken, *A Domestic Drama*, pp. 17, 48-50; Grimsted, "Uncle Tom from Page to Stage," pp. 239-40; John Daniel Collins, "American Drama in Anti-Slavery Agitation, 1792–1861" (Ph.D. diss., State University of Iowa, 1963), pp. 320-21.

17. *UTC*, 1:93-94; Aiken, *A Domestic Drama*, pp. 15-16; *World's Greatest Hit*, pp. 306-28.

18. Aiken, *A Domestic Drama*, p. 68; *UTC*, 2:283.

19. *UTC*, 2:279-81; Aiken, *A Domestic Drama*, p. 68.

20. *UTC*, 2:299-303; Aiken, *A Domestic Drama*, p. 68; HBS, *The Christian Slave*, pp. 65-67.

21. *Troy* (N.Y.) *Budget*, 19 October 1852; *Troy* (N.Y.) *Daily Times*, 28 September 1852, quoted in *World's Greatest Hit*, pp. 51-53; Fletcher, "Illustrations for Uncle Tom," p. 169.

22. *World's Greatest Hit*, pp. 60-63, 69-70; "Famous First Nights," *Theatre Magazine* 50 (August 1929): 65.

23. *World's Greatest Hit*, pp. 75-76; Adolphus M. Hart, *Uncle Tom in Paris; or, Views of Slavery Outside the Cabin, Together with Washington's Views of Slavery* (Baltimore: Taylor & Co., 1854), pp. 5-6; *New York Atlas*, 16 October 1853, quoted in Bernard Hewitt, *Theatre U.S.A.: 1665 to 1957* (New York: McGraw-Hill Book Co., 1959), pp. 174-75.

24. *New York Tribune,* quoted in *National Anti-Slavery Standard,* 20 August 1853.

25. *World's Greatest Hit,* pp. 70-71. The cartoon from *Yankee Notions* is reproduced on p. 71; *National Anti-Slavery Standard,* 20 August 1853.

26. "'Uncle Tom' on the Stage," *Liberator,* 8 September 1853; Garrison, *Letters,* 4:251; Grimsted, "Uncle Tom from Page to Stage," p. 241; Theodore Parker was speaking of another dramatic adaptation of *Uncle Tom's Cabin,* probably one which he saw in Boston; see *World's Greatest Hit,* pp. 110-11.

27. Henry James, *A Small Boy and Others* (New York: C. Scribner's Sons, 1913), pp. 158-63.

28. *New York Herald,* 3 November 1852, cited in Montrose J. Moses and John Mason Brown, eds., *The American Theatre as Seen by Its Critics: 1752–1934* (New York: W. W. Norton & Co., 1934), pp. 72-75. Charles Taylor wrote this adaptation of the novel for the stage but apparently it was never printed; see "Famous First Nights," p. 65.

29. *New Orleans Weekly Picayune,* 30 August 1852.

30. *World's Greatest Hit,* pp. 86-91.

31. Ibid., pp. 88-89.

32. Ibid., p. 87.

33. *New York Tribune,* 12 November 1852, p. 7. For a similar castigation, see *Liberator,* 16 December 1853; Aiken, *A Domestic Drama,* p. 52.

34. *New Orleans Daily Delta,* 29 January 1854, quoted in Hirsch, "Uncle Tom's Companions," p. 369; Toll, *Blacking Up,* p. 93.

35. *World's Greatest Hit,* p. 142; "Interview with Sam Sanford," *Boston Globe,* 28 October 1882, clipping, Boston Public Library, cited in Toll, *Blacking Up,* pp. 94-95; Alexander Saxton, "Blackface Minstrelsy and Jacksonian Ideology," *American Quarterly* 27 (March 1975): 19-20.

36. John E. Owens's letter quoted in Cordelia Howard Macdonald, "Memoirs of the Original Little Eva," *Educational Theatre Journal,* 8 (December 1956): 274; *World's Greatest Hit,* pp. 112, 141-42.

37. *World's Greatest Hit,* pp. 113-14.

38. *UTC,* 1:49, 2:140; *New York Daily Times,* 27 July 1853.

39. *World's Greatest Hit,* pp. 41-42. The reviewer in the *National Anti-Slavery Standard* thought that the G. C. Howard troupe was making a mistake in not recruiting blacks to play the parts of black characters in the play. "We hope to live to see colored actors in this great drama personated," he said, "not by white men with faces besmeared with lampblack, but by real negroes, mingling on terms of equality with white associates. Not until then will the full power of the drama be realized." See *National Anti-Slavery Standard,* 20 August 1853.

40. *New York Atlas,* 16 October 1853, quoted in Barnard Hewitt, *Theatre U.S.A.,* pp. 175-76. Germon himself went on to play Uncle Tom, however, for the remaining years of his acting career. See *World's Greatest Hit,* pp. 41-42.

41. For reviewers who saw Uncle Tom as an old man, see review of *UTC, Westminster Review* 58 (1852): 283; Woodward, *Review of Uncle Tom's Cabin,* p. 81; [Simms], review of *Key to UTC,* p. 252. For an account of the portrayal of elderly blacks in minstrel shows, see Toll, *Blacking Up,* pp. 77-80. A reproduction of the photograph of David Belasco in the role of Uncle Tom is in *World's Greatest Hit,* p. [222]; Alex Haley, "In Uncle Tom Are Our Guilt and Hope," *New York Times Magazine,* 1 March 1964, p. 23.

42. *New Orleans Daily Delta,* 16 and 17 February 1854, quoted in Joseph P. Roppolo, "Uncle Tom in New Orleans: Three Lost Plays," *New England Quarterly* 27 (June 1954): 220.

43. Maria Ward Brown, *The Life of Dan Rice* (Long Beach, N. J.: privately published, 1901), p. 438; *New Orleans Daily Picayune,* 31 March, 1 April, 2 April 1854 (The comment was made in all three issues), quoted in Roppolo, "Uncle Tom

in New Orleans," p. 222; *Charleston* (S. C.) *Standard*, quoted in *National Anti-Slavery Standard*, 16 November 1853; *World's Greatest Hit*, p. 139.

44. *World's Greatest Hit*, pp. 144-65; Mark Lemon and Tom Taylor, *Slave Life; or, Uncle Tom's Cabin: A Drama in Three Acts* (London: Webster & Co., [1852?]), pp. 12, 61, 63; Frank S. Arnett, "Fifty Years of Uncle Tom," *Munsey's Magazine* 27 (September 1902): 897-903.

45. Edmond Texier et L. de Wailly, *L'Oncle Tom: Drame en Cina Actes et Neuf Tableaux* (Paris: Michel Lévy, Frères, 1853); Philippe François Pinel Dumanoir et A. P. D'Ennery, *La Case de l'Oncle Tom: Drame en Huit Actes* (Paris: Michel Lévy, Frères, 1853).

XV. STOWE AND ANTISLAVERY: 1853–1856

1. *Key to UTC*, p. [5].

2. Ibid., pp. [5]-46; Daniel B. Corley, *A Visit to Uncle Tom's Cabin* (Chicago: Laird & Lee, 1892), p. 3.

3. [Theodore Weld], *American Slavery as It Is: Testimony of a Thousand Witnesses* (New York: American Anti-Slavery Society, 1839). HBS is said to have told Angelina Grimké Weld that she slept with this book under her pillow while she was writing *Uncle Tom's Cabin*. Its influence on the novel is not readily apparent, but it did strongly influence *A Key to Uncle Tom's Cabin*. Benjamin P. Thomas says that *A Key to UTC* contains twenty-one quotations or references to *American Slavery as It Is*. See Thomas, *Theodore Weld: Crusader for Freedom* (New Brunswick: Rutgers University Press, 1959), pp. 222-23; Kenneth S. Lynn, "Introduction," HBS, *Uncle Tom's Cabin* (Cambridge: Harvard University Press, Belknap Press, 1962), p. xvii.

4. *Key to UTC*, pp. 133-43.

5. *Key to UTC*, p. 100; *Charleston* (Va.; now W. Va.) *Free Press*, quoted in *Alexandria* (Va.) *Gazette*, 23 October 1852.

6. [Holmes], review of *Key to UTC*, pp. 327-38; William R. Manierre, "A Southern Response to Mrs. Stowe: Two Letters of John R. Thompson," *Virginia Magazine of History and Biography* 69 (January 1961): 91-92.

7. *Key to UTC*, p. 92. For the charge that Stowe had shown ignorance of the laws of Louisiana in having Cassy's master sell her daughter away from her even though the daughter was only nine years old, see [Thompson], review of *UTC*, p. 638; *New York Courier and Enquirer*, quoted in "Slavery and Its Abuses—Mrs. Stowe and the N. York Courier and Enquirer," *National Era* 6 (21 October 1852): 170.

8. Said one northern reviewer, "[F]or Heaven's sake, Mrs. Stowe! wife of one clergyman, daughter of another, and sister to half a dozen, respect the cloud of black cloth with which you are surrounded," review of *UTC*, *Literary World* 10 (24 April 1852): 292. For other attacks on Stowe's alleged unfairness to clergymen, see *New York Observer*, quoted in review of *UTC*, *Independent* 5 (9 June 1853): 90; [Holmes], review of *UTC*, p. 731; Rev. Mr. George W. Bethune to John Brydon, July 1853, quoted in Abraham Rynier Van Dest, *Memoir of Rev. George W. Bethune, D.D.* (New York: Sheldon & Co., 1867), p. 290.

9. *Key to UTC*, p. 38.

10. Samuel Brooke, *The Slave-Holder's Religion* (Cincinnati: Sparkhawk & Lytle, 1845), p. 28; Rev. Mr. William Meade (1789–1862) was the Protestant Episcopal Bishop of Virginia; *Key to UTC*, pp. 249, 199.

11. Souther *v.* Commonwealth, 48 Va. (7 Gratt.) 338 (1851); *Key to UTC*, p. 81; Acts 28:5. Rev. E. J. Stearns was quick to seize upon Stowe's momentary departure from a belief in the primacy of law. Mrs. Stowe, he said, "would not have allowed . . .[Souther] the benefit of a trial at all. . . . Now what is this but the very spirit of *lynch law* against which Mrs. Stowe is, elsewhere so virtuously indignant, when the abolitionists are the victims! And this is from one of the softer sex!" Stearns, *Notes on Uncle Tom's Cabin*, pp. 194-95.

12. *Key to UTC,* pp. 254, 252.

13. John L. Thomas, a modern scholar, paraphrases the southern proslavery response to the charges of the abolitionists. Proslavery thinkers did little to refute specific arguments. Charges against slavery were conceived by them to be "not so much untrue as utterly unreal, a tissue of moral absolutes woven with diabolical cleverness into successive syllogisms to prove that any institution not perfect ought to be destroyed. Mrs. Stowe's indictment [proslavery writers thought] struck at the heart of all community." See Thomas, "Antislavery and Utopia," in Martin Duberman, ed., *The Antislavery Vanguard: New Essays on the Abolitionists* (Princeton: Princeton University Press, 1965), p. 242.

14. Review of *Key to UTC, DeBow's Review* 15 (1853): 496; Stearns, *Notes on Uncle Tom's Cabin,* pp. 30-35, 203-4. For other defenses of southern slave codes, see review of *UTC, United States Review* 32 (April 1853): 313-14; Woodward, *Review of Uncle Tom's Cabin,* pp. 70-71; [Holmes], review of *Key to UTC,* pp. 214-15; A. Beatty, review of *Key to UTC, Western Journal and Civilian* 10 (September 1853): 38.

15. HBS to Wendell Phillips, 23 February 1853, Crawford Blagden Collection, Houghton Library, Harvard University; Garrison and Garrison, *William Lloyd Garrison,* 3:363n.; Luke 10: 29.

16. HBS to William Lloyd Garrison, [November 1853], Garrison and Garrison, *William Lloyd Garrison,* 3:396; W. L. Garrison to HBS, 30 November 1853, *Letters,* 3:282; Garrison's quotation is from Thomas Jefferson's "First Inaugural Address," 1801.

17. W. L. Garrison to HBS, 30 November 1853, *Letters,* 4:238-84; HBS, "William Lloyd Garrison: Men of Our Times," *Christian Watchman and Reflector* 47 (17 May 1866), [1].

18. *Thirteenth Annual Report of the American and Foreign Anti-Slavery Society. Presented at New-York, May 11, 1853; with the Addresses and Resolutions* (New York: American and Foreign Anti-Slavery Society, 1853), pp. 192-93.

19. HBS, *Sunny Memories,* 2:87-88.

20. Ibid., 1:302-3. For critics of the Duchess of Sutherland, see H. C. Carey, *The Slave Trade: Domestic and Foreign* (Philadelphia: A. Hart, 1853), p. 203; Donald M'Leod, *Donald M'Leod's Gloomy Memories in the Highlands of Scotland versus Mrs. Harriet Beecher Stowe's Sunny Memories in (England) a Foreign Land* (Toronto: Thompson & Co., 1857), passim; Karl Marx castigated the Duchess of Sutherland for the inconsistency between her antislavery views and her attitude to the removal of the tenants from the Sutherland estates. See *New York Daily Tribune,* 9 February 1853, p. 6. For the attitudes of modern scholars to the removal of the tenants, see Rosalind Mitchison, *A History of Scotland* (London: Methuen & Co., 1970), p. 376; William Ferguson, *Scotland: 1689 to the Present* (Edinburgh and London: Oliver & Boyd, 1968), pp. 276-77.

21. HBS, *Sunny Memories,* 1:302-3.

22. Harriet Martineau, quoted in *Life and Letters,* p. 216; [George Eliot], review of *Dred, Westminster Review* 66 (October 1856): 313-14; Queen Victoria's opinion is paraphrased in *Life and Letters,* p. 226.

23. *Dred,* 1:[7-8], 143; review of *Dred, Edinburgh Review* 104 (October 1856): 585. For other unfavorable reactions to Nina, see review of *Dred, Blackwood's Magazine* 80 (December 1856): 694; review of *Dred,* (London) *Times,* 18 September 1856, p. 10; Nassau W. Senior, *Essays on Fiction* (London: Longman, Green, Longman, Roberts & Green, 1864), p. 481.

24. James C. Derby, *Fifty Years among Authors: Books and Publishers* (New York: G. W. Carleton & Co., 1884), p. 459; William Styron to *New York Review of Books* 15 (19 November 1970): 52.

25. *Dred,* 1:18-19; review of *Dred, Blackwood's Magazine* 80 (December 1856): 694; review of *Dred, Irish Quarterly Review* 6 (1856): 77-78; review of *Dred,* (London) *Times,* 18 September 1856, p. 10; review of *Dred, New Englander* 14

(November 1856), p. 521. Stowe believed that it was one of the missions of woman to soften the supposedly rugged and unfeeling "masculine" traits of men. To be the highest type of hero, she thought, a man should exhibit some of the qualities usually attributed to women. On one occasion she argued that since the father of Jesus was God himself, his mother was "[a]ll that was human in him . . . ; it was the union of the divine nature with the nature of a pure woman. Hence there was in Jesus more of the pure feminine element than in any other man. It was the feminine element exalted and taken in union with divinity." HBS, *Footsteps of the Master* (New York: J. B. Ford & Co.).

26. Shields McIlwaine, *The Southern Poor-White from Lubberland to Tobacco Road* (Norman: University of Oklahoma Press, 1939), p. 36; *Dred*, 2:184-87.

27. *Dred*, 1:107-8. For comparisons of Tiff to Uncle Tom, see review of *Dred*, (London) *Times*, 18 September 1856, p. 10; review of *Dred*, *Dublin University Magazine* 48 (December 1856) : 677; review of *Dred*, *New Englander* 14 (November 1856) : 521; William Peterfield Trent and John Erskine, *Great American Writers* (New York: Henry Holt & Co., 1912), pp. 209-10; Alexander Cowie, *The Rise of the American Novel* (New York: American Book Co., 1948), p. 453; Adams, *Harriet Beecher Stowe*, p. 70. In 1967, Richard Beale Davis wrote a defense of Tiff. "Old Tiff is held by some critics to be merely a variant, by others to be a superior version, of Uncle Tom. Actually his situation is entirely different from Tom's, and what he shows primarily is attachment to the children of the blue-blooded mistress who had married a poor white, a resourcefulness in time of need, a tendency to giggle, and withal a genuine, quiet dignity." See Davis, "Mrs. Stowe's Characters-in-Situations and a Southern Literary Tradition," in Clarence Ghodes, ed., *Essays on American Literature in Honor of Jay B. Hubbell* (Durham: Duke University Press, 1967), p. 16.

28. *Dred*, 1:98.

29. Ibid., 1:109.

30. Ibid., 2:336-37.

31. Ibid., 1:253. See Chapter 5 of this work, pp. 67-69.

32. *Dred*, 2:215-18, 6-7, 1:90-91.

33. *Dred*, 1:60; George Washington Cable, *The Grandissimes: A Story of Creole Life* (New York: Charles Scribner, 1880), pp. 215-59.

34. Review of *Dred*, *Southern Literary Messenger* 27 (October 1858): 284; review of *Dred*, *New Englander* 14 (November 1856): 517; review of *Dred*, *Quarterly Review* 101 (April 1857): 334-35; *Dred*, 2:126; review of *Dred*, *Tait's Edinburgh Review*, 26 n.s. (November 1859): 642.

35. *Dred*, 2:237-38.

36. Ibid., 2:46.

37. Ibid., 2:59, 67.

38. Ibid., 2:70-74.

39. Ibid., 2:49-51.

40. Ibid., 2:271.

41. Ibid., 2:330-31.

42. Review of *Dred*, *Blackwood's Magazine* 80 (December 1856): 693.

XVI. THE CIVIL WAR

1. HBS, "Letter from Mrs. Stowe, Florence, January 1, 1860," *Independent* 12 (16 February 1860): 1.

2. Francis Bacon, *Selected Writings*, ed. Hugh G. Dick (New York: Modern Library, 1955), p. 15; HBS, "Pencilings from Home," *Independent* 12 (3 May 1860): 1; HBS, "To 'the Affectionate and Christian Address of Many Thousands of Women of Great Britain,'" *Atlantic Monthly* 11 (January 1863): 122.

3. HBS, "What Hath God Wrought!" *Independent* 12 (15 November 1860): 1.

4. Ibid; Psalms 14: 1.

5. HBS, "Getting Ready for a Gale," *Independent* 13 (25 April 1861): 1.

6. Abraham Lincoln to Horace Greeley, 22 August 1862, in *Collected Works*, ed. Roy P. Basler, 9 vols. (New Brunswick: Rutgers University Press, 1953–1955), 5:388-89; HBS, "Will You Take a Pilot?" *Independent* 14 (11 September 1862): 1.

7. HBS, "Letter from Andover," *Independent* 13 (13 June 1861): 1; HBS, "Letter from Andover," *Independent* 13 (20 June 1861): 1.

8. HBS to James T. Fields, 13 November 1862, MS letter, FI 4012, Huntington Library, San Marino, Cal.

9. Annie Fields attributed the account of Lincoln's comment to Stowe's daughter, Harriet. See *Life and Letters*, p. 269. For opinions on whether Stowe was or was not the one chiefly responsible for the Civil War, see Paul Hamilton Hayne in Charles Roberts Anderson, "Charles Gayarré and Paul Hayne: The Last Literary Cavaliers," in David Kelly Jackson, ed., *American Studies in Honor of William Kenneth Boyd* (Durham: Duke University Press, 1940), pp. 232-33; Frank A. Shoup, "*Uncle Tom's Cabin* Forty Years After," *Sewanee Review* 2 (November 1893): 104; Review of *Life and Letters of Harriet Beecher Stowe: The Academy* 53 (12 February 1898): 169; Paul Laurence Dunbar, "Harriet Beecher Stowe," [poem] *Century Magazine* 37 n.s. (November 1898): 61; Thomas Dixon, Jr., *The Leopard's Spots: A Romance of the White Man's Burden—1865–1900* (New York: Doubleday, Page & Co., 1902), p. 262; Grant C. Knight, *American Literature and Culture* (1932; reprint, New York: Cooper Square Publishers, 1972), p. 132; James Truslow Adams, ed., *Album of American History*, 5 vols. (New York: C. Scribner's, 1945), 2:394; Joseph Chamberlain Furnas, *Goodbye to Uncle Tom* (New York: William Sloane Assoc., 1956), p. 30; Kenneth S. Lynn, "Mrs. Stowe and the American Imagination," *New Republic* 148 (29 June 1963): 21; Burgess, "Making de White Boss Frown," p. 54.

10. HBS, "To 'the Affectionate and Christian Address,'" pp. 123-24.

11. Ibid.; Alexander H. Stephens, "Speech Delivered on the 21st of March, 1861, in Savannah [Ga.]," in *Alexander H. Stephens in Public and Private, with Letters and Speeches Before, During, and Since the War*, ed. Henry Cleveland (Philadelphia: National Publishing Co., [1866]), p. 723.

12. HBS, "To 'the Affectionate and Christian Address,'" pp. 125, 122.

13. Ibid., pp. 103-32.

14. HBS to the Duchess of Argyll, 31 July 1862, Harriet Beecher Stowe Collection (#6318-c), Clifton Waller Barrett Library, University of Virginia Library; HBS [Christopher Crowfield, pseud.], "Woman's Sphere," *The Chimney-Corner* (Boston: Ticknor & Fields, 1868), pp. 29-30.

15. HBS to the Duchess of Argyll; HBS, "To 'the Affectionate and Christian Address,'" p. 132.

16. HBS, *Sunny Memories*, 2:161; Nathaniel Hawthorne to James T. Fields, 3 May 1863, quoted in Fields, *Yesterdays with Authors* (Boston: Houghton Mifflin Co., 1899), p. 105; HBS to James T. Fields, 3 November 1863, Huntington Library, San Marino, Cal.

17. HBS, "Dress; or, Who Makes the Fashions," *Atlantic Monthly* 17 (April 1866): 497; HBS, "The Inner Chamber," *Independent* 14 (4 September 1862): 1.

18. HBS, "Prayer," *Independent* 14 (28 August 1862): 1.

19. HBS, "The Chimney-Corner," *Atlantic Monthly* 15 (January 1865): 114-15.

20. Ibid.

21. HBS, *Men of Our Times*, pp. 75-76, 88.

XVII. RECONSTRUCTION AND BEYOND

1. Stowe disclosed that Lady Byron had told her the reason for her break with Lord Byron. Lady Byron discovered Byron's incestuous relationship with his half-sister, Augusta Leigh, with whom he had fathered a child. See HBS, "The True Story of Lady Byron's Life," *Atlantic Monthly* 24 (September 1869): 295-313; HBS, *Lady*

Byron Vindicated: A History of the Byron Controversy from its Beginning to the Present Times (Boston: Fields, Osgood & Co., 1870). On this issue, Stowe caused almost as much comment as she had in writing *Uncle Tom's Cabin*. This time, however, the response was largely unfavorable, especially so in Great Britain. Byron had many defenders who argued that the charges were untrue, but many reviewers were angry with Stowe because they did not regard it as suitable for such charges to be made public, especially by a woman, even if they were true. Later evidence has suggested that the charges were indeed true, and Byron's sexual relationship with Augusta Leigh is now accepted as a fact by his modern biographers.

2. HBS, "The Noble Army of Martyrs," *Atlantic Monthly* 16 (1865): 235-36. The essay was published while the Civil War was still going on, but it was reprinted in January of 1866 in a collection of articles and stories, an indication that Stowe had not relaxed her feeling of bitterness toward the South. See HBS, *Little Foxes*.

3. HBS, "The Noble Army of Martyrs," p. 236; HBS, *Men of Our Times*, p. 86.

4. HBS, *Men of Our Times*, pp. 115-16.

5. See Paxton Hibben, *Henry Ward Beecher: An American Portrait* (New York: George H. Doran Co., 1927), pp. 199-200.

6. HBS to the Duchess of Argyll, 19 February 1866, Harriet Beecher Stowe Collection (#6318-c), Clifton Waller Barrett Library, University of Virginia Library.

7. Ibid.; HBS to Charles Beecher, 1866, in C. E. Stowe, *Life of Harriet Beecher Stowe*, p. 400.

8. HBS, "An Eventful Week in Rome," *Independent* 12 (19 April 1860): 1.

9. HBS, "Being a Family Talk on Reconstruction," *Atlantic Monthly* 17 (January 1866): 89, 91.

10. Ibid., pp. 90-91.

11. *Crusader in Crinoline*, pp. 481, 497, 515, 527, 533; L. B. Stowe, *Saints, Sinners and Beechers*, p. 233; Mary B. Graff, *Mandarin on the St. Johns* (Gainesville: University of Florida Press, 1953), pp. 48-49. A number of writers have discussed the question of whether Stowe was to blame for the alcoholism of Frederick Stowe. See James Branch Cabell and A. J. Hanna, *The St. Johns: A Parade of Diversities* (New York: Farrar & Rinehart, 1943), pp. 211-26; Furnas, *Goodbye to Uncle Tom*, p. 40; Wagenknecht, *Harriet Beecher Stowe*, pp. 67-71; F. Bruce Kirkham, "Andover, Gettysburg, and Beyond: The Military Career of Frederick M. Stowe," *Essex Institute Historical Collections* 109 (January 1973): 95.

12. HBS, "What Is to Be Done with Them?" *Independent* 14 (21 August 1862): 1.

13. HBS, *Palmetto Leaves*, pp. 280-83.

14. Ibid., pp. 283, 317.

15. HBS, "The Colored Labor of the South," *Hearth and Home* 1 (3 July 1869): 440.

16. HBS, *Palmetto Leaves*, pp. 270-78.

17. HBS, "Letter from Florida," *Christian Union* 4 (7 February 1877): 122. George Franklin Drew was the governor of Florida at the time Stowe made this comment.

18. HBS, "The Colored Labor of the South," p. 440.

19. C. E. Stowe and L. B. Stowe, *Harriet Beecher Stowe*, p. 218.

20. HBS, "The Education of Freedmen," *North American Review* 128 (1879): 609.

21. HBS, "A Brilliant Success," *Independent* 10 (30 September 1858): 1; *Dred*, 2:331.

22. HBS, "The Colored Labor of the South," p. 441.

23. HBS to Mary Estlin, 7 April 1869, Estlin Papers 24.123 (4) [copy], Dr. Williams' Library, London; HBS to Mary Estlin, 7 May [1869], 24.123.5, cited in Alex L. Murray, "Harriet Beecher Stowe on Racial Segregation in the Schools," *American Quarterly* 12 (Winter 1960): 518-19; see also, Christine Bolt, *The Anti-*

Slavery Movement and Reconstruction: A Study in Anglo-American Co-operation, 1833–77 (New York: Oxford University Press, 1969), pp. 129-30.

24. HBS to Miss Wigham, 4 June 1869, Estlin Papers, 24.123.6, cited in Murray, "Harriet Beecher Stowe on Racial Segregation in the Schools," pp. 518-19; see also Bolt, *Anti-Slavery Movement and Reconstruction,* pp. 129-30.

25. HBS to Lucy Perkins, 5 December 1876, Stowe-Day Foundation, Hartford, Conn.

26. HBS, "Letter from a Verandah," *Christian Union* 12 (8 December 1875): 466; Ezekiel 37:22.

27. HBS, "The Education of Freedmen," p. 610.

28. HBS, quoted in "The Birthday Garden Party to Harriet Beecher Stowe," *Atlantic Monthly Supplement* 50 (August 1882): 10.

XVIII. THE REPUTATION OF UNCLE TOM'S CABIN, THE NOVEL: 1865–1940

1. Grace Seiler, "Harriet Beecher Stowe," *College English* 11 (December 1949): 135.

2. [John W. De Forest], "The Great American Novel," *Nation* 6 (9 January 1868): 28-29; De Forest, undated letter in "The Birthday Garden Party to Harriet Beecher Stowe," p. 11.

3. John W. De Forest, *Miss Ravenel's Conversion from Secession to Loyalty* (New York: Harper Bros., 1867), pp. 267-68.

4. James, *A Small Boy,* pp. 158-59; James, "Notes for an Essay on Mr. and Mrs. Fields," *The American Essays,* ed. Leon Edel (New York: Vintage Books, 1956), p. 281.

5. [William Dean Howells], review of *Uncle Tom's Cabin, Atlantic Monthly* 43 (March 1879): 407-8; *New York Sun,* 6 February 1898.

6. George Washington Cable, quoted in "The Birthday Garden Party to Harriet Beecher Stowe," p. 12; Mark Twain, quoted in Edith Colgate Salsbury, ed., *Susy and Mark Twain: Family Dialogues* (New York: Harper & Row, 1965), p. 242; Twain, *The Man that Corrupted Hadleyburg and Other Stories and Sketches* (New York: Harper Bros., 1900), p. 22.

7. Barrett Wendell, *A Literary History of America* (New York: C. Scribner's Sons, 1900), p. 354.

8. Constance Rourke, *Trumpets of Jubilee* (New York: Harcourt, Brace & Co., 1927), pp. 104-5.

9. Rhodes, *History of the United States from the Compromise of 1850,* 1:279.

10. *Life and Letters,* p. 269; William Hand Browne to Paul Hamilton Hayne, 30 July 1870, 11 September 1871, quoted in Jay B. Hubbell, *The South in American Literature: 1607–1900* (Durham: Duke University Press, 1954), p. 751.

11. Paul Hamilton Hayne to Charles Gayarré, 4 February 1885, Paul Hamilton Hayne Papers, Duke University, cited in Anderson, "Charles Gayarré and Paul Hayne," pp. 232-33; Hayne, "A Character," *Poems of Paul Hamilton Hayne* (Boston: D. Lothrop & Co., 1882), p. 284.

12. Grace King, *Memories of a Southern Woman of Letters* (New York: Macmillan Co., 1932), pp. 76-77.

13. William Lyon Phelps, *Howells, James, Bryant, and Other Essays* (New York: Macmillan Co., 1924), pp. 199-200; William Alexander Percy, *Lanterns on the Levee: Recollections of a Planter's Son* (New York: Alfred A. Knopf, 1941), p. 121.

14. Raymond Allen Cook, *Thomas Dixon* (New York: Twayne Publishers, 1974), p. 51; Thomas Dixon, Jr., *The Clansman: An Historical Romance of the Ku Klux Klan* (New York: Doubleday, Page & Co., 1905), passim; Everett Carter, "Cultural History Written with Lightning: The Significance of *Birth of a Nation*," *American Quarterly* 12 (1960): 347-57.

15. Dixon, *The Leopard's Spots*, pp. 242, 117; see Maxwell Bloomfield, "Dixon's *The Leopard's Spots*: A Study in Popular Racism," *American Quarterly* 16 (1964): 387-401.

16. Dixon, *The Leopard's Spots*, p. 86.

17. Allen, " 'Uncle Tom' at Home in Kentucky," pp. 858, 863.

18. Ibid., pp. 853-54.

19. Joel Chandler Harris, *Joel Chandler Harris: Editor and Essayist, Miscellaneous Literary, Political, and Social Writings*, ed. Julia Collier Harris (Chapel Hill: University of North Carolina Press, 1931), pp. 115-16; Harris, *Uncle Remus: His Songs and His Sayings* (New York: D. Appleton & Co., 1881), p. 4; Thomas P. Riggio, "Uncle Tom Reconstructed: A Neglected Chapter in the History of a Book," *American Quarterly* 28 (Spring 1976): 60.

20. Thomas Nelson Page, *Red Rock: A Chronicle of Reconstruction* (New York: Charles Scribner, 1898), passim; Hubbell, *The South in American Literature*, p. 702; Page, *The Negro: The Southerner's Problem* (New York: Charles Scribner, 1904), p. 236.

21. Thomas Nelson Page, *The Old South: Essays Social and Political* (New York: C. Scribner's Sons, 1912), pp. 341-42.

22. Stark Young, "Uncle Tom's Measure," *New Republic* 76 (4 October 1933): 212-13.

23. Ibid.; Stark Young, "Sweet River," *New Republic* 89 (18 November 1936): 78.

24. Jefferson Davis, *Jefferson Davis, Constitutionalist: His Letters, Papers and Speeches*, ed. Dunbar Rowland, 10 vols. (Jackson: Mississippi Department of Archives and History, 1923), 9:372.

25. Woodrow Wilson, *A History of the American People*, 5 vols. (New York: Harper Bros., 1902), 4:160; Wilson, *Division and Reunion, 1829–1889* (New York: Longmans, Green & Co., 1893), pp. 127, 181.

26. Shoup, *"Uncle Tom's Cabin,"* pp. 89-91.

27. Ibid., pp. 97-98; *UTC*, 2:49.

28. Shoup, *"Uncle Tom's Cabin,"* pp. 103-4.

29. Thomas Pearce Bailey, *Race Orthodoxy in the South and Other Aspects of the Negro Question* (New York: Neale Publishing Co., 1914), pp. 177-78, 195; *UTC*, 1:47, 304.

30. Bailey, *Race Orthodoxy in the South*, pp. 178, 199-200, 203.

31. Ulrich B. Phillips, *Life and Labor in the Old South* (Boston: Little, Brown & Co., 1930), pp. 7-8; *UTC*, 1:20.

32. Dumas Malone, *Saints in Action* (New York: Abingdon Press, 1939), pp. 93-94, 89.

33. See HBS, "The True Story of Lady Byron's Life," *Atlantic Monthly* 24 (September 1869): 295-313; HBS, *Lady Byron Vindicated*, passim.

34. George Eliot to Sara Sophia Hennell, 15 May 1877, *George Eliot Letters*, 6:371-72; Charles Dickens to James T. Fields, 6 October 1869, quoted in Mark Antony DeWolfe Howe, ed., *Memories of a Hostess: A Chronicle of Eminent Friendships Drawn Chiefly from the Diaries of Mrs. James T. Fields* (Boston: Atlantic Monthly Press, 1922), p. 191; Algernon Charles Swinburne to Paul Hamilton Hayne, 2 May 1877, in *Letters*, ed. Cecil Y. Lang, 6 vols. (New Haven: Yale University Press, 1959–1962), 3: 331-32.

35. Julian Hawthorne and Leonard Lemmon, *American Literature: An Elementary Text-Book for Use in High Schools and Academies* (Boston: D. C. Heath & Co., 1891), pp. 89-90; Agnes Repplier, *Points of View* (Boston: Houghton Mifflin Co., 1892), pp. 75-77.

36. John Erskine, *Leading American Novelists* (New York: Henry Holt & Co., 1910), pp. 291-92.

37. Ibid., pp. 292-94.

38. *New York Times*, 21 May 1903; *World's Greatest Hit*, pp. 367-68.

39. Vernon L. Parrington, *Main Currents in American Thought*, 3 vols. in 1 (New York: Harcourt, Brace & Co., 1927–30), 2:376-78; Norman Foerster, ed., "Harriet Beecher Stowe," in *American Poetry and Prose*, rev. and enl. ed. (Boston: Houghton Mifflin Co., 1934), p. 794; Fred Lewis Gattee, *The First Century of American Literature, 1770–1870* (New York: D. Appleton-Century Co., 1935), pp. 572-73; Sinclair Lewis, "Foreword," Paxton Hibben, *Henry Ward Beecher: An American* (1927; reprint, New York: Press of the Readers Club, 1942), pp. viii-ix.

40. James Truslow Adams, *America's Tragedy* (New York: C. Scribner's Sons, 1934), p. 127; Adams, ed., *Album of American History*, 5 vols. (New York: C. Scribner's Sons, 1944–1949), 3:394; J. G. Randall, *The Civil War and Reconstruction* (Boston: D. C. Heath & Co., 1937), pp. 169-70.

41. Albion W. Tourgée, "The Literary Quality of 'Uncle Tom's Cabin,'" *Independent* 48 (20 August 1896): 1127.

42. Ibid.

43. Ibid., p. 1128.

44. Frederick Douglass, quoted in "The Birthday Garden Party to Harriet Beecher Stowe," pp. 12-13.

45. Paul Laurence Dunbar, "Harriet Beecher Stowe," *Century* 57 (November 1898): 61.

46. W. E. B. Du Bois, *Book Reviews by W. E. B. Du Bois*, comp. and ed. Herbert Aptheker (Millwood, N. Y.: KTO Press, 1977), pp. 17-18. Du Bois said nothing about Uncle Tom or the other black characters in the novel. It is at least possible that he did not object to the supposed racial traits of the black characters in *Uncle Tom's Cabin*. His own conception of the innate traits of blacks was different from that of Stowe, but he did share at least some of her ideas on this subject. "This race [the blacks]," said Du Bois, "has the greatest of the gifts of God, laughter. It dances and sings; it is humble; it longs to learn; it loves men; it loves women. It is frankly, baldly, deliciously human in an artificial and hypocritical land." See W. E. B. Du Bois, *Dusk of Dawn: An Essay toward an Autobiography of a Race Concept* (New York: Harcourt, Brace & Co., 1940), p. 148.

47. George W. Williams, *History of the Negro Race in America from 1619 to 1880* (New York: G. P. Putnam & Sons, 1883), pp. 546-47.

48. James Weldon Johnson, *The Autobiography of an Ex-Colored Man* (Boston: Sherman, French & Co., 1912), pp. 38-40.

49. *New York World*, 7 August 1920, quoted in Melvin Drimmer, *Black History: A Reappraisal* (Garden City, N. Y.: Doubleday & Co., 1968), p. 391.

XIX. UNCLE TOM'S CABIN, THE PLAY: 1865–1940

1. Mark Twain, *Mark Twain's Travels with Mr. Brown*, ed. Franklin Walker and G. Ezra Dane (New York: A. A. Knopf, 1940), p. 84.

2. Quoted in T. Henry Foster, "America's Most Famous Book," *Book Collector's Packet* 4, No. 5 (1946): 5; *New York Times*, 5 September 1869, p. 4.

3. J. Frank Davis, "Tom Shows," *Scribner's* 77 (April 1925): 350-60; "Famous First Nights," pp. 26, 65; "The Pioneer Uncle Tomers: By One of Them," *Theatre* 4 (February 1904): 44; *World's Greatest Hit*, pp. 213-19; John Seely Hart, *A Manual of American Literature* (Philadelphia: Eldredge & Bro., 1873), p. 494; Chester E. Jorgenson, comp., *Uncle Tom's Cabin as Book and Legend: A Guide to an Exhibition* (Detroit: Friends of the Detroit Public Library, 1952), pp. 29-30; Odie B. Faulk, *Tombstone: Myth and Reality* (New York: Oxford University Press, 1972), p. 117.

4. *World's Greatest Hit*, pp. 233-35, 315-16, 355; Ralph Eugene Lund, "Trouping with Uncle Tom," *Century* 115 (January 1928): 329-37; Davis, "Tom Shows," p. 356; Jorgenson, *Uncle Tom's Cabin as Book and Legend*, p. 32.

5. Quoted in Richard Moody, "Uncle Tom, the Theatre, and Mrs. Stowe," *American Heritage* 6 (October 1955): 103.

6. Joseph Francis Daly, *The Life of Augustin Daly* (New York: Macmillan Co., 1917), p. 277; Harry Thurston Peck, "*Uncle Tom's Cabin* in Liverpool," *Bookman* 6 (December 1897): 310-16.

7. Quoted in *World's Greatest Hit*, pp. 285, 263.

8. A. M. Drummond and Richard Moody, "The Hit of the Century: *Uncle Tom's Cabin*—1853–1952," *Educational Theatre Journal* 4 (December 1952): 319-20; *World's Greatest Hit*, pp. 355-56, 333; Fletcher, "Illustrations for Uncle Tom," p. 172; Charles Townson [playwright], *Uncle Tom's Cabin: A Melodrama in Five Acts* (New York: Wehman Bros., 1889), p. 4.

9. *World's Greatest Hit*, p. 333.

10. Arnett, "Fifty Years of Uncle Tom," p. 898; *World's Greatest Hit*, pp. 388-89; Drummond and Moody, "Hit of the Century," p. 315; Frank Rahill, "America's Number One Hit," *Theatre Arts* 36 (October 1952): 18.

11. Davis, "Tom Shows," p. 352.

12. MacDonald, "Memoirs of the Original Little Eva," p. 281.

13. Henry Clay Trumbull, *War Memories of an Army Chaplain* (New York: C. Scribner's Sons, 1898), p. 411.

14. *World's Greatest Hit*, pp. 280-82, 228, 270.

15. Ibid., p. 283.

16. Ibid., pp. 339-40.

17. *New Orleans Daily Picayune*, 18 February 1883, quoted in Joseph P. Roppolo, "Harriet Beecher Stowe and New Orleans: A Study in Hate," *New England Quarterly* 30 (September 1957): 361.

18. *World's Greatest Hit*, pp. 340, 368; Joseph M. Rogers, "*Uncle Tom's Cabin* in Kentucky," *Era* 10 (September 1902): 262.

19. Isaac F. Marcosson and Daniel Frohman, *Charles Frohman: Manager and Man* (New York: Harper Bros., 1916), p. 42; Bernard Sobel, ed., *Theatre Handbook and Digest of Plays* (New York: Crown Publishers, 1940), p. 169; 16 Kentucky Revised Statutes, Chapter 437.100 (1973); repealed, 16 Kentucky Revised Statutes, 437.100 (1975).

20. *World's Greatest Hit*, p. 373.

21. Furnas, *Goodbye to Uncle Tom*, p. 15; Frank William Boreham, *The Gospel of Uncle Tom's Cabin* (London: Epworth Press, 1956), pp. 7-8.

22. Foster, *The Rungless Ladder*, p. viii; Bernard Hewitt, "Uncle Tom and Uncle Sam: New Light on an Old Play," *Quarterly Journal of Speech* 37 (February 1951): 65-69.

23. Fletcher, "Illustrations for Uncle Tom," p. 172; Hewitt, "Uncle Tom and Uncle Sam," pp. 65-69; Davis, "Tom Shows," pp. 352-53; *World's Greatest Hit*, p. 331.

24. Richard Fraiherr von Krafft-Ebing, *Psychopathia Sexualis*, trans. Charles G. Chaddock (Philadelphia: F. A. Davis Co., 1892), p. 105.

25. *World's Greatest Hit*, pp. 247-48, 331.

26. Ibid., pp. 330-31.

27. Ibid., p. 355.

28. Ibid., pp. 162-63.

29. Ibid., p. 220, 329; Davis, "Tom Shows," p. 355.

30. Charles Morton [playwright], *Uncle Tom's Cabin: A New Dramatization in Five Acts of Mrs. Harriet Beecher Stowe's Celebrated Story* [mimeographed] (Chicago: Chicago Manuscript Co., 1912), p. 12.

31. Lund, "Trouping with Uncle Tom," p. 335.

32. Phelps, *Howells, James, Bryant*, pp. 188-89.

33. Elizabeth F. Corbett, "A Footnote to 'The Drama,'" *Drama* 16 (19 May 1926): 285-86.

34. *World's Greatest Hit*, p. 318; Arnett, "Fifty Years of Uncle Tom," p. 902.

35. Peter Noble, *The Negro in Films* (1948: reprint, New York: Arno Press, 1970), pp. 31-32; *World's Greatest Hit*, pp. 393-410; Eileen Landay, *Black Film Stars* (New York: Drake Publishers, 1973), pp. 17-18.

36. Noble, *The Negro in Films*, pp. 32-33; *World's Greatest Hit*, pp. 398-401.

37. Thomas Cripps, *Slow Fade to Black: The Negro in American Film, 1900–1942* (New York: Oxford University Press, 1977), pp. 159-61; Edith Isaacs, "The Middle Distance: 1890–1917," *Theatre Arts* 26 (August 1942): 530; Noble, *The Negro in Films*, pp. 31-33; *Amsterdam* (N. Y.) *News*, 31 August 1927, 7 September 1927, 2 November 1927, 9 November 1927, 21 March 1928, cited in Cripps, *Slow Fade to Black*, p. 161.

38. "The Death of Uncle Tom," *Outlook* 157 (January 1931): 89; Bill Sachs [repertoire editor of *Billboard*] to Samuel Selden, 10 January 1935, quoted in Anne Blanche Stewart, "A Critique of *Uncle Tom's Cabin*" (master's thesis, University of North Carolina, 1937), p. 14n; L. Berne Slout [manager of Slout Players] to Samuel Selden, 12 January 1935, *idem*, p. 15.

39. Richard Dana Skinner, "The Players Revive Uncle Tom," *Commonweal* 18 (9 June 1933): 160.

40. Stark Young, "Sweet River," p. 78.

41. Edward Estlin Cummings, *Tom* (Santa Fe, N. M.: Rydal Press, 1935), pp. 11, 12, 21, 32-34.

42. Ouyang Yu-chien, "The Modern Chinese Theatre and Dramatic Tradition," *Chinese Literature* 11 (November 1959): 103; Walter J. Meserve and Ruth I. Meserve, "*Uncle Tom's Cabin* and Modern Chinese Drama," *Modern Drama* 17 (1974): 57-66.

43. "Uncle Tom in Russia," *Literary Digest* 114 (2 July 1932): 16-17.

XX. CRITICAL RECEPTION OF UNCLE TOM'S CABIN: 1941 TO THE PRESENT

1. Fern Marja Eckman, *The Furious Passage of James Baldwin* (New York: M. Evans & Co., 1966), p. 41; Lyle Glazier, "Pointing Upward," *Hacettepe Bulletin of Social Sciences and Humanities* 3 (1971): 34.

2. *UTC*, 2:25; James Baldwin, "Everybody's Protest Novel," *Partisan Review* 16 (June 1949): 578, essay reprinted in Baldwin, *Notes of a Native Son* (Boston: Beacon Press, 1955), pp. 13-24.

3. Baldwin, "Everybody's Protest Novel," p. 581.

4. Glazier, "Pointing Upward," pp. 34-35; *UTC*, 1:43.

5. Glazier, "Pointing Upward," p. 36.

6. Ibid.; *UTC*, 2:94-95.

7. Furnas, *Goodbye to Uncle Tom*, pp. 51, 63-64.

8. Ibid., pp. 77-78. Furnas misreads Thomas J. Wertenbaker. British immigrants encountered greater financial obstacles in the South than they did in the North, but they came from fundamentally the same social class as did immigrants in the North. See Thomas J. Wertenbaker, *The Planters of Colonial Virginia* (Princeton: Princeton University Press, 1922), pp. 82, 137-40; Wertenbaker, *The First Americans, 1607–1690* (New York: Macmillan Co., 1929), pp. 43-44.

9. Furnas, *Goodbye to Uncle Tom*, pp. 76-77, 171.

10. Ibid., pp. 56-57, 40-41.

11. For criticism of the opinions of Furnas concerning Stowe, see Paul Pickrel, review of *Goodbye to Uncle Tom*, *Harper's* 213 (July 1956): 88-89; reply by J. C. Furnas, 213 (September 1956): 6; reply by Paul Pickrel, *Harper's* 213 (September 1956): 619; Wagenknecht, *Harriet Beecher Stowe*, pp. 4-5; Thomas Graham, "Harriet Beecher Stowe and the Question of Race," *New England Quarterly* 46 (1973): 614-22.

12. Furnas, *Goodbye to Uncle Tom*, pp. 303-4; *Key to UTC*, p. 50.

13. Addison Gayle, Jr., *The Way of the New World: The Black Novel in America*

(Garden City, N. Y.: Anchor Press/Doubleday, 1975), p. 6; LeRoi Jones [Aman Baraka], "Uncle Tom's Cabin: Alternate Ending," *Tales* (New York: Grove Press, 1967), pp. 35-40.

14. Donald Chaput, "Uncle Tom and Predestination," *Negro History Bulletin* 27 (March 1964): 143; *UTC*, 1:141; Arlene A. Elder, *The "Hindered Hand": Cultural Implications of Early African American Fiction* (Westport, Conn.: Greenwood Press, 1978), p. 6.

15. "Classics by the Pound," *Harper's* 265 (August 1982): 73.

16. *Crusader in Crinoline*; Foster, *The Rungless Ladder*; Kirkham, *The Building of Uncle Tom's Cabin.*

17. Allan Nevins, *Ordeal of the Union*, 8 vols. (New York: Charles Scribner, 1947), 1:408.

18. Ibid., 1:408-9.

19. Edmund Wilson, "No! No! No! My Soul An't Yours, Mas'r," *New Yorker* 24 (27 November 1948): 134. Wilson expanded this paragraph in *Patriotic Gore*, pp. 5-6.

20. Wilson, "No! No! No!" p. 38; see also Wilson, *Patriotic Gore*, p. 6.

21. Wilson, "No! No! No!" p. 38; see also Wilson, *Patriotic Gore*, pp. 9-10.

22. Lionel Trilling, "*Uncle Tom's Cabin* by Harriet Beecher Stowe," in Eric Larrabee, ed., *American Panorama: Essays by Fifteen American Critics on 350 Books Past and Present Which Portray the U.S.A. in Its Many Aspects* (New York: New York University Press, 1957), p. 318; Lynn, "Introduction," HBS, *Uncle Tom's Cabin*, p. xi.

23. David Levin, "American Fiction as Historical Evidence: Reflections on *Uncle Tom's Cabin*," *Negro American Literature Forum* 5 (Winter 1972): 132.

24. Ibid., p. 133.

25. Ibid., p. 134; *UTC*, 1:64.

26. Levin, "American Fiction as Historical Evidence," p. 154; *UTC*, 2:251.

27. Levin, "American Fiction as Historical Evidence," p. 154.

28. Jones, "Introduction," HBS, *Uncle Tom's Cabin*, p. vii; Matt. 5:44.

29. Kenneth Rexroth, "*Uncle Tom's Cabin*," *The Elastic Retort: Essays in Literature and Ideas* (New York: Seabury Press, 1973), pp. 103-7.

30. William Faulkner, *Faulkner at West Point*, ed. Joseph L. Fant III (New York: Random House, 1964), pp. 103-4.

31. Robert Penn Warren, quoted in Herbert Mitgang, "Writers Hail Reissuing of Classics," *New York Times*, 14 May 1982, Section B, p. 1.

32. Florence Ryerson and Colin Clements, *Harriet: A Play in Three Acts* (New York: Charles Scribner, 1943); *Time* 43 (13 March 1944): 54; Richard Rodgers and Oscar Hammerstein, 2nd. *The King and I, Based on the Novel Anna and the King of Siam by Margaret Landon* (New York: Random House, 1951).

33. John Mason Brown, "Topsy-Turvy Uncle Tom's Cabin Barred in Bridgeport and New Haven," *Saturday Review of Literature* 28 (6 October 1945): 24, reprinted as "Is *Uncle Tom's Cabin* Anti-Negro? No." *Negro Digest* 4 (January 1946): 69-70; Phyllis Rauch Klotman, *Frame by Frame—a Black Filmography* (Bloomington: Indiana University Press, 1979), p. 395.

34. Mel Gussow, "A Stoic Dignified Uncle Tom Is Portrayed on Stage," *New York Times*, 27 February 1975, Section C, p. 30.

35. Adrian Hall and Richard Cumming, *Uncle Tom's Cabin: A History* [stage adaptation], Trinity Square Repertory Co., Providence, Rhode Island, typewritten MS, 1980, pp. 76-77.

36. Joe Butler, "Feature Working Well," *Taunton* (Mass.) *Daily Gazette*, 8 November 1978; Carolyn Clay, "Renovation 'Uncle Tom's Cabin,' " *Boston Phoenix*, 7 November 1978; R. M., "Trinity's 'Uncle Tom' Shows Artistic Flair," *Sippican* (Mass.) *Sentinel*, 16 November 1978; Kevin Kelly, " 'Uncle Tom' at Trinity Square," *Boston Globe*, 2 November 1978.

37. *Books in Print: 1983–1984. Authors* (New York: R. R. Bowker Company, 1983), 2:4212; *Les Livres Disponsibles: 1982* (French Books in Print). *Auteurs* (Paris: Cercle de la Librairie, 1981), p. 1641; Frederick H. Jackson, "*Uncle Tom's Cabin* in Italy," *Symposium* 7 (November 1953): 323-32.

38. George May, "Forty Months in Red Hungary," *Harper's* 206 (June 1953): 87.

39. Tien Han, "A Talk on 'Sorrows of the Negro Slave,'" *Survey of China Mainland Press*, No. 2555 (10 August 1961): 7-16.

40. Ibid.

41. Ibid.

Bibliography

WORKS BY HARRIET BEECHER STOWE

[STOWE, HARRIET BEECHER.] *Primary Geography for Children on an Improved Plan.* By C. and H. Beecher. Cincinnati: Corey, Webster & Fairbank, 1833. Catharine Beecher's name was listed first because she was better known then as an author, but apparently Harriet wrote the book.

STOWE, HARRIET BEECHER. *The Mayflower; or, Sketches of Scenes and Characters among the Descendants of the Pilgrims.* New York: Harper Bros., 1843.

————. *Uncle Tom's Cabin; or, Life among the Lowly.* 2 vols. Boston: J. P. Jewett & Co.; Cleveland: Jewett, Proctor & Worthington, 1852.

————. *Uncle Tom's Cabin; or, Life among the Lowly. With a preface by the author written expressly for this edition.* London: T. Bosworth, 1852.

————. *Uncle Tom's Cabin: With a new preface expressly written for this edition.* 2 vols.; also 2 vols. in 1. Leipzig: B. Tauchnitz, 1852.

————. *A Key to Uncle Tom's Cabin: Presenting the Original Facts and Documents upon Which the Story Is Founded.* Boston: J. P. Jewett, 1853.

————. *Uncle Sam's Emancipation; Earthly Care, a Heavenly Discipline; and Other Sketches.* Philadelphia: W. P. Hazard, 1853.

————. *Sunny Memories of Foreign Lands.* 2 vols. Boston: Phillips, Sampson & Co., 1854.

————. *The Christian Slave: A Drama Founded on a Portion of "Uncle*

Tom's Cabin." Dramatized by Harriet Beecher Stowe, Expressly for the Readings of Mrs. Mary E. Webb. Boston: Phillips, Sampson & Co., 1855.

————. *First Geography for Children.* Edited by Catharine E. Beecher. Boston: Phillips, Sampson & Co.; New York: J. C. Derby, 1855. A revision of *Primary Geography for Children.*

————. *Dred: A Tale of the Great Dismal Swamp.* 2 vols. Boston: Phillips, Sampson & Co., 1856.

————. *The Minister's Wooing.* New York: Derby and Jackson; Boston: Brown, Taggard & Chase, 1859.

———— [Christopher Crowfield, pseud.]. *The Little Foxes.* Boston: Ticknor & Fields, 1866.

————. *Men of Our Times; or, Leading Patriots of the Day.* Hartford, Conn.: Hartford Publishing Co.; New York: J. D. Denison; Chicago: J. A. Stoddard, 1868.

————. *Oldtown Folks.* Boston: Fields, Osgood & Co., 1869.

————. *Lady Byron Vindicated: A History of the Byron Controversy from its Beginning to the Present Times.* Boston: Fields, Osgood & Co., 1870.

————. *Pink and White Tyranny: A Society Novel.* Boston: Roberts Bros., 1871.

————. *The Lives and Deeds of Our Self-Made Men.* Hartford, Conn.: Worthington, Dustin & Co., 1872. A revision of *Men of Our Times.*

————. *Oldtown Fireside Stories.* Boston: J. R. Osgood & Co., 1872.

————. *Palmetto Leaves.* Boston: J. R. Osgood & Co., 1873.

————. *We and Our Neighbors; or, The Records of an Unfashionable Street.* New York: J. B. Ford & Co., 1875.

————. *Poganuc People: Their Loves and Lives.* New York: Fords, Howard & Hulbert, 1878.

————. *Uncle Tom's Cabin.* New ed. *With illustrations, and a bibliography of the work by George Bullen, together with an introductory account of the work.* Boston: Houghton Mifflin Co., 1879.

————. *The Writings of Harriet Beecher Stowe.* Riverside Edition. 16 vols. Boston: Houghton Mifflin Co., 1896.

SELECTED BIBLIOGRAPHY

AARON, DANIEL. *The Unwritten War: American Writers and the Civil War.* New York: A. A. Knopf, 1973.

"Abolition Dramatized." *New York Tribune,* reprinted in *National Anti-Slavery Standard* 14 (1853): 49.

ADAMS, FRANCIS COLBURN. *Uncle Tom at Home: A Review of the Reviewers and Repudiators of Uncle Tom's Cabin by Mrs. Stowe.* Philadeldephia: W. P. Hazard, 1853.

ADAMS, JOHN R. "Harriet Beecher Stowe." *American Literary Realism* 2 (1969): 160-64.

————. *Harriet Beecher Stowe.* New York: Twayne Publishers, 1963.

————. "Structure and Theme in the Novels of Harriet Beecher Stowe." In *Long Fiction of the American Renaissance: A Symposium on Genre.* Edited by Paul McCarthy. Hartford: Transcendental Books, 1974.

[ADAMS, NEHEMIAH.] *The Sable Cloud: A Southern Tale, with Northern Comments.* Boston: Ticknor & Fields, 1861.

ADAMS, NEHEMIAH. *A South-Side View of Slavery; or, Three Months at the South in 1854.* Boston: T. R. Marvin & B. B. Mussey Co., 1854.

AIKEN, GEORGE L. *Uncle Tom's Cabin or Life among the Lowly: A Domestic Drama in Six Acts.* New York: Dick & Fitzgerald, Publishers, n. d.

ALLEN, JAMES LANE. "Mrs. Stowe's 'Uncle Tom' at Home in Kentucky." *Century* 34 (1887): 852-69.

American and Foreign Anti-Slavery Society. Thirteenth Annual Report of the American and Foreign Anti-Slavery Society. Presented at New York, May 11, 1853; with the Addresses and Resolutions. New York: American and Foreign Anti-Slavery Society, 1853.

AMES, EDGAR W. "The First Presentation of *Uncle Tom's Cabin* at Troy Museum, Troy, New York, Sept. 27, 1852." *Americana* 6 (1911): 1045-52.

AMMONS, ELIZABETH. "Heroines in *Uncle Tom's Cabin.*" *American Literature* 49 (1977): 161-79.

"Anti-Slavery Drama." *National Anti-Slavery Standard* 14 (1853): 50.

ARCHER, LEONARD COURTNEY. *Black Images in the American Theatre: NAACP Protest Campaigns—Stage, Screen, Radio & Television.* New York: Pageant-Poseidon, 1973.

ARNETT, FRANK S. "Fifty Years of Uncle Tom." *Munsey's Magazine* 27 (1902): 897-903.

AUSTIN, JAMES C., ed. "Harriet Beecher Stowe." In *Fields of the Atlantic Monthly: Letters to an Editor, 1861–1870.* San Marino, Cal.: Huntington Library, 1953.

BAILEY, THOMAS PEARCE. "'Uncle Tom's Cabin' Sixty Years After." In *Race Orthodoxy in the South and Other Aspects of the Negro Question.* New York: Neale Publishing Co., 1914.

BALDWIN, JAMES. "Everybody's Protest Novel." *Partisan Review* 16 (1949): 578-85. Reprinted in *Notes of a Native Son.* Boston: Beacon Press, 1955.

BEATTY, A. "The Evils of Slavery." *Western Journal and Civilian* 10 (1853): 319-28.

————. Review of *A Key to Uncle Tom's Cabin. Western Journal and Civilian* 10 (1853): 388-98.

————. Review of *Uncle Tom's Cabin. Western Journal and Civilian* 9 (1852): 133-39.

BEECHER, CATHARINE E. *An Essay on Slavery and Abolitionism with Reference to the Duty of American Females.* Philadelphia: Henry Perkins; Boston: Perkins & Martin, 1837.

BEECHER, EDWARD. *Narrative of Riots at Alton: In Connection with the Death of Rev. Elijah P. Lovejoy.* Alton, Ill.: George Holton, 1838.

BEECHER, HENRY WARD. *Norwood; or, Village Life in New England.* New York: Charles Scribner & Co., 1868. A novel.

BEECHER, LYMAN. *Autobiography, Correspondence, etc. of Lyman Beecher, D.D.* Edited by Charles Beecher. 2 vols. New York: Harper Bros., 1864. Sections of the book were written by Harriet Beecher Stowe.

BIBB, HENRY. "American History Coming to Light." *Voice of the Fugitive* 2 (1852): 2.

BIRDOFF, HARRY. *The World's Greatest Hit: Uncle Tom's Cabin.* New York: S. F. Vanni, 1947.

"The Birthday Garden Party to Harriet Beecher Stowe." *Atlantic Monthly Supplement* 50 (1882): 1-16.

BLACKFORD, LAUNCELOT MINOR. "*Uncle Tom's Cabin.*" In *Mine Eyes Have Seen the Glory: The Story of a Virginia Lady, Mary Berkeley Minor Blackford, 1802–1896.* Cambridge: Harvard University Press, 1954.

BOLT, CHRISTINE. *The Anti-Slavery Movement and Reconstruction: A Study in Anglo-American Co-operation, 1833–77.* New York: Oxford University Press, 1969.

BOREHAM, FRANK WILLIAM. *The Gospel of Uncle Tom's Cabin.* London: Epworth Press, 1956.

BRACKENRIDGE, H. M. "Slavery in the South: *Uncle Tom's Cabin*," *National Intelligencer.* Reprinted in *National Anti-Slavery Standard* 13 (1853): 129.

BRADFORD, GAMALIEL. "Harriet Beecher Stowe." *Atlantic Monthly* 122 (1918): 84. Reprinted in *Portraits of American Women.* Boston: Houghton Mifflin Co., 1919.

BRADY, KATHLEEN. "The Sources, Reputation, and Influence of *Uncle Tom's Cabin.*" Master's thesis, University of Minnesota, 1935.

BRAITHWAITE, WILLIAM STANLEY. "The Negro in American Literature." In *The New Negro.* Edited by Alain Locke. New York: A. & C. Boni, 1925.

BRANDSTADTER, EVAN. "Uncle Tom and Archy Moore: The Antislavery Novel as Ideological Symbol." *American Quarterly* 26 (1974): 160-75.

[BRIGGS, CHARLES.] "Uncle Tomitudes." *Putnam's Monthly* 1 (1853): 97-102.

BRIMBLECOMB, NICHOLAS, ESQ. [pseud.] *Uncle Tom's Cabin in Ruins! Triumphant Defence of Slavery! In a Series of Letters to Harriet Beecher Stowe.* Boston: Charles Waite, 1853. A satire of proslavery arguments.

"British Philanthropy and American Slavery. By a Southern Lady." *DeBow's Review* 14 (1853): 258-80.

BROOKS, VAN WYCK. "Introduction," *Uncle Tom's Cabin.* London: J. M. Dent & Sons, Ltd.; New York: E. P. Dutton, 1961.

BROWN, DOROTHY S. "Thesis and Theme in *Uncle Tom's Cabin.*" *English Journal* 58 (1969): 1330-34, 1372.

BROWN, JOHN MASON. "Topsy-Turvy; *Uncle Tom's Cabin* Barred in Bridgeport and New Haven." *Saturday Review of Literature* 28 (1945): 24-25.

BROWN, STERLING A. "The American Race Problem as Reflected in American Literature." *Journal of Negro Education* 8 (1939): 275-90.

―――――. "A Century of Negro Portraiture in American Literature." *Massachusetts Review* 7 (1966): 73-96.

―――――. "Negro Character as Seen by White Authors." *Journal of Negro Education* 2 (1933): 179-203.

BROWNE, MARGARET A. "Southern Reactions to *Uncle Tom's Cabin.*" Master's thesis, Duke University, 1941.

BRUCE, MRS. WILLIAM LIDDELL [Andasia Kimbrough Bruce]. *Uncle Tom's Cabin of To-Day.* New York: Neale Publishing Co., 1906. An anti-*Uncle Tom's Cabin* novel.

BURGESS, ANTHONY. "Making de White Boss Frown." *Encounter* 27 (1966): 54-58.

BURNETT, FRANCES HODGSON. *The One I Knew Best of All.* New York: C. Scribner's Sons, 1893, pp. 237-38.

BURTON, RICHARD. "The Author of 'Uncle Tom's Cabin.'" *Century* 52, n.s. (1896): 698-704.

BUTT, MARTHA HAINES. *Antifanaticism: A Tale of the South.* Philadelphia: Lippincott, Grambo & Co., 1853. An anti-*Uncle Tom's Cabin* novel.

CAIRNS, WILLIAM B. "'Uncle Tom's Cabin' and Its Author." *Dial* 50 (1911): 465-70.

CANADAY, NICHOLAS, JR. "The Antislavery Novel Prior to 1852 and Hildreth's *The Slave* (1836)." *College Language Association Journal* 17 (1973): 175-91.

CARLISLE, GEORGE WILLIAM FREDERICK HOWARD, 7th Earl of. "Introduction." HBS, *Uncle Tom's Cabin.* London: G. Routledge & Co., 1852.

CASKEY, MARIE. *Chariot of Fire: Religion and the Beecher Family.* New Haven: Yale University Press, 1978.

CASSARA, ERNEST. "The Rehabilitation of Uncle Tom: Significant Themes in Mrs. Stowe's Antislavery Novel." *College Language Association Journal* 17 (1973): 230-40.

CAYTON, HORACE. "Is *Uncle Tom's Cabin* Anti-Negro? Yes." *Negro Digest* 4 (1946): 71-72.

CHAPUT, DONALD. "Uncle Tom and Predestination." *Negro History Bulletin* 27 (1964): 143.

CHASE, LUCIEN B. *English Serfdom and American Slavery; or, Ourselves—as Others See Us.* New York: H. Long & Bro., 1854. An anti-*Uncle Tom's Cabin* novel.

CHESNUT, MARY BOYKIN (MILLER). *Mary Chesnut's Civil War.* Edited by C. Vann Woodward. New Haven: Yale University Press, 1981.

COLLINS, JOHN DANIEL. "American Drama in Anti-Slavery Agitation, 1792–1861." Ph.D. diss., State University of Iowa, 1963.

COOK, RAYMOND ALLEN. *Fire from the Flint: The Amazing Careers of Thomas Dixon.* Winston-Salem, N. C.: John F. Blair, 1968.

CORBETT, ELIZABETH F. "A Footnote to 'The Drama.'" *Drama* 16 (1926): 285-86.

————. "Uncle Tom Is Dead." *Theatre Guild Magazine* 8 (1931): 16.

COWIE, ALEXANDER. *The Rise of the American Novel.* New York: American Book Co., 1948.

COX, J. M. "Humor and America: The Southwestern Bear Hunt, Mrs. Stowe, and Mark Twain." *Sewanee Review* 16 (1975): 732-45.

CRISWELL, ROBERT. *"Uncle Tom's Cabin" Contrasted with Buckingham Hall, the Planter's Home; or, A Fair View of the Slavery Question.* New York: D. Fanshaw, 1852. An anti-*Uncle Tom's Cabin* novel.

CROSS, BARBARA M. "Harriet Beecher Stowe." In *Notable American Women, 1607–1950: A Biographical Dictionary.* Edited by Edward T. James. Vol. 3. Cambridge, Mass.: Harvard University Press, Belknap Press, 1971.

CROW, MARTHA FOOTE. *Harriet Beecher Stowe: A Biography for Girls.* New York: D. Appleton & Co., 1913.

CROZIER, ALICE C. *The Novels of Harriet Beecher Stowe.* New York: Oxford University Press, 1969.

CUMMINGS, EDWARD ESTLIN. *Tom.* Santa Fe, N. M.: Rydal Press, 1935. A ballet.

DANA, RICHARD HENRY, JR. *The Journal.* Edited by Robert F. Lucid. 3 vols. Cambridge: Harvard University Press, Belknap Press, 1968.

DAVIS, J. FRANK. "Tom Shows." *Scribner's* 77 (1925): 350-60.

DAVIS, RICHARD BEALE. "Mrs. Stowe's Characters in Situations and a Southern Literary Tradition." In *Essays on American Literature in Honor of Jay B. Hubbell.* Edited by Clarence Gohdes. Durham: Duke University Press, 1967.

DAY, KATHERINE SEYMOUR. "Harriet Beecher Stowe." *Lincoln Herald* 48 (1946): 15-18.

[DE FOREST, JOHN W.] "The Great American Novel." *Nation* 6 (1868): 27-29.

DEGLER, CARL N. *The Other South: Southern Dissenters in the Nineteenth Century.* New York: Harper & Row, 1974.

DELANY, MARTIN R. *Blake or the Huts of America.* With an Introduction by Floyd J. Miller. Boston: Beacon Press, 1970. An anti-*Uncle Tom's Cabin* novel with the thesis that *Uncle Tom's Cabin* is not a sufficiently strong attack on slavery.

DEMPSEY, DAVID. "Uncle Tom, Centenarian." *New York Times Magazine*, 3 June 1951, pp. 55-56.

DENMAN, THOMAS (Lord). *Uncle Tom's Cabin, Bleak House, Slavery and Slave Trade. Seven Articles by Lord Denman.* London: Longman, Brown, Green & Longmans, 1853.

DICKENS, CHARLES. *The Nonesuch Dickens.* 23 vols. Bloomsbury (London): The Nonesuch Press, 1937–1938.

[DICKENS, CHARLES, and HENRY MORLEY.] "North American Slavery." *Household Words* 6 (1852): 1-6.

[DIX, JOHN.] *Transatlantic Tracings; or, Sketches of Persons and Scenes in America.* London: W. Tweedie, 1853.

DIXON, THOMAS, JR. *The Leopard's Spots: A Romance of the White Man's Burden—1865–1900.* New York: Doubleday, Page & Co., 1902.

DOUGLASS, FREDERICK. "A Day and a Night in *Uncle Tom's Cabin.*" *Frederick Douglass' Paper*, 4 March 1853.

————. "John Brown and Mrs. Stowe." In *Life and Times of Frederick Douglass.* Hartford, Conn.: Park Publishing Co.; Cleveland: G. M. Rewell & Co.; Chicago: J. S. Goodman & Co.; San Francisco: Phillips & Hunt, 1882.

————. "*The Key to Uncle Tom's Cabin.*" *Frederick Douglass' Paper*, 29 April 1853.

————. "To Harriet Beecher Stowe." Letter in *Proceedings of the Colored National Convention Held in Rochester, July 6th, 7th, and 8th, 1853.* Rochester, N. Y.: Printed at the office of F. Douglass' Paper, 1853.

DRUMMOND, A. M., and RICHARD MOODY. "The Hit of the Century: *Uncle Tom's Cabin—1853–1952.*" *Educational Theatre Journal* 4 (1952): 315-22.

DU BOIS, W. E. B. *Book Reviews by W. E. B. Du Bois.* Compiled and edited by Herbert Aptheker. Millwood, N. Y.: KTO Press, 1977.

DUNBAR, PAUL LAURENCE. "Harriet Beecher Stowe." *Century* 57 (1898): 61. A poem.

DUVALL, SEVERN. "*Uncle Tom's Cabin*: The Sinister Side of the Patriarchy." *New England Quarterly* 36 (1963): 3-22. Reprinted in *Images of the Negro in American Literature.* Edited by Seymour Gross and John Hardy. Chicago: University of Chicago Press, 1966.

————. "W. G. Simms' Review of Mrs. Stowe." *American Literature* 30 (1958): 107-17.

EASTMAN, MARY H. *Aunt Phillis's Cabin; or, Southern Life as It Is*. Philadelphia: Lippincott, Grambo & Co., 1852. An anti-*Uncle Tom's Cabin* novel.

ELIOT, GEORGE. *The George Eliot Letters*. Edited by Gordon S. Haight. 9 vols. New Haven: Yale University Press, 1954–1978.

_____. Review of *Dred*. *Westminster Review* 66, n.s. 10 (1856):571-73.

ERSKINE, JOHN. *Leading American Novelists*. New York: Henry Holt & Co., 1910, pp. 274-323.

[ESTES, MATTHEW.] *Tit for Tat: A Novel by a Lady of New Orleans*. New York: Garret & Co., 1856. An anti-*Uncle Tom's Cabin* novel.

FIEDLER, LESLIE A. *Love and Death in the American Novel*. Cleveland: Criterion Books, World Publishing Co., 1960.

FIELDS, ANNIE. "Days with Mrs. Stowe." *Atlantic Monthly* 78 (1896): 145-56.

_____, ed. *The Life and Letters of Harriet Beecher Stowe*. Boston: Houghton Mifflin Co., 1897.

FISHER, G. P. Review of *Dred*. *New Englander* 14 (1856): 515-26.

[FISHER, SIDNEY G.] "The Possible Amelioration of Slavery." *North American Review* 78 (1853): 466-93.

FLANDERS, MRS. G. M. *The Ebony Idol, by a Lady of New England*. New York: D. Appleton & Co., 1860. A pro-slavery novel.

FLETCHER, EDWARD G. "Illustrations for Uncle Tom." *Texas Quarterly* 1 (1958): 166-80.

[FORMAN, W. H.?] "*Uncle Tom's Cabin*." *Manhattan* 1 (1883): 28-31.

FOSTER, CHARLES H. *The Rungless Ladder: Harriet Beecher Stowe and New England Puritanism*. Durham: Duke University Press, 1954.

FOSTER, THOMAS HENRY. *America's Most Famous Book: A Dissertation on Harriet Beecher Stowe, "Uncle Tom's Cabin," and Uncle Tom Shows*. Cedar Rapids, Iowa: Torch Press, 1947.

FREDERICKSON, GEORGE M. *The Black Image in the White Mind: The Debate on Afro-American Character and Destiny, 1817–1914*. New York: Harper & Row, 1971.

FRENCH, EARL A., and DIANA ROYCE, eds. *Portraits of a Nineteenth Century Family*. Hartford: Stowe-Day Foundation, 1976.

FRUTH, MARY ANN. "Scenery and Staging of *Uncle Tom's Cabin*: Allegory and Ohio River Scenes." *Theatre Studies*, no. 19 (1963): 31-39.

FURNAS, JOSEPH CHAMBERLAIN. *Goodbye to Uncle Tom*. New York: William Sloan Assoc., 1956.

GAINES, FRANCIS PENDLETON. "Introduction." HBS, *Uncle Tom's Cabin*. New York: Macmillan Co., 1926.

_____. *The Southern Plantation: A Study in the Development and the Accuracy of a Tradition*. New York: Columbia University Press, 1925.

GARDINER, JANE. "The Assault upon Uncle Tom: Attempts of Pro-Slavery Novelists to Answer *Uncle Tom's Cabin,* 1852–1860." *Southern Humanities Review* 12 (1978): 313-24.

GARRISON, WENDELL PHILLIPS, and FRANCIS JACKSON GARRISON. *William Lloyd Garrison, 1805–1879: The Story of His Life Told by His Children.* 4 vols. New York: Century Co., 1885–1889.

GARRISON, WILLIAM LLOYD. *The Letters of William Lloyd Garrison.* Edited by Walter M. Merrill and Louis Rachames. 6 vols. Cambridge: Harvard University Press, Belknap Press, 1971–1981.

[GARRISON, WILLIAM LLOYD.] Review of *Uncle Tom's Cabin. Liberator* 22 (1852): 50.

GEBO, DORA R. "*Uncle Tom's Cabin* and Biblical Ideas of Freedom and Slavery." *Negro History Bulletin* 19 (1955): 11-13.

GERSON, NOEL B. *Harriet Beecher Stowe: A Biography.* New York: Praeger, 1976.

GILBERTSON, CATHARINE P. *Harriet Beecher Stowe.* New York: D. Appleton-Century Co., 1937.

GLAZIER, LYLE. "Pointing Upward." *Hacettepe Bulletin of Social Sciences and Humanities* 3 (1971): 34-39.

GRAFF, MARY B. *Mandarin on the St. Johns.* Gainesville: University of Florida Press, 1953.

GRAHAM, THOMAS. "Harriet Beecher Stowe and the Question of Race." *New England Quarterly* 46 (1973): 614-22.

GRAYSON, WILLIAM J. *The Hireling and the Slave, Chicora and Other Poems.* Charleston, S. C.: McCarter & Co., 1856. "The Hireling and the Slave" is a proslavery poem.

GRIMSTED, DAVID. "Uncle Tom from Page to Stage: Limitations of Nineteenth-Century Drama." *Quarterly Journal of Speech* 56 (1970): 235-44.

GROSS, SEYMOUR, and JOHN HARDY, eds. *Images of the Negro in American Literature.* Chicago: University of Chicago Press, 1966.

GUERRY, WILLIAM A. "Harriet Beecher Stowe." *Sewanee Review* 6 (1898): 335-44.

GYSIN, BRION. *To Master—A Long Goodnight: The Story of Uncle Tom, a Historical Narrative.* New York: Creative Age Press, 1946.

HADLEY, B. "*Uncle Tom's Cabin* in Brazil." *Inter-America* 2 (1940): 26-27.

HALE, NANCY. "What God Was Writing." *Texas Quarterly* 1 (1958): 35-40.

HALE, SARAH JOSEPHA, ed. *Liberia; or, Mr. Peyton's Experiments.* New York: Harper Bros., 1853. An anti-*Uncle Tom's Cabin* novel.

HALEY, ALEX. "In Uncle Tom Are Our Guilt and Hope." *New York Times Magazine,* 1 March 1964, pp. 23, 90.

HALL, BAYNARD R. *Frank Freeman's Barber Shop: A Tale*. New York: C. Scribner, 1852. An anti-*Uncle Tom's Cabin* novel.

HALL, D. D. "A Yankee Tutor in the Old South." *New England Quarterly* 33 (1960): 89-90.

HAN, TIEN. "A Talk on 'Sorrows of the Negro Slave.'" *Survey of China Mainland Press*, no. 2555 (1961): 7-16.

HARRIS, JOEL CHANDLER. *Joel Chandler Harris: Editor and Essayist. Miscellaneous Literary, Political, and Social Writings*. Edited by Judith Collier Harris. Chapel Hill: University of North Carolina Press, 1931.

HART, ADOLPHUS. *Uncle Tom in Paris; or, Views of Slavery Outside the Cabin, Together with Washington's Views of Slavery*. Baltimore: Taylor & Co., 1854.

HAYNE, BARRIE. "Yankee in the Patriarchy: T. B. Thorpe's Reply to *Uncle Tom's Cabin*." *American Quarterly* 20 (1968): 180-95.

HAYNE, PAUL HAMILTON. "A Character," *Poems of Paul Hamilton Hayne*. Boston: D. Lothrop & Co., 1882, p. 284.

[HELPS, ARTHUR.] *"Uncle Tom's Cabin."* *Fraser's Magazine* 46 (1852): 237-44. Revised and reprinted in Arthur Helps, *A Letter on Mrs. Harriet Beecher Stowe's Novel, "Uncle Tom's Cabin."* London: n. p., 1852; reprint, Cambridge, Mass.: John Bartlett, 1852.

HENRY, STUART C. *Unvanquished Puritan: A Portrait of Lyman Beecher*. Grand Rapids, Mich.: William B. Eerdman's Publishing Co., 1973.

[HENSON, JOSIAH.] *Father Henson's Story of His Own Life*. With a Preface by Harriet Beecher Stowe. Boston: J. P. Jewett & Co., 1858.

HENSON, JOSIAH. *The Life of Josiah Henson, Formerly a Slave, Now an Inhabitant of Canada, as Narrated by Himself*. Boston: A. D. Phelps, 1849.

HENTZ, CAROLINE LEE. *The Planter's Northern Bride: A Novel*. 2 vols. Philadelphia: A. Hart, 1854. An anti-*Uncle Tom's Cabin* novel.

HEWITT, BERNARD. "Uncle Tom and Uncle Sam: New Light on an Old Play." *Quarterly Journal of Speech* 37 (1951): 63-70.

HIGGINSON, THOMAS WENTWORTH. *Cheerful Yesterdays*. Boston: Houghton Mifflin Co., 1898.

————. "Harriet Beecher Stowe." *Nation* 63 (1896): 24-26. Obituary.

————. "Introduction." HBS, *Uncle Tom's Cabin*. New York: D. Appleton & Co., 1898.

HILDRETH, RICHARD. *Archy Moore, the White Slave; or, Memoirs of a Fugitive*. New York: Miller, Orton & Co., 1857.

[HILDRETH, RICHARD.] *Brief Remarks on Miss Catharine E. Beecher's Essay on Slavery and Abolitionism: By the Author of Archy Moore*. Boston: I. Knapp, 1837.

HILDRETH, RICHARD. *The Slave; or, Memoirs of Archy Moore*, 2nd ed. 2 vols. in 1. Boston: Whipple & Damrell, 1840.

_____. *The White Slave; or, Memoirs of a Fugitive*. Boston: Tappan & Whittemore; Milwaukee: Rood & Whittemore, 1852. A revision of *The Slave; or, Memoirs of Archy Moore*.

HILL, HERBERT. "'Uncle Tom,' an Enduring American Myth." *Crisis* 72 (1965): 289-95.

HIRSCH, STEPHEN ALEXANDER. "Uncle Tom's Companions: The Literary and Popular Reaction to *Uncle Tom's Cabin*." Ph.D. diss., State University of New York at Albany, 1975.

[HOLMES, GEORGE FREDERICK.] Review of *A Key to Uncle Tom's Cabin*. *Southern Literary Messenger* 19 (1853): 321-38.

_____. Review of *Uncle Tom's Cabin*. *Southern Literary Messenger* 18 (1852): 721-31.

HOVET, THEODORE R. "Christian Revolution: Harriet Beecher Stowe's Response to Slavery and the Civil War." *New England Quarterly* 47 (1974): 535-49.

_____."The Church Diseased: Harriet Beecher Stowe's Attack on the Presbyterian Church." *Journal of Presbyterian History* 52 (1974): 167-87.

_____. "Harriet Beecher Stowe's Holiness Crusade Against Slavery." Ph.D. diss., University of Kansas, 1970.

How Do You Like Uncle Tom? Cambridge, Mass.: J. Bartlett, 1852.

HOWARD, JOHN RAYMOND. "Harriet Beecher Stowe, a Sketch." *Outlook* 54 (1896): 138-43.

_____. *Remembrance of Things Past*. New York: Thomas Y. Crowell Co., 1925, pp. 284-95.

HOWE, JULIA WARD. "Harriet Beecher Stowe." *Reader Magazine* 5 (1905): 613-17.

[HOWELLS, WILLIAM DEAN?] "Recent Literature." *Atlantic Monthly* 43 (1879): 407-8.

HUBBELL, JAY B. "Literary Nationalism in the Old South." In David Kelly Jackson, ed. *American Studies in Honor of William Kenneth Boyd*. Durham: Duke University Press, 1940.

_____. *The South in American Literature, 1607–1900*. Durham: Duke University Press, 1954, pp. 385-93, 962.

_____. *Southern Life in Fiction*. Athens: University of Georgia Press, 1960.

HUDSON, BENJAMIN F. "Another View of 'Uncle Tom.'" *Phylon* 24 (1963): 79-87.

HUGHES, LANGSTON. "Introductory Remarks and Captions." HBS, *Uncle Tom's Cabin*. New York: Dodd, Mead & Co., 1952.

IGLESIAS, A. "Classic Blend in Literature: *Uncle Tom's Cabin*." *Saturday Review of Literature* 33 (1950): 6, 31-32.

JACKSON, FREDERICK H. "*Uncle Tom's Cabin* in Italy." *Symposium* 7 (1953): 323-32.

JACKSON, PHYLLIS WYNN. *Victorian Cinderella; The Story of Harriet Beecher Stowe.* New York: Holiday House, 1947.

JACOBSON, DAN. "Down the River." *New Statesman* 44 (1962): 490-91.

JAFFE, ADRIAN. "Uncle Tom in the Penal Colony: Heine's View of *Uncle Tom's Cabin.*" *American-German Review* 19 (1953): 5-6.

JAMES, HENRY. *A Small Boy and Others.* New York: C. Scribner's Sons, 1913.

JERROLD, WALTER. "The Author of 'Uncle Tom,' Some Centenary Notes." *Bookman* (London) 40 (1911–1912): 241-45.

JOHNSON, JAMES WELDON. *The Autobiography of an Ex-Colored Man.* Boston: Sherman, French & Co., 1912.

JOHNSTON, JOHANNA. *Runaway to Heaven: The Story of Harriet Beecher Stowe.* Garden City, N. Y.: Doubleday & Co., 1963.

JONES, HOWARD MUMFORD. "Introduction." HBS, *Uncle Tom's Cabin.* Columbus: Charles E. Merrill Publishing Co., 1969.

JORGENSON, CHESTER E., comp. *Uncle Tom's Cabin as Book and Legend: A Guide to an Exhibition.* Detroit: Friends of the Detroit Public Library, 1952.

KASPIN, ALBERT. "*Uncle Tom's Cabin* and Uncle Akim's Inn: More on Harriet Beecher Stowe and Turgeniev." *Slavic and East European Journal* 9 (1965): 47-55.

KAYE, JOSEPH. "Famous First Nights: 'Uncle Tom's Cabin.'" *Theatre Magazine* 50 (1929): 26, 65.

KER, LEANDER. *Slavery Consistent with Christianity, with an Introduction Embracing a Notice of the "Uncle Tom's Cabin" Movement in England.* Weston, Mo.: Finch & O'Gorman, 1853.

KINMONT, ALEXANDER. *Twelve Lectures on the Natural History of Man, and the Rise and Progress of Philosophy.* Cincinnati: U. P. James, 1839.

KINNEY, JAMES JOSEPH. "The Theme of Miscegenation in the American Novel to World War I." Ph.D. diss., University of Tennessee, 1972.

KIRKHAM, E. BRUCE. *The Building of Uncle Tom's Cabin.* Knoxville: University of Tennessee Press, 1977.

————. "Harriet Beecher Stowe and the Genesis, Composition and Revision of *Uncle Tom's Cabin.*" Ph.D. diss., University of North Carolina, 1968.

KLINGBERG, F. J. "Harriet Beecher Stowe and Social Reform in England." *American Historical Review* 43 (1938): 542-52.

LITWACK, LEON F. *North of Slavery: The Negro in the Free States, 1790–1860.* Chicago: University of Chicago Press, 1961.

LUCAS, EDITH E. *La Littérature Anti-Esclavagiste au Dix-Neuvième Siècle. Étude sur Madame Beecher Stowe et son Influence en France.* Paris: E. de Boccard, 1930.

LUND, RALPH EUGENE. "Trouping with Uncle Tom." *Century* 115 (1928): 329-37.

LYNN, KENNETH S. "Introduction." *Uncle Tom's Cabin.* Cambridge, Mass.: Harvard University Press, Belknap Press, 1962.

————. "*Uncle Tom's Cabin.*" In *Visions of America: Eleven Literary Historical Essays.* Westport, Conn.: Greenwood Press, 1973.

[McCORD, MRS. LOUISA S.] Review of *Uncle Tom's Cabin. Southern Quarterly Review* 23 (1853): 81-120.

McCRAY, FLORINE THAYER. *The Life-Work of the Author of Uncle Tom's Cabin.* New York: Funk & Wagnalls, 1889.

MacDONALD, CORDELIA HOWARD. "Memoirs of the Original Little Eva." *Educational Theatre Journal* 8 (1956): 267-82.

McDOWELL, J. H. "Original Scenery and Documents for Productions of *Uncle Tom's Cabin.*" *Revue d'Histoire du Théatre* 15 (1963): 71-79.

————. "Scenery and Staging of *Uncle Tom's Cabin*: Selected Scenes." *Theatre Studies; The Journal of the Ohio State University Theatre Research Institute,* no. 10 (1963): 19-30.

McDOWELL, TREMAINE. "The Use of Negro Dialect by Harriet Beecher Stowe." *American Speech* 6 (1931): 322-26.

McINTOSH, MARIA J. *The Lofty and the Lowly; or, Good in All and None All-Good.* 2 vols. New York: D. Appleton & Co., 1853. An anti-*Uncle Tom's Cabin* novel.

MacLEAN, GRACE EDITH. *Uncle Tom's Cabin in Germany.* New York: D. Appleton & Co., 1910.

M'LEOD, DONALD. *Donald M'Leod's Gloomy Memories in the Highlands of Scotland versus Mrs. Harriet Beecher Stowe's Sunny Memories in (England) a Foreign Land.* Toronto: Thompson & Co., 1857.

McLOUGHLIN, WILLIAM G. *The Meaning of Henry Ward Beecher: An Essay on the Shifting Values of Mid-Victorian America, 1840–1870.* New York: Alfred A. Knopf, 1970.

McPHERSON, JAMES M. "A Brief for Equality: The Abolitionist Reply to the Racist Myth, 1860–1865." In Martin Duberman, ed. *The Antislavery Vanguard: New Essays on the Abolitionists.* Princeton: Princeton University Press, 1965.

MANIERRE, WILLIAM R. "A Southern Response to Mrs. Stowe: Two Letters of John R. Thompson." *Virginia Magazine of History and Biography* 69 (1961): 83-92.

MAROTTA, KENNY RALPH. "The Literary Relationship of George Eliot and Harriet Beecher Stowe." Ph.D. diss., Johns Hopkins University, 1974.

MARX, KARL. An article on the Highland clearances and the Duchess of Sutherland. *New York Tribune*, 9 February 1853.

MATTHEWS, BRANDER. "American Fiction Again." *Cosmopolitan* 12 (1892): 636-40.

MAURICE, A. B. "Famous Novels and Their Contemporary Critics." *Bookman* 16 (1903): 23-30.

MAY, HENRY F. "Introduction." HBS, *Oldtown Folks*. Cambridge: Harvard University Press, Belknap Press, 1966.

MERIDETH, ROBERT. *The Politics of the Universe: Edward Beecher, Abolition, and Orthodoxy*. Nashville: Vanderbilt University Press, 1968.

MESERVE, WALTER J., and RUTH I. MESERVE. "*Uncle Tom's Cabin* and Modern Chinese Drama." *Modern Drama* 17 (1974): 57-66.

MILLER, RANDALL M. "Mrs. Stowe's Negro: George Harris' Negritude in *Uncle Tom's Cabin*." *Colby Library Quarterly* 10 (1974): 521-26.

MOERS, ELLEN. *Harriet Beecher Stowe and American Literature*. Hartford, Conn.: Stowe-Day Foundation, 1978.

_____. "Mrs. Stowe's Vengeance." *New York Review of Books* 15 (1970): 25-32. A review of Alice C. Crozier's *The Novels of Harriet Beecher Stowe*.

_____. "Nat Turner and Dred." *New York Review of Books* 15 (1970): 52. A reply to a letter by William Styron.

MOODY, RICHARD. "Uncle Tom, the Theatre, and Mrs. Stowe." *American Heritage* 6 (1955): 29-33, 102-3.

MORROW, JOHN C. "The Harmount Company: Aspects of an *Uncle Tom's Cabin* Company." *Theatre Studies*, no. 10 (1963): 10-18.

"The Most 'Harmful' Book." *Literary Digest* 45 (1912): 1225-26.

"Moving Novel Sixty Years After." *Outlook* 98 (1911): 286-87.

"Mrs. Stowe and *Dred*." *Southern Literary Messenger* 27 (1858): 284-86.

"Mrs. Stowe's Drama." *Liberator* 25 (1855): 199. A review of a reading by Mrs. Mary E. Webb of *Uncle Tom's Cabin* as adapted by Harriet Beecher Stowe.

MURRAY, ALEX L. "Harriet Beecher Stowe on Racial Segregation in the Schools." *American Quarterly* 12 (1960): 518-19.

NDU, POL. "From 'Jegar Adhadutha' to Gary, Indiana: Uncle Tomism and the Black Literary Revolution." *Ufahamu* 4 (1973): 119-33.

"Negro History and the Modern 'Uncle Tom.'" *Negro History* 27 (1964): 134-35.

NELSON, JOHN HERBERT. *The Negro Character in American Literature*. Lawrence: Department of Journalism Press, University of Kansas, 1926.

_____. "A Note on the Genesis of Mrs. Stowe's *Dred*." In *Studies in English in Honor of Raphael Dorman O'Leary and Selden Lincoln Whitecomb by the Members of the English Department, University of Kansas.* Lawrence: University of Kansas Press, 1940.

"A New *Uncle Tom's Cabin* for England." *DeBow's Review* 22 (1857): 484-86.

A news story concerning an attempt in New York City to drop *Uncle Tom's Cabin* from an approved reading list in the public schools. *New York Times,* 21 May 1903, p. 5.

NICHOLAS, H. G. "*Uncle Tom's Cabin,* 1852–1952." *Georgia Review* 8 (1954): 140-48.

NICHOLS, CHARLES. "The Origins of *Uncle Tom's Cabin.*" *Phylon* 19 (1958): 328-34.

NOBLE, PETER. *The Negro in Films.* London: S. Robinson, 1948; reprint, New York: Arno Press, 1970.

"The Novel that Overruled the Supreme Court." *Current Literature* 51 (1911): 208-10.

OAKS, HAROLD RASMUS. "An Interpretative Study of the Effects of Some Upper Mid-West Productions of Uncle Tom's Cabin as Reflected in Local Newspapers Between 1852 and 1860." Ph.D. diss., University of Minnesota, 1964.

OKOGBUE, C. "The Negro Slave and 'Black-Assed' Feeling in American Fiction." *Muse: Literary Journal of the English Association of Nsukka* 8 (1976): 57-60.

OLIVER, EGBERT S. "The Little Cabin of Uncle Tom." *College English* 26 (1964–65): 355-61.

OLMSTED, FREDERICK L. *A Journey in the Seaboard Slave States, with Remarks on Their Economy.* New York: Dix & Edwards; London: Low, Son & Co., 1856.

OUYANG, YU-CHIEN. "*Sorrows of the Negro Slave.*" *Chu Pen,* No. 11 (1959). A Chinese dramatic adaptation of *Uncle Tom's Cabin.*

PAGE, JOHN W. *Uncle Robin in His Cabin in Virginia, and Tom without One in Boston.* Richmond, Va.: J. W. Randolph, 1853. An anti-*Uncle Tom's Cabin* novel.

PALMER, JACLYN. "Images of Slavery: Black and White Writers." *Negro History Bulletin* 41 (1978): 888-89.

PARKER, THEODORE. "Speech of Theodore Parker at the Annual Meeting of the Massachusetts Anti-Slavery Society." *National Anti-Slavery Standard* 13 (1853): 158-59.

PARRINGTON, VERNON L. *Main Currents in American Thought.* 3 vols. in 1. New York: Harcourt Brace & Co., 1927–30, 2:371-78, 3:62-64.

The Patent Key to Uncle Tom's Cabin; or, Mrs. Stowe in England, By a Lady in New York. New York: Pudney & Russell, 1853. An anti-*Uncle Tom's Cabin* poem.

PEASE, WILLIAM H., and JANE H. PEASE, "Uncle Tom and Clayton: Fact, Fiction, and Mystery." *Ontario History* 50 (1958): 61-73.

PECK, HARRY THURSTON. "*Uncle Tom's Cabin* in Liverpool." *Bookman* 6 (1897): 310-16.

PERKINS, HOWARD C. "The Defense of Slavery in the Northern Press on the Eve of the Civil War." *Journal of Southern History* 9 (1943): 501-31.

PERRY, THOMAS SERGEANT. "American Novels." *North American Review* 115 (1872): 370-71.

PHELPS, ELIZABETH S. (WARD). *Chapters from a Life*. Boston: Houghton Mifflin Co., 1897.

PHELPS, WILLIAM LYON. "*Uncle Tom's Cabin*." *Howells, James, Bryant, and Other Essays*. New York: Macmillan Co., 1924.

PHILLIPS, WENDELL. "Explanation and Defense." *National Anti-Slavery Standard* 13 (1853): 173.

PICKENS, DONALD K. "Uncle Tom Becomes Nat Turner: A Commentary on Two American Heroes." *Negro American Literary Forum* 3 (1969): 45-48.

"The Pioneer Uncle Tomers: By One of Them." *Theatre* 4 (1904): 44.

POLLARD, EDWARD A. *Black Diamonds Gathered in the Darkey Homes of the South*. New York: Pudney & Russell, 1859.

[PRINGLE, EDWARD J.] *Slavery in the Southern States. By a Carolinian*. 2nd ed. Cambridge, Mass.: J. Bartlett, 1852. "An answer to the question, What do you think of *Uncle Tom's Cabin* at the South?"

PURCELL, J. M. "Mrs. Stowe's Vocabulary." *American Speech* 13 (1938): 230-31.

QUARNSTROM, I. BLAINE. "Early Twentieth-Century Staging of *Uncle Tom's Cabin*." *Theatre Studies*, no. 15 (1968): 32-42.

"The Queen's Dream—A Sequel to *Uncle Tom's Cabin*." *DeBow's Review* 15 (1853): 95-105. A satire.

RAHILL, FRANK. "America's Number One Hit." *Theatre Arts* 36 (1952): 18-24.

RAMMELKAMP, CHARLES H. "Harriet Beecher Stowe's Reply." *Mississippi Valley Historical Review* 19 (1932): 261.

RANDOLPH, J. THORNTON [Charles Jacobs Peterson, pseud.]. *The Cabin and Parlor; or, Slaves and Masters*. Philadelphia: T. B. Peterson, 1852. An anti-*Uncle Tom's Cabin* novel.

REED, KENNETH T. "*Uncle Tom's Cabin* and the Heavenly City." *College Language Association Journal* 12 (1968): 150-54.

Review of *Dred*. *DeBow's Review* 21 (1856): 662.

————. *Southern Literary Messenger* 27 (1858): 284-86.

Review of *A Key to Uncle Tom's Cabin*. *Southern Literary Messenger* 19 (1853): 321-30.

Review of *Uncle Tom's Cabin. Jefferson* (Mo.) *Inquirer.* 23 October 1852.

———. *Literary World* 10 (1852): 291-92.

———. *New Englander* 10 (1852): 588-613.

———. *New Orleans Weekly Picayune,* 30 August 1852.

———. *New York Tribune,* 8 August 1853. A review of a dramatic production of *UTC.*

———. *Raleigh Weekly North Carolina Standard,* 2 June 1852.

———. *Western Journal and Civilian* 9 (1852): 133-39.

REXROTH, KENNETH. "*Uncle Tom's Cabin.*" *Saturday Review* 52 (1969): 71. Reprinted in *The Elastic Retort: Essays in Literature and Ideas.* New York: Seabury Press, 1973.

[RICHARD, HENRY.] *English Anti-Slavery and the American War: A Letter to Harriet B. Stowe.* London: R. Barrett, [1863?].

RIDGELY, JOSEPH V. "*Woodcraft*: Simms's First Answer to *Uncle Tom's Cabin.*" *American Literature* 31 (1960): 421-33.

RIGGIO, THOMAS P. "Uncle Tom Reconstructed: A Neglected Chapter in the History of a Book." *American Quarterly* 28 (1976): 56-70.

ROGERS, JOSEPH M. "*Uncle Tom's Cabin* in Kentucky." *Era* 10 (1902): 262-68.

ROPPOLO, JOSEPH P. "Harriet Beecher Stowe and New Orleans: A Study in Hate." *New England Quarterly* 30 (1957): 346-62.

———. "Uncle Tom in New Orleans: Three Lost Plays." *New England Quarterly* 27 (1954): 213-26.

ROSE, R. BURTON. "Death of *Uncle Tom's Cabin.*" *Overland Monthly and Outwest Magazine,* n.s. 89 (1931): 14, 24.

ROSSI, JOSEPH. "*Uncle Tom's Cabin* and Protestantism in Italy." *American Quarterly* 11 (1960): 416-24.

ROURKE, CONSTANCE. *Trumpets of Jubilee.* New York: Harcourt, Brace & Co., 1927.

RUGOFF, MILTON. *The Beechers: An American Family in the Nineteenth Century.* New York: Harper & Row, 1981.

[RUSH, CAROLINE E.] *The North and South; or, Slavery and Its Contrasts.* Philadelphia: Crissy & Markley, 1852. An anti-*Uncle Tom's Cabin* novel.

SAND, GEORGE [Amandine Lucie Aurore Dupin, Baroness Dudevant, pseud.]. Introduction to Henriette [*sic*] Beecher Stowe, *La Case de l'Oncle Tom.* Paris: G. Barba, 1853.

———. Review of *Uncle Tom's Cabin. La Presse* (Paris) 17 December 1852.

SAXTON, ALEXANDER. "Blackface Minstrelsy and Jacksonian Ideology." *American Quarterly* 27 (1975): 5, 19-20.

SCHOOLCRAFT, MRS. HENRY R. [MARY HOWARD SCHOOLCRAFT]. *The Black Gauntlet: A Tale of Plantation Life in South Carolina*. Philadelphia: J. B. Lippincott Co., 1860. An anti-*Uncle Tom's Cabin* novel.

SEILER, GRACE. "Harriet Beecher Stowe." *College English* 11 (1949): 127-37.

SENIOR, NASSAU W. "American Slavery." *Quarterly Review* 101 (1857): 324-25.

[SENIOR, NASSAU W.] "Slavery in the United States." *Edinburgh Review* 101 (1855): 293-331. Reprinted in revised form as *American Slavery*. London: Longman, Brown, Green, Longmans & Roberts, 1856.

"The 'Senior Editor' [of the *New York Observer*] against *Uncle Tom's Cabin*." *Independent* 5 (1853): 94.

SHEPPERSON, GEORGE. "Harriet Beecher Stowe and Scotland, 1852–53." *Scottish Historical Review* 32 (1953): 40-46.

SHOUP, FRANK A. "*Uncle Tom's Cabin* Forty Years After." *Sewanee Review* 2 (1893): 88-104.

[SIMMS, WILLIAM GILMORE.] "*A Key to Uncle Tom's Cabin*." Review in *Southern Quarterly Review*, n.s. 7 (1853): 214-54.

SIMMS, WILLIAM GILMORE. *Woodcraft or Hawks about the Dovecote: A Story of the South at the Close of the Revolution*. Rev. ed. New York: J. S. Redfield, 1854. A proslavery novel, probably a reply to *Uncle Tom's Cabin*.

SKINNER, RICHARD DANA. "Players Revive Uncle Tom." *Commonweal* 18 (1933): 160.

SKLAR, KATHRYN KISH. *Catharine Beecher: A Study in American Domesticity*. New Haven: Yale University Press, 1973.

Slavery Past and Present; or, Notes on Uncle Tom's Cabin. Edited by a Lady. London: Longman, Brown, Green & Longmans, 1852.

SLOUT, WILLIAM L. "*Uncle Tom's Cabin* in American Film History." *Journal of Popular Film* 2 (1973): 137-51.

SMITH, WILLIAM L. G. *Life at the South; or, "Uncle Tom's Cabin" as It Is: Being Narratives, Scenes, and Incidents in the Real "Life of the Lowly."* Buffalo, N. Y.: George H. Darby & Co., 1852. An anti-*Uncle Tom's Cabin* novel.

SMYLIE, JAMES H. "*Uncle Tom's Cabin* Revisited: The Bible, the Romantic Imagination, and the Sympathies of Christ." *Interpretation* 27 (1973): 67-85.

[SMYTHE, JAMES M.] *Ethel Somers; or, The Fate of the Union*. Augusta: H. D. Norrell, 1857.

"Southern Slavery and Its Assailants. *The Key to Uncle Tom's Cabin*. By a Lady of Georgia." *DeBow's Review* 15 (1853): 486-96; 16 (1854): 46-62.

STARKE, CATHERINE JUANITA. *Black Portraiture in American Fiction: Stock Characters, Archetypes, and Individuals.* New York: Basic Books, [1971].

STEARNS, REV. E. J. *Notes on Uncle Tom's Cabin: Being a Logical Answer to its Allegations and Inferences against Slavery as an Institution.* Philadelphia: Lippincott, Grambo & Co., 1853.

STEELE, THOMAS J., S.J. "Tom and Eva: Mrs. Stowe's Two Dying Christs." *Negro American Literary Forum* 6 (1972): 85-90.

STERN, PHILIP VAN DOREN. "Introduction" and "Notes." HBS, *The Annotated Uncle Tom's Cabin.* New York: Paul S. Eriksson, 1964.

STONE, HARRY. "Charles Dickens and Harriet Beecher Stowe." *Nineteenth-Century Fiction* 12 (1957): 198-202.

STOWE, CHARLES EDWARD. "Harriet Beecher Stowe: Friend of the South." *Outlook* 98 (1911): 300-303.

_____. "How My Mother Wrote *Uncle Tom's Cabin.*" *Ladies Home Journal* 28 (1911): 9.

_____. *Life of Harriet Beecher Stowe Compiled from Her Letters and Journals.* Boston: Houghton Mifflin Co., 1889.

STOWE, CHARLES EDWARD, and LYMAN BEECHER STOWE. *Harriet Beecher Stowe: The Story of Her Life.* Boston: Houghton Mifflin Co., 1911.

_____. "How Mrs. Stowe Wrote *Uncle Tom's Cabin.*" *McClure's Magazine* 36 (1911): 604-21.

STOWE, LYMAN BEECHER. *Saints, Sinners and Beechers.* Indianapolis: Bobbs-Merrill Co., 1934.

STROUT, CUSHING. "*Uncle Tom's Cabin* and the Portent of Millenium." *Yale Review* 57 (1968): 375-85.

STYRON, WILLIAM. "Nat Turner and Dred." Letter to *New York Review of Books* 15 (1971): 52. See reply by Ellen Moers, ibid.

SUCKOW, RUTH. "An Almost Lost American Classic." *College English* 14 (1953): 314-25.

SURGHNOR, Mrs. M. W. *Uncle Tom of the Old South: A History of the South in Reconstruction Days.* New Orleans: L. Graham & Son, 1897. An anti-*Uncle Tom's Cabin* novel.

TANDY, JEANNETTE REID. "Pro-Slavery Propaganda in American Fiction of the Fifties." *South Atlantic Quarterly,* pt. 1, 21 (1922): 41-50; pt. 2 (1922): 170-78.

TAYLOR, WALTER FULLER. *A History of American Letters.* Boston: American Book Co., 1936.

TAYLOR, WILLIAM R. *Cavalier and Yankee: The Old South and American National Character.* New York: George Braziller, 1961.

_____. "The Plantation Novel and the Sentimental Tradition." In *Intellectual History in America.* Edited by Cushing Strout. 2 vols. New York: Harper & Row, 1968, 1:219-30.

TEXIER, EDMOND, and L. DE WAILLEY. *L'Oncle Tom. Drame en Cinq Actes et Neuf Tableaux.* Paris: Michel Lévy, Frères, 1853. A dramatization.

[THOMPSON, JOHN REUBEN.] "*Uncle Tom's Cabin.*" Review in *Southern Literary Messenger* 18 (1852): 630-38.

THORPE, THOMAS B. *The Master's House; or, Scenes Descriptive of Southern Life.* 3rd ed. New York: J. C. Derby, 1855. An ambiguous novel, partially pro- and partially anti-*Uncle Tom's Cabin.*

TILTON, THEODORE. "Out of Jail. The Black Man Who Was Imprisoned for Reading *Uncle Tom's Cabin.*" *Liberator* 32 (1862): 108.

TOLL, ROBERT C. *Blacking Up: The Minstrel Show in Nineteenth-Century America.* New York: Oxford University Press, 1974.

TOMPKINS, JANE P. "*Uncle Tom's Cabin* and the Politics of Literary History." *Glyph* 8 (1981): 79-102.

TOURGÉE, ALBION W. "The Literary Quality of 'Uncle Tom's Cabin.'" *Independent* 48 (1896): 1127-28.

TURNER, LORENZO DOW. *Anti-Slavery Sentiment in American Literature Prior to 1865.* Washington, D.C.: Association for the Study of Negro Life and History, 1929.

"'Uncle Tom' among the Bowery Boys." *New-York Daily Times.* Reprinted in *National Anti-Slavery Standard* 14 (1853): 41. A review of a performance of the play.

"'Uncle Tom' and His Followers." *Norton's Literary Gazette* 2 (1852): 168.

"The Uncle Tom Epidemic." *Literary World* 11 (1852): 355-58.

Uncle Tom in England; or, A Proof that Black's White. An Echo to the American "Uncle Tom." New York: A. D. Failing, [1852]. An anonymous English novel defending Great Britain against the charge that its laborers were materially worse off than American slaves.

"'Uncle Tom' in Philadelphia, *The Liberator.*" Reprinted in *National Anti-Slavery Standard* 14 (1853): 74. A review of a dramatic production.

"'Uncle Tom' Literature." *Norton's Literary Gazette* 11 (1852): 212-13.

Uncle Tom's Cabin. Directed by Harry Pollard. With James B. Lowe, George Sugmann, Margarita Fischer, Arthur Edmund Carew. Universal, 1927. A movie.

"*Uncle Tom's Cabin.*" *The Friend* (Philadelphia). 28 (1853): 159; 29 (1853): 294-95.

————. *Literary World* 10 (1852): 291-92.

————. *New York Observer,* 23 September 1852.

"*Uncle Tom's Cabin* and Its Opponents." *Eclectic Review,* n.s. 4 (1852): 717-44.

"*Uncle Tom's Cabin* and Slavery in the Southern States by a Carolinian." *New York Quarterly Review* 1 (1853): 470-78.

"*Uncle Tom's Cabin*: Is It a Novel?" *Andover Review* 4 (1885): 363-67.

"*Uncle Tom's Cabin*: The Most Influential Novel Ever Written." *Nation* 92 (1911): 619-20.

"Uncle Tom's Message: The Book of War and Freedom." (London) *Times Literary Supplement* 4 (1963): 777-78.

VAN DOREN, CARL. *The American Novel*. New York: Macmillan Co., 1921.

————. "Mrs. Stowe." *The Cambridge History of American Literature*. New York: Macmillan Co., 1921.

VAN WHY, JOSEPH S., and E. BRUCE KIRKHAM. "A Note on Two Pages of the Manuscript of *Uncle Tom's Cabin*." *Papers of the Bibliographical Society of America* 66 (1973): 433-34.

VEACH, CARSON WARD. "Harriet Beecher Stowe: A Critical Study of Her Early Novels." Ph.D. diss., University of Indiana, 1968.

VIDI [pseud.]. *Mr. Frank: The Underground Mail-Agent*. Philadelphia: Lippincott, Grambo & Co., 1853. An anti-*Uncle Tom's Cabin* novel.

A Voice from the Motherland, Answering Mrs. H. Beecher Stowe's Appeal, by Civis Anglicus. London: Trübner & Co., 1863.

WADDELL, JAMES A. "*Uncle Tom's Cabin*" Reviewed; or, American Society Vindicated from the Aspersions of Mrs. Harriet Beecher Stowe*. Raleigh, N. C.: Southern Weekly Post, 1852.

WAGENKNECHT, EDWARD. *Harriet Beecher Stowe: The Known and the Unknown*. New York: Oxford University Press, 1965.

WAN CHAI-PAO [Tsao Yu]. "The Modern Chinese Theatre." *National Reconstruction Journal* 7 (1946): 33-48.

WARD, JOHN WILLIAM. "Afterword," *Uncle Tom's Cabin*. New York: New American Library, 1966.

————. "The Meaning of History in *Uncle Tom's Cabin*." *Red, White, and Blue: Men, Books, and Ideas in American Culture*. New York: Oxford University Press, 1969.

————. "*Uncle Tom's Cabin*, as a Matter of Historical Fact." *Columbia University Forum* 9 (1967): 42-47.

WARNER, CHARLES DUDLEY. "The Story of *Uncle Tom's Cabin*." *Atlantic Monthly* 78 (1896): 311-21.

WATSON, CHARLES S. "Simms's Answer to *Uncle Tom's Cabin*: Criticism of the South in *Woodcraft*." *Southern Literary Journal* 9 (1976): 78-90.

————. "Simms's Review of *Uncle Tom's Cabin*." *American Literature* 48 (1976): 365-68.

[WELD, THEODORE.] *American Slavery As It Is: Testimony of a Thousand Witnesses*. New York: American Anti-Slavery Society, 1839.

————. *Letters of Theodore Dwight Weld, Angelina Grimké Weld and Sarah Grimké: 1822–1844*. Edited by Gilbert H. Barnes and Dwight L. Dumond. 2 vols. 1934; reprint, Gloucester, Mass.: Peter Smith, 1965.

WHITTIER, JOHN GREENLEAF. *The Letters of John Greenleaf Whittier.* Edited by John B. Pickard. 3 vols. Cambridge: Harvard University Press, Belknap Press, 1975.

WILLIAMS, GEORGE W. *History of the Negro Race in America from 1619 to 1880.* New York: G. P. Putnam & Sons, 1883.

WILSON, EDMUND. "'No! No! No! My Soul An't Yours, Mas'r.'" *New Yorker* 24 (1948): 134ff.

————. *Patriotic Gore: Studies in the Literature of the American Civil War.* New York: Oxford University Press, 1962.

WILSON, [ROBERT] FORREST. *Crusader in Crinoline: The Life of Harriet Beecher Stowe.* Philadelphia: J. B. Lippincott Co., 1941.

WOODRESS, JAMES. "*Uncle Tom's Cabin* in Italy." In *Essays in American Literature in Honor of Jay B. Hubbell.* Edited by Clarence Gohdes. Durham: Duke University Press, 1967.

WOODS, JOHN A. "Introduction." HBS, *Uncle Tom's Cabin.* London: Oxford University Press, 1965.

WOODWARD, A. *A Review of Uncle Tom's Cabin; or, An Essay on Slavery.* Cincinnati: Applegate & Co., 1853.

WRIGHT, HENRY C. "*Uncle Tom's Cabin*—Objectionable Characteristics." Letter in the *Liberator* 22 (1852): 111. Reply by William Lloyd Garrison, *Liberator*, 17 September 1852.

YELLIN, JEAN FAGAN. *The Intricate Knot: Black Figures in American Literature.* New York: New York University Press, 1972.

YOUNG, STARK. "Gentle Mrs. Stowe." *New Republic* 108 (1944): 381.

————. "Sweet River." *New Republic* 89 (1936): 78.

————. "Uncle Tom's Measure." *New Republic* 76 (1933): 212-13.

ZANGER, JULES. "The 'Tragic Octoroon' in Pre-Civil War Fiction." *American Quarterly* 18 (1967): 63-70.

ZINN, HOWARD. "Abolitionists, Freedom-Riders, and the Tactics of Agitation." In Martin Duberman, ed. *The Antislavery Vanguard: New Essays on the Abolitionists.* Princeton: Princeton University Press, 1965.

BIBLIOGRAPHIES

ASHTON, JEAN W. *Harriet Beecher Stowe: A Reference Guide.* Boston: G. K. Hall & Co., 1977.

HASKELL, JOHN D., JR. "Addenda to Hildreth: Harriet Beecher Stowe." *Papers of the Bibliographical Society of America* 72 (1978): 348.

HILDRETH, MARGARET HOLBROOK. *Harriet Beecher Stowe: A Bibliography.* Hamden, Conn.: Shoe String (Archon), 1976.

MAIR, MARGARET GRANVILLE, comp. *The Papers of Harriet Beecher Stowe.*

Edited by Earl A. French, Librarian Diana Royce. Hartford: Stowe-Day Foundation, 1977.

Radcliffe College, Harvard University. Women's Archives. Beecher-Stowe Collection of Family Papers, 1798–1956. Cambridge, Mass., 1962.

Stowe-Day Foundation. Hartford, Conn. Collection of Stowe and Beecher materials.

VAN WHY, JOSEPH. "Letters of Harriet Beecher Stowe." *Bulletin of the Stowe-Day Foundation* 1 (1961): 2-14.

Acknowledgments

Adams, James Truslow. *America's Tragedy.* © 1934, Charles Scribner's Sons; copyright renewed Kathryn Seeley Adams. Reprinted with the permission of Charles Scribner's Sons, New York.

Brown, John Mason, and Montrose J. Moses, eds. *The American Theatre as Seen by Its Critics, 1752–1934.* © 1934, W. W. Norton & Co., Inc., New York. Permission given by Mr. Meredith M. Brown, estate of John Mason Brown.

Davis, Richard Beale. "Mrs. Stowe's Characters in Situations and a Southern Literary Tradition." In *Essays on American Literature in Honor of Jay B. Hubbell.* Edited by Clarence Gohdes. © 1967, Duke University Press, Durham, North Carolina.

Eaton, Clement. *Freedom of Thought in the Old South.* © 1940, Duke University Press, Durham, North Carolina.

Eckman, Fern Marja. *The Furious Passage of James Baldwin.* © 1966, M. Evans & Co., Inc., New York. Reprinted by permission of the publisher.

Foster, Charles H. *The Rungless Ladder: Harriet Beecher Stowe and New England Puritanism.* © 1954, Duke University Press, Durham, North Carolina.

Gussow, Mel. "A Stoic Dignified Uncle Tom Is Portrayed on Stage." © 1975, New York Times Company. Reprinted by permission.

Hubbell, Jay B. *The South in American Literature: 1607–1900.* © 1954, Duke University Press, Durham, North Carolina.

Jackson, David Kelly, ed. *American Studies in Honor of William Kenneth Boyd.* © 1940, Duke University Press, Durham, North Carolina.

Kenner, Hugh. "Classics by the Pound." © *Harper's Magazine.* Reprinted from the August 1982 issue by special permission.

James, Henry. *A Small Boy and Others.* © 1913, 1941, Charles Scribner's Sons, New York.

Johnson, James Weldon. *The Autobiography of an Ex-Colored Man.* © 1912, Sherman, French & Co., Boston. Permission granted by Alfred A. Knopf, Inc., New York.

Moody, Richard. "Uncle Tom, the Theatre, and Mrs. Stowe." © 1955. Reprinted by permission of American Heritage Publishing Co., Inc., New York.

Murray, Alex L. "Harriet Beecher Stowe on Racial Segregation in the Schools." *American Quarterly.* © 1960, University of Pennsylvania, Philadelphia.

Nevins, Allan. *Ordeal of the Union.* © 1947, 1975, Charles Scribner's Sons, New York.

Page, Thomas Nelson. *The Old South: Essays Social and Political.* © 1912, 1940, Charles Scribner's Sons, New York.

Saxton, Alexander. "Blackface Minstrelsy and Jacksonian Ideology." *American Quarterly.* © 1975, University of Pennsylvania, Philadelphia.

Simms, William Gilmore. Quotations from letters, reprinted with permission of the publisher, from *The Letters of William Gilmore Simms*, Volume III, edited by Mary C. Simms Oliphant et al. © 1972, University of South Carolina Press, Columbia, South Carolina.

Stowe, Harriet Beecher, and members of the Beecher families, various letters. Reprinted with the permission of the Stowe-Day Foundation, Hartford, Connecticut.

Stowe, Harriet Beecher, letter to Dr. Gamaliel Bradley, 9 March 1851. By permission of the Boston Public Library.

————, letter to George Eliot, 18 March 1876. Henry W. and Albert A. Berg Collection, New York Public Library. Astor, Lenox and Tilden Foundations.

————, letter to James T. Fields, 13 November 1862. Huntington Library, San Marino, California. Number FI 4012.

Styron, William. Reprinted with permission of the *New York Review of Books.* © 1970, Nyrev, Inc., New York.

Swinburne, Charles Algernon, letter to Paul Hamilton Hayne, 2 May 1877. Henry W. and Albert A. Berg Collection, New York Public Library. Astor, Lenox and Tilden Foundations.

Ward, John William. "Afterword," *Uncle Tom's Cabin.* © 1966. Reprinted by arrangement with The New American Library, Inc., New York.

Index